# HANDBOOK OF POPULATION AND FAMILY ECONOMICS
## VOLUME 1A

# HANDBOOKS
# IN
# ECONOMICS

14

*Series Editors*

## KENNETH J. ARROW
## MICHAEL D. INTRILIGATOR

**ELSEVIER**
AMSTERDAM · LAUSANNE · NEW YORK · OXFORD · SHANNON · TOKYO

# HANDBOOK OF POPULATION AND FAMILY ECONOMICS

## VOLUME 1A

*Edited by*

## MARK R. ROSENZWEIG
*University of Pennsylvania*

and

## ODED STARK
*University of Oslo and University of Vienna*

1997

ELSEVIER

AMSTERDAM · LAUSANNE · NEW YORK · OXFORD · SHANNON · TOKYO

ELSEVER SCENCE B.V.
Sara Burgerhartstraat 25
P.O. Box 211, 1000 AE Amsterdam, The Netherlands

ISBN Volume 1A: 0 444 82645 9
ISBN Volume 1B: 0 444 82646 7
ISBN Set (1A & 1B): 0 444 89647 3

3 2280 00641 4262

# INTRODUCTION TO THE SERIES

The aim of the *Handbooks in Economics* series is to produce Handbooks for various branches of economics, each of which is a definitive source, reference, and teaching supplement for use by professional researchers and advanced graduate students. Each Handbook provides self-contained surveys of the current state of a branch of economics in the form of chapters prepared by leading specialists on various aspects of this branch of economics. These surveys summarize not only received results but also newer developments, from recent journal articles and discussion papers. Some original material is also included, but the main goal is to provide comprehensive and accessible surveys. The Handbooks are intended to provide not only useful reference volumes for professional collections but also possible supplementary readings for advanced courses for graduate students in economics.

# CONTENTS OF THE HANDBOOK

# PREFACE TO THE HANDBOOK

When the idea for a compendium on economic demography was conceived, we had to persuade ourselves that there was a sufficient body of economics literature on population and the family to support a *Handbook;* that the compendium could be sensibly divided into main areas and well-defined chapter topics; that there was a group of scholars able and willing to take critical stock of each area in a coordinated enterprise; and that there was a reasonable likelihood that those assigned to write chapters would deliver drafts within a finite time. We believe that the resulting product – the *Handbook of Population and Family Economics* – shows that our original affirmative assessments of at least the first three of these ex ante conditions were correct, although we had not anticipated that our comprehension of many demographic events such as mismarriage, miscarriage, and overdue births would also be enriched by this experience. We are indebted to the *Handbook* chapter authors who were waiting (while updating) long and patiently for their fellow authors to complete the write-ups of their drafts. Our pinched nerves notwithstanding, we also thank the late-coming authors for finally heeding our pleas and noncredible threats, so that by the Spring of 1996, completed drafts of all the chapters were in hand.

At the outset it seemed to us that the task of providing a comprehensive reference source divided into survey chapters that summarize frontier areas of research, elucidate new theoretical developments, and review the existing evidence, would be made considerably easier if we could bring together the authors of the *Handbook* chapters at the stage at which detailed chapter outlines were in hand. Such a meeting would acquaint all authors with each other's planned work, assist in filling gaps, help achieve appropriate coverage, identify interconnections, and limit unwarranted duplications. We are indebted to the Ford Foundation and its Reproductive Health and Population Division for providing us, through a grant to Harvard University and the University of Pennsylvania, with financial support for our authors' conference. We believe that the conference was highly conducive to transforming the *Handbook* into a product more valuable than the sum of its parts. We are also grateful to Ann Facciola, Janet Conway, and Claudia Napolilli for competent assistance in coordinating the conference and subsequent author and editor communications. We will know that our efforts and theirs were worthwhile if the *Handbook of Population and Family Economics* contributes to increasing the population of economists involved in research on population and the family, and if the family of social science disciplines more readily adopts the thinking of economists on population and family issues.

MARK R. ROSENZWEIG
ODED STARK

# CONTENTS OF VOLUME 1A

## PART III: MORTALITY AND HEALTH

*Chapter 9*

New Findings on Secular Trends in Nutrition and Mortality: Some Implications for Population Theory

ROBERT WILLIAM FOGEL

# Chapter 1

# INTRODUCTION: POPULATION AND FAMILY ECONOMICS

MARK R. ROSENZWEIG

*University of Pennsylvania*


ODED STARK

*University of Oslo and University of Vienna*

*Handbook of Population and Family Economics. Edited by M.R. Rosenzweig and O. Stark*
*© Elsevier Science B.V., 1997*

The rationale, contents, and organization of the *Handbook of Population and Family Economics* evolve from three premises. First, the family is the main arena in which population outcomes are forged. A review and stock-taking of economists' contributions to the understanding of demographic phenomena thus mandates specific attention to the family – its organization, composition, and constraints, including those associated with technology and incentive structures. Second, there are important interactions and significant causal links across all demographic phenomena. Demographers have constructed models that demonstrate how the size of a population and its growth rate, as well as the age composition of the population, depend on age-specific fertility, mortality, and net migration rates; these three "vital rates" also interact within families and households. A useful way to capture and assess these latter linkages is through the study of household and family behavior. Third, the study of the size, composition, and growth of a population can benefit from the application of economic methodology and tools. To the extent that economics provides useful tools for studying human behavior and linking aggregate phenomena, economics should contribute to the understanding of demographic behavior. Conversely, because of the strong interactions between demographic phenomena and economic variables, economics can be amply enriched by an improved grasp of demographic phenomena. Indeed, economic analyses and economic policy formulation devoid of a sound grasp of population economics may be seriously flawed.

In the last twenty-five years, many economists have focused their attention on the determinants and consequences of demographic processes and outcomes. The availability of *household* data sets, in both low- and high-income countries, played a large role in the birth and growth of the "new" household economics of the 1970s where fertility, contraception, marriage, divorce, the production of health, and mortality captured attention. To some extent, in the 1970s household economic demography was a subfield of that part of labor economics concerned with labor supply and human capital, with its emphasis on household modeling and use of survey data for empirical analysis. However, more recently population issues have become a fundamental component of both microeconomics and macroeconomics. Indeed, it is increasingly recognized that the disregard of family behavior and demographic relationships can lead to a seriously incomplete understanding of economic phenomena, as well as to erroneous forecasts and policy prescriptions. Examples abound, and many are provided in the *Handbook* chapters. To mention just a few: the effects of targeted welfare programs have been shown to depend significantly on relationships across and within households; the efficacy of macro policies has been shown to be conditioned by the

2

extent and character of intergenerational family linkages; the costs of welfare policies supporting children depend on the extent to which fertility and marriage decisions respond to economic incentives; and changes in the aggregate amounts of savings and human capital in an economy, as well as income distribution, are influenced significantly by changes in the age structure, which of course reflect changes in fertility and mortality.

Mainstream economics has been substantially influenced by family and demographic considerations. The study of labor supply and consumer behavior, which used to take household structure as given, has been transformed by attention to the determinants of household formation and consideration of intrahousehold distribution. Theories of the family have provided a more solid basis for applied work on all family and household behavior, just as theories of the firm support empirical studies of firm behavior. An important example is migration, where a better understanding of remittances arose from attention placed on family behavior and in which new insights into migration patterns stemmed from a better understanding of marital behavior. Outside of economic demography, models of economic growth which take population change as exogenous are no longer significantly guiding development policy, the incidence of government programs and taxes are increasingly viewed from the perspective of models that highlight intergenerational family linkages, and welfare analysis which considers the consequences of population growth on natural resources and the environment no longer ignores family decisions about family size.

Finally, a better understanding of the family and households not only provides new and better insights into the outcomes of family decisions that have a major long-run impact on the aggregate behavior of an economy, but also the changing structure of households, the interdependencies of kin-linked households, and the increasing changeability of households have important implications for the design of survey data and the utility of descriptive statistics and estimates pertinent to the economic models that are obtained from them. For example, conventional household-based sampling frames may provide misleading pictures of family behavior at a given point in time if household behavior depends on the circumstances of other households not sampled, as new research on the family suggests. Time-series of household-based income or other measures of wellbeing (for example, median household income) can lead to erroneous inferences about the evolution of the distribution of individual wellbeing over time, particularly if household size and structure is responsive to economic change. To the extent that developments in economic theory depend in part on inferences from data, inattention to population and family economics in data collection efforts can impede the progress of economics generally.

The collection of chapters in the *Handbook* and their organization reflect the most recent developments in economics pertaining to population issues and the family. Reflecting a *Handbook* theme that the family must be an important focus in demographic research, the first section of the *Handbook* begins with four chapters examining the family. Theodore Bergstrom's opening chapter traverses the burgeoning theoretical literature concerned with understanding the rationale for, the formation, structure and dissolution of, and resource allocations within families and households. The chapter shows how the building blocks of modern microeconomics, preferences, and technology can be used to productively study families, employing modern concepts and tools such as public goods, transferable utility, cooperative, noncooperative, and evolutionary game theory, and programming methods. Bergstrom shows how these concepts contribute to an understanding of whether the family can be considered as a single unified decision maker, how resources are allocated among members of a household, the matching of individuals in the marriage market (the assignment problem), how the marriage market influences within-household decisions, the age of marriage of men and women, nonmonogamous household structures, and the strength of the intergenerational linkages among family members. Among the important concepts discussed in this chapter are those that arise because of the close interactions of family members These include the concepts of altruism, envy, paternalism, and interdependence which are given rigorous definitions and whose implications for behavior and for welfare analysis are elucidated.

Yoram Weiss' chapter focuses on family formation and dissolution. The chapter begins with explanations of family formation and marriage, including rationales based on the technology of household production, imperfect intertemporal markets, household public goods, and risk. The chapter then goes on to discuss the question of how a set of individuals in a household can make collective decisions. The roles and contributions of transferable utility, altruism, and cooperative and noncooperative behavior in reaching collective decisions are illuminated and described as are the efficiency and behavioral implications of the different models that emphasize family attributes. The next part of the chapter describes the marriage market, with particular emphasis on the search for marital partners and on how the marriage market influences activities within the families which are the outcomes of the marriage market equilibrium. Weiss discusses how the problem of limited information in the marriage market, that gives rise to search, also contributes to an understanding of the breakup of families. In this context Weiss discusses marital transfers, the limitations on pre-nuptial agreements, post-divorce transfers inclusive of child custody, and the effects of enforcement costs on within-marriage investments and child wellbeing. While the emphasis of the chapter is on theory, Weiss carefully draws out the testable implications of many of the models discussed and points to some of the available evidence pertinent to the models.

The chapter by Jere Behrman focuses on models that describe the allocation of resources among members of households and the empirical evidence on intrahousehold distribution. The chapter begins with descriptions of specific static models of intrahousehold distribution that give rise to a number of implications concerning the role of families in altering the distribution of incomes and wealth across generations. Behrman next discusses the available evidence in terms of how well the studies cope with such common and important empirical problems as the existence of unmeasured endowments of individuals that play a prominent role in models of intrahousehold

distribution, the absence of direct information on individual-specific resource allocations within the household, and imperfect measurement of outcomes. Evidence is reviewed on such issues as whether the allocation of resources across children in a family is sensitive to price differentials, whether parents reinforce or compensate for differences in endowments of ability or health across children, and whether households
are unified and/or allocate resources efficiently. The empirical studies reviewed include those examining behavior in both high- and low-income countries, and many of
the studies employ novel family-based sampling frames including samples of sisters
and identical and nonidentical twins. These studies examine differences in mortality
across male and female children, gender differentials in the allocation of time, the
relationship between work activities, health endowments, and intrahousehold food
distribution, and the role of endowment differentials in allocating schooling within the
family.

The fourth chapter in the section pertaining to the family, by John Laitner, examines the kin-based linkages among adult family members who do not coreside in
households. These linkages are principally manifested in financial transfers across
households as well as transfers of time and services. The first part of the chapter describes overlapping generations models incorporating altruism, which is one assumption that gives rise to intergenerational transfers in the form of both inter vivos transfers and bequests. Alternative models that explain the existence and behavior of interhousehold transfers are also considered, and the differences in the implications of the
models are drawn out. The policy implications of cross-household economic linkages
are described, including the implications for the efficacy of both macroeconomic fiscal policy and targeted public assistance transfers. Laitner also reviews the empirical
evidence on interhousehold family links. These studies are categorized by whether
they examine directly inter vivos interhousehold transfers and bequest behavior, or
whether they draw inferences about such behavior indirectly based on information
describing asset accumulation and consumption patterns. The chapter also considers
models of two-sided altruism, sophisticated general equilibrium models incorporating
(one-way) altruism, and single-sided altruism models incorporating human capital
formation. In the final section of the chapter, Laitner considers the theory of, and evidence on, how households interact when markets fail, or are incomplete, and the roles
of exchange and altruism in such transactions.

The second and third parts of the *Handbook* are concerned with the economics literature that examines fertility, infant mortality and adult mortality, and the interactions between mortality and fertility. The first chapter in the section on fertility, by
Bernard Van Praag and Marcel Warnaar, addresses a topic which has a long history in
economics – how to measure the costs of children. One of the practical reasons for the
attention paid to this issue is that public programs designed to redistribute income seek
to take into account the direct and "welfare" costs imposed by children. As pointed
out by the authors, the approaches taken to quantify the costs of children and the belief that wellbeing is lower, for those with more children among otherwise identical

families, rest on the assumption that fertility is not the outcome of a welfare-maximizing decision process – families are assumed not to choose fertility. The economics of children in this literature is thus quite different from that discussed in the fertility chapters by Joseph Hotz, Jacob Klerman and Robert Willis, and by T. Paul Schultz, as well as in other chapters in this *Handbook,* in which children's contribution to wellbeing and fertility is assumed to be a choice variable. Both sets of literature have in common the fact that they utilize a variety of sophisticated consumer demand models, and the contrast between them illuminates thinking about the role of children in welfare analyses, the evaluation of public programs, and the power of economic reasoning for understanding the family.

After defining terms and concepts, Van Praag and Warnaar first discuss some simple ("naive") methods of calculating child costs that, while without foundation in economic theory, are used in practice. The limitations of these measures, which add up direct and opportunity costs that appear to be reasonably related to children based on descriptive statistics, are made clear by the subsequent discussions that review methods based on consumer demand models. Among the consumer-demand methods discussed and evaluated are those based on the household consumption of "adult" goods, the use of Engel's Law and food consumption, and equivalence scales based on the incorporation of demographic effects in demand systems. The latter are estimated from econometric implementations of demand systems, and these empirical studies are reviewed by the authors. The difficulties in estimating such systems are discussed. In particular, the quality of the cost of children estimates derived from demand system estimates depend on the accuracy of the estimated models, which for reasons of tractability incorporate many auxiliary assumptions (for example, functional forms) not necessarily grounded in evidence or theory. The final section provides a discussion of an alternative approach to comparing the wellbeing of households with different incomes and numbers of children that does not rely on demand system estimation. This approach is based on survey techniques that elicit directly from households' subjective measures of their wellbeing. The relationships between the households' self-evaluations and their incomes and demographic compositions permit, under certain assumptions, measurement of child costs and wellbeing comparisons, again under the assumption that children do not themselves provide utility, and family size is not determined jointly with other consumption goods.

The second *Handbook* chapter in the fertility section, by Hotz, Klerman, and Willis, focusses on the contributions of microeconomic theory to the understanding of the determinants of various aspects of fertility, including family size, in developed countries. The chapter begins with an overview of major fertility trends and other prominent characteristics of fertility behavior in developed countries that have motivated many economic analyses of fertility. Among the salient stylized facts of developed countries over the last fifty years, upon which many fertility analyses have focused, are the long-term decline in birth rates, the availability of new contraceptive devices (the "contraceptive revolution"), the post-World War II temporary increase in birth rates (the "baby boom"), increases in teenage childbearing, and rising out-of-wedlock births. Following the descriptive section there is a review of static models of fertility behavior, beginning with an analysis of how standard price theory concepts can potentially illuminate a number of important dimensions of fertility behavior, including the effects of contraceptive costs, taxes, child care availability, and subsidized abortion. Examples are also described that provide cautions about how the prices that affect fertility can be measured and their effects identified. A major question addressed in this section, relating to the descriptive evidence from the first part of the chapter, is how the negative time-series and cross-sectional empirical relationship between income and fertility can be explained without resorting to the assumption that children are inferior goods. This discussion encompasses analyses of the roles of the "quality" of children, the cost of women's time, an assessment of the evidence, and econometric difficulties pertinent to the identification of these aspects of fertility behavior. The section on static models concludes with a review of studies focusing on the relationship between fertility and marriage. This subsection addresses the questions of how the welfare state impinges on both marriage and fertility decisions, and how the role of welfare benefits affects nonmarital fertility. The next section of the chapter discusses dynamic models of fertility that seek to explain the timing and spacing of births as well as completed family size. Among the models discussed are those that incorporate different assumptions about capital markets, uncertainty with respect to fertility and contraception, fecundity constraints, human capital investments, income uncertainty, and fluctuations in aggregate labor demand. New work relating fertility behavior to the riskiness of marriage and marriage disruption concludes the chapter.

Schultz's chapter reviews the literature on the microeconomics of fertility emphasizing its relevance for understanding fertility behavior and population growth in low-income countries and the effects of economic development on population growth. Schultz's chapter begins with a presentation of descriptive statistics on the relationships across low-income countries among fertility, the level of economic development, and family planning efforts. This section is followed by a review of microeconomic fertility models. While a number of fertility behavior aspects are similar across low-income and industrialized countries, including the distinct effects of variations in male and female wages and the importance of changes in the costs and returns to schooling, there are distinguishing features of low-income economies that also have implications for fertility behavior in those environments. Among these are the positive and significant contributions of children to family income, particularly in agricultural settings; biases in parental sex preferences; the prominent role of family planning programs; imperfect and absent markets; and relatively high risks of infant death. Schultz's review focuses on both the theoretical and empirical literature that shed light on the fertility consequences of these attributes of low-income countries. As a way of summarizing and assessing the findings from the microeconomic studies, Schultz's chapter concludes with an empirical analysis, making use of the microeconomic perspective, applied to aggregate data describing low-income countries. The purpose is to identify the principal determinants of fertility change and variation. Consideration is given to characterizing in a theoretically appropriate way the exogenous constraints influencing families using such data, with particular attention to the endogeneity of both child mortality and family planning resource allocations. A provocative result of this exercise is that while variations in the level and sex composition of schooling, the decline of the importance of agriculture, and reductions in mortality associated with economic development explain a substantial part of cross-country fertility differentials and changes in fertility over time within countries, there is little evidence of the influence of family planning programs.

The section of the *Handbook* examining mortality and health begins with a historical overview by Robert Fogel who makes use of the latest evidence and methods from the economics, biomedical, and demography literature to elucidate the relationships among economic growth, medical advances, and life expectancy. In this chapter both the historical evidence on the relationship between economic variables and mortality, and the evolution of thought about this relationship are reviewed. The principal aim of the chapter is to explain the marked secular decline in mortality experienced by the Western World after 1750 and more recently, in newly industrialized countries. The chapter reviews the evidence on the relationship between anthropomorphic measures – height and body mass – and morbidity and mortality. Based on energy cost accounting, it is shown that variations in body size are an equilibrating factor when there are changes in the productivity of food production. It is shown that because the availability of food (calories) affects the ability of individuals to expend energy, it substantially affects labor productivity for a given body mass. Therefore, the relationship between economic growth, morbidity, and mortality is complex – increases in agricultural productivity enhance labor productivity and also lower mortality. Fogel also considers the evidence on the relationship between nutritional intake at young ages and the subsequent health and mortality of adults. This relationship not only has important implications for the targeting of nutritional and health policies but also impacts the future increases in life expectancy in countries that have recently experienced improvements in health and nutrition.

Kenneth Wolpin's chapter focuses on infant mortality using a microeconomic perspective. The first half of the chapter is concerned with the relationship at the household level between infant mortality and fertility. This relationship has long been of concern to demographers because the secular decline in Europe's mortality ("the demographic transition"), discussed in detail in Fogel's chapter, was accompanied by a dramatic fall in fertility rates, as Wolpin shows in the introduction to his chapter. Understanding to what extent the mortality decline influenced fertility is of major relevance for today's developing economies. Wolpin reviews static and more recent dynamic models of family decision-making that elucidate the distinct ways in which infant deaths and changes in the risk of infant deaths affect fertility. In the light of those models, Wolpin then reviews the empirical methods that have been used by both economists and demographers to estimate how infant mortality affects family size.

Estimation problems associated with unobserved heterogeneity in mortality risk and biological feedback mechanisms of fertility and infant mortality are discussed. The second part of Wolpin's chapter is concerned with understanding the causes of observed variations in infant mortality based on the biomedical, demographic, and economics literature assessed from the perspective of economics. Particular attention is paid to distinguishing empirically the consequences for infant health and mortality of a variety of parental behaviors, changes in constraints, and variation in unmeasured biological factors. Among the behaviors that potentially affect infant health that are discussed in detail are breast-feeding, prenatal care, and maternal age. This discussion includes a review of the literature on teenage childbearing and the different econometric methods applied to family-based data – cousins and siblings – that have been used to identify how maternal age and other behaviors affect birth outcomes.

Robin Sickles and Paul Taubman review in their chapter the literature on the determinants of morbidity and mortality among adults in developed countries, with particular focus on the elderly. As discussed in the chapter by David Weil, changes in adult life expectancy can have important consequences for aggregate savings, capital investments, and the sustainability of pay-as-you-go intergenerational transfer schemes such as social security. The chapter begins with an overview of trends in, and cross-sectional country comparisons of, life expectancy and mortality in the twentieth century. Associations among mortality and aggregate income per capita, sex, ethnicity, and health care systems are described. Sickles and Taubman then review the structural microeconomic models that economists have used to characterize the determination of adult health status. In the theoretical sections of the chapter, the alternative ways in which adult mortality is endogenized in a choice-theoretic framework are discussed. The basic structure of these models is used to assess the empirical studies of the relationships between adult health and schooling level, occupation, marital status and such "lifestyle" variables as smoking, exercise, and alcohol consumption. Considerable space is devoted to assessing the adequacy of data sources on adult health and mortality. The problem of measuring health or "quality of life" is considered and particular attention is paid to the use and validity of subjective measures of health that are found in survey-based data. In the final section of the chapter, Sickles and Taubman review the literature on the statistical modeling of mortality.

The coverage of migration in the *Handbook* is divided into four chapters. This reflects closely the broad topics which have occupied migration research: migration in developed economies, migration in developing economies, the labor market performance and impact of migrants, and international migration. The dividing lines between research on migration in developed and developing economies arise largely from the underlying process of which migration is considered a co-variate: in developing economies, migration, especially rural-to-urban migration, has been viewed as an integral part of the development process and hence has been studied as being *specific* to that process. In developed economies, however, where sectoral adjustment and redistribution have largely run their course, the main emphasis in migration research has been on the causes and consequences of the mobility of workers between highly developed *labor* markets.

Michael Greenwood's chapter on migration in developed countries emphasizes the impact of local unemployment on the migration decisions of both the unemployed and new job seekers, an impact that is significant in some developed economies, notably the United States, but not in others, notably much of Europe. Recent micro and longitudinal data have been particularly useful in highlighting this relationship. Greenwood also discusses what we have learned about the *speed* at which the unemployed react through migration. Here the link with family characteristics such as marital status and, if married, the employment status of the spouse (for example, a wife's employment discourages migration) is of much relevance, as is the institutional setting, for example, the prevalence of unemployment insurance. Thus, in low-income economies, where formal or governmental support arrangements are not in place, the links between migrants and their families are much more prevalent as is reflected, for example, by family co-insurance arrangements and remittance flows – themes taken up in Robert Lucas' chapter. Greenwood intimates that recent data also facilitate careful testing of simple versions of the human capital model through estimation of earning equations; these tests typically reveal that this simple model does not provide a powerful explanation of migration, especially because of apparent earning losses, spanning over several years, consequent upon migration. Greenwood points to the need to incorporate additional nonconventional variables such as location-specific amenities, tax structures, and leisure in analyses of migration. The subject of return migration, an area of research in need of considerable more work, is briefly addressed by Greenwood. He argues that those who are unemployed prior to migration are more likely to return than those who are employed. Greenwood's chapter also illustrates well the interaction between the timing of migration and the occurrence of demographic events, discussed in considerable detail in other chapters of the *Handbook,* such as the birth and aging of children, changes in marital status, and retirement. However, Greenwood laments the relative paucity of evidence on the fertility consequences of migration. While welcoming the surge in the availability of micro and longitudinal data over the last two decades or so and the ensuing micro research, Greenwood urges a more balanced approach comprised of close attention to macro data such as characteristics of the communities in which people live and to which they consider migrating.

In his chapter on migration in developing countries, the two main themes taken up by Robert Lucas are (i) the causes of migration, where close attention is paid to family strategies, information, financing, and the contextual setting, as well as to the conventional variables of earning opportunities and job search, and (ii) the economic consequences of migration for rural, especially agricultural, production, for national output, and for inequality in the distribution of income by size. Lucas provides a detailed account of the migration process that has attracted most of the attention in this context: rural-to-urban migration. Among the main findings highlighted are that wage differentials are not the only factor influencing rural-to-urban migration and that the family plays a particularly important role in explaining migration by individuals. He shows that these two findings can be principally explained by the absence of markets and institutions, the existence of which is taken for granted in developed countries. Indeed, Lucas intimates that in developing countries migration appears to enable families to straddle two sectors of the economy rather than substitute one sector for another. Lucas weaves together the insights gained from the study of the causes and consequences of internal migration in low-income countries to summarize policy implications. In particular, he concludes that the apparent preoccupation with policy measures to reduce rural-to-urban migration may be largely misplaced because there are good reasons to believe, as can be discerned from his review of both the determinants and the repercussions of migration, that rural-to-urban migration is socially beneficial.

In countries receiving large numbers of migrants, such as the United States, Canada, and Australia, the impact of migration on the labor market, the extent to which migrants assimilate in the labor market, and the burden migrants place on the social welfare system are of much concern. Robert LaLonde and Robert Topel review and synthesize the large literature that addresses these three issues. Their main broad findings are remarkably straightforward. First, migrants have a modest impact on the receiving country's labor market. The resulting change in the factor distribution of income is not large, the wage depressing effect is largely confined to other migrants, and the effect on the employment and earnings of native workers is small. This latter effect is due partly, and quite interestingly, to the fact that native workers themselves migrate internally in response to adverse labor market conditions. This migration by natives thus dissipates the local impact of the initial in-migration and spreads it across the receiving economy. Second, there is significant assimilation of migrants in some countries (United States), somewhat less in others (Australia, Canada). In the United States it appears that within a generation or less, migrants' earnings approach those of comparably skilled and ethnically similar natives. The key underlying process is acquisition of country-specific skills. Interestingly, the extent of the assimilation – the returns to time spent in the host country – is inversely related to the skill similarity with the natives upon arrival. Third, the use by migrants of the social welfare system is subject to two competing processes: need and familiarity. The puzzling finding that the use of public transfer payments by migrants rises with time – as do their earnings – is explained by the fact that on average migrants' knowledge of entitlements and rights increases with residence in the home country faster than their overall eligibility for public support declines. LaLonde and Topel also show that to properly conduct a burden–contribution analysis of immigration, it is necessary to co-calculate the benefits that natives receive from migrants' tax payments and the cost of migrants' claims on the social welfare system. Their conclusion is that, at least in the United States, migrants confer modest net benefits upon the natives.

The four-chapter section on migration concludes with the contribution of Assaf Razin and Efraim Sadka who study the relationship between international trade and migration, a topic the importance of which appears to be inversely related to the attention it has received. Razin and Sadka begin with a natural premise: just like any trade activities in well-functioning markets, migration is beneficial to all parties involved. Yet markets usually do not function well, and migration is the movement of an unusual composite "commodity": labor, skills, consumption preferences. Razin and Sadka investigate the conditions under which trade in goods between countries can narrow the inter-country wage gap thereby reducing the incentive to migrate. They show that when commodity trade and labor mobility are perfect substitutes, factor prices including wage rates are equalized. However, when trade in goods is insufficient to equalize factor prices, trade in commodities may even widen the wage gap. They also show that the simple analogy between skilled labor and capital breaks down when it is recognized that capital embodied in workers – human capital – has unique external effects in that it raises the productivity of other workers – as well as that of capital. Hence migration by skilled workers can exacerbate inter-country wage differentials and induce further migration.

Razin and Sadka also confront the difficult issue of determining the efficient volume of migration. In particular, they discuss the considerations that impinge on the calculation of optimal migration flows and the factors that confer advantage and disadvantages to size. (There is a separate discussion of optimal population size elsewhere in the *Handbook*, notably in the last chapter.) Razin and Sadka also provide a set of conditions that identify clearly which economic groups gain from migration and which ones lose. Indeed, they show that such losses, which can arise either from distortions brought about by wage rigidity or from the generosity and nonexcluding nature of the typical income redistribution systems in the destination economy, could explain an economic-based resistance to migration in many developed economies. The novel nature of much of this chapter invites considerable empirical work. Future work, both empirical and theoretical, would also lie at the very frontier of migration research if it were to study closely skill formation in the countries of origin as a consequence of international migration possibilities, return migration, migration dynamics, and international remittances.

Three chapters in the *Handbook* discuss aging – of individuals and of populations. These chapters appear after the chapters that examine fertility behavior, not only because birth must precede aging for an individual, but also because an aggregate population that has experienced a change in fertility will subsequently experience a faster or slower rate of aging. Many countries of the world have experienced fertility declines in recent decades, and in some countries the declines are dramatic. These countries are already experiencing the consequences of population aging. To the extent that anti-natalist policies in low-income countries and successful economic development policies bring down fertility in such countries, the world at large will be experiencing population aging for the foreseeable future. It is important therefore to understand both how aging affects behavior and the behavior of the aged as their numbers increase in relative terms; and to understand the aggregate consequences of an aging population, including effects on the distribution of income.

Michael Hurd studies three key issues pertaining to individual aging: the optimal timing of retirement, the optimal level of consumption when retired, and the economic wellbeing of the elderly. The decisions when to retire and how much to save for retirement are of great significance to an economy at large as they impinge on the size and structure of the labor force, and on the fraction of the population to which transfers, both private and public, need to be made. The literature on individual aging in developed economies, notably the United States, reveals that an increasing proportion of life is spent in retirement, and that the timing of retirement does not reflect a gradually changing taste for leisure. Hurd discusses several factors that impinge on the timing of retirement and on the incentives to retire, in particular social security provisions, private pensions, and personal wealth holdings (resources acquired during working life). Quite surprisingly, social security appears to have a small effect. While consumption in old age is associated with dissaving, it, and wellbeing in general, depend significantly on transfers to and from children, a subject taken up in considerable detail by Laitner in Chapter 5. Indeed, it is possible that parents who transfer resources to their children end up consuming more than nonparents largely because grateful children act as providers of insurance "against" very long life and against very weak health. Whether the marked improvement in the economic status of the elderly in the last two and half decades in countries such as the United States is also due to greater support from children who received, or expect to receive, more from their parents is an open research question. What is clear though is that the poverty rate among the elderly has strongly and negatively been affected by the prevalence and structure of social security and private pensions, and that it can be expected to continue to decline. Hurd lists several interesting topics for future research including the demand for aged workers. A somewhat surprising fact is that while in some sense a worker at the age of 65, when life expectancy is 80, is as "young" as a worker at the age of 55, when life expectancy is 68, employers usually treat the 65-year-old as an old worker, but not so the 55-year-old.

David Weil in his chapter assesses the aggregate consequences for economies whose age structure changes in favor of the old. He shows that it is important to differentiate between aging arising from a decline in fertility and aging which is due to a fall in mortality, not only because the dynamics of changes in dependency ratios differs, but also because only a decline in mortality affects the fraction of an individual's life spent in each age group. Aging affects the ratio of the working-age population to the "dependent" population (children and elderly) and thereby influences production and consumption in the economy as a whole. There are other effects as well. For example, if aging which arises from reduced mortality (a lower probability of dying at any give age) and a reduction in life-ending diseases is also associated with a reduction in disabling diseases, the health of people at each age, including working age, improves and the productivity of the working population rises. However, Weil is unable to marshal strong evidence in support of this nexus.

Although population aging is largely viewed as a costly phenomenon, it is often coupled, as in recent US history, with per capita output growth; to an extent yet to be determined, the latter is not causally independent of the former. Weil stresses the increasing role of government as a channel of transfers to the elderly which he contrasts with the role of the family as the source of support for children. Fertility reduction that increases population aging has important effects on these support "assignments": although the decline in fertility eases the burden on families whose age is sufficiently young so that they are not providing transfers to elders, the burden on governments is increased because when it comes to supporting the elderly, the age of providing is substantially younger than the age of receiving. The difference in the source of population aging also impacts on the political economy of government behavior. Aging due to a reduction in mortality enlarges the constituency supporting government aid (social security benefits) to the elderly more than aging which is due to a reduction in fertility.

Changes in the age distribution of an economy, whatever its vital rate source, affect not only the aggregate performance of the economy but also the distribution of resources across individuals, families, and households. Since not only do family constraints and opportunities change over the life-cycle but also earnings, a change in the population age structure can significantly affect measures of aggregate income inequality and inferences about changes in economic wellbeing. David Lam's chapter considers the relationships between all demographic variables and income inequality with particular attention to the effects of age-composition on income inequality. He shows that the analytics of stable population theory provides a number of insights for understanding how aging affects the distribution of income through compositional changes that influence within-group and between-group income inequality. In most cases these effects counteract so that the net effect of population aging on inequality is an empirical matter. Lam then reviews evidence from both low- and high-income countries which shows conflicting results on the inequality effects of population aging, results that are not inconsistent with the analytics of the theory. Lam also considers the more complex question of how the composition of households affects inequality comparisons across time and space. He shows that measures of income inequality are sensitive to changes in both marital sorting and within household labor supply decisions. This underscores once again the importance of studying the family. Lam also discusses how fertility differentials by income affect measures of the intergenerational "transmission" of inequality and reviews evidence on the effects of population growth on inequality. Lam concludes that the inequality literature is not sufficiently sensitive to the fact that population growth is itself endogenously related to moments of the income distribution; identification of population effects requires better models integrating endogenous population into growth models.

As suggested in the chapters by Lam and Weil, a great deal of the evidence on the aggregate effects of population change is weakened by the lack of an adequate, or in many cases, any theoretical foundation. The last section of the *Handbook* examines questions about the dynamic behavior of economies based on models that link fertility decisions and mortality outcomes with the dynamics of aggregate population and economic movements, both in the short and long run. The section begins with a chapter by Ronald Lee who reviews models of population equilibrium to explore how short-term demographic and economic shocks affect demographic behavior, aggregate economic activity, and population size. He presents classical models of demographic-economic equilibrium in order to examine the short-term dynamics of population growth and aggregate economic activity, and examines the historical evidence on these relationships based on measures of population size, prices, and wage rates from time-series data. Lee reviews the econometric problems pertaining to such data and the sensitivity of results to assumptions about the properties of the data as well as the models underlying the specifications. Lee tentatively concludes that in preindustrial Europe, swings in population growth played an important role in the movements of the aggregate economy and conformed somewhat to classical models of population equilibrium. Lee also considers evidence on demographic responses to economic shocks such as famines and epidemics. He concludes that the evidence indicates similar reactions in both pre-industrial European societies and in contemporary low-income countries, with fertility always falling in response to economic crises. Lee speculates that the reason such relationships are far less clear-cut for high-income societies is the heightened role of the state in providing social insurance. Lee also considers population oscillations brought about by generational cycles that result from the age-compositional effects of fluctuations in fertility, such as those associated with the post World War II baby boom, and the consequences of these for fluctuations in the aggregate economy due to age-compositional effects of consumption, savings, and labor supply.

Marc Nerlove and Lakshmi Raut tackle in their chapter the difficult question of why in some contexts and not in others, as income grows both fertility and mortality fall, and per capita human capital and physical capital increase. The dynamics of these interactions are complicated to model, and in general, there are multiple equilibria with not much in hand to distinguish which is more likely to be obtained. Furthermore, the role of initial conditions is not all that clear. (These very same problems are encountered in the subsequent chapter by James Robinson and T.N. Srinivasan, which focuses on the role of resource constraints and environmental impacts.) The modeling difficulties are compounded by the fact that fertility decisions and decisions pertaining to how much to invest in children are made within the family, while the resulting human and physical capital stocks are economy-wide state variables. To make their chapter self-contained Nerlove and Raut find it necessary to review in considerable detail the value parents attach to the number of children (fertility) and to the quality of children (human capital), topics largely covered in the chapter by Hotz, Klerman, and

Willis, and also in the chapter by Behrman. Nerlove and Raut emphasize these family decisions because they seek to unravel the interactions between, and the causal paths that link, fertility and human capital formation, on the one hand, and short- and long-run income growth in the economy at large, on the other hand. Nerlove and Raut view the family as the main sphere where human capital is produced, and they believe that it is investment in nutrition, health, skills, and knowledge that leads first to a surge in economic and population growth, and subsequently to a decline in population growth upon a substitution of further human capital investments for the number of children. For this substitution to occur, though, the existence of opportunities and the absence of obstacles to additional investments in human capital are crucial. In the light of these considerations Nerlove and Raut discuss only briefly the literature on economic growth in which population is endogenous in the sense that its rate of change over time depends mechanically on real wages or on per capita consumption (without explicit consideration of fertility choices by optimizing parents). Nerlove and Raut turn most of their reviewing energy to theories and models of parents' choices that determine the human capital and the financial and physical endowments of their children. The discussion enables Nerlove and Raut to connect familial allocations with variables that determine the evolution of the economy over time. The loop is nicely closed as the human and physical capital formed within families is transformed through production technologies and distribution and tax policies into per family income and rates of return to various familial investments, these being key variables (along, of course, with rates of child and infant mortality) to which families respond in making their allocative decisions.

The last chapter of the *Handbook* is the longest and was perhaps the most difficult to produce. Modeling the joint endogeneity of population and technical change in the presence of natural and environmental resources (both exhaustible and renewable) is extremely complicated. Although the proper framework for studying population growth, technological change, resource use, and the environment must obviously be dynamic, there is considerable uncertainty about the nature of the dynamics due, among other considerations, to nonlinearities, threshold effects, and irreversibilities. Robinson and Srinivasan track the evolution of thinking about the relationship between the finiteness of natural resources and the bounds they place, or need not place, on per capita income. They show how general concerns about the implications of population and income growth for the global environment replaced a confidence that with proper production technologies and technical change, societies could substitute man-made for natural capital to allow sustained growth in living standards. They also point out that the interaction between the environment and population growth that developing economies face differs in kind rather than in degree from the interactions which pertain to developed economies. In the former, the solution to many key environmental problems lies in economic development. Improving the environment, influencing population growth (initiating and speeding up the demographic transition), and promoting economic development are *complementary*. Not so in developed economies. Moreover, and this is both a recurrent theme throughout the chapter and a key conclusion of the chapter, in the case of developing economies a fundamental cause of underdevelopment is dysfunctional social and political institutions (in particular, ownership structures and property rights) and highly imperfect capital markets (which, coupled with low life expectancy and poverty, lead to strong impatience and heavy discounting of the future). In short, in economies where markets are complete and competitive, efficient equilibrium allocations have been reached and therefore per capita consumption of physical commodities, aggregate population, and environmental resources need to be traded off. In economies with incomplete markets and inadequate institutions, no trade-offs need to be encountered until gross inefficiencies are eliminated. An additional main theme of the chapter, which links it with the opening chapters of the *Handbook*, is that an understanding of both population growth and natural resource use needs to start with an analysis of the motivation of families and households, the nature of inter-family links, and the forces that shape and govern intergenerational and dynastic preferences.

The diversity and depth of the work reviewed and presented in the *Handbook* conveys both the progress that has been made by economists in understanding the forces shaping population processes, including the behavior of families, and the many questions, empirical and theoretical, that still remain. One intriguing set of questions pertains to the dynamic interaction between families and the population of which they are constituent parts: when and how do familial characteristics and preferences convert into population traits and norms? For example, does altruism within the family confer an evolutionary advantage such that the entire population consists of altruists? Another set of questions pertains to the demographic response of families to their economic environment and to the impact of this environment on family demography: how sensitive is family behavior, organization, and structure to changes in prices and incomes? To what extent do family relationships reflect and affect the consequences of public policies? Relatedly, to what extent does the behavior both of families and of the aggregate population reflect a biological legacy and biological constraints? As new forms of data emerge, shaped in part by new theories, and as economists continue to incorporate ideas and concepts from other fields as well as develop their own economic approaches, it is likely that population and family economics will continue its progress and remain a lively field within economics, and beyond.

# PART I

# THE FAMILY

*Chapter 2*

# A SURVEY OF THEORIES OF THE FAMILY

THEODORE C. BERGSTROM*

*University of Michigan*

## Contents

*Thanks to Maria Cancian, Matz Dahlberg, John Laitner, David Lam, Robert Pollak, Robert Schoeni, Oded Stark, Yoram Weiss, and Robert Willis for welcome encouragement and useful advice.

*Handbook of Population and Family Economics. Edited by M.R. Rosenzweig and O. Stark*
*© Elsevier Science B.V., 1997*

# 1. Introduction

To a labor economist or an industrial organization economist, a family looks like "a little factory". To a bargaining theorist, a husband and wife are "two agents in a relation of bilateral monopoly". To an urban economist or a public choice theorist, a family looks like "a little city", or perhaps "a little club". To a welfare economist, a family is an association of benevolently interrelated individuals. Each of these analogies suggests useful ways in which the standard tools of neoclassical economics can aid in understanding the workings of a family. The second section of this review draws on the analogies to a little factory and to a little city. It explores the theory of household technology and the household utility possibility frontier. The third section concerns decision theory within the household. This discussion applies standard consumer decision theory as well as bargaining theory and the theory of public choice. The fourth section of this paper deals with family formation and the choice of mates. This theory is analogous to "Tiebout theory" in urban economics, where the objects of choice include not only the public goods supplied in each city, but which individuals live together. An aspect of family life that has fewer parallels in the economics of market economies is intrafamilial love and altruism. The final section of this paper reviews a growing theoretical literature on love, altruism and the family.

## 2. Household technology and utility possibility frontiers

### 2.1. Household production functions

In his *Treatise on the Family*, Becker (1981) emphasizes the importance of division of labor and gains from specialization. Drawing on his 1965 paper, "A Theory of the Allocation of Time", Becker endows households with *household production functions* which describe the possibilities for producing "household commodities". Becker's household commodities are nonmarket goods that are the outputs of production processes that use market goods and the labor time of household members as inputs. His examples of household commodities include "children, prestige and envy, health, and pleasures of the senses". He suggests that the number of household commodities is typically much smaller than the number of market goods.

The concept of production function, borrowed from the theory of the firm, has been a fruitful source of insight into the workings of families. Becker exploits this analogy as he examines such issues as specialization within the household, comparative advantage, returns to scale, factor substitution, human capital and assortative mating. Each individual in Becker's household can use time either for household labor or market labor. The family can purchase *market goods* and either consume them directly or use them as inputs into household production.

Pollak and Wachter (1975) develop the formal structure of Becker's household production model and show that if household commodities are produced with constant returns to scale and no joint production, then "shadow prices" for these commodities are determined by the prices of market goods and the wage rates for market labor – independently of the quantities demanded. This means that the household's production possibility set, like an ordinary competitive budget set, has a linear boundary with marginal rates of transformation that are independent of the quantities chosen.[1] If production possibility sets have this property, then the household production model allows a neat separation of production and consumption activities. Pollak and Wachter observe that with joint production or with nonconstant returns to scale, this separation of production and consumption is lost since the shadow prices of commodities depends on the quantities produced and the boundary of the production possibility set is "curved". Pollak and Wachter argue that unless the production of "household commodities" permits separation of production and consumption activities, there is little to be gained from adding unobservable household commodities to the model. Instead they recommend studying the demand for market goods and leisure directly as functions of wages and the prices of market goods. Pollak and Wachter also maintain that tastes and technology are likely to be confounded by treating nonmeasurable aggregate variables such as "child quality" as commodities. They recommend more narrowly defined child-related commodities such as "scores on standardized tests" or "number of dental cavities".

As Pollak and Wachter point out, even with very general technologies, there will be well-defined demand functions for market goods and supply functions of labor which could in principle be determined from household utility. Rader (1964) establishes general conditions under which "induced preferences" for trades inherit such properties as convexity, continuity and homogeneity from the production functions and the preferences for produced commodities. Muth (1966) shows that even if the output of a household commodity is not directly observable, the assumption that this commodity is produced with constant returns to scale can have interesting testable implications. If, for example, two or more market goods are used as inputs for this good and no other goods, then it must be that the income elasticities of demand for the two goods will be identical. A detailed discussion of the theory of household production and additional references can be found in Deaton and Muellbauer (1980).

## 2.2. Household public goods

A unit of private goods consumed by one person cannot be consumed by another. But some goods, such as living space, household heating and lighting and shared auto-

---

[1] This result is essentially the generalized Samuelson non-substitution theorem for the "small-country case" where factors can be purchased at constant prices (see Samuelson, 1961; Varian, 1984).

mobile trips are jointly consumed and are best modeled as local public goods which enter simultaneously into the utility functions of all family members.

While Becker (1981) did not explicitly distinguish *household public goods* from private goods, his household technology model could certainly be used to describe production of household public goods as well as ordinary private goods. Manser and Brown (1980) and McElroy and Horney (1981) were among the first to introduce household public goods as an integral part of their models of family behavior. These authors emphasize the benefits of shared public goods as a reason that marriage yields a utility surplus over living separately. Weiss and Willis (1985), in their economic study of divorce and child-support payments, treat the well-being of children as a household public good that enters the utility of both parents whether these parents are married or divorced. Lam (1988) suggests that the presence of household public goods will favor positive assortative mating by income.

Household public goods are modeled as follows. Consider a household with $h$ members. Each household member $i$ has a utility function $U_i(x_i, y)$ where $x_i$ is the vector of private goods consumed by $i$ and where $y$ is the vector of household public goods. A *household allocation* is a vector $(x_1, \ldots, x_h, y)$ that specifies the consumption of private goods by each household member and the vector of household public goods. The household budget and household technology determine a *household production possibility set S* which specifies all possible aggregate consumptions of public and private goods for the household. A *feasible allocation* for the household is an allocation $(x_1, \ldots, x_h, y)$ such that $(x, y) \in S$, where $x = \sum_{i=1}^{h} x_i$.

## 2.3. The household utility possibility frontier

The *utility possibility frontier* is an analytic tool that illuminates many issues in the theory of the family.[2] Consider a household with $h$ members and a household production possibility set $S$. To each feasible allocation $(x_1, \ldots, x_h, y)$, corresponds a distribution of utilities among household members in which person $i$ gets utility $U_i(x_i, y)$. The set of all utility distributions that can be constructed in this way is called the utility possibility set. The "upper" boundary of the utility possibility set is known as the utility possibility frontier. By construction, the utility possibility frontier consists of all utility distributions that are Pareto optimal for the household.

For any fixed vector $y$ of public goods, it is possible to construct a conditional utility possibility set $UP(y)$, such that $UP(y)$ corresponds to all of the distributions of utility that can be achieved by some feasible allocation in which the vector of public goods is $y$. The *conditional utility possibility frontier* corresponding to $y$ is the upper

---

[2] The utility possibility frontier seems to have been introduced to the economic literature by Samuelson (1950), who presents this idea in a section of his paper titled *The Crucially Important Utility Possibility Function*.

boundary of $UP(y)$. In general, the conditional utility possibility frontiers corresponding to different public goods vectors may cross each other. The utility possibility frontier for the household will be the outer envelope of the conditional utility possibility frontiers corresponding to all feasible choices of $y$.

### 2.3.1. Examples of utility possibility frontiers for households with public goods

*Example 1.* A household has two members. There is one private good and one household public good. Total household income is $3. The quantity of the household public good must be either zero or one unit. The price of the private good is $1 per unit and the cost of a unit of the public good is $2. Person 1 has utility function $U_1(X_1, Y) = X_1(Y + 1)$ and Person 2 has utility function $U_2(X_2, Y) = X_2(Y + 1)^2$.

If $Y = 0$, then $U_1 = X_1$ and $U_2 = X_2$. Since in this case, the household budget constraint is $X_1 + X_2 = 3$, the conditional utility possibility set $UP(0)$ is the set $\{(U_1, U_2) \mid U_1 + U_2 \leq 3\}$. In Fig. 1, $UP(0)$ is bounded by the line $CD$.

If $Y = 1$, then $U_1 = 2X_1$ and $U_2 = 4X_2$. Since the cost of one unit of the public good is $2, the household budget constraint is now $X_1 + X_2 = 3 - 2 = 1$, the utility possibility set $UP(1)$ is the set $\{(U_1, U_2) \mid \frac{1}{2}U_1 + \frac{1}{4}U_2 \leq 1\}$. This is the set bounded by the line $AB$ in Fig. 1.

The utility possibility set for the household is the union of the sets $UP(0)$ and $UP(1)$, and the household utility possibility frontier is the thick broken line running from $A$ to $E$ to $D$. Notice that in this example, some Pareto optimal allocations for the household are achieved by supplying no household public goods and others are achieved by supplying one unit of household public goods.

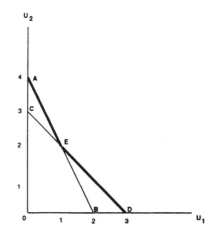

Fig. 1.

*Example 2.* A household has two members. There is one private good and one household public good. Total income available to the household is \$10. The price of private goods is \$1 per unit and the price of public goods is \$1 per unit. The household can choose any allocation $(X_1, X_2, Y) \geq 0$ such that $X_1 + X_2 + Y \leq 10$. Person 1 has the utility function $U_1(X_1, Y) = X_1 + Y^{1/2}$ and Person 2 has the utility function $U_2(X_2, Y) = X_2 + 3Y^{1/2}$.

An allocation in which both consumers consume positive amounts of the private good will be Pareto optimal if and only if the sum of their marginal rates of substitution between public and private goods equals the price ratio of public to private goods. (This is sometimes known as the Samuelson condition, in honor of Samuelson's (1954) construction of the theory of public goods.) This condition implies that $\frac{1}{2} Y^{-1/2} + \frac{3}{2} Y^{-1/2} = 1$ or equivalently that $Y = 4$. Therefore the set of Pareto optimal allocations in which both household members have positive consumption of private goods consists of all allocations $(X_1, X_2, 4) > 0$ such that $X_1 + X_2 = 10 - 4 = 6$. When $Y = 4$, it must be that $U_1 = X_1 + 2$ and $U_2 = X_2 + 6$. Therefore along the part of the utility possibility frontier corresponding to allocations where both consume positive amounts of private good, it must be that $U_1 + U_2 = X_1 + X_2 + 8$. Since for these allocations, $X_1 + X_2 = 6$, it follows that this part of the utility possibility frontier lies on the line $U_1 + U_2 = 14$. If both consumers are consuming positive amounts of the public good, then it is also true that $U_1 > 2$ and $U_2 > 6$. Therefore the part of the utility possibility frontier corresponding to positive consumption of private goods for both household members is the line segment *BC* in Fig. 2. There are other Pareto allocations where only one of the consumers consumes positive amounts of private goods. These allocations correspond to the curved lines *AB* and *CD* in Fig. 2. At these points, the Samuelson conditions do not apply and the amount of public good supplied is less

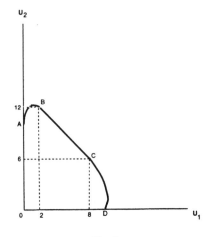

Fig. 2.

than four units. This part of the story is explained in detail by Bergstrom and Cornes (1983) and by Campbell and Truchon (1988).

In Example 2, all Pareto optima such that both consumers have positive consumption of private goods must have the same output of public good. Moreover, for all such allocations, the utility possibility frontier is a straight line. Every Pareto optimal household allocation has the property that $(X_1, X_2, Y)$ could be found by maximizing the sum of utilities, $U_1(X_1, Y) + U_2(X_2, Y)$, subject to the household feasibility constraint $X_1 + X_2 + Y = 10$.

## 2.4. Transferable utility in the household

The term *transferable utility* seems to have originated in game theory, but the idea that it represents is familiar to all economists. Roughly speaking, transferable utility means that utility can be "redistributed", like apples or bananas. If one distribution of utility is possible then so is any other distribution of utilities where individual utilities sum to the same number. The assumption of transferable utility has powerful and interesting implications in the theory of the household. Therefore it is worthwhile investigating this assumption carefully.[3]

This rough definition of transferable utility needs to be extended and clarified. One issue arises in Example 2, where the utility possibility frontier is not a straight line over its entire range, but is a straight line for all utility allocations that are achieved with a positive amount of private good for each consumer. Since this is the part of the utility possibility frontier that is relevant for most analysis, economists usually define transferable utility to include cases like Example 2, where the utility possibility frontier is linear over the "relevant" range of utility distributions.

Another, more subtle aspect of the definition needs clarification. For the utility functions that are specified in Example 1, the utility possibility frontier is not a straight line, but it would be possible to make a monotonic transformation of each person's utility in such a way that with the new utility representation, the utility possibility frontier is a straight line. In fact this is possible whenever the utility possibility frontier is downward-sloping.[4] Transferable utility becomes a nontrivial property

---

[3] The domain of applicability of transferable utility is not as widely understood as it should be. Some economists and game theorists think there is more transferable utility than there really is and some think there is less. Some believe that transferable utility obtains whenever preferences are continuous and there exists a divisible and fully exchangeable good that is desired by all consumers. Others believe that transferable utility applies only in the very special case of "quasilinear utility", where utility is linear in the quantity of some commodity. As we will show, neither view is correct.

[4] Consider any utility possibility frontier in the positive orthant, defined by an equation $U_2 = F(U_1)$, where $F$ is a strictly decreasing function. Define the functions $g_1(U) = U/(U + F(U))$ and $g_2(U) = U/(U + F^{-1}(U))$. The functions $g_1$ and $g_2$ are well defined and strictly monotone increasing. Let $V_1(x) = g_1(U_1(x))$ and $V_2(x) = g_2(U_2(x))$. Then the $V_i$'s are increasing transformations of the $U_i$'s, and for the utility possibility frontier with utilities measured by the functions, $V_i$ is described by $V_1(x) + V_2(x) = 1$.

*direct* utility function of the form $U_i(x_i, y) = f(y)x_i + g_i(y)$, where $x_i$ is the amount of the private good received by person $i$ and $y$ is the $n$-vector of public goods in the household. One special case is the quasilinear utility representation, $U_i(x_i, y) = x_i + f_i(y)$ (see, for instance, Example 2). In this example, a consumer's willingness to pay for public goods is independent of his income. But there are also examples in this class of utility functions where willingness to pay depends on income. For example, let each consumer $i$ have a utility function of the generalized Cobb–Douglas form $U_i(x_i, y) = x_i(y + b_i)^c$ where $c > 0$ and where the $b_i$'s are arbitrary constants.

The Bergstrom–Cornes result can be combined with the Bergstrom–Varian results on transferable utility with several private goods to characterize transferable utility when there is any number of private goods and any number of public goods. Let us define an *extended indirect utility function* with public goods in the same way that indirect utility is defined when there are no public goods except that utility depends on the amount of public goods as well as on the price vector and on income. Define $V_i(p, m_i, y)$ as the maximum of $U_i(x_i, y)$ subject to the constraint that $px_i = m_i$. It can be shown that there will be transferable utility in a household if and only if this indirect utility function is of the form $V_i(p, m_i, y) = \alpha(p, Y)m_i + \beta_i(p)$.

The utility possibility frontiers in households where utility is of the Bergstrom–Cornes form have the following properties:

- The conditional utility possibility frontiers $UPF(y)$ and $UPF(y')$, corresponding to any two different quantities of public goods $y$ and $y'$ will not cross each other. One of these two frontiers lies strictly to the northeast of the other.
- The utility possibility frontier is a straight line segment with slope $-1$. All points on the utility possibility frontier that correspond to interior Pareto optima are achieved with the same amount of public goods, $y = y^*$. The end points of the utility possibility frontier correspond to the two utility distributions in which one consumer gets $x^* = W - py^*$ units of private goods, and the other gets no private goods.

### 2.4.3. Transferable utility and mate selection

An important conceptual building block for economic theories of marriage is the utility possibility frontier that any couple would face if they were to marry each other. Shapley and Shubik (1972) and Becker (1974) suggested that this problem could be modeled as a linear programming assignment problem. The linear programming assignment model requires that there be transferable utility within each possible marriage. Here we explore the degree of generality that can be accommodated by transferable utility within this framework.

The notion of household public goods is well-suited for analyzing the issues of compatibility that arise in possible marriages. The public goods model of course applies to such jointly consumed household commodities as heat, light, and a well-tended garden. It is also suitable to the many important joint decisions that a married couple must make. If two people marry each other, they must marry on the same date. They must also agree about where to live, how many children to have, how to educate their children and what size of estate to leave them. Each of these variables can be modeled as a pure public good that enters the utility function of both partners.

Suppose that male $i$ marries female $j$ and they choose private consumption $X_i$ for him, $X_j$ for her, and the vector $Y$ of household public goods. Assume that their utility functions are of the following functional form: $U_i = A(Y)X_i + B_i(Y, j)$ and $U_j = A(Y)X_j + B_j(Y, i)$.

These utility functions indicate three things that a person must consider when he or she contemplates a potential marriage: (i) the vector $Y$ of public choices that would be made in this marriage; (ii) the amount of private goods that he or she would get to consume in that marriage; and (iii) his or her feelings about the intrinsic desirability of the other person as a marriage partner. The third effect is registered by the fact that the functions $B_i(Y, j)$ and $B_j(Y, i)$ depend not only on $Y$ but also on who one has as a partner.

The consumption options available to a potential pair of spouses depend on their joint economic productivity. In particular, let $F_{ij}(Y)$ be the total amount of private good that would be available to male $i$ and female $j$ if they chose to have the vector $Y$ of household public goods. (The function $F_{ij}(Y)$ would incorporate the effect on the household budget of public goods that must be purchased. It could also include the effects of household public goods that influence household income, like location or education of household members.) The set of affordable combinations of private consumptions and public choices is the set of vectors $(X_i, X_j, Y)$ which satisfy the equation $X_i + X_j < F_{ij}(Y)$.

In this case, for any couple, $i$ and $j$, the part of the utility possibility frontier corresponding to allocations where both persons get positive consumptions of private goods is described by the linear equation $U_i + U_j = A_{ij}$ where $A_{ij}$ is the maximum of $A(Y)X + B_i(Y, j) + B_j(Y, i)$ subject to the constraint $X \le F_{ij}(Y)$. In this case, the problem of finding Pareto efficient allocations within a potential marriage reduces to a constrained maximization problem in the aggregate quantities $X$ and $Y$. If they were to marry, there would be transferable utility between any pair $i$ and $j$, with utility possibility frontier for this pair consisting of utilities that add to $A_{ij}$.

## 3. Decision-making in the family

After proving that in general there do not exist "social indifference curves" that rationalize aggregate demand, Samuelson (1956) worries that

But haven't I in a sense proved too much? Who after all is the consumer in the theory of consumer's (not consumers') behavior? Is he a bachelor? A spinster? Or is he a "spending unit" as defined by statistical pollsters and recorders of budgetary spending? In most of the cultures actually studied by modern economists, the fundamental unit on the demand side is clearly the "family" and this consists of a single individual in but a fraction of cases.

Economists are not the only social scientists to be concerned about whether the family should be treated as a decision-making agent. The issue is nicely posed by the sociologist, James Coleman (1990: p. 580):

> The family has always been an entity within which multiple activities are carried out: economic production, joint consumption, procreation, socialization of children, and leisure pursuits. Generally it cannot be regarded as a purposive actor ... for it cannot usually be described as having a purpose for which it acts. It is, like society as a whole but on a smaller scale, a system of action composed of purposive actors in relation. Yet in some capacities the family may be usefully regarded as a purposive actor for it is an entity in terms of whose perceived interests natural persons act; for example some persons say they are acting to "uphold the honor of the family." And in some cases a family does act as a unit, to attain ends that can be described as purposes or goals of the family. It may be useful to clarify when and for what purposes a system of actions should be called an actor. For example, in a swarm of insects hovering in the summer air, each insect is darting this way and that, apparently either randomly or in pursuit of its own ends. But the swarm as a whole will move this way or that, hover expand or contract, and then fly off no less coherently than if it were a single organism. ... Thus just as a swarm of insects may be considered an actor, the family may – sometimes – be considered an actor.

## 3.1. Unitary theories of family decision-making

At least until recently, empirical studies of household demand have routinely assumed that a family acts as if it were maximizing a "family utility function".[5] That they should have done so is understandable since most of the available cross-sectional data on household consumption consists of household aggregates which do not distinguish either the incomes or the consumptions of individual family members. The reservations that Samuelson (1956) raised about this approach were amplified by the work of Manser and Brown (1980) and McElroy and Horney (1981), who showed that if the allocation of resources within the family is determined by Nash bargaining, then

---

[5] Good surveys of this work can be found in Deaton and Muellbauer (1980) and Browning (1992).

household aggregate demand functions cannot in general be rationalized by maximization of a family utility function.

Theories in which household demand can be rationalized by a family utility function have at various times been called "single-agent", "common preference", "consensus", "altruistic", or "benevolent dictator" theories.[6] But this does not mean that the natural course of neoclassical economics is to assume that families act like single agents. We follow the suggestion of Chiappori et al. (1992), who designate these models as unitary models. The classification "unitary" is sufficiently broad to encompass the several different models of family structure that predict that a family in aggregate behaves "as if" it is maximizing a family utility function.

### 3.1.1. Unitary models with transferable utility

Consider a household with private goods but no public goods, where indirect utility functions are of the Gorman polar form. If each family member is given an income and all face the same competitive prices, then the total amount of each good consumed by household members is determined by prices and total family income. Changes in the way that income is distributed within the household would have no effect on total household consumption. Gorman (1953) described this situation as the presence of "community preference fields". In this case, household demand can be rationalized as maximizing the utility of a single consumer. Suppose that an econometrician had access to a time series of commodity prices and to this household's time path of total income and total consumption, but could not observe consumption by individual household members. The econometrician would not be able to reject the hypothesis that all household decisions were made by a single rational consumer (who spends the entire household budget on himself).

Conversely, if preferences are not of the Gorman form, total household consumption will, in general, depend on the distribution of income within the household. Therefore if changes in the distribution of household income occur during the course of the time series, an econometrician might detect a violation of the weak axiom of revealed preference in household consumption data. This would enable her to con-

---

[6] Some economists refer to single-agent theories of the family as the "neoclassical theory of the family". Chiappori (1992) suggests that this is not an appropriate name. Although neoclassical economists sometimes treat the family as a single maximizing agent, more pluralistic theories of the family fall squarely within the neoclassical tradition. A distinctive feature of neoclassical microeconomics is "methodological individualism". When faced with fundamental questions about group behavior, neoclassical economists typically take a reductionist approach that seeks to explain group behavior not as a choice of a single rational agent, but rather as the result of the interplay of actions by group members with distinct objectives. It is true that neoclassical economists such as Gorman (1953), Samuelson (1956), and Becker (1974) have explored special assumptions on preferences under which families act as maximizing agents. It is also true that econometricians have often tried to simplify the task of applying neoclassical theory to household data by assuming that they act like a single agent.

clude that the household does not act like a single rational decision-maker. (Of course the data might not be rich enough so that the econometrician could detect violations of the weak axiom, even though the actual household decisions are not consistent with the unitary model.)

It is a consequence of the second fundamental theorem of welfare economics that if preferences are convex and there are no consumption externalities, then any household that allocates marketable private goods efficiently among its members will act as if each household member is given a personal income and is allowed to spend it as he or she wishes (see Chiappori, 1988, 1992). Combining this fact with our previous discussion, we see that if preferences in a household are convex and if indirect utility is of the Gorman polar form, then an efficiently operating household will act as if all household decisions were made by a single utility-maximizing consumer.

The results of Bergstrom and Cornes (1981, 1983) allow us to extend this result to the case where there are public goods as well as private goods. In particular, if indirect utility is of the form $V(p, m_i, y) = \alpha(p, y)m_i + \beta_i(p, y)$ and if the household chooses a Pareto optimal allocation in which all household members consume some private goods, then the vector of public goods selected and the vector of total household consumption of private goods is independent of the distribution of income within the household. As in the case of private goods with Gorman polar form utility, an observer of the response of household aggregates respond to prices and household income would not be able to reject the hypothesis of decision-making by a single rational consumer.

### 3.1.2. Unitary models with a household social welfare function

Samuelson (1956) and Varian (1984) point out that if income distribution within the family is itself the result of an optimizing choice rather than arbitrarily determined as in our previous discussion, then even for very general individual preferences, aggregate household demand will behave as if it is the demand of a single maximizer. Suppose that each household member $i$ has a quasi-concave utility function of the form $U_i(x_i, y)$ and that income distribution within the family is decided by a benevolent dictator who has a utility function of the form $W(U_1(x_1, y), \ldots, U_n(x_n, y))$. The dictator could solve for the allocation $(x_1^*, \ldots, x_n^*, y^*)$ which maximizes $W(U_1(x_1, y), \ldots, U_n(x_n, y))$ subject to $px\sum_{i \in H} x_i + p_y y \le W$ and implement this outcome by providing the family with the vector $y^*$ of public goods and giving the family member an income of $px_i^*$, which $i$ would use to purchase $x_i^*$. If we define the function $V(x, y)$ to be the maximum of $W(U_1(x_1, y), \ldots, U_n(x_n, y))$ subject to $\sum x_i = x$, then it will be the case that aggregate demand in this family is always chosen in order to maximize $V(x, y)$ subject to the family budget constraint. Samuelson suggests that even if a family is not a dictatorship, it might be that

> preferences of the different members are interrelated by what might be called a 'consensus' or 'social welfare function' which takes into account the deservingness

or ethical worths of the consumption levels of each of the members. The family acts *as if* it were maximizing their joint welfare function.

The joint welfare function that Samuelson has in mind is a function of the form $W(U_1(x_1, y), ..., U_n(x_n, y))$ where $W$ is an increasing function of each family member's utility. A utility function of this kind is known as a Bergson–Samuelson social welfare function.[7]

If a family chooses allocations to maximize a Bergson–Samuelson social welfare function subject to a family budget constraint, then the family's aggregate consumption is rationalized by some utility function $V(x, y)$ where $V(x, y)$ is the maximum of $W(U_1(x_1, y), ..., U_n(x_n, y))$ subject to the constraint that $\sum_i^N x_i = x$. Therefore it is impossible using data on total family consumption to distinguish the behavior of a family that maximizes a social welfare function from the behavior of a single rational consumer. If $W$ is a concave function of the $x_i$'s then it will also be true that the consumption of each family member is uniquely determined by aggregate family income.

Eisenberg (1961) discovered that if each family member always gets the same fraction of income and if all family members have homothetic, but not necessarily identical, preferences then family demand can be rationalized as the choice of a single individual. This idea was clarified and generalized by Chipman (1974), Shafer (1977), and Shapiro (1977).

### 3.1.3. Unitary models with the Rotten Kid Theorem

Becker's "Rotten Kid Theorem" (1974, 1981) establishes another set of circumstances under which households act as if they were governed by a single, utility-maximizing decision maker. In Becker's model, there is one consumption good and no public goods. There is a single, benevolent parent and $n$ selfish "kids", who care only about their own consumptions. The parent's utility is given by $U(x_0, ..., x_n)$ where $x_0$ is the parent's consumption and $x_i$ is the $i$th kid's consumption. Each kid $i$ has an income, $m_i$. The parent's income $m_0$ is much larger than that of the kids and he chooses to make "gifts" to each of them. Since the parent wants to make gifts to each kid, the post-gift distribution of consumption in the family is the vector $(x_0^*, ..., x_n^*)$, that maximizes the parent's utility, $U(x_0, ..., x_n)$ subject to $\sum_{i=0}^n x_i = \sum_{i=0}^n m_i$. If each kid's consumption enters the parent's utility function as a "normal good", then each kid's consumption is an increasing function of total family income. If each person in the family chooses an action $a_i$ that influences the income of other family members but does not influence their utility directly, then it follows that all persons in the family seek to maximize total family income. The problem of choosing the actions $a_i$ is there-

---

[7] A social welfare function of this type was introduced to economics by Bergson (1938) and further developed by Samuelson (1947).

fore of the type that Marshak and Radner (1972) describe as a problem in "team theory".

It should be recognized that Becker's results are not a trivial consequence of the household head being a "dictator". As Becker (1974) remarks, although the head is able to choose consumption distributions, he is *not* able to dictate the actions $a_i$ that determine individual incomes. Nevertheless, because of the head's distributional actions, all individuals in the family will agree on the same objective function to pursue in their choices of the $a_i$'s, namely maximization of total family income.

Lindbeck and Weibull (1988) and Bruce and Waldman (1990) show that parental altruism can lead to inefficiency in a multi-period model. A similar source of inefficiency in the context of government welfare programs was called the "Samaritan's Dilemma" by Buchanan (1975).[8] In the Bruce–Waldman model, if parents make transfers to their children in the second period, then children will do too little saving. But if parents confine their transfers to the first period, then children will have no incentive to maximize joint family income in the second period. Lindbeck and Weibull extend the analysis to cases where there is mutual benevolence between "parent" and "child". They also point out that an important instance of this problem is the case of children supporting indigent parents. Parents will have too little incentive to save for their old age if the support they will receive from their children is a decreasing function of the aged parents' resources.

Bergstrom (1989a) showed that the Rotten Kid Theorem depends critically on an implicit assumption of transferable utility.[9] The need for this assumption is illustrated by the following example taken from Becker – *the case of the controversial nightlight*. A husband likes to read at night, but the light interferes with his wife's slumber. The husband controls the family budget, but he loves his wife and gives her a generous bundle of consumption goods. He is aware that the nightlight annoys her and because he wants her to be happy, he turns the light out earlier than he otherwise would. But he still uses the nightlight more than she would like him to. One day, while the husband is away, an electrician drops by and offers to disconnect the nightlight in such a way that the husband would not be able to use it again. The wife is convinced that the husband would never know the reason that the nightlight was disconnected. But although she is entirely selfish and dislikes the nightlight, she decides to refuse the electrician's offer. Becker reasons as follows. Although the husband will not *blame* the wife for the loss of the nightlight, he will be made worse off. This will change his utility-maximizing gift to his wife in such a way as to make her worse off, despite her gain in utility from elimination of the nightlight. The effect, according to Becker, is like a loss in family income. If the wife's utility is a "normal good" for the husband, then the

---

[8] The biblical New Testament parable of the "Prodigal Son", Luke XV 11–32, seems more appropriate to this problem than the parable of the "Good Samaritan".

[9] Johnson (1990) has independently obtained similar results.

effect of a loss in family income is to choose a gift level that leaves her with a lower utility than she had before the nightlight was eliminated.

Bergstrom shows by an example that Becker's conclusion is not in general correct. For a reasonable choice of utility functions for husband and wife, it turns out that even after the husband adjusts his behavior in response to the loss of the nightlight, the wife is better off than before it was disconnected. The reason this happens, is that removal of the nightlight does not necessarily shift the household utility possibility frontier representing private preferences toward the origin in a parallel fashion. Elimination of the nightlight may also change the slope of this utility possibility frontier in such a way that there is a "substitution effect" which induces the husband to give her a higher total utility than she had when the nightlight was available.

## 3.2. The family with pluralistic decision-making

Just as it is possible in general competitive equilibrium theory to construct useful models without assuming that there is only one consumer, there are many ways to build interesting economic theories of "pluralistic" households. In this section we consider examples of such theories.

### 3.2.1. Proportional sharing rules

One of the simplest possible models of household consumption assumes that household income is always divided in prespecified proportions between household members and that there are no public goods. Each household member chooses his or her own consumption bundle to maximize utility subject to the resulting budget constraint. Samuelson (1956) calls this division rule an example of a shibboleth and points out that in general, dividing income in proportions that do not change when prices change would be inconsistent with maximizing the utility of a benevolent parent or with maximizing a well-defined social welfare function.[10]

### 3.2.2. Cooperative Nash bargaining solutions

Manser and Brown (1980) and McElroy and Horney (1981) applied the Nash cooperative bargaining model to marriages. These authors modeled marriage as a static bilateral monopoly in which a married couple can either remain married or divorce. There are potential gains for both parties from remaining married rather than getting

---

[10] As Samuelson acknowledges, demands resulting from proportional income division would be rationalizable as the demand of a single consumer if preferences were identical and homothetic. As remarked above, Eisenberg (1961) showed that this would be the case even if different household members had different preferences so long as everyone's preferences are homothetic.

divorced. These authors propose that the division of potential gains from marriage is determined by the symmetric Nash bargaining model, where the *threat point* is that they dissolve the marriage.

Specifically, they propose the following model. If they remain married, each partner has a utility function $U_i(x_i, y)$ where $x_i$ is $i$'s vector of consumption of private goods (including leisure) and $y$ is the vector of household public goods that they share. There is a vector of prices $p_x$ for private goods and $p_y$ for public goods. The set of possible household allocations consists of all vectors $(x_1, x_2, y)$ such that $p_x x_1 + p_x x_2 + p_y y = W_1 + W_2$, where $W_i$ is the "full income" of household member $i$.[11] Given this information, it is possible to construct the utility possibility set within this marriage. The utility that each person can achieve if the marriage is dissolved depends on prices and on his or her full income. Where $V_i$ is $i$'s utility if the marriage is dissolved, the symmetric Nash bargaining solution is the utility distribution $(U_1^*, U_2^*)$ that maximizes $(U_1 - V_1)(U_2 - V_2)$ on the utility possibility set.[12]

If the threat points $V_1$ and $V_2$ were independent of prices and individual incomes, then in a household governed by Nash bargaining, aggregate demand could be rationalized by the family utility function $W(x_1, x_2, y) = (U_1(x_1, y) - V_1)(U_2(x_2, y) - V_2)$. Aggregate demand would obey the Slutsky conditions and the revealed preference axioms. But in the model proposed by Manser and Brown and by McElroy and Horney, the threat points $V_i$ represent the utility levels that each person could achieve if he or she were not married. These threat points generally will depend both on prices and on individual incomes. Since the parameters $V_j$ depend on prices and incomes, the family aggregate utility function $\tilde{U}$, unlike the utility function of ordinary neoclassical consumers, depends on prices and on the distribution of incomes as well as on consumption. McElroy and Horney work out the "generalized Slutsky matrix" that corresponds to this situation and show that it will not in general be symmetric; thus total demand would not satisfy the revealed preference axioms, and family demand could not be explained as the behavior of a single rational consumer.

Woolley (1988) questions the assumption that divorce is the appropriate threat point for Nash bargaining between spouses. Woolley examines a model in which the threat point is a noncooperative Nash equilibrium within marriage and another model in which the threat point is a "consistent conjectural equilibrium". Lundberg and Pollak (1993) propose a threat point that is not necessarily a noncooperative equilibrium, but a "division of labor based on socially recognized and sanctioned gender roles". Lundberg and Pollak point out that their model (and Woolley's model) predict an em-

[11] When we treat leisure as a commodity, full income is the value at market prices of a person's initial endowment of nonhuman wealth plus the value of the total amount of labor the person could supply to the market.

[12] This expression is sometimes known as the Nash product. Nash (1950) proposed a set of axioms for resolution of static two-person bargaining games such that the only outcomes that satisfy the axioms maximize the Nash product on the utility possibility set.

pirical outcome that differs strikingly from divorce-threat models and from Becker's Rotten Kid model. If government child-care allowances are paid to mothers rather than to fathers in two-parent households, the threat point envisioned by Lundberg–Pollak and by Woolley is likely to shift in the mothers' favor. Accordingly, the outcomes of cooperative bargaining within households are likely to be more favorable to women. By contrast, in divorce-threat models, the outcome of bargaining depends only on the total resources available to the household and on the utilities that each would receive if they divorced. Whether the nominal recipient of child-care allowances in a marriage is the husband or wife would have no effect on total resources available to the married couple nor would it change the resources available to either spouse if they were to divorce. Therefore the divorce-threat model predicts that such differences would have no effect on allocation within married households. Similarly in Becker's Rotten Kid model, the well-being of each household member is determined by total family income, independently of intrafamily income distribution.

### 3.2.3. *Empirical tests of the unitary model based on private-goods consumption*

McElroy (1990) observed that it is possible in principle to test the unitary model of family decision-making, even if one cannot observe consumption of individual household members, using observations of aggregate household consumption and of other variables that could affect an individual's threat point; for example the wage rates and unearned incomes of each household member. If, holding prices and incomes constant, the distribution of income within the household has significant effects on demand, then one would reject the unitary hypothesis.

Stronger tests will be possible if it is possible to determine which household member is the ultimate consumer. For most commodities, this is very difficult to obtain, but there are some interesting exceptions. Sometimes data are available about the amount of leisure consumed by each household member. For a useful discussion and an extensive description of the data available from time-allocation studies in Canada, Europe, Japan, see Juster and Stafford (1991). Ingenious use has also been made of studies in which the nature of the goods strongly suggests the gender of the ultimate consumer.

Schultz (1990) found that in Thailand, an increase in a woman's unearned income from outside the household will have a larger negative effect on the probability that she joins the labor force than does an equal increase in her husband's unearned outside income. According to Browning et al. (1992), in Canada the shares of the family budget devoted to men's clothing and to women's clothing are positively related to the shares of family income earned respectively by men and women. Using data from a household survey from the Cote d'Ivoire, Haddad and Hoddinott (1994) and Hoddinott and Haddad (1995) report that "increases in the proportion of cash income accruing to women significantly raise the budget share of food and lower those of alcohol and cigarettes".

The results found by Schultz, Browning et al., and Hoddinott and Haddad would not be observed in a unitary model of household demand. Schultz is able to peek inside the family black box and observe separate consumptions of leisure by husbands and by wives. Hoddinott and Haddad do not directly observe which household members consume the food or the alcohol and cigarettes, nor do Browning and his co-workers know who wears the trousers in Canadian families. The finding that an increase in the wife's share of family income tends to increase consumption of food and women's clothes and an increase in the husband's share tends to increase consumption of cigarettes, alcohol, and men's clothes is, however, indirect evidence that men in Cote d'Ivoire consume more cigarettes and alcohol than women, and that people in Canada tend to wear gender-appropriate clothing.

### 3.2.4. The well-being of children, household public goods, and Pareto efficiency

Thomas (1990) found evidence that in Brazilian families, unearned income of the mother has a much stronger positive effect on fertility and on measures of child health such as caloric intake, weight, height, and survival probability than unearned income of the father. For fertility and measures of caloric intake, the effect of mothers' income is about eight times as large as that of fathers' income. For survival probability, the effect of mothers' income is nearly 20 times as large. Hoddinott and Haddad find that in Cote d'Ivoire, children's height for age is positively related to the share of family wealth controlled by their mothers. Schultz finds that in Thailand, an increase in a woman's unearned income tends to increase her fertility while an increase in her husband's unearned income does not.

The results of Thomas, Hoddinott and Haddad, and Schultz on child welfare and fertility, suggest that the distribution of control of resources within the family influences the composition of household demand. But unlike the commodities, leisure, clothing, and alcohol and tobacco discussed above, child health and fertility are *household public goods* jointly "consumed" by both the husband and wife. In the case of private goods, the theory suggested as an alternative to the unitary theory is that the distribution of earnings within the household determines the way in which household expenditure budgets are divided between household members. As Woolley (1988) observed, where the commodity in question is a household public good, even if the wife values the commodity more than her husband, it does not follow that more of the public good will be supplied at Pareto optimal allocations that distribute more utility to the wife.

Suppose, for example, that the household always chooses a Pareto efficient allocation and that utility functions are of the form $U_i(x_i, y) = A(y)x_i + B_i(y)$, where $y$ is child welfare and $x_i$ is $i$'s private consumption. According to Bergstrom and Cornes (1981, 1983), when utility functions are of this form, the Pareto efficient choice of child welfare will be independent of the distribution of income within the household. This will be the case, even if $B'_w(y) > B'_h(y)$ for all $y$, an assumption that implies that the wife is more concerned about child welfare than the husband, and even if $A'(y) > 0$, an assumption that implies that child care is a normal good for both husband and wife.[13] This is not to say that the results of Thomas, Schultz, and Haddad–Hoddinott are inconsistent with Pareto efficient allocations within the household. Alternative utility functions can be found such that Pareto efficient allocations that give higher utility to the wife are allocations with greater amounts of child welfare. But it is important to realize that if this is the explanation, it rides on stronger assumptions on household preferences than the assumptions that child welfare is a normal good and the wife is more concerned about child welfare than the husband.

An alternative to assuming that allocation is efficient within households is the hypothesis that public goods like child care are provided by voluntary contributions in a noncooperative equilibrium. Woolley (1988) proposed this model of family decision-making as the threat point for Nash bargaining and investigated its comparative statics under the assumption of Stone–Geary utility. Bergstrom et al. (1986) explore the general comparative statics of Nash equilibrium in voluntary public goods supply. Weiss and Willis (1985) suggest that divorced couples, because they are not able to monitor each other's activities, are likely to reach an inefficient, noncooperative equilibrium in supplying resources to their children. In contrast, married couples (who plan to stay married) are likely to be able to sustain an efficient outcome because of the repeated nature of their interaction and because they are able to observe each others' actions closely.

If a household public good is supplied as a noncooperative Nash equilibrium between husband and wife, there are three possible equilibrium regimes: (i) the wife supplies a positive amount and the husband supplies none; (ii) the husband and wife each supply a positive amount; (iii) the husband supplies a positive amount and the wife supplies none. According to Bergstrom et al. (1986), if equilibrium is in regime (i) an increase in wife's wealth relative to husband's would increase expenditures on the public good. If equilibrium is in regime (iii) an increase in wife's wealth relative to husband's would decrease expenditures on the public good, and if the equilibrium is in regime (ii), income redistribution within the family would have no effect on the equilibrium supply of the public good.

One way to explain the finding that redistribution of income toward wives has a strong positive effect on child welfare is to argue that the families observed by Thomas, Shultz, and Haddad and Hoddinott are in noncooperative Nash equilibria where the wife is the only contributor to the public good, child welfare. It would be interesting to find direct evidence that bears on whether the explanation lies here or whether

---

[13] The reason for this rather puzzling result is that a transfer of private consumption from husband to wife would typically increase her marginal willingness to pay for the public good, child care, and would decrease his. To assume that her marginal rate of substitution between child care and private consumption is higher than his is not sufficient to imply that a transfer of income from him to her will *increase* her marginal rate of substitution by more than it will reduce his.

outcomes in the families reflect a difference in the amount of child care appropriate to different points on the utility possibility frontier.

### 3.2.5. *Testing the hypothesis of Pareto efficiency with private goods*

The evidence of Schultz, Browning et al., and Haddad and Hoddinott on private goods tends to support rejection of the unitary hypothesis on household demand, but these results provide no direct evidence about whether households allocations are Pareto efficient. Chiappori (1988, 1992) points out that a cooperative Nash solution with divorce as the threat point is not the only alternative to the unitary hypothesis of family decision-making, even if the assumption of Pareto efficiency within households is maintained. Chiappori proposes to test the weaker hypothesis that a family chooses some efficient point on the household utility possibility frontier, using only data on household aggregate consumption. He studies a model in which each member of a married couple consumes a "Hicksian composite" private good and leisure. The two household members are assumed to be "price-takers" both in the goods market and the labor market and are free to work as many hours as they choose. Household aggregate demand is therefore formally the same as aggregate demand in a competitive economy with two consumers and three commodities. According to Diewert (1977), competitive equilibrium in an economy with more commodities than consumers must obey certain empirically falsifiable restrictions. In his 1988 paper, Chiappori spells out Diewert's restrictions as applied to his two-consumer, three-commodity model, both in parametric form and in a nonparametric, revealed-preference form.

### 3.2.6. *Noncooperative bargaining theory*

The Nash cooperative solution predicts that the outcome of a static, two-person bargaining game will be the outcome that maximizes the product of the two persons' *utility gains* over the *threat point* that would obtain in the absence of agreement. But deciding the appropriate threat point is problematic. Should the threat point be divorce as in Manser and Brown (1980) and McElroy and Horney (1981)? Should it be an uncooperative marriage in which spouses revert to socially sanctioned gender roles for uncooperative spouses as in Lundberg and Pollak (1993, 1994)? If either party to a marriage has the right to divorce the other, should the threat point for each person be the maximum of his or her utility from divorce and from a noncooperative marriage?

The Nash axioms are of no direct help in deciding the appropriate threat point in specific models. But recent work on the noncooperative foundations of bargaining theory offers useful guidance on this question. Rubinstein (1982) developed an extensive form multiperiod bargaining game for two agents in which a cake is to be partitioned only after the players reach agreement. Players alternate in proposing how to divide the cake, with one time period elapsing between each offer. Both agents are impatient; player $i$ discounts future income by the discount factor $\delta_i$. Thus, the utility to player $i$ of receiving $w$ units of cake in period $t$ is $w\delta_i^t$. Rubinstein proved that in the limit as the time between proposals becomes small, the only subgame perfect equilibrium is for the cake to be divided in the first period with player $i$'s share of the cake being $\alpha_i = \delta_i/(\delta_1 + \delta_2)$. More generally, if agent $i$'s utility from receiving $w_i$ units of cake in period $t$ is $u_i(w_i)\delta_i^t$ where $u_i$ is a concave function, then the only perfect equilibrium is the allocation that maximizes the "generalized Nash product", $u_1^{\alpha_1} u_2^{\alpha_2}$ on the utility possibility set $\{(u_1(w), u_2(1-w) \mid 0 \le w \le 1)\}$. In the case where the two agents have equal discount rates, this outcome is the same as the symmetric Nash equilibrium corresponding to the threat point $(0, 0)$.

Binmore (1985) shows how the Rubinstein model can be extended to the case where each of the bargaining agents has access to an "outside option". Binmore's model is like the Rubinstein model, except that each agent $i$ has the option of breaking off negotiations at any time and receiving a payoff of $m_i$ units of cake, in which case the other player receives no cake. If agreement is not reached and neither agent exercises an outside option, the utility outcome would be $(0, 0)$ as in the standard Rubinstein model. One might expect that the introduction of outside options would move the threat point to $(m_1, m_2)$. (If negative values of $m_i$ are considered, this conjecture might be amended to $(\max\{0, m_1\}, \max\{0, m_2\})$. Binmore finds, however, that this is not the answer. Instead, it turns out that the only perfect equilibrium for the game with outside options is an agreement in the first period on the utility distribution $(u_1, u_2)$ that maximizes the Nash product $u_1^{\alpha_1} u_2^{\alpha_2}$ on the utility possibility set $\{u_1(w), u_2(1-w) \mid 0 \le w \le 1\}$ subject to the constraint that $u_i \ge m_i$ for each $i$. In general, this solution is not the same as maximizing $(u_1 - m_1)^{\alpha_1}(u_2 - m_2)^{\alpha_2}$ on the utility possibility set, which would be the outcome of shifting the threat point to $(m_1, m_2)$. A similar argument is made by Sutton (1987) and the argument is presented in more detail in a paper by Binmore et al. (1989). The latter paper reports on laboratory tests of a Rubinstein bargaining game with outside options. The laboratory results were better predicted by the Binmore model than by a competing model in which the outside option is the threat point.

Binmore's model of bargaining with an outside option has an interesting interpretation for bargaining models of marriage. Consider a married couple who expect to live forever in a stationary environment. Suppose that in any period, there is transferable utility with the utility possibility frontier $\{(u_1, u_2) \mid u_1 + u_2 = 1\}$. Each spouse has an intertemporal utility function that is a discounted sum of the period-by-period utility flows. Spouse $i$ evaluates the time path $(u_1, ..., u_t, ...)$ of period utilities by the utility function $\sum_{t=1}^{\infty} u_t \delta_i^t$, where $\delta_i < 1$ is $i$'s discount factor. Let $b_i$ be the utility that spouse $i$ would get in any period where the couple stays married, but does not reach agreement and suppose that if they divorce, then spouse $i$ will get a utility of $v_i$ in every subsequent period. Assume that $b_1 + b_2 = b < 1$ and $m_1 + m_2 = m < 1$. This means that there are potential gains for both persons in reaching an agreement about how to divide utility.

As in Rubinstein, the spouses alternate in making offers of feasible utility distributions. Following Binmore's argument, one finds that in the limit as the time between offers approaches zero, the only subgame perfect equilibrium is one in which the spouses agree immediately to distribute utility in every period in such a way as to maximize the Nash product $(u_1 - b_1)(u_2 - b_2)$ subject to $u_1 + u_2 = 1$ and subject to $u_i \geq m_i$ for $i = 1,2$. Depending on the parameters $m_i$ and $b_i$, there are three possible types of solution:

(i) Neither of the outside option constraints $u_i \geq v_i$ is binding. In this case, the outcome is $u_1 = b_1 + (1 - b)/2$ and $u_2 = b_2 + (1 - b)/2$. Neither outside option is binding if $b_i + (1 - b)/2 \geq m_i$ for $i = 1$ and $i = 2$.

(ii) The outside option is binding for person 1, but not for person 2. In this case the solution is $u_1 - v_1$ and $u_2 = 1 - v_1$. This happens if $b_1 + (1 - b)/2 < m_1$.

(iii) The outside option is binding for person 2, but not for person 1. In this case the solution is $u_2 = v_2$ and $u_1 = 1 - v_2$. This happens if $b_2 + (1 - b)/2 < m_2$.

The first of these cases corresponds to the Lundberg–Pollak cooperative solution where the threat point is not divorce, but a noncooperative marriage. In the other two cases, the divorce threat is relevant, but notice that the outcome is never the outcome predicated by the Manser–Brown and McElroy–Horney models. When the divorce threat is relevant, there is not an equal split of the gains from being married rather than divorced. Instead one partner enjoys all of the surplus and the other is indifferent between being divorced and being married.

In the absence of agreement one might expect harsh words and burnt toast until the next offer is made. If the couple were to persist in noncooperative behavior forever, the outcome might be worse for one or both persons than being divorced. But divorce (as we have modeled it) is irrevocable, while a bargaining impasse need last only as long as the time between a rejected offer and acceptance of a counter offer. So long as the gains from marriage are divided in such a way that both are better off being married than being divorced, a threat of divorce is not credible. But for many divisions of utility, a threat of delayed agreement and a later counter proposal is credible. In fact the Rubinstein theorem tells us that there is only one equilibrium division of utility in which no such threat is credible.

Rubinstein's original bargaining model can be relaxed in the direction of realism without altering the main results. Binmore (1985) shows that one can relax the assumption that the two parties take turns making offers and that the period between offers is of fixed length. Qualitatively similar results obtain when the length of time between offers and the person whose turn it is to make the next offer are randomly determined after every refusal. It is straightforward to add a constant probability of death for each partner without seriously changing the model. On the other hand, stationarity of the model seems to be necessary for Rubinstein's beautifully simple result. This stationarity is lacking in a model where children grow up and leave the family and where the probability of death increases with age. It would be useful to know more about the robustness of the Rubinstein results to more realistic models of the family. Some interesting beginnings for such an investigation are found in Lundberg and Pollak (1994).

## 4. Theories of the marriage and household membership

### 4.1. Matching models

#### 4.1.1. The Gale–Shapley stable marriage assignment

Gale and Shapley (1962) introduced the concept of a *stable marriage assignment* and presented a courtship algorithm that leads to a stable assignment of marriage partners for arbitrary configurations of preference rankings of the opposite sex as possible marriage partners. This model has been extended and developed by several authors (see Roth and Sotomayor (1990) for an excellent survey of this work). Here we follow Roth and Sotomayor in presenting a slightly modified version of Gale and Shapley's model that allows the option of remaining single to persons who do not want anyone who will have them.

Consider a population consisting of $n$ men and $p$ women. Each person $i$ in the population is able to rank all members of the opposite sex as possible marriage partners and also to determine which members of the opposite sex he or she would be willing to marry if remaining single were the only alternative. All persons satisfying the latter condition are said to be *acceptable to i*. A monogamous assignment of marriage partners is said to be *stable* if no two people of opposite sexes would prefer each other to their assigned partners, if no married person would prefer being single to being married to his or her spouse and if no two single people would prefer being married to each other over being single.

The men-propose version of the Gale–Shapley algorithm has each man propose to his favorite woman. Each woman rejects the proposal of any man who is unacceptable to her, and if she receives more than one proposal, she rejects the proposal of any but the most preferred of these. To her most preferred suitor she says "maybe". At each step in the procedure, men who have been rejected move to their next choice so long as there are any acceptable women to whom they have not proposed. Women reject proposals from unacceptable men and from any but the best of their current suitors, including any man to whom she said "maybe" on the previous step. The algorithm continues until a step is reached where no man is rejected. At this point, all women marry the last man to whom they said "maybe".

In general, the assignment resulting from the men-propose version of the Gale–Shapley algorithm is different from that produced by the women-propose version. The difference between these outcomes reveals a remarkable polarity of interest between men and women. When all men and women have strict preference orderings over the opposite sex, the men-propose assignment turns out to be at least as good for *every* man as any other stable marriage assignment and to be at least as bad for every woman as any other stable assignment. Conversely, the women-propose assignment is at least as good for every woman and at least as bad for every man as any other stable assignment. In general there can be other stable assignments besides the men-propose and the women-propose assignments. Where there are more than two stable assignments, the binary relations "is at least as good for all women" and "is at least as good for all men", defined over the set of stable matchings, have the following "lattice property". For any two stable matchings *A* and *B*, there is a stable matching *C* that is at least as good for all women as *A* and as *B*. This matching *C* will be no better for any man than either *A* or *B*.[14] Roth and Sotomayor prove some interesting general comparative statics results, including the proposition that adding more women to the marriage market or enlarging some women's lists of acceptable men will (if it has any effect at all) help some men and harm no men and harm some women and help no women.

### 4.1.2. Marriage markets as a linear programming assignment

Shapley and Shubik (1972) and Becker (1974) suggest that the market for marital partners can be posed formally as the classic *linear programming assignment problem*.[15] The assignment problem is one of the early showcase applications of linear programming techniques (Danzig, 1951). Not only does linear programming offer powerful algorithms for finding an optimal assignment, it also yields dual variables which can serve as "shadow prices" to guide decentralized implementation of the optimum as a market solution. Koopmans and Beckmann (1957) developed the assignment problem model as an economic tool. Their model has *n* workers and *n* jobs. Each worker can be assigned to one and only one job. The value of output from worker *i* in job *j* would be a specified amount, $a_{ij}$. An efficient assignment maximizes the total value of output from all workers subject to the constraint that each worker can only have one job and each job must be done by only one worker. The dual solution to this linear program yields a vector of shadow prices for workers and jobs. If $w_i$ is the shadow price for worker *i* and $r_j$ is the shadow price for job *j*, it happens that $w_i + r_j \geq a_{ij}$ for all workers *i* and jobs *j* and if the optimal solution assigns *i* to *j*, then $w_i + r_j = a_{ij}$.

The dual variables to the assignment problem can be given a market interpretation as follows. Imagine that each job has an owner who wants to maximize his profits net of wages and who has to pay any worker his shadow price. If the owner of job *j* hires worker *k*, her net profit is $a_{ik} - w_k$. Since $w_k + r_j \geq a_{kj}$ for all *k* and $w_i + r_j = a_{ij}$ for the worker assigned to firm *j* by the assignment problem algorithm, it must be that the profit maximizing choice of worker for firm *j* is the same one assigned to her by the assignment problem algorithm. A similar argument establishes that if workers rather than firms were the residual claimants after paying the shadow prices $r_k$ for jobs, the

---

[14] A proof of this result, and a nice illustrative example is found in Roth and Sotomayor (1990: p. 37).

[15] A thorough discussion of the assignment model and its extensions is found in Roth and Sotomayor (1990).

profit maximizing choice of job for each worker would be the same one that is assigned to him by the linear programming solution.

The Koopmans–Beckmann model can also be interpreted as a problem of optimal marriage assignments, where one sex plays the formal role of workers and the other the role of firms. For each male, $i$, and each female, $j$, there is a number $a_{ij}$ which measures the amount of "marital bliss" that would be produced if $i$ married $j$. Each male is only allowed to marry one female and each female is only allowed to marry one male. The solution to the assignment problem determines not only who is assigned to whom, but also how the jointly produced marital bliss is "divided" between the partners of the marriages that form. This division is determined by the "prices" in the dual linear program, just as wages and rents are found in the Koopmans–Beckman interpretation.

Shapley and Shubik developed a cooperative game-theoretic interpretation of the assignment model of marriage. Consider the transferable utility game in which the only coalitions that yield nonzero payoffs consist of exactly one man and exactly one woman. The payoff from the coalition consisting of man $i$ and woman $j$ is $a_{ij}$. An allocation in which partners are assigned by solution of the linear programming assignment problem and payoffs are equal to the corresponding dual shadow prices will be in the *core* of this game. The core of this game consists of the set of allocations such that no two people could improve on their current situation by abandoning their current partners, forming a new partnership and dividing their joint payoff in some way. Shapley and Shubik show that the set of core allocations has the same lattice property that was found for the stable marriage assignments in the Gale–Shapley model.

### 4.1.3. Marriage assignments with and without transferable utility

The special ingredient that makes it possible to model the matching of marital partners as an assignment problem is transferable utility. The interpretation of marriage as an assignment problem has it that for each male, $i$, and female, $j$, there is a number $a_{ij}$ such that if $i$ marries $j$ they will produce $a_{ij}$ units of "bliss" which can be divided between them in any way such that the sum of $i$'s bliss and $j$'s bliss is $a_{ij}$. On the face of it, the assumption that the total utility from a marriage could be redistributed between the partners just like money or jelly beans seems crude and unreasonable. But, as we showed in the model of transferable utility and mate selection in Section 2.4, a transferable utility framework can accommodate a wide range of interesting and subtle interactions between marital partners.

The Gale–Shapley model is at the opposite extreme from transferable utility. The model contains no allowance for altering the terms of marriage. Since there are no "side-payments", the utility possibility frontier available to any two potential spouses is just a single point. If it is possible for potential marriage partners to draw up premarital contracts which determine in advance the household's choice of public goods and division of private goods, then the Gale–Shapley model is very unrealistic. But if credible and binding premarital contracts are not possible then, as we will see, there are reasonable models in which the relevant part of the utility possibility frontier for any pair is a single point.

Crawford and Knoer (1981) present an ingenious extension of the Gale–Shapley algorithm that works when monetary side-payments can be made but which does not require transferable utility.[16] In their model side-payments are measured in discrete units. Individuals rank options that are specified not only by whom one mates but also by the size of promised side-payments. In the initial round, the side-payment of each member of the proposing sex is restricted to a low level. Proposals, refusals and may-bes proceed as in the Gale–Shapley algorithm, but each time a member of the proposing sex is refused, the side-payment that he is allowed to offer to the refusing individual increases by one unit. This process continues until no proposal is rejected. The outcome is a stable assignment of partners. Demange and Gale (1985) show that general models with side-payments but without transferable utility share the lattice property found for the Gale–Shapley model and for the assignment model. These results are well summarized by Roth and Sotomayor (1990).

Kaneko (1982) also analyzes general models of "two-sided exchange economies" that include both the Gale–Shapley model and the transferable utility model as well as markets where there are side-payments without transferable utility. Kaneko shows that for his model, the core is nonempty and coincides with the set of competitive equilibria.

### 4.1.4. Strategic issues in stable matching

Roth and Sotomayor (1990) present several interesting results about the extent to which assignment mechanisms can be manipulated. If marriages were assigned by the Gale–Shapley algorithm with males proposing to females, then unless there is only one stable matching for the population, there will be at least one woman who will be better off if she misrepresents her preferences. More generally, there exists no stable matching algorithm which would make truth-telling a dominant strategy for all members of the population. In the Gale–Shapley algorithm, with males proposing, it is dominant strategy for the males to reveal their preferences truthfully. In general, a woman would need a great deal of information about others' preferences in order to know how to improve her outcome by deceptive play. But suppose that each woman knew who her match would be in the women-propose version of the Gale–Shapley algorithm and suppose that in the play of the men-propose algorithm, each woman declares a man to be unacceptable if she likes him less well than the mate that she

---

[16] The Crawford–Knoer results are generalized by Kelso and Crawford (1982).

would be assigned in the women-propose outcome. This configuration of strategies would be a strong Nash equilibrium.[17]

## 4.2. Household allocation in the shadow of the marriage market

### 4.2.1. Gifts, commitment, and divorce

Carmichael and MacLeod (1993) propose a theory of gifts as a commitment device in long term relationships. Their theory offers a partial answer to such questions as: Why are courting males expected to offer "inefficient" gifts such as cut flowers, or gift-wrapped, perishable chocolates? What explains seemingly wasteful expenditures on such commodities as engagement rings, wedding rings, and expensive weddings? Carmichael and MacLeod consider an overlapping generations model in which individuals find a partner with whom they will play repeated prisoners' dilemma. After each round in the game, each player has the option of abandoning his or her current partner or offering to play another round. If either partner chooses to abandon, then both must return to the matching market to acquire a new mate. All players who return to the marriage market are assumed to find a match for the next period. At the beginning of a new match, there is no information available regarding an individual's play in previous matches.

In games of repeated prisoners' dilemma, where abandonment is not a possible action, it is well known that for a large range of parameter values, cooperative behavior can be sustained in a subgame perfect equilibrium by "punishment strategies" that offer cooperation so long as one's partner cooperates, and defection for at least some period of time if the partner should defect (see, e.g., Axelrod, 1984). But, as Carmichael and MacLeod demonstrate, if abandonment is possible, there cannot be an equilibrium in which new relationships begin costlessly and all agents cooperate in every period. The reason is simple. If all other agents cooperate at each stage, a player could defect on his partner in the first round, abandon her, and play the same trick on a new partner in the next round.[18] Such a defector would receive the benefits of defecting against a cooperating partner in every round of the game. Carmichael and MacLeod suggest that in such an environment, lasting cooperation could be sustained by a convention in which at the beginning of a new relationship, each partner is expected to give a gift at the beginning of the relationship. In the equilibrium proposed by Carmichael and MacLeod, nobody will be willing to start a new relationship with

---

[17] A strong Nash equilibrium is a Nash equilibrium that has the additional property that no subgroup of the players would all benefit by changing their actions if the actions of players outside this subgroup are left unchanged.

[18] The model presented by Carmichael and MacLeod is a one-sex model. The main idea extends readily to the two-sex case, but it would be interesting to consider the effects of asymmetries between the sexes, especially asymmetries in the cost of being abandoned.

someone who does not offer the conventional gift. If the cost of the gift is large enough, cooperative behavior can be sustained in Nash equilibrium if everyone chooses the strategy of making the conventional gift and playing *cooperate* so long as his or her partner plays *cooperate* and by abandoning the partner if the partner ever plays *defect*. In such an environment, it does not pay to defect against your partner because if you do, the partner will leave you and you will have to reenter the matching market and present a new gift in order to attract a mate. If the required gift is large enough relative to the gains from defecting on your partner, defection will not be worthwhile. The authors point out that for the gifts to serve this purpose, they should be expensive, but of little benefit to the recipient and certainly not resellable.[19] Otherwise, the cost of buying a gift for your new partner would be nullified by the benefit of receiving a gift when you reenter the marriage market.

### 4.2.2. Household equilibrium without perfect information

Roth (1992) develops a model of a potentially long-lived partnership in which the partners do not know with certainty how "good" the partnership will be relative to their outside opportunities. If the partnership were known with certainty to be a "good one", the partners would understand that it will be long-lived and will both invest substantial resources in it. As time passes, the partners learn about the quality of their partnership by observing current and past outcomes. The greater the amount of investment in the partnership, the more likely that good realizations will occur in each period. The more good realizations that are observed, the more likely the partners are to invest. In the model as formulated by Roth, no matter how much is invested, "bad" partnerships will eventually be discovered to be bad, but some "good" partnerships are dissolved by rational decision-makers because a run of bad luck has led the partners to think that the partnership will not last and hence the partners do not invest. Roth develops an iterative procedure suggested by dynamic programming which enables him to compute and characterize sequential equilibria for this game.

### 4.2.3. Divorce as a threat point in bargaining

In the bargaining models discussed in Section 3.2, the payoff from being divorced is determined outside the model. For many people who consider divorce, the utility of the divorce option depends on the utility of forming a second marriage.[20] But the util-

---

[19] Brinig (1990) offers intriguing evidence that the demand for diamond engagement rings increased dramatically with the abolition in the 1930s of state laws enabling women to bring lawsuits for "breach of promise to marry". Brinig suggests that the engagement rings were "part of an extralegal contract guarantee", which were a prerequisite to premarital sexual intimacy for many couples.

[20] Weiss and Willis (1993) report that in a sample taken in 1985 of Americans who had graduated from high school in 1972, about 60% of those persons who divorced during the period since high school had remarried.

ity of a second marriage must be determined as part of the same theory that determines the distribution of utility within all marriages. Rochford (1984) defines an equilibrium which she calls a symmetrically pairwise-bargained allocation (SPB) that captures this idea. Rochford's model has transferable utility within households. She defines an SPB to be an assignment of partners and an allocation of payoffs within marriages such that the division of utility within each marriage is determined by bargaining, where the threat point is determined by the utility each spouse would get from divorce and remarriage. A person's threat point in a marriage is the highest utility that he or she could achieve as a Nash cooperative solution in some other marriage where the threat points in the other marriage are the utilities the two hypothetical partners get in their current marriages. Rochford proposes an iterative process that is guaranteed to converge to an SPB. Moldevanu (1990) considers a model of trading partners and formulates an equilibrium concept similar to Rochford's. He is able to extend her results to economies without transferable utility.

The models proposed by Rochford and by Moldevanu do not include explicit costs of divorce. While the costs of switching from one partner to another may be small for trading partners, this is not likely to be the case for marriage partners, who are likely to have invested significant amounts of "marriage-specific capital" that will be lost if they divorce. If the partners have children, then arrangements for sharing the costs and joys of child care become difficult and inefficient.[21] In societies where divorce is unusual, divorced people are sometimes ostracized or at least suspected of being unusually difficult to live with.

The introduction of costs of divorce will markedly affect the workings of the formal model. As Moldevanu points out, in a model like Rochford's, if each person has at least one "clone", then any core allocation, including the symmetrically pairwise-bargained allocations would have the property that identical people must be equally well off. In this case, the SPB allows no scope for bargaining within households. In equilibrium, each married couple would correspond to another couple just like them with the same payoffs. The threat point of each individual would be the same as the utility he or she obtains in equilibrium. In the absence of clones, if there were very close substitutes for each person in the society, spouses would not have much surplus to bargain over, once each is given at least his or her outside option.

### 4.2.4. Household bargaining with outside options

Shaked and Sutton (1984) discuss a model of labor and management which is formally similar to a model of a marriage in which divorce is costly. In their model, the firm has a current work force which it cannot replace immediately or costlessly. They impose these costs by putting a restriction on the timing of offers in a Rubenstein bar-

---

[21] See Weiss and Willis (1985) for a discussion of incentive problems that arise for child care in divorce settlements.

gaining model. This leads to an outcome that is intermediate between a bilateral monopoly outcome where neither side has an outside option and the "Walrasian" outcome, which would obtain if there were no costs to a firm from changing its work-
force.

Rubinstein and Wolinsky (1985) have a model of transactions between pairs of
agents who meet randomly and bargain if they meet. Their model, viewed as a model
of marriage, offers an interesting interpretation of the "costs of divorce". There are
two types of agents, buyers and sellers. All agents of a given type are identical. At the
beginning of each time period, there is a matching stage, where each agent tries to find
a new partner. Some agents will find partners, some will not. Any buyer and seller
who meet will start to bargain according to a noncooperative iterative bargaining
scheme. If these two agents reach agreement, a transaction occurs and they leave the
market. If they do not reach agreement in this period, there is a chance that one or
both of them will meet another agent of the opposite type. If this happens, the agent
ceases bargaining with his or her current bargaining partner and starts bargaining with
the newly met partner. If neither meets a new partner, the current partners proceed
together to the next round of bargaining. The cost of not reaching agreement in the
current period is now twofold. If agreement is ultimately reached with the current
partner, there is a cost of delay. In addition there is the risk that one's current bargaining partner will meet someone else before the next round of offers. If one is abandoned by one's current partner, one will not be sure to meet anybody to bargain with
in the next period. When the number of buyers does not equal the number of sellers, it
takes longer on average for the abundant type to find a new partner than it does for the
scarce type. Because of this, the abundant type will be willing to concede a larger
share of the gains from agreement than will the scarce type.

Binmore's version of the Rubinstein model with outside options, discussed in the
previous section, has strong and interesting implications if all people who divorce
eventually remarry, but face a transactions cost in the process. Consider the special
case of a large population of identical males and of identical females. A male and female who marry and who reach agreement can achieve any constant flow of utility
$(u_m, u_f)$ such that $u_m + u_f = 1$. Utilities are normalized so that the utility flow while the
partners are in disagreement is 0 for each. At any stage in the bargaining process, either spouse can either accept the other person's offer, reject the other person's offer
and make a counter offer, or ask for a divorce. If the two spouses have equal time rates
of discount, then in equilibrium, according to Binmore's results, the outcome will be
an allocation of utility $(u_m, u_f)$ that maximizes the Nash product $u_m u_f$ subject to the
constraints that $u_m + u_f = 1$, and that each person gets a utility at least as high as his or
her outside option. The utility distribution $(\bar{u}_m, \bar{u}_f) = (1/2, 1/2)$ maximizes $u_m u_f$ subject to $u_m + u_f = 1$. Given that the equilibrium distribution of utility in a marriage is
$(\bar{u}_m, \bar{u}_f)$ a person who divorces and remarries will have to bear a divorce cost of $c_m$ if
he is male and $c_f$ if she is female. Therefore the utility of a male who takes the outside
option of divorce and remarriage is $\bar{u}_m - c_m < \bar{u}_m$ and the utility of a female who

chooses this option is $\bar{u}_f - c_f < \bar{u}_f$. Therefore so long as divorce costs are positive for both parties, the presence of the outside option does not influence the bargaining outcome.

In this model, unlike the Rubinstein–Wolinsky model, the distribution of utility within marriages does not depend on the relative supplies of males and females, but only on their impatience and on the position of the utility possibility frontier relative to the noncooperative outcome within marriage. The difference seems to lie in the fact that in the Rubinstein–Wolinsky model, an individual who "meets a stranger" of the opposite sex can abandon his or her spouse without bearing any transaction cost (although the abandoned spouse may be in for a long wait before another offer appears). In the variant of the Binmore model just proposed, a threat by either party to abandon the current marriage is not credible because persons who divorce would have to pay the transactions cost of divorce and remarriage and when they are done with this, would be in no better bargaining situation than they were before divorcing. These ideas can readily be extended to a community with many types of males and females and very general utility possibility frontiers within each possible marriage.

When there are divorce costs to both parties, the Binmore argument implies the striking conclusion that even though technology and preferences allow transferable utility, the nature of bargaining determines that there is only one possible distribution of utility between any two people if they should marry. This outcome is the Nash cooperative solution with uncooperative marriage as the threat point. Despite the presence of side-payments and the availability of remarriage as an outside option, the original Gale–Shapley model without side-payments then applies. This means that the marriage market suffers from rigidity of a "price" which may be important for clearing the marriage market. If it were possible to settle the distribution of utility within possible marriages in advance by a binding contract, then the distribution of utility between males and females within marriages would respond to competitive forces in such a way as to tend to equilibrate the number of males and the number of females who choose to marry at any time. If, on the other hand, the distribution of utility within marriages is determined by a threat point such as uncooperative marriage, which is independent of market forces, then changes in the terms of marriage cannot be expected to equalize imbalances in supplies of the two sexes in the marriage market.

## 4.3. Age at marriage

### 4.3.1. Classical one-sex population theory

Classical Stable Population Theory as developed by Lotka (1922), shows that if current age-specific fertility and mortality rates for females remain unchanged, then, in the long run, the age distribution of the population would asymptotically approach some constant distribution, and therefore raw birth rates and population growth rates would approach constancy. This fact has encouraged demographers to project hypothetical long run population growth rates implied by current age-specific female fertility. Since every baby has a father as well as a mother, it is possible (in societies that have good data on paternity) to construct tables of age-specific rates at which the current population of males father children. These data can be used to make an alternative projection of long run population growth rates parallel to the projections made using a female one-sex model. Perhaps surprisingly, when the male one-sex model is applied to actual populations, the predictions are often quite different from those found by applying it to females. For example, using 1968 data in a one-sex model for US males would predict a long term population growth rate of 10.1 per 1000 population, while the female one-sex model would predict a long term population growth rate of 5.7 per 1000 population (Das Gupta, 1973). Since every child that is born, must have exactly one mother and one father, it is simply numerically impossible that both sexes would maintain the same age-specific fertility and mortality rates after 1968 as did the population surveyed in 1968. Since every wedding also involves one male and one female, the same logical difficulty is present in efforts to predict future marriage rates of males and of females separately, by projecting current age and sex-specific marriage rates into the future.

### 4.3.2. Two-sex theories of mating

Modern demographers (Keyfitz, 1971; Das Gupta, 1973) have responded to this discrepancy by building two-sex models based on "marriage functions" which ensure the necessary parity between male and female parents or wedding partners. As applied to marriages, these models predict that the number of marriages between a female of age $i$ and a male of age $j$ in year $t$ should depend at least on the number of males and the number of females present in year $t$. McFarland (1972) criticizes these models because they do not adequately reflect the possibilities for substitution among various cohorts. To allow these possibilities, the number of marriages between a female of age $i$ and a male of age $j$ should depend on the numbers of males and females of other ages in the population as well. McFarland suggests an iterative procedure (which bears an interesting similarity to the Gale–Shapley model) for dealing with these effects.

Pollak (1986, 1987, 1990) reformulates the "two-sex problem" by replacing the constant age-specific fertility schedule of the classical theory with two more fundamental relationships. These are a "birth matrix" and a "mating rule". The birth matrix postulates an expected number of births per period from a marriage of an age $i$ male to an age $j$ female. The mating rule is a function that determines the number of marriages of type $i$ males to type $j$ females for all $i$ and $j$ as a function of the vector listing the numbers of males and females of each age in the population. Pollak shows that if these fundamental relationships remain constant over time and if the mating rule follows certain natural conditions, the resulting dynamical system will converge to a constant equilibrium growth rate, yielding a constant equilibrium age structure. Pollak imposes only certain very general conditions on the mating function such as nonnegativity, homogeneity, continuity, and that the number of persons of a given age and sex who marry must not exceed the number of persons of that age and sex in the population.

### 4.3.3. Transferable utility model suitable for empirical estimation

Pollak's mating rule is a "reduced form" description of the dependence on the outcome of a marriage market on supplies and demands of the two sexes from various cohorts. Bergstrom and Lam (1989a,b) construct a model of the marriage market that rationalizes Pollak's mating rule. Their work concentrates on reconciling the numbers of males and females who are willing to marry in any given year. In the absence of side-payments, two arbitrarily selected persons would usually disagree about their preferred wedding date. Suppose, for example that all males prefer marrying at age 25 and all females prefer marrying at age 23. A male and a female will agree about the best time for them to marry only if the male was born two years earlier than the female. But in a population where cohort sizes change over time, there will not always be an equality between the number of females of one cohort and the number of males of a cohort born two years earlier. If males prefer to marry at an older age than do females, then if there is a "baby boom", females in the boom generation will find a shortage of males who want to marry when they do. Males born at a time when the birth rate is falling will find a shortage of females two years younger, who will want to marry when these males are 25. When members of one sex and cohort are in excess supply relative to their "natural partners", there will be readjustments in which some of the abundant group postpone marriage and some of the scarce group marry earlier than they otherwise would.

Bergstrom and Lam propose a simple overlapping-generations model of the marriage market, designed to deal with this problem. This model has enough special structure so that its parameters can be empirically estimated. Utility is assumed to be linear in consumption and quadratic in age at marriage. Utility of a person whose preferred age at marriage is $a^*$ and who consumes $c$ units of consumption good and marries at age $a$ is $c - (a - a^*)^2$. In the simplest form of this model, suppose that all males have preferred age of marriage $a_m^*$ and all females have preferred age at marriage $a_f^*$. Suppose also that the income that each individual brings to a marriage is independent of whom he or she marries. Suppose that male $i$ has income $I_i$ and was born in year $b_i$ while female $j$ has income $I_j$ and was born in year $b_j$. If they marry, they will both have to choose the same date of marriage, so the date of their marriage is a "household public good". The assumption of quasilinear utility implies that there is a unique Pareto optimal wedding date for this couple. Given the quadratic specifications of utility of age at marriage, this date is the midpoint between the two partners' preferred wedding dates. The preferred wedding date of male $i$ is $b_i + a_m^*$, the preferred wedding date of female $j$ is $b_j + a_f^*$, and the Pareto optimal date for their wedding is $(b_i + a_m^*)/2 + (b_j + a_f^*)/2$.

Let us define $d_{ij}$ to be the number of years that separate the preferred wedding dates of male $i$ and female $j$. Then $d_{ij} = |(b_j + a_f^*) - (b_i + a_m^*)| = |(b_j - b_i) - (a_f^* - a_m^*)|$. Each partner's actual wedding date will differ from his or her preferred wedding date by $d_{ij}/2$. The feasible consumption allocations $(c_i, c_j)$ for this couple must satisfy the equation $c_i + c_j = I_i + I_j$. Therefore the couple's utility possibility frontier is described by the equation $u_i + u_j = a_{ij}$ where $a_{ij} = I_i + I_j - d_{ij}^2/2$.

Let the numbers of surviving males and females born in year $i$ be $M_i$ and $F_i$. The linear programming assignment model predicts that the pattern of marriages will solve the following maximization problem: Where $X_{ij}$ represents the number of marriages between males born in year $i$ and females born in year $j$, solve for the values of $X_{ij}$ that maximize $\sum_i \sum_j a_{ij} X_{ij}$ subject to the constraints, $\sum_i X_{ij} = F_j$ for all $j$ and $\sum_j X_{ij} = M_i$ for all $i$. Since we have assumed that incomes are independent of whom one marries, the optimizing solution for the $X_{ij}$'s is independent of the distribution of incomes and can be determined by minimizing $\sum_i \sum_j d_{ij}^2 X_{ij}$ subject to the constraints $\sum_i X_{ij} = F_j$ for all $j$ and $\sum_j X_j = M_i$ for all $i$.

In the simple model proposed here, the only parameters to be estimated are the preferred marriage ages $a_m^*$ and $a_f^*$ of males and females. Any specification of these parameters determines the matrix of $d_{ij}$'s. This information together with an empirically observed distribution of age-cohorts by sex will determine an optimal assignment of marriage partners by cohort. Estimation can proceed by choosing the values of $a_m^*$ and $a_f^*$ that best predict the patterns of actual marriages. More flexible functional forms and some variation of preferences among individuals can also be accommodated within this model, in fairly obvious ways. Bergstrom and Lam (1989a) applied this technique to Swedish historical data on marriage rates in the 19th and 20th centuries.

### 4.3.4. Why do women marry older men?

One of the strongest demographic regularities is the observation that men marry later in life than women. In a study conducted by the United Nations,[22] the average age of marriage for males exceeded that for females in each of 90 countries and in every time period studied between 1950 and 1985. The age difference tends to be larger in traditional societies than in modern industrial countries and has diminished over time in most industrial countries.

Bergstrom and Bagnoli (1993) proposed an explanation for this difference. They suggest that, at least in traditional societies, women are valued as marriage partners for their ability to bear children and manage a household, while men are valued for their ability to make money. Information about how well a male will perform economically

---

[22] *Patterns of First Marriage: Timing and Prevalence* (1990).

– whether he is diligent and sober – becomes available at a later age than the relevant information about how well a female would perform her household roles. This leads to an "intertemporal lemons model", in which males who expect to do poorly in later life will seek to marry at a relatively young age and males who expect to prosper will postpone marriage until their success becomes evident to potential marriage partners. Females, on the other hand, marry relatively early, with more desirable females marrying the successful, older males who postponed marriage and the less desirable females marrying the young males who want to marry young. In equilibrium, a young male who attempts to marry is signaling a lack of confidence in his future economic prospects. While the most desirable females would not accept such males, the less desirable females have no better alternatives in the marriage market and hence are willing to marry young males.

This theory implies not only that males tend to marry later in life than females, but also that males who marry young will tend to be less prosperous in later life than males who postpone marriage. Bergstrom and Schoeni (1992) investigate the empirical relationship between age-at-first-marriage and lifetime income, for males and for females. Using 1980 US Census data, they plot wage income of males in later life as a function of the age at which they married. Income is highest for those who marry in their late 20s. Men who marry at age 28 or 29 have average earnings about 20% higher than men who marry at 18.

## 4.4. Alternative household structures

Most of the work by economists on the theory of the household has concerned either single-person households or monogamous couples, with or without children. There is, however, considerable evidence that nonmonogamous modes of household organization are too significant to ignore.

### 4.4.1. Polygyny in marriage markets

Becker (1981) devotes a chapter of his *Treatise on the Family* to "Polygamy and Monogamy in marriage markets". Becker's analysis of polygamy is more than a clever curiosum; it extends methods of economic analysis to a major social institution that has received all too little attention from economists. Although overt polygamy is rare in our own society, it is a very common mode of family organization around the world. Polygyny (men having multiple wives) is prevalent in 850 of the 1170 societies recorded in *Murdock's Ethnographic Atlas* (Murdock, 1967), while official polyandry (women having multiple husbands) is prevalent in only a handful of societies (Hartung, 1982).

One of the first economic issues that must be confronted by a polygynous society is the question of how are wives allocated. Not surprisingly (to economists at least), the price system usually comes into play. Becker suggests that theory would predict higher incomes for women under polygyny than under monogamy. He reasons that relaxing the constraint that a man can have only one wife would shift the demand schedule for wives upward, leading to higher bride prices with polygyny than with monogamy. The argument that polygyny leads to higher bride prices is theoretically compelling and appears to be supported by anthropological evidence.[23] It does not, however, follow that higher bride prices imply welfare gains for females. If "property rights" to an unmarried female lie with her family, it seems plausible that her family would use the proceeds from the sale of a bride to purchase a wife or an additional wife for one of her male siblings. This theoretical prediction appears to be strongly supported by anthropological field studies (see Goody, 1973).

### 4.4.2. Unwed parents

Economic theorists have done little work on extending bargaining models of sexual relationships and child support to noncohabiting, unmarried parents. This neglect might have been excusable 30 years ago on the grounds that the most children were born into households with two cohabiting adults. Recent statistics show that unwed parenthood is no longer rare. In the United States in 1960, only 5% of all births occurred out of wedlock. In 1990, more than 25% of births were to unwed parents. (About 30% of the unwed parents in 1990 were cohabiting couples.) The proportion of all children who live in single-parent, mother-only households has risen from 8% in 1960 to 23% in 1990. For Black Americans, the statistics are even more dramatic. In 1990, two-thirds of births were out of wedlock and more than half of all children live in single-parent households.[24]

Willis (1994) studies some of the interesting theoretical issues that arise in the analysis of unwed parenthood. Willis begins with an analysis of fertility decisions and child care expenditures for a single mother who is not able to identify the father(s) of her children. He then considers an equilibrium model of child support for noncohabiting parents. In this model, the father's identity is known and both parents care about the well-being of a child. Since they do not live together, it is difficult for them to monitor each other's behavior sufficiently to sustain efficient cooperative arrangements for child support. Willis examines a noncooperative Stackelberg equilibrium where the mother has custody of the child and the father can influence expenditure on the child only by transferring income to the mother. This equilibrium will not in general be efficient. Marriage, Willis argues, is likely to lead to more efficient, cooperative arrangements for child care between mother and father. The question arises: If it

---

[23] According to Gaulin and Boster (1992), about two-thirds of the societies found in Murdock's *Ethnographic Atlas* have positive bride prices, while in only about 3% of these societies is it the case that brides must pay a dowry to the husband. Moreover, according to Gaulin and Boster, almost all of the societies with dowries are monogamous.

[24] These statistics and many interesting related facts are reported by DaVonza and Rahman (1994).

is more efficient for the two parents of a child to live together than apart, why is un-wed motherhood so common? Willis suggests some possible reasons. One force for unwed parenthood that leads to a particularly interesting analysis is imbalance be-tween the number of marriageable women and the number of marriageable men. This explanation seems particularly compelling for the Black population. Wilson (1987) argues that women's search for partners will be confined primarily to a pool of "marriageable males" – males who would bring resources to a marriage. For statistical purposes, he identifies this pool with males who are currently employed. Wilson found that in 1980, the ratio of black marriageable males aged 20–44 to black females aged 20–44 was about 0.56 in the Northeast and North Central states of the US. (In 1960, this ratio was about 0.67.) The corresponding ratio of white marriageable males to females was about 0.85. Following Wilson's suggestion, Willis works out an equilib-rium model in which men choose between monogamy and a polygynous life in which they father children by several women but marry none of them. Monogamous men are confined to a single mate. A polygynous life will have some advantages, because a man may father children by more women, and some disadvantages, including the in-efficiencies in child care arrangements that arise when parents do not live together. In Willis's model, there is a threshold expected number of partners $P$ such that men will be indifferent between monogamy and a polygynous life if their expected number of partners in polygyny is equal to $P$. Suppose that there are more women who want to have children than the number of marriageable males available to them, but suppose that there are not enough marriage females so that every male could have $P$ partners. Then there would be an equilibrium in which some marriageable males (and an equal number of females) are monogamous and some marriageable males do not marry, but father children by $P$ different women. As Willis shows, this model leads to an interest-ing algebra of a society with a mixture of monogamy and unofficial polygyny.

## 5. Interdependent preferences within families

### 5.1. Benevolence and other forms of unselfishness

#### 5.1.1. Preferences on allocations

If household members love each other, copy each other, envy each other or annoy each other, then individuals care not only about their own consumptions, but also about the consumptions of other members. In the most general case, each member's utility would depend on the amount of each private good consumed by each member of the household as well as about the amount of each household public good.

It is often useful to consider a model of household interdependence that is inter-mediate between a fully general model of interdependence and the case where con-sumers care only about their own consumptions of private goods and the vector of household public goods. An interesting and much-studied assumption is that preferences on allocations are "weakly separable" between one's own consumption and that of others.[25] The assumption that consumer $i$'s preferences are separable with respect to his own consumption means that $i$'s preferences among alternative bundles $(x_i, y)$ of private goods and household public goods are not changed by changes in the consumption bundles of others. In this case, a person may *care* about what other family members consume, but their consumption does not influence one's preferences about one's own consumption. In this case, each individual $i$ has a well-defined "private utility function" $v_i(x_i, y)$ that represents $i$'s preferences on private goods for himself given the vector $y$ of public goods.

In a model with private goods only, Winter (1969) and Bergstrom (1971a,b) define preferences of consumer $i$ to be benevolent (nonmalevolent) if there is weak separability and every family member favors (does not object to) a change in another family member's consumption that ranks higher in that person's private preferences. If there is benevolence (nonmalevolence), then preferences of every person $i$ can be represented by a utility function of the Bergson–Samuelson form, $U_i(v_1(x_1, y), \ldots, v_h(x_h, y))$. where $U_i$ is an increasing (nondecreasing) function of $v_j$. Archibald and Donaldson (1976) define preferences that can be represented by utility functions of the form $U_i(v_1(x_1, y), \ldots, v_h(x_h, y))$ where $U_i$ is not necessarily monotone increasing in its arguments to be *nonpaternalistic preferences*. They point out that nonpaternalistic preferences permit not only nonmalevolence and benevolence, but also malevolence as well as preferences for equity such that $U_i$ may not be monotonic.

## 5.2. Interdependent utility functions

When family members love (or hate or envy) each other, their interlinked joys and sorrows may feed on each other in curious ways. No matter how these feelings are entwined, economists concerned with resource allocation are likely to be more interested in derived "reduced form" preferences over allocations of goods than in a tangle of interrelated preferences about the happiness of others. Therefore, although preferences over household allocations may be founded on interrelated preferences, economists are likely to want to disentangle the interrelated utilities of family members and find the corresponding derived preferences on allocations. This problem has been addressed by several economists, including Bergstrom (1971b, 1988, 1989b), Barro (1974), Becker (1974), Pearce (1983), Kimball (1987) and Bernheim and Stark (1988).

Bergstrom (1989, 1990) studies models in which there is a group of consumers whose happiness depends on their own consumption and on their perceptions of the happiness of other members of the group. Then the happiness of each person can only

---

[25] A thorough treatment of a variety of separability assumptions is found in Blackorby et al. (1978).

be determined if one knows the happiness of each of the others. One resolution of this paradoxical simultaneity is to suppose that each individual's happiness is observable by others, but with a lag. Each person's current happiness depends on his or her own current consumption and on her observation of the happiness of all other family members in the previous period. With this structure, the time path of happiness for each person is determined as a system of difference equations.[26]

As a concrete example, consider a family with $h$ members. Let $c_i(t)$ be family member $i$'s consumption bundle at time $t$ and let $U_i(t)$ be $i$'s utility at time $t$. Suppose that utility interdependence takes the additive form

$$U_i(t) = u_i(c_i(t)) + \sum_{j \neq i} a_{ij} U_j(t-1),$$

where the constant $a_{ij}$ represents the marginal effect of person $j$'s happiness in the previous period on person $i$'s current happiness. This system of difference equations can be written as a matrix equation $U(t) = u(c(t)) + AU(t-1)$, where $c(t) = (c_1(t), ..., c_h(t))$, $u(c(t)) = (u_1(c_1), ..., u_h(c_h))$, $U(t) = (U_1(t), ..., U_h(t))$ and $A$ is the matrix with zeroes on the diagonal and with $A_{ij} = a_{ij}$ for $i \neq j$.

Let us evaluate the path of utilities in the case where each family member receives a constant consumption over time so that $c(t) = c$ in every period. Suppose that in period 0, family members start with an arbitrary distribution of utilities $(U_1(0), ..., U_h(0))$. If the eigenvalues of the matrix $A$ all have absolute values less than unity, the distribution of utilities will converge to a constant vector that we will define to be $U(c)$. This equilibrium distribution of utilities must satisfy the equation $U(c) = (I - A)^{-1} u(c)$. As Pearce (1983) and Bergstrom (1988) observe, when utility interdependence is nonmalevolent, the matrix $A_{ij}$ is nonnegative and the formal structure of the model is the same as that of Leontief input–output matrices. The theory of productive Leontief matrices[27] can be borrowed to good effect. A nonnegative matrix $A$ is said to be *productive* if there exists some positive vector $x$ such that $(I - A)x$ is a strictly positive vector. Gale proves the following properties of productive matrices:
(i) If $A$ is a nonnegative, productive matrix, the matrix $(I - A)^{-1}$ exists and is nonnegative in every element.
(ii) A nonnegative matrix $A$ is productive if and only if all eigenvalues of $A$ are smaller than one in absolute value.
From property (i), it follows that if $A$ is a productive matrix, then where the allocation $c$ of consumption over time is constant, there must be a unique limiting distribution of

---

[26] In a paper which proposes several interesting models of interdependent utility, Pollak (1976) introduces the idea of using lagged, rather than simultaneous independence.

[27] For an elegant treatment of productive matrices, see Gale (1960). An equivalent condition is known as the Hawkins–Simon condition. Yet another equivalent condition is that the matrix $I - A$ be "dominant diagonal". See McKenzie (1960).

utility $U(c)$ such that $U(c) = u(c) + Au(c)$. Thus $U(c) = (I - A)^{-1}u(c)$. Writing out in full, the implied utility functions on allocations, we have $U_i(c_1, \ldots, c_h) = \sum_{j=1}^{h} a_{ij}b_{ij}u_j(c_j)$ where $b_{ij} \geq 0$ is the $ij$th element of the matrix $(I - A)^{-1}$.

The requirement that $A$ be a productive matrix limits the strength of benevolent interdependence. For example, in a two-person family, $A$ will be a productive matrix if and only if $a_{12}a_{21} < 1$. Bergstrom (1971b, 1989b) shows that for two persons, a system of *superbenevolent* interdependent utilities in which $a_{12}a_{21} > 1$ has the property that at all Pareto optimal allocations, disagreements between the two persons take the form of each wanting the other to have the better part.[28] In the case where there are more than two persons, the matrix $A$ will be productive if $\sum_{j=1}^{h} a_{ij} < 1$ for all $i$. If there is nonmalevolence and the matrix $A$ is not productive, then the dynamical system implied by the equation $U(t) = u(c) + AU(t-1)$ is not stable. This would imply that starting from certain configurations of utility, although consumption of each consumer is constant, the interrelated happinesses would feed on each other and diverge. The dynamics of unstable utility interactions have not yet been studied by economists.

## 5.3. Intergenerational utility interdependence

Utility interdependence in families does not begin and end with a single nuclear family. Everyone's parents were children of parents who were children of parents and so on.[29] Samuelson (1958) pioneered formal modeling of an "overlapping generations" economy, in which a new generation appears in every time period, and each generation ages and dies. In Samuelson's model, there is no benevolence between parents and offspring. Each newborn enters the world, not as a helpless baby, but as a rational decision-maker aware that she has a specific pattern of endowments of labor to sell over the course of her life. Her encounters with preceding and subsequent generations are entirely commercial – borrowing or lending to smooth her lifetime consumption.[30]

Strotz (1955) argues that individual preferences need not be time-consistent in the sense that if one makes an optimal lifetime consumption plan from the viewpoint of the present, one's "future self" may choose not to abide by this plan. In the absence of time-consistency, Strotz suggests two possible theories of consumer behavior. These theories, which are clarified and refined by Pollak (1968) and by Blackorby et al. (1978), are known as theories of "naive" strategies and of "sophisticated" strategies. A person with a naive strategy takes the first step of the intertemporal consumption plan

[28] Matzkin and Streufert (1991) present an interesting example in which *supermalevolence* leads to paradoxes similar to those induced by superbenevolence.

[29] It is tempting to say that every child will be a parent of children who will be parents, but of course not everyone has children. Most economic models of overlapping generations do not, however, take this fact into account.

[30] Diamond (1965a,b) extends this model to allow accumulation of capital and to study the effects of national debt.

that is optimal given his current preferences while making the (incorrect) assumption that in the future he will stick to this plan. In an equilibrium of sophisticated strategies, a person with intertemporally inconsistent plans chooses his current consumption, knowing that in the next period, his preferences over the future will not be consistent with his current preferences. If he knows what these preferences will be, then in equilibrium, each period's choice will be optimal for that period based on what he knows will be chosen in future periods.

As Phelps and Pollak (1968) and Blackorby et al. (1978) suggest, the Strotz model is a natural starting point for a theory of interaction between benevolent parents and their descendants. Let $c_t$ be the consumption vector of generation $t$ and $_tc$ be the vector $(c_t, c_{t+1},...)$ specifying the consumption of generation $t$ and each subsequent generation. Then a person in generation $t$ has preferences represented by a utility function of the form $U_t(_tc)$. The Strotz model would allow a member of any generation $t$ to choose its own $c_t$ and to leave an inheritance to its successor generation. The next generation in turn is allowed to choose its consumption and the inheritance it leaves to its successor. A mother who follows a naive strategy chooses consumption and saving based on the (generally incorrect) assumption that her descendants will dispose of her inheritance in the same way she would wish them to. A mother who follows a sophisticated strategy chooses her preferred amount of saving in the knowledge that her daughter will spend her inheritance in a way that is optimal from the daughter's point of view.

Koopmans (1960) studied conditions on utility functions that guarantee time-consistency. Where $_tc$ is the vector $c_t, ..., c_m$ of consumption in time periods from $t$ until the end of the decision-maker's life, Koopmans showed that if preferences are stationary, additively separable between time periods and time consistent, then (subject to some technical conditions) it must be that preferences of the individual in time $t$ are representable by a "time-discounted" utility function of the form $U_t = \sum_{\tau=t}^{m} \alpha^\tau u(c_\tau)$. If weak separability rather than additive separability is assumed and if the time horizon is infinite, then time consistent utility functions must take the recursive form $U_t(_tc) = V(c_t, U(_{t-1}c))$.

Naive application of single-person intertemporal models to family dynasties lack one important feature of modern economic life: the illegality of slavery. It is natural in a single-consumer model to allow the consumer to borrow on future income, even if he is not able to commit his future selves to a particular course of action. In the intergenerational interpretation, people are allowed to leave positive inheritances, but they are not allowed to sell the future labor services of their descendants and thus enhance their current consumption. Laitner (1979a,b, 1988, 1990) published a series of papers that explore bequests, saving and debt in models where parents cannot extract wealth from their descendants, under various assumptions about mating patterns.

One of the most influential applications of recursive intergenerational utility is Barro's (1974) paper, "Are Government Bonds Net Wealth?". Barro argues that if utility functions take the form $U_t(_tc) = V(c_t, U(_{t-1}c))$ and if each generation voluntarily leaves an inheritance to its successor, then government programs which impose intergenerational transfers (for example subsidized education, social security, and government debt) will be offset by corresponding changes in inheritance.

Barro finds neutrality in a model where reproduction is asexual or the only mating is between siblings. There are no marriages and no connections between family lines. Bernheim and Bagwell (1988) suggest that if Barro's model is to be taken seriously, then it must also apply in a model with intermarriage between families. Bernheim and Bagwell argue that if a daughter from one family marries a son from another family and if both parental families leave inheritance to the bride and groom, then a small income transfer from one parental family to another would be undone by offsetting changes in the inheritances of the two sides of the family. But this is only the beginning. If the bride and groom each have a sibling who marries someone else, then the two families that were directly linked by marriage will be indirectly linked to a third and fourth family, which in turn will be linked to other families. Since transfers between directly linked families are offset by changes in gifts, income transfers between indirectly linked families will likewise be fully offset, through a chain reaction of changes in gifts along the path of marriages relating these families.

Bernheim and Bagwell apply simulations and offer corroborating arguments from random graph theory to show that with reasonable models of mate selection, there is a very high probability that any two families in large finite populations will be indirectly linked by marriage where the links connecting people span only two generations. If it were the case that for all marriages, both sets of parents-in-law left inheritance to their offspring, then with very high probability, almost any small governmental income redistribution would be undone by offsetting private actions. Bernheim and Bagwell find this implausible and suggest that it is likely that there are large numbers of breaks in the chain, that is instances where one or both sets of parents-in-law do not leave estates to their children. Where there are many breaks in the intergenerational chain of giving, Barro's neutrality result cannot be expected to apply.

Laitner (1991) proposes a model in which marriage is not random but strongly assortative on income so that persons who expect large inheritances will marry others who expect similarly large inheritances. In Laitner's model, the cross-sectional neutrality found by Bernheim and Bagwell is absent because marriages between children from families of significantly different income levels are rare and when they do occur, typically the less wealthy parental family will leave no estate to the young couple.

An economically and mathematically interesting structure arises when each generation cares not only about its own consumption and the utility of its successor but also about the utility of its parent generation. Kimball (1987), models "two-sided altruism" by assuming that preferences of generation $t$ take the additively separable form

$$U_t = u_t(c_t) + aU_{t-1} + bU_{t+1},$$

where $a$ and $b$ are positive constants. Kimball was the first to solve this system of in-

terdependent utility functions for the equivalent set of utilities defined over allocations. Hori and Kanaye (1989) and Hori (1990) study extensions of the two-sided altruism model to cases where the interaction are of the nonadditively separable form
$U_t = V(U_{t-1}, c_t, U_{t+1})$.

Bergstrom (1988) examines Kimball's model of two-sided altruism within the more
general class of interdependent utilities that are expressed by the matrix equation
$U = u + AU$ where $A$ is a nonnegative matrix. In the overlapping generations model,
there are infinitely many future generations. This fact threatens to pose formidable
mathematical problems. While many of the fundamental results of finite dimensional
linear algebra carry over to denumerable matrices and vectors, there are some nasty
surprises. Among these surprises are the fact that matrix multiplication is not, in general, associative and the fact that a matrix may have more than one inverse (for a good
exposition of this theory, see Kemeny et al., 1966). Fortunately, it turns out that denumerable productive matrices are much better behaved than denumerable matrices in
general and in fact share all of the desirable properties of finite productive matrices
(see Bergstrom, 1988).

In Kimball's case, the matrix $A$ has values $a$ everywhere on the first subdiagonal, $b$
everywhere on the first superdiagonal and zeros everywhere else. It turns out that the
matrix $I - A$ is dominant diagonal if and only if $a + b < 1$. In this case, the interdependent utility functions can be untangled by matrix inversion to yield simple, but
very interesting utility functions defined over allocations of consumption. Kimball and
Bergstrom both find that the generation $t$'s utility for an infinite consumption stream
over the past and future is given by

$$U_t = \sum_{j=1}^{\infty} \alpha^j u_{t-j}(c_{t-j}) + u_t(c_t) + \sum_{j=1}^{\infty} \beta^j u_{t+j}(c_{t+j}),$$

where $\alpha$ and $\beta$ are constants, such that $0 < \alpha < 1$, $0 < \beta < 1$ and $\alpha/\beta = a/b$.

In this formulation, a person born in period $t$ cares not only about her own consumption and the consumption of her dependents, but also about the consumption of
her ancestors. While it may be true that she can do nothing to change the consumption
of her ancestors, it could be that her preferences about her own consumption and that
of her descendants would be shaped by what had happened to her ancestors. As it
happens, preferences on allocations that are derived from the two-sided altruism
model are additively separable between the consumption of one's ancestors, one's own
consumption and that of one's descendants. Hence for this case, one can study preferences over future generations without investigating family history. This observation
illustrates the usefulness of disentangling preferences on allocations from preferences
on utilities. When one simply looks at the structure of two-sided altruistic preferences
over utilities, it is not obvious without the mathematics that preferences on allocations
will be additively separable across generations. One might also want to ask whether it

is realistic to assume a preference structure that implies additive separability between one's preferences over the consumption pattern of ancestors and the consumptions of one's descendants. For example, in some families it is important not to leave a smaller estate to one's children than has been the norm for previous generations.

The utility function over allocations that is derived from two-sided altruism implies a time-consistency property which is an interesting generalization of the Strotz–Koopmans property. Consider two generations in the same family line, $t$ and $t'$ where $t < t'$. Generation $t$ and $t'$ will have identical preferences about the allocation of consumption among generations that come after $t'$ and about generations that come before $t$. They will, however, in general disagree about income transfers among generations in the interval between $t$ and $t'$.

Laitner (1988) studies gift and bequest behavior in a model of two-sided altruism where bequests must be positive and voluntary and where there are random differences in wealth between generations. As Laitner points out, in reasonable models of intergenerational preferences, there will be gifts from parents to children if the parents are much richer than their children and gifts from children to parents if the children are much richer than their parents, and over some (quite possibly large) intermediate range of relative incomes, there will not be gifts in either direction. Thus there is a positive (and possibly high) probability that in any generation, the chain of voluntary gift-giving necessary to sustain neutrality as in the Barro model or the Bernheim–Bagwell model will be broken.

## 5.4. Pareto optimality of competitive equilibrium in households with utility interdependence: the First Welfare Theorem

It is reasonable to ask what kind of decentralized allocation mechanisms can achieve Pareto efficient allocation in a household. A competitive equilibrium allocation within the household should certainly be included in any roundup of the usual suspects. But if there are benevolent consumers, there is in general no reason to expect that competitive equilibrium is Pareto optimal. If we define competitive equilibrium so as to exclude the possibility of gifts, then even in a two-person family a competitive equilibrium can fail to be Pareto optimal. The reason is simply that with benevolence it may be possible for both donor and recipient to benefit from a gift.[31]

The problem in the previous example could be fixed by extending the notion of competitive equilibrium to allow for voluntary "gifts". This approach is taken in Bergstrom (1971b), who shows that for two-person families, a competitive gift equi-

---

[31] For example, consider a family with two persons and one good. Utility functions $U_1(x_1, x_2) = x_1^2 x_2$ and $U_2(x_1, x_2) = x_1 x_2^2$, where $x_i$ is the amount of good consumed by person $i$. Person 1 has an initial endowment of five units of the private good and person 2 has one unit. The initial endowment (5, 1) is a competitive equilibrium, but it is not Pareto optimal, since both persons would prefer the allocation where person 1 gets four units and person 2 gets two units.

librium is Pareto optimal. But for households in which more than one person cares about the consumption of others, a competitive gift equilibrium in which individuals decide independently how much to give each other is not Pareto optimal. The reason is that the well-being of someone who is loved by more than one person becomes a "public good". Purely bilateral gift arrangements will not result in a Pareto optimal allocation. In such an environment, Pareto efficiency requires multilateral coordination among those who are benevolent toward the same individual. Bergstrom (1971a) explores a Lindahl equilibrium in which those who are benevolent toward an individual each pay some share of the cost of that individual's consumption and all agree on the quantities, given their cost shares.

In Becker's Rotten Kid model (1974), competitive equilibrium with gifts leads to a Pareto optimal allocation in the household. However, this optimality is purchased with a very strong assumption. In particular it is assumed that there is one benevolent family member who makes voluntary gifts to each of the other family members, while no other family members choose to make gifts. Since by assumption, the head of the family is making gifts to all other family members, the allocation that results is the household head's favorite allocation among all allocations which cost no more than total family income.[32]

In an overlapping generations model where each generation has a property right to its own labor, the assumption that a current household head is willing to make positive gifts to all future generations is not attractive. But for families in which preferences are characterized by the recursive structure $U_t = U_t(c_t, U_{t+1})$, competitive equilibrium with voluntary inheritance turns out to be Pareto optimal even if some generations choose to leave nothing to their successors. There seems to be neither a statement nor a proof of this proposition in the literature, but for a family with a finite horizon, proving this proposition is a fairly easy exercise in backward induction.[33] One uses the recursive structure of preferences to show that if an allocation is at least as good for all family members and preferred by some family members to a competitive equilibrium, then the total cost of the proposed allocation to the family dynasty exceeds the total cost of the family's competitive allocation. The remainder of the proof mimics the Arrow–Debreu proof of the Pareto optimality of competitive equilibrium.

### 5.4.1. The efficiency of competitive equilibrium with nonbenevolence

According to the First Welfare Theorem, under very weak assumptions, a competitive equilibrium is Pareto optimal for selfish consumers. It seems plausible that this result

---

[32] Although in the simplest version of the Rotten Kid theorem, family members other than the head are assumed to be selfish, the optimality of competitive equilibrium would extend to the case where more than one family member is benevolent if it is assumed that the utility of the head depends positively on the overall utility of each family member.

[33] The proof extends to an infinite horizon if there is sufficient "impatience" so that the present value of resources to appear in the distant future converges to zero.

would extend to the case of malevolent (or nonbenevolent) preferences. Parks (1991) demonstrates that this conjecture holds for a broad class but not for all nonbenevolent preferences. Where all family members have preferences of the Bergson form

$$U_i(v_1(x_1), \ldots, v_n(x_n)),$$

Parks defines the $n$ by $n$ matrix $G(v_1, \ldots, v_n)$ to be the Jacobean matrix whose $ij$th element is $\partial U_i(v_1, \ldots, v_n)/\partial v_j$. He shows that a competitive equilibrium will necessarily be a local Pareto optimum if the matrix $G^{-1}$ is a nonnegative matrix.[34] As Parks observes, in the case of nonbenevolence the off-diagonal elements of $G$ are nonpositive and the diagonal elements are positive. In addition, as this matrix has the dominant diagonal property (McKenzie, 1960), it will be true that $G^{-1}$ is a nonnegative matrix.

The matrix $G$ will fail to be dominant diagonal if malevolence is too intense. In this case, a competitive equilibrium is not necessarily Pareto optimal. Consider for example a pure exchange economy with two consumers and one private good and suppose that free disposal is possible. Each consumer has an initial endowment of two units of the good. Consumer 1 has utility $U_1(x_1, x_2) = x_1 - x_2^2$ and consumer 2 has utility $U_2(x_1, x_2) = x_2 - x_1^2$, where $x_i$ is consumption by consumer $i$. The no-trade outcome where $x_1 = x_2 = 2$ is a competitive equilibrium. In this case, each consumer has a utility of $-2$. But this outcome is evidently not Pareto optimal. For example, if $x_1 = x_2 = 1/2$, each consumer will have a utility of $1/4$. In this example, the conditions of Parks' theorem fail since the matrix $G$ turns out not to be dominant diagonal when $x_1 = x_2 = 2$.

### 5.5. Sustainability of Pareto optimality as competitive equilibria: the Second Welfare Theorem

Winter (1969) observed that the Second Welfare Theorem (with convex preferences, every Pareto optimum can be sustained as a competitive equilibrium) extends without modification to the case of nonmalevolent preferences. This result has an interesting application to the theory of family consumption because it suggests that in families where nonmalevolence reigns, consumption decisions can be efficiently decentralized by giving each family member an allowance to spend on personal consumption.

Winter's result, however, is not quite as powerful as it might first appear. Competitive equilibrium as defined by Winter requires that each family member spend his income only on himself. A more useful theorem for decentralization in a benevolent

---

[34] Parks' proof is as follows. A local Pareto improvement is possible only if $G \, dv > 0$ for some vector $dv$. If $G^{-1}$ is nonnegative, then $G \, dv > 0$ implies $dv > 0$. But as in the proof of the First Welfare Theorem without externalities, it must be that starting from a competitive equilibrium, there is no feasible change in allocation for which $dv > 0$.

family would state that in a "competitive equilibrium with gifts", where people are allowed to choose their best combination of personal consumption and money transfers to others, every Pareto optimum is a competitive equilibrium. But this result is not true without some qualification. For example, consider the case where $U_1(x_1, x_2) = x_1 x_2^2$ and $U_2(x_1, x_2) = x_1^2 x_2$ and consider the allocation $(3, 3)$, which is Pareto optimal. If no gifts are permitted, then this is a competitive equilibrium, but if gifts are allowed, person 1 would want to give one unit to person 2 and accept no gifts from her. If person 2 were allowed to choose, she would give one unit to person 1 and accept nothing from him. Thus there will be no equilibrium in which each is allowed to determine his or her net gift to the other. We could rescue the situation by defining a gift equilibrium to be one in which nobody wants to make a gift which other persons are willing to accept, or alternatively by assuming that persons are "selfish enough" so that it never happens that one person wants to make a gift that the other will not accept. More complicated versions of this problem arise when several generations have interconnected utility functions (see Bergstrom, 1971b; Pearce, 1983).

Archibald and Donaldson (1976) show that with certain restrictions, the Second Welfare Theorem extends to nonpaternalistic preferences which are not monotonic increasing in all of the $v_j$'s. Their argument is based on the observation that the standard first-order conditions for Pareto optimality in an economy with nonpaternalistic preferences require that individuals all have the same marginal rates of substitution between goods. Given sufficient convexity, and given that the constrained optimality problem determining a Pareto optimum satisfies the appropriate constraint qualifications so that the standard first-order conditions are necessary for Pareto optimality, the Archibald–Donaldson conclusion follows.

### 5.5.1. Public goods and benefit–cost analysis in benevolent families

If family members want each other to be happy and if they share some household public goods, how do we determine a Pareto efficient expenditure on these public goods? For example, consider a married couple without children who are deciding whether to get a new car. The price of a new car is $P$. Suppose that the husband is willing to pay $H_1$ for the enjoyment he would get from using the car and $H_2$ for the enjoyment his wife would get from using the car. The wife is willing to pay $W_1$ for the enjoyment she would get from using the car and $W_2$ for the enjoyment the husband would get from using the car. How much should the couple be willing to pay in total for the car?

In the presence of "pure" nonmalevolence, there is a very simple and perhaps surprising answer to this question. Even though each person is willing to pay something for the other's enjoyment of the car, they should buy the car if and only if the sum $H_1 + W_1 \geq P$. This result is an instance of a very general result that also applies to multiperson families and to cases where the public goods are supplied continuously rather than discretely.

Consider a family with $n$ members where the utility of each household member $i$ can be expressed as $U_i(u_1(c_1, y), ..., u_n(c_n, y))$ where $c_i$ is the vector of private consumption goods consumed by $i$ and where $y$ is the vector of household public goods consumed by the family. The assumption of nonmalevolence means that $U_i$ is an increasing function of $u_i$ and a nondecreasing function of $u_j$ for all $j \neq i$. Therefore if an allocation is Pareto optimal (in terms of the $U_i$'s), it must be that this allocation would also be Pareto optimal for an economy of selfish people in which each $i$ has a utility function $u_i(x_i, y)$. But this means that any conditions which are necessary conditions for optimality in this selfish family are also necessary conditions for optimality in the actual benevolently related family.

For our example of the husband, wife, and car, it is easy to see that if $P < H_1 + W_1$, they can achieve a Pareto improvement by buying the car and dividing the costs so that the husband gives up less than $H_1$ dollars worth of private goods and the wife gives up less than $W_1$ dollars worth of private goods. Now suppose that $P > H_1 + W_1$. Imagine for the moment that husband and wife are selfish with private utilities $u_i(c_i, y)$. Then buying the car would be inefficient in the following sense. For any household allocation that they could afford if they buy the car, there will be another household allocation in which they do not buy the car and both of their private utilities will be higher. But since their preferences are benevolent, the fact that they can improve both of their private utilities by not buying the car implies that they can both increase the utilities that represent their benevolent preferences by not buying the car. If the couple were to use a decision rule such as "Buy the car if $P < H_1 + W_1 + H_2 + W_2$" they would act inefficiently whenever $P < H_1 + W_1 + H_2 + W_2$ but $H_1 + W_1 < P$.

Where the quantity of public goods is a continuous variable and consumers are selfish, the fundamental benefit–cost result for efficient supply of public goods in an economy is the Samuelson first-order condition (Samuelson, 1954) which requires that the sum of all individuals' marginal rates of substitutions between the public good and their own private consumption equals the marginal cost of public goods in terms of private goods. Since the Samuelson condition is a necessary condition for Pareto optimality in the selfish family where individual preferences are $u_i(c_i, y)$, and since Pareto efficiency in this selfish family is necessary for Pareto efficiency in the corresponding benevolent family, the Samuelson conditions measured from the selfish utility functions must be satisfied in order for there to be efficiency in the benevolent family.

Although the problem of benefit–cost analysis of household public goods in benevolent families seems interesting and important, it does not seem to have received much attention in the literature. The issue does, however, arise fairly frequently in discussions in the public policy literature about how to value persons' lives. If family members love each other, then the survival of each is a household public good. Jones-Lee (1991, 1992) has recently organized and clarified this discussion. According to Jones-Lee, the traditional prescription for evaluating a public project that saves "statistical lives" is that the evaluation should include not only people's willingness to pay for their own safety, but the sum of the amounts people would be willing to pay for improvements in the safety of others.[35] As Jones-Lee points out, Bergstrom (1982) claims this prescription is inappropriate if altruism takes the form of pure concern for other people's utility. Bergstrom's (1982) argument is essentially the same as the argument made above for household public goods, but was specialized to the analysis of risks to life.

Jones-Lee discusses the alternative case of "safety-focused altruism" in which people's only concern with the well-being of others is with their survival probabilities. In this case, he shows that it is appropriate in benefit–cost analysis to add people's willingness to pay for other people's survival probabilities to their willingness to pay for their own. Jones-Lee (1992) also suggests a model of interdependent preferences, which he calls paternalistic preferences, in which each person is "benevolent" towards others, but instead of accepting the other person's relative valuation of survival probability and wealth, the paternalistic individual wishes to impose his *own* relative values on the recipient.

## 5.6. Evolutionary models of benevolence with the family

In recent years, evolutionary biologists have developed a body of formal theory of the amount of altruism that can be expected to emerge among relatives in sexually reproducing species. Haldane (1955) remarked that according to evolutionary theory, one should be prepared to rescue a sibling from drowning if the likelihood of saving the sibling's life is at least twice the risk to one's own. To induce one to take the same risk for a first cousin, the likelihood of saving the cousin's life must be at least eight times the risk of drowning oneself.

Hamilton's remarkable papers (1964a,b) were the first to work out a formal justification for Haldane's calculus of altruism. Hamilton's main result has come to be known as "Hamilton's Rule". Hamilton states his rule as follows:

> The social behavior of a species evolves in such a way that in each distinct behavior-evoking situation the individual will seem to value his neighbors' fitness against his own according to the coefficients of relationship appropriate to that situation. (1964b: p. 19)

According to Hamilton's rule, natural selection will favor genes that lead a creature to be willing to exchange its own expected number of offspring for those of a relative so long as $c/b < r$, where $c$ is the cost of the action in terms of ones own expected off-

---

[35] This prescription is advanced in Mishan's (1971) classic paper on the evaluation of human life and safety as well as in papers by Needleman (1976), Jones-Lee (1976), and Viscusi et al. (1988).

spring, $b$ is the gain to the relative and $r$ is the "coefficient of relatedness" between the individual and his relative. For diploid, sexually reproducing species with random mating, $r$ is 1/2 for offspring and full siblings, 1/4 for grandchildren and half-siblings, 1/8 for great grandchildren and first cousins, and so on.

Dawkins' book *The Selfish Gene* (1976) popularized Hamilton's theory in a way that many economists have found accessible and stimulating. Dawkins advocates the viewpoint that the replicating agent in evolution is the *gene* rather than the animal. If a gene carried by one animal is likely to appear in its relatives, then a gene for helping one's relatives, at least when it is cheap to do so, will prosper relative to genes for totally selfish behavior. Trivers' book *Social Evolution* (1985) explores numerous applications of the theory of the evolution of altruism and conflict between relatives. This book is a pleasure to read, with a fascinating mixture of theories and applications of the theories throughout the animal kingdom.

Hamilton's rule is intriguing because it not only predicts a limited degree of altruism toward relatives, but makes explicit predictions of the degree of altruism as a function of the degree of relationship. Since the environments that shaped our genes are hidden in the distant past, most economists are skeptical about the usefulness of evolutionary hypotheses for explaining human preferences. Still, such fundamental features of family life as mating, child-rearing, and sibling relations are remarkably similar across existing cultures[36] and are likely not to have changed drastically over the millennia. This suggests that evolutionary theory can be expected to enrich the economics of the family.[37]

Trivers (1985) applies the Hamilton theory to parent–offspring conflict and to sibling rivalry and sibling conflict. According to Hamilton's theory, in a sexually reproducing diploid species, full siblings (who on average have half of their genes in common) will tend to value each other's survival probability half as much as they value their own. Parents, on the other hand, will value the survival probabilities of each offspring equally. Trivers illustrates these theoretical problems with field observations of feeding conflicts between mother and offspring and among siblings in several species of birds and mammals.

Hamilton proves his propositions only for environments where costs and benefits are purely additive. That is, each individual's survival probability can be expressed as a sum of "gifts" given to or received from relatives. Bergstrom (1995) extends the Hamilton model of altruism between siblings in order to allow general interactions in which benefits and costs from helping others may be nonlinear and nonseparably interactive.

Bergstrom and Stark (1993) offer a series of models in which altruism between

---

[36] For an anthropologist's view of the near-universality of much family structure, see for example, Stephens (1963).

[37] This view seems to be shared by Becker (1976) and Hirshleifer (1977, 1978). Hirshleifer's 1978 paper contains an engaging manifesto on behalf of an evolutionary theory of preference formation.

siblings and neighbors persists under evolutionary pressures. In these models, inheritance may be either genetic or "cultural".

## 5.7. Conscious choice of altruism

### 5.7.1. When is more love not a good thing?

In evolutionary models, the degree of altruism is selected endogenously by forces of natural selection. Bernheim and Stark (1988) consider some issues that arise if people are able to make conscious choices about how much to love others. Choices of this kind are especially pertinent to courtship and marriage. The metaphor "falling in love" suggests a certain lack of control of the process, but even here, one has some choice in choosing which precipices to approach.

Bernheim and Stark find interesting examples in which an increase in love by one individual may be bad for both the lover and the beloved. They parameterize love as a particular kind of interdependence of utility functions and show that altering the amount of love in a relationship can have surprising effects. For example, suppose that one member of a couple is naturally unhappy. If his partner were to increase her love for him, she would share his unhappiness and become visibly less happy herself. To make matters worse, her unhappy beloved would become even more miserable when he observes her reduced happiness.

Bernheim and Stark find further paradoxes in the application of noncooperative game theory to people who love each other. Consider two players in a nonzero-sum game. Suppose that an increase in one person's love is defined as making that person's payoff a convex combination of his own and his partner's payoff with an increased weight on the partner's payoff. In the Nash equilibrium for the resulting game, an increase in love may turn out to decrease rather than increase the payoffs of one or both partners. Bernheim and Stark also show that increased love may make both parties worse off in multi-stage games, where an increase in love may eliminate certain punishment strategies as credible threats and hence result in a Pareto inferior equilibrium.

### 5.7.2. Maximizers and imitators

Cox and Stark (1992) suggest that selfish people may choose to be kind to their aged parents because with some probability this behavior will be "imprinted" on their own children, who when the time comes will treat their own parents as they saw their parents treat their grandparents. Parents would then find it in their self-interest to treat their parents as they would like to be treated themselves when they are old.

Bergstrom and Stark (1993) remark that there is an incongruity in assuming that each generation rationally selects its behavior towards its parents, but believes that its children will copy their parents rather than make their own rational choices. Bergstrom and Stark suggest a model in which some fraction of children turn out to be imitators, while the others are maximizers. They assume that the environment is stationary, so that maximizers in any generation have the same utility functions and face the same probabilities that their children will be maximizers. A maximizer, although she may be entirely selfish, realizes that if her child is an imitator, then the help that she gives to her aged parents will be rewarded when she, herself, is old, by her child who has learned to treat aged parents generously. If, however, the child is a maximizer, the child's best action is independent of the way her mother acted. Bergstrom and Stark describe the optimizing conditions for maximizers in this situation and show that the more likely children are to be imitators, the better people will treat their aged parents. Since the behavior of imitators is ultimately copied from an ancestor who is a maximizer, the same analysis predicts the behavior of imitators.

# References

Archibald, G.C. and D. Donaldson (1976), "Non-paternalism and the basic theorems of welfare economics", Canadian Journal of Economics 9: 492–507.

Axelrod, R. (1984), The evolution of cooperation (Basic Books, New York).

Barro, R. (1974), "Are government bonds net wealth?", Journal of Political Economy 82: 1095–1117.

Becker, G. (1965), "A theory of the allocation of time", Economic Journal 75: 493–517.

Becker, G. (1974), "A theory of social interactions", Journal of Political Economy 82: 1063–1094.

Becker, G. (1976), "Altruism, egoism, and fitness: economics and sociobiology", Journal of Economic Literature 14: 817–826.

Becker, G. (1981), A treatise on the family (Harvard University Press, Cambridge, MA).

Bergson, A. (1938), "A reformulation of certain aspects of welfare economics", Quarterly Journal of Economics 52: 310–334.

Bergstrom, T. (1971a), "A 'Scandinavian consensus' solution for efficient allocation with non-malevolent preferences", Journal of Economic Theory 2: 383–398.

Bergstrom, T. (1971b), "Interrelated consumer preference and voluntary exchange", in: A. Zarley, ed., Papers in quantitative economics (Kansas University Press, Lawrence, KS) pp. 79–94.

Bergstrom, T. (1988), "Systems of benevolent utility interdependence", Working paper (University of Michigan, Ann Arbor, MI).

Bergstrom, T. (1989a), "A fresh look at the rotten kid theorem", Journal of Political Economy 97: 1138–1159.

Bergstrom, T. (1989b), "Love and spaghetti, the opportunity cost of virtue", Journal of Economic Perspectives 3: 165–173.

Bergstrom, T. (1995), "On the evolution of altruistic ethical rules for siblings", American Economic Review 85: 58–81.

Bergstrom, T. and M. Bagnoli (1993), "Courtship as a waiting game", Journal of Political Economy 101: 185–202.

Bergstrom, T. and R. Cornes (1981), "Gorman and Musgrave are dual – an antipodean theorem on public goods", Economics Letters 7: 371–378.

Bergstrom, T. and R. Cornes (1983), "Independence of allocative efficiency from distribution in the theory of public goods", Econometrica 51: 1753–1765.

Bergstrom, T. and D. Lam (1989a), "The effects of cohort size on marriage markets in twentieth century Sweden", in: The family, the market, and the state in industrialized countries (Oxford University Press, Oxford).

Bergstrom, T. and D. Lam (1989b), "The two-sex problem and the marriage squeeze in an equilibrium model of marriage markets", Working paper (University of Michigan, Ann Arbor, MI).

Bergstrom, T. and R. Schoeni (1992), "Income prospects and age of marriage", Working paper (Economics Department, University of Michigan, Ann Arbor, MI).

Bergstrom, T. and O. Stark (1993), "How altruism can prevail in an evolutionary environment", American Economic Review (Papers and Proceedings) 83: 149–155.

Bergstrom, T. and H. Varian (1985), "When do market games have transferable utility", Journal of Economic Theory 35: 222–233.

Bergstrom, T., L. Blume and H. Varian (1986), "On the private supply of public goods", Journal of Public Economics 29: 25–49.

Bernheim, B.D. and K. Bagwell (1988), "Is everything neutral?", Journal of Political Economy 96: 308–338.

Bernheim, B.D. and O. Stark (1988), "Altruism within the family reconsidered: do nice guys finish last?", American Economic Review 78: 1034–1045.

Binmore, K.G. (1985), "Bargaining and coalitions", in: A. Roth, ed., Game-theoretic models of bargaining (Cambridge University Press, Cambridge) pp. 259–304.

Binmore, K.G. (1987), "Perfect equilibrium in bargaining models", in: K. Binmore and P. Dasgupta, eds., The economics of bargaining (Blackwell, Oxford).

Binmore, K., A. Shaked and J. Sutton (1989), "An outside option experiment", Quarterly Journal of Economics 753–770.

Blackorby, C., D. Primont and R.R. Russell (1978), Duality, separability and functional structure: theory and economic applications (North-Holland, New York).

Brinig, M. (1990), "Rings and promises", Journal of Law, Economics, and Organization 6: 203–215.

Browning, M. (1992), "Children and household economic behavior", Journal of Economic Literature 30: 1434–1475.

Browning, M., F. Bourguignon, P.-A. Chiappori and V. Lechene (1992), "A structural empirical model of within household allocation", Working paper (McMaster University, Hamilton, Ontario).

Bruce, N. and M. Waldman (1990), "The rotten-kid theorem meets the Samaritan's dilemma", Quarterly Journal of Economics 105: 155–165.

Buchanan, J. (1975), "The Samaritan's dilemma", in: E. Phelps, ed., Altruism, morality, and economic theory (Russell Sage Foundation, New York) pp. 71–85.

Campbell, D. and M. Truchon (1988), "Boundary optima and the theory of public goods supply", Journal of Public Economics 35: 241–250.

Carmichael, H.L. and W.B. MacLeod (1993), "Gift giving and the evolution of cooperation", Working paper (Economics Department, Queens University, Kingston, Ontario).

Chiappori, P.-A. (1988), "Rational household labor supply", Econometrica 56: 63–90.

Chiappori, P.-A. (1992), "Collective labor supply and welfare", Journal of Political Economy 100: 437–467.

Chiappori, P.-A., L. Haddad, J. Hoddinot and R. Kanbur (1992), "Unitary versus collective models of the household: time to shift the burden of proof", Paper presented at the 1993 American Economics Meetings.

Chipman, J. (1974), "Homothetic preferences and aggregation", Journal of Economic Theory 8: 26–28.

Coleman, J. (1990), Foundations of social theory (Harvard University Press, Cambridge, MA).

Cox, D. and O. Stark (1992), "Intergenerational transfers and the demonstration effect", Mimeo. (Boston College, Chestnut Hill, MA).

Crawford, V. and A. Kelso (1982), "Job matching, coalition formation, and gross substitutes", Econometrica 50: 1483–1504.

Crawford, V. and E. Knoer (1981), "Job matching with heterogeneous firms and workers", Econometrica 49: 437–451.

Danzig, G. (1951), "Application of the simplex method to the transportation problem", in: T.C. Koopmans, ed., Activity analysis of production and allocation (Wiley, New York).

Das Gupta, P. (1973), "Growth of the U.S. population, 1940–1971, in the light of an interactive two-sex model", Demography 10: 543–565.

DaVonza, J. and M.O. Rahman (1994), "American families: trends and correlates", Population Index 59: 350–386.

Dawkins, R. (1976), The selfish gene (Oxford University Press, New York).

Deaton, A. and J. Muellbauer (1980), Economics and consumer behavior (Cambridge University Press, Cambridge).

Demange, G. and D. Gale (1985), "The strategy structure of two-sided matching models", Econometrica 53: 873–888.

Diamond, P. (1965), "National debt in a neoclassical growth model 2", American Economic Review 55: 1126–1149.

Diamond, P. (1965), "The evaluation of infinite utility streams", Econometrica 33: 170–17.

Diewert, E. (1977), "Generalized Slutsky conditions, for aggregate consumer demand functions", Journal of Economic Theory 15: 333–336.

Eisenberg, E. (1961), "Aggregation of utilities", Management Science 7: 337–350.

Gale, D. (1960), The theory of linear economic models (McGraw-Hill, New York).

Gale, D. and L. Shapley (1962), "College admissions and the stability of marriage", American Mathematical Monthly 69: 9–15.

Gaulin, S. and J. Boster (1992), "Dowry as female competition", American Anthropologist 92: 994–1005.

Goody, J. (1973), "Bridewealth and dowry in Africa and Eurasia", in: J. Goody and S. Tambiah, eds., Bridewealth and dowry (Cambridge University Press, Cambridge) pp. 1–57.

Gorman, W.M. (1953), "Community preference fields", Econometrica 21: 63–80.

Haddad, L. and J. Hoddinott (1991), "Household expenditures, child anthropomorphic status and the intra-household division of income: evidence from the Cote d'Ivoire", Discussion paper 155 (Research Program in Development Studies, Princeton University, Princeton, NJ).

Haddad, L. and J. Hoddinott (1994), "Womens' income and boy–girl anthropometric status in the Cote d'Ivoire", World Development 22: 543–553.

Haldane, J.B.S. (1955), "Population genetics", New Biology 18: 34–51.

Hamilton, W.D. (1964a), "The genetical evolution of social behavior. I", Journal of Theoretical Biology 7: 1–16.

Hamilton, W.D. (1964b), "The genetical evolution of social behavior. II", Journal of Theoretical Biology 7: 17–52.

Hartung, J. (1982), "Polygyny and inheritance of wealth", Current Anthropology 23: 1–12.

Hicks, J.R. (1956), A revision of demand theory (Clarendon Press, Oxford).

Hirshleifer, J. (1977), "Economics from a biological viewpoint", Journal of Law and Economics 1–52.

Hirshleifer, J. (1978), "Natural economy versus political economy", Journal of Social and Biological Structures 1: 319–337.

Hoddinott, J. and L. Haddad (1995), "Does female income share influence household expenditure? Evidence from Cote d'Ivoire", Oxford Bulletin of Economics and Statistics 57: 77–96.

Hori, H. (1990), "Utility functionals with nonpaternalistic intergenerational altruism: the case where altruism extends to many generations", Working paper.

Hori, H. and S. Kanayo (1989), "Utility functionals with nonpaternalistic intergenerational altruism", Journal of Economic Theory 49: 241–255.

Johnson, D.S. (1990), "Team behavior in the family: an analysis of the rotten kid theorem", Working paper (Bureau of Labor Statistics).

Jones-Lee, M. (1991), "Altruism and the value of other people's safety", Journal of Risk and Uncertainty 4: 213–219.

Jones-Lee, M. (1992), "Paternalistic altruism and the value of statistical life", The Economic Journal 102: 80–90, 102.

Juster, F.T. and F.P. Stafford (1991), "The allocation of time: empirical findings, behavioral models, and problems of measurement", Journal of Economic Literature 29: 471–522.

Kaneko, M. (1982), "The central assignment game and the assignment markets", Journal of Mathematical Economics 10: 205–232.

Kemeny, J., J. Snell and A. Knapp (1966), Denumerable Markov chains (Van Nostrand, Princeton, NJ).

Keyfitz, N. (1971), "The mathematics of sex and marriage", in: Proceedings of the sixth Berkeley symposium on mathematical statistics and probability, Vol. IV (University of California Press, Berkeley, CA).

Kimball, M. (1987), "Making sense of two-sided altruism", Journal of Monetary Economics 20: 301–326.

Koopmans, T. (1960), "Stationary ordinal utility and impatience", Econometrica 28: 287–309.

Koopmans, T. and M. Beckman (1957), "Assignment problems and the location of economic activities", Econometrica 25: 53–76.

Laitner, J. (1979a), "Household bequests, perfect expectations, and the national distribution of wealth", Econometrica 47: 1175–1194.

Laitner, J. (1979b), "Bequests, golden-age capital accumulation and government debt", Economica 46: 403–414.

Laitner, J. (1988), "Bequests, gifts, and social security", Review of Economic Studies 55: 275–299.

Laitner, J. (1990), "Intergenerational preference differences and optimal national saving", Journal of Economic Theory 22: 56–66.

Laitner, J. (1991), "Modeling marital connections among family lines", Journal of Political Economy 99: 1123–1141.

Lam, D. (1988), "Marriage markets and assortative mating with household public goods", Journal of Human Resources 23: 462–487.

Lindbeck, A. and J. Weibull (1988), "Altruism and efficiency, the economics of fait accompli", Journal of Political Economy 96: 1165–1182.

Lotka, A. (1922), "The stability of the normal age distribution", Proceedings of the National Academy of Sciences USA 8: 339.

Lundberg, S. and R. Pollak (1993), "Separate spheres bargaining and the marriage market", Journal of Political Economy 101: 988–1011.

Lundberg, S. and R. Pollak (1994), "Noncooperative bargaining models of marriage", American Economic Review 84: 132–137.

Manser, M. and M. Brown (1980), "Marriage and household decision theory – a bargaining analysis", International Economic Review 21: 21–34.

Marshack, J. and R. Radner (1972), Economic theory of teams (Yale University Press, New Haven, CT).

Matzkin, R. and P. Streufert (1991), "On interdependent utility", Working paper (University of Wisconsin, Madison, WI).

McElroy, M. (1990), "The empirical content of Nash-bargained household behavior", Journal of Human Resources 25: 559–583.

McElroy, M. and M. Horney (1981), "Nash-bargained decisions: toward a generalization of the theory of demand", International Economic Review 22: 333–349.

McFarland, D. (1972), "Comparison of alternative marriage models", in: T.E. Greville, ed., Population dynamics (Academic Press, New York) pp. 89–106.

McKenzie, L. (1960), "Matrices with dominant diagonals and economic theory", in: K. Arrow, K.S. Karlin and P. Suppes, eds., Mathematical methods in the social sciences (Stanford University Press, Stanford, CA).

Mishan, E.J. (1971), "Evaluation of life and limb: a theoretical approach", Journal of Political Economy 79: 687–705.

Moldevanu, B. (1990), "Stable bargained equilibria for assignment games without side-payments", International Journal of Game Theory 19: 171–190.

Murdock, G.P. (1967), Ethnographic atlas (University of Pittsburgh Press, Pittsburgh, PA).

Muth, R. (1966), "Household production and consumer demand functions", Econometrica 34: 699–708.

Nash, J. (1950), "The bargaining problem", Econometrica 18: 155–162.

Needleman, L. (1976), "Valuing other people's lives", Manchester School 44: 309–342.

Parks, R. (1991), "Pareto irrelevant externalities", Journal of Economic Theory 54: 165–179.

Pearce, D. (1983), "Nonpaternalistic sympathy and the inefficiency of consistent intertemporal plans", Working paper (Cowles Foundation, Yale University, New Haven, CT).

Phelps, E. and R. Pollak (1968), On second-best national saving and game-equilibrium growth, Review of Economic Studies 35: 185–200.

Pollak, R. (1968), "Consistent planning", Review of Economic Studies 35: 201–208.

Pollak, R. (1976), "Interdependent preferences", American Economic Review 66: 309–320.

Pollak, R. (1986), "A reformulation of the two-sex problem", Demography 23: 247–259.

Pollak, R. (1987), "The two-sex problem with persistent unions: a generalization of the birth matrix-mating rule model", Theoretical Population Biology 32: 176–187.

Pollak, R. (1990), "Two-sex demographic models", Journal of Political Economy 98: 399–420.

Pollak, R. and M. Wachter (1975), The relevance of the household production function and its implications for the allocation of time", Journal of Political Economy 68: 349–359.

Rader, T. (1964), "Edgeworth exchange and general economic equilibrium", Yale Economic Essays 4: 133–180.

Rochford, S. (1984), "Symmetrically pairwise-bargained allocations in an assignment market", Journal of Economic Theory 34: 262–281.

Roth, D. (1992), "A theory of partnership dynamics, learning, specific investment, and dissolution", Working paper (University of Michigan, Ann Arbor, MI).

Roth, A. and M. Sotomayor (1990), Two-sided matching (Cambridge University Press, Cambridge).

Rubinstein, A. (1982), "Perfect equilibrium in a bargaining model", Econometrica 50: 97–109.

Rubinstein, A. and A. Wolinsky (1985), "Equilibrium in a market with sequential bargaining", Econometrica 53: 1133–1150.

Samuelson, P. (1947), Foundations of economic analysis (Harvard University Press, Cambridge, MA).

Samuelson, P. (1950), "Evaluation of real national income", Oxford Economic Papers II: 1–20.

Samuelson, P. (1954), "The pure theory of public expenditures", Review of Economics and Statistics 36: 387–389.

Samuelson, P. (1956), "Social indifference curves", Quarterly Journal of Economics 70: 1–22.

Samuelson, P. (1958), "An exact consumption-loan model of interest with or without the social contrivance of money", Journal of Political Economy 66: 467–482.

Samuelson, P. (1961), "A new theorem on nonsubstitution", in: Money, growth and methodology, Published in honor of Johan Akerman (Lund Social Science Studies, Lund, Sweden) pp. 407–423.

Schultz, T.P. (1990), "Testing the neoclassical model of family labor supply and fertility", Journal of Human Resources 25: 599–634.

Shafer, W. (1977), "Revealed preference and aggregation", Econometrica 45: 1173–1182.

Shaked, A. and J. Sutton (1984), "Involuntary unemployment as a perfect equilibrium in a bargaining model", Econometrica 52: 1351–1364.

Shapiro, P. (1977), "Social utility functions", Journal of Economic Theory 16: 475–480.

Shapley, L. and M. Shubik (1972), "The assignment game I: the core, International Journal of Game Theory 1: 111–130.

Stephens, W.N. (1963), The family in cross-cultural perspective (Holt, Rinehart, Winston, New York).

Strotz, R. (1955), "Myopia and inconsistency in dynamic utility maximization", Review of Economic Studies 23: 165–180.

Sutton, J. (1986), "Noncooperative bargaining theory: an introduction", Review of Economic Studies 53: 709–724.

Thomas, D. (1990), "Intra-household resource allocation: an inferential approach", Journal of Human Resources 25: 635–696.

Trivers, R. (1985), Social evolution (Benjamin/Cummings, Menlo Park, CA).

Varian, H. (1983), "Nonparametric tests of consumer behavior", Review of Economic Studies 50: 99–110.

Varian, H. (1984), "Social indifference curves and aggregate demand", Quarterly Journal of Economics 99: 403–414.

Viscusi, W.K., W.A. Magat and A. Forest (1988), "Altruistic and private valuations of risk reduction", Journal of Policy Analysis and Management 7: 227–245.

Weiss, Y. and R. Willis (1985), "Children as collective goods in divorce settlements", Journal of Labor Economics 3: 268–292.

Weiss, Y. and R. Willis (1993), "Transfers among divorced couples: evidence and interpretation", Journal of Labor Economics 11: 629–679.

Willis, R. (1994), "A theory of out-of-wedlock childbearing", Working paper (University of Chicago, Chicago, IL).

Wilson, W.J. (1987), The truly disadvantaged (University of Chicago Press, Chicago, IL).

Winter, S. (1969), "A simple remark on the second optimality theorem of welfare economics", Journal of Economic Theory 1: 99–103.

Woolley, F. (1988), "A non-cooperative model of family decision making", Working paper TIDI/125 (London School of Economics, London).

*Chapter 3*

# THE FORMATION AND DISSOLUTION OF FAMILIES: WHY MARRY? WHO MARRIES WHOM? AND WHAT HAPPENS UPON DIVORCE

YORAM WEISS*

*Tel-Aviv University*

**Contents**

*I received helpful comments from G. Becker, T. Bergstrom, S. Grossbard-Shechtman, P. Chiappori, R. Michael R. Pollak, R. Willis and A. Wolinsky.

*Handbook of Population and Family Economics. Edited by M.R. Rosenzweig and O. Stark*

# 1. Introduction

This survey summarizes the main ideas that economists bring to the analysis of marriage and divorce. It is fair to say that most of the work on these issues has been done outside economics. The new perspective of economists is that marriage, when viewed as a voluntary union of rational individuals, is subject to the same tools of analysis as other economic phenomena. In particular, economists rely heavily on the similarity between the job market, where workers and firms combine to produce marketable goods, and the marriage market where husbands and wives combine to produce non-marketable household goods. In both cases the forces of competition determine the assignment and the associated division of the proceeds between the partners.

As usual, analogies can be extremely helpful or totally misplaced. In this survey applications of simple economic analysis are presented. The intention is to illustrate how economists think about the issues of marriage and divorce. However, economic considerations do not dominate the picture. A successful theory which is capable of explaining the data on marriage and divorce must incorporate ideas from sociology biology and other fields. Yet, an understanding of the economic point of view can be helpful in the construction of a unified approach.

This survey does not enumerate individual contributions and does not provide an exhaustive list of empirical facts. Instead, the reader is exposed to the main ideas in an integrated fashion, using simple models. Empirical findings are mentioned, briefly, only to the extent that they bear on these ideas. Such a presentation of the literature can be useful to students and researchers who are curious about what can economics say on "noneconomic" subjects such as marriage and divorce (Becker, 1991). Mortensen (1988) provides an excellent survey of part of the material. A recent survey with similar objectives but somewhat different coverage than the present one is Cigno (1991). Several aspects of the interactions between the labor and marriage markets are discussed by Grossbard-Shechtman (1993).

# 2. Economic reasons for marriage

From an economic point of view, marriage is a partnership for the purpose of joint production and joint consumption. The production and rearing of children is the most commonly recognized role of the family. But there are other important functions:
(1) Division of labor to exploit comparative advantage or increasing returns. For instance, one partner works at home and the other works in the market.
(2) Extending credit and coordination of investment activities. For example, one partner works when the other is in school.
(3) Sharing of collective (nonrival) goods. For instance, both partners enjoy the same child and share the same home or the same information.

(4) Risk pooling. For example, one partner works when the other is sick or unemployed.

None of the above must really happen within families. If all goods and work activities are marketable, there is no need to form marriages to enjoy increasing returns or to pool risks. In fact, the role of the family varies depending on market conditions and vice versa. For instance, with good medical or unemployment insurance one does not need to rely on one's spouse. Sex and even children can be obtained commercially. Nevertheless, household production persists because it economizes on search, transaction costs and monitoring. However, to fully exploit these advantages requires a durable relationship. This shifts attention to the question which types of partnerships are likely to last.

Gains from human partnerships need not be confined to a couple of the opposite sex. One also observes "extended families" of varying structures which coordinate the activities of their members and provide self-insurance. The prevalence of male–female partnerships has to do with sexual attraction which triggers some initial amount of blind trust. (The Bible is quite right in puzzling over why "shall a man leave his father and mother and cleave unto his wife".) Equally important is a strong preference for own (self-produced) children. These emotional and biological considerations are sufficient to bring into the family domain some activities that could be purchased in the market. Then, the accumulation of specific "marital capital" in the form of children, shared experience and personal information increases the costs of separation and creates incentives for a lasting relationship. In this sense, there is an accumulative effect where economic considerations and investments reinforce the natural attachment. Other glues, derived from cultural and social norms also support lasting relationships. But in each case customs interact with economic considerations. The weaker the market, the more useful is the extended family, and social norms (commands) are added to the natural glue.

Some simple examples are provided which illustrate the potential gains from marriage.

## 2.1. Increasing returns

There is a household production function where purchased goods, $x$, and time spent at home, $t$, are combined to produce a commodity, $z$, which can be consumed and transferred within the household but cannot be sold. Since it takes about the same time to produce a meal for two as for one, using twice the materials, we shall use a production function of the form

$$z = xt. \tag{2.1}$$

This production function displays increasing returns to scale in the sense that doubling all inputs raises output by a factor of four. However, increasing returns do not cause indeterminacy of household actions because household time cannot be bought directly. The only way to get more household time is to work less in the market. Therefore, it is not feasible to increase both $x$ and $t$.

For a single person we can assume, without loss of generality, that utility is measured by total output. His objective, therefore, is to maximize $z$. If we use the budget constraint

$$x = wh, \tag{2.2}$$

and the time constraint

$$t + h = 1, \tag{2.3}$$

we see that a single person will choose $t = h = 1/2$, resulting in optimal output $z^* = w/4$.

Now consider a marriage between two people a and b with wages $w_a$ and $w_b$, respectively. Assume that each person's utility is simply his share, $z_i$ in total family output. In this case, the household's objective will be to maximize the joint output

$$z = [(w_a(1 - t_a) + w_b(1 - t_b)](t_a + t_b). \tag{2.4}$$

Observe that total output is determined by the aggregate time spent at home by both partners and the total amount of goods purchased by the family in the market. This expression is maximized by setting the home time of the high-wage person to zero and the home time of the low-wage person to one, yielding a joint output

$$z^* = \text{Max}[w_a, w_b]. \tag{2.5}$$

Comparing the results for a single person household and a couple, we see that there is always a positive gain from marriage. If the two wages are equal, $w_a = w_b = w$, the gain from marriage, $w/2$, is purely due to increasing returns. If $w_a \neq w_b$ the gain is even larger, reflecting the added gains from specialization according to comparative advantage.

As emphasized by Becker (1991: Ch. 2), even in the absence of ex-ante differences between the partners, comparative advantage can be developed via differential investments. Whether at the market or at home, human capital is more useful if it is used more intensely. Within marriage each party can use his capital to a larger extent. For instance, a wife can specialize in household capital and a husband in building a career.

There is ample evidence for division of labor within the household. Married men work longer hours in the market and have substantially higher wages than unmarried men. Married women have lower wages and work more at home than unmarried women (see Gronau, 1986; Daniel, 1992; Korenman and Neumark, 1992).

## 2.2. Imperfect credit market

Consider two potential partners denoted by a and b. Each person lives for two periods which we denote by 1 and 2. Utility in each period is derived from consumption only

$$u_{it} = U(c_{it}). \tag{2.6}$$

Each person has a given earning capacity which he can augment by schooling:

$$y_{i2} = y_{i1}(1 + \gamma\lambda_{i1}), \tag{2.7}$$

where $\gamma$ is a parameter indicating learning capacity, $\gamma > 1$, and $\lambda$ is the rate of investment, $0 \leq \lambda \leq 1$. Investment at a rate $\lambda$ implies a loss of potential earnings $\lambda y$ and a direct cost $\lambda d$, where $d$ denotes the per period tuition costs. The gain in future earnings is given by $y\gamma\lambda$. Thus, the rate of return for investment in human capital is

$$\rho_i = \gamma y_{i1}/(y_{i1} + d) - 1. \tag{2.8}$$

Because of the linear technology, the rate of return is independent of the level of investment. Because of the presence of direct costs, a person with higher earning capacity (higher $y_{i1}$) will have a higher rate of return for investment in human capital.

Consider first a perfect capital market where each person can borrow and lend freely at a fixed interest rate, $r$. Under a perfect capital market, production and consumption decisions can be separated. Schooling is chosen to maximize wealth. Each person will specialize in schooling in the first period if $\rho_i > r$ and invest nothing if $\rho_i < r$. This simple investment rule holds whether or not a marriage occurs. Consider now an imperfect capital market where a person can save (at a real interest rate of $r$) but cannot borrow against his future labor income. In this case, consumption and production cannot be separated and the investment rule will depend on marital status. In particular, person $i$ in isolation cannot invest more than $y_{1i}/(d + y_{1i})$ since this would imply negative consumption. However, if two people facing a borrowing constraint marry, they can transfer consumption good within the family and support an optimal investment policy.

To illustrate, let us simplify further assuming a linear utility function, $U_i(c_{it}) = c_{it}$, and setting $r = 0$. In this case, a single person with initial earning capacity $y_{i1}$ obtains a life time utility (consumption) given by

$$u_i = y_{i1} + y_{i1} \text{Max}[1, \gamma y_{i1}/(y_{i1} + d)].$$                       (2.9)

A family consisting of two individuals with initial incomes $y_a$ and $y_b$, such that $0 \leq y_a, y_b \leq d$, can obtain

$$u_{ab} = y + y \text{Max}[1, \gamma y_a/(y_a + d), \gamma y_b/(y_b + d)],$$              (2.10)

where $y = y_a + y_b$. That is, the family invests only in the schooling of the person with the higher rate of return, i.e. the person with the higher earning capacity. The other person works in the market and finances this investment. At a lower cost of schooling, where $y_a, y_b \geq d$, it may be profitable to send both partners to school, but again most of the resources will be invested in the person with the higher earning capacity. In any case, because of the substitution within marriage towards the person with higher earning capacity we must have $u_{ab} \geq (u_a + u_b)$. In this model, there is no gain from marriage for partners with equal earning capacity. More generally, if individuals vary in their ability as investors for reasons which are unrelated to earning capacity (i.e. have different $\gamma$) there would be gains from marriage even if incomes are equal.

Evidence of implicit credit arrangements within marriage is sometimes revealed at the time of divorce, when the wife claims a share of her ex-husband's earnings on the grounds that she supported him in school (see Borenstein and Courant, 1989).

### 2.3. Sharing collective goods

Some of the consumption goods of a family are nonrival and both partners can share them. Expenditures on children or housing are clear examples. If all goods within marriage are collective goods, the gains from marriage are obvious. If a person with income $y_i$ lives alone, his utility is $U_i(y_i)$, $i = a,b$. If two such persons marry, each member $i$ of the union will have a utility $U_i(y_a + y_b)$, which exceeds his utility in the single state.

There is no need to assume that all family income is spent on public goods. In fact, the presence of any amount of collective goods generates gains from marriage. To see that, let

$$u = U_i(c_i, q_i),$$                                                                  (2.11)

where $c_i$ is private consumption and $q_i$ expenditure on a sharable good. When each partner is single, $q$ is treated like a private good and the budget constraint is

$$c_i + q_i = y_i.$$                                                                     (2.12)

Each person alone will maximize his utility subject to his budget constraint. Let us denote the optimal choices by $c_i^*$, $q_i^*$ and the resulting utility by $u_i^*$.

Now consider a marriage between two individuals a and b. Without loss of generality, assume that $q_b^* \geq q_a^*$. Consider the maximization

$$\text{Max } U_a(c_a, q), \tag{2.13}$$

subject to

$$c_a + c_b + q \leq y_a + y_b \tag{2.14}$$

and

$$U_b(c_b, q) \geq u_b^*. \tag{2.15}$$

Observe that in this maximization, the same quantity $q$ appears in both utilities. This reflects the public good aspect of $q$. The allocation $c_a = c_a^*$, $c_b = c_b^*$ and $q = q_b^*$ satisfy Eq. (2.15) as an equality and Eq. (2.14) as an inequality. It also makes person a at least as well off as in the original single state. Therefore, by increasing consumptions to the point where Eq. (2.14) is binding, person a can be made strictly better off, while person b is as well off as in the his single state. Implicit in this proof is the assumption that an increase in the marginal utility from the public good is positive for both partners. Clearly, there is a loss from marriage if one of the partners views $q$ as a nuisance, and would not have consumed it on his own.

To illustrate, let preferences be represented by

$$u_i = c_i q_i, \quad i = a, b. \tag{2.16}$$

Each person separately maximizes $u_i = (y_i - q)q$ with respect to $q$, yielding $q_i^* = y_i/2$ and $u_i^* = y_i^2/4$. Maximizing the utility of partner a subject to the family budget constraint (2.14) and the efficiency requirement $c_b q \geq y_b^2/4$ yields $q = y/2$ and $u_a^{**} = y^2/4 - y_b^2/4 > y_a^2/4$.

The share of public goods in family expenditures can be substantial. For instance, Lazear and Michael (1980) estimate that two single individuals can almost double their purchasing power by forming a union. Sometimes the partners can share productive inputs rather than consumption goods. It has been observed, for instance, that the wife's schooling enhances her husband's wages (see Benham, 1974).

## 2.4. Risk sharing

Consider two risk averse partners with uncertain incomes. Acting alone each partner will have an expected utility given by $E(U_i(y_i))$. Acting together they can trade consumption in different states of nature. To see the potential gains from trade, consider the maximization

$$\text{Max } E(U_a(c_a)), \tag{2.17}$$

subject to

$$E(U_b(y_a + y_b - c_a)) \geq E(U_b(y_b)). \tag{2.18}$$

Clearly, setting in each state $c_a = y_a$ is a feasible solution which will imitate the allocations in the single state. However, the optimal risk sharing rule is

$$U_a'((c_a) = \lambda U_b'(c_b) \tag{2.19}$$

where $\lambda$ is a positive constant. That is, the slope of the utility frontier (given by $-U_a'(c_a)/U_b'(c_b)$) is equalized across states. Otherwise, both partners can be made better off by transferring resources to a person in a state where his marginal utility of consumption is relatively high, taking resources away from him in another state where his marginal utility is relatively low. Following this optimal rule, both partners can be made strictly better off, provided that their incomes are not perfectly correlated.

Depending upon the particular risk, the potential gains from mutual insurance can be quite large. For instance, Kotlikoff and Spivak (1981) who consider the risk of uncertain life, in the absence of an annuity market, estimate that the gains that a single person can expect upon marriage are equivalent to 10–20% of his wealth. In a different application, Rosenzweig and Stark (1989) show that marriages in rural India are arranged between partners who are sufficiently distant to significantly reduce the correlation in rainfall, thereby generating gains from insurance.

Keeping these examples in mind, we can now return to the question which activities will be carried out within the family. One argument is that the family simply fills in gaps in the market system, arising from thin markets, or other market failures (see Locay, 1990). Another line of argument (see Pollak, 1985) is that the family has some intrinsic advantages in monitoring (due to proximity) and in enforcement (due to access to nonmonetary punishments and rewards). A related but somewhat different argument is that family members have already paid the (sunk) costs required to acquire information about each other (see Ben-Porath, 1980). Thus, credit for human capital investments may be supplied internally either because of a lack of lending institutions, or because a spouse recognizes the capacity of her partner to learn and is able to monitor the utilization of his human capital better than outsiders. Similarly, annuity insurance is provided internally, either because of lack of annuity markets or because married partners have a more precise information on their spouse's state of health than the market at large. It is clear that these three considerations interact with each other and cannot be easily separated. The main insight is that the gains from marriage depend on the state of the market and must be determined in a general equilibrium context.

## 3. How families solve their economic problems

The existence of potential gains from marriage is not sufficient to motivate marriage and to sustain it. Prospective mates need to form some notion as to whether families realize the potential gains and how they are divided. This section discusses mainly the implications of efficiency and altruism to the family's allocation problem. As a preliminary, the family's allocation problem is examined in the case of transferable utility, a simplifying assumption that plays a crucial role in the literature.

### 3.1. Transferable utility

In comparing alternative marriages it is useful to define an output measure that characterizes the marriage. In general, associated with each marriage, there is a set of feasible actions. Each action yields an outcome which is the utility values (payoffs) of the two partners. In a special case, the set of utility payoffs is characterized by a single number, which can be naturally defined as the output of the marriage. This substantial simplification occurs if there exists a commodity (usually called money) which, upon changing hands, shifts utilities between the partners at a fixed rate of exchange.

Formally, let $X$ be a set of possible actions for the family. Let $x \in X$ be a particular action and let $U_a(x)$ and $U_b(x)$ represent the preferences of the two partners with respect to these actions. Suppose that preferences can be represented by

$$U_a(x) = \alpha x_1 g(x_2, x_3, \ldots, x_n) + V_a(x_2, x_3, \ldots, x_n) \tag{3.1}$$

and

$$U_b(x) = -\beta x_1 g(x_2, x_3, \ldots, x_n) + V_b(x_2, x_3, \ldots, x_n). \tag{3.2}$$

Note that for both partners the marginal utility of $x_1$ is independent of $x_1$. By assumption, the marginal utility is $\alpha g(x_2, x_3, \ldots, x_n)$ for one partner and $-\beta g(x_2, x_3, \ldots, x_n)$ for the other. In this sense, $x_1$ can be viewed as a tool for transferring utility between the partners.

Now consider any action $x$ which is Pareto efficient. That is, for some feasible $u_0$, $x$ solves the program

$$\text{Max } U_a(x), \tag{3.3}$$

subject to

$$U_b(x) \geq u_0.$$

It is easy to verify that the sub vector $(x_2^*, x_3^*, \ldots, x_n^*)$ which maximizes the weighted sum of the two utility functions, given by

$$f(x_2, x_3, \ldots, x_n) = \beta V_a(x_2, x_3, \ldots, x_n) + \alpha V_b(x_2, x_3, \ldots, x_n), \tag{3.4}$$

will be a component of any such solution. Hence, if we restrict attention to efficient outcomes, $(x_2^*, x_3^*, \ldots, x_n^*)$ will be adopted by the couple independently of the distribution of utilities within the family (i.e. independent of $u_0$). A change in $u_0$ will affect only $x_1$, the sole variable which regulates the distribution. We may define $z^* = f(x_2^*, x_3^*, \ldots, x_n^*)$ to be the output of the marriage. For any feasible action, the individual utility levels $u_a = U_a(x)$ and $u_b = U_b(x)$ satisfy

$$\beta u_a + \alpha u_b \leq z^*. \tag{3.5}$$

Eq. (3.5) defines a linear utility frontier with a slope of $-\beta/\alpha$.

The assumption of transferable utility serves two distinct purposes: (i) It simplifies the description of the family choices in the presence of conflict. In particular, it assures that a single commodity (e.g. money) is used to regulate the conflict between the two partners, while all other actions are chosen to maximize a common goal. The family decision process can be described as: choose an action which yields the highest utility frontier, then choose a point on the frontier to regulate the division. The assumptions on preferences ensure that these two steps are separable. (ii) The existence of an output measure allows each person to compare the gains from marriage that he may acquire with various potential mates. As we shall see, the distribution of outputs across marriages is sufficient information for the determination of the equilibrium outcome.

Some of the examples discussed in the previous section satisfy the requirements for transferable utility and the existence of an output measure. In the first example with household production the utility of each partner was assumed to be linear in terms of an abstract nonmarketable good. In the example with imperfect capital market, a family output measure exists when the utility of both partners is linear in the marketable consumption good. In this case, the family's objective is to maximize aggregate household consumption summed over partners and periods. A somewhat less standard case arises in the example with public goods where preferences are represented by $u_i = c_i q$ for $i = a, b$. Although utility is not strictly linear, the private consumption goods can be used to transfer utility across partners at a fixed rate of exchange. The couple will, therefore, maximize the utility sum $u_a + u_b = (y - q)q$ and choose $q = y/2$. Thus, $u_a + u_b = z^* = y^2/4$.

It should be noted that except for the function $g(x_2, x_3, ..., x_n)$, which is assumed to be comparable, it is generally not necessary to require comparability across members of the household. Thus, if we double the units of utility for person a, keeping the units for person b unaffected, the function $f(x_2, x_3, ..., x_n)$ defined in Eq. (3.4) will also double in order to keep the choice of $(x_2^*, x_3^*, ..., x_n^*)$ unaffected. Similarly, condition (3.5) will change to reflect the change in units. In particular, we can normalize $\alpha$ and $\beta$ to unity.

One may question the empirical relevance of transferable utility. It is clear that the family relationship involves multiple exchanges and quid pro quo rather than the transfer of a mean of exchange. The main role of this assumption is to capture in a simple way the idea that each partner can be compensated for his actions or traits. The simplification is that such compensations can be made without affecting total resources.

## 3.2. The role of altruism

As stated in Section 2, sexual attraction is an important ingredient in explaining why human partnerships take a rather special form. By the same view, love or altruism helps married couples to solve their allocation problem, and is therefore conducive for a lasting relationship. Specifically, altruism diminishes the need for bargaining and facilitates efficient mechanism designs which rely on informal commitments.

Consider, first, the simple case of transferable utility where the two issues of efficiency and distribution can be separated. As we have seen, there is in this case a well-defined set of actions which maximizes joint output. How are those actions actually enforced? One possibility is that bargaining takes place at the outset of marriage, some sort of binding agreement is signed and then carried out. With perfect information, one may presume that the outcome of this bargaining is efficient in the sense that the partners will agree at the outset on the set of actions which maximize marital output. However, if the partners are altruistic towards each other, their feelings of love generate implicit commitments. This can be exploited in the design of mechanisms which implement an efficient outcome and are self-enforcing.

One such scheme (see Becker, 1991: Ch. 8) is to select a principal (a family head) who is given control over family resources and can make transfers as he sees fit. The only requirement is that the principal should care about all family members in the sense that their utility enters his own preferences as normal goods. Once this scheme is put in place, each person is allowed to choose his own actions selfishly. It had been observed by Becker that such a mechanism is efficient and each participant voluntarily acts in the interest of the group. The reason is that any productive action which increases total output is rewarded by an increased transfer from the principal. Conversely, any destructive action is punished by reduced transfers. In this way the interests of the group are internalized by every member. Note that it is immaterial who the principal is and that the gains from the transfer activities can be eliminated by a lump sum at the outset. The crucial aspect is that every partner should trust the principal to truly care about all family members and that he should be able to fully control the distribution of income (including negative transfers).

Even in the absence of transferable utility, altruism can reduce the range of disagreement. That is, the parties, if they had power to determine the outcome unilaterally, will choose actions which are relatively close. This factor also diminishes the incentives to bargain (Stark, 1993).

To illustrate these two general points, let us first define altruism or caring, as it is most commonly used. Consider a couple with interrelated preferences given by

$$U_a(x) = W_a(u_a(x_a), u_b(x_b)),$$

(3.6)

$$U_b(x) = W_b(u_a(x_a), u_b(x_b)).$$

(3.7)

Thus, the aggregate (social) utility of each partner is a function of the "person specific" (private) utility indices $u_a(x_a)$ and $u_b(x_b)$, where $x_a$ and $x_b$ denote the components of the family action which directly affect each spouse. (The vectors $x_a$ and $x_b$ may include some separate components such as consumption of private goods by the two partners and some common components, such as public goods.) Caring of a for b is represented by a positive impact of $u_b$ in $W_a(.,.)$. Selfishness is represented by $u_b$ having zero marginal effect in $W_a(.,.)$. One might also write a different formulation, where a cares about the social preferences of b rather than his private ones, in which case $W_b$ would appear as an argument in a's social welfare function. That is, a takes into account that b cares for a who cares for b and so on. In this case, Eqs. (3.6) and (3.7) are the reduced form solutions of the infinite regress (see Bernheim and Stark, 1988). Operationally, the main restriction embedded in this system is that each partner is indifferent between all private actions that his spouse considers equivalent, and does not care how a given level of utility aggregate is obtained by his spouse. An immediate implication of this restriction is that a necessary condition for Pareto efficiency in terms of social preferences is Pareto efficiency in terms of private preferences. That is, to be socially efficient, the actions $x_a$ and $x_b$ must be such that $u_a(x_a)$ is maximized given $u_b(x_b)$.

To illustrate the working of the "head mechanism", let each spouse have two private actions: consumption and work. Time not spent at work is used to produce a household good which is a public good (e.g. child quality). Let us assume transferable utility and write the person specific utility as $u_i(x_i) = qc_i = \varphi(t_a, t_b)c_i$ and let the budget constraint be $c_a + c_b = (1 - t_a)w_a + (1 - t_b)w_b$, where $c_i$ denotes consumption, $t_i$ denotes time at home, and $w_i$ is the wage, $i = a,b$. Applying the results on transferable utility, it is easy to verify that any Pareto efficient allocation must maximize the "pie" [(1 −

$t_a)w_a + (1 - t_b)w_b]\varphi(t_a, t_b)$. To show that this is an equilibrium outcome of the "head mechanism", we solve the problem backwards. In the last stage, the levels of $t_a$ and $t_b$ are given and so is total family income. Given family resources, the head chooses transfers (i.e. consumption levels) for each partner in order to maximize his social welfare function. Because of transferable utility, this problem of the head translates into a choice of utility levels for each spouse given a linear constraint $u_a + u_b \leq z$, where $z$ is the size of the pie. Assuming that private utilities enter $W_a(.,.)$ as normal goods, he will increase (decrease) the person specific utilities whenever total resources at his disposal increase (decrease). Anticipating that, each person (including the head himself) will select the actions in the first stage to maximize the pie.

It has been shown by Bergstrom (1989) that, in the presence of public goods, transferable utility is necessary to obtain efficiency. If all goods are private goods and preferences are altruistic as in Eqs. (3.6) and (3.7) then there are many efficient mechanisms, even in the absence of transferable utility. For instance, let each person decide on his work and use the proceeds to purchase his own consumption.

To illustrate the narrowing of the bargaining range, let us take an even simpler case with only one consumption good for each spouse. Assume diminishing marginal utility (i.e. the person specific utilities $u_i(c_i)$ are strictly concave). In this simple case, the family has only two decisions to make, $c_a$ and $c_b$. Using the family budget constraint to eliminate $c_b$ and substituting into Eqs. (3.6) and (3.7), we can write the social welfare functions of the two partners as function of a single variable, $c_a$:

$$U_a(x) = W_a(u_a(c_a), u_b(y - c_a)), \tag{3.8}$$

$$U_b(x) = W_b(u_a(c_a), u_b(y - c_a)). \tag{3.9}$$

Now consider the allocation $c_a = y$, $c_b = 0$. This allocation would be efficient if both partners are selfish. However, under altruism a small increase in $c_b$ will make both partners better off. The reason is that b has at this point a relatively high marginal utility of consumption and a who cares about b will be more than compensated for the reduction in his private utility. By the same argument, the allocation $c_a = 0$, $c_b = y$, which is efficient under selfishness, will be inefficient if b cares about a. In general, the higher the degree of caring, the narrower will be the range of conflict. That is, both partners will agree to delete extremely unequal distributions from the family's choice set.

Note, however, that in some cases altruism may increase conflicts. Consider, for instance, the following model:

$$U_a(x) = qc_a + \beta c_b, \tag{3.10}$$

$$U_b(x) = qc_b + \beta c_a, \tag{3.11}$$

where $c_a$ and $c_b$ are husband's and wife's consumptions and $q$ is a public good. The parameter $\beta$, $0 < \beta < 1$, may be interpreted as a measure of altruism, but in this case each partner cares only about a particular good that his partner consumes not his total utility. Such goods are called "merit goods". In this example, the consumption goods have been chosen to be the merit goods. Although these merit goods are formally indistinguishable from public goods, the source of interdependence is different. The public good aspect arises from the technology of consumption (both a and b can consume the same good), the merit good aspect arises from the structure of preferences. It is easy to show that, in this case, an increase in $\beta$ will reduce the expenditure on the public good $q$ and will, therefore, increase the range of conflict in terms of consumption goods.

### 3.3. Modes of family decision-making

We may distinguish three general modes of family decision-making. The first mode arises when the family has no internal conflict, the second mode arises when a conflict exists but the partners manage to cooperate (i.e., they reach a binding agreement), the third mode arises when the conflict is resolved by a self-enforcing set of actions where no one wishes to deviate unilaterally (an equilibrium). Let us first describe these three modes for a household with two decisions for each member, consumption and work. To maintain a general framework, let us assume that each partner may care about all of the family decision variables.

### 3.3.1. A common objective

The traditional approach to the analysis of household decisions, such as labor supply of family members, was to describe the family as maximizing a "family utility function". A prototype formulation is

P1:   Max $V(c_a, c_b, l_a, l_b)$,

s.t.

$$c_a + c_b = w_a(1 - l_a) + w_b(1 - l_b) + y_a + y_b,$$

where, $c_i$, $l_i$, $w_i$ and $y_i$ denote, respectively, consumption, leisure, wage and nonwage income of partner $i$, $i = $ a,b.

Throughout the survey, we viewed a marriage as a union of two independent decision makers who may or may not cooperate. This raises the question: what is the source of the common utility function $V(\cdot)$ imposed in P1? One possible interpretation is that it relies on some (unobserved) private good to transfer utility, so that there is no real conflict in terms of observable actions. Alternatively, one may think of $V(\cdot)$ as representing the preferences of the altruistic head who, by agreement, or by custom, obtained the power to pool resources and who via transfers or other means, is capable of manipulating the actions of all family members.

### 3.3.2. Cooperation

Consistent with our general approach, let us endow the two partners with separate utility functions and assume that via bargaining, or otherwise, they reach a Pareto efficient allocation. In this case, family decisions solve the problem P2:

P2:  Max $U_a(c_a, c_b, l_a, l_b)$,

s.t.

$$c_a + c_b = w_a(1 - l_a) + w_b(1 - l_b) + y_a + y_b,$$

$$U_b(c_a, c_b, l_a, l_b) \geq u_b(w_a, w_b, y_a, y_b).$$

Here, $U_i(x)$ represent the preferences of partner $i$ over possible family actions, $i = a,b$. Each of the utility indicators depends on all family decisions since we allow for any sort altruism. By allowing $u_b$ to depend on $w_1$, $y_1$, $w_2$ and $y_2$ we can apply explicit bargaining mechanisms to select the point on the utility frontier. For instance, $u_b$ is likely to increase in $w_b$ since a higher wage for b may improve her opportunities outside marriage and, therefore, increase her share within marriage (see Manser and Brown, 1988). The crucial assumption of the cooperative model is that, whatever the mechanism for selecting the point on the efficiency frontier, the partners can always agree on and enforce an efficient outcome.

### 3.3.3. Noncooperation

One can think of family members as being linked via externalities but acting non-cooperatively. That is, each person determines the variables under his control unilaterally, taking the decisions of his spouse as given. In the single period framework discussed here, the equilibrium to this "game" satisfies

P3:  $c_a, l_a \in \underset{c,l}{\text{Argmax}}\, U(c, c_b, l, l_b)$,

s.t.

$$c = w_a(1 - l) + y_a,$$

and

$$c_b, l_b \in \operatorname*{Argmax}_{c,l} U_b(c_a, c, l_a, l),$$

s.t.

$$c = w_b(1 - l) + y_b.$$

The crucial feature of the equilibrium outcome is that it is self-enforcing. However, in contrast to the cooperative outcome, the solution need not be efficient (see Lundberg and Pollak, 1993).

### 3.4. Tests of the family's modes of behavior

Each mode of family behavior is not merely an analytic tool but a testable hypothesis. In standard demand theory one can derive restrictions on the demand function based on the assumption that the consumer maximizes some utility function subject to a budget constraint. Moreover, given information on choices at different price–income situations, one may recover the preference structure of the consumer. Similarly, in the theory of the household, one may obtain restrictions on observed demand based solely on the assumption that the allocation is efficient or self-enforcing, which hold for any pair of utility functions. Again, given data on the resources of family members, the prices they face and their consumption of private and collective goods, we may, under some conditions, recover the preferences of the partners.

In general, the fact that two individuals are linked imposes some cross-equation restrictions on their demand functions. The nature of the restrictions vary according to the particular mode of family decision-making.

With a common objective function, the demand functions solving P1 are

$$x_j = D_j(w_a, w_b, y) \tag{3.12}$$

where $x_j$ denotes one of the four decision variables $(c_a, c_b, l_a, l_b)$, and $y = y_a + y_b$ is nonwage family income. The cross-equation restrictions are embodied in the requirement that the matrix of substitution effects must be symmetric and negative semi-definite (the Slutzky conditions). For instance, the labor supply functions, derived from P1, must satisfy the symmetry condition

$$\partial h_1/\partial w_2 - h_2 \partial h_1/\partial y = \partial h_2/\partial w_1 - h_1 \partial h_2/\partial y. \tag{3.13}$$

Under cooperation, we can write the demand functions in the form

$$x_j = D_j(w_a, w_b, y, \mu(w_a, y_a, w_b, y_b)), \tag{3.14}$$

where $\mu$ is the Lagrange multiplier associated with the efficiency constraint in P2. Holding $\mu$ constant, one obtains the same demand functions as in the common objective case. Indeed, $\mu$ is constant if there is transferable utility or if one of the partners is a dictator. In general, $\mu$ varies with prices and individual incomes and the Slutzky conditions fail to hold (see McElroy, 1990). However, efficiency is indicated by the presence of the common (unknown) function which appears in all demands. Exploiting this common factor one can obtain the appropriate cross equation constraints. Consider, for instance, the demands for consumption and leisure by person a. Holding $y$ constant and differentiating with respect to the private incomes $y_a$ and $y_b$, one obtains

$$\left( \frac{\partial l_a / \partial y_a}{\partial c_a / \partial y_a} \right) = \left( \frac{\partial l_a / \partial y_b}{\partial c_a / \partial y_b} \right). \tag{3.15}$$

That is, the ratios of the marginal propensity to consume of the two goods are independent of the source of income (see Browning et al., 1994).

In the noncooperative case, demands will be of the form

$$x_{ja} = D_{ja}(w_a, y_a, f_b(w_b, y_b)) \tag{3.16}$$

and

$$x_{jb} = D_{jb}(w_b, y_b, f_a(w_a, y_a)), \tag{3.17}$$

where $x_{ji}$ denotes one of the two actions (consumption or leisure) for person $i$, $i = $ a,b. The restrictions arise because, in the solution of P3, variations which do not affect b's behavior do not influence a's behavior and vice versa.

An interesting special case arises when the links across partners depend only on the sum of their consumption levels. That is,

$$U_i(x) = U_i(c, l_i), \tag{3.18}$$

where $c = c_1 + c_2$. In this example, the sum of the consumptions constitute a public good and $l_i$ are private goods. In this case, as long as both partners consume at a positive level, the demand curves induced by the Nash equilibrium will depend only on the sum of the incomes of the two partners. That is,

$$x_{ji} = D_{ji}(w_b, w_a, y_a + y_b). \tag{3.19}$$

This result emerges because the effective constraint on the levels of the public good and private good chosen by each individual is

$$c = w_i(1 - l_i) + y_i + c_j, \quad i \neq j. \tag{3.20}$$

Note that person $i$ influences $c$ through his private contribution $c_i$, taking the contribution of $j$ as given. There is, therefore, an additional constraint facing $i$, namely $c > c_j$ which we assume not to bind. Thus, if a dollar is transferred from b to a and $c_b$ is reduced by a dollar, then a, facing the same budget constraint, will choose the same level of public good, $c$. But this means that he raises his own contribution by a dollar and, therefore, person b will be in fact satisfied with reducing his contribution by a dollar. Hence, after the redistribution all demands will be unaffected (see Bergstrom et al., 1986).

Recently, there have been attempts to test some of these restrictions. Special attention has been given to the restrictions implied by income pooling. A household with a joint objective would be influenced only by total family income. As we have seen, the same restriction also holds, in some circumstances, if the partners act noncooperatively. This prediction seems to be rejected by findings that husbands and wife's (nonwage) income have different effects on the allocation of family resources (see Horney and McElroy, 1988; Schultz, 1990; Thomas, 1994). The separate role of individual incomes is consistent with both cooperation and noncooperation. However, cooperation severely restricts the role of independent incomes as all appear through the common factor $\mu$. Browning et al. (1994) who analyze the effects of husband's and wife's (labor) income on spending on women's clothes find that pooling is rejected but efficiency is not.

In the context of uncertainty, efficiency has some further implications. Since the ratio of marginal utilities from consumption of the two partners are equalized across states of nature (see Eq. (2.19)), the consumption levels of the two partners are tied together. In particular, if there is only one consumption good and utilities are state independent then, holding aggregate consumption constant, the consumption of partner $i$ is independent of idiosyncratic shocks such as fall into unemployment or bad health. Stated differently, with risk sharing, all individuals in the household are affected by a random shock to any individual income and all consumptions move together. Testing for efficient insurance within the household is complicated by the problems in assigning family consumption to individual members. Therefore, most often the tests involve coinsurance across larger units such as villages (Townsend, 1994) or extended families (Altonji et al., 1992). Not surprisingly, the data reject efficient risk sharing at this level of aggregation. Shocks to individual households do matter.

One may well argue that efficiency or lack of it is not the main issue which separates the three modes of behavior. For example, if we restrict attention to altruistic utility functions of the form

$$U_i(x) = W_i(u_a(c_a, l_a), u_b(c_b, l_b)), \quad i = a,b, \tag{3.21}$$

then, because of separability, each of the three modes of behavior can be reduced to a single principle; divide family incomes between the two partners and let them select their own level of consumption and leisure. Efficiency, in this case, simply means that each person maximizes his specific utility, given the budget allotted to him, yielding

$$w_i U_c^i(c_i, l_i) = U_l^i(c_i, l_i), \quad i = a,b. \tag{3.22}$$

These efficiency conditions will be satisfied in all the three cases discussed above, however, they will hold at different allocations of family resources and the comparative statics with respect to changes in incomes and wages will differ. In this case, it is mainly, the division of family resources which is influenced by the mode of family decision-making (see Chiappori, 1988, 1993).

The most easily observed aspect of within family allocation is the labor supply of the two partners. Lundberg (1988) reports that in families with no young children, labor supplies are independent of their spouse wage, which is consistent with non-cooperation under separable preferences. On the other hand, among families with children, an increase in husband's wage or nonwage income reduces her hours of work. These results are consistent with either cooperation or joint maximization. As one would expect, the presence of children creates scope for division of labor and enhances cooperation. In some cases one might assign some goods to a particular partner. Browning et al. (1994) assume that women's clothes, which women presumably like, do not affect husbands directly (i.e. they are not merit goods or public goods). With this assumption one can derive the sharing rule of total family income only from observations on incomes and expenditures on clothes. They find that an increase in the wife's share in family income increases her share in total family expenditures. Similarly, Thomas (1994) reports that health outcomes for daughters and sons depend on educational differences among parents. When the wife is relatively more educated than her husband, more resources are transferred to daughters relative to sons. These findings seem to suggest that an increase in earning power increases the wife's bargaining power and her share in family resources.

## 4. The marriage market

Individuals in society have many potential partners. This situation creates competition over the potential gains from marriage. In modern societies, explicit price mechanisms are not observed. Nevertheless, the assignment of partners and the sharing of the gains from marriage can be analyzed within a market framework. The main insight of this approach is that the decision to form and maintain a particular union depends on the whole range of opportunities and not only on the merits of the specific match.

## 4.1. Stable matching

Marriage can be viewed as a voluntary assignment of males to females. We can say that an assignment is stable if:
(i) there is no married person who would rather be single;
(ii) there are no two (married or unmarried) persons who prefer to form a new union.

The interest in stable marriage assignments arises from the presumption that an assignment which fails to satisfy (i) and (ii) either will not form or will not survive.

It is relatively easy to apply the criteria for stability in the case of transferable utility, where a unique "output" measure can be associated with each marriage. In this case, a stable assignment must maximize total output over all possible assignments. To understand this result, consider the simplest possible case. Let there be two people of each sex. We use the indices $i$ and $j$ to refer to a particular male or female, $i, j = 1, 2$. Assuming that marriage dominates the single state (i.e. if any two remain unattached they can gain by forming a union), there are two possible assignments: man 1 is married to woman 1 and man 2 is married to woman 2, or man 1 is married to woman 2 and man 2 is married to woman 1. These assignments can be presented by matrices with zero or one entries, depending upon whether or not male $i$ is married to female $j$. We wish to determine which of these assignments is stable.

An output matrix with entries $z_{ij}$ which specifies the total output of each marriage provides all the information required for the determination of stable outcomes. However, to show this result we need to consider the possible divisions of the gains from marriage. Let $v_{ij}$ be the share of total output that male $i$ receives if he marries woman $j$. The woman's share in this marriage is $u_{ij} = z_{ij} - v_{ij}$. In testing for stability we treat the totals as given and the divisions as variables. Suppose that the matrix with ones on the opposite diagonal represents a stable assignment. Then, the following inequalities must hold:

$$v_{21} + u_{12} \geq z_{22}, \tag{4.1}$$

$$z_{12} - u_{12} + z_{21} - v_{21} \geq z_{11}. \tag{4.2}$$

If the first inequality does not hold then man 2 and woman 2, who are presently not married to each other, can form a union and reassign utilities so as to improve over any possible values of $v_{21}$ and $u_{12}$. If the second inequality fails to hold then male 1 and female 1, who are currently not married to each other, can form a union with an assignment of utilities which will improve upon any possible values of $v_{12}$ and $u_{21}$. Adding conditions (4.1) and (4.2), we obtain

$$z_{12} + z_{21} \geq z_{11} + z_{22}. \tag{4.3}$$

By a similar argument an assignment along the main diagonal will be stable only if (4.3) is reversed.

Condition (4.3) is not only necessary but also sufficient for stability of the off diagonal assignment. For, if it is satisfied, we can find values of $u_{12}$ and $v_{21}$ such that (4.1) and (4.2) hold. Such imputations support the stability of the assignment since it is then impossible for both partners to gain from reassignment.

Our main interest lies in the following question. Suppose each male is endowed with a single characteristic, $m$, and each female is endowed with a single characteristic, $f$, which positively affects the family's output (gains from marriage), would a stable assignment associate males with a high marital endowment to females with high marital endowment or, to the contrary, associate highly endowed males with lowly endowed females? The answer follows immediately from the observation that a stable assignment must maximize total output. Let

$$z_{ij} = Z(m_i, f_j). \tag{4.4}$$

Let us rank males and females by their marital endowment (i.e. $m_2 > m_1$ and $f_2 > f_1$). Then Eq. (4.3) can be rewritten as

$$Z(m_1, f_2) - Z(m_1, f_1) \geq Z(m_2, f_2) - Z(m_2, f_1). \tag{4.5}$$

That is, the contribution to output of the female's attribute is diminishing with the male's attribute. By a similar rearrangement, the impact of the male's attribute diminishes in the female's attribute. In other words, there is a negative interaction between the two sex-specific traits. We conclude that a negative (positive) interaction in the production of marital output leads to a negative (positive) assortative mating. Thus, if $m$ stands for money and $f$ stands for beauty then, with a negative interaction, the wealthy male will not marry the pretty woman, since, whichever way they divide their gains from marriage, either he is bid away by the less pretty woman or she is bid away by the poorer man.

Associated with a stable matching is a division of the gains from marriage. Thus the quantity $u_{ij}$ can be interpreted as the implicit wage or the bride-price that women $j$ receives for marrying man $i$. Similarly, $v_{ij}$ may be interpreted as the implicit wage or the dowry that man $i$ receives if he marries woman $j$. Eqs. (4.1) and (4.2) restrict these prices but, in general, do not determine them uniquely. In some cases, however, the within marriage division is uniquely determined by market forces. For instance, suppose that both men have the same endowment, $m_1 = m_2$, but women differ and $f_1 < f_2$. Since both men can produce more with woman 2, one would expect that competition will bid her share up and she will get a higher share within marriage than woman 1. Indeed, it is easily verified that, for this example, Eqs. (4.1)–(4.3) hold as equalities, that is, both diagonals are a stable matching, and in each matching woman 2 receives the whole marital output, while woman 1 receives nothing. Alternatively, if all females have the same endowment of the marital characteristic, $f$, and if the number of women exceeds the number of men, then a matching in which any woman gets more than the (common) value of being single cannot be stable. Even if the division within marriage is not fully determined, some qualitative properties of the division can be derived from information on the joint distribution of male and female characteristics together with a specification of household production function (Eq. (4.4)) (see Parsons, 1980).

### 4.1.1. Examples

(1) Consider the example in Section 2.1 where division of labor leads to a total output $Z(w_i, w_j) = \text{Max}[w_i, w_j]$. Since a high-wage person is more useful to a low-wage person, we generally get negative sorting. The assignment also depends on the location of the income distribution for each gender. If the two distributions are identical, then, in the 2 by 2 case, the maximal output is obtained on the opposite diagonal, where a low-wage person is matched to a high-wage person. If there are more couples, the opposite diagonal is still a solution but other solutions which are close to the diagonal exist too. If the distributions differ, there might be substantial departures from negative sorting. As an extreme case, let the worst woman have a higher wage than the best man. Then in all marriages the female wage determines the outcome and all assignments are equally good.

(2) Consider the example in Section 2.2 where, because of imperfect capital market, one partner finances the schooling investment of the other. In this case, marital output as a function of earning capacities is given by $Z(y_i, y_j) = y + y \text{ Max}[1, \gamma y_i/(y_j + d), \gamma y_j/(y_j + d)]$, implying a positive interaction, except in the region where the two partners have similar earning capacity. Since the family invests in the schooling of the person with high earning capacity, it is most efficient to match the investor with a spouse who is most productive among the less productive than the investor himself, in order to permit the maximal investment at the highest rate of return. On the whole, one would expect, therefore, to obtain positive sorting. For the case of symmetric income distributions by gender, since the gains from marriage exist only among unequals, the assignment cannot be on the main diagonal. However, as the number of couples increases, the stable assignment approaches the diagonal. If the distributions are displaced (e.g., by a translation) the assignment on the diagonal is stable.

(3) Consider, finally, the example in Section 2.3 where the partners share public goods and $Z(y_i, y_j) = (y_i + y_j)^2/4$. In this case, there is a positive interaction everywhere leading to positive sorting.

Generally speaking, one would expect negative sorting on wages and positive sorting on nonwage income (see Becker, 1991: pp. 130–134). Empirical findings suggest positive sorting on both wage and nonwage income. In particular, there is a substantial correlation in the schooling achievements of partners to marriage. In the US about half of the couples have the same level of schooling for both partners (see Mare, 1991). It is possible to rationalize such findings by combining together elements of household production and joint consumption (see Lam, 1988). For instance, similarity in schooling may lead to similarity in tastes and facilitate the allocation of public goods.

## 4.2. Nontransferable utility and the Gale–Shapley algorithm

In some cases there is no commodity which the couple can transfer within marriage. In this case a marriage generates an outcome for each partner which is fully deter-mined by the individual traits of the partners. This outcome cannot be modified by one partner compensating the other for his deficient traits. However, an undesired mar-riage can be avoided or replaced by a better one. Although there is no scope for trade within marriage, there is margin for trade across couples.

Consider again a model with equal number of females and males. Each man has a preference ranking over all women and vice versa. Such rankings can be represented by a matrix with two utility entries in each cell. A column $u_j$ describes the preference ordering of woman $j$ over all feasible males. A row $v_i$ describes the preference order-ing of man $i$ over all feasible women. We may incorporate the rankings of the single state by adding a column and a row to the matrix. In contrast to the previous analysis the entries $u_{ij}$ and $v_{ij}$ are datum for the analysis (of course, they are only unique up to monotone transformations). Given the preferences, the problem is to identify stable assignments in such a matrix.

Gale and Shapley (1992) suggested the following algorithm: To start, each man proposes marriage to his most favored woman. A woman rejects any offer which is worse than the single state, and if she gets more than one offer she rejects all the dominated offers and keeps all the undominated offers. The nonrejected proposals are put on hold (engagement). In the second round each rejected man proposes to the best of the women who did not reject him. Women will reject all dominated offers, includ-ing the ones on hold. The process stops when no male is rejected. Convergence is en-sured by the demand that no woman is approached more than once by the same man. The process must yield a stable assignment because women can hold all previous of-fers. So if there is some pair not married to each other it is only because either the man did not propose or that he did and was rejected. A different stable assignment is ob-tained if women make the offers and men can reject or store them. It can be shown that the stable matching obtained when men make the proposal is weakly preferred by all men to the stable matching that is obtained when women propose first.

*Example.* Recall the example in Section 2.3 and suppose that all goods within the family are public, implying $u_{ij} = U_j(y_i + y_j)$ and $v_{ij} = U_i(y_i + y_j)$. That is, the utility of each partner from the marriage is determined by the sum of the incomes of the two partners. In this case, there is no mean for transferring utility. Thus, for all women the ranking of men is the same, the higher his income the better. Similarly all men rank women in the same order. In this special case, there is a unique stable marriage assignment which is independent of whether men or women propose first. The only stable assignment is to associate people in a positive assortative matching along the main diagonal. To see that, suppose that men propose first. In the first round all men will propose to the woman with the highest income and she will reject all offers but the one from the best man. In the second round all remaining men will propose to the second best woman and she will reject all but the second best man and so on. The situation when women propose first is identical.

In addition to the identification of stable assignments, one can use the Gale–Shapley algorithm to obtain simple comparative static results. Allowing for unequal number of man and women, it can be shown that a change in the sex ratio has the anticipated effect. An increase in the number of women increases the welfare of men and harms some women. The same result holds in many to one assignments (polygamy). The model can be further extended to allow transfers in which case transferable utility is just a special case. Thus, if $X_{ij}$ is some feasible set of actions and $x$ is a member of this set we can define $u_{ij}(x)$ and $v_{ij}(x)$ as the utility of members $i$ and $j$, respectively, if they marry each other and action $x \in X_{ij}$ is taken. A particular action is for $i$ to transfer consumption goods to $j$. If marginal utilities are constant we are back to the case of transferable utility. In this more general framework stability is defined with respect to an assignment together with a specified action for each couple. Such an outcome is stable if no pair who is currently not married can marry and choose an action which yields a result which is better for both than their lot under the existing assignment and associated set of actions. Observe that the assignment and the actions are simultaneously restricted by this definition. (It is only under transferable utility that the two aspects can be separated). The comparative static results concerning the addition of player hold in this more general case (see Roth and Sotomayor, 1990: Ch. 6; Crawford, 1991).

## 4.3. Search

The process of matching in real life is characterized by scarcity of information about potential matches. The participants in the process must spend time and money to locate their best options. The realized distribution of matches and the division of the gains from each marriage are therefore determined in an equilibrium which is influenced by the costs of search and the search policies of other participants.

The main ingredients of the search model are as follows. There is a random process which creates meetings between members of society of the opposite sex. When a meeting occurs, the partners compare their characteristics and evaluate their potential gains from marriage. Each partner anticipates his share in the joint marital output. If the gains for both partners from forming the union exceed their expected gain from continued search, then these partners marry. Otherwise, they depart and wait for the next meeting to occur.

· Meetings occur according to a Poisson process. That is, the waiting times between successive meetings are i.i.d. exponential variables with mean $1/\lambda$. Within a short period $h$, there is a probability of a meeting given by $\lambda h + o(h)$ and a probability of no meeting given by $1 - \lambda h + o(h)$, where, $o(h)/h$ converges to zero as $h$ approaches zero. The arrival rate $\lambda$ is influenced by the actions of the participants in the marriage market. Specifically, imagine an equal number of identical males and females, say $N$, searching for a mate. Let $s_{im}$ denote the "search intensity" (i.e. number of meetings per period) initiated by a particular male. If all females search at the same intensity $s_f$ they will generate $Ns_f$ contacts per period distributed randomly across all males. In this case, the probability that male $i$ will make a contact with some female, during a short interval, $h$, is $(s_{im} + s_f)h$. If all males search at a rate $s_m$ and all females at a rate $s_f$ then the rate of meetings between agents of opposite sex is

$$\lambda = s_m + s_f. \tag{4.6}$$

The key aspect in Eq. (4.6) is that activities on both side of the market determine the occurrence of meetings. A limitation of the linear meeting technology is that the number of searchers, $N$, has no effect on the arrival rate $\lambda$ (see Diamond and Maskin, 1979, 1981).

Each participant who searches actively and initiates meetings must bear a monetary search cost given by $c_i(s)$, $i = m,f$ where we allow the costs of search to differ by sex. The total and the marginal costs of search increase as search intensity increases. (Specifically, $c(0) = c'(0) = 0$, $c'(s) > 0$ for $s > 0$ and $c''(s) > 0$.)

When a meeting occurs the marital output (quality of match) that the partners can generate together is a random variable, $z$, drawn from some fixed distribution, $F(z)$. Having observed $z$, the couple decides whether or not to marry. With transferable utility, the decision to marry is based on the total output that can be generated by the couple within marriage relative to the expected total output if search continues. Hence, a marriage occurs if and only if

$$z \geq v_m + v_f, \tag{4.7}$$

where $v_m$ and $v_f$ denote the value of continued search for the male and female partners, respectively. These values depend, in equilibrium, on the search intensity that will be chosen if the marriage does not take place. Specifically, for $i, j = m,f$,

$$rv_i = \text{Max}\{(s + s_j)\int_{v_m+v_f}^{\infty} (w_i(z) - v_i)\, df(z) - c_i(s)\}, \quad i \neq j, \tag{4.8}$$

where $w_i(z)$ denote the share of the gains of marital output that male and female partners expect. By definition,

$$w_m(z) + w_f(z) = z. \tag{4.9}$$

Eq. (4.8) states that the value of being an unattached player arises from the option to sample from offers which arrive at a rate $s + s_j$ and are accepted only if Eq. (4.7) holds. Each accepted offer yields a surplus of $w_i(z) - v_i$ for partner $i$ and integrating over all acceptable offers, weighting by $dF(z)$ (or the density $f(z)$ if it exists), we obtain the expected gain from search. Since each participant controls his own intensity of search he will choose the level of $s$ which maximizes his value in the unattached state. Therefore, with identical males and females,

$$\int_{v_m+v_f}^{\infty} (w_i(z)-v_i)\, dF(z) = c'_i(s_i), \quad i = \text{m,f}. \tag{4.10}$$

The marginal benefits from a search, the left-hand side of Eq. (4.10), depend on the share that a person of type $i$ expects in prospective marriages. As $w_i(z)$ rises, holding $z$ constant, he or she searches more intensely. Hence, the equilibrium outcome depends on the sharing rules that are adopted.

The literature examined two types of sharing rules. One class of sharing rules relies on Nash's axioms and stipulates

$$w_i(z) = v_i + \theta_i(z - v_m - v_f), \tag{4.11}$$

where $\theta_i > 0$ and $\theta_m + \theta_f = 1$, $i = \text{m,f}$.

The parameter $\theta_i$ allows for asymmetry in the bilateral bargaining between the sexes due to preferences or social norms. The crucial aspect of this assumption, however, is that outside options, reflected in the market determined values of $v_m$ and $v_f$, influence the shares within marriage. Wolinsky (1987) points out that a threat to walk out on a potentially profitable partnership is not credible. Rather than walking away, the partners exchange offers. When an offer is rejected, the partners search for an outside opportunity that would provide more than the expected gains from an agreement within the current marriage. Hence, during the bargaining process each partner search at an intensity given by

$$\int_y^{\infty} (w_i(z)-w_i(y))\, d(F(z)) = c'_i(s_i), \quad i = \text{m,f}, \tag{4.12}$$

where $y$ is the quality of the current marriage and $w_i(y)$ is the expected share in the current marriage if an agreement is reached. Since $y \geq v_m + v_f$ and $w_i(y) \geq v_i$, a person who searches for better alternatives during a bargaining process will search less intensely and can expect lower gains than an unattached person. The threat of each partner is now influenced by two factors: the value of his outside opportunities (i.e., the value of being single), which enters only through the possibility that the other partner will get a better offer and leave; the value of continued search during the bargaining process, including the option of leaving when an outside offer (whose value exceeds the value of potential agreement) arrives. Therefore, the threat points, $v_i$, in Eq. (4.11) must be replaced by a weighted average of the value of remaining without a partner and the value of continued search during the bargaining (the weights are the probabilities of these events). Given these modified threat points, the parameter $\theta_i$ which determines the shares depends on the respective discount rates of the partners and the probabilities of their exit from the bargaining process. The logic behind this type of formula, due to Rubinstein (1982), is that each person must be indifferent between accepting the current offer of his partner or rejecting it, searching for a better offer and, if none is received, return to make a counter offer that the partner will accept.

Given a specification of the share formulae, one can solve for the equilibrium levels of search intensities and the values of being unattached. For instance, if the shares are determined by Eq. (4.11) and $\theta_i$ is known, then Eqs. (4.8) and (4.10) determine unique values for $s_m$, $s_f$, $v_m$ and $v_f$. Because of the linear meeting technology, these equilibrium values are independent of the number of searchers. Observe that although the share formulae depends on institutional considerations the actual share of marital output that each partner receives depends on market forces and is determined endogenously in equilibrium.

We can close the model by solving for the equilibrium number of unattached participants relative to the population. Suppose that each period a new flow of unattached persons is added to the population. To maintain a steady state, this flow must equal the flow of new attachments which were formed from the current stock of unattached. The rate of transition into marriage is given by the product of the meeting rate $\lambda$ and the acceptance rate $1 - F(z_0)$, where $z_0$ is the reservation quality of match. Using Eqs. (4.6) and (4.7), we obtain

$$u(s_m + s_f)(1 - F(v_m + v_f)) = e, \tag{4.13}$$

where $u$ is the endogenous, steady state, rate of nonattachment and $e$ is the exogenous constant rate of entry.

The meeting technology considered thus far has the unsatisfactory feature that attached persons "do not participate in the game". A possible extension is to allow matched persons to consider offers from chance meetings initiated by the unattached, while maintaining the assumption that married people do not search. In this case divorce becomes an additional option. If an unattached person finds a married person who belongs to a marriage of quality $z$ and together they can form a marriage of quality $y$ then a divorce will be triggered if $y > z$. The search strategies will now depend on the relative numbers of attached and unattached persons. Specifically, Eq. (4.8) is replaced by

$$rv_i = \text{Max}\{u(s+s_j)\int_{v_m+v_f}^{\infty}(w_i(z)-v_i)\,dF(z)$$

$$+(1-u)s\int_{v_m+v_f}^{\infty}\int_{t}^{\infty}(w_i(z)-v_i)\,dF(y)\,dG(z)-c_i(s)\}, \quad i,j=m,f \text{ and } i \neq j, \tag{4.14}$$

where $G(z)$ is the distribution of quality of matched couples. Observe that the expected returns from meeting an attached person are lower than those of meeting with an unmarried one. Therefore, the higher is the aggregate rate of nonattachment the higher are the private returns for search.

Assuming that partners are ex-ante identical, the search models outlined above do not address the question who shall marry whom. Instead, they shift attention to the fact that, in the process of searching for a mate, there is always a segment of the population which remains unmatched, not because they prefer the single state but because matching takes time. A natural follow up to this observation is the question whether or not there is "too much" search. Clearly, the mere existence of waiting time for marriage does not imply inefficiency since time is used productively to find superior matches. However, the informational structure causes externalities which may lead to inefficiency. One type of externality arises because, in deciding on search intensity, participants ignore the higher chance for meetings that others enjoy. This suggests that search is deficient. However, in the extended model which allows for divorce there is an additional externality operating in the opposite direction. When two unattached individuals reject a match opportunity with $z \leq v_m + v_f$ they ignore the benefits that arise to other couples from a higher nonattachment rate. Thus, as in a related literature on unemployment, it is not possible to determine whether there is too much or too little nonattachment.

An important aspect of Eq. (4.14) is the two-way feedback between individual decisions and market outcomes. The larger is the proportion of the unattached the more profitable is search and each unattached person will be more choosy, further increasing the number of unattached. As emphasized by Diamond (1981) such reinforcing feedbacks can lead to multiplicity of equilibria. For, instance, the higher is the aggregate divorce rate the more likely it is that each couple will divorce. Therefore, some societies can be locked into an equilibrium with a low aggregate divorce rate while others will settle on a high divorce rate.

There are some additional features which characterize the search for a mate and can be incorporated into the analysis. First, as noted by Mortensen (1988), the quality of marriage is revealed only gradually. Moreover, each partner may have private information which is useful for predicting the future match quality (see Bergstrom and Bagnoli, 1993). Second, as noted by Oppenheimer (1988), the offer distribution of potential matches varies systematically with age, as the number and quality of available matches changes, and the information about a person's suitability for marriage sharpens. Finally, meetings are not really random. Unattached individuals select jobs, schools and leisure activities in order to affect the chances of meeting a qualified person of the opposite sex (see Goldin, 1992).

## 4.4. The division of the gains from marriage

The marriage market influences not only the assignment of partners but also the division of resources and activities within the family. At a given market situation, one would expect that a partner with more marketable traits will command a higher share of the gains from marriage. As market conditions change and a shortage of suitable partners of a particular kind is created, such partners will receive a larger share of the gains from marriage.

In traditional societies the transfer takes the form of an up-front payment in the form of a dowry or bride-price, with a possible reversed payment in the event of divorce. The data on dowries in such societies provide some evidence on the working of market forces. Grossbard (1978) brings evidence that polygamy, which raises the demand for women, tends to increase the bride-price. Rao (1993) shows that an increase in the demand for men created by faster population growth, combined with the tendency of men to marry younger women (a marriage squeeze), has led to an increase of dowries in rural India.

In modern societies, up-front payments are rare, so that the effects of market forces are mostly revealed by the division of labor within families. Grossbard-Shechtman (1993: Ch. 6) finds that a low ratio of males to females tends to increase labor force participation of married women and interprets this as a reduction in the female share in the gains from marriage. Examining recent trends in patterns of time use, Juster and Stafford (1991) observe that women reduced their total work (in the market and at home) more than men, while shifting hours from household chores to the market. In the same time, the marriage premium for males has declined (see Blackburn and Korenman, 1994). It has been argued that these shifts indicate, in part, an increase in the female share in gains from marriage. One can link the redistribution of shares to more liberal divorce laws (see Carlin, 1991) and other forms of government intervention, such as child allowances. Of course, legal changes and policy changes are to a large extent an outcome rather than a cause of market changes. Becker (1991: Ch. 2) argues that the main driving force is the higher earning capacity of women associated with modernization and changing industrial structure.

Additional information on the (expected) gains from marriage is contained in the decisions to enter marriage and to stay married. One might argue that a party who expects higher gains from marriage will decide to marry earlier and will be less likely to divorce. Keeley (1977) finds that a high wage induces men to have an early marriage while it induces women to postpone their marriages. This seems to be consistent with the view that, given the usual division of labor within the household where men work mostly in the market and women at home, high-wage men and low-wage women stand to gain more from marriage. Similarly, Weiss and Willis (1996) find that high expected earning capacity of males stabilizes the marriage, while high earning capacity of females is destabilizing. Brien (1991) finds evidence that local sex ratios (at the county level) influence the decisions to enter marriage and to have children out of wedlock. In particular, he finds support to Wilson's (1987) claim that an imbalance in the marriage market, i.e. a shortage of eligible black males in the US is a major reason for the lower rates of entry into marriage of black females relative to white females.

## 5. Divorce and its economic consequences

### 5.1. Determinants of divorce

As we have seen in the previous section, the search model allows for divorce in quite a natural way. Since couples meet randomly, a matched person can find a better match than his current match. Another important cause for divorce is uncertainty about the quality of the match and other marriage related characteristics of the partners. In this section a simple framework for a dynamic analysis of the marriage relationship is presented which incorporates the acquisition of new information. At the time of marriage, the two spouses have only limited information on the determinants of the gains from marriage. As time passes, new information on the success of their joint venture and on the outside options of each partner is accumulated and the couple decides whether to dissolve the partnership or to continue the marriage. Divorce occurs endogenously whenever the couple cannot find an allocation within marriage that dominates the divorce allocation.

The gains from marriage can be specified with the aid of a household production function. Household production in each period depends on the characteristics of the two partners (e.g., family background, schooling and earning capacity), the quality of their match (which is usually unobserved), and the accumulation of marital capital (e.g., children and common property). Some of these variables may vary as the marriage evolves. Denote the time since the marriage was formed by $t$, $t = 1, 2, \ldots, T$; the spouses' personal characteristics by $x_{it}$, $i = h,w$; the quality of match by $\theta_t$; and marital capital by $k_t$. The household production function is written as

$$g_t = G(x_{ht}, x_{wt}, k_f, \theta_t). \tag{5.1}$$

Although household production is also influenced by the allocation of time and goods within the household, we only consider the outcome after these activities are "maximized out", the production function only in terms of the current state variables. (Such a two-stage procedure is only valid if time allocation has no impact on future states; investment activities are introduced in the subsequent section). In general, one expects the gains of marriage to be a nonlinear function of the partners' characteristics. This nonlinearity reflects variety of potential interactions between the spouses characteristics. For instance, it was shown in Section 2 that if the partners pool their incomes and share in a public good, their incomes will be complements in the household's production function.

Each partner has alternatives outside their particular marriage, as a single person. The value of being in the single state includes the option value of becoming remarried. It is assumed that the value of these outside alternatives can be described as a linear function of the characteristics of each partner:

$$A_{it} = \zeta_i' x_{it} + v_{it}. \tag{5.2}$$

Once a marriage is formed, dissolving it is costly. First, there are legal costs associated with the divorce process and the division of property. Secondly, marriage-specific capital such as information about the preferences of one's spouse is lost. Thirdly, if the couple has children, separation can lead to an inefficiently low level of child care expenditures. This is because the custodial parent does not internalize the preferences of his or her ex-spouse for expenditure on children (see Weiss and Willis, 1985). The extent of these costs depends on the nature of the divorce settlement and on the assignment of custody. For instance, if the husband fails to pay child support to the custodial mother, there will tend to be under provision of child expenditures and, assuming that both value the children's welfare, both partners will suffer. Let $C_t$ denote the costs of divorce. Then

$$C_t = \gamma' k_t + \eta' s_t + \omega_t, \tag{5.3}$$

where $s_t$ represents the various components of the divorce settlement (e.g., child support and alimony).

Each of the exogenous variables, $x_{ht}$, $x_{wt}$, $k_t$, $\theta_t$, is governed by a stochastic difference equation. Let us indicate the "state" at time $t$ by the vector $y = (x_{ht}, x_{wt}, k_t, \theta_t)$ then

$$y_t' = B y_{t-1}' + \mu_t, \tag{5.4}$$

where $B$ is a matrix of coefficients and $\mu_t$ is a vector of unanticipated shocks.

In this dynamic framework the decision whether to marry and whether to stay married are characterized with the aid of the "value function". Let $V_t(y_t)$ denote the expected gain from being married in period $t$, conditioned on the current state $y_t$ and on behaving optimally from $t$ all the way to $T$ (the end of the horizon). The value function is defined recursively by

$$V_t(y_t) = G(y_t) + \beta E_t \operatorname{Max}[V_{t+1}(y_{t+1}), A_{w,t+1} + A_{h,t+1} - C_{t+1}] \tag{5.5}$$

where $\beta$ is a discount factor, $\beta < 1$, and the expectation is taken over all possible realizations of the unanticipated shocks $\mu_{t+1}$.

A couple will stay married at time $t$ if the value of marriage exceeds the sum of outside opportunities at the time of marriage,

$$V_t(x_{ht}, x_{wt}, k_t, \theta_t) \geq A_{wt} + A_{ht} - C_t, \tag{5.6}$$

and divorce otherwise. Observe that divorce occurs whenever the value of marriage falls below the sum of the husband's and wife's outside opportunities. That is, divorce occurs endogenously whenever the couple cannot find an allocation within marriage that dominates the divorce allocation. This rule for "efficient divorce" holds as long as utility is transferable across spouses whether or not mutual consent of the couple is required by law (see Becker, 1991: Ch. 10; Mortensen, 1988).

Solving for $V_t(\cdot)$ by backward recursion, one can find the divorce rule. In general, it will depend on the realized values of $x_{ht}$, $x_{wt}$, $s_t$, $k_t$ and $\theta_t$. The quality of match, $\theta_t$, is observed only by the couple and therefore, the researcher can only predict the probability of divorce, conditioned on observable characteristics of the partners. This type of reasoning leads to estimable models in which the researchers explain the probability of divorce or marriage in the sample.

The model outlined above yields several testable implications:

(1) It is the unanticipated changes in the characteristics of the partners or the quality of match which trigger divorce. It is clear that a reduction in $\theta$, that is, falling out of love can cause divorce. It is less obvious how an unanticipated change in personal attributes, such as earning capacity, influence divorce. An increase (decrease) in earning capacity of a spouse influences both his/her contribution to the current marriage and his/her outside opportunities. Due to interactions in household production, the impact within marriage depends on the attributes of the current partner. Since the partners were matched based on their (predicted) earning capacity at the time of marriage, any surprise leading to an unanticipated rise or decline in earning capacity, can cause divorce (see Becker et al., 1977).

(2) If the gains from marriage are substantial, small shocks will not lead to divorce. Therefore, the probability of divorce will be lower amongst couples who are well matched. Anticipating that, couples sort into marriage according to characteristics which are likely to enhance the stability of the marriage.

(3) The costs of divorce, due to loss of specific marital capital, and the costs of searching for a mate are two sources of friction which mitigate the impact of unanticipated shocks on marital dissolution.

Several authors have attempted to test these implications. Weiss and Willis (1996) use data on a single cohort which finished high school in 1972 (age 18) and was subsequently followed up to 1986 (age 32). They report that unexpected changes in earning capacity strongly influence the probability of divorce. Specifically, an unexpected increase in the husband's earning capacity reduces the divorce hazard while an unexpected increase in the wife's earning capacity raises the divorce hazard. However, expectations of earning capacity which are formed at the time of marriage do not influence divorce. Thus, surprises concerning the earning capacity of the partners are more important than the differences in gains from marriage resulting from initial sorting based on expected earning capacity. Becker et al. (1977) report a cross-section relationship where the husband's income first reduces then increases the divorce hazard. Their interpretation of this finding is that unexpectedly high as well as unexpectedly low male earnings trigger divorce. Additional support to the claim that positive surprises can trigger divorce is provided by finding that unexpected subsidy (through a negative income experiment) increased the divorce hazard among the recipients (see Groenenveld et al., 1980; Cain and Wissoker, 1990).

There is ample evidence for a strong influence of sorting based on educational attainment. Couples with similar schooling attainments at the time of marriage are less likely to divorce and individuals are more likely to marry if they have a similar amount of schooling (the correlation in schooling attainments of the two spouses at the time of marriage is about 0.6). Likewise, similarity in religion and ethnicity, reduces the probability of divorce and a large proportion of all marriages are to individuals of the same ethnicity or religion. The finding that initial predictions of earning capacity do not influence subsequent divorce rates is consistent with the absence of sorting based on these predictions. (The correlation between the predicted earning capacities of husband and wife at the time of marriage is only 0.2 (see Weiss and Willis, 1996).)

The important roles of search and costs of divorce is indicated by the findings that higher age at marriage has a stabilizing effect, the divorce hazard is initially increasing with the duration of marriage, the presence of children and high levels of property stabilize the marriage (see Becker et al., 1977; Lillard and Waite, 1993; Weiss and Willis, 1993).

Somewhat more controversial is the role of divorce laws, in particular whether the legal possibility to unilaterally walk away from a marriage increases the divorce rate. The compensation principle implicit in the rule of efficient divorce suggests that such legal changes should only affect the shares in the gains from marriage but not the decision to separate. However, to the extent that legal rules affect the joint cost of divorce either in legal fees or through the impact on the expenditure on children, the legal environment may be relevant. There is weak evidence suggesting that divorce rates are higher in states where "fault" is not a prerequisite for divorce (see Allen, 1992; Peters, 1992; Weiss and Willis, 1996).

## 5.2. Divorce transfers

The presence of uncertainty together with risk aversion raises the issue of risk sharing. In the absence of appropriate mechanisms for risk sharing, divorce can have a substantial effect on the welfare of the partners. It has been observed that divorced husbands, even if relatively well-to-do, fail to support their ex-wives and their children at the standard to which they were accustomed during marriage. Consequently, divorced women and children in their custody seem to suffer a large decline in economic well-being (see Hoffman and Duncan, 1988). There are three possible explanations for this phenomenon. One is the lack of binding marriage contracts. The second is the inability of noncustodial parents to monitor expenditures by the custodian. Finally, fathers who live apart from their children may lose interest in them.

Following Weiss and Willis (1985), consider a simple two-period framework, where the only role of time is the resolution of uncertainty. The marriage is formed and children are born at time zero when the partners are still uncertain of the quality of their match. In the second period the quality of match is realized, the partners re-evaluate their original decision and decide whether or not to stay married. To abstract from issues of search, assume that remarriage is not an option.

If the marriage continues, the utility of each partner is given by

$$u_i = u_i(q, c_i) + \theta, \quad i = h, w, \tag{5.7}$$

where $q$ is the expenditure on children, $c_i$ is the consumption level of partner $i$ and $\theta$ is the quality of the match. If divorce occurs, the utility of each partner is given by Eq. (5.7) with $\theta$ set to zero. Observe that the same quantity $q$ appears in both utilities, reflecting the assumption that child quality is a collective good for their parents.

When the partners meet they will form a union if the expected quality of the match is positive. Later on, having observed $\theta$, the partners must decide whether or not to divorce. If the partners could cooperate in the divorce state then the marriage would break if and only if the partners can jointly produce more in the divorce state than in the marriage state, i.e. if and only if $\theta < 0$. However, if divorce also detracts from the efficiency of the allocation of family resources, then the marriage may continue even if $\theta < 0$. This is due to the presence of children whose maintenance is a collective good for the parents. We may assume that, within marriage, the allocation on the public good is determined in a cooperative fashion, while if they live apart the allocation will be determined noncooperatively.

A common arrangement in the event of divorce is that one partner is selected as custodian who determines the expenditure on the public good. The noncustodian can transfer resources to the custodian but cannot monitor the allocation of expenditures. If the wife is the custodian, the allocation is determined by

$$\underset{s \geq 0}{\text{Max}} \; u_h(q^-, y_h - s), \tag{5.8}$$

subject to

$$q^- = \underset{q}{\text{Argmax}} \; u_w(q, y_w + s - q). \tag{5.9}$$

Another possibility is that both partners contribute independently to the child. In this case

$$q_i = \underset{q \geq 0}{\text{Argmax}} \; u_i(q + q_j, y_i - q), \quad i, j = h, w \text{ and } i \neq j. \tag{5.10}$$

The Stackelberg model, given by Eqs. (5.8) and (5.9), is probably more appropriate when the husband transfers money to his wife who then serves as an agent in transferring resources to the child. The Cournot model, described by Eq. (5.10), may be more appropriate if the partners can transfer directly to their child, as in the case of college education or other child-specific expenses.

Common to both models is an ex-post inefficiency in the allocation of family resources. If the wife controls the expenditure on children (i.e., she is the custodian) then, most likely, she will not take account of the impact of her choices on the welfare of her ex-husband. In the Stackelberg model, this can interpreted as an agency problem. Out of every dollar transferred to the custodial wife with the intention of raising the welfare of the child, she uses part for her own consumption. The father is thus facing a price for child quality which exceeds the true resource cost. Hence, he will reduce his transfer and under provision of child care arises. In the Cournot case, the problem can be viewed as a free rider problem. Here, both partners underpay hoping to shift the load to the other partner. Thus, in both cases, the quality of children falls short of the efficient level given by the Samuelson condition for an efficient allocation of collective goods,

$$\left(\frac{\partial u_h / \partial q}{\partial u_h / \partial c_h}\right) + \left(\frac{\partial u_w / \partial q}{\partial u_w / \partial c_w}\right) = 1. \tag{5.11}$$

In addition to being inefficient ex-post, the self-enforcing transfer is inefficient from an ex-ante point of view. It does not share risks optimally. To simplify the presentation of ex-ante efficiency, assume now that the quality of the match $\theta$ obtains only two values: $\theta^+$ with probability $p$ and $\theta^-$ with probability $1 - p$. Suppose that the husband cannot monitor the expenditure on children in the divorce state but can make a binding contract to pay the wife a certain amount, $s^-$ in the event of divorce. Suppose further, that for any $s^-$, if the event $\theta = \theta^-$ occurs then there is no distribution within marriage which is preferable to both partners so that divorce is imminent. In this case, the ex-ante efficient allocation is determined from

$$\text{Max } E(u_h) = (1 - p)u_h(q^-, y_h - s^-) + p[u_h(q^+, y_h - s^+) + \theta^+], \tag{5.12}$$

subject to the constraints

$$E(u_w) = (1 - p)u_w(q^-, y_w + s^- - q^-) + p[u_w(q^+, y_w + s^+ - q^+) + \theta^+] \geq u^*, \tag{5.13}$$

$$u_w(q^+, y_w + s^+ - q^+) + \theta^+ \geq u_w(q^-, y_w + s^- - q^-), \tag{5.14}$$

$$u_h(q^+, y_h - s^+) + \theta^+ \geq u_h(q^-, y_h - s^-), \tag{5.15}$$

$$q^- = \underset{q}{\text{Argmax}}\, u_w(q, y_w + s^- - q). \tag{5.16}$$

Instead of the consumption levels, we view the within-family transfers as the decision variables for the maximization above. We denote the transfer from the husband to the wife by $s^j$, and the transfers to the child by $q^j$, $j = +,-$. We denote by $y_i$ the income of partner $i$, $i = $ h,w, and total family income, $y_h + y_w$, is denoted by $y$.

The participation constraint, Eq. (5.13) states that the wife is willing to join the partnership when it is formed only if her expected gains from marriage exceed her next best alternative, $u^*$. More generally, $u^*$ is any feasible level of expected utility that the wife obtains through bargaining at the time of marriage. The incentive compatibility constraints, Eqs. (5.14) and (5.15), require that, given the promised divorce and marriage transfers, the wife or the husband do not wish to walk out of the marriage if the realization is $\theta^+$. The constraint, Eq. (5.16), reflects the assumption that in the event of divorce the wife becomes the custodian.

If $\theta^+$ is sufficiently large to make the constraints (5.14) and (5.15) nonbinding, then the first-order conditions for the maximization imply that the slopes of the utility frontiers are equated in the divorce and marriage states. Thus, the main feature of ex-ante efficiency is that it ties the divorce transfer to the wife to the standard of living to which she and the child were accustomed within the marriage. We refer to these ties as the insurance motive in divorce settlements. In contrast, the ex-post transfers determined by Eqs. (5.8) and (5.9) or by (5.10) pay no attention to the options within marriage and therefore do not share risks optimally.

The inherent problem of the ex-ante marriage contract is that it is not self-enforcing. Intervention by the court is required to maintain efficiency. However, in most countries the law does not intervene in within-marriage allocations and its intervention in post-marriage allocations is limited to some general guidelines or formulae relating to child support, alimony and property division to the partners' incomes and to considerations such as the needs of children, investments in the marriage, and the accustomed standard of living. While this form of intervention certainly affects the bargaining power of the two partners and the post-divorce allocation (see Mnookin and Kornhouser, 1979), the upshot of this legal situation is that divorce can cause a substantial reduction in economic welfare. The amount that husbands transfer to their ex-wives falls short of the efficient level (see Weiss and Willis, 1993). The transfers would be larger if ex-ante contracts would be enforced, but legal intervention cannot resolve the ex-post inefficiency due to difficulties in monitoring the within household allocation. The problem of underprovision is exacerbated by the apparent loss of altruism towards the child by the noncustodian father. Seltzer (1991) reports a reduction in contacts between father and son following divorce. In addition, she found a clear association between child support payments and frequency of contacts.

## 5.3. Defensive investments

With deficient transfer mechanisms, the partners must prepare for the event of divorce. One important instrument is the allocation of time within marriage. By investing in human capital each partner can be less dependent on transfers in the event of divorce. However, such investments may detract from marital output. For instance, a wife who works is better defended against divorce but has less time to spend on children. Indeed, it appears that women tend to increase their investment in market work in anticipation of divorce (see Johnson-Skinner, 1986). Thus, lack of enforcement of divorce transfers reduces the welfare of children not only in the divorce state but also within marriage.

To analyze this phenomenon, let us use a slight variation on the previous model and assume that child quality is produced at home rather then purchased in the market. Specifically, in each period $j$, $j = 1,2$, child quality $q_j$ is determined by the household production function

$$q_j = (\alpha t_{hj} + \beta t_{wj})^{\gamma} e_j^{1-\gamma}, \tag{5.17}$$

where $t_{ij}$ is time spent at home by partner $i$, $i =$ h,w, and $e_j$ are market goods devoted to home production. Let us assume transferable utility, where, for each partner

$$u_{ij} = q_j c_{ij} + \theta_j. \tag{5.18}$$

The quality of match $\theta_j$ is set to zero if the partners are not married. Time now plays two roles; as time passes, information is gathered and investments mature. When the partners marry in period 1, the initial wages $w_{ij}$ are given and $\theta_1$ is known (without loss of generality, let $\theta_1 = 0$). In the second period, a new value for $\theta$ is realized and new wages are determined according to

$$w_{i2} = W_{i2}(h_{i1}), \tag{5.19}$$

where $h_{i1}$ is time spent at work by partner $i$ in the first period and $W_{i2}(h_{i1})$ is a monotone increasing function of $h_{i1}$. This relationship represents a process of learning by doing where current work in the market affects future wages. Let the wife have the comparative advantage in home production, $\beta/w_{wj} > \alpha/w_{hj}$ for $j = 1,2$. To simplify further, assume that saving and borrowing is not an option. Otherwise, all previous assumptions are maintained including the assumption that the wife is the custodian in the case of divorce.

We solve the family's problem backwards, starting in the second (and last) period. Having observed $\theta_2$ and given the new wages, there are two possible states. Either the partners remain married or they decide to separate. If the partners remain married then the husband will specialize in market work and the wife will spend part of her time working at home. This division of labor reflects her comparative advantage in home production. (The wife will specialize in home production if her wage is sufficiently low relative to the husband, i.e. if $w_{h2}/w_{w2} > (2 - \gamma)/\gamma$, but it is assumed that the difference in wages is such that the wife is in an interior solution.) The total family utility is given by

$$u_{h2} + u_{w2} = \kappa w_{w2}^{-\gamma}(w_{h2} + w_{w2})^2 + 2\theta_2, \tag{5.20}$$

where $\kappa$ is a constant which depends on the parameters. Note that an increase in the wife's wage has a positive income effect and a negative substitution effect on child quality. This is reflected in the opposing effects for $w_{w2}$ in Eq. (5.20). However, the total effect of an increase in $w_w$ on family utility is positive.

If the partners divorce, then the wife will obtain custody and the outcome will be determined by Eqs. (5.8) and (5.9). Specifically, the wife will spend time on her children according to $w_{w2}t_{w2} = \gamma(w_{w2} + s)/2$, and other expenditures according to $e_2 = (1 - \gamma)(w_{w2} + s)/2$, where $s$ is the payment that she gets from her husband. Taking this reaction function $s$ as given, the husband will choose $s$ to maximize his own utility, implying $s = (w_{h2} - w_{w2})/2$. The implied utilities are $u_{i2} = \kappa_i w_{w2}^{-\gamma}(w_{h2} + w_{w2})^2$, where $\kappa_i$ are constants that depend on the parameters. It is easily verified that $\kappa_w + \kappa_h < \kappa$ and $\kappa_h > \kappa_w$. That is, the wife obtains a lower utility than her husband in the divorce state and aggregate utility in the divorce state is lower than the utility in the marriage state, with $\theta = 0$. These outcomes reflect the loss of efficiency in the allocation of the public good and the under payment by the husband resulting from the lack of control on the wife's expenditures.

The divorce rule which emerges from the results above is that the couple will remain married for realizations of $\theta_2$ satisfying

$$\theta_2 \geq w_{w2}^{-\gamma}(w_{h2} + w_{w2})^2[\kappa_h + \kappa_w - \kappa]/2 \tag{5.21}$$

and divorce otherwise. Note that the partners remain married for some negative values of $\theta_2$. That is, to avoid the loss of efficiency, the partners will stay married despite the "failure" of their marriage, provided, of course, that the negative shock is not too large. The higher is the wife's or the husband's wage in the second period, the lower is the probability of divorce. This happens because the loss in efficiency is larger at higher wages.

Anticipating the possibility of divorce, the partners need to decide on their respective work effort in the market (and at home) in the first period, when the future value of $\theta$ is still unknown. If the partners can coordinate their work activities, they will maximize the sum of their expected utilities,

$$\sum_i E \sum_j u_{ij} = (\beta t_{w1})^\gamma e_1^{1-\gamma}(w_{h1} + w_{w1}(1 - t_{w1}) - e_1) +$$

$$+ [(1 - F(\theta^*))\kappa + F(\theta^*)(\kappa_h + \kappa_w)]w_{w2}^{-\gamma}(w_{h2} + w_{w2})^2 + 2\int_{\theta^*}^\infty \theta \, dF(\theta), \qquad (5.22)$$

where $\theta^*$ is the reservation value of $\theta_2$ at which Eq. (5.21) holds as an equality, $F(\theta)$ is the distribution of $\theta$, and we exploit the assumption on the husband's comparative advantage and set his work at home to zero. Recall that, by Eq. (5.19), the second-period wages are positively affected by current work in the market. Therefore, the wife's work at home (market) in the first period will be set below (above) the level that maximizes the current family utility. We may refer to this adjustment as the investment effect on labor supply. The risk of divorce, and the associated loss of utility affect the incentives for investment. In particular, if divorce does not cause a loss of efficiency ($\kappa = \kappa_h + \kappa_w$), there will be a higher probability of divorce, and less work at home than in the case with costly divorce ($\kappa > \kappa_h + \kappa_w$). In this sense, the anticipation of a higher divorce probability is associated with more market work by the wife in the initial period of the marriage.

This analysis can be extended to the choice of the number of children. The larger the number of children, the higher will be the costs of divorce and the anticipation of divorce will reduce fertility. The analysis suggests that changes in the divorce law that would enforce transfers and make divorce less costly may increase the amount spent on children within marriage. However, changes in the law which facilitate divorce, but do not enforce transfers may have the opposite effect. Indeed, some studies find a positive impact of no-fault divorce laws on female participation in the labor force and the amount of work at home (see Peters, 1986; Carlin, 1991).

The analysis in this section was substantially simplified by the assumption of transferable utility which implies that the partners have a mutual interest to coordinate their work activities if they stay married. It was shown that defensive actions will be taken even in this case, simply because both partners anticipate the difficulties which would arise if divorce becomes imminent. Clearly, the problem of defensive investments will be exacerbated if the partners cannot cooperate in the marriage state (see Cohen, 1987). In any case, the main insight is that the developments in employment fertility and divorce are interrelated. An exogenous change which reduces the incentive to specialize in the household will increase divorce and reduce fertility. Similarly, an exogenous change which increases the divorce risk will increase labor market participation and reduce fertility (see Grossbard-Shechtman, 1984, 1993: Ch. 10; Ermisch, 1994).

## 6. The future of the family

The oldest of all Societies, and the only natural one, is that of the family; yet children remain tied to their father by nature only as long as they need him for their preservation. As soon as this need ends, the natural bond is dissolved. Once the children are freed from the obedience they owe their father, and the father is freed from his responsibilities towards them, both parties equally gain their independence. If they continue to remain united, it is no longer nature, but their own choice, which unites them; and the family as such is kept in being only by agreement.

Jean-Jacques Rousseau, The Social Contract, Ch. 2.

Despite its firm roots in nature and its antiquity in human society, the future of the family institution has been recently put into question. The recent trends of declining marriage rates, declining fertility, higher divorce rates and the rise in alternative arrangements such as cohabitation, single-person households and single-mother families, are common to many western societies. The economist can wisely relate these trends with the changes in the market place, in particular increased participation of female workers, and in the nature of government intervention in the form of taxes and subsidies and in the laws regulating marriage and divorce. The demographer can relate the weakening of the family to changes in the technology of producing children, in particular, lower mortality rates and more effective birth control. The sociologist may point to the relation with the erosion of religious and political authority and the rise of individual freedom (see Lesthaeghe, 1983; Bumpass, 1990; Goldscheider and Waite, 1991; Espenshade, 1985). From a casual reading of the literature, there is a sense that social scientists in each of these disciplines agree that gains can be made by the interweaving of social economic and demographic considerations. However, no single discipline seems capable of providing such a synthesis.

Examining the economic contributions, the main obstacle is the scarcity of equilibrium models which carefully tie the individual behavior with market constraints and outcomes. Consequently, we do not yet have a convincing model which would explain the aggregate changes in family formation and dissolution (see Michael, 1988). In a broad sense, this research agenda has a long tradition in economics, dating back to Malthus. For instance, Easterlin (1987) argues that if the offsprings' cohort is large relative to the parents' cohort (e.g. the baby boomers), then economic pressures, combined with a desire to imitate their parents consumption standards, will force the youngsters to postpone marriage and have smaller families. This line of argument suggests that the current pressures on the family are cyclical in nature and will diminish as fertility declines. A weakness of this model, however, is its failure to address the apparent increase in the wife's share in the gains from marriage. For this purpose, one needs to introduce additional feedbacks from the labor and marriage markets to family decision-making (see Becker, 1992). Hopefully, the ideas and models summarized in this survey may help to establish such links, but much remains to be done.

## References

Allen, D. (1992), "Marriage and divorce: comment", American Economic Review 82: 679–685.

Altonji, J., F. Hayashi and L. Kotlikoff (1992), "Is the extended family altruistically linked? Direct tests using microdata", American Economic Review 82: 1177–1198.

Becker, G. (1991), A treatise on the family (enlarged edition) (Harvard University Press, Cambridge, MA).

Becker, G. (1992), "Fertility and the economy", Journal of Population Economics 5: 158–201.

Becker, G., E. Landes and R. Michael (1977), "An economic analysis of marital instability", Journal of Political Economy 85: 1141–1187.

Benham, L. (1974), "Benefits of women education within marriage", Journal of Political Economy 81: S57–S71.

Ben-Porath, Y. (1980), "The F-connection: families, friends, firms and the organization of exchange", Population and Development Review 6: 1–30.

Bergstrom, T. (1989), "A fresh look at the rotten kid theorem – and other household mysteries", Journal of Political Economy 97: 1138–1159.

Bergstrom, T. and M. Bagnoli (1993), "Courtship as a waiting game", Journal of Political Economy 101: 185–202.

Bergstrom, T., L. Blume and H. Varian (1986), "On the private provision of public goods", Journal of Public Economics 29: 25–49.

Bernheim, D. and O. Stark (1988), "Altruism within the family reconsidered: do nice guys finish last", American Economic Review 78: 1034–1045.

Blackburn, M. and S. Korenman (1994), "The declining marital-status earnings differential", Journal of Population Economics 7: 247–270.

Borenstein, S. and P. Courant (1989), "How to carve a medical degree: human capital assets in divorce settlements", American Economic Review 79: 992–1009.

Brien, M. (1991), "Economic determinants of family structure: an examination of black and white differences", Ph.D. dissertation (University of Chicago, Chicago, IL).

Browning, M., F. Bourguignon, P. Chiappori and V. Lechene (1994), "Incomes and outcomes: a structural model of intra-household allocation", Journal of Political Economy 102: 1067–1096.

Bumpass, L. (1990), "What's happening to the family? Interactions between demographic and institutional change", Demography 27: 483–498.

Cain, G. and D. Wissoker (1990), "A reanalysis of marital stability in the Seattle–Denver income-maintenance experiment", American Journal of Sociology 95: 1235–1269.

Carlin, P. (1991), "Intra-family bargaining and time allocation", Research in Population Economics 7: 215–243.

Cigno, A. (1991), Economics of the family (Oxford University Press, Oxford).

Chiappori, P. (1988), "Rational household labor supply", Econometrica 56: 63–90.

Chiappori, P. (1992), "Collective labor supply and welfare", Journal of Political Economy 100: 437–467.

Cohen, L. (1987), "Marriage, divorce, and quasi rents; or I gave him the best years of my life", Journal of Legal Studies 16: 267–303.

Crawford, V. (1991), "Comparative statics results in matching markets", Journal of Economic Theory 54: 389–400.

Daniel, K. (1992), "Does marriage make men more productive?", Working paper no. 92-2 (Economic Research Center, NORC).

Diamond, P. (1981), "Mobility costs, frictional unemployment, and efficiency", Journal of Political Economy 89: 798–812.

Diamond, P. and E. Maskin (1979), "An equilibrium analysis of search and breach of contract, I: Steady states", Bell Journal of Economics 10: 282–316.

Diamond, P. and E. Maskin (1981), "An equilibrium analysis of search and breach of contract, II: A non steady state example", Journal of Economic Theory 25: 165–195.

Easterlin, R. (1987), Birth and fortune: the impact of numbers on personal welfare, 2nd edn. (Basic Books, Chicago, IL).

Ermisch, J. (1994), "Economie, politique et changement familial", Population 49: 1377–1388.

Espenshade, T. (1985), "Marriage trends in America: estimates, implications, and underlying causes", Population and Development Review 11: 193–245.

Gale, D. and L. Shapley (1962), "College admission and the stability of marriage", American Mathematical Monthly 69: 9–15.

Goldin, C. (1992), "The meaning of college in the lives of American women: the past hundred years", Working paper no. 4099 (NBER, Cambridge, MA).

Goldscheider, F. and L. Waite (1991), New families, no families? (University of California Press, Berkeley, CA).

Groenenveld, L., M. Hannan and N. Tuma (1980), "The effects of negative income tax programs on marital dissolution", Journal of Human Resources 14: 654–674.

Gronau, R. (1986), "Home-production – a survey", in: O. Ashenfelter and R. Layard, eds., Handbook of labor economics (North-Holland, Amsterdam).

Grossbard, A. (1978), "Towards a marriage between economics and anthropology and a general theory of marriage", American Economic Review 68: 33–37.

Grossbard-Shechtman, A. (1984), "A theory of allocation of time in markets for labor and marriage", Economic Journal 94: 863–882.

Grossbard-Shechtman, S. (1993), On the economics of marriage: a theory of marriage labor, and divorce (Westview Press, Boulder, CO).

Hoffman, S. and G. Duncan (1988), "What are the economic consequences of divorce", Demography 25: 641–645.

Horney, M. and M. McElory (1988), "The household allocation problem: empirical results from a bargaining model", Research in Population Economics 6: 15–38.

Johnson, W. and J. Skinner (1986), "Labor supply and marital separation", American Economic Review 76: 455–469.

Juster, T. and F. Stafford (1991), "The allocation of time: empirical findings, behavioral models and problems of measurement", Journal of Economic Literature 29: 471–522.

Keeley, M. (1977), "The economics of family formation", Economic Inquiry 15: 238–250.

Korenman, S. and D. Neumark (1992), "Marriage, motherhood, and wages", Journal of Human Resources 27: 233–255.

Kotlikoff, L. and A. Spivak (1981), "The family as an incomplete annuity market", Journal of Political Economy 89: 372–391.

Lam, D. (1988), "Marriage markets and assortative mating with household public goods: theoretical results and empirical implications", Journal of Human Resources 23: 462–487.

Lazear, E. and R. Michael (1980), "Family size and the distribution of real per capita income", American Economic Review 70: 91–107.

Lesthaeghe, R. (1983), "A century of demographic and cultural change in western Europe: an exploration of underlying dimensions", Population and Development Review 9: 411–435.

Lillard, L. and L. Waite (1993), "A joint model of marital childbearing and marital disruption", Demography 30: 653–681.

Locay, L. (1990), "Economic development and the division of production between households and markets", Journal of Political Economy 98: 965–982.

Lundberg, S. (1988), "Labor supply of husbands and wives: a simultaneous equations approach", Review of Economics and Statistics 70: 224–235.

Lundberg, S. and R. Pollak (1993), "Separate spheres bargaining and the marriage market", Journal of Political Economy 101: 988–1010.

Manser, M. and M. Brown (1980), "Marriage fertility and household decision-making: a bargaining analysis", International Economic Review 21: 31–44.

Mare, D. (1991), "Five decades of educational assortative mating", American Sociological Review 56: 15–32.

McElroy, M. (1990), "The empirical content of the Nash bargained household behavior", Journal of Human Resources 25: 559–583.

Michael, R. (1988), "Why did the U.S divorce rate double within a decade?", Research in Population Economics 6: 367–399.

Mnookin, R. and L. Kornhouser (1979), "Bargaining in the shadow of the law: the case of divorce", Yale Law Journal 88: 950–997.

Mortensen, D. (1982), "The matching process as a noncooperative bargaining game", in: J. McCall, ed., The economics of information and uncertainty (University of Chicago Press, Chicago, IL).

Mortensen, D. (1988), "Matching: finding a partner for life or otherwise", American Journal of Sociology 94, Supplement: S215–S240.

Oppenheimer, V. (1988), "A theory of marriage timing", American Journal of Sociology 94: 563–591.

Parsons, D. (1980), "The marriage market and female economic well-being", Journal of Mathematical Sociology 7: 113–138.

Peters, E. (1986), "Marriage and divorce: informational constraints and private contracting", American Economic Review 76: 437–454.

Peters, E. (1992), "Marriage and divorce: reply", American Economic Review 82: 686–693.

Pollak, R. (1985), "A transaction costs approach to families and households", Journal of Economic Literature 23: 581–608.

Rao, V. (1993), "The rising price of husbands: a hedonic analysis of dowry increases in rural India", Journal of Political Economy 101: 666–677.

Rosenzweig, M. and O. Stark (1989), "Consumption smoothing, migration, and marriage: evidence from rural India", Journal of Political Economy 97: 905–926.

Roth, A. and M. Sotomayor (1990), Two sided matching: a study in game-theoretic modeling and analysis (Cambridge University Press, Cambridge).

Rubinstein, A. (1982), "Perfect equilibrium in a bargaining model", Econometrica 50: 97–109.

Schultz, P. (1990), "Testing the neoclassical model of family labor supply and fertility", Journal of Human Resources 25: 599–634.

Seltzer, J. (1991), "Relationships between fathers and children who live apart; the father's role after separation", Journal of Marriage and the Family 53: 79–101.

Stapleton, D. (1991), "Implicit marriage markets with collective goods", Mimeo. (Lewin-VHI, Fairfax, VA).

Stark, O. (1993), "Non-market transfers and altruism", European Economic Review 37: 1413–1424.

Thomas, D. (1994), "Like father, like son; like mother, like daughter: parental resources and child height", Journal of Human Resources 29: 950–988.

Townsend, R. (1994), "Risk and insurance in village India." Econometrica 62: 539–592.

Weiss, Y. and R. Willis (1985), "Children as collective goods", Journal of Labor Economics 3: 268–292.

Weiss, Y. and R. Willis (1993), "Divorce settlements: evidence and interpretation", Journal of Labor Economics 11: 629–679.

Weiss, Y. and R. Willis (1996), "Match quality, new information and marital dissolution", Journal of Labor Economics, in press.

Wilson, W. (1987), The truly disadvantaged (University of Chicago Press, Chicago, IL).

Wolinsky, A. (1987), "Matching, search, and bargaining", Journal of Economic Theory 42: 311–333.

# Chapter 4

# INTRAHOUSEHOLD DISTRIBUTION AND THE FAMILY

JERE R. BEHRMAN*

*University of Pennsylvania*

## Contents

*The author acknowledges the help of and thanks the editors and an anonymous referee and various colleagues (some of whom were co-authors on papers related to the topics discussed in this chapter), including Harold Alderman, Nancy Birdsall, Angus Deaton, Anil Deolalikar, Andrew Foster, Edward Funkhouser, Arthur Goldberger, Victor Lavy, Jonathon Morduch, Mark Pitt, David Ross, Richard Sabot, Paul Schultz, John Strauss, Duncan Thomas, Terence Wales, Kenneth Wolpin, Barbara Wolfe and particularly Robert A. Pollak, Mark Rosenzweig, and Paul Taubman.

*Handbook of Population and Family Economics. Edited by M.R. Rosenzweig and O. Stark*
© *Elsevier Science B.V., 1997*

# 1. Introduction

Casual observations and systematic analysis both suggest that what happens within households has important implications for time allocations, human resource investments, wages and other economic outcomes.[1,2] Intergenerational correlations in schooling attainment in a number of societies are of the magnitude of 0.3–0.4. Intergenerational correlations in earnings or income in the US are of the magnitude of 0.4 or greater. Same-sex sibling correlations in schooling and adult earnings in the US are about 0.5 for brothers and 0.4–0.5 for sisters, with sibling schooling correlations as high as 0.8 for identical twins. Numerous estimates suggest that observed and unobserved family background components affect substantially outcomes for children over their life-cycles in different societies. The magnitudes of these intergenerational and intragenerational associations and estimated family endowment effects suggest that what happens in families has important and persistent effects on the economic options and outcomes of children throughout their lifetimes.

But casual observations and systematic analysis also suggest that what happens within families does not result in equal outcomes for all family members. There are claims that within-household allocations result in less satisfactory outcomes for females than for males, for higher than for lower birth order children, and for the elderly than for prime-age adults. For instance, Sen (1990) states that over 100 million women are missing in Asia and North Africa because of relatively high female mortality due in considerable part to intrahousehold allocations that are not favorable to

---

[1] The terms "families" and "households" can refer to a range of institutions. Nuclear families constitute parents and their children. Nuclear families may be extended vertically (e.g., including in addition grandparents) or horizontally (e.g., including in addition siblings of the household head or spouse) or both. Households usually are defined by co-residence or by sharing the same "hearth" or "pot". Family members may or may not be in the same household. Households may be composed only of family members, only individuals who are not related by blood or legal bonds or may include both family members and nonrelated individuals. Much of the economic literature treats the terms "family" and "household" as if they both refer to a nuclear family that constitutes a household, though at times there is explicit reference to other types of families or households. This chapter follows the practice in most of the economic literature of using family and household to refer to a situation consistent with a nuclear family that constitutes a household.

[2] Examples of studies that are summarized in this paragraph are: intergenerational correlations of earnings with control for measurement error; Behrman and Taubman (1990), Solon (1992), Zimmerman (1992) (previous estimates without such controls, as summarized in Becker and Tomes (1986) and Behrman and Taubman (1985), averaged about half as large correlations); sibling correlations in schooling attainment and earnings (generally without control for measurement error); Altonji and Dunn (1991, 1995), Behrman et al. (1980, 1995a), Griliches (1979), Jencks and Brown (1977), Lykken et al. (1990), Olneck (1977); and impact of family endowments; Altonji and Dunn (1991, 1995), Ashenfelter and Krueger (1994), Behrman et al. (1980, 1994, 1995), Behrman and Wolfe (1984, 1989), Chamberlain and Griliches (1975), Griliches (1979), Herrnstein and Murray (1994), Jencks and Brown (1977), Miller et al. (1995), Olneck (1977), Quisumbing (1994a,b), Rosenzweig and Schultz (1987).

females. There also are claims that who controls resources in households affects importantly the nature of intrahousehold allocations with, for example, children faring better the more their mothers control resources, ceteris paribus. Descriptions of the extent of variance in intrahousehold allocations from systematic socioeconomic data sets are limited because many data sets take the household as the unit of observation for most of the information that they collect. But there are some data that suggest that within-household variances are fairly large. Several studies, further, find that individual endowments account for substantial shares of variations in earnings and other outcomes, with these endowment effects in some cases amplified by intrahousehold allocations.[3]

The focus of this chapter is on intrahousehold allocations, and what are the roles in such allocations of endowments, preferences, human resource investment prices, household resource levels, labor market opportunities, and marriage markets.[4] These intrahousehold allocations are of interest from an economic perspective for at least four major reasons. *First*, given critical roles of households in human capital investments and time use, whether such allocations are efficient socially, or even Pareto-optimal for family members, may be important. If such allocations are determined through noncooperative bargaining, for example, they may be neither Pareto-optimal nor socially efficient even if there are no market failures outside of households. *Second*, intrahousehold allocations may have important effects on distribution. Households may act either to increase inequalities by allocating resources so as to reinforce endowment differences or to decrease inequalities by allocating resources so as to compensate for endowment differences. *Third*, the nature of human capital allocations may have important implications for analysis of other outcomes, such as the impact of schooling in labor markets. If such allocations are responsive to endowments that also affect labor market success, for example, then it may be critical to control for such endowments in order to be able to obtain consistent estimates of the effects of schooling on wages. *Fourth*, the nature of intrahousehold allocations may alter the effectiveness of policies ranging from transfer programs directed towards particular types of household members (e.g., infants and small children, school-aged children, pregnant and nursing women, elderly) to the effectiveness of macro policies (e.g., the relevance of Ricardian equivalence, as in Barro (1974)).

---

[3] Large within-household variances are reported, for example, in Behrman (1992), Behrman and Lavy (1995), Behrman et al. (1995a), Haddad and Kanbur (1990, 1992), Harriss (1990), Kanbur and Haddad (1994), Strauss et al. (1993) and Tauchen et al. (1991). Important individual endowment effects, in addition, are found in Behrman et al. (1994, 1995), Pitt et al. (1990), Quisumbing (1994b) and Rosenzweig and Wolpin (1988).

[4] Closely related questions are why do families play such roles, what causes the formation and dissolution of families, and what are the nature of interhousehold relations among relatives including parents and children and siblings. These topics are addressed in other chapters in this volume by Bergstrom, Laitner and Weiss.

## 2. Consensus parental preference models of intrahousehold allocations

Economists have developed several one-period models of intrahousehold allocations based on constrained maximization of consensus parental preferences.[5] The defining characteristic of consensus parental preferences models is the assumption that parents act as if they are maximizing a single utility function, subject to appropriate constraints. Most consensus models treat parents' preference as a primitive and make no attempt to derive them from the underlying preferences of husbands and wives. These models focus on the intrahousehold allocation among children of parent-provided resources,[6] which can take the form either of human resource investments or transfers, given family size.[7] The parental utility function reflects the preferences of the parents, not the children, although the parents are assumed to be "altruistic" in the sense that their utility depends on the levels and distribution of their children's utility or income. The traditional analysis assumes that the children are passive, and denies them an independent role as decision makers (e.g., Becker and Tomes, 1976, 1979; Behrman et al., 1982: Section 2.1). In some other models, parents have consensus preferences, but the children are active, independent decision makers (e.g., "exchange" models such as Bernheim et al. (1985), Pollak's (1988) "paternalistic preferences" model). Under some conditions, nevertheless, Becker's "Rotten Kid Theorem" shows that altruistic parents can maximize their preferences subject to the *family* budget constraint and the active, purely selfish behavior of their children (Section 2.2).

---

[5] Different terms are used to describe these models: "family utility model" (Lundberg, 1988), "common preference model" (Thomas, 1990), "neoclassical models" (McElroy and Horney, 1981; McElroy, 1990; Schultz, 1990), "unitary models" (Alderman et al., 1994; Hart, 1994) and "altruistic models" (McElroy, 1992), because of the underlying Becker altruism that is often used to rationalize these models, but McElroy's Nash models have altruistic preferences because the utility of one household member depends on the consumption or utility of another). In Section 4 nonconsensus models of intrahousehold allocations are considered.

[6] Although in some applications such consensus preference models have been used to explore allocations among adults as well as children. See, for example, Pitt et al. (1990) (Section 3.2.2).

[7] Earlier models considered the determination of the number of children and of average child "quality" together with parental consumption, but not differences among children within a family (see references in Becker (1991); also see Willis (1973)). The literatures concerning, respectively, the determination of the number of children and the distribution of resources among children have not been integrated. Therefore there is an implicit assumption that unobserved heterogeneities related to the determination of the number of children do not also affect intrahousehold allocations among children. Empirical tests of integration of these two concerns would be difficult, particularly if adult outcomes of children are required for the analysis because longitudinal data over long periods may be necessary. One can conceive of situations, however, in which this maintained assumption of separability between the two concerns is violated. For example, suppose that there is unobserved heterogeneity in parents' desires to assure substantial social advancement for at least one offspring. Those whose preferences weight heavily this outcome may be more likely both to have fewer children and to concentrate their resources on more promising children than those who weight this outcome less.

## 2.1. Consensus parental preference models with passive children

Altruistic parents maximize their consensus utility function,[8]

$$U = U(C_P, Y_1, Y_2, ..., Y_n, T_1, T_2, ..., T_n), \tag{1}$$

where $C_P$ is the parents' (and offsprings' childhood) consumption, $Y_j$ is the adult earnings of the $j$th child,[9] and $T_j$ are transfers (the sum of inter vivos gifts and bequests) given by the parents to the $j$th child.[10] Relation (1) is written so that the parents are altruistic; their utility function includes as arguments the levels and the distributions of the sources of income of their children when they become adults. The most transparent formulation explicitly includes two sources of the children's income when they become adults: a human-capital-dependent component called "earnings" and another component called "transfers". Earnings are "full" earnings to value leisure and allow for endogenous labor supplies.

To determine the optimal level of parental consumption, of earnings by each child, and of transfers to each child, the parental utility function is maximized subject to two types of constraints: the budget constraint and an earnings production function for each child.[11] The budget constraint requires that the present value of parental expenditures on their own consumption and investments in their children's human capital not exceed their total resources – the sum of their own full earnings minus the net transfers that the parents give. The earnings production function states the adult earnings of the $j$th child that are produced by human resource investments in that child ($H_j$) and that child's endowments ($G_j$):

$$Y_j = Y(H_j, G_j). \tag{2}$$

---

[8] This utility function is written in terms of children's incomes. If parental utility instead depends on children's utilities, the estimated preference parameters discussed below (e.g., Section 3.2.1) reflect both parental preferences and the relation between child utilities and child income.

[9] $Y_j$ can be considered more broadly to be (in Behrman et al. (1986) terminology) the "human-capital-dependent" income of the children. If, for example, there is assortative mating on human capital investments such as schooling, beyond ones' own earnings the spouse's earnings are part of this broader definition. All of the wealth and earnings possibility frontiers that are discussed below are consistent with this broader definition. But for convenience and to be consistent with most of the literature, "earnings" is used rather than the "human-capital-dependent income".

[10] Because we are focussing on intrahousehold allocation of resources among children, for simplicity attention is limited to transfers from parents to children, ignoring other transfers (taxes), public and private. In principle it would be easy to extend the model to include other transfers by specifying the relevant transfer functions.

[11] In some applications there may be other human resource outcomes in the preferences, such as health, and there may be other production functions among the constraints, such as health production functions.

The endowment includes all determinants of earnings that are predetermined prior to the human capital investment process. Endowments include various genetically inherited characteristics that are rewarded directly or indirectly (through their interaction with human capital investments) in labor and marriage markets. Across different markets over time and space, different endowed attributes may be valued different. Endowments related to physical strength and stamina, for example, may be relatively highly valued in comparison with endowments related to intelligence given the low level of technology in some contexts with low levels of development. If there are differences in labor market rewards to individuals depending on their gender, moreover, a person's sex is an endowment for the purpose of this framework. This general parental consensus model places few restrictions on the allocation of human resource investments and transfers to and among children. Two special cases of this model, the wealth model of Becker and Tomes (1976, 1979), Becker (1991) and Becker and Murphy (1988) and the SET (separable earnings–transfers) model of Behrman et al. (1982), make stronger assumptions and yield sharper conclusions. The wealth model and the SET model both take the total resources that parents allocate to their children as given when examining the allocation among children. They both assume that parents make human resource investment decisions for their children and that imperfect capital markets mean that it is not assured that such investments can take place to the point at which the expected rate of return on such investments equals the market rate of interest on financial assets. These two special cases of the consensus parental preference model differ in their implications regarding whether parents allocate resources to compensate for or to reinforce differences in endowments.

### 2.1.1. The wealth model

Becker and Tomes (1976) assume that parents are concerned with each child's total wealth but are unconcerned with the sources of wealth – that is, parents are indifferent between earnings and transfers as components of the wealth of their children. In terms of the parents' utility function, the wealth model collapses each child's income and transfer into a single term, their sum: $Y_j + T_j = W_j$.

The wealth model, and other models of consensus parental preferences, is often further specialized by assuming "equal concern". Equal concern means that all children receive equal weight in the parents' utility function so that the utility function is symmetric in the space of children's wealth.

Becker and Tomes analyze a particular case of the wealth model in which parents allocate sufficient resources to their children so that all children receive transfers. In this case, with equal concern and the additional assumption that investments in human capital are subject to diminishing returns, they conclude that parents invest in human capital for each child until the marginal rate of return on human capital investment in that child equals the return available on financial investments. This wealth-maximizing level of human capital is denoted by $H^*$. Any additional resources allocated to a child beyond the point at which the child's human capital is at $H^*$ takes the form of transfers.

Becker and Tomes claim that in the wealth model, under the above assumptions, reinforcement depends on whether the second cross partial derivative of the earnings production function with respect to human capital investments and endowments is positive (i.e., $\partial^2 Y/\partial G\partial h > 0$). If the better endowed child obtains higher returns from a given investment in human capital, parents respond by investing more in this child, thus increasing the difference in siblings' earnings beyond that due to endowment differentials alone. Parents then use transfers to equalize the wealth of their children, fully offsetting the earnings differentials. The assumption that the parents' utility function exhibits equal concern, together with the assumption that in equilibrium all children receive transfers from the parents, implies that parents equalize the wealth of their children, despite differences in their earnings.

In summary, Becker and Tomes claim that under the above assumptions:
- parents are likely to allocate human resource investments so as to reinforce endowment differentials among their children.
- human resource investments in the children are socially efficient (i.e., Pareto optimal) and privately efficient (i.e., wealth-maximizing) and,
- parents obtain equality in the children's wealth by distributing transfers among their children so as to offset earnings differences, whether these arise from differences in endowments or differences in human resources.

These implications of the wealth model have shaped the way most economists view intrahousehold allocation and investment in human capital.[12] But Behrman et al. (1995b) note that these conclusions depend on three crucial assumptions beyond those noted above.

*First*, the social efficiency conclusion depends on the absence of externalities and on perfect capital markets. This conclusion, while holding for parental allocations of children within the household, also holds equally if individuals make all of their own schooling investment decisions. As such, it has nothing to intrahousehold allocations per se.

*Second*, the conclusion regarding the reinforcement of endowment differentials depends upon parents devoting "enough" resources to their children in the sense that is elaborated in the next point and on restrictions on the earnings production function. To see the latter, consider a family with two children. For a given interest rate, the children can be ranked in terms of the resources required to give them the wealth-maximizing level of human resources. Designate the child for whom more resources are required to provide that child with the wealth-maximizing level of human re-

---

[12] For example, Cox and Rank (1992) have the wealth model in mind when they refer to altruistic models, apparently not recognizing that the wealth model is one, but not the only, specialized case of general altruistic models of parental behavior.

sources as "more educable".[13] If the schedule of the marginal returns to human resource investments for one child always lies above the corresponding schedule for the
other child, the identity of the "more educable" child is independent of the rate of interest. There is, however, no reason why these schedules cannot intersect. If they intersect and if both children receive the wealth-maximizing level of human resources,
the more educable child need not be the child with higher earnings: higher *marginal*
returns need not imply higher *average* returns to human resources. Thus, even if parents devote enough resources to their children to attain the wealth-maximizing levels
of human resource investments, the Becker and Tomes conclusion that the allocation
of educational resources tends to "reinforce" differences in endowments rather than
"compensate" for them depends crucially on the assumption that the earnings production function is such that the child with higher marginal returns to human resources
also has higher average returns to human resources.

*Third*, all of the conclusions depend on the assumption that parents devote
"enough" resources to their children. Parents who are insufficiently wealthy or insufficiently altruistic (i.e., those who fail to place "sufficient" weight on their children's
wealth in their own utility function) fail to provide their children with the socially
efficient, wealth-maximizing levels of human resources, and fail to equalize their children's wealth. Whether such parents reinforce or compensate for endowment differentials, moreover, may depend on preference parameters in addition to the second cross
derivative of the earnings production function. Becker and Tomes recognize that there
is a problem if parents do not devote enough resources to the children, and Becker
(1991) discusses the issue and cites research indicating that less than 40% of US families make significant financial (as opposed to human resource) transfers to their children.[14] Becker and Tomes do not, however, explore the consequences of less generous
provision of resources by parents for their children for within-sib allocations or for
reinforcement or compensation.

Behrman et al. (1995b) examine the implications of the wealth model in cases ignored by Becker and Tomes, cases in which parents allocate an "intermediate" level of
resources to their children. They begin with a separability assumption regarding paren-

---

[13] This is the designation used by Behrman et al. (1995b). This terminology seems clear for education,
but less so for other human resource investments such as in health and nutrition. Nevertheless, "more
educable" is used as a convenient short-hand expression for the child for whom the wealth-maximizing
human resource is greater at a given interest rate.

[14] Becker and Murphy (1988) argue that the possibility that parental poverty and selfishness result in
less than the optimal provisions of human capital for their children can be overcome by universal public
education coupled with Social Security. Public education, they argue, is likely to induce more schooling
for children in such families since it lowers the price. Social Security is likely to increase the resources that
such families devote to their children since it lowers the need for the parents to save for their old age.
Their discussion, however, is within a framework in which there is either one child or concern about the
average or representative child, not a concern about the intrahousehold distribution among children. It also
is not clear that these policies lead to efficient levels of education.

tal consumption versus child wealth that is now standard in models based on parental altruism in order to focus the analysis on the distribution of resources among children:

$$U = U^*[C_P, V(W_1, \ldots, W_n)], \tag{3}$$

where $V$ is the *parental welfare function*. Becker and Tomes generally make the assumption that all children receive the same weight in the parents' utility function, the assumption that Behrman et al. call "equal concern".[15] This assumption means that $V(W_1, \ldots, W_n)$ is symmetric around the 45° ray from the origin. Equal concern does not ensure equal wealth because it does not ensure equal labor market opportunities since endowments differ among children. For the rest of this section equal concern is a maintained assumption.

Behrman et al. note the following implications of the wealth model that hold regardless of the level of resources that parents devote to their children. Transfers are never provided to any child receiving less than the wealth-maximizing level of human resources; no child is ever provided with more than the wealth-maximizing level of human resources;[16] and any child receiving positive transfers receives the wealth-maximizing level of human resources.

Behrman et al. then consider how the implications of the Becker and Tomes wealth model depend upon the parental resources allocated to the children by considering the maximization of the parental welfare function subject to the wealth possibility frontier with simple diagrams in child wealth space. The wealth possibility frontier is determined by the total level of resources that parents devote to the children, the children's endowments, and the earnings production function in relation (2). Fig. 1 has a wealth possibility frontier that corresponds to the "very high resource case" in which parents are "rich enough and altruistic enough" so that the Becker and Tomes results hold. For the $j$th child, $Y_j^n$ designates the earnings level if there are no human resource investments in that child (i.e., if $H_j = 0$) and $Y_j^*$ designates the earnings level if human resource investments in that child are at the wealth-maximizing level (i.e., if $H_j = H_j^*$). The earnings production function is assumed to have continuous first derivatives with respect to human resource investments and diminishing marginal returns to human resource investments given fixed endowments. In the very high resource case, for a fixed level of resources devoted to children, the wealth possibility frontier has three regions: (i) the northwest region between $Y_1^n$ and $Y_1^*$ in which

---

[15] Becker and Tomes refer to "neutrality". If children have different consumption "needs" due to disabilities, this definition of equal concern or neutrality may be awkward (though perhaps less so if child utilities are considered instead of child wealth).

[16] Human resource investments above the wealth-maximizing levels are possible in the SET model (Section 2.1.2) if, for example, parents prefer that their children "earn" income rather than clip coupons if such investments are warranted to obtain the earnings distribution that the parents want. In Pollak's (1988) paternalistic preference model, parents may invest beyond the wealth-maximizing level if they consider education to be a "merit good".

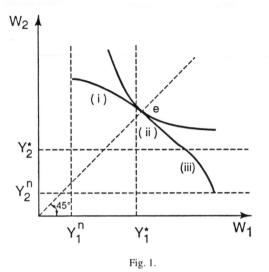

Fig. 1.

child 2 receives both the wealth-maximizing level of human resources and transfers, while child 1 receives less than the wealth-maximizing level of human resources and no transfers, (ii) the central region between $Y_1^*$ and $Y_2^*$, in which the frontier is linear with a slope of minus one, in which both children receive the wealth-maximizing levels of human resources and both receive transfers, and (iii) the southeast region between $Y_2^*$ and $Y_2^n$ in which child 1 receives the wealth-maximizing level of human resources and transfers, while child 2 receives less than the wealth-maximizing level of human resources and no transfers.[17] Regions (i) and (iii) both are convex to the origin because of diminishing returns to human resource investments. For simplicity, it is assumed here and in the rest of this section that child 1 is more educable than child 2 at all interest rates, so the wealth possibility frontier is elongated in the direction of wealth for child 1.[18] The assumption that parents devote a "very high" level of resources to their children ensures that the 45° ray from the origin intersects (at point *e*) and is perpendicular to the linear segment of the frontier (region ii). The assumption that the parental welfare function exhibits equal concern ensures that this intersection

---

[17] If children with no education have positive earnings, there are two additional regions starting at the axes that are of secondary importance for this analysis.

[18] If which child is more educable depends on the interest rate, as noted above, the child with the highest average earnings need not be the child with the highest marginal earnings so the wealth possibility curve need not be elongated in the direction of the child with the greater endowments (see Behrman et al., 1995b).

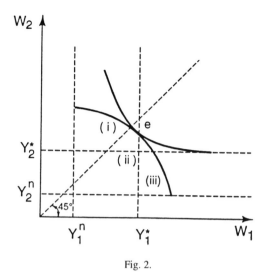

Fig. 2.

is the point of utility maximization.[19] Hence, in the very high resource case with equal concern, parents (a) provide each child with the efficient (i.e., wealth-maximizing) level of human resources (i.e., $Y_1 = Y_1^*$ and $Y_2 = Y_2^*$) and (b) use transfers to equalize the children's wealth, offsetting fully differences in earnings resulting from differences in endowments and human resources (i.e., $Y_1^* - Y_2^* = T_2 - T_1$). Given the assumption that child 1 is more educable at all interest rates, the earnings from human resource investments are greater for this child (i.e., $Y_1^* > Y_2^*$), and the other child receives more transfers in equilibrium (i.e., $T_2 > T_1$).

But Behrman et al. maintain that these results do not necessarily hold if parental resources are not "very high" (where "very high" means that the 45° ray from the origin passes through the linear region (ii) in Fig. 1). As parental resources allocated to the children are reduced ceteris paribus, the wealth possibility frontier moves closer to the origin and the linear region shrinks (since there are less resources left over for transfers after paying for the wealth-maximizing human resource investments for both children) until it disappears. Fig. 2 illustrates a case in which there still is a region (ii) but it does not intersect the 45° ray from the origin, and Fig. 3 illustrates a case in which there is no region (ii) and in fact parental resources are "very low" in the sense that they are not sufficient to attain the wealth-maximizing human resource investment for either child. It is immediately clear from these figures that the Becker and Tomes result that parents with equal concern equalize wealth among their chil-

---

[19] Any welfare function that causes parents to select a point on the linear segment of the frontier implies that each child receives the wealth-maximizing level of education.

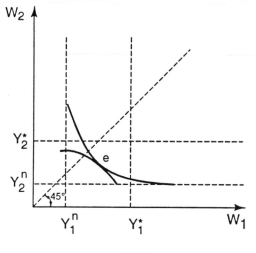

Fig. 3.

dren generally does not hold if parents do not allocate sufficient resources to their children (except in the limiting case in which the parental welfare function is L-shaped). Instead, the more educable child has the higher wealth ($W_1 > W_2$) because the equilibrium tangency is below the 45° ray from the origin.[20] It also is clear that for the cases below the very high resource case, at most one child receives transfers at the equilibrium (i.e., in Fig. 2, $T_2 > 0 = T_1$ and in Fig. 3, $T_2 = T_1 = 0$), which contrasts with the Becker and Tomes implicit very high resource assumption in which both children receive transfers. It also is clear that, if parents do not provide enough resources for the very high resource case, human resource investments in at least one child are below the wealth-maximizing level (i.e., in Fig. 2, $H_1 < H_1^*$ even though $H_2 = H_2^*$ and in Fig. 3, $H_1 < H_1^*$ and $H_2 < H_2^*$), so the Becker and Tomes conclusion about human resource investments being socially efficient does not hold even if private marginal rates of return to such investments are the same as social marginal rates of return at the wealth-maximizing levels of human resources investments. Finally, which child receives the greater human resource investment may depend on parental preferences in addition to the properties of the earnings production function – again in contrast to the claim by Becker and Tomes. This can be seen by considering the very low re-

[20] This tangency must be below the 45° ray from the origin under these assumptions since the parental welfare function is perpendicular to that ray where it intersects with that ray (given equal concern) but the wealth possibility frontier is less steep than the preference function where it intersects that ray (given that the intersection is not in region (ii) where both children receive transfers it must be in region (i) in which the marginal impact of equal human resource investments in the two children must be higher for child 1 than for child 2 if child 1 is more educable at all interest rates).

source case in Fig. 3 with the modification (not drawn) of parental preferences with extreme inequality aversion (L-shaped) so the equilibrium point *e* is on the 45° ray from the origin; this implies greater human resource investment in child 2 even though that child is less educable and the second cross derivative of the earnings production function is positive. Thus, consideration of the wealth model for the less than very high resource case on which Becker and Tomes concentrate suggests that the implications that Becker and Tomes draw may hold only for the very high resource case.

These considerations about the wealth model lead to several possible tests of the model conditional on equal concern: If all children in a sibship receive transfers from their parents, do the differences in transfers received offset differences in earnings? If all children in a sibship receive transfers from their parents, do they all have the same marginal rate of return to human resource investments and is this rate of return equal to the rate of return on financial assets? If one child in a sibship does not receive transfers and at least one child does receive transfers from their parents, does the child that receives the transfer have less earnings but a higher marginal rate of return to human resource investments than does the child who does not receive transfers and is this rate of return for the latter child equal to the rate of return on financial assets? If no child in a sibship receives transfers from their parents, are the marginal rates of return to human resource investments higher for the children with smaller earnings and are all of these rates of return greater than the rate of return on financial assets? Unfortunately, these tests are very difficult to implement because of problems in estimating marginal rates of return to human resource investments for different individuals in a sibship with a framework that is consistent with the wealth model (see start of Section 3) and because of the difficulty of obtaining data on all transfers from parents to children, including inter vivos gifts and bequests. Nevertheless there is some suggestive evidence that is summarized in Section 3.4.

### 2.1.2. The separable earnings–transfers (SET) model

Behrman et al. (1982) introduced the "separable earnings–transfers" (SET) model. This model, like the wealth model discussed in Section 2.1.1, is a special case of the general consensus parental model. The SET model assumes that the parental welfare function is separable – that preferences among earnings distributions are independent of the distribution of transfers and that preferences among transfer distributions are independent of the distributions of earnings:

$$U = U^{**}(C_P, V^*(Y_1, \ldots, Y_n), V^{**}(T_1, \ldots, T_n)), \tag{4}$$

where $V^*$ is the parental subwelfare function defined over their children's earnings, and $V^{**}$ is the parental subwelfare function defined over the parental transfers to their children. The assumption that earnings distributions enter into the parental welfare

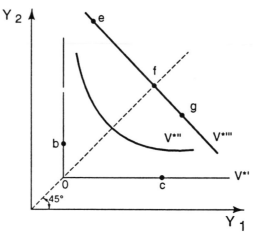

Fig. 4.

function separably from transfers may be rationalized because parents value a dollar that their children earn in the labor market more (or at least differently) than a dollar received from assets because, for example, a person may be valued more who "earns his or her way". The separability assumption enables the analysis of the distribution of human resource investments among children without regard to the magnitude or distribution of transfers. Thus, the predictions of the SET model about earnings distributions coincide with those of the wealth model with zero transfers with the exception that the SET model does not predict that the level of human resource investments must be less than or equal to the wealth-maximizing level. That is, for the SET model, there is a figure similar to Fig. 3, but with earnings measured on the axis (not wealth) and with the location of $Y_1^*$ and $Y_2^*$ not specified necessarily to be greater than the maximum wealth possible given the wealth possibility frontier constraint.

Two features of the earnings subwelfare function, $V^*$, are of particular interest: the equity–productivity tradeoff and equal concern. Fig. 4 illustrates the range of possibilities for the equity–productivity tradeoff in the two-child case with equal concern. At one extreme, parents may be concerned exclusively with equity; in this case the subwelfare function indifference curve is L-shaped, as is $V^{*\prime}$, indicating that there is no welfare gain if, from an initially equal earnings distribution such as at point a, there is a movement to a point such as *b* or *c* by increasing the earnings of one child while maintaining those of the other unchanged. At the other extreme, parents may be concerned solely with productivity, so that the subwelfare function indifference curve is linear, as is $V^{*\prime\prime\prime}$. In this case, the parents are not concerned with the distribution of earnings among their children, but only with the sum of their children's earnings.

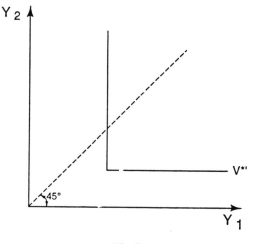

Fig. 5.

Hence, they are indifferent among distributions such as $e$, $f$, and $g$.[21] Between these two extremes are intermediate cases in which parents trade off equity against productivity, such as $V^{*''}$. Conditional on the validity of the model, the magnitude of the equity–productivity tradeoff implicit in parental allocations is an empirical issue (see Section 3.2.1).

The second feature of the earnings subwelfare function, equal concern, already has been discussed in conjunction with the wealth model in Section 2.1.1. Unequal concern might be based on a variety of characteristics: sex, birth order, beauty, cuteness, brightness, energy, health. In Fig. 5, $V^{*'}$ illustrates an indifference curve which places greater weight on the earnings of child 1 than child 2. Empirical estimates of the extent of unequal concern, again conditional on the validity of the model, are summarized in Section 3.3.1 below.

The equity–productivity tradeoff and the extent of equal concern are distinct features of the earnings subwelfare function. Parents may exhibit substantial concern with equity (reflected in indifference curves that are nearly L-shaped), but exhibit unequal concern (so the indifference curves are asymmetric around the 45° ray). Or parents may be primarily interested in productivity (so that their indifference curves are almost linear), but have equal concern (so that the indifference curves are sym-

---

[21] The exclusive concern with productivity in this case suggests a link with the human capital investment model of Becker (1967), but without the implication that the rate of return on schooling equals the market interest rate.

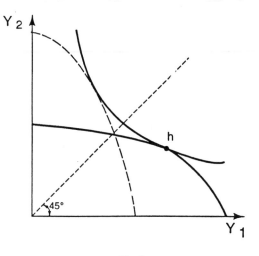

Fig. 6.

metric). Thus, there is no necessary link between equal concern and concern with equity in the equity–productivity tradeoff.

In the SET model, human resource investments in children and thus the children's earnings capacities are determined by maximizing the subwelfare function $V^*$ subject to an earnings production function as in relation (2) and a budget constraint on human resource investments in the children,

$$\sum p_{H_j} H_j \leq R^*, \tag{5}$$

where $p_{H_j}$ is the price per unit of human resource investments for the $j$th child and $R^*$ is the parental resource constraint on human resource investments in their children. Fig. 6 illustrates the solution for constrained maximization of the parental subwelfare function $V^*$ in relation (4) subject to relations (2) and (5). A parental subwelfare curve is indicated by $W^*$. With equal concern, this curve is symmetric around the 45° ray. The budget constraint, the earnings production functions, and the given endowments ($G_j$'s) and human resource investment prices ($p_{H_j}$'s) imply an earnings possibility production frontier. In general, this frontier is not symmetrical around the 45° ray because endowments and the human resource investment prices may differ among children. In this figure the solid earnings possibility frontier is drawn as if child 1 has greater endowments and/or faces lower human resource investment prices. Constrained maximization leads to a point such as $h$, where the indifference curve of the parental subwelfare function is tangent to the earnings possibility frontier. Even with equal concern, the maximizing outcome is not in general equal earnings for the children because the frontier is *not* symmetric. Instead, the more educable child (if one child is more educable at all interest rates)[22] and/or the child facing lower human resource investment prices has higher earnings.[23] If parents are concerned solely with equity, then their indifference curves are L-shaped. If, in addition, they have equal concern, then unequally endowed children receive equal earnings. If parents have unequal concern, the parental subwelfare function is shifted in the direction of the favored child.[24]

Fig. 6 also can be used to educate one's intuition about identifying the curvature and asymmetry of the parental subwelfare functions. In general for any pair of children in the same or different families, relative child endowments differ. For a second pair of children, for example, the earnings possibility frontier might look like the dashed line. By examining the tangencies between a whole set of earnings possibility frontiers for different pairs of children with the same parental subwelfare curve, the curvature and the asymmetry of the parental subwelfare function can be traced out, conditional on the earnings production function and on the parental subwelfare function being homothetic.

Behrman et al. (1982) also use specific functional forms to derive tractable expressions for the relative human resource investments and relative earnings of siblings. The parental subwelfare function defined over their children's earnings is CES:

$$V^* = \left(\sum h_j Y_j^d\right)^{1/d}, \quad -\infty < d \le 1. \tag{6}$$

The budget constraint is given above in relation (5). The earnings production function in relation (2) is log-linear or Cobb–Douglas (with diminishing returns to human resource investments and to endowments):

$$Y_j = f H_j^\alpha G_j^\lambda, \quad 0 < \alpha < 1, \quad 0 < \lambda < 1, \quad 0 < f, \quad j = 1,2. \tag{7}$$

The equilibrium ratio of the two siblings' human resource investments and earnings are

$$(H_1/H_2) = [(h_1 p_{H_2})/(h_2 p_{H_1})]^{1/(1-\alpha d)}(G_1/G_2)^{\lambda d/(1-\alpha d)}, \tag{8}$$

$$(Y_1/Y_2) = [(h_1 p_{H_2})/(h_2 p_{H_1})]^{\alpha/(1-\alpha d)}(G_1/G_2)^{\lambda/(1-\alpha d)}. \tag{9}$$

---

[22] As is discussed in Section 2.1.1, if this condition is not satisfied the child with the higher marginal rate of return may not have higher average returns.

[23] Human resource investment prices may be functions of endowments if, for example, merit scholarships are important. See Behrman et al. (1989) that is summarized below in Section 3.1.2.

[24] This suggests the possibility of a borderline case in which equal earnings result because parents prefer the less-well endowed child just enough to offset the impact of differential endowments on the earnings possibility frontier.

What does the SET model with these specific functional form assumptions imply about compensation and reinforcement? The implications are most clear when human resource investment prices are the same for all children (i.e., $p_{H_j} = p_H$) and parents have equal concern (i.e., $h_j = h$). Under these assumptions, the expressions in brackets [ ] are unity, so parents reinforce the children's endowment differentials if and only if $d > 0$ and compensate if and only if $d < 0$. The borderline case separating reinforcement from compensation is a Cobb–Douglas parental subwelfare function ($d = 0$); in this case, parents are neutral, neither compensating nor reinforcing endowment differentials among their children, so that the earnings ratio is proportional to the endowments ratio raised to the power $\lambda$. These conclusions differ from those of the wealth model (Section 2.1.1) for values of $d \leq 0$. The cross partial derivatives of the earnings production function (7) are given by $\partial^2 Y/(\partial G \partial H) = \alpha \lambda f H^{\alpha-1} G^{\lambda-1}$, which is strictly positive since $f$, $\alpha$ and $\lambda$ are positive; hence, the wealth model implies reinforcement in all cases.

When transfers to all children are zero, the SET model and the wealth model imply that the distribution of human resources among children is found by maximizing the same objective function subject to the same constraints. Thus, the Becker–Tomes criterion for reinforcement or compensation is incorrect for some families for some functional forms. The Behrman et al. specific results, however, are functional form dependent. For example, if the earnings production function is CES with an elasticity of substitution of $b$, rather than a Cobb–Douglas, then the relation between two siblings' ratios of human resource investments and earnings is

$$\ln(H_1/H_2) = [(d-1)/(b-1)] \ln(Y_2/Y_1). \tag{10}$$

This expression points to the difficulty of identifying the parental subwelfare curvature parameter ($d$) from the production function curvature parameter ($b$).

What effect does unequal concern have in the SET model? With unequal concern, $h_1 \neq h_2$ in the brackets at the front of the right-hand side of relations (8) and (9). As one would expect, unequal concern shifts resources toward the child with greater preference weight and increases the absolute and relative earnings of the preferred child. The greater the product $\alpha d$, the greater are these shifts. This product is greater, in turn, the greater is the concern about productivity (or, equivalently, the less is the concern about equity) and the greater is the elasticity of earnings with respect to human resource investments.

*2.1.3. The returns to schooling and the relation of schooling to child quality in the wealth and SET models*

The intrahousehold allocations in the wealth model and the SET model have implications for estimates of returns to schooling and for the interpretation of schooling as child quality which is now briefly summarized. More extensive discussions are in Behrman (1987a,b).

*Identifying the returns to schooling.* Parents invest in their children not only with expenditures on schooling but also with time and goods allocated to health, nutrition, and general development. In poor societies, the value of the resources devoted to these nonschooling investments may exceed those devoted to schooling. This observation raises the question, whether an investigator can distinguish between the effect of schooling investments and the effects of nonschooling investments? The answer is that identification of the effect of schooling is difficult, and in some cases, not possible. For example, consider the low resource case of the wealth model or equivalently the SET model with an earnings production function in relation (2) that is CES in schooling, nonschooling investments and endowments. In this case for those children for whom the prices for human capital investments are the same (i.e, those in the same region), schooling and nonschooling investments are perfectly correlated across children regardless of differences in their endowments. In such a case, the impact of schooling on earnings or other outcomes can not be identified even if all nonschooling investments are observed. More generally, the correlation between schooling and nonschooling investments may be high, though not one, so that estimates of schooling effects that do not control for nonschooling investments (such as most earnings function estimates) attribute to schooling the correlated effects of nonschooling investments. But note that, though identifying the effect of schooling may be difficult if there are nonschooling investments, the more correlated are schooling and nonschooling investments, the better schooling represents total human resource investments in studies of the intrahousehold allocation of resources.

*Child quality.* Child quality plays a critical role in the analysis of fertility and investments in children's human capital in the dominant model in economic demography, the "quantity–quality" model of Becker and Lewis (1973) and Willis (1973). Child quality also is of considerable interest because of its relation to well-being and productivity. In the theoretical literature, child quality is sometimes defined as a set of desirable characteristics that appear as arguments of parents' utility functions, sometimes defined as expected adult earnings or income (e.g., Becker, 1991) and, too often, not defined at all. In empirical studies, child quality is usually treated as an unobserved variable and is represented by child schooling (or, occasionally, by some other variable, such as health).[25] For example, in her presidential address to the Population Association of America, Blake (1981) explicitly equates child quality with child schooling. The widespread practice in empirical work of equating child quality and schooling raises the question: how good a proxy for child quality is child schooling?

---

[25] For example, see Blake (1981), DeTray (1977), Leibowitz (1974), and Rosenzweig and Wolpin (1980).

Assume that child quality is the command over resources, and schooling is an input into the production of earnings, which together with transfers determines the command over resources. First assume in addition that the wealth model of Section 2.1.1 applies. For the very high resource case emphasized by Becker and Tomes, the intrahousehold association between schooling and quality so-defined is zero. If all children receive positive transfers, all households face the same marginal costs of funds for schooling investments and the same relative prices for schooling, and there is no association between child endowments and the total resources devoted to children, then the wealth model also implies that the interfamily association between schooling and quality also is zero. For lower levels of resources devoted to the children within the wealth model, the intra- and interhousehold associations between schooling and quality may be positive, negative, or zero. Likewise, within the SET model, if child quality is the total command over resources (i.e., wealth) or the command over resources obtained from labor (i.e., earnings), the intra- and interhousehold associations between schooling and quality may be positive, negative, or zero depending on the extent of reinforcement versus compensation due to underlying parental preferences regarding equity versus productivity and the extent to which for different children the relative prices for schooling versus nonschooling human resource investments vary.

Hence, the use of schooling as a proxy for child quality must be interpreted carefully. Clarity probably would be increased if schooling were simply called "schooling" in empirical work. If a representation of child quality is required to test some hypothesis, then the relevant concept of child quality should be defined explicitly, as well as its relation to the representation used. Under the assumptions of the wealth and SET models, as noted, such considerations may imply that schooling is not a very good indicator of child quality and may not even be positively correlated with child quality.

## 2.2. Active children and Becker's "Rotten Kid Theorem"

The wealth model and the SET model assume that children are passive in the sense that they do not have independent roles as decision makers. Some other models, such as the intergenerational exchange models (that are summarized in the chapter by Laitner in this volume), assume that children are active, independent decision makers.[26]

---

[26] In the Bernheim et al. (1985) model, for example, the parents influence the behavior of their (active) children by holding wealth in bequeathable form and by conditioning the division of bequests among their children (and perhaps others) on the beneficiaries' actions (e.g. providing attention to the parents). If parents credibly can precommit, they can reap all the surplus from the intergenerational interchange. While this model considers only financial transfers to adult children from parents in exchange for attention, conceptually the approach could be extended to incorporate intrahousehold allocations of human resource investments in children as part of the intergenerational interactions. Such an extension would be consistent in spirit with the inclusion of both intrahousehold resource allocations and intergenerational transfers in

Becker (1974, 1991) argues in his "Rotten Kid Theorem" that variations in transfers to selfish, active children force such children to consider their parents' interests. Each beneficiary, no matter how selfish, behaves so that utility of the altruistic benefactor is maximized subject to the total family income constraint. The essence of this model is captured by considering the nature of intrahousehold allocations between one child and parents with consensus preferences rather than among children, though there may be implications for the allocations among children. Assume that the parents' preferences depend on their own consumption and on the child's utility, but that the child is selfish in the sense that the child's utility depends only positively on the child's consumption and negatively on the child's income (since child income generation involves foregone leisure):

$$U^P = U^P(C^P, U^C(C^C, Y^C)), \quad \text{with } U^P_1 > 0 \text{ and } U^P_2 > 0, \tag{11}$$

$$U^C = U^C(C^C, Y^C), \quad \text{with } U^C_1 > 0 \text{ and } U^C_2 < 0. \tag{12}$$

Also assume that the parental budget constraint indicates that parental income must be equal to or greater than parental consumption plus transfers from parents to the child and that the child's budget constraint indicates that the child's own-generated income plus transfers from the parents must be equal to or greater than the child's income:

$$Y_P \geq C_P + T, \tag{13}$$

$$Y_C + T \geq C_C. \tag{14}$$

The child maximizes her/his utility in relation (12) by choosing her/his own income generation effort and consumption given transfers received from the parents subject to the income constraint in (14). If the parents choose the transfers to the child, they maximize their utility in relation (11) by choosing their own consumption and transfers to the child subject to the budget constraint in relation (13) and the child's behavior. In this case, the Rotten Kid Theorem states that the child chooses own consumption and income generation levels that the parents would choose were they to maxi-

the wealth model discussed in Section 2.1.1. The Bernheim et al. model and most exchange models generally do not, however, include endowments that are central to the intrahousehold models discussed above. Another example of active children is in Pollak's (1988) model of paternalistic parental preferences. In this model transfers are tied; for example, parents may pay for college tuition, but not for a junket around the world. The tied transfers model assumes that the child's ability or willingness to untie transfers is limited, perhaps because of transaction costs or because parents and child play a repeated game. Pollak notes that this model may be consistent with some observations about parental–child behavior that are consistent neither with a pure parental altruism model nor with an exchange model, though he does not offer suggestions about how one might test systematically the implications of this model.

mize their utility in relation (11) subject to the family budget constraint, $Y_P + Y_C \geq C_P + C_C$. In both cases,

$$U_1^P = U_2^P U_1^C = -U_2^P U_2^C. \tag{15}$$

A critical assumption is that the parents choose the transfers to the child, which is plausible for positive transfers from the parents to the child. It is also the case that a forced transfer from the parents to the child has no effect on either the parents' or the child's consumption as long as the parents still make positive transfers to the child above the forced level, which is the basis of the Ricardian equivalence theorem (Barro, 1974).

The Rotten Kid Theorem may not hold for at least three reasons. *First*, as Hirshleifer (1977, 1985) points out, parents must have some way of forcing children to respond as the parents wish, such as the parents making their transfer after the child makes all his/her actions that affect family income. If not, the selfish child can maximize his/her utility at the expense of the parents. *Second*, Bergstrom (1989) and Bernheim et al. (1985) point out that the theorem may not hold if utility does not depend solely on transferable commodities. *Third*, Bruce and Waldman (1990) show that the theorem may not hold in a two-period model with savings. If the parents make transfers only in the second period, the child chooses efficient income-generating actions in both periods without the need for parents to engage in retaliatory strategies, but consumes too much and saves too little in the first period in order to be more impoverished and receive greater transfers in the second period (i.e., the "Samaritan's dilemma"). If the parents precommit by making sufficiently large transfers in the first period so that the second-period transfer is inoperable, the child no longer has incentives to save too little in the first period but the Rotten Kid Theorem is not operable in the second period. Therefore, if parents can not behave in a retaliatory fashion, they must chose between an operative second-period transfer with a Samaritan dilemma-type inefficiency and a nonoperative second-period transfer with a Rotten Kid-type inefficiency. In either case the family unit does not achieve the Pareto frontier.

## 3. Empirical explorations of single-period consensus preference models

The models that are reviewed in Section 2 have some important implications for understanding intrahousehold allocations, their implications for efficiency and equity, whether such allocations tend to reinforce or compensate for endowment differentials, and even for other considerations such as Ricardian equivalence and thereby the efficacy of macro-economic policies. But empirical explorations of these and related models are difficult because of data limitations. *First*, individual endowments generally are not observed in socioeconomic data sets, so direct estimates of the impact of differential endowments among household members usually is not possible. *Second*, the intrahousehold distribution of transfers and of consumption and investments goods rarely are directly observed, with the exception of schooling, certain types of purchased health goods and services, non labor market time, non schooling time, and, in a very few data sets, food or child–parental contact. *Third*, data that are available usually cover fairly short time periods, but in some important cases the relevant concepts are for lifetime variables, such as the flows of transfers (inter vivos and bequests) between children and their parents or lifetime earnings. *Fourth*, many data sets do not link adults who are not co-resident with their siblings, so the impact of childhood intrahousehold allocations on adult outcomes can not be investigated even for variables such as wages that are collected in many socioeconomic data sets (though increasingly special data sets have become available with such linkages). *Fifth*, many outcomes that are affected by intrahousehold allocations are not (e.g., rates of return to human resource investments for siblings within a family) or rarely (e.g., nonpecuniary aspects of jobs, health outcomes) observed or estimable. *Sixth*, the extent of measurement error in observed variables often is difficult to assess.

Despite these data problems, some interesting empirical explorations have been undertaken that permit some insights in some cases into the relative merits of some of these models and in other cases into the implications of the models. These explorations also reveal the difficulties of undertaking empirical research in this area due in substantial part to the data problems just summarized.

## 3.1. Intrahousehold human resource allocation responses to prices related to individual endowments

The parental consensus models in Section 2.1 generally[27] imply greater resource investments in children for whom endowments are such that the earnings possibilities frontiers are more elongated in the direction of their earnings. Similar predictions arise if parents are not altruistic but reap all of the gains from investments in their children, or if the investment in each child reflects pure investment decisions with perfect credit markets.[28] In all of these cases, the distribution of endowments among the children in a family affects the relative human resource investments in those children.

Some important dimensions of endowments, as noted at the start of Section 2.1, may relate to prices that depend on such endowments. One example is that expected returns in labor markets may depend on endowments such as sex because of discrimi-

---

[27] With the exceptions of the case in which parental preferences reflect extreme inequality aversion in the SET model and the case in which parental preferences reflect extreme inequality aversion and parental resources provided to children are very low in the wealth model.

[28] But, as noted above in Section 2.1.1, the more-educable child at the margin given interest rates does not necessarily have greater earnings.

nation or gender specialization in those markets.[29] Another example is that prices for schooling may depend on family size if access to capital markets for schooling investments vary with family size or if there are merit scholarships related to endowments.

### 3.1.1. Indian male–female infant and child mortality differentials and labor markets

There has been considerable interest and concern about differences in male and female mortality, particularly in Asia and North Africa (e.g., Sen, 1990). Rosenzweig and Schultz (1982) analyze the determinants of male–female differentials in child survival rates in rural India, using both 1971 rural household and 1961 district level data. They argue that the male–female survival differential depends upon the expected relative returns to male and female labor because those expectations influence parental investments in sons and daughters. They use predicted employment rates of current men and women as proxies for the economic returns to investing in boys and girls under the assumption of static expectations which they suggest is plausible in the pre Green Revolution period from which their data come. They argue (not entirely persuasively) that wage rates may not reflect the value of time as well as do employment rates because cultural factors such as religion and caste may prevent women from equalizing the marginal products of market and household labor, so the use of employment rates is preferable to the use of wage rates.[30] They do not observe that where employment rates are higher for current women, the opportunity cost of women's time in child care is likely to be higher, which would tend to work in the opposite direction of their posited effects. In both the household and the district level samples, they find predicted female (but not male) employment rates to be a significant negative determinant of the male–female child survival differential. They interpret these results to imply that children who seem likely to become more economically productive adults receive a greater share of family resources and therefore have a greater propensity to survive than other children. In a comment on this article Folbre (1984) suggests that these results are supportive of a model in which women who have greater income have greater influence in intrahousehold allocations which leads to greater investments in daughters, which is in the spirit of the nonconsensus models of household behavior

---

[29] But, as Behrman and Deolalikar (1995) note, higher wages for males does not necessarily imply higher rates of returns for investing in education of males than for females. Their estimates suggest, in fact, that in Indonesia the rates of return to time spent in schooling by females are higher than for males so that the gender gap in wages favoring males declines with schooling levels. They also suggest that the opportunity costs of attending school are higher for females, perhaps in part because of gender division of tasks in the household such as the care for younger sick siblings that Pitt and Rosenzweig (1990) explore (see Section 3.3.3).

[30] Further, as Pitt et al. (1990: p. 1143) observe with regard to their model discussed below in Section 3.2.2, "it is not market work time (or even the average wage rate) that matters for food allocation (as in Rosenzweig and Schultz, 1982), but the type of activity engaged in, as defined by the wage-effort-health association".

that are discussed below in Section 4. Rosenzweig and Schultz (1984) respond by observing that the available data do not permit one to identify whether the underlying allocations reflect such a bargaining model versus responses to differential expected returns.

### 3.1.2. Sibship similarity and variance in schooling prices

Behrman et al. (1989) focus on equality of access to resources for financing college education, what they call "equal access". Equal access prevails if all individuals, regardless of differences in family background and parental wealth, face the same marginal cost schedule for resources for college. Equal access at the college level would occur if there were a student loan program that made resources available to all high school graduates at the same interest rate, provided none of them could borrow elsewhere at a lower rate.[31] With diminishing returns to schooling and equal access to resources, every high school graduate could and presumably would pursue further education until the marginal rate of return to schooling equals this interest rate if the child is the decision maker. If this interest rate were no higher than the rate of return on financial assets and if parents and children were solely interested in expected wealth maximization, then neither parents nor children, however rich, would invest in education beyond the point at which the expected marginal return equaled the marginal cost of funds. (Some parents or children, however, may invest more to achieve nonmarket returns.)

Behrman et al. use the SET model (Section 2.1.2) to analyze the extent of sib schooling and earning similarities in large and small families.[32] They argue that a larger sibship size implies less sib schooling similarity unless there is equal access to financing. They argue that, within the SET model, the effect of an increase in sibship size on the variation in schooling is best understood by considering a "preference displacement effect", which implies that larger sibships are associated with less variability in education, and a "price effect", which implies that larger sibships are associated with greater variability in education.

The preference displacement effect arises because parental resources for schooling investment per child tend to decrease as sibship size increases, moving the earnings possibility frontier toward the origin in Fig. 6. Let the translation of the parental CES parental subwelfare function from the 0 origin be given by $b_j$'s, which refer to "subsistence levels" only above which parents make tradeoffs among their children's

---

[31] Even with equal access and similar genetic endowments among children, family environment or family resources might make substantial differences in children's life chances. For example, inequalities in lifetime earnings might result from differences in family environment or resources available during childhood. Thus, equal access does not imply equality of opportunity.

[32] Though they present their arguments in terms of the SET model, their points also hold for the wealth model in Section 2.1.1 (which should not be surprising for at least the very low resource case of the wealth model that is equivalent to the SET model).

expected earnings. Because the inward movement of the earnings possibility frontier toward the origin with more children places the tangency with the parental welfare function closer to the levels indicated by the *b*'s and because parents make trade-offs among their children's earnings only above the *b*'s, the preference displacement effect tends to reduce the variation in investment in schooling among the children in a family as the sibship size increases.[33] Under the assumption that the marginal schooling price is identical for all children in all families, the preference displacement effect by itself tends to lead to greater sib schooling similarity as sibship size increases.[34] Empirically, however, the values of *b* are very small for the two generations that Behrman et al. (1982, 1986) and Behrman and Taubman (1986) consider, so the preference displacement effect is likely to be weak.

The price effect tends to cause sib schooling variability – and, therefore, earnings variability – to increase with sibship size (under the assumption that $d > -\infty$, so the reference functions are not at the Rawlsian extreme). Families with larger sibship size are more likely to be eligible for scholarships and thus more likely to face schooling prices that vary with their children's endowments. The price effect operates alone when the displacement parameters are zero; in this case the first-order conditions can be solved to obtain the explicit expressions for the two siblings' ratios of years of schooling and of earnings in Eqs. (8) and (9), conditional on the particular functional forms that underlie these relations. These expressions imply that variations in sib schooling and earnings are greater if prices vary inversely with children's endowments. They also imply that increased sibship size does not result in more variation in schooling when the schooling price is the same for all children in the family and, a fortiori, when that price is the same for all children in all families.

To explore the importance of equal access, Behrman et al. compare the experience of World War II veterans, who were eligible for the considerable educational benefits of the G.I. Bill, with the experience of the subsequent generation, which faced sub-

---

[33] The interpretation of the *b*'s as subsistence parameters rather than bliss points is equivalent to assuming that the parameter *d* relating to the curvature of the parental subwelfare function in relation (6) (with $Y_j' = Y_j - b_j$ replacing $Y_j$) is $\leq 1$; for further discussion, see Behrman et al. (1982: p. 66, n. 13). The estimates that are summarized in Section 3.3.1 suggest that *d* is significantly less than 1.

[34] This discussion assumes that intrafamilial variations in child endowments and thus in demand functions for schooling are independent of sibship size. Behrman et al. (1989) note, however, that there are at least two reasons to expect wider diversity in the distribution of demand functions in larger families than in smaller. First, larger families are more likely to include children born to older mothers, and such children are more likely to have birth defects. Although fraternal twins are born more frequently to older mothers, identical twins are not. Thus comparing identical and fraternal twins sheds some light on this possible source of greater demand diversity in larger families. In the NAS-NRC Twin sample, however, they find little evidence of greater demand diversity in larger families. Second, if there are liquidity constraints, families with more children are likely to have such children over more variegated parts of the parents' life-cycle income path and thus have more variation in the budget constraint than families with fewer children. The estimates in Behrman and Taubman (1990) suggest that liquidity constraints may be important in explaining patterns of schooling at the margin. This is one of the reasons that they focus on adjacent sib pairs in the regression analysis in the study being summarized.

stantially less generous governmental programs for financing their college educations. Their analysis hinges on the relationship between sibship size, on the one hand, and sib schooling similarity and earnings similarity, on the other. Their empirical results are basically consistent with their theoretical expectations. In the National Academy of Science–National Research Council (NAS-NRC) Twins Offspring sample for which less generous governmental programs for financing college education were available, there are strong and statistically significant positive associations of sibship size with work while at college and the use of loans, and a significant negative association with parental aid to finance college education (all with control for birth order, parents' ages, mother's education, and parents' income). In that sample for both schooling attainment and earnings the family means and intraclass correlations (i.e., the proportion of the total variance that is attributable to differences in family means) fall, and the within-family standard deviations rise with sibship size. Sibship similarity as indicated by the $R^2$ or the coefficient estimate for a regression of a child's schooling or earnings on the same variable for the next older sib also tends to decline with sibship size. In contrast, for the NAS-NRC Twins sample that was eligible for the G.I. Bill educational benefits, though there is some decline of mean schooling with sibship size, the association of sibship similarity (measured in the same way) with sibship size is much weaker than for the offspring generation. Behrman et al. also provide a rough estimate of how important unequal access would have been for World War II veterans in the absence of the G.I. Bill within a variance components framework.[35] They estimate that, among white males, unequal access would have accounted for 25–30% of the variance in the natural log of earnings without the G.I. Bill, more than twice the estimate of 12% reported in Behrman et al. (1980) for a group eligible for the G.I. Bill.

## 3.2. Estimates of reinforcement or compensation of endowments

One of the issues that the models in Section 2.1 raise is whether parental allocations of human resources among children in a family tend to reinforce or compensate for endowment differentials among the children. The Becker and Tomes (1976) presentation of their wealth model claims that such allocations are reinforcing because of positive effects of greater endowments on the marginal product of human resource investments in the earnings production function. (However, as discussed in Section 2.1.1, the more-educable child at the margin is not necessarily the child with greater endow-

---

[35] Their estimates summarized to this point use very simple methods to describe associations (and not to determine causality). Their estimates based on the variance decomposition, however, are based on stronger assumptions and greater approximations that they discuss in some detail, for which reason their estimates are characterized here as "rough".

ments on the average and for cases in which parental resources allocated to their children are less than "very high" preference parameters as well as production function parameters enter into this decision.) The Behrman et al. (1982) SET model, in contrast, posits that such investments may be reinforcing, compensating, or neutral, depending on the extent of equity–productivity tradeoff in parental preferences and the properties of the earnings production function.

This section summarizes three different sets of estimates of whether reinforcement or compensation prevails. These estimates are reviewed in chronological order, which also is in order of relaxing a priori assumptions on the structure of the analysis.

### 3.2.1. SET model estimates

Section 2.1.2 develops the general SET model and discusses many of its implications. It also presents an empirically tractable version of the SET model conditional on the specific functional form assumptions that the parental subwelfare function defined over their children's expected earnings is CES as in relation (6) and that the earnings production function is Cobb–Douglas as in relation (7). Let realized earnings $(Y')$ also be related to expected earnings $(Y)$ as follows:

$$Y' = Y e^v, \tag{16}$$

where $v$ is a stochastic disturbance term with expected value of zero that refers to unanticipated market luck and accidents and that is orthogonal to $Y$. The first-order conditions for the constrained maximization of the parental subwelfare function with equal concern imply

$$\ln(H_1/H_2) = (d - 1) \ln(Y'_2/Y'_1) + u, \tag{17}$$

where $u = (1 - d) (v_1 - v_2)$. An advantage of this expression is that the unobserved Lagrangian for the budget constraint in relation (5) and the unobserved genetic endowments $(G_j)$ that enter into the earnings production function in relation (7) do not enter directly. Therefore, if relation (17) can be estimated, the curvature of the parental subwelfare function (related to $d$) can be estimated. As is discussed in Section 2.1.2, conditional on these functional forms, parents reinforce children's endowment differentials if and only if $d > 0$ and compensate if and only if $d < 0$, with the neutral borderline case if $d = 0$. With respect to the equity–productivity tradeoff, thus, equity is weighed more heavily in parental preferences if $d < 0$ and productivity is weighed more heavily if $d > 0$. As $d \rightarrow -\infty$, only equity matters and the subwelfare function becomes Rawlsian. As $d \rightarrow 1$, only productivity matters, and parents allocate resources to their children's human resources to maximize the sum of their children's expected earnings with no concern about the distribution of those expected earnings among their children.

To estimate relation (17) requires a sample of adult siblings with at least both human resource investments (such as years of school) and earnings data. Note that the sample restriction to households with at least two adult children with labor market earnings does not cause selectivity bias if the underlying selectivity rule for such households depends on parental household factors since relation (17) effectively is a within-household expression that controls for unobserved household fixed effects. Behrman et al. (1982, 1986) and Behrman and Taubman (1986) present estimates of relation (17) for two United States samples with such data – the NAS-NRC Twin Sample and the NAS-NRC Twin Offspring sample. The estimates for $d$ range from 0.03 to 0.12, depending on the exact details of the specification (e.g., whether unequal concern is allowed or not) and the sample, but generally are significantly greater than 0.0 and significantly less than 0.5.[36] This range of estimates indicates basic stability in parental inequality aversion across these two United States generations and implies substantial concern about equity (since the estimates are significantly less than one) and therefore challenges the spirit of the wealth model and of pure investment models of human resource investments. That all of their estimates of $d$ are significantly less than 0.5 also implies that human capital investments are distributed more equally than is the impact of the endowments in a relation such as (9) above (also see Behrman et al., 1986).

However, there are at least three problems with these estimates of relation (17).

*First*, schooling and expected earnings are determined simultaneously in this model in response to unobserved endowments. If data were available on the endowments ($G_j$), these data could be used to instrument the earnings in this relation in order to avoid simultaneity bias. But generally such data are not available so that the estimates presented in these studies are based on ordinary least squares (OLS). However, Behrman and Taubman (1986) demonstrate that OLS in this context bias upward the estimate of $d$ (i.e., towards the productivity end of the spectrum). This means that the estimates that are summarized above are not definitive regarding whether there is compensation or reinforcement even conditional on functional forms since the upward-biased estimates are (by asymptotic $t$ tests assuming no biases) significantly above the neutral value of zero, so consistent estimates may be above or below this value. But this direction of bias does not affect the challenge that these estimates offer to the spirit of the wealth model, nor the conclusion regarding the more equal distribution of human resource investments than of endowments.

*Second*, the modeling in Section 2.1.2 refers to lifetime full earnings. However the data that are used are for actual annual earnings. The use of annual rather than lifetime earnings by itself probably causes classical measurement error bias towards zero,

---

[36] Behrman (1988a,b) estimates a SET model with anthropometric measures of health as the outcome and nutrients as the inputs (instead of earnings and schooling, respectively) for rural South India. He reports lower estimates of $d$ (implying compensation) in the surplus season when food is relatively available, but much higher values (close to the pure productivity case) for the lean season when food is relatively scarce. See Section 3.3.1.

away from emphasis on productivity in parental preferences. As is well-known, moreover, within estimates exacerbate the bias due to random measurement error (Bishop, 1976; Griliches, 1979), though a consideration that works in the other direction is that components of transitory fluctuations to which both siblings are exposed, such as macro shocks, are controlled in the within estimates. The bias caused by the use of actual rather than full earnings depends on the relation between time spent in nonmarket activities and the time spent in labor market activities (again, with control to the extent that this relation is similar for the siblings).

*Third*, years of schooling is used in these estimates to represent human resource investments. But, as noted in Section 2.1.3, only under special assumptions are years of schooling a perfect proxy for all human resource investments. Once again, however, these estimates control for the common components of other human resource investments between the siblings – such as the common school quality for schools that both siblings attended. Therefore this problem is not as great as it would be in individual estimates.

### 3.2.2. Intrahousehold distributions of nutrients, health, work effort and endowments in a poor subsistence economy

Pitt et al. (1990) develop and estimate a model that incorporates linkages among nutrition, labor-market productivity, health heterogeneity, and the intrahousehold distribution of food and work activities in a subsistence economy. This model builds on and integrates several literatures, including that on the productivity impact of health and nutrition in such societies and on gender variations in intrahousehold allocations (see Behrman, 1992), as well as the more general literature on intrahousehold allocations.

A household is assumed to have individuals in $m$ classes (defined by age and sex so that within a class the health and wage production functions are the same for all members of the household). The household maximizes its consensus preference function that is defined over the health, food consumption, and work effort of each individual (with positive effects of health and food consumption and negative effects of work effort). The constraints on this maximization include (i) a budget constraint that posits that income from labor and other sources must be greater than or equal to expenditures on food and other consumption and (ii) production functions for health and wages for each class:

$$H_j^k = h^k(N_j, E_j, G_j), \tag{18}$$

$$W_j^k = w^k(H_j, E_j), \tag{19}$$

where $H_j^k$ is the health of the $j$th individual in the $k$th class, $N_j$ is the nutrient or food consumption of the $j$th individual, $E_j$ is the work effort of the $j$th individual, $G_j$ is the health endowment of the *j*th individual (i.e., that component of health influenced neither by nutrient intakes nor by work effort) that is observed by the household members but not by social scientists, and $W_j^k$ is the wage rate for the *j*th individual in the *k*th class.[37] Nutrients and endowments are posited to have a positive effect on health, health a positive effect on wage rates, and effort a negative effect on health and a positive effect on wage rates. Health is assumed to increase the marginal product of effort in producing wages, with all the endowments effects working through health.

The first-order conditions indicate that the marginal cost of allocating nutrients at the margin to an individual is lower the greater the extent to which that person's health improves with more nutrition and that person's wage increases with better health. If different classes of individuals participate in different work, as appears widely to be the case in South Asia with respect to gender, and the wage effects of health vary across types of work, the marginal costs of food allocated to different classes of individuals may vary substantially. Within a class the distributions of food and work effort across individuals depend on the distribution of endowments among those individuals.

Compensation or reinforcement can be examined by investigating the first derivative of health with respect to endowments, which includes the partial effects on health through both work effort and nutrient intakes. In the case in which endowments enter additively in the health production relation, there is compensation (reinforcement) if the sum of these two partial effects is negative (positive). The cross effect of *j*'s endowment on *i*'s nutrient consumption is more negative if the household preference function is nonlinear with the consumption of *i* and *j* as substitutes the stronger is the relation between health and effort productivity for *j*.

To explore empirically whether there is compensation or reinforcement, estimates of the endowments first must be obtained. To do so, the health production function is estimated directly and, based on the parameter estimates and the actual nutrients consumed and work effort expended by each individual, individual-specific endowments are calculated. There are two problems that must be dealt with in this "residual" endowment method. *First*, since endowments are not observed by social scientists and they influence household allocations, OLS estimates of the health production technology are not consistent. Pitt et al. therefore use as instruments "food prices, labor-market variables reflecting labor demand, and exogenous components of income" under the assumption that such variables "determine resource allocations but do not directly affect health status, given food and activity levels" (p. 1145). *Second*, the residually derived endowments are likely to be measured with systematic error because of random measurement error in the observed inputs into the health

---

[37] Work time is assumed to be the same for all individuals because there are no data on time allocations and because casual observations suggest that there is very little leisure in the sample area.

production function such as individual nutrients, which carry over to cause errors in the estimated endowments that in turn causes biases in the estimated impact of the endowments on allocated variables. These biases tend to make households appear more compensatory than they really are.[38] To obtain consistent estimates Pitt et al. use instrumental variables in the form of estimated health endowments for weight-for-height, mid-arm circumference, and skinfold thickness from other survey rounds than the one for which the allocation estimate is being made under the assumption that the period-specific measurement errors are not correlated across time periods.

The data requirements for this study are considerable: individual-specific observations on nutrient intakes, health outcomes, and work effort; sufficient cross-sectional variation in exogenous instruments needed for consistent estimation of the health production function; and repeated observations on individuals to purge estimated endowments of measurement errors. They use data from the 1981–1982 Bangladesh Rural Nutrition Survey of 385 households in 15 villages, though with intrahousehold nutrient data available for about half of these households and longitudinal data on intrahousehold allocations available for a further subset. They use Food and Agricultural Organization/World Health Organization (FAO/WHO) classifications of the 14 occupations provided in the data as "very active" and "exceptionally active" to characterize higher than normal work effort and control for whether women were lactating or pregnant in the sample period to control for nonwork nutrient use.

Estimates of the health production function for weight-for-height suggest that the impact of calories is understated and the signs of the coefficients of the work effort variables wrong if OLS is used instead of simultaneous estimators. Then the residual endowments obtained from the consistently estimated health production technology were used for the households with longitudinal data to obtain consistent estimates of the impact of individual endowments on individual nutrients. These estimates suggest reinforcement in the sense that individuals with better endowments receive more nutrients once there is control for the measurement error problem noted above (which, if not controlled, leads to estimates that are opposite in sign, suggesting compensation); these effects are about ten times larger for males than for females, which is consistent with their model, given that their data indicate that women do not participate in energy-intensive activities. Within-household estimates by gender with age-specific endowment effects suggest that reinforcement is significant for males 12 years of age or older and for both males and females in the 6–12 year age range, but that compensation may occur for those under six years of age of both sexes (though the standard

---

[38] Pitt et al. show that, if the true impact of such endowments on nutrients is positive, the estimated impact will be downward biased. But if the true impact is negative, the classical measurement error bias is towards zero (and therefore positive) while the bias due to the correlation of the estimated endowment with the measurement error in nutrients is negative, so the overall effect is indeterminate.

errors are large); for females 12 years of age or older the sign of the coefficient is positive but the magnitude is very small and the standard error very large. Next, Pitt et al. explore what the impact of (instrumented) endowments is on household income and on participating in an exceptionally active occupation (in the absence of data on individual wage rates or earnings). Their estimates suggest that there is a pecuniary return to health and effort, that adult males with higher endowments are more likely to undertake exceptionally energy-intensive work, and that adult female health endowments are relatively unimportant (in comparison with those for adult males) in determining activity choices or household income. Finally, the net effect of a change in own endowments on own health are calculated from the estimated health production functions and the estimated endowment effects on the nutrient and work effort variables in those production functions; the elasticities of own health with respect to own endowments are 0.88 for adult males and 0.97 for adult females. Thus, on net Bangladeshi households exhibit compensatory behavior with respect to adult health endowments so that these elasticities are less than one, with adult males being "taxed" to the benefit of other household members more than females.

Limitations in the data mean that some qualifications are appropriate. The use of the instruments for the health production function to obtain consistent estimates of the production function coefficients and of the residual endowments depends upon the assumption that there are no allocated inputs into the production of health that are not observed, which seems to be a strong assumption. If women's time in household production (not observed), for example, has an effect on health, instrumented nutrients and work effort may be representing in part the impact of women's time allocations since such allocations presumably respond to the same set of exogenous instruments.[39] The assumption that measurement errors in nutrient intakes are not correlated across periods, moreover, may be strong if the intrahousehold allocation of food was altered to favor certain groups identified by age or sex because of the presence of outside dietary investigators. The measure of work effort based on 14 occupational categories, finally, is quite crude, ignores what probably are substantial variations within such categories, and may impart a gender bias since some have claimed that the FAO/WHO estimates understate energy used in various household activities performed primarily by females.

Nevertheless, this study is the most thorough available study to my knowledge of intrahousehold allocations that builds in part explicitly on the estimation of structural relations. As such, it is a model for emulation in a number of respects, including its wide perspective about what allocations are interlinked, its care with regard to estimation issues, and its use of especially rich cross-sectional and panel data in a systematic and integrated manner.

---

[39] Behrman and Lavy (1995) explore the assumption that there are no unobserved allocated inputs in production function estimates in another context and find that it affects substantially the estimates that they obtain.

### 3.2.3. *Endowments and the allocation of schooling in the family and in the marriage market*

Behrman et al. (1994) show how information on own earnings and own and spouse's schooling of monozygotic ("identical" or MZ) and dizygotic ("fraternal" or DZ) twins drawn from the same sampling frame can be used to identify the effects of individual endowments in the household and in the marriage market under a very limited set of assumptions. Such estimates test whether families reinforce or compensate for individual differences in earnings endowments and whether marital sorting leads to a division of labor in households, with high-earnings men marrying women with lower propensities for labor market participation. They also show that such estimates reveal the patterns of endowment responses in the family and in the marriage market in some cases without the need to make any assumptions about the degree of measurement error in schooling, while in other cases it is possible to bound meaningfully the estimates of endowment responses, given upper-bound estimates about the degree of measurement errors in schooling reports.[40] They further explore to what extent actual measurement error in the data and labor market luck during the schooling years influence the estimates of the returns to schooling and the endowment responses.

They begin with a statistical model of the family allocation of schooling that incorporates endowment heterogeneity and that is consistent with theoretical models of the intrafamily allocation of resources. Consider the following linear representation of an equation relating log earnings $H_{ij}$ for the $i$th member of family $j$ to his or her schooling $S_{ij}$ and to three sets of unobserved variables representing (i) genetic endowments $g_j$ that are common among all children of family $j$, (ii) the component of endowments or "ability" that is specific to child $i$ in $j$ ($a_{ij}$), and (iii) a random earnings shock that is specific to $i$ in $j$, inclusive of measurement errors in earnings, represented by $v_{ij}$:

$$H_{ij} = \beta S_{ij} + g_j + a_{ij} + v_{ij,} \tag{20}$$

where $\beta$ is the effect of schooling. There is a parallel expression for the $k$th child (and, to explore the allocations between the $i$th and $k$th child, the impact of other children is absorbed in the family components of the allocation rules below).

$S_{ij}$ is itself a function of unobserved variables that pertain to the family and to the $i$th and $k$th children in the family as expressed in the following linear family allocation rule (again, with a parallel relation for the $k$th child):

---

[40] Previous economics studies of twins have focused either on the estimating the returns to schooling with control for endowments or on variance decompositions between "nature" and "nurture" (e.g., Ashenfelter and Krueger, 1994; Behrman et al., 1980; Miller et al., 1995). The importance of measurement error in schooling in biasing estimates towards zero has been emphasized for twins (and other within siblings) studies (e.g., Griliches, 1979; Ashenfelter and Krueger, 1994).

$$S_{ij} = \alpha_1 a_{ij} + \delta g_j + s_j + \alpha_2 a_{kj} + u_{ij}, \tag{21}$$

where $\alpha_1$ and $\alpha_2$ are the own and the cross effects of the child-specific earnings endowments associated with each of the two siblings; $s_j$ represents the joint influence of exogenous features of the family environment, including prices, family income, and parents' human capital characteristics; $\delta$ is the effect of the family-specific earnings endowment of the child $g_j$ on schooling investment, and $u_{ij}$ is a disturbance that affects $S_{ij}$ but not $H_{ij}$ except indirectly through $S_{ij}$. For the moment, assume that schooling is measured without error. The genetic endowments of siblings are drawn from the same distribution, so that $\text{var}(a_{ij}) = \text{var}(a_{kj})$. In addition, if both siblings face drawings from the same distributions for the stochastic earnings and schooling shocks, $\text{var}(v_{ij}) = \text{var}(v_{kj})$ and $\text{var}(u_{ij}) = \text{var}(u_{kj})$.

If the family allocates schooling so as to reinforce endowments, $\alpha_1 > 0$ and $\alpha_2 < 0$, while if the family compensates for child-specific endowment differences, $\alpha_1 < 0$ and $\alpha_2 > 0$. However, if schooling decisions are individualistic, are made by individuals solely on the basis of their own endowments, then $\alpha_2 = 0$ and $\alpha_1 = \delta$. In that case, there is only the "own" endowment effect, the distinction between the family and individual-specific components of that endowment are irrelevant, and compensation or reinforcement is reflected solely in $\alpha_1$.

As is well known, the parameter $\beta$ is not identified in Eqs. (20) and (21) if $\alpha_1$ or $\delta$ is not zero even if schooling is measured precisely. That is, $\beta$ is estimated with bias if Eq. (20) is estimated across individuals with different values of $g_j$ and $a_{ij}$. With no further assumptions placed on the set of equations (20) and (21) and the parallel relations for the $k$th child, it is clear that neither $\beta$, the returns to schooling, nor the $\alpha$ or the $\delta$ schooling allocation parameters, are identified even if sibling-pair data are used to control in the estimation of $\beta$ for the covariant common components of the endowment and environment $g_j$ and $s_j$. This is because of the existence of the specific components of the endowments $a_{ij}$ and $a_{ik}$. As long as families or individuals respond to individual-specific differences in endowments, and such differences are important, then sibling estimators may not be very useful.

Combined MZ and DZ twin data, however, permit estimation of critical parameters. For MZ twins, $a_{ij} = a_{kj} = 0$, so the within-family variances and covariances are (where the superscript M refers to MZ twins):

$$\text{Var}(\Delta H^{\text{M}}) = 2\beta^2 \sigma_u^2 + 2\sigma_v^2, \tag{22}$$

$$\text{Var}(\Delta S^{\text{M}}) = 2\sigma_u^2, \tag{23}$$

$$\text{Cov}(\Delta H^{\text{M}}, \Delta S^{\text{M}}) = 2\beta\sigma_u^2. \tag{24}$$

It can be seen that dividing Eq. (24) by Eq. (23), which is the expression for the within-MZ estimator $b_{MZ^w}$, yields $\beta$, and expressions (22) to (24) also provide information on the specific variances of $u$ and $v$.

While MZ twin-pairs can be used, based on the model described, to identify the return to schooling $\beta$, such data obviously cannot be used to estimate how families respond to within-family endowment differences. Information on dizygotic DZ twin-pairs combined with information on MZ twin-pairs drawn from the same sampling frame, however, can be used to identify both the schooling return and the schooling responses to individual-specific endowments that are not observed directly in the data. This is because there are additional cross-equation restrictions implied by the twins "experiment".

There are two plausible restrictions that are critical for drawing behavioral inferences from the comparison of DZ and MZ twin-pairs: First, that the returns to schooling $\beta$ are the same for all individuals of the same sex and race, as is commonly assumed, and second that the *individual-specific* stochastic disturbances are drawn from the same distributions for MZ twins as for other siblings including DZ twins. It is not necessary to assume anything about the common endowment components for MZ or DZ twins. Indeed, these will not be identical as the common endowment for the former group includes what are both the common and the specific genetic components for other siblings (including DZ twins) and DZ twins are more likely to occur among older mothers in poorer households compared to MZ twins (Cavalli-Sforza and Bodmer, 1971). Thus, although $\mathrm{var}(g_j^D) \neq \mathrm{var}(g_j^M)$ and $\mathrm{var}(s_j^D) \neq \mathrm{var}(s_j^M)$, $\mathrm{var}(u_{ij}^D) = \mathrm{var}(u_{ij}^M)$, where the superscript D refers to DZ twins. Moreover, if DZ and MZ twins are surveyed with a common survey instrument, any errors in measurement, in this case in earnings, should have the same distribution; i.e., $\mathrm{var}(v_{ij}^D) = \mathrm{var}(v_{ij}^M)$.

The DZ variances and covariance differ from those for MZ twins only because of terms related to the variance of specific endowments $(\sigma_a^2)$:

$$\mathrm{Var}(\Delta H^D) - \mathrm{Var}(\Delta H^M) = 2(1 + \beta\alpha_1 - \beta\alpha_2)^2\sigma_a^2, \tag{25}$$

$$\mathrm{Var}(\Delta S^D) - \mathrm{Var}(\Delta S^M) = 2(\alpha_1 - \alpha_2)^2\sigma_a^2, \tag{26}$$

$$\mathrm{Cov}(\Delta H^D, \Delta S^D) - \mathrm{Cov}(\Delta H^M, \Delta S^M) = 2(\alpha_1 - \alpha_2)(1 + \beta\alpha_1 - \beta\alpha_2)\sigma_a^2. \tag{27}$$

Because the left-hand sides of these last three relations are observed moments prima facie it might appear that these three expressions could be used to solve for $\alpha_1 - \alpha_2, \beta$, and $\sigma_a^2$. But this is not the case since only two of these expressions are independent. However, given $\beta$, division of Eq. (27) by Eq. (26) yields $\alpha_1 - \alpha_2$, the difference between the own and cross effect of child-specific endowment differentials, and $\sigma_a^2$, the variance in the child-specific component of endowments.

While it can be seen that the individual own, $\alpha_1$, and cross, $\alpha_2$, endowment effects cannot be identified if there are intrafamily responses to endowments, the estimate of

$\alpha_1 - \alpha_2$ is sufficient to identify whether or not parents (or individuals) compensate or reinforce innate or exogenous endowment differences, because of the different sign patterns for the individual parameters $\alpha_1$ and $\alpha_2$ associated with family-based reinforcement and compensatory behavior. Given those sign patterns, if there are intrafamily responses and the estimated difference is negative (positive), compensation (reinforcement) characterizes family behavior. If there is no family behavior, then $\alpha_2 = 0$, and the own endowment effect $\alpha_1$ is identified directly. Although compensatory or reinforcing behavior can thus be identified by combining MZ and DZ twinpairs whether or not schooling is allocated within a family context, such data do not yield information on the common endowment response $\delta$ without further restrictions (e.g., that $\text{cov}(h, s) = 0$). It is therefore not possible to test with such data the restriction implied by individualistic behavior that $\alpha_1 = \delta$.

The MZ-DZ model can be estimated for a vector of outcomes. By estimating sets of outcome equations jointly, it is possible additionally to (i) compare the responsiveness of schooling investments and of marital outcomes to different types of ability/environment endowments, (ii) identify covariances among outcome-specific ability and family environmental-ability components, and (iii) ascertain if there are common (across outcomes) variance components to all family and individual specific factors.

Random measurement error in a regressor variable, in this case schooling, biases regression coefficient estimates towards zero. Moreover, within-sibling (twin) estimates are likely to suffer more from measurement error than individual estimates (Bishop, 1976; Griliches, 1979). If true schooling $S_{ij}$ is measured with random error $w$, $\sigma_w^2$ is added to relation (23) so that $\beta$ is not identified. But Behrman et al. (1994) note that random measurement error in schooling does not affect the moment expressions involving the *differences* between the MZ and DZ within-estimators (22)–(24) or (25) and (26), as long as the measurement errors are drawn from the same distributions for both types of twins. As a consequence it is possible to identify (i) whether there is compensation with respect to own schooling for individual-specific endowment differences and (ii) whether there is positive assortative mating with respect to spouse's schooling and earnings endowments without any additional information on the accuracy with which schooling is measured. If the estimates are consistent with reinforcement under the assumption of no measurement error in schooling, it is possible to find the *maximum* proportion of measurement error in observed schooling that would lead to the rejection of the conclusion that there is compensation. An alternative procedure if measurement error is suspected is to obtain additional measures of schooling whose measurement errors are not correlated. It can be easily shown that with one additional measure of schooling for each sibling (twin) and orthogonality across the measurement errors of all four schooling indicators, the true return to schooling $\beta$ is identified.

Behrman et al. use two independent twin data sets to estimate the model: 689 MZ and 593 DZ married male twin pairs in the NAS-NRC Twin and Offspring Samples (also used for the studies summarized in Section 3.2.1 above) and 557 MZ and 438 DZ married male twin pairs in the Minnesota Twin Registry (MTR) of all twins born in Minnesota between 1936 and 1955. The use of two independent twin data sets permits both the assessment of the robustness of the estimates and also the testing of important assumptions about the model since each data set has some special information (see below).

Estimates of the variability and effects of endowments were obtained from a multigroup variance components model applied to these two twins samples. Despite different eligibility criteria, the samples yielded similar results: (i) individual-specific earnings and health endowments are important components of earnings and health, with these components making up as much as 27% of the total variance in log earnings and 42% of the total variance in a measure of obesity (body-mass index, BMI), (ii) allocations of schooling reinforce specific endowments for both earnings and health, and (iii) there is a negative association between the individual-specific earnings endowments of men and, net of their own schooling, their spouses' schooling and probabilities of participating in the labor market, consistent with the hypothesis that marital sorting tends to increase the division of labor by sex in households, at least for married couples in which the husband was born as late as 1956.

Behrman et al. (1994) further exploit special features of the two data sets to investigate the empirical relevance of measurement error in schooling (by using the twins' children's report on the twins' schooling as an instrument) and of individual-specific earnings shocks (by using birth weight to capture differential environments in the womb) for the estimated impact of schooling. They find that the estimated schooling effects on earnings are biased downwards by measurement error in schooling, but appear to be robust to the influence of individual-specific shocks that are orthogonal to endowments. Moreover, the level of measurement error estimated is not sufficient to alter conclusions about the existence of intrafamily reinforcement behavior or negative assortative mating with respect to earnings endowments. Based on their best estimates of schooling effects on earnings and spouse schooling, the calculations of the effects of endowment variations gross of schooling effects indicate that positive reinforcement of endowments in the home increases by about 80% absolute earnings differentials among siblings that emanate from pre-school individual-specific endowment differentials. Siblings with higher earnings endowments also marry women with lower labor force participation probabilities but with only trivially lower schooling because the positive impact on spouse schooling of such endowments through own schooling offsets the negative direct impact. Further exploration of the MZ-DZ model with female twins in new data collected from the MTR in Behrman et al. (1995) indicates that for women (i) individual-specific earnings endowments are important components of earnings and (ii) allocations both of years of college and of resource-intensive college characteristics reinforce specific endowments.

## 3.3. Other evidence on gender and birth-order effects

The previous two sections contain some systematic analysis of gender and birth-order (or at least age) effects in intrahousehold allocations, particularly the extent to which in some contexts they are responses to gender specializations in labor markets and related endowment differentials. But such topics have been among the more emphasized in the intrahousehold literature, so some additional studies are summarized here on these topics.

### 3.3.1. SET model estimates with unequal concern

The SET model with unequal concern under the assumptions about specific functional forms that are discussed in Section 2.1.2 leads to an expression like relation (17) with, in addition, an additive term that is ln of the ratio of the unequal concern parameters (i.e., the $h_j$'s in expression (6)). Estimates can be made with this extended version of relation (17) of the dependence of unequal concern on observed characteristics of the children. Such estimates have been presented for the United States and for India.

For the United States, Behrman and Taubman (1986) and Behrman et al. (1986) estimate the extent of unequal concern by child age (relative birth order) and by child sex, respectively, using the NAS-NRC Twin Offspring Sample. The former study finds that older children are favored significantly over younger children. The latter study first develops a "generalized" SET model in which earnings is replaced by "human-capital-dependent income" that includes, in addition to own earnings, the expected earnings of one's spouse given assortative mating on human capital. The restrictions that reduce this generalized model with unequal concern to the original SET model with equal concern are rejected at the 5% level. This supports the composite hypothesis that marriage markets and unequal concern are important in intrahousehold allocations of investments in children. Within the generalized model the nonlinear maximum likelihood estimates suggest unequal concerning favoring daughters (at least at the 10% level), which works in the opposite direction from gender differences in labor market returns that favor males.

For rural South India, Behrman (1988a,b) uses the International Crops Research Institute for the Semi Arid Tropics (ICRISAT) panel data on 240 households to estimate extensions of the SET model with the output(s) being health (with anthropometric indicators) and the inputs being individual nutrient intakes. These papers consider two extensions of the SET model: one in which there is but one latent output ("health") and one latent input ("nutrients") but multiple indicators of each and a second alternative in which the basic SET model is generalized to include multiple outputs and multiple inputs. For both approaches the data are divided between the lean season in which food is relatively scarce and the surplus season in which food is relatively available since seasonal variations are strong and allegedly important in this region. Nonlinear maximum likelihood estimates suggest that there are significant differences between the seasons, that in the surplus season there is significant inequality aversion and equal concern, and that in the lean season, when food is scarce, the parental equity–productivity tradeoff is close to the pure productivity case and unequal concern significantly favors older children over younger children and sons over daughters. Therefore, during the lean season the combination of relatively little concern about equity and preference weights that favor older children and sons may leave the more vulnerable younger children and daughters at considerable nutritional risk.

### 3.3.2. Health and nutrition demand variations

The previous subsection summarizes some evidence about systematic differences in preferences by birth order and sex of children, conditional on specific functional forms. Such differences can be one source, but not the only possible source (since production function differences also could have such an effect), of differences in reduced-form demand relations for different types of household members. Three studies of different reduced-form demand relations by types of family members for three different societies are now summarized.

Behrman and Deolalikar (1990) estimate separate nutrient demand relations for men, women, girls and boys for the rural south India ICRISAT sample introduced in the previous subsection. This exploration depends, of course, on the presence of individual food consumption in this data set. These estimates suggest that nutrient price responses are significantly smaller algebraically for females than for males. This means that females eat less when food is scarce and the marginal value of food is high, even if there are corresponding increases in their food intake when food prices are low (but when the marginal value of nutrients also is lower). This is consistent with the lean season results for preference parameters with unequal concern favoring sons that is discussed in the previous subsection. They do not find, however, significant evidence of systematic differences by age groups.

Pitt and Rosenzweig (1985) use data on 2347 Indonesian farm households (from the 1978 SUSENAS socioeconomic survey) to estimate separate "illness demand" ordered probits for husbands and wives, and a fixed effect logit for the difference between the husband's illness and the wife's illness. The right-hand side variables in these functions are the prices of thirteen consumption goods (foods and nonfoods); source of drinking water; availability of hospitals, family-planning clinics, public lavatories, and clinics; land ownership; farm profits (treated as predetermined based on a Wu–Hausman test); and the age and education of the husband and the wife. They find relatively few significant determinants of health, but the fixed effects logit estimates suggest that there are some differences in the effects on men versus women. The presence of clinics and the price of vegetables, for example, significantly increases the health of women relative to that for men, while the opposite is the case for the price of fish. Pitt and Rosenzweig attribute the lack of precise estimates to measurement problems: illness was reported by the sick themselves (or by the household head or spouse), and hence subject to differences in sensitivity to symptoms and in propensities to report them and was recorded over a period of only one week.

Horton (1988) analyzes the demand for individual health outcomes with 1978 data on approximately 2000 predominantly rural Filipino children (in the Bicol region) aged 15 or less. To control for family preferences (particularly with respect to child quality and quantity) and other unobserved family fixed effects, Horton explores the differences in weight-for-height and height-for-age among children *within* each family in terms of age, sex, and birth order. She also allows some household-specific variables to enter her health demand function indirectly by specifying that the coefficient on birth order depends on maternal education and total household expenditure per capita. Her results suggest that higher birth order significantly lowers height-for-age and weight-for-height, with the effect reinforced for larger sibship sizes for weight-for-height but reduced with larger sibship sizes for height-for-age.[41] Sons also are significantly below daughters in weight-for-height.

Deaton (1989, 1994, 1995b), Subramanian and Deaton (1991) and Ahmad and Morduch (1993) apply an idea of Rothbarth (1943) to use expenditures on adult goods to measure the costs of children to investigate allocations to boys versus girls for a number of data sets: the World Bank's 1985 Living Standard Measurement Survey for Cote d'Ivoire, the 1981 Thai Socioeconomic Survey, the 1988 Bangladeshi Household Expenditure Survey, the 1984 Pakistani Household Income and expenditure Survey, and the 1983 Maharashtran sample of the Indian National Sample Survey. The method basically is to estimate the share of expenditures on adult goods (e.g., alcohol, tobacco, adult clothing) on the logarithm of total expenditure per household member, the logarithm of household size, the shares of household members in various age–sex categories, and other relevant variables. A comparison then can be made between how much in terms of adult goods is given up for sons versus daughters to see if there is gender discrimination. The results from these estimates indicate little evidence of gender discrimination, with the possible except of those from Maharashtra, even though for some of the populations studied other evidence suggests important gender differences in access to household resources. Deaton (1994) discusses this "puzzle". He concludes that some explanations (e.g., endogenous labor–leisure choices, intertemporal choices related to dowries) would not seem to account for the lack of significant empirical evidence of gender differences in this approach if in fact there is gender discrimination, but that more attention to dynamic considerations might help resolve this puzzle. Despite the considerable literature on fertility and mortality choices (e.g., Chapter 8 in this volume; Strauss and Thomas, 1995), Deaton does not consider whether exogenous fertility and mortality choices, particularly at the margin in light of

---

[41] Maternal education tends to weaken the birth order effects, but with coefficient estimates that are significantly nonzero only at the 25% level.

the sex composition of those previously born, might confound the results in estimates that treat household size and structure as predetermined right-hand side variables.

All of the studies reviewed in this subsection share two limitations. First, if there is selective mortality by gender, there may be gender discrimination that is not reflected in the distribution of household resources among the survivors. Rose (1995), for example, presents evidence that favorable weather shocks increase the probability of daughters surviving to school age in rural India relative to the probability of sons surviving. Second, reduced-form demand approaches do not permit identification of whether there are preference weights that favor some children over others ("unequal concern") versus differential market incentives by gender that induce greater resource allocation to some children (which could induce differential resource allocation by gender even if there is no preference discrimination).

### 3.3.3. Child health and gender inequality in time allocation

In most societies there is gender specialization in the provision of home health care, with females providing most such care. Pitt and Rosenzweig (1990) develop and implement a method for estimating the effects of infant morbidity on the differential allocation of time of family members within the context of a household model in which health is determined simultaneously. They note that identification of the effects of the health of person $k$ on the behavior of person $j$ when the behavior of person $j$ may affect the health of person $k$ (e.g., through child care) is not easy in part because it is difficult to find instruments that directly affect $i$'s health but not directly that of $j$ (net of any indirect effects through $i$'s health). They develop a method, based on some strong simplifying assumptions, to estimate how older siblings and mothers reallocate their time in response to an infant's morbidity.

They assume that households have a consensus preference function defined over the home time and health of each household member and a composite jointly-consumed consumption commodity with heterogeneity in such preferences across households. This preference function is maximized subject to a budget constraint (which includes the wage for each household member type as well as nonlabor earnings) and a health production function (which includes the home time of each household member, the health of every other household member to allow for intrafamily health externalities inclusive of contagion and/or health efficiency effects on home time, and private health-related goods and services). As noted above, the absence of exogenous person-specific health prices makes the consistent direct estimation of the health production functions difficult. By imposing more structure, however, Pitt and Rosenzweig are able to obtain estimates of the impact of the health of one family member on time allocations of other household members. They posit that the linearized demand relations for home time of household members $i$ and $j$ conditional on the health of household member $k$ in which the coefficients on price of private health-related goods is the same for $i$ and for $j$ (e.g., if the health production function is the same for $i$ and $j$). The differenced version of these relations then gives the difference in the home time of $i$ and $j$ as a function of the difference in their wage rates, any difference in the impact of the price of the jointly-consumed composite commodity price on their home time use, and any difference in the impact of the health of $k$ on their time use. Conditional on the assumptions underlying this relation, a consistent estimate of the impact of the health of $k$ on the difference in home time use between $i$ and $j$ can be obtained by using the prices of health-related goods as instruments.

The data requirement for estimating such relations are severe: information on child health, the activities of all household members, and the prices of health-related goods, as well as a large enough sample so that there are enough families with the family types of interest with whom the within estimates can be made (i.e., mothers, teenage daughters and sons, and infants). The 1980 Indonesian Socioeconomic Survey (SUSENAS) linked with other information on prices and health programs has such data for 5831 households. However, for both health and time allocations what is available in this data set are discrete indicators (dichotomous for health, trichotomous for activities – labor force, school, home time), which complicates the estimation. Pitt and Rosenzweig adopt a fixed effects or within-family logit procedure that is parsimonious in terms of parameters to be estimated, permits identification, and controls for possible selectivity of households into this subsample. The estimates obtained indicate that teenage daughters were significantly more likely to increase their participation in household care activities and to reduce their participation in market activities and at school in comparison with teenage sons in response to increased morbidity of infant siblings. Moreover, such estimates differed markedly from the estimates obtained if there was not control for the simultaneity of child health determination and time uses of household members, though the conclusions need to be qualified because the critical identifying assumption seems to be a strong one.

### 3.4. Sibling differences in earnings and transfers

Some critical predictions of the Becker and Tomes (1976) wealth model with equal concern (Section 2.1.1) are: (1) for the very high resource case with equal concern the differences in transfers from parents to their children fully offset differences in earnings among the children and (2) for other cases in which less than very high resources are provided to the children only the lowest earning child receives transfers. The Behrman et al. (1982) SET model (Section 2.1.2) implies that differences in transfers to siblings are orthogonal to differences in earnings among the siblings, and, with equal concern, transfer differences are zero.

To explore the first prediction noted above of the wealth model, it is useful to know what are the magnitudes of earnings differentials between siblings. Behrman et al. (1995b) present mean absolute differences in sibling earnings (which eliminates common shocks, such as from the macro economy) by gender for identical twins, fra-

ternal twins, sib pairs (of the same sex), and the twins' offspring from the NAS-NRC
Twin and Offspring samples, and sibling offspring (of the same sex) in the Panel
Study of Income Dynamics (PSID).[42] For the PSID, earnings differences are presented
for one year and for the average over 6 years, while for the NAS-NRC samples only
the values for one year are available. These data suggest that the mean earnings differentials are: (i) greater for fraternal than for identical twins, presumably because their
endowment differences are greater; (ii) greater for males than for females, apparently
reflecting that fewer females have very high earnings; (iii) greater for nontwin siblings
than for fraternal twins, presumably because the twins have a greater common environment than siblings born at different times;[43] and (iv) somewhat less for 1982–1987
averages than for 1987 alone for brothers and for sisters from the PSID, presumably
because of some smoothing of transitory fluctuations. These patterns are consistent
with what one would expect from the wealth model, as well as from the SET model
with less than infinite inequality aversion. The mean absolute differences for males in
the various samples are in the range of $7000–12 000, while those for females are in
the range of $7000–8000.[44] The respective values for the PSID over six years are
$9272 and $6842. Such values imply that if there were to be equal wealth as in the
very high resource case of the wealth model with equal concern, and if transfers took
the form of annual inter vivos gifts, then the difference in such gifts would have to
average this order of magnitude.[45] Alternatively, if transfers were to take the form
only of bequests, the difference in bequests to children must be of the order of magnitude of $35 000–150 000 depending on the children's ages.[46]

Transfers by parents to children may take the form of inter vivos gifts or bequests.
It is difficult to test empirically some of the predictions regarding transfers of the
wealth model, the SET model and the strategic bequest model because data are required on the present discounted value of all transfers from parents to children over a

---

[42] Their PSID offspring sample uses children who were less than 19 years old in 1968 who lived with
their parents then, but who set up or joined another household before 1988. Up to 10% of the children did
not leave their parents households in this time period. The children who stayed at home received inter
vivos gifts if they did not pay their marginal cost to their parents plus any explicit inter vivos gifts from
their parents.

[43] Perhaps also because the offspring and PSID data are from earlier points in the life-cycle and, hence,
contain more noise due to search and human capital investments. With the exception of the female offspring of the twins, the coefficients of variation are not larger for the younger offspring and the PSID
samples than for the prime-age twin samples as might have been expected.

[44] Parents may respond to the "full earnings" rather than actual earnings of their children. For those
samples with relevant data, the coefficient of variation is generally slightly higher using full earnings
calculated from average wage rates rather than actual earnings. With progressive tax rates, the after-tax
differences are somewhat smaller.

[45] The magnitude required for one-time rather than annual inter vivos gifts is the same as for bequests
except for discounting to reflect timing differences.

[46] If annuity payments are used to finance only consumption differences, a 40-year annuity at 6% requires $5.05 in transfers to purchase the annuity per dollar of earnings differential to be offset; a 20-year
annuity requires $11.47.

period of decades and transfers often are made in large lump sums at infrequent and irregular intervals. Examples include transfers for purchases of major consumer durables (e.g., automobiles, houses) and education for grandchildren. A further problem is that bequests may be much different than expected because of realizations regarding health and age of death different than anticipated. For these reasons, the available data with which to test the alternative models are limited, but some studies yield insights nonetheless.

Hurd and Mundaca (1987) examine the relative importance of bequests and inter vivos gifts to households' wealth in the 1964 Survey on the Economic Behavior of the Affluent (in which the probability of being in the sample was "roughly proportional to 1961 income", p. 5).[47] They find that bequests on average account for about twice as large a share of wealth as inter vivos gifts.[48] If this holds in other samples, then the magnitudes of sibling differences in bequests received tells much of the story about the extent to which differences in transfers offset differences in earnings as the wealth model predicts. They also summarize these data as showing that "most people even in the high income classes received no inheritances" (p. 7). Thus, for "most" households bequests could not be fulfilling the function of compensating for earnings differentials (as suggested by the wealth model in all but the lowest resource cases).

Pechman (1987: p. 350) reports that in the late 1970s, about 8% of US decedents had estates of at least $60 000 so that a federal estate tax return had to be filed; in the mid-1980s, the filing limit was raised to $300 000 and filings fell to 1.5% of the decedents. The limit was subsequently raised in 1986 and filings fell below 1%. For most parents, therefore, total bequests alone are not large enough to offset very large earnings differentials among their children, especially if they have more than two children.

Are bequest patterns consistent with the wealth model's predictions of transfers fully offsetting earnings inequalities at very high resource levels and disinheritance of some siblings at lower resource levels? Are they consistent with the SET model with equal concern of equal bequests? Several studies provide data on the division of bequests among siblings.

Menchik (1980), using data from Connecticut for the period 1930–1945, studies the division of large estates among siblings. He finds that estate shares were independent of estate size, and that equal sharing predominated.[49] Tomes (1981) examines estate shares using a sample of beneficiaries drawn from Cleveland probate records for

[47] This sample only has data on individual households, without sibling matches so sibling differences can not be investigated with them.

[48] These shares apparently refer to the original dollar value of the gift or bequest divided by the household's current net worth. Because they do not adjust for timing differences and there has been inflation, they probably understate the importance of inter vivos gifts relative to bequests.

[49] This conclusion holds regardless of whether he included inter vivos transfers and imputed grandparents' bequests to grandchildren to their parents. Gifts over $3000 were to be reported on the Connecticut estate tax return.

the period 1964–1965. His data include all estate sizes. Using data on bequests collected from the recipients in 1970 by mail questionnaires and interviews, Tomes finds that less than half the sibs reported receiving equal amounts. Menchik (1988) contradicts these results. Menchik studied a random sample of wills from the Cleveland probate records for the same period as Tomes. He finds that about 80% of sibships shared the estate equally. Tomes' results well may reflect recall error, perhaps arising from the five to six years that elapsed between the bequest and the survey.

Wilhelm (1996) uses a 1982 Federal Estate Tax return, in which gross estates exceeded the filing minimum of $300 000 and which was then matched by Social Security numbers to decedents' and beneficiaries' 1981 federal income tax return.[50] There are 5777 decedents whom he studies who came from about the richest 3% of US adults and who own about 30% of US personal wealth. He reports (p. 880), "Over two-thirds (68.6 percent) of the decedents divided their estates exactly equally among their children.... Eighty-eight percent divided their estates approximately equally".

Thus, limited empirical evidence suggests that in the US the typical pattern is equal bequests, and the differences are not related to variations in children's income. Therefore, the available data on bequests in the US fail to support the hypothesis that, when parents have very high resource levels, they use bequests to offset earnings differentials. More to the point, the data fail to support the wealth model's implication that at lower resource levels some siblings are disinherited while others receive bequests. The data are much more consistent with the SET models' prediction that transfers are orthogonal to earnings than with the wealth model's predictions.

Of course, transfers can be made via inter vivos gifts rather than bequests. Behrman et al. (1995b) examine the sibling cross-tabulation of the 1982–1987 average "help from relatives" reported by offspring in the PSID. As an alternative, in one case they add to the recorded monetary flow of help from relatives the annual imputed rental value of housing purchased with help from relatives. The PSID includes data on whether an occupied house was purchased with help from a relative. For respondents who indicated that their house was purchased with help from a relative, they include 7% of the value of the house as part of the current average imputed income from such housing. This is likely to be an underestimate of the frequency of help from relatives through aid in purchasing a house because individuals may have had help from relatives in purchasing a first house, which they then sold when they purchased subsequent houses. In such cases the respondents probably did not indicate that they had help from relatives in purchasing their current houses even though part of the asset value of their first houses that was used to purchase subsequent houses indeed come from help from relatives.[51] On the other hand, for those cases in which the PSID does indicate help from relatives in purchasing housing, Behrman et al.'s procedure proba-

---

[50] Cases were dropped if the 1981 income tax returns were not found for any beneficiary.

[51] The question refers to help in purchasing their current houses, but does not indicate whether those are their first houses nor if they received help in purchasing any earlier houses.

bly overstates the value of that help because they attribute the rent for the entire house to such help even through frequently relatives only provide a portion of the initial purchase price, most typically part of the downpayment. The first and most important point about these transfers is that they are small, less than $200 annually per child in 1987. Moreover, help from relatives is relatively uncommon: for over 56% of the sib pairs neither sib received cash help from relatives during the six-year period and for almost 90% of the sib pairs at least one sib did not receive cash help during this period. With imputed rental value on houses included, these percentages drop to 43 and 83, respectively. Thus, even with the housing adjustment, the conclusion holds that help from relatives is small and relatively uncommon. Therefore help from relatives cannot do much to offset the average annual sib earnings differentials of $6000–9000, as would be required at least for the very high resource case of the wealth model.

Is the pattern of help from relatives received by siblings more consistent with the wealth model or the SET model? A crude indicator is whether lower-earnings sibs receive more help from relatives than higher-earning sibs. For help from relatives alone, 23.0% of the sibling pairs have only the lower-earning sib receiving help and 12.8% have only the higher-earning sib receiving transfers; the corresponding figures if imputed rent is included are 30.8% and 17.8%. These figures provide some support for the wealth model relative to the SET mode, but the support is fairly weak since it depends primarily on the distribution of cases in which one sib receives less than $500 and the other zero. In terms of the overall income levels of these households and the average earnings differentials, these transfer differences are small and therefore not far from being consistent with the SET model of basically equal transfers. Within-sibling regressions for differences in help from relatives provide further evidence. They have a negative but insignificant coefficient estimate of −0.0007 for the difference in earnings; if the imputed rent also is included the coefficient becomes significant, but remains quite small in absolute value at −0.0060. Once again, the signs are consistent with the wealth model, but the magnitudes are so small as to indicate very little offsetting effects of transfers for observed earnings differentials.

It would be interesting, of course, to explore more directly intrahousehold patterns of human resource allocations together with bequests. As noted above, data problems generally have precluded such examinations. An exception is Quisumbing (1994a). She examines schooling, land and nonland asset transfers from parent to children in 344 households in five rice villages in Central Luzon and Panay Island in the Philippines using retrospective survey data. Analysis of a subsample with completed inheritance decisions indicates that daughters are not disadvantaged in schooling at least at the 5% significance level, but receive significantly less land and total inheritance, with partial compensation through receiving greater nonland assets. Thus these results suggest equal concern by gender with regard to human resources though unequal concern favoring males for land transfers and overall inheritances. In this case there does not seem to be compensation between human resource investments and physical and financial transfers at least with regard to gender, which is consistent with the SET model but not the wealth model.

## 4. Nonconsensus models of household behavior

Micro-economic theory traditionally has considered the household (or at least the parents) as the basic decision-making unit, with well-defined consensus preferences maximized subject to budget and production function constraints as in Section 2 above. This traditional approach, however, is being challenged increasingly by advocates of nonconsensus approaches to household behavior that treat the household members (or, more usually, the adult household members) as distinct individuals with conflicting as well as common interests.

Nonconsensus approaches view household behavior as the outcome of a noncooperative or a cooperative game, although the game itself is often not fully specified. Advocates of nonconsensus approaches argue that the traditional consensus approach either ignores differences in the interests and preferences of the individuals who comprise a household or provides an unsatisfactory account of how such differences are reconciled. The weaknesses of the consensus approach are particularly evident in dealing with household formation and dissolution because these issues cannot be approached without recognizing that different individuals have different interests and preferences; but distribution within marriage raises similar difficulties as does distribution between parents and children. Thus far nonconsensus models have generally focused on interactions between husbands and wives rather than those between parents and children or among children.

Among nonconsensus models, an important distinction is between those that are rooted in cooperative game theory and those that are rooted in noncooperative game theory. Cooperative models often allow only Pareto optimal outcomes, while noncooperative models often allow nonoptimal outcomes. Chiappori (1988, 1992a,b) and Bourguignon et al. (1992, 1993) have developed nonconsensus models that assume household allocations are Pareto optimal but avoid specifying a particular bargaining game or collective decision process.

### 4.1. Nash bargaining models of intrahousehold allocations

Manser and Brown (1980) and McElroy and Horney (1981) introduced nonconsensus models of distribution within marriage that rely on the Nash bargaining solution, a leading solution concept from cooperative game theory. The Nash bargaining model generalizes the comparative statics of the consensus model by allowing changes in the "threat point" to affect household behavior. In the Nash bargaining approach, the threat point corresponds to the utility that each individual would obtain in the absence of agreement. In Manser and Brown and in McElroy and Horney these threat points correspond to the utility of divorce, while in the separate spheres bargaining model of Lundberg and Pollak (1993) they correspond to a noncooperative equilibrium in marriage specified in terms of traditional gender roles (also see Ulph, 1988). In the Nash bargaining solution, the surplus from cooperation is shared so that the household maximizes, subject to the appropriate constraints, the product of the gains to cooperation, where the gains are measured from the threat point. The result is a system of "demand" equations for goods and leisure that depend on prices, broadly defined, and on the resources that each spouse controls.

In her recent writings, McElroy (1990, 1992) emphasizes that individual nonearned income and "extrahousehold environmental parameters" (EEPs) shift the threat point. As examples of EEPs, she proposes: "parameters that describe marriage markets, parameters that characterize the legal structure within which marriage and divorce occur, and parameters that characterize government taxes and government or private transfers that are conditioned on marital or family status" (1990: p. 567). McElroy (1992) summarizes the empirical tests of the bargaining model to date as including tests of across-equations restrictions (which she characterizes as "few and inconclusive") and single-equation tests of income pooling (which she characterizes as having "produced strong results favoring the bargaining models" [pp. 11–12]). Tests for income pooling are considered in Section 4.2.

McElroy (1990: pp. 575–576) also proposes a procedure for obtaining estimates with which to test the Nash versus the consensus restrictions hypotheses on across-equation restrictions and on income pooling. This procedure basically consists of estimating probits for marital state separately for men and for women, using these probits to control for marital selection in estimates of demand systems derived from indirect utility functions separately for men and women, using these probits to estimate the Nash demand function for married couples derived from the Nash criterion function and the threat points (indirect utilities) from the nonmarried estimates, and comparing the Nash demand system estimates with estimates based on a consensus model for married individuals to test across-equation restrictions and pooling. It would appear to me, however, that this procedure is not straightforward because it is not clear what could identify the marital selection rules. McElroy (p. 576) simply states that "sample selectivity corrections are well-trod territory that will not be reviewed here...", but provides no guidance regarding what variables possibly could affect the divorce decisions that are not incorporated into the threat points so that they could identify the selectivity correction.

If the procedure is implementable, then several, in some cases interrelated, features merit emphasis. *First*, this procedure and the resulting tests are conditional on the specification of the threat points so the tests are of compound hypotheses (i.e., that the threat points are divorce or separation and that Nash bargaining occurs). With different threat points such as the noncooperative outcomes suggested by Ulph (1988) and Lundberg and Pollak (1993), it is hard to know how such a procedure could be used to identify the threat points since noncooperation within a marriage does not obviously bring into the picture a set of usually observed prices parallel to McElroy's EEPs. *Second*, this procedure uses estimated threat points but does not consider the implications of measurement error, which – as illustrated in the Pitt et al. (1990) study that is summarized above in Section 3.3.3 – may cause considerable problems in efforts to obtain consistent parameters of the relations underlying household demand systems. *Third*, as generally applied, tests of symmetry depend on functional forms, so again the tests are of a compound hypotheses (Varian (1982) is an exception in which nonparametric tests are presented; also see Pollak and Wales (1992)). *Fourth*, the Nash intrafamily literature in general and this procedure in particular ignores the possible roles of heterogeneity in unobserved endowments that underlie critically the wealth and SET models of intrahousehold allocation in Section 2 above and some of the more interesting empirical explorations in Section 3 above. The lack of attention to such endowments may cause serious problems of interpretation in the estimation of threat points and the household demand systems, as well as in the interpretation of the coefficients of variables such as "unearned" income (see Section 4.2 below for elaboration). This same problem, in fairness to the literature on Nash household bargaining models, plagues other efforts at nonconsensus household modeling and much (though not all – see Sections 2 and 3) of the literature based on consensus preferences.

## 4.2. Tests of income pooling in demand relations

There have been several recent studies that purport to test whether male and female nonearned income can be pooled. Two of these studies are summarized here.

Thomas (1990) explores whether there are different effects of men's and women's unearned income on child survival rates, anthropometric measures and nutrient intakes for children using 1974/1975 Estudo Nacional da Despesa Familiar (ENDEF) Brazilian data for over 25 000 urban households. Unearned income (not wages) is used and parents' education is controlled in order to focus on the income effects alone, without the price effects that wages would entail. The estimates indicate a much larger effect on child survival and child anthropometric measures of women's unearned income than of men's, with some further gender differentiation in that mothers' unearned income has greater impact on daughters than on sons, while fathers' unearned income has greater impact on sons.[52] He also reports that the estimated effects of both women's and men's unearned income are positive, but decline as income increases.

---

[52] There are some possible anomalies, such as the indication that unearned income of non-parents has much greater impact on anthropometric measures for boys than either mothers' or fathers' unearned income. Also in the household demand relation for calories, other unearned income has a possibly puzzling negative estimated impact, declining with income.

But the estimated impact of women's unearned income is about seven times of that for men's, for both calories and proteins. Thomas concludes that these results reject the consensus preference model of households often used for economic analysis,[53] and suggest that mothers' income is much more important in shaping children than is fathers' income.

Schultz (1990) explores whether there are different effects of men's and women's unearned income on female labor supply and recent fertility using over 8000 households with adults between 25 and 54 in age from the 1980/1981 Thai Socioeconomic Survey (SES). He finds that women's nonearned income has significantly different effects (i.e., reducing more) than men's nonearned income on women's labor supply, but not for men's labor supply. He also finds that women's nonearned income has a significant positive effect on the number of co-resident children under five years of age (a proxy for recent fertility) but men's unearned income does not. However he notes that his relation may reflect reverse causality if women with more children are likely to receive more transfers from their families and other sources. Schultz concludes that this paper "has rejected one of the restrictions implied by the neoclassical model of family demand behavior, that for female labor supply" (and, with more qualifications, perhaps that for fertility).[54]

What do these studies mean with regard to the consensus preference model and nonconsensus alternatives? McElroy (1992: p. 12) interprets these and related studies to be part of the "strong results favoring bargaining models." Schultz and Thomas both claim that their evidence rejects one of the restrictions implied by the consensus preference model, but agree with Bourguignon and Chiappori (1992) that such evidence does not thereby support any particular nonconsensus model. Alderman et al. (1994) suggest that such results imply that it is "time to shift the burden of proof" to those who favor the consensus assumption.

But there are problems with the interpretation that these results reject the pooling assumption of the consensus preference model. To test that assumption what one would like to do would be to conduct an experiment in which extra income were distributed randomly to males and females and then to observe whether the marginal propensities to use such income differed depending upon who is the recipient. However neither Schultz or Thomas (nor, to my knowledge, anyone else) uses such data for these tests of micro income pooling.[55] Instead they use individual "unearned" income. They explicitly use unearned income rather than earned income or total income

---

[53] Though he notes that ratios of income effects are not significantly different form each other, which is consistent with the common preference model if income is measured with error, as well as consistent with differential intrahousehold preferences that are homogenous in the relative preference weights that mothers and fathers have for the health outcomes.

[54] He also notes that sample selectivity for conducting such tests only on co-habitating couples appears to cause selectivity biases in the Thai case.

[55] Lundberg et al. (1994) provide some provocative more aggregative evidence that raises questions about pooling by examining the impact of changes in child benefit laws on intrahousehold allocations.

in order to abstract from price (i.e., opportunity cost of time) or preference effects that wages would represent. But is there any reason to think that unearned income is orthogonal to wages and unobserved productivity and preferences? The answer depends in part on what are the sources of unearned income. In the data for both studies the sources are largely pensions and social security, both of which are related to past wages and productivity. Even earnings from assets may reflect past wages and productivity if such assets were acquired out of past labor earnings. Therefore unearned income may in part represent preferences regarding time use and productivity in labor market activities associated with household activities pertaining to health, nutrition, fertility and time allocations. If so, these results do not necessarily mean that shifting income to women would have more positive effects on, say, child health than shifting equal income to men, but simply that more productive women or women with different preferences have more positive effects on their children's health. These results, in fact, are consistent with the true effects involving income pooling, but unearned income coefficient estimates being biased differentially by proxying for unobserved productivity and preference endowments given gender specialization in household tasks.

## 4.3. Pareto-efficient collective household models

Chiappori (1988, 1992a,b) and co-authors (e.g., Bourguignon et al., 1992, 1993) have developed cooperative nonconsensus household models – that they call "collective household models" – that only assume that allocations are Pareto efficient, but do not assume any explicit solution process. Thus this approach is more general than those that are based on particular cooperative game theory equilibrium concepts.

Bourguignon and Chiappori (1992) survey this still rapidly evolving line of research. This section is based on their survey, supplemented by reference to the underlying articles. Bourguignon and Chiappori begin by criticizing the consensus preference model and then asking, what should we require from a collective theory of household behavior? They answer with three criterion, the first two of which also apply to traditional models with consensus preference functions:
(i) it must generate *testable restrictions* that potentially can be falsified by empirical observations (i.e, the *testability* requirement);
(ii) it must allow the *recovery of structural components* (such as preferences) from observed behavior and thereby suggest interpretations for empirical results and provide a formal basis for normative recommendations (i.e., the *integrability* requirement); and
(iii) it must solve the *assignability problem* of deducing individual consumption from the data on aggregate household consumption that usually are available.
They then define a general framework regarding preferences, distinctions among private consumption goods, the decision process, and income sharing rules.

Preferences: Consider a household with two members, M and F, each of whom can consume $n$ private goods in the vector $x^M$ (or $x^F$) and $N$ public goods in the vector $X$ so that the utility functions of these two individuals in the most general case of altruism as in McElroy and Horney (1981) are: $U^M = U^M(x^M, x^F, X)$ and $U^F = U^F(x^M, x^F, X)$. The most specialized case is if there is no altruism (i.e., an egoistic case) and all goods are privately consumed as in Chiappori (1992a) so that $U^M = U^M(x^M)$ and $U^F = U^F(x^F)$. An intermediate case is Becker's (1981) notion of caring in which each household member has a welfare function that depends on both own and companion's egoistic utilities, $W^M[U^M(x^M, X), U^F(x^F, X)]$ and $W^F[U^M(x^M, X), U^F(x^F, X)]$, which is less general than altruism because of the separability assumption.

*Distinctions among types of private consumption goods.* A good is exclusive if it is consumed by one member only, such as an individual's leisure (if it has no public good characteristics). A nonexclusive good is assignable if each member's consumption can be observed independently (and otherwise it is nonassignable).

*Decision processes.* A basic distinction is between cooperative and noncooperative settings, as discussed in the introduction to this section. The literature has emphasized more the cooperative settings, though – as noted above – the noncooperative settings have been suggested as possibly establishing threat points for game theory models.

*Income sharing rules.* All cooperative models have an income sharing rule interpretation in that any efficient decision process can be interpreted as one in which household members allocate the total income (minus that devoted to public goods) by some sharing rule that may depend on income and prices (e.g., F receives $1(p, y)$ and M receives $y - 1(p, y)$) and then each member maximizes her/his utility conditional on the level of pubic goods subject to the budget constraints so defined.

Bourguignon and Chiappori then review recent results based on the efficiency approach. These results use cross-sectional data in which prices are assumed to be the same for all households, though wages and nonlabor income may vary across households. Preferences are assumed to be egoistic or caring, and all goods are private. Two classes of models are considered.

First, each member's labor supply is freely chosen, observable, and exclusive. (Note that the assumption that labor supply is observable is not innocuous and in fact not usually satisfied in most data sets if labor supplied to household production is included, not just a simple dichotomy between labor supplied to the labor market and "leisure" – inclusive of all other time, including that devoted to household production.) Chiappori (1988, 1992b) considers the simplest case with a single aggregate consumption good and proves:

– If individuals are egoistic, conditions can be derived both from parametric (e.g., partial differential equations on labor supplies) and nonparametric ("revealed preference" type conditions) perspectives. These conditions are totally independent from "neoclassical" ones, so empirical tests may be performed to compare the two settings.

—　The sharing rule can be recovered from labor supplies except for an additive constant. Each individual's utility also can be recovered, up to the same additive constant. The key intuitive point is that, under the exclusive good assumption, each individual household member's wage and common nonearning income only can have income effects through the sharing rule on the spouse's behavior. For instance, if a 10% increase in the husband's wage and a 5% increase in common nonlabor income both have the same effect on the wife's behavior, this provides the bases for estimating the marginal rate of substitution between the husband's wage and common nonlabor income in the sharing rule (and vice versa for the wife's wage), so the partials in the sharing rule can be recovered (up to a constant). These results can be extended to the case of several consumption goods, each of which generate additional empirically testable restrictions. For nonassignable consumption goods, individual consumptions can be recovered up to a constant.

If individuals have altruistic preferences, what can be said depends upon the number of goods relative to the number of household members. Any finite set of labor supply data can be exactly rationalized by adequately defined preferences, even if the sharing rule is known ex ante, for a two-member household with only one positive labor supply and one consumption good. If, all else equal, there is a second labor supply, nonparametric conditions can be identified. It is not known whether nonparametric restrictions can be obtained in more general settings such as if there are several goods, though Chiappori's conjecture is that they can.

Second, consumption models are considered with exogenous incomes for different household members, with the following implications:

—　Consumption may depend independently on the separate incomes.

—　Testable implications can be derived.

—　The sharing rule can be recovered up to an increasing transformation if one household member's private consumption of one good can be observed and up to a constant if a private consumption good can be observed for both household members (an assignable good, or two exclusive goods). In the latter case individual consumption also can be recovered up to a constant for nonassignable goods.[56]

Bourguignon and Chiappori conclude their survey: "The collective approach described above is still in a preliminary stage. Several theoretical issues remain unsolved; and the empirical work only begins. We however believe that it constitutes a

---

[56] The intuition is similar to that described for the first set of models. For a sharing rule in which F receives $\theta(y^F, y^M)$ and M receives $y^F + y^M - \theta(y^F, y^M)$, the demands for the assignable good (subscript 1) are $x_1^F = f_1[\theta(y^F + y^M)]$ and $x_1^M = f_1^M[y^F + y^M - \theta(y^F, y^M)]$, so that $\partial\theta/\partial y^F$ and $\partial\theta/\partial y^M$ can be recovered from $[(\partial x_1^F/\partial y^F)/(\partial x_1^F/\partial y^M)] = [(\partial\theta/\partial y^F)/(\partial\theta/\partial y^M)]$ and $[(\partial x_1^F/\partial y^F)/(\partial x_1^F/\partial y^F)] = [(1 - \partial\theta/\partial y^F)/(1 - \partial\theta/\partial y^M)]$. Next, the demand for any nonassignable good $i$ is $x_i^F = f_i^F[\theta(y^F, y^M)] + f_i^M[y^F + y^M - \theta(y^F, y^M)]$, so $\partial x_i/\partial y^F = (f_i^F - f_i^M)/(\partial\theta/\partial y^F) + f_i^M$ and $\partial x_i/\partial y^M = (f_i^F - f_i^M)/(\partial\theta/\partial y^M) + f_i^M$, from which it is possible to recover both Engel curves.

coherent and promising research program, which is likely to be pursued in the forthcoming years" (p. 9).

An assessment of this research program, of course, must be tentative because it appears to be developing fairly rapidly with much work still underway or projected for the future. The effort to elucidate exactly what can and what cannot be estimated about a number of dimensions of intrahousehold behavior, such as clarifying the conditions under which individual consumption of nonassignable goods can be recovered, under the general assumption of Pareto-efficient collective household behavior, is to be applauded. The stated intent to link rigorously modeling of household behavior with empirical testing is to be applauded, and efforts to undertake the empirical testing with the same rigor demonstrated in the theoretical modeling should be encouraged. The goal of seeing how much can be said with fairly minimal assumptions about the collective decision process is to be applauded.

Nevertheless, how positively one assesses the results to date relates to the old saw about whether the glass is a half full or half empty. Some of the results are impressive, such as the development of income sharing rule approaches that empirically under some conditions allow the estimation of individual household member Engel curves for nonassignable goods. On the other hand, a more pessimistic view is that the results to date suggest how difficult it is to make progress in this area since the assumptions must be very strong to make the headway made in various alternative and partial models to date, e.g., that households face varying wages but the same prices, that leisure has no public good characteristics (it would seem that solitaire has its limitations), that household production activities are leisure, that income is fixed. Also, at least for some societies, there is evidence that production inputs are not distributed efficiently among different household members (i.e., men versus women; Jones (1983), Udry (1996)), in which case household activities can not be Pareto optimal as is assumed in cooperative approaches to collective household behavior. Finally, the papers in this genre to date and the limited empirical work that has been undertaken do not show sensitivity to the estimation problems involved if there are unobserved heterogeneities in productivities and preferences that are at the heart of much of the more interesting analysis of consensus preference models (as discussed at the end of Section 4.2), but appears naively implicitly to assume away these difficult empirical problems.

## 5. Conclusions

Intrahousehold allocations appear to be quite important in the determination of time use, human resource investments, and intra- and intergenerational transfers. The nature of such allocations have potentially significant implications for efficiency, equity, and the efficacy of micro- and macro-economic policies, as well as for the analysis of the impact of human resources on economic outcomes.

In the past decade and a half there has been substantial progress in modeling intra-household allocations in ways that lead to testable propositions despite enormous data limitations regarding the nature of the allocations of unobserved variables and the impact of unobserved heterogenous endowments. This progress has been made by using better data, by increasing the rigor of the relation between the modeling and the empirical estimation, and by assuming away possibly important aspects of the data problems. In contrast to many areas of economics, many of the most interesting studies in the economic analysis of intrahousehold allocations have been for developing countries because of the recent expanded availability of interesting micro household data sets for such countries. Different researchers, or different groups of researchers, have made different assumptions and have focused on different dimensions of intra-household allocations.

Most of the analytical modeling and most of the empirical work has been within a one-period framework with consensus parental preferences. The best of the studies within this framework have elaborated on and tested hypotheses about the role of un-observed heterogenous endowments in intrahousehold allocations within the context of labor, product and marriage markets. Their results suggest that controlling for such unobserved heterogeneity indeed is critical for understanding the nature of and the impact of intrahousehold allocations. These studies have tended to deal with an ever-widening range of issues in more integrated ways with increasing sensitivity to esti-mation issues. But even the best studies in this tradition are characterized by some strong maintained hypotheses, though with some variance regarding the exact as-sumptions (implicit and explicit) in different studies: consensus household, or at least parental, preferences, perhaps with additional strong assumptions regarding separabil-ity; no problems with dynamics or with imperfect information;[57] all of the relevant choice variables are observed in the estimation of household production functions; the determinants of household structure are not addressed and are assumed not to be criti-

---

[57] A rare exception to this generalization regarding dynamics and learning is Rosenzweig and Wolpin (1988). They develop a simple dynamic model of child health that incorporates unobserved heterogeneity among households and uncertainty regarding unobserved heterogeneity in each child's health endowments prior to birth. They compare estimates using OLS versus fixed-effect procedures to control for heteroge-neity in child health relations based on data from 109 Colombian households. The dependent variables are the age-standardized weights of the children at birth, and within six months of birth. The right-hand side variables include birth order, birth spacing and timing, per capita family food consumption, DPT inocula-tions, breastfeeding, maternal age, and the sex of the children, all except the last of which are treated as endogenous in lagged instrumental variable fixed-effect estimates. Control for unobserved heterogeneity alters the statistical inferences substantially. They then use their estimated relations to calculate unob-served family- and child-specific endowments. They find that family health environments are significantly correlated with parental education (as well as with family income), which implies that estimates of child health outcomes that do not control for such endowments have upward-biased coefficients because such variables are partially proxies for uncontrolled health endowments. Their results, though quite imprecise, also are suggestive of possible upward biases in the estimates of the effects of parents' schooling (as well as breastfeeding and family income) on child weight if there is no control for unobserved heterogeneity.

cal;[58] restraints such as credit market imperfections are assumed to prevail; estimates of structural relations are conditional on functional forms; and the demand relations estimated may not be integrable to obtain even locally unique preferences.

The nonconsensus models of household behavior emphasize that different household members, usually husband and wife, may have different preferences and different command over resources. On the basis of casual observations, this seems an important feature of households in many societies. It also, in some cases, leads to an integration of concern about intrahousehold allocations with concern about household formation/dissolution. Interesting theoretical results have been derived concerning under what conditions income sharing rules and allocations of nonassignable goods can be derived. But there are many limitations in this literature to date. The nonconsensus models of household behaviors literature is static, with no consideration of dynamic processes and learning. This literature abstracts from the possibly important roles of household production. Progress to date in developing empirically tractable models has been conditional on strong assumptions, such as there being a small number of perfectly observed assignable goods or there being wage but not other price variation. Perhaps most important, both the theoretical and the empirical studies in this literature (usually implicitly) ignore the role of unobserved heterogeneous endowments. The limited empirical studies that are part of this literature to date also tend to pay but limited attention to other econometric problems, such as those related to measurement errors. For such reasons, the limited empirical results in this strain of analysis are not very persuasive even on the topic on which most work has been done, that is, whether there is income pooling within households.

So, while progress has been considerable regarding the economic analysis of intrahousehold allocations, the present generation of economic graduate students hardly need despair because all of the interesting topics already have been examined satisfactorily. To the contrary, as suggested by the limitations noted above, there is considerable potential for making advances in this area. There might be interesting possibilities, for example, for integration into studies on collective household decision-making of unobserved heterogeneity that has been the focus of studies that assume consensus preferences, for integration of concerns about intrahousehold allocations with those on intergenerational parent–child exchange, for expansion of the analysis of intrahousehold allocations into frameworks that consider as well the determination and mainte-

---

[58] Foster (1995) is an exception that explores the implications of the marriage selection process on Bangladeshi intergenerational gender links in human resources such as have been emphasized by King and Lillard (1987) and Thomas (1994) for Brazil, Ghana, Malaysia, the Philippines and the United States. Handa (1996) also attempts to control for determination of marital status in his investigation of the Jamaican expenditure patterns as they relate to children. Quisumbing (1994b) further considers intrahousehold allocations within the context of extended families within the Philippines. But such exceptions are rare. And some aspects of households in some other societies, such as the child fostering that is widespread in some parts of Africa that Ainsworth (1992) describes, that have not yet been subject to very satisfactory analysis.

nance of household structure; and for incorporation of learning and dynamics into analyses. The most useful advances probably will further the recent research in this area in which theoretical modeling, special data including that on "natural experiments,"[59] and appropriate econometric techniques are carefully integrated with explicit recognition of missing data and imperfectly measured variables.

## References

Ahmad, A. and J. Morduch (1993), "Identifying sex bias in the allocation of household resources: evidence from linked household surveys from Bangladesh", Discussion paper no. 1636 (Harvard Institute of Economic Research, Harvard University, Cambridge, MA).

Ainsworth, M. (1992), "Economic aspects of child fostering in Côte D'Ivoire", Working paper no. 92 (Living Standards Measurement Study, World Bank, Washington, DC).

Alderman, H., P.-A. Chiappori, L. Haddad, J. Hoddinott and R. Kanbur (1994), "Unitary versus collective models of the household: time to shift the burden of proof?", Mimeo. (DELTA, Paris).

Altonji, J.G. and T.A. Dunn (1991), "Relationships among the family incomes and labor market outcomes of relatives", in: R.G. Ehrenberg, ed., Research in labor economics, Vol. 12 (JAI Press, Greenwich, CT) pp. 269–310.

Altonji, J.G. and T.A. Dunn (1995), "The effects of school and family characteristics on the return to education", Mimeo. (Northwestern University, Evanston, IL).

Ashenfelter, O. and A. Krueger (1994), "Estimates of the economic return to schooling from a new sample of twins", American Economic Review 84: 1157–1174.

Barro, R. (1974), "Are government bonds new wealth?", Journal of Political Economy 82: 1063–1093.

Becker, G.S. (1967), "Human capital and the personal distribution of income: an analytical approach", Woytinsky Lecture, Ann Arbor: University of Michigan; Republished in: G.S. Becker (1975), Human capital, 2nd edn. (NBER, New York) pp. 94–117.

Becker, G.S. (1974), "A theory of social interactions", Journal of Political Economy 82: 1063–1093.

Becker, G. (1991), A treatise on the family, 2nd edn. (Harvard University Press, Cambridge, MA).

Becker, G.S. and H.G. Lewis (1973), "On the interaction between the quantity and quality of children", Journal of Political Economy 81: S279–S288.

Becker, G.S. and K.M. Murphy (1988), "The family and the state", Journal of Law and Economics 31: 1–17.

Becker, G. and N. Tomes (1976), "Child endowments and the quantity and quality of children", Journal of Political Economy 84: S143–S162.

Becker, G.S. and N. Tomes (1979), "An equilibrium theory of the distribution of income and intergenerational mobility", Journal of Political Economy 87: 1153–1189.

Becker, G.S. and N. Tomes (1986), "Human capital and the rise and fall of families", Journal of Labor Economics 4: S1–S39.

Behrman, J.R. (1987a), "Is child schooling a poor proxy for child quality?", Demography 24: 341–359.

Behrman, J.R. (1987b), "Schooling and other human capital investments: can the effects be identified?", Economics of Education Review 6: 301–305.

Behrman, J.R. (1988a), "Nutrition, health, birth order and seasonality: intrahousehold allocation in rural India", Journal of Development Economics 28: 43–63.

---

[59] For example, Rosenzweig and Wolpin (1980) utilize the fact of unanticipated multiple births to explore the impact of exogenous increases in child quantities on child quality. Also see Deaton (1995a,b), Rosenzweig (1990) and Strauss and Thomas (1995).

Behrman, J.R. (1988b), "Intrahousehold allocation of nutrients in rural India: are boys favored? do parents exhibit inequality aversion?", Oxford Economic Papers 40: 32–54.

Behrman, J.R. (1992), "Intrahousehold allocation of nutrients and gender effects: a survey of structural and reduced-form estimates", in: S.R. Osmani, ed., Nutrition and poverty (Oxford University Press, Oxford).

Behrman, J.R. and A.B. Deolalikar (1990), "The intrahousehold demand for nutrients in rural South India: individual estimates, fixed effects and permanent income", Journal of Human Resources 25: 665–696.

Behrman, J.R. and A.B. Deolalikar (1995), "Are there differential returns to schooling by gender? the case of Indonesian labor markets", Oxford Bulletin of Economics and Statistics 57: 97–118.

Behrman, J.R. and V. Lavy (1995), "Production functions, input allocations and unobservables: the case of child health and schooling success", Mimeo. (University of Pennsylvania, Philadelphia, PA).

Behrman, J.R. and P. Taubman (1985), "Intergenerational earnings mobility in earnings in the US: some estimates and a test of Becker's intergenerational endowments model", Review of Economics and Statistics 67: 144–151.

Behrman, J.R. and P. Taubman (1986), "Birth order, schooling and earnings", Journal of Labor Economics 4: S121–S145.

Behrman, J.R. and P. Taubman (1990), "The intergenerational correlation between children's adult earnings and their parents' income: results from the Michigan Panel survey of income dynamics", Review of Income and Wealth 36: 115–127.

Behrman, J.R. and B.L. Wolfe (1984), "The socioeconomic impact of schooling in a developing country", Review of Economics and Statistics 66: 296–303.

Behrman, J.R. and B.L. Wolfe (1989), "Does more schooling make women better nourished and healthier? Adult sibling random and fixed effects estimates for Nicaragua", Journal of Human Resources 24: 644–663.

Behrman, J.R., R.A. Pollak and P. Taubman (1982), "Parental preferences and provision for progeny", Journal of Political Economy 90: 52–73.

Behrman, J.R., R.A. Pollak and P. Taubman (1986), "Do parents favor boys?", International Economic Review 27: 31–52.

Behrman, J.R., R.A. Pollak and P. Taubman (1989), "Family resources, family size, and access to financing for college education", Journal of Political Economy 97: 398–419.

Behrman, J.R., R.A. Pollak and P. Taubman (1995a), From parent to child: intrahousehold allocations and intergenerational relations in the United States (University of Chicago Press, Chicago, IL).

Behrman, J.R., R.A. Pollak and P. Taubman (1995b), "The wealth model: efficiency in education and equity in the family", in: J.R. Behrman, R.A. Pollak and P. Taubman, eds., From parent to child: intrahousehold allocations and intergenerational relations in the United States (University of Chicago Press, Chicago, IL).

Behrman, J.R., M.R. Rosenzweig and P. Taubman (1994), "Endowments and the allocation of schooling in the family and in the marriage market: the twins experiment", Journal of Political Economy 102: 1131–1174.

Behrman, J.R., M.R. Rosenzweig and P. Taubman (1995c), "Individual endowments, college choice and wages: estimates using data on female twins", Mimeo. (University of Pennsylvania, Philadelphia, PA).

Behrman, J.R., Z. Hrubec, P. Taubman and T.J. Wales (1980), Socioeconomic success: a study of the effects of genetic endowments, family environment and schooling (North-Holland, Amsterdam).

Bergstrom, T. (1989), "A fresh look at the rotten kid theorem – and other household mysteries", Journal of Political Economy 97: 1138–1159.

Bernheim, B.D., A. Shleifer and L. Summers (1985), "The strategic bequest motive", Journal of Political Economy 93: 1045–1076.

Bishop, J. (1976), "Reporting errors and the true return to schooling", Mimeo. (University of Wisconsin, Madison, WI).

Blake, J., 1981, "Family size and the quality of children", Demography 18, 421–442.

Bourguignon, F. and P.-A. Chiappori (1992), "Collective models of household behavior: an introduction", European Economic Review 36: 1–10.

Bourguignon, F., M. Browning, P.-A. Chiappori and V. Lechene (1992), "Intrahousehold allocation of consumption: some evidence on Canadian data", Mimeo. (DELTA, Paris).

Bourguignon, F., M. Browning, P.-A. Chiappori and V. Lechene (1993), "Intrahousehold allocation of consumption: some evidence on French data", Annales d'Economie et de Statistiques 29: 137–156.

Bruce, N. and M. Waldman (1990), "The rotten-kid theorem meets the Samaritan's dilemma", Quarterly Journal of Economics 105: 155–166.

Cavalli-Sforza, L.L. and W.F. Bodmer (1971), The genetics of human populations (W.H. Freeman, San Francisco, CA).

Chamberlain, G. and Z. Griliches (1975), "Unobservables with a variance components structure: ability, schooling, and the economic success of brothers", International Economic Review 16: 442–449.

Chiappori, P. (1988), "Rational household labour supply", Econometrica 56: 63–89.

Chiappori, P. (1992a), "Collective labor supply and welfare", Journal of Political Economy 100: 437–467.

Chiappori, P. (1992b), "'Traditional' versus 'collective' models of household behavior: what can data tell us?", Mimeo. (DELTA, Paris).

Cox, D. and M.R. Rank (1992), "Inter-vivos transfers and intergenerational exchange", Review of Economics and Statistics 74: 305–314.

Deaton, A. (1989), "Looking for boy–girl discrimination in household expenditure data", World Bank Economic Review 3: 1–15.

Deaton, A. (1994), "Inequality within and between households in growing and aging economies", in: M.G. Quibria, ed., Critical issues in Asian development (Oxford University Press, Oxford).

Deaton, A. (1995a), "Data and econometric tools for development analysis", in: J.R. Behrman and T.N. Srinivasan, eds., Handbook of development economics, Vol. 3 (North-Holland, Amsterdam).

Deaton, A. (1995b), The analysis of household surveys: microeconometric analysis for development policy (Johns Hopkins University Press for the World Bank, Baltimore, MD).

DeTray, D.N. (1977), "Child quality and the demand for children", Journal of Political Economy 81: S70–S90.

Folbre, N. (1984), "Market opportunities, genetic endowments, and intrafamily resource distribution of resources: comment", American Economic Review 74: 518–520.

Foster, A. (1995), "Schooling aspirations when human capital is a public good within marriage: evidence from rural Bangladesh", Mimeo. (University of Pennsylvania, Philadelphia, PA).

Griliches, Z. (1979), "Sibling models and data in economics: beginning of a survey", Journal of Political Economy 87: S37–S64.

Haddad, L. and R. Kanbur (1990), "How serious is the neglect of intra-household inequality?", Economic Journal 100: 866–861.

Haddad, L. and R. Kanbur (1992), "Intrahousehold inequality and the theory of targeting", European Economic Review 36: 372–378.

Handa, S. (1996), "Expenditure behavior and children's welfare: an analysis of female headed households in Jamaica", Journal of Development Economics 50: 165–188.

Harriss, B. (1990), "The intrahousehold distribution of hunger", in: J. Dreze and A. Sen, eds., The political economy of hunger, Vol. I (Clarendon Press, Oxford).

Hart, G. (1994), "Gender and household dynamics: recent theories and their implications", in: M.G. Quibria, ed., Critical issues in Asian development: theories, experiences and policies (Oxford University Press, Oxford).

Herrnstein, R.J. and C. Murray (1994), The bell curve: intelligence and class structure in American life (The Free Press, New York).

Hirshleifer, J. (1977), "Shakespeare vs. Becker on altruism: the importance of having the last word", Journal of Economic Literature 15: 500–502.

Hirshleifer, J. (1985), "The expanding domain of economics", American Economic Review 75 (Supplementary issue): 53–68.

Horton, S. (1988), "Birth order and child nutritional status: evidence on the intrahousehold allocation of resources in the Philippines", Economic Development and Cultural Change 36: 341–354.

Hurd, M. and B. Mundaca (1987), "The importance of gifts and inheritances among the affluent", Working paper 2415 (National Bureau of Economic Research, Cambridge, MA).

Jencks, C. and M. Brown (1977), "Genes and social stratification: a methodological exploration with illustrative data", in: P. Taubman, ed., Kinometrics: determinants of socioeconomic success within and between families (North-Holland, Amsterdam).

Jones, C. (1983), "The mobilization of women's labor for cash crop agriculture: a game theoretic approach", American Journal of Agricultural Economics 65: 1049–1054.

Kanbur, R. and L. Haddad (1994), "Are better-off households more unequal or less unequal: a bargaining theoretic approach to the 'Kuznets effect' at the micro level", Oxford Economic Papers (July).

King, E.M. and L.A. Lillard (1987), "Education policy and schooling attainment in Malaysia and the Philippines", Economics of Education Review 6: 167–181.

Leibowitz, A. (1974), "Home investments in children", Journal of Political Economy 82: S111–S131.

Lundberg, S. (1988), "Labor supply of husbands and wives: a simultaneous equations approach", Review of Economics and Statistics 70: 224–235.

Lundberg, S. and R.A. Pollak (1993), "Separate spheres bargaining and the marriage market", Journal of Political Economy 6: 988–1010.

Lundberg, S.J., R.A. Pollak and T.J. Wales (1994), "Do husbands and wives pool their resources? Evidence from the U.K. child benefit", Mimeo. (University of Washington, Seattle, WA).

Lykken, D.T., T.J. Bouchard, Jr., M. McGue and A. Tellegen (1990), "The Minnesota twin family registry: some initial findings", Acta Geneticae Medicae et Gemellologiae 39: 1.

Manser, M. and M. Brown (1980), "Marriage and household decision-making: a bargaining analysis", International Economic Review 21: 31–44.

McElroy, M. (1990), "The empirical content of Nash-bargained household behavior", Journal of Human Resources 25: 559–583.

McElroy, M. (1992), "The policy implications of family bargaining and marriage markets", Mimeo. (Duke University, Durham, NC).

McElroy, M. and M. Horney (1981), "Nash-bargained household decisions: toward a generalization of the theory of demand", International Economic Review 22: 333–349.

McElroy, M. and M. Horney (1988), "The household allocation problem: empirical results from a bargaining model", in: T.P. Schultz, ed., Research in population economics, Vol. 6 (JAI Press, Greenwich, CT).

Menchik, P. (1980), "Primogeniture: equal sharing and the US distribution of wealth", Quarterly Journal of Economics 95: 299–315.

Menchik, P. (1988), "Unequal estate division: is it altruism, reverse bequests or simply noise?", in: D. Kessler and A. Masson, eds., Modelling the accumulation and distribution of wealth (Oxford University Press, Oxford).

Miller, P., C. Mulvey and N. Martin (1995), "Family characteristics and the returns to schooling: evidence on gender differences from a sample of Australian twins", Mimeo. (University of Western Australia, Nedlands).

Olneck, M. (1977), "On the use of sibling data to estimate the effects of family background, cognitive skills, and schooling: results from the Kalamazoo brothers study", in: P. Taubman, ed., Kinometrics: determinants of socioeconomic success within and between families (North-Holland, Amsterdam) pp. 125–163.

Pechman, J. (1987), Federal tax policy, 5th edn. (Brookings Institution, Washington, DC).

Pitt, M.M. and M.R. Rosenzweig (1985), "Health and nutrient consumption across and within farm households", Review of Economics and Statistics 67: 212–223.

Pitt, M.M. and M.R. Rosenzweig (1990), "Estimating the behavioral consequences of health in a family context: the intrafamily incidence of infant illness in Indonesia", International Economic Review 31: 969–989.

Pitt, M.M., M.R. Rosenzweig and M.N. Hassan (1990), "Productivity, health and inequality in the intrahousehold distribution of food in low-income countries", American Economic Review 80: 1139–1156.

Pollak, R. (1988), "Tied transfers and paternalistic preferences", American Economic Review 78: 240–244.

Pollak, R. and T.J. Wales (1992), Demand system specification and estimation (Oxford University Press, New York).

Quisumbing, A.R. (1994a), "Intergenerational transfers in Philippine rice villages: gender differences in traditional inheritance customs", Journal of Development Economics 43: 167–196.

Quisumbing, A.R. (1994b), "The extended family and intrahousehold allocation: inheritance and education in the rural Philippines", Mimeo. (World Bank, Washington, DC).

Rose, E. (1995), "Consumption smoothing and excess female mortality in rural India", Mimeo. (University of Washington, Seattle, WA).

Rosenzweig, M.R. (1990), "Population growth and human capital investments: theory and evidence", Journal of Political Economy 98: S38–S71.

Rosenzweig, M.R. and T.P. Schultz (1982), "Market opportunities, genetic endowments, and intrafamily resource distribution: child survival in rural India", American Economic Review 72: 803–815.

Rosenzweig, M.R. and T.P. Schultz (1984), "Market opportunities, genetic endowments, and intrafamily resource distribution of resources: reply", American Economic Review 74: 521–522.

Rosenzweig, M.R. and T.P. Schultz (1987), "Fertility and investments in human capital: estimates of the consequences of imperfect fertility control in Malaysia", Journal of Econometrics 36: 163–184.

Rosenzweig, M.R. and K.J. Wolpin (1980), "Testing the quantity–quality model of fertility: results of a natural experiment – twins", Econometrica 48: 227–240.

Rosenzweig, M.R. and K.J. Wolpin (1988), "Heterogeneity, intrafamily distribution, and child health", Journal of Human Resources 23: 437–461.

Rothbarth, E. (1943), "Note on a method of determining equivalent income for families of different composition", in: C. Madge, ed., War time pattern of saving and spending, Occasional paper number 4, Appendix 4 (National Institute of Economic and Social Research, London).

Schultz, T.P. (1990), "Testing the neoclassical model of family labor supply and fertility", Journal of Human Resources 25: 599–634.

Sen, A.K. (1990), "More than 100 million women are missing", New York Review of Books 37: 61–66.

Solon, G.R. (1992), "Intergenerational income mobility in the United States", American Economic Review 82: 393–408.

Strauss, J. and D. Thomas (1995), "Human resources: empirical modeling of household and family decisions", in: J.R. Behrman and T.N. Srinivasan, eds., Handbook of development economics, Vol. 3 (North-Holland, Amsterdam).

Strauss, J., P. Gertler, O. Rahman and K. Fox (1993), "Gender and life-cycle differentials in the patterns and determinants of adult health", Journal of Human Resources 28: 791–837.

Subramanian, S. and A. Deaton (1991), "Gender effects in Indian consumption patterns", Sarvekshana 14: 1–12.

Tauchen, H.V., A. Dryden Witte and S.K. Long (1991), "Violence in the family: a non-random affair", International Economic Review 32: 491–511.

Thomas, D. (1990), "Intra-household resource allocation: an inferential approach", Journal of Human Resources 25: 635–664.

Thomas, D. (1994), "Like father, like son; like mother, like daughter: parental resources and child height", Journal of Human Resources 29: 950–989.

Tomes, N. (1981), "The family, inheritance, and the intergenerational transmission of inequality", Journal of Political Economy 89: 928–958.

Udry, C. (1996), "Gender, agricultural production and the theory of the household", Journal of Political Economy 104: 1010–1046.

Ulph, D. (1988), "A general non-cooperative Nash model of household consumption behavior", Mimeo. (University of Bristol, Bristol).

Varian, H. (1982), "The nonparametric approach to demand analysis", Econometrica 50: 945–973.

Wilhelm, M. (1996), "Bequest behavior and the effect of heirs' earnings: testing the altruistic model of bequests", American Economic Review 86: 874–892.

Willis, R.J. (1973), "A new approach to the economic theory of fertility behavior", Journal of Political Economy 81: S14–S64.

Zimmerman, D.J. (1992), "Regression toward mediocrity in economic stature", American Economic Review 82: 409–429.

*Chapter 5*

# INTERGENERATIONAL AND INTERHOUSEHOLD ECONOMIC LINKS

JOHN LAITNER

*University of Michigan*

## Contents

*Handbook of Population and Family Economics. Edited by M.R. Rosenzweig and O. Stark*
*© Elsevier Science B.V., 1997*

# 1. Introduction

This chapter discusses two theoretical frameworks which economists use to analyze links between households. The first is based on altruistic preferences (e.g., Becker, 1974, 1991). The idea is that one household, say, a parent household, may transfer money, time, or services to a second, say, a grown child. The reason the parent unit "transfers" resources rather than selling them is that the child household's well-being directly affects the parent's felicity. The second framework falls under the heading "transactions cost approach" (e.g., Williamson, 1979; Pollak, 1985). In it, two households may share or exchange services, or provide credit or insurance to one another, not because, or strictly because, one's utility depends on the other's consumption, but rather on the basis of mutual perceived advantage in transacting, or engaging in joint production, outside of normal market channels.

# 2. Altruism

Asked to describe a consumer's behavior, an economist thinks of an entity which, within limits imposed by budgetary and institutional constraints, acts to maximize its well-being. Sections 2 and 3 attempt to address the issue of what the "entity" is; Section 4 considers the latitude which the institutional environment may provide.

Economists sometimes anoint the "household" – parents plus minor children living in a common domicile – as the locus of consumer decision-making (generally setting aside questions of distribution within that group). A prominent alternative, often associated with Gary Becker, however, proposes a broader unit: people care about their relatives, taking special notice of the households of their grown-up children; thus, parents may attempt to maximize a combination of the lifetime well-being of their own household and the well-being of their mature children. This is our concept of "altruism". Inter vivos gifts and bequests are means through which altruism is expressed.

Altruism raises complications for modeling behavior. In a simple case, households in a line of descent all care about each other as much as they care about themselves. Unanimity of purpose follows, and the appropriate entity of behavior becomes the family line. In another simple case, altruistic attachments are more restrained, but one household in a linked group is preeminent and can dictate behavior to the remainder. Other possibilities are more difficult to model. Households in the same line of descent may care about each other, but less strongly than about themselves, and none may be able to dictate behavior to the rest. Game theoretic issues may then arise, with strategic planning and counterplanning becoming distinct possibilities. Actions which would otherwise seem unnecessary, or irrational, may be contemplated. Likewise, if an altruistic parent sympathizes only with his/her own blood relations, marriages may entangle different family lines' sympathies.

There are policy considerations at stake. If households navigate in isolation, they may be buffeted by shocks against which little insurance protection is available. Also, if young households want to acquire human capital for the sake of their future earnings but cannot borrow funds without tangible collateral, insufficient investment in human capital may follow and the overall efficiency of the economy may suffer. Altruism can modify the environment. It ties households together, thereby allowing risks to be pooled. Government help may be less essential than it would otherwise appear, as it will merely substitute for private alternatives. Young households may be able to depend, at least in part, on the support of their parents to secure efficient human investments. The effects of altruistic sharing are often labeled "neutrality results".

Also at stake is a question of the nature of modern society. Plant and equipment must be financed. Government could help by collecting taxes in excess of its current spending, using the surplus for investment. In practice, however, savings from the consumer sector are often the economy's primary source of financial capital. The "life-cycle" model stresses the potential role of independent households in this process: each household passes through a period of earnings followed by an interval of retirement; a household must save during the former period to be ready for the latter. This is in some ways a comforting theory: all households participate in national wealth accumulation, roughly in proportion to their earnings. On the other hand, whether life-cycle saving finances modern capital formation, or is the major source of the financing, remains a controversial issue. Some investigators suggest that bequest-motivated saving is quite important. If so, it is worth noting that theoretical analysis (see below) suggests that saving to create bequeathable estates may have a less democratic character than life-cycle wealth accumulation: only the highest earners may engage in estate building. Which theory of saving is more relevant may then determine whether modern capital accumulation depends on the thrift of numerous middle class household units, or on the disproportionate accumulation of a small percentage of high earners with dynastic planning horizons.

## 2.1. A simple altruistic model

This section develops a bare-bones model illustrating what we mean by "altruism". We have a sizable literature from which to draw (e.g., Becker, 1974; Becker and Tomes, 1979; Laitner, 1979a,b, 1992; Loury, 1981; Tomes, 1981; Ioannides, 1986; Cox, 1987; Kimball, 1987; Weil, 1987 and others).

Our model envisions an economy which lasts just two periods (time being discrete). It is populated with parent households and, in the second period, the households of adult children. A parent lives through both periods, having (fixed) labor earnings $y^p$ in the first, and zero earnings in the second. In period 1, each parent raises a single child; in period 2, the child forms its own household – which only lasts the period. The child household (i.e., the "descendant") has earnings $y^d$, which are exogenously given. There is only one good to consume at any time, and its price per unit is always one. The quantity of this good that the parent household chooses to consume in period $i = 1,2$ is $c_i^p$; the adult child consumes $c^d$ in its single period of life. For simplicity, set the interest rate to zero; assume that the parent has no resources to spend other than $y^p$; that the grown child's resources are equal to $y^d$ plus the transfer received from its parent; and, that when the child is young, its consumption needs relative to an adult's are trivially small. Finally, let the utility flow to any household in any period be the logarithm of its current consumption.[1]

Economists model households as maximizing utility subject to budget constraints and use the implied consumption, saving, and transfers to describe behavior. We follow most of the literature in assuming that each parent–child pair plays a noncooperative game and reaches a Nash equilibrium – in other words, that each parent (child) maximizes utility taking the actions of its child (parent) as given.[2]

For the child household above, the setup is especially straightforward:

$$\max_{c^d}\{\ln(c^d)\},$$

$$\text{subject to: } c^d \leq y^d + t^p,$$

(1)

where $t^p$ is the parent's transfer, taken as given by the child. Clearly the child's solution is to consume as much as possible:

$$c^d = y^d + t^p.$$

The utility of the child household is thus

$$\ln(y^d + t^p).$$

The parent in this formulation has more choices. Under one prominent approach, the "life-cycle" or "overlapping generations" model (e.g., Modigliani and Brumberg, 1954; Samuelson, 1958), the parent household has no interest in making transfers. Its lifetime problem is

---

[1] We choose the logarithm because of its familiarity and simplicity. The crucial properties of utility functions for the analysis here are monotonicity and concavity.

[2] Kotlikoff et al. (1990), in contrast, consider a cooperative game framework of analysis. Note also that while "noncooperative game" and "altruism" seem like contradictory terms, they are compatible here: in the models below, the parent cares about its child but the child does not care about the parent – so that interests of the parties conflict. Section 3.1 broadens the concept of altruism – though parent–child conflicts generally remain.

$$\max_{c_1^p, c_2^p, t^p} \{\ln(c_1^p) + \rho \ln(c_2^p)\},$$

subject to: $c_1^p + c_2^p + t^p \leq y^p,$ \hfill (2)

$$c_1^p \geq 0, \quad c_2^p \geq 0, \quad t^p \geq 0,$$

where $\rho > 0$ embodies the parental preference ordering's weight for future utility flows relative to the first period; i.e., the parent's "subjective discount factor". (If $\rho = 1$, the parent assigns equal weight to utility flows from both periods of its life; if $\rho < 1$, the parent is "impatient" in the sense of valuing early flows more.) The solution to (2) is

$$c_1^p = \frac{y^p}{1+\rho}, \quad c_2^p = s_1^p = \frac{\rho \cdot y^p}{1+\rho}, \quad t^p = 0, \hfill (3)$$

where $s_1^p$ is the parent household's saving in its youth.

A principal focus of this chapter is the alternative to (2) in which the parent household is "altruistic" toward its grown child. "Altruism" means that the parent's objective function includes a term reflecting empathy toward the household of its grown child (e.g., Becker, 1991).[3] Specifically, in our terminology, in addition to its own lifetime consumption, an "altruistic" parent cares about the consumption, or the well-being, of its grown child. A simple variant with one-sided altruism leaves (1), the child's setup, the same, but replaces (2) with

$$\max_{c_1^p, c_2^p, t^p} \{\ln(c_1^p) + \rho \cdot \ln(c_2^p) + \lambda^p \cdot \ln(c^d)\},$$

subject to: $c_1^p + c_2^p + t^p \leq y^p,$

$$c^d = y^d + t^p, \hfill (4)$$

$$c_1^p \geq 0, \quad c_2^p \geq 0, \quad t^p \geq 0,$$

where $t^p$ is the parent's transfer. Just as $\ln(c_2^p)$ receives a weight $\rho$ in the objective function, $\ln(c^d)$ receives a weight $\lambda^p \geq 0$. If $\lambda^p = \rho$, the parent values the consumption

---

[3] In the words of Becker and Tomes (1979: p. 1155), "The economic approach to social interactions ... views an individual not in isolation but as part of a family whose members span several generations. ... The current generation can increase its consumption at the expense of future generations but is discouraged from doing so by its concern for the interests of its children and perhaps of other future family members". Note also that in the work of Becker, altruism is sometimes synonymous with parental concern for offspring "quality".

of the adult child, $c^d$, in the same way as its own at the same time; if $\lambda^p < \rho$, the child receives less weight. Framework (2) is seen to be a special case of (4) with $\lambda^p = 0$ and $t^p = 0$. The objective function of (4) could have arisen in one of two ways: (i) the parent's felicity might include own utility from lifetime consumption plus a weight times the felicity of its grown child, or (ii) the parent's direct utility function might have arguments $c_1^p$, $c_2^p$, and $c^d$ – with (4) being a specific example. In other words, the parent might care about the utility the child perceives, or it might care about the child's consumption.[4] Implied behavior when the constraint $t^p \geq 0$ does not bind is

$$c_1^p = \frac{y^p + y^d}{1 + \rho + \lambda^p}, \quad c_2^p = \frac{\rho \cdot (y^p + y^d)}{1 + \rho + \lambda^p}, \quad t^p = \frac{\lambda^p \cdot (y^p + y^d)}{1 + \rho + \lambda^p} - y^d,$$

$$c^d = \frac{\lambda^p \cdot (y^p + y^d)}{1 + \rho + \lambda^p}, \quad s_1^p = y^p - \frac{y^p + y^d}{1 + \rho + \lambda^p}.$$

$$(5)$$

A two-step method of solving (4) begins by deriving (5), which ignores the non-negativity constraint on transfers. If $t^p \geq 0$ in (5), the constraint is nonbinding and we are done. If $t^p < 0$ in (5), the constraint on transfers does bind in the original problem. Then $t^p = 0$ and $c_i^p$ are as in (3). The constrained outcome is likely if the child's earnings are high relative to the parent's. In fact, (5) shows that the constraint binds when

$$\frac{\lambda^p \cdot (y^p + y^d)}{1 + \rho + \lambda^p} - y^d < 0 \quad \Leftrightarrow \quad y^p < \frac{(1+\rho) \cdot y^d}{\lambda^p}.$$

$$(6)$$

The theoretical distinction between the life-cycle and altruistic frameworks of (2) and (4) arises from the connection between parents and their grown children. In either

---

[4] In more complex treatments this distinction becomes important. Suppose, for example, that the child values its consumption, $c^d$, and its leisure time, $l^d$, and that the child's objective function is $\ln(c^d) + 2 \ln(l^d)$ rather than (1). If the parent has preferences over $(c_1^p, c_2^p, c^d, l^d)$, its utility function might, for example, be $\ln(c_2^p) + \rho \ln(c_2^p) + \lambda[2 \ln(c^d) + \ln(l^d)]$, whereas if it values its own lifetime consumption plus its child's utility, the term in brackets would have to be $\ln(c^d) + 2 \ln(l^d)$. In the former instance – which Pollak (1988) or Hori and Kanaya (1989) would label "paternalistic" preferences – the child and parent will disagree about how the child should deploy its resources (i.e., the child will want more leisure than the parent desires for it). The parent might be able to influence the child's resource division, say, by making transfers of non-fungible consumption goods rather than money. If "tied transfers" are not possible, the parent will have to condition its bequest on the child not behaving as it would most prefer (e.g., Phelps and Pollak, 1968; Laitner, 1980). See also Section 4.3 below.

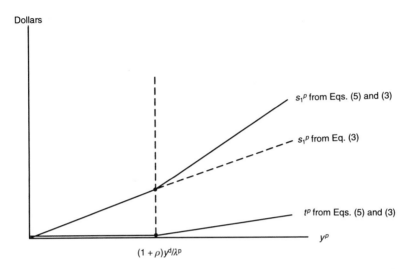

Fig. 1. Savings and altruistic transfers as functions of parental earnings.

case, parents provide support for their young offspring.[5] In the simple life-cycle model, when children reach maturity, their role in parents' utility functions abruptly ends. Presuming that parent–child affections do not adjust so precipitously, the modeling must implicitly assume a compartmentalization: emotional ties among family members must be separate from economic responsibilities, with the latter perhaps emanating from social norms, the norms decreeing parental financial responsibility up to but not beyond some prespecified age. In the altruistic formulation, a parent can treat young and grown children the same way, which we will presume to be the case with $\lambda^p = \rho$ in (4). Or, even with altruism there can be differential treatment of mature children, for example, with $\lambda^p$ smaller than $\rho$.

The relative height of the two savings curves in Fig. 1 gives our first result: altru-

---

[5] We have omitted this above, assuming young children have trivial consumption needs. Tobin (1967), for example, gives a detailed presentation. He has $c_i^p$ register consumption per "equivalent adult". Suppose that a young child's "needs" are 50% as large as an adult's and that our parent household internally allocates its expenditures to reflect this. Tobin would rewrite the budget in (2) as $\$1.5c_1^p + c_2^p \leq y^p$. In words, with one parent and one child in the household in the first period, one unit of spending in $c_1^p$ requires one unit for the adult and 0.5 unit for the young child. Tobin's criterion would be $\$1.5 \ln(c_1^p) + \rho \ln(c_2^p)$. The new 1.5 factor weights per capita utility more when the household has more members, seemingly consistent with the intertemporal specification. In the end, total parent-household consumption will be higher until children grow up. The same complications could be added to the $c_1^p$-terms of (2) and (4).

ism should tend to increase average wealth holdings.[6] Whether this is of major or minor empirical significance remains a controversial issue (see Section 2.4).

Second, the graph shows a linear relation between average lifetime wealth and lifetime resources, $y^p$, in the life-cycle case – and this would remain true with more general homothetic preferences – but a steepening relation with altruism. The intuition is that with altruism and a positive transfer all consumption figures (i.e., $c_i^p$ and $c^d$) depend on family-line resources $y^p + y^d$. A 10% increase in $y^p$, ceteris paribus, raises combined resources less than 10%, say, 6%. With homothetic preferences, that implies a 6% rise in $c_1^p$; hence, more than a 10% increase in $s_1^p = y^p - c_1^p$. Another way of stating this is to say that altruism makes parental wealth holdings behave like a "luxury good" with respect to $y^p$. Conceivably this is part of the reason that economists sometimes characterize savers and consumers as two different groups (e.g., Carroll and Summers, 1991; Avery and Kennickell, 1991): according to the model, young parent households with lifetime earnings $y^p < (1 + \rho)y^d/\lambda^p$ engage in life-cycle saving alone, while those with higher earnings save more than proportionately more.[7]

## 2.2. Altruistic and nonaltruistic transfers

Although the basic observable difference between models (2) and (4) is the possibility in the altruistic case of positive intergenerational transfers, that difference depends on the stringent simplifications of the preceding section. We now examine cases in which transfers can arise without altruism. We then develop an empirical basis for distinguishing between intergenerational transfers which are motivated by altruism and those which are not.

In practice, the time of death is uncertain. Returning to life-cycle model (2), suppose that a fraction of all parents, say, Prob{*death*}, die after a single period of life and that early death is equally likely for all. This complicates a parent's first-period planning: the probability of living necessitates some period 1 saving for consumption during retirement, but in the event of early death the sum saved will go to waste (becoming an "accidental bequest"). Insurance companies can help by marketing annuities. In this context, an actuarially fair annuity is a security a unit of which sells for $1(1 − Prob{*death*}) in period 1 and pays a bearer who survives $1 in period 2, there

---

[6] Section 3 warns, however, that while this is likely, it need not always be true: if a grown child is altruistic toward its parent, the parent may in some circumstances reduce its life-cycle saving, relying on future support from the child.

[7] Empirical evidence that prosperous households in the US save a larger fraction of their income than poor households goes back at least to the 1930s (see, for example, the discussion in Evans (1969)) – and it stimulated "relative" and "permanent income" theories of consumption behavior. Modigliani (1986: p. 307) makes assumptions to guarantee that bequests in his (nonaltruistic) model rise more than proportionately with cross-sectional earnings. He writes, "The most casual observation suggests that the planning and leaving of bequests is concentrated in the upper strata of the distribution of life resources ...".

being no payout if the bearer dies. Incorporating this into model (2), and modifying the objective function to expected utility, one has

$$\max_{c_1^p, c_2^p}\{\ln(c_1^p) + \rho \cdot (1 - \text{Prob}\{death\}) \cdot \ln(c_2^p)\},$$

$$\text{subject to: } c_1^p + (1 - \text{Prob}\{death\}) \cdot c_2^p \le y^p, \tag{2'}$$

$$c_1^p \ge 0, \quad c_2^p \ge 0.$$

The concavity of preferences implies risk aversion, so the parent will fully annuitize second-period consumption. Utility maximizing choices are (e.g., Yaari, 1965)

$$c_1^p = \frac{y^p}{1 + \rho \cdot (1 - \text{Prob}\{death\})}, \quad s_1^p = \frac{\rho \cdot (1 - \text{Prob}\{death\}) \cdot y^p}{1 + \rho \cdot (1 - \text{Prob}\{death\})},$$

$$c_2^p = \frac{\rho \cdot y^p}{1 + \rho \cdot (1 - \text{Prob}\{death\})}. \tag{3'}$$

In model (4), saving earmarked for $c_2^p$ would be fully annuitized, although, of course, saving for $t^p$ would not be annuitized at all.

Empirical observation shows households making surprisingly little use of annuities outside of pensions and social security. It seems likely that the price of annuities is driven up by insurance companies' costs of doing business and by adverse selection: different groups may have different mortality rates, and people may have private information about the group to which they belong (the private information perhaps being knowledge of their ancestors' longevity). Nevertheless, within our pure life-cycle framework, a parent should fully annuitize its consumption whether or not annuities are actuarially fair, provided only that they pay some premium over other financial investments. One possible explanation of observed behavior is that many households have a degree of altruism. Faced with expensive annuities, such households may choose to self-insure, reasoning that they can derive some satisfaction out of knowing that if they die young their heirs will benefit from the resulting "accidental bequest" (e.g., Friedman and Warshawsky, 1990; Bernheim, 1991). A second possibility is that family lines tend to insure their own members (see Section 4). A third is that people have a variety of uninsured risks in old age, centering on illness, nursing care, etc. This may make them reluctant to commit the principal of their wealth in illiquid securities of any type (e.g., Friedman and Warshawsky, 1990: p. 153).

Following Davies (1981), think about an extreme case with no annuities available. Our life-cycle model is then

$$\max_{c_1^P, c_2^P}\{\ln(c_1^P) + \rho \cdot (1 - \text{Prob}\{death\}) \cdot \ln(c_2^P)\},$$

subject to: $c_1^P + c_2^P \le y^P,$ \hfill (2'')

$$c_1^P \ge 0, \quad c_2^P \ge 0.$$

The solution is not much different from (3'):[8]

$$c_1^P = \frac{y^P}{1 + \rho \cdot (1 - \text{Prob}\{death\})}, \quad c_2^P = s_1^P = \frac{\rho \cdot (1 - \text{Prob}\{death\}) \cdot y^P}{1 + \rho \cdot (1 - \text{Prob}\{death\})}. \tag{3''}$$

However, first-period saving, $s_1^P$, becomes a transfer (here a bequest) if the parent dies before period 2 (e.g., Davies, 1981; Abel, 1985; Eckstein et al., 1985; Kotlikoff et al., 1986).

Nonaltruistic transfers can occur for reasons not related to time of death. A frequently employed version of (2) is (e.g., Yaari, 1965; Blinder, 1974; Atkinson, 1971; Hurd, 1987, 1989)

$$\max_{c_1^P, c_2^P}\{\ln(c_1^P) + \rho \cdot \ln(c_2^P) + \lambda^P \cdot \ln(t^P)\},$$

subject to: $c_1^P + c_2^P + t^P \le y^P,$ \hfill (2''')

$$c_1^P \ge 0, \quad c_2^P \ge 0, \quad t^P \ge 0.$$

Call this the "egoistic" model: the parent household of (2''') derives pleasure from making a transfer $t^P$, but, in contrast to (4), the usefulness of the transfer to the recipient does not modulate the donor's joy. In different words, consider a parent making a transfer of $10 000 to its adult child. If the child has high earnings, it may benefit little in terms of utility or consumption from an extra $10 000. A child with very low earnings, on the other hand, might derive a great increment to its well-being from the sum. In setup (4), a parent sets its $t^P$ in light of its child's neediness; in (2'''), the child's earnings have no bearing on parental planning.

---

[8] This apparent similarity is partly a consequence of our logarithmic functional forms. Suppose the flow of utility from consumption $c$ comes from the more general isoelastic class: $[c]^\beta/\beta$, $\beta < 1$, $\ne 0$. A common calibration has $\beta < -1$. Define $\sigma \equiv 1/(1 - \beta)$. First-period life-cycle saving with annuities is $y^P \cdot \rho^\sigma \cdot [1 - \text{Prob}\{death\}]/(1 + \rho^\sigma \cdot [1 - \text{Prob}\{death\}])$; without them it is $y^P \cdot \rho^\sigma \cdot [1 - \text{Prob}\{death\}]^\sigma/(1 + \rho^\sigma \cdot [1 - \text{Prob}\{death\}]^\sigma)$. If $\sigma$ is a small fraction, these formulas show that life-cycle saving can be much higher in the absence of annuities.

While both altruistic and nonaltruistic transfers constitute economic links between households, Section 2.3 shows that the two have quite different implications for the overall economy and for public policy.

Although we can now see that the mere presence of transfers between households is not evidence of altruism, a comparison of (3) and (5) still yields an empirical basis for disputing or validating alternative modeling frameworks: in the absence of altruism, a parent's behavior should be independent of $y^d$. The latter independence holds whether accidental bequests or egoistic transfers occur or not. In contrast, if a parent is altruistic, and if nonnegativity constraints do not bind, the parent's consumption, saving, and transfer will depend on the earnings of its grown descendant as well as its own. Formally, with altruism

$$t^P > 0 \quad \Rightarrow \quad \frac{\partial c_1^P}{\partial y^d} > 0, \quad \frac{\partial c_2^P}{\partial y^d} > 0, \quad \frac{\partial t^P}{\partial y^d} < 0, \quad \frac{\partial s_1^P}{y^d} < 0. \tag{7}$$

Line (7) provides the basis for the empirical work of Tomes (1981), Cox (1987), Altonji et al. (1992), and others discussed below. The practical challenge of using this logic to identify altruism and to measure its consequences is evident: studying the relation between parent behavior and offspring earnings requires a data set with observations on more than one generation per family line.

## 2.3. Economic linkages

Altruistic and nonaltruistic transfers can link together households, most likely households of different generations within the same family line. If child households are formed through marriage, more extensive connections are imaginable. This section turns to these topics. It also considers the way an altruistic parent household with many children would divide its estate.

A fundamental feature of the outcomes of all of the models above is "consumption smoothing": with concave utility, unit increases in consumption yield felicity gains which are smaller than the losses from unit decreases; hence, evenness over time is desired, although this proclivity must be balanced against impatience (i.e., subjective discounting). In our simple overlapping generations case (i.e., (2)), the parent receives all of its earnings in youth – it is retired thereafter. With linear utility, the household would willingly let its consumption follow the same pattern, $c_1^P = y^P$ and $c_2^P = 0$. Because the logarithmic function is concave, on the other hand, a line drawn for (3) yields a much more level time path. In fact, when $\rho = 1$, the parent chooses $c_1^P = c_2^P$. To implement smoothing, a household uses its wealth as a buffer to separate earnings and consumption trajectories: the parent saves in years when resource flows are high (i.e., period 1 above) and dissaves when the opposite is true (i.e., period 2).

If smoothing is working as in (3), government policies which shift household resources from one period of life to another while leaving their present value unchanged may have little effect on consumption or well-being. For example, the initiation of a fully funded social security system which taxes $X from a parent in period 1 and returns a benefit of the same present value in period 2 would not alter the parent's consumption choices. The parent would carry $X less private wealth (i.e., a lower $s_1^p$) into period 2 but the corresponding funding in the social security system would keep national wealth unchanged. Similarly, if the government provides all parents a period-1 transfer payment of $X, to be financed with a tax of the same present value on the same group in period 2, the effect on household consumption is nil: utility-maximizing consumption choices in (2) remain as before.

The same logic shows that if there are year-to-year fluctuations for which full market insurance is not available, households have some capacity for self-protection. For instance, if moral hazard precludes complete insurance against spells of unemployment, personal savings (or reliance on other family members; see Section 4) can serve as a buffer (e.g., Deaton, 1991; Aiyagari, 1994).

Barro (1974) extends the same reasoning to the altruistic model. When the non-negativity constraint on transfers does not bind in (4), consumption smoothing expands to the dynastic realm: for example, if $\rho = \lambda^p = 1$, then $c_1^p = c_2^p = c^d$ and all three depend on the sum $y^p + y^d$. Suppose we initiate period-1 government transfers of $X to parents, to be paid for by period-2 taxes on grown children, the government borrowing the funds to make the transfers in period 1 and repaying its debt from tax revenues in period 2. Consider a family line which would have had a positive transfer in the old regime. Although the new government policy enhances the parent's lifetime budget and makes the child household's less favorable, the family line's combined resources are unaffected, remaining $y^p + y^d$. Thus the consumer choices in (5) still characterize utility-maximizing behavior, so that $c_1^p$, $c_2^p$, and $c^d$ should stay as before. The parent merely adds the period-1 government transfer to its saving, passing it along in its private transfer $t^p$; the grown child uses the increment in $t^p$ to pay the new taxes it faces. There are not even any indirect effects: the new saving finances the temporary government debt in the bond market, and this increment to savings disappears exactly as the debt is being liquidated; hence, overall financing for investments in physical capital need never change. Since private actions fully offset the economic influence of the policy, we say the model exhibits "Ricardian neutrality".

In the case of accidental bequests from incomplete annuitization, neutrality will be largely absent: if government borrows to give $X to each parent household in period 1 and announces that taxes on adult children will rise in period 2 to repay the public debt, life-cycle parents will have no desire to share their $X with their descendants, although as parents are made richer, accidental bequests will tend to rise slightly. Egoistic parents will share part of their $X, provided private transfers are normal goods in (2$'''$).

A number of implications follow. First, in a more sophisticated framework there would be random elements such as temporary unemployment or sickness. There would be random differences in lifetime earnings as well: some children are born with high earning abilities, and others are less favorably endowed or happen to chose unprofitable careers. To the extent that adverse selection and moral hazard make market insurance costly, unavailable, or partial, dynastic altruism can help: an unlucky child may draw a larger transfer from its parents. Such assistance is absent in models with only accidental or egoistic bequests. Thus, altruistic transfers can offset innate earning-ability differences (see Section 3) and provide protection against short-term risks. Although this will not iron out all inter-household consumption differences – because insurance pools are small (operating only within family lines), their workings are limited by the degree to which parents are altruistic, and, in the case of poor parents, they are restricted by the nonnegativity constraint on transfers, it can at least partially replace missing insurance markets.

Second, public assistance programs may benefit their recipients less than amounts spent might seem to indicate, and they may benefit households other than the ones actually receiving money from the government (see Becker and Tomes, 1976; Lampman and Smeeding, 1983). For example, suppose that an altruistic parent provides $X per month of support for its disabled child. If the government begins an assistance program making public transfers to the child, the parent may reduce, or stop, its contributions. The child then ends up with a smaller gain than the public transfers seem to imply, and the parent, whom the public program may not have been designed to help, gains perhaps as much as the child or more.[9]

A third implication does not depend on random elements: actual families live many periods, and their earnings typically rise until retirement. If financial institutions will not extend loans without tangible collateral, life-cycle households may lose utility by not being able to attain consumption levels as high early in life as later (see Hubbard and Judd, 1987). Altruistic transfers from parents may help: a middle aged parent may be far enough in its life cycle of earnings to escape the need to borrow, and it may therefore be willing to give to its child as an inter vivos gift a sum which in the absence of borrowing constraints on the child it would have bequeathed at death (see Cox, 1990).

Even with altruism, Ricardian neutrality and self-insurance by dynastic families depend on avoiding binding nonnegativity constraints on private transfers. Suppose a parent is at a corner $t^p = 0$ in (4). Absent any constraint, the parent would choose a negative transfer, expropriating some of the adult child's resources for itself. Our deficit-financed public transfer above facilitates just this. If in period 1 the government gives $X to each parent, promising to raise taxes on children a similar amount in period 2, the parent would raise its consumption, setting $c_i^p$ as in (3) with $y^p + X$ in place of $y^p$. Its child would be left to pay the tax bill, with $c^d = y^d - X$. The government

---

[9] Note, however, that recent work by Cox and Jakubson (1993) suggests that the empirical magnitudes of this class of effects may be small.

program would not be neutralized: the intergenerational distributions of consumption and utility would change; at the aggregate level, first-period saving would not rise in step with government issues of bonds, so physical investment would tend to be crowded out.

A question arises as to whether we would expect the constraint on private transfers to bind in problem (4). We have already seen that (6) provides the condition for a corner solution; Barro (1974) would call (6) the condition for an "inoperative transfer". The factors likely to lead to an operative transfer are plain. One is a high degree of altruism: (6) is more likely to fail with a large $\lambda^p$. High earnings for the parent relative to the grown child are another. Laitner (1979b, 1992) (also Feldstein, 1988) studies a model with an exogenous distribution of (lifetime) earnings in each generation. When a parent has a high earning ability relative to its child, an operative transfer occurs; in a family line where the child has relatively high earnings, the nonnegativity constraint on bequests binds. In the economy as a whole, some parent–child pairs will be connected through open bequests, but others not (see Section 3).[10]

A surprising outcome in the same vein arises for members of the same generation if we modify the altruistic model to include marriage of adult children (e.g., Bernheim and Bagwell, 1988; Kotlikoff, 1989: Ch. 3). To illustrate, assume that when two children marry, they combine their resources and each consumes half. Let the lower-case parent below have a son who marries the daughter of the upper-case parent. Given the daughter's earnings, $Y^d$, and transfer, $T^p$, the son's parent solves an altered version of (4):

$$\max_{c_1^p, c_2^p, t^p} \left\{ \ln(c_1^p) + \rho \cdot \ln(c_2^p) + \lambda^p \cdot \ln\left( \frac{y^d + t^p + Y^d + T^p}{2} \right) \right\},$$

subject to: $c_1^p + c_2^p + t^p \le y^p,$  (8)

$$c_1^p \ge 0, \quad c_2^p \ge 0, \quad t^p \ge 0.$$

Given the son's earnings, $y^d$, and transfer, $t^p$, the daughter's parent solves[11]

---

[10] Bernheim (1987) provides a survey of the extensive literature on Ricardian neutrality. Kotlikoff et al. (1990) consider the case in which the child plays a more aggressive role – in effect saying to its parent, "If you don't give me a big enough estate, then I won't take anything at all". Since the parent cannot help caring about the child, the latter has leverage for manipulation. The authors abandon our noncooperative game setup and examine a Nash bargaining solution. The bequest tends to be larger and Ricardian neutrality, in strict terms at least, fails for a different reason: a government transfer program, for example, will modify the "threat point" of the bargaining problem, typically changing the distribution of utilities in the outcome.

[11] Although the parameters $\lambda^p$ and $\rho$ are the same in (8) and (8′), that is not essential for the gist of the arguments below.

$$\max_{c_1^p, c_2^p, T^p} \left\{ \ln(C_1^p) + \rho \cdot \ln(C_2^p) + \lambda^p \cdot \ln\left(\frac{Y^d + T^p + y^d + t^p}{2}\right) \right\},$$

subject to: $C_1^p + C_2^p + T^p \leq Y^p,$ \hfill (8′)

$$C_1^p \geq 0, \quad C_2^p \geq 0, \quad T^p \geq 0.$$

In each case, the parent values only the consumption of its own adult child, not that of the child's spouse or the spouse's parent, and the earnings–transfer characteristics of an adult child's spouse are assumed to be known in advance. Call the lower-case parent's desired transfer, conditional on earnings and the inheritance of its daughter-in-law $\bar{t}(y^p, y^d, Y^p, T^p)$; let the same for the upper-case parent be $\overline{T}(Y^p, Y^d, y^p, y^d, t^p)$. We are interested in the Nash equilibrium case, where $t^p$ and $T^p$ simultaneously satisfy

$$t^p = \bar{t}(y^p, y^d, Y^p, Y^d, Y^p) \quad \text{and} \quad T^p = \overline{T}(Y^p, Y^d, y^p, y^d, t^p). \hfill (9)$$

An intratemporal neutrality result can then emerge. Suppose that in the Nash equilibrium the transfers of both parents are positive and greater than 1. Recompute the equilibrium after the following change: in the first period, the government, or chance, imposes a lump-sum tax of $1 on the upper-case parent and gives the $1 to the lower-case parent. Consider a prospective solution in which each parent maintains the same lifetime consumption as before, the lower-case parent appends its $1 from the government to its former $t^p$, and the upper-case parent reduces its former $T^p$ by the tax it now faces, $1. Each child then has the same consumption as before. Indeed, all consumption figures remain unchanged. Thus, the original first-order conditions for (8)–(8′) hold, as does (9). This is the neutrality result: after the lump-sum change, overall consumption and saving are the same as before (note that upper case parent's saving in youth declines $1 but lower case parent's rises $1). A more realistic setup would yield broader results: suppose parents each have two children, a boy and a girl. If the son of parent A marries the daughter of B, and the son of B marries the daughter of C, a redistribution from parent C to A can be neutralized under the same logic.

This is another incarnation of consumption smoothing: lump-sum transfers across a set of parents have no effect on the distributions of consumption and utility, or on aggregate financing available for physical investment, provided the parents have operative private transfers and are connected to one another through their children's marriages. The problem is that while counterintuitive results can often reveal the power of a model, this goes too far: the scope of neutrality has become implausibly broad, calling into question the altruistic theoretical framework itself. Further, under our equal-sharing rule within marriage at least, equilibrium parental consumption levels are not only invariant to the intra-family distribution of resources but equal! For, consider again formulation (7)–(9). Let $u(c) \equiv \ln(c)$. With open bequests and a Nash equilibrium, the lower- and upper-case parents have first-order conditions, respectively

$$u'(c_1^p) = \rho \cdot u'(c_2^p) = \frac{\lambda^p}{2} \cdot u'\left(\frac{y^d + t^p + Y^d + T^p}{2}\right)$$

and                                                                               (10)

$$u'(C_1^p) = \rho \cdot u'(C_2^p) = \frac{\lambda^p}{2} \cdot u'\left(\frac{y^d + t^p + Y^d + T^p}{2}\right).$$

Combining the two lines

$$c_1^p = C_1^p \quad \text{and} \quad c_2^p = C_2^p.$$

With more children per parent and correspondingly wider intragenerational links, this equalization would carry over more generally.

The story so far, of course, neglects the nonnegativity constraint $t^p \geq 0$. As in the previous discussion, a parent with modest earnings relative to its offspring will tend not to have an operative transfer (see also Section 3). Binding constraints cut economic links, potentially reducing the extent of intragenerational neutrality. Marriage itself may cause constraints to hold more often: if the offspring of the lower-case parent marries into a wealthy family line, $T^p$ may be sufficiently large to drive $t^p$ to 0.

Laitner (1991) raises an additional issue: all of the modeling above presupposes behavior consistent with rational calculations of self-interest, and he argues that the same presumption would lead one to expect assortativity rather than randomness in mating patterns. A child with high earning ability and/or the potential of receiving a large transfer is a desirable mate, at least in one significant dimension, and ceteris paribus such a child will be able to attract a spouse with similar characteristics. In fact, if all of a person's attributes can be assigned monetary values and these summed to an index, we might expect the eligible man and woman having the highest indices to marry, the man and woman each standing second to marry, and so on. Only very homogeneous groups of parents may experience Bernheim–Bagwell links therefore. Marital connections would not cross between groups. (A limited number of deviations from rigid assortativity need not alter this result. For example, if the son of parent A marries into a high-index group while his sister does not, the parent may transfer exclusively to the daughter. Average resources of the high-index group as a whole are not much affected, and the high group's wealth cannot cascade down through the single channel – from the son, to parent A, to the daughter – because of the nonnegativity constraint on the parent's transfer its son. Another possibility is that the parent of the son's spouse will use transfers of goods and services, or trusts, to prevent its largess from ever finding its way to parent A.)

With assortative mating, neutrality with respect to time-1 intragenerational government transfers may be irrelevant. Consider two similar family lines. Let the government expropriate money from one parental household and give to the other. The child of a parent benefiting from the transfer might well climb to a more favorable mating group; the child of a parent suffering expropriate might drop to a lower one. With the children moving to different mating groups, the possibility of neutralization disappears. In the end, Laitner (1991) argues that a seemingly highly stylized altruistic model in which each household (in every generation) has one adult and one offspring, with no mating, may provide predictions about behavior and utility that mimic an elaborate model with two adults and two children per household unit and assortative mating. The remainder of this chapter follows that lead.

Reverting to a model without marital complications, another issue in the literature is the division of a parent's total bequest between several children. To illustrate, modify (4) to give the parent two, equally loved offspring, one with period-2 earnings $y^d$, and the other with $y^{dd}$. The parent solves

$$\max_{c_1^p, c_2^p, t^p, t^{pp}} \left\{ \ln(c_1^p) + \rho \cdot \ln(c_2^p) + \lambda^p \cdot \ln(y^d + t^p) + \lambda^p \cdot \ln(y^{dd} + t^{pp}) \right\},$$

subject to: $c_1^p + c_2^p + t^p + t^{pp} \leq y^p,$

$$c_1^p \geq 0, \quad c_2^p \geq 0, \quad t^p \geq 0, \quad t^{pp} \geq 0,$$

where $t^p$ and $t^{pp}$ now stand, respectively, for parental transfers to the two offspring. If nonnegativity constraints do not bind, chosen transfers are

$$t^p = \lambda^p \cdot \left[ \frac{y^p + y^d + y^{dd}}{1 + \rho + 2 \cdot \lambda^p} \right] - y^d, \quad t^{pp} = \lambda^p \cdot \left[ \frac{y^p + y^d + y^{dd}}{1 + \rho + 2 \cdot \lambda^p} \right] - y^{dd}.$$

In other words, theory predicts a higher transfer to the descendant with lower earnings. In fact, the prediction is even stronger: if both transfers are positive, they should fully equalize the consumption of the two descendant households.

Menchik (1980, 1988) and Tomes (1981) study this issue. Although there is some disagreement, empirical evidence seems to point to equal division of estates among siblings. In a sample of 269 estates from Cleveland, Tomes (1981) uses very similar data), Menchik (1988) finds 115 with a positive bequest for at least one child. Among the latter, almost 88% exhibit approximate equality (for testate cases, 81%). It is hard to construe this as supporting the altruistic model. On the other hand, in a sample of 379 large estates from Connecticut, Menchik (1980) uncovers near equality among children less frequently, for 50–65% of the cases.

There are, of course, a number of possible rationalizations. For example, (i) most of the estates in the Cleveland studies are small relative to the lifetime earnings of the recipients. Such sums may be tokens of remembrance, or accidents stemming from incomplete annuitization, rather than serious contradictions of the altruistic model. Although the sample from Connecticut has larger estates, the evidence there is more ambiguous and Menchik (1980) does not have recipients' earnings for comparison with their inheritances when the latter are unequal. (ii) Section 2.4 suggests that the importance of inter vivos gifts may outweigh bequests at death for many families, yet Menchik's Cleveland sample did not cover gifts. Although the Connecticut study had some information, it was deemed "much less reliable and complete than the inheritance data" (p. 305). (iii) Even if a number of the features of the altruistic model are basically correct, an additional element in practice may be social norms demanding equal or nearly equal division of each household's transfers to its children. Such rules might promote efficiency by curbing rent seeking behavior on the part of siblings competing for a larger share of parental resources, and they might help to preserve peace within family lines.

### 2.4. Empirical evidence on interfamily transfers

This section briefly reviews empirical findings on the magnitude and nature of intergenerational transfers. Rather than presenting a comprehensive survey, it attempts to highlight difficulties in implementing tests based upon Eq. (7).

Perhaps the best known empirical paper is Kotlikoff and Summers (1981). Kotlikoff and Summers attempt to measure the quantitative importance of bequest-motivated saving. They do not distinguish among accidental, egoistic, and altruistic transfers.

Kotlikoff and Summers split overall US private wealth accumulation into two components: one comes from intergenerational transfers between households, and the other from life-cycle saving. The authors attempt to measure the two components independently. They assess the first by developing a synthetic distribution of bequests: they multiply average wealth for households in different age groups, as measured in the 1962 *Survey of Consumer Finances*, by the mortality rate for each age, and then they multiply by empirical estate division percentages from a Washington, DC, inheritance tax file. The present value of lifetime net transfers received by each existing household, plus an estimate of bequeathed life insurance payouts, parental support for college, and trusts, is wealth originating from intergenerational transfers. The reported sum seems to explain about one half of private wealth.

Kotlikoff and Summers next turn to an accounting relation: apart from intergenerational transfers, a household's net worth equals the present value of its earnings, plus government transfers, less taxes, and less consumption. Kotlikoff and Summers use this present value as their measure of life-cycle wealth. They derive life-cycle earnings patterns from social security data, and they estimate consumption spending at different ages from the 1960 and 1972 *Consumer Expenditure Surveys*. Aggregating across households in the US economy in 1974, they conclude that less than 20% of national wealth is due to life-cycle saving – and 80% is a second estimate of the part of national wealth due to intergenerational transfers.

Modigliani (1988) proposes major upward revisions in Kotlikoff and Summers' share of private wealth stemming from life-cycle saving. Three principal revisions are:

treating purchases of consumer durable goods as investments (hence as additions to saving), including interest on inheritances as part of life-cycle saving, and excluding college expenses from measurements of intergenerational transfers. The original article and these suggestions remain controversial (see also Modigliani, 1986; Kotlikoff, 1988; Carroll and Summers, 1991). For example, if purchases of consumer durables are to be treated as investments, the stock of durables must be added to the total of other private wealth. Thus, unless durables tend to be purchased early in adulthood, their inclusion will not make as much of a difference as one might at first imagine. The categorization of interest on inheritances seems to be a matter of one's definition of life-cycle saving. The treatment of college-aged children raises a similar issue: in the pure life-cycle model, parents willingly finance the consumption of their young children, but they take no responsibility for their grown descendants. So, the age at which offspring become grown-ups must somehow be specified as part of the theory – indeed as part of the description of parental preference orderings.

A second set of papers tests the altruistic model using data on interfamily transfers. Tomes (1981) has a sample of 659 probated estates from Cleveland, 1964/65. The data contain inheritance amounts; information on the heirs, including current income and schooling; and limited information on decedents, including education and occupation. From the latter Tomes imputes decedents' permanent incomes. Using the subsample with inheritances above $250, Tomes then regresses inheritance amount on recipient income and decedent permanent income. The estimates conform with the altruistic model – see (7): the coefficient on recipient income is negative, and the coefficient on decedent income is positive. The altruistic model predicts that purchases of schooling for children will have priority over transferring assets in a bequest (see Section 3 below), and this is also borne out.

Menchik and David (1983) use a sample of inheritance tax records for males from Wisconsin, 1960–1964. They match the records with income tax returns from, 1946–1964. Thus, the data include both inheritances and decedents' incomes, with a usable sample of about 1400. The data do not contain information on recipient earnings, however. When Menchik and David regress estate size on lifetime permanent income of the decedent, the marginal propensity to bequeath from permanent income is positive and rising (see, for example, their Table 7) – reminiscent of Fig. 1 above.

Parental transfers may include lifetime (i.e., inter vivos) gifts as well as bequests at death. Cox (1987) analyzes data from the 1979 *President's Commission on Pension Policy* survey (see also Kurz, 1984; Cox and Raines, 1985). The survey covers about 4600 families and includes fairly detailed information on inflow and outflow of current private transfers.[12] Inheritances constitute one measured category, but Cox and Raines (1985: Table 13.4) show that they only account for about 25% of the value of

---

[12] Nonmonetary transfers, such as transfers of time and housing services (1100–1200 of the families live with relatives), are not measured. Note also that children over 18 are classified as separate families – even if they continue to live with their parents.

total transfer receipts. In other words, in this data inter vivos gifts seem to be three times as large as inheritances.

Cox and Raines present various summary tables: about 16% of sample report making a transfer (in 1979), about 12% report receiving at least one, and the largest 10% of the transfers account for about 55% of the total (for either transfers given or received). In terms of magnitudes, Cox (1987, Table B1) shows the mean income among transfer recipients is about $13 000, and the mean transfer receipt is about $800. Cox and Raines (1985, Table 13.7) show about two thirds of transfers given (received) going to (coming from) younger (older) people, with most of the rest transferred to people of the same age.

Cox and Raines (1985) present Tobit results for transferred amounts showing a significantly positive coefficient on the donor's income. This is consistent with the altruistic model. For transfer sums received, recipient's income has a significantly negative coefficient in some specifications – which is consistent with the altruistic model – but significantly positive in others. In the end, the altruistic model receives only mixed support. As in the cases of Tomes and Menchik and David, Cox and Raines' transfer equations generally have either the donor's income or the recipient's, but not both. One exception is Table 13.14, where the sample is restricted to non-education transfers for multiple households at the same address. Then in a regression of transfer amounts received by "secondary" households, the recipient's income has a significantly positive coefficient and the "primary" household's income has an insignificantly positive coefficient.[13] The positive coefficient on recipient's income stands in contradiction to the altruistic model.

Cox (1987) confronts Eq. (7) more directly. To do this, however, he must use the mean income in the recipient's neighborhood as a substitute for donor's income. Obviously many assumptions are needed to justify this proxy variable. His probit estimates (see his Table 2) show receipt of a transfer more likely when the recipient's income is low and the neighborhood income is high – both consistent with either the altruistic model or the exchange models of Section 4 below. In his Tobit equation for amount of transfers received, the neighborhood income is still positive, but the recipient's income also has a significantly positive coefficient. The latter is not consistent with the simple altruism model – although it is not inconsistent with exchange models.

Cox (1990) views the same data in a somewhat different way. Limiting the analysis to transfer recipients, he attempts to distinguish between a recipient's current and permanent income. The latter is deduced from recipient characteristics, current income, and panel results from the existing literature. Probit equations (see Cox's Tables III–IV) find that the receipt of a transfer is positively dependent on neighborhood mean income (still a proxy for donor's income), positively dependent on the recipient's permanent income, and negatively dependent on the recipient's current income. Re-

---

[13] Note that the primary (i.e., parent) household's income is an appropriate regressor only if we can assume that the primary household is the origin of the secondary unit's transfers.

gressions of transfer amounts (see Cox's Table V) find significantly positive coefficients on neighborhood income, but insignificant coefficients on recipient-income variables. These results do not support the simple altruistic model – for which recipient permanent income should negatively affect transfer probability and amount – nor do they necessarily suggest an exchange model (see Section 4). Instead, they suggest that transfers – especially inter vivos transfers – may primarily be a means of lifting temporary liquidity constraints on young families.

Many other studies try to make deductions about transfer behavior without observations of transfer amounts.

For example, Hurd (1987) uses wealth and income data from the *Longitudinal Retirement History Survey*. His sample includes singles and couples aged 58–63 in 1969. He follows "bequeathable wealth", private net worth excluding pensions and social security, for retired households. He has measurements of wealth at two-year intervals over 1969–1979. Hurd's idea is that if some households are altruistic and some are not, then the altruistic ones will tend to decumulate wealth more slowly in retirement than the others. In practice, his approach is to divide his sample of households into groups with and without children, assuming that those without children will not be altruistic. Checking rates of wealth decumulation at two-year intervals, if altruism is important, he expects to find slower decumulation for households with children.

Hurd does not find slower wealth decumulation during retirement for households with children than for those without children. This remains true even when the sample is stratified on the basis of households' initial wealth. He concludes, "The most straightforward interpretation of the results of this paper is that in the *Retirement History Survey* any bequest motive is not an important determinant of consumption decisions and wealth holdings" (p. 307).

Hurd (1989) approaches the same data (although limited to single parents) with a structural model. The model allows life-cycle saving and egoistic bequests – although a restriction is that the latter are zero for any household without living children. In the structural model, annuities are available only through social security and pensions. Nonlinear least squares estimates show statistically significant evidence of desired bequests in only one specification. Even then, average desired bequests are less than $1000.

Bernheim (1991) uses the 1975 cross section of the same data set, again focusing on retired households. He uses social security earnings histories to compute social security benefits and lifetime resources (i.e., the present value of lifetime earnings). His model has the following form: let *LTR* be a household's lifetime resources and *SSB* its social security retirement benefit flow. Let $f(LTR)$ give a retired household's planned income flow from annuities. We would expect $f'(\cdot) > 0$. If $f(LTR)$ exceeds *SSB*, a household demands annuities – a demand assumed accommodated in practice through private pensions. If $f(LTR)$ is smaller than *SSB*, social security over-annuitizes the household – a situation which the household can correct through the purchase of term life insurance. The latter situation seems most plausible if the household desires to leave a bequest.

Bernheim sets retirees' demand for life insurance, say, $D^{LI}$, and for private pensions, say, $D^{PP}$, equal to

$$D^{LI} = \zeta \cdot SSB - \omega \cdot LTR + \text{error} \quad \text{and} \quad D^{PP} = \omega \cdot LTR - \zeta \cdot SSB + \text{error},$$

where $\omega = f'(LTR)$. In a sense, the model cannot be strictly consistent with the data: a number of households in the survey have both private pensions and life insurance. Nevertheless, proceeding with the two equations separately, the estimates of $\zeta$ tend to be positive and highly significant, and the estimates of $\omega$ are often positive and significant as well. Bernheim (p. 924) reaches a conclusion opposite to Hurd: "... strong bequest motives are evidently quite common. For close to 30% of households with children, desired bequests substantially exceeded the value of conventional assets".

While both Hurd and Bernheim consider evidence for and against intentional bequests, neither specifically looks for altruistic transfers. Altonji et al. (1992), in contrast, use the *Panel Study of Income Dynamics* (PSID) to confront (7) head-on. The PSID has followed a panel of families for several decades, and as children of the original families have formed their own households, the survey has tried to incorporate them into the sample. The 1985 survey wave which Altonji et al. employ includes several thousand "split-off" households, and in those cases earnings for at least two different generations in the same family line are available.

Altonji et al. use their data as follows. Given altruism in (4), and given a non-binding constraint on transfers, line (5) shows that a parent and child's concurrent consumption will both depend on the sum $y^p + y^d$, although not on $y^p$ or $y^d$ separately. Hence,

$$\ln(c_2^p) - \ln(c^d) = \ln(\rho) - \ln(\lambda^d). \tag{11}$$

The authors in effect regress the left-hand side of Eq. (11) on a constant and $\ln(y^p)$ (or $\ln(y^d)$). With altruism and operative transfers, the coefficient on earnings should be zero. Results (see their Tables 3–4) show the opposite: the coefficient on $\ln(y^d)$ is positive and highly significant. The authors then test a pure life-cycle model. For that case, our solution (3) implies

$$\ln(c_2^p) = \ln\left(\frac{\rho}{1+\rho}\right) + \ln(y^p). \tag{12}$$

Altonji et al. add a $\ln(y^d)$ term to the right-hand side of Eq. (12). While the new term is irrelevant according to the pure life-cycle model, Tables 5 and 6 in Altonji et al. show $\ln(y^d)$ enters with a nonzero coefficient – although the coefficient's magnitude and significance level tend to be less impressive than for the case of $\ln(y^p)$ in Eq. (11). The authors (p. 1196) conclude that "the key prediction of the operative altruism model" is overwhelmingly rejected by the PSID data and that "extended-family member resources have at most a modest effect on marginal household consumption decisions after one has controlled for the fact that extended-family resources help predict a household's own permanent income".

Note that despite the high quality of the PSID data, the PSID does not measure total household consumption. Altonji et al. are therefore forced to use food consumption as a proxy for our $c_2^p$ and $c^d$.[14] Also note that even if households are altruistic, Eq. (11) only holds when transfer constraints do not bind. If constraints bind for a portion of the sample, the strong rejections in Altonji et al.'s Tables 3 and 4 are only evidence against universally operative transfers. (The authors do begin to address this issue by regressing Eq. (11) for a sample restricted to parents above median parent-income and children below median child-income – see the fifth row of their Table 3 – and their outcomes are unchanged.)

Laitner and Juster (1993) examine a sample of 1000 retirees in the TIAA-CREF retirement system. The data include 1988 net worth (including private pension equity), a lifetime earnings history, a history of gifts and inheritances received, a question of how well-off the retiree thinks his children will be relative to himself, and questions about the importance (to the retiree) of leaving an estate. Three results are: (i) almost half the sample views leaving an estate as "very/quite important"; (ii) among those who say that leaving an estate is important, a regression of the respondent's net worth on his assessment of his children's well-being relative to his own shows the sign pattern predicted in (7) – while a similar regression for the remainder of the sample reveals a small and (generally) insignificant coefficient on the child-prosperity variable; and (iii) at age 65, retirees who value leaving an estate have net worth about $400 000 (1988 dollars) higher than those who do not. Unlike the PSID or *Retirement History Survey*, the TIAA-CREF sample is almost entirely upper middle class. Even in this group, however, only half seem interested in leaving intentional bequests.

Returning to Hurd's assumption that families without living children would not be altruistic, Laitner and Juster's Table 3.2 provide a breakdown of sentiments on leaving an estate for retirees with and without children: 46% of those with children rate leaving an estate "very" or "quite important"; 23% of those without children answer the same way. Hurd therefore seems vindicated in the sense that leaving an estate is more likely to be important to households with children. On the other hand, households without children may display altruism toward siblings, nieces and nephews, or charities, and in the TIAA-CREF data, inclinations toward leaving an estate are by no means absent for such households.

## 2.5. Conclusion

We can see that bequests are not prima facie evidence of altruism. Conversely, even if altruism is widespread, for many households binding nonnegativity constraints may

---

[14] See, for instance, the discussion in Runkle (1991) and Altonji and Siow (1987).

block its manifestation.

To the extent that altruistic transfers do take place, they have a dual nature: on the one hand, Fig. 1 suggests that they will tend to be quite unequal – and in that sense they will tend to promote inequality between families; on the other hand, within family lines they should smooth consumption – redistributing resources to generations with the highest marginal utilities.

In terms of empirical results, the aggregate magnitude of bequest-motivated saving remains an open question. Deciding whether observed bequests are accidental, egoistic, altruistic, or motivated by exchange (see Section 4) presents difficulties. Indeed, the data requirements for implementing a thorough test of condition (7) are severe. Existing evidence does seem to indicate that among family lines intentional bequests are far from universal. Inter vivos gifts may be more common. They are almost certainly intentional – although whether they are motivated by altruism or exchange remains unclear.

## 3. More sophisticated models with altruism

Section 3 discusses three more sophisticated frameworks with intergenerational altruism: one allows two-sided altruism, the second provides a general equilibrium setup, and the third incorporates investments in human capital. The three sections are independent of one another and may be read in any order.

### 3.1. Two-sided altruism

As in much of the existing literature, the discussion in Section 2 assumes that altruism is one-sided – that parents care about their children but that children do not care about their parents. If altruistic behavior stems from affection, the one-sided paradigm would seem to be overly restrictive. Accordingly, this section proceeds to two-sided altruism, examining several new issues.

The easiest two-sided specification to analyze is the polar one in which parents care as much about their grown children as they do about themselves and likewise children care as strongly about their parents as about themselves.[15] To illustrate, keep the demographic details of (4), but add the possibility of the grown child making a transfer back to the parent. All transfers occur at the start of the second period. Call the parent's transfer, if any, to the child a "bequest", $b^p$. Call the descendant's transfer, if any, to its parent a "gift", using the notation $g^d$. Retain the assumption of an interest rate of 0. Set $\rho = 1$ for simplicity, assuming that the parent and child both have the

---

[15] Bernheim and Stark (1988) would label this the "perfect" altruism case. See also Stark (1989) and Laitner (1992).

objective function $\ln(c_1^p) + \ln(c_2^p) + \ln(c^d)$. Then both the parent and the child will want to solve

$$\max_{c_1^d, c_2^d, b^p, g^d} \left\{ \ln(c_1^p) + \ln(c_2^p) + \ln(c^d) \right\},$$

subject to: $c_1^p + c_2^p + b^p \leq y^p + g^d,$ (13)

$$c^d \leq y^d + b^p - g^d,$$

$$c_1^p \geq 0, \quad c_2^p \geq 0, \quad b^p \geq 0, \quad g^d \geq 0.$$

Finding the solution is not difficult. Define $n^p \equiv b^p - g^d$ as the "net transfer" from the parent household. Substitute it into the objective function and the budget constraint of (13). Noticing that $n^p$ can take either sign, maximization yields

$$c_1^p = c_2^p = c^d = \frac{y^p + y^d}{3}, \quad s_1^p = y^p - \frac{y^p + y^d}{3}. \tag{14}$$

We can easily recover the desired individual transfers:

$$b^p = \begin{cases} 0, & \text{if } n^p < 0 \\ n^p, & \text{if } n^p \geq 0 \end{cases} \quad \text{and} \quad g^d = \begin{cases} -n^p, & \text{if } n^p < 0 \\ 0, & \text{if } n^p \geq 0 \end{cases}.$$

Here the parent and child pool their resources under all circumstances. If the child's earnings are high relative to the parent's earnings, the child shares through a gift (i.e., $g^d > 0$ and $b^p = 0$); if the opposite pattern holds, transfers move from parent to child (i.e., $g^d = 0$ and $b^p > 0$). There is never a conflict: when either party makes a transfer, the amount is exactly what the recipient desires.

The case in which the parent and child care about each other less than about themselves is possibly more realistic, but trickier. Continue to set $\rho = 1$. A seemingly straightforward approach is as follows. Assuming the parent weighs its descendant's flow of utility with $\lambda^p < 1$, let the parent solve, taking $g^d$ as given,

$$\max_{c_1^p, c_2^p, b^p} \left\{ \ln(c_1^p) + \ln(c_2^p) + \lambda^p \cdot \ln(y^d + b^p - g^d) \right\},$$

subject to: $c_1^p + c_2^p + b^p \leq y^p + g^d,$ (15)

$$c_1^p \geq 0, \quad c_2^p \geq 0, \quad b^p \geq 0.$$

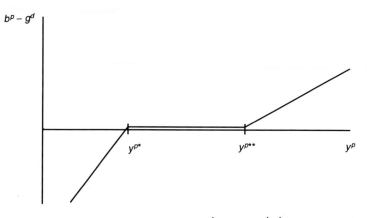

Fig. 2. Nash equilibrium net transfers given $y^d$ ($y^{p*} = 2 \cdot \lambda^d \cdot y^d$ and $y^{p**} = [2/\lambda^p] \cdot y^d$).

Assuming the adult child weighs its parent's utility flow with $\lambda^d < 1$, let the child household solve

$$\max_{g^d \geq 0}\{\lambda^d \cdot [\ln(c_1^p) + \ln(c_2^p)] + \ln(y^d + b^p - g^d)\}, \tag{16}$$

taking $c_1^p$, $c_2^p$, and $b^p$ as given. If the maximizing bequest for the parent is $\overline{b}(g^d, y^p, y^d)$ and the maximizing gift for the child is $\overline{g}(b^p, y^p, y^d)$, a bequest–gift pair simultaneously satisfying

$$b^p = \overline{b}(g^d, y^p, y^d) \quad \text{and} \quad g^d = \overline{g}(b^p, y^p, y^d)$$

constitutes a Nash equilibrium (e.g., Blanchard and Fischer, 1989: p. 109). In words, each household is maximizing given what the other choses to do. Fig. 2 shows a set of possible outcomes: if the child household's earnings are very high relative to the parent's, the child makes a gift (although not as large a gift as the parent would like); if the child's earnings are low relative to the parent, the parent makes a bequest (although not as large a bequest as the child would like); and in the middle, each party would like a transfer from the other, and none is made.

A criticism of the above approach is that the parent takes its child's second-period gift as given when setting its first-period consumption. This would be appropriate if the child could irrevocably commit in period 1 to $\overline{g}^d$. In practice, however, the parent might reason that in the second period all agents will do the best that they can conditional on what transpires in the first (e.g., Bernheim and Stark, 1988; Laitner, 1988; Lindbeck and Weibull, 1988; Bruce and Waldman, 1990). Then the child's gift will depend on the parent's first-period savings behavior, a circumstance the parent may be able to exploit. Specifically, a relatively poor parent might set $c_1^p$ higher than otherwise in order to present itself to its grown child in period 2 destitute (i.e., with a very high marginal utility for money) – thereby extracting an especially large gift. Such strategic behavior induces what Buchanan (1975), Bernheim and Stark (1988) and Bruce and Waldman (1990) call the "Samaritan's dilemma".[16] The new behavior can be consistent with Nash equilibrium, but generally a different equilibrium from the one constructed above – one satisfying the refinement of subgame perfection (e.g., Selten, 1975).

A subgame perfect equilibrium takes into account the sequencing of decisions: in period 1 of the model above, the parent sets its own consumption, $c_1^p$, and saving, $s_1^p$; in period 2, the child and the parent choose their transfers – taking $s_1^p$ and $c_1^p$ as given.[17] To find a subgame perfect equilibrium, work backward. In period 2, think of the parent as solving the remaining portion of (15):

$$\max_{b^p \geq 0} \{\ln(s_1^p + g^d - b^p) + \lambda^p \cdot \ln(y^d + b^p - g^d)\},$$

given $g^d$ and given its own first-period saving, $s_1^p$. Similarly, think of the child as solving the remaining part of (16):

$$\max_{g^d \geq 0} \{\lambda^d \cdot \ln(s_1^p + g^d - b^p) + \ln(y^d + b^p - g^d)\},$$

conditional on $b^p$ and $s_1^p$. Thus, at time 2 each party selects a utility-maximizing transfer conditional on the current behavior of the other and on what happened in the first period. Since the parent weighs its own lifetime utility flow more heavily than its child's, and since the child weighs its own lifetime flow more heavily than its parent's, the parent will desire a positive bequest only when the child desires a zero gift, and the child will desire to make a positive gift only when the parent's desired bequest is 0. Fig. 3 illustrates the possibilities: when $s_1^p > y^d/\lambda^p > y^d$, the parent wants to make a bequest and the child is at a corner solution $g^d = 0$; thus the net transfer from the parent to the child is

$$n^p \equiv b^p - g^d = b^p = s_1^p - \frac{s_1^p + y^d}{1 + \lambda^p},$$

---

[16] More generally, the "Samaritan's dilemma" is said to arise when a benefactor's generosity encourages beneficiaries to be less self sufficient (e.g., Buchanan, 1975).

[17] As in Section 1, we assume here that the parent's earnings, $y^d$, which occur in period 1, and the child's earnings, $y^d$, which occur in period 2, are both known in period 1 to the parent and to the child. If $y^d$ only becomes known in period 2, the analysis in period 1 requires the maximization of expected utility (e.g., Laitner, 1988).

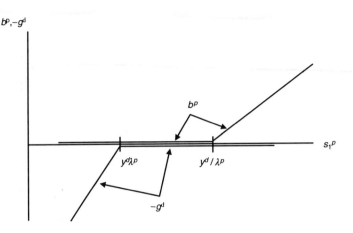

Fig. 3. Second-period choices conditional on $s_1^p$ and $y^d$.

if $s_1^p < \lambda^d \cdot y^d < y^d$, the child wants to make a gift, and the parent is at a corner solution $b^p = 0$; thus the net transfer should be

$$n^p \equiv b^p - g^d = -g^d = -\left[ \lambda^d \cdot \frac{s_1^p + y^d}{1 + \lambda^d} - s_1^p \right]$$

and, if $\lambda^d \cdot y^d < s_1^p < y^d/\lambda^p$, the parent and the child are both at corner solutions; so

$$n^p = b^p - g^d = 0.$$

Call the second-period net-transfer outcome $n^p(s_1^p, y^d)$. The parent's second-period utility will then be

$$v(s_1^p, y^d) \equiv \ln(s_1^p - n^p(s_1^p, y^d)) + \lambda^p \cdot \ln(y^d + n^p(s_1^p, y^d)). \qquad (17)$$

Anticipating $y^d$ and that the second-period outcome will follow Eq. (17), the parent adjusts its first-period saving to solve

$$\max_{s_1^p \geq 0} \{\ln(y^p - s_1^p) + v(s_1^p, y^d)\}.$$

Laitner (1988) studies the subgame perfect solution of such a model. One result is that transfers from parent to child or from child to parent are both possible, as are the zero-transfer outcomes in the middle section of Fig. 3. (In fact, if earning abilities are random samplings from a stationary distribution, twin corner solutions tend to have a long-run inevitability within every family line.) Second, the function $v(\cdot)$ can easily fail to be concave because of the complicated nature of $n^p(s_1^p, y^d)$. Convex regions in

$v(., y^d)$ give parents incentives to invest their first-period savings in lotteries – the analogue of playing a "mixed strategy" in a conventional game. In other words, a young parent foreseeing second-period outcomes resembling the left end of Fig. 3 might rationally seek a risky outlet for its saving $s_1^p$, reasoning that good luck would eliminate dependence on the child's (limited) generosity, while bad luck would be partially offset by a larger gift than otherwise from the child. In practice, this might lead parents to participate in riskier business ventures than they would otherwise find attractive. Or, it might lead to passive risk taking in the form of not buying adequate life insurance and annuities – counting on help from grown children as a backstop.

In a more realistic model the life spans of parents and their adult children would overlap for many periods, of course. Children, as well as parents, would then have opportunities for stategic behavior. For example, children might undertake inefficiently risky ventures under the "cover" of parent-provided, altruistically induced insurance. Or, children might consume large amounts of leisure – reasoning that the less that they earn, the more generous will be their inheritance.

Finally, note that strategic behavior can lead away from Pareto efficiency – with parents saving too little (e.g., Bernheim and Stark, 1988) or taking on entirely unnecessary risks. Laitner (1988) proposes that the US social security system may help out in this regard. The idea is that the system in effect compels saving during working years, via payroll taxes, yet forbids borrowing with future benefits as collateral. Thus, it limits the strategy space for parents, possibly leaving only privately sustainable outcomes close to society's utility possibilities frontier.

As stated, much of the existing literature on altruism assumes single sidedness, with parents caring about their grown children but the children not concerned about their parents. One reason for this assumption is the simpler nature of one-sided models. Another reason may be the suspicion that transfers from parents to children are larger in practice (recall Section 2.4), at least in current times, and hence are of a higher priority for modeling.[18]

## 3.2. General equilibrium

This section expands our altruistic model to a general equilibrium framework and an enduring economy. The reformulation endogenizes the distribution of wealth and the occurrence of binding nonnegativity constraints on interhousehold transfers. For a general equilibrium model with accidental transfers, see, for example, Abel (1985) and Eckstein et al. (1985); for one with egoistic transfers, see, for example, Blinder (1974).

The model follows Laitner (1979b, 1992) and has two key features: (i) each household has an innate earning ability and such abilities differ among households, even among households in the same family line; and, (ii) parents care about the well-being

---

[18] Yet another reason may be the logic of genetics. See, for example, Bergstrom and Stark (1993).

of their descendants. For simplicity, the discussion assumes single-sided altruism (although Laitner (1992) uses two-sided, perfect altruism), and there is neither technological change nor international trade.

Think of each family line as consisting of an endless sequence of two-period-lived households. Let every household have one adult and one offspring. Generations in a family line overlap for one period, a child reaching maturity and forming its own household as its parent begins old age. A household supplies $\mu$ "effective" units of labor in youth and 0 in old age. Different households can have different $\mu$'s, reflecting Nature's idiosyncrasies. The wage per "effective labor unit" is $w$, the interest rate is $r$, and we restrict our attention to steady states in which both $w$ and $r$ are independent of time. We must keep track of transfers received as well as those given.

An adult household born at date $j$, having earning ability $\mu_j$, receiving (at the start of its first period) a transfer of $t_{j-1}$ from its parent, and making (at the start of its second period) a transfer of $t_j$ to its adult child, gains utility $U(t_{j-1}, t_j, \mu_j, r, w)$ from its lifetime consumption:

$$U(t_{j-1}, t_j, \mu_j, r, w) \equiv \max_{c_j^1, c_j^2 \geq 0} \{\ln(c_j^1) + \rho \cdot \ln(c_j^2)\},$$

(18)

$$\text{subject to: } c_j^1 + \frac{c_j^2}{1+r} + \frac{t_j}{1+r} \leq w \cdot \mu_j + t_{j-1}.$$

A family line has one elderly and one young household alive at each time. Let $\lambda \leq 1$ register the degree of (one-sided) altruism, and assume that a household started at date $i$ wants the transfer it makes, and the transfers of all of its descendants, to solve

$$\max_{t_j \geq 0} \left\{ \sum_{j=1}^{\infty} \lambda^j \cdot U(t_{j-1}, t_j, \mu_j, r, w) \right\}.$$

(19)

In other words, a household derives utility from its own lifetime consumption and also from the consumption of all of its future descendants, with geometrically declining weights.[19]

Let every household's $\mu$ be an independent draw from a random variable $\tilde{\mu}$ having a fixed, exogenous distribution.[20] Then if a family line solves (19), the utility maximizing transfer for a household at date $j$ will be a function, say, $\bar{t}(\ )$, of the house-

---

[19] Extending the criterion into the future in this way – as opposed to sticking with the two-generation utility function of (4) – actually provides the simplification of avoiding time consistency problems which would otherwise tend to emerge in an enduring economy.

[20] In practice, of course, a child's earning ability is correlated with its parent's – see, for example, Solon (1992) and Zimmerman (1992). Becker and Tomes (1979) and Ioannides (1986), for example, study intergenerational transfer models with such correlations.

hold's current financial resources and of the factor prices that it faces (e.g., Laitner, 1979b, 1992; Stokey and Lucas, 1989):

$$t_j = \bar{t}(t_{j-1}, \mu_j, r, w). \tag{20}$$

Returning to corresponding lifetime allocations, (18) and (20) determine a function $\bar{s}(\cdot)$ giving the same household's utility-maximizing first-period-of-adulthood saving $s_j$ (i.e., the wealth it desires to carry from youth to retirement):

$$s_j = \bar{s}(t_{j-1}, \mu_j, r, w). \tag{21}$$

Eq. (20) determines a Markov transition rule for private transfers between generations: the probability that a household receiving transfer $t_{j-1}$ choses to leave a transfer $t_j$ falling in interval $T_j$ is

$$\Pr\{\tilde{\mu} : \bar{t}(t_{j-1}, \tilde{\mu}, r, w) \in T_j\}. \tag{22}$$

Laitner (1979b, 1992) generates a steady-state equilibrium with the following steps. Let $N$ be the number of family lines – assumed to be unchanging, with reproduction just covering replacement; let $K$ be the aggregate capital stock; and let $k$ be the ratio of capital to "effective" labor. With an aggregate production function and competitive factor pricing, a value of $k$, say, $k^*$, determines wage and interest rates. Laitner shows that a unique stationary distribution of transfers follows from Eq. (22) – hence a unique stationary distribution of private wealth from Eq. (21). The law of large numbers allows us to treat average wealth as nonrandom. In a closed economy this average wealth must equal the amount of capital per household, $\sum_{x=1}^{N} s_x/N$, where the index $x$ covers households currently alive. The corresponding economywide ratio of capital-to-"effective" labor is

$$\frac{\sum\limits_{x=1}^{N} s_x}{\sum\limits_{x=1}^{N} \mu_x} = \frac{\sum\limits_{x=1}^{N} s_x / N}{\sum\limits_{x=1}^{N} \mu_x / N}. \tag{23}$$

The denominator of (23) is nonrandom by the law of large numbers. Varying $k^*$ until it equals the ratio in (23), we have a steady-state general equilibrium.

Most of the existing general equilibrium literature divides into two polar cases. One has models with just life-cycle saving – corresponding to $\lambda = 0$ in (19) – with no altruism and no intergenerational transfers. Examples include Diamond (1965), Tobin (1967) and Auerbach and Kotlikoff (1987). The second maintains $\lambda > 0$ but eliminates the randomness of $\tilde{\mu}$. This is the "representative agent" model of Ramsey (1928), Barro (1974) and many others (see Blanchard and Fischer, 1989: Ch. 2). With no exogenous randomness, the steady-state equilibrium of a representative agent model tends to preserve indefinitely the initially given distribution of wealth among family lines. Laitner (1992: Fig. 2) relates outcomes for formulations with and without heterogeneous earning abilities to corresponding differences in equilibrium interest rates.

Returning to the framework of this section, one question of interest is whether the model can reach a steady-state equilibrium at per capita wealth levels broadly similar to US data – after all, Section 2.4 suggested that the pure life-cycle model had difficulties in this regard. Laitner (1992) presents several simulations. In the simulations, adult life spans are 52 years; the distribution of $\tilde{\mu}$ is set from Census data; the patterns of lifetime earnings and of social security taxes and benefits are empirically based, as are the costs of raising minor children; there are personal income taxes on wages and on interest income; and, altruism is two-sided but "perfect" (recall Section 3.1).[21] The time of death is certain. With $\lambda$ set to 0, the model condenses to a pure life-cycle framework with no intergenerational transfers, and simulations fail to yield a long-term equilibrium with realistic interest rates.[22] Indeed, household wealth accumulations seem on average only about one-third as large as observable levels. In contrast, with $\lambda = \rho$ – the altruistic case in which parents, in effect, care as much about their grown children as about themselves – the simulations always attain a steady-state equilibrium with realistic average private wealth accumulations and aftertax interest rates of 2–4.5% per annum. The study interprets the simulations as attributing 57–67% of overall wealth accumulation to saving motivated by intergenerational altruism.

In the same vein, data suggest that households' savings are less equal than households' consumption (e.g., Avery, 1991; Carroll and Summers, 1991; Hubbard et al., 1994). The general equilibrium model with altruism and idiosyncratic earning abilities predicts just such an outcome and hence may provide part of the explanation. In the model, because of intergenerational transfers, the highest earners in any cross section may be observed saving the most, causing their wealth to build more than proportionately higher than other households'; low earners tend to be at corner solutions with regard to making transfers – so incentives to build estates may not operate at all for them.

The general equilibrium model can address the question of what fraction of households will have binding transfer constraints. Section 1.3 shows that binding constraints block intertemporal neutrality results for public policy. More generally, during periods with a binding transfer constraint, a household, even if it has altruistic preferences, is entirely preoccupied with life-cycle concerns. Laitner (1979b, 1992) shows that altruistic behavior and uncertainty about $\mu$ leads to lower steady-state interest rates than

---

[21] In the results, transfers from children to their parents tend to be small, however.

[22] The simulations consider variants of the model with and without non-negativity constraints on each family's net worth at every age.

would otherwise prevail, and this, in turn, requires (i) that some households in any cross section have inoperative intergenerational transfers and (ii) that over long enough time periods, inoperative transfers emerge in every family line. In other words, exceptional earning abilities tend to stimulate positive intergenerational transfers, through which the lucky household shares with its descendants; however, links between generations in any given family line are broken at intervals, as bad luck inevitably emerges. The simulations reported in Laitner (1992: Table II) show 30–40% of all households facing binding transfer constraints at least once in their lives. Had the model assumed a lower degree of altruism the fraction would have been even larger.

A third question is what difference intergenerational transfers make to the equality of economic circumstances among households. Inheritances are frequently maligned as a source of disparity and unfairness (see the references in Menchik (1988) for example). There are varying perspectives, however, from which to view this issue. On the one hand, children who are lucky enough to have well-off parents may be the only ones to receive transfers. On the other, earning abilities seem themselves to have a substantial degree of heritability – see Becker and Tomes (1979), Solon (1992) and Zimmerman (1992) – and the inheritance of an extraordinary earning potential may not be more fair than receipt of a large financial legacy. On the one hand, Fig. 1 suggests that transfers will be nonlinear functions of parental resources, with the nonlinearities leading to a distribution of inheritances in which parental resource disparities are amplified. On the other hand, looking at the preceding generation of households, only the most well-off parents will have made transfers at all, and the amounts transferred will have varied more than proportionately to donor resources. Thus, consumption amounts that parents spent on themselves might, in the end, have been equalized.[23] Put in other words, problems controlling moral hazard prevent the formation of insurance markets for lifetime earnings, so a baby cannot buy an insurance policy protecting him/her against an unfavorable $\mu$. In the altruistic model, family lines step forward to provide private insurance to their members. Intergenerational transfers are the mechanism through which this operates: households with high samplings from $\tilde{\mu}$ make transfers to descendants with average or low realizations. This does not eliminate all consumption and utility differences; nevertheless, to the extent that self-insurance is successful it can alleviate extreme outcomes.

Finally, children not receiving transfers may make inefficiently low investments in their own human capital (e.g., Becker, 1967; Drazen, 1978; Loury, 1981 and others). That, however, may be more a reason to augment private transfers than to fault them.

The model of this section endogenizes the distribution of inheritances. It can be employed, therefore, to study the distribution's features – see, for example, Becker and Tomes (1979), Loury (1981) and Ioannides (1986). In particular, such a frame-

---

[23] Laitner (1979a) shows theoretically in a greatly simplified formulation that the coefficient of variation of the overall distribution of consumption can be reduced by altruistic intergenerational transfers.

work can be employed to study the distributional consequences of various tax policies, as well as their implications for overall saving and for factor prices.

### 3.3. Human capital

Returning to single-sided altruism and a partial equilibrium framework, this section presents a structure which allows several different forms of intergenerational transfer. Human capital investments make an appearance and are seen to have a potentially important role.

Again, we frame our discussion in the context of a specific model. There are households from two generations: parent households, which start at time 1, and (grown) child households, which start at time 2. Each lives three periods and has one adult. At time 1, every parent household has one young child. As before, the young child's consumption needs are miniscule. At time 2 the child, having matured, forms its own household, passing youth and middle age as the parent proceeds through its second and third periods. There are no subsequent generations; the analysis terminates after period 4.

In the first variant, a household inelastically supplies $e_i$ units of labor in its period of life $i = 1,2,3$. Earnings manifest a "life cycle": $e_2$ is higher than $e_1$, perhaps because of on-the-job training and experience, and $e_3$ is small because of retirement – we assume $e_3 = 0$. As before, there is one consumption good, the good has price 1 in each period, and preferences are logarithmic. The wage rate per labor unit is $w$ and the interest rate is $r$, both being time invariant.

A parent has opportunities to make two transfers: an inter vivos gift at the start of middle age, say, $g$, and a "bequest" at the start of old age, say, $b$. Conditional on the gift and bequest which it receives, $G$ and $B$, and those it gives, a household's lifetime utility is $U$:

$$U(g,b,G,B) \equiv \max_{c_1,c_2,c_3} \{\ln(c_1) + \rho \cdot \ln(c_2) + \rho^2 \cdot \ln(c_3)\},$$

$$\text{subject to: } c_1 + \frac{c_2}{1+r} + \frac{c_3}{(1+r)^2} + \frac{g}{1+r} + \frac{b}{(1+r)^2} \leq w \cdot e_1 + \frac{w \cdot e_2}{1+r} + G + \frac{B}{1+r},$$

$$c_1 \geq 0, \quad c_2 \geq 0, \quad c_3 \geq 0, \tag{24}$$

$$w \cdot e_1 + G - c_1 \geq 0,$$

$$[w \cdot e_1 + G - c_1] \cdot (1+r) + [w \cdot e_2 + B - c_2] - g \geq 0.$$

The last two nonnegativity constraints are new. They presuppose that the household can neither consume nor give beyond its own periodic resources – because of bankruptcy laws, financial markets do not allow borrowing without collateral; a household's financial net worth can never slip below zero. If either or both of the new restrictions bind, we say the household is "liquidity constrained".

Without altruism (and we rule out accidental transfers here), one could set all gifts and bequests to zero in (24). That would yield the life-cycle model with nonnegativity restrictions on net worth of Mariger (1986), Hubbard and Judd (1987), Hubbard et al. (1994) and others. A substantial body of literature finds empirical support for binding lifetime liquidity constaints (e.g., Hall and Mishkin, 1982; Mariger, 1986; Zeldes, 1989; Campbell and Mankiw, 1990; Jappelli, 1990). In our formulation, constraints cannot bind in the second period of life because $e_3 = 0$ – a household would never want to leave itself with $c_3 = 0$. Constraints can, however, bind in a household's first period. When liquidity constraints bind on a youthful household, the household will consume all of its current resources, saving nothing. In other words, a constrained household's marginal propensity to consume current resources will be one. This has macroeconomic implications for the amplification and transmission of business-cycle shocks. In terms of welfare, it leaves the household's marginal utility of consumption highest in youth: if $u(c) \equiv \ln(c)$, first-order conditions (the so-called "Euler equations") for a constrained household are

$$u'(c_1) > (1+r) \cdot \rho \cdot u'(c_2) = (1+r)^2 \cdot \rho^2 \cdot u'(c_3). \tag{25}$$

When Eq. (25) holds, taking a dollar from resources in old age and providing $1/(1 + r)^2$ in youth, or taking a dollar from resources in middle age and providing $1/(1 + r)$ in youth, would cause the household to consume more in its first period and would raise its overall utility – despite the fact that the present value of its lifetime resources would be unchanged. Intra-lifetime neutrality therefore fails. In fact, a voting constituency for deficit finance emerges: a young household will be glad to have a government transfer payment even if it is financed with future tax liabilities of the same present value. (Hubbard and Judd (1987) point out, for example, that the US social security system, which taxes households in youth and returns benefits in old age, tends to do exactly the wrong thing in this context, potentially making liquidity problems worse.)

Human capital accumulation can further exacerbate liquidity difficulties. Suppose that "effective" labor supply is an increasing, concave function of human capital investments (i.e., college education) at the onset of maturity: if $H$ is human capital, let

$$e_1 = h^1(\mu, H) \quad \text{and} \quad e_2 = h^2(\mu, H)$$

where $\mu$ registers innate ability. Rephrase (24) accordingly:

$$U(G, B, g, b; \mu) \equiv \max_{c_1, c_2, c_3, H} \{\ln(c_1) + \rho \cdot \ln(c_2) + \rho^2 \cdot \ln(c_3)\},$$

$$\text{subject to: } c_1 + \frac{c_2}{1+r} + \frac{c_3}{(1+r)^2} + \frac{g}{1+r} + \frac{b}{(1+r)^2} + H$$

$$\leq w \cdot h^1(\mu, H) + \frac{w \cdot h^2(\mu, H)}{1+r} + G + \frac{B}{1+r},$$

$$c_1 \geq 0, \quad c_2 \geq 0, \quad c_3 \geq 0, \quad H \geq 0, \tag{24'}$$

$$w \cdot h^1(\mu, H) + G - c_1 - H \geq 0,$$

$$[w \cdot h^1(\mu, H) + G - c_1 - H] \cdot (1+r) + [w \cdot h^2(\mu, H) + B - c_2] - g \geq 0.$$

To preserve the characteristic age profile of earnings, assume

$$h^1(\mu, H) < h^2(\mu, H) \quad \text{for all } \mu, H. \tag{26}$$

Absent altruism, if scholarships and government education loans (not requiring collateral) fully fund human capital, we can separate human investments from consumption, dealing with each alone. Children would then choose human capital satisfying

$$1 = w \cdot \frac{\partial h^1(\mu, H)}{\partial H} + \frac{w}{1+r} \cdot \frac{\partial h^2(\mu, H)}{\partial H}. \tag{27}$$

Fixing $H$ to satisfy this condition, the present value of the marginal return to a 1 dollar investment in human capital is 1. Then (24') collapses to (24). If, on the other hand, investments in education face the same credit market problems as consumption, separation may not be possible: human capital needs then raise chances for a binding liquidity constraint in the first period of life, and the condition for efficient overall investment in human capital is unlikely to hold (e.g., Becker, 1967).

Now add one-sided altruism (e.g., Drazen, 1978; Loury, 1981; Cox, 1990; Galor and Zeira, 1993; Laitner, 1993). Assume the parent generation receives no gift or bequest but may choose to leave $g^p$ and $b^p$; grown children make no transfers themselves (they have been assumed to have no children of their own and they are not altruistic toward their parents). Consider any family line. Suppose the parent wants to maximize

$$\ln(c_1^p) + \rho \cdot \ln(c_2^p) + \rho^2 \cdot \ln(c_3^p) + \lambda^p \cdot [\ln(c_1^d) + \rho \cdot \ln(c_2^d) + \rho^2 \cdot \ln(c_3^d)],$$

subject to its budget and nonnegativity constraints, where $c_i^p$ is the parent's period $i$ consumption, $c_i^d$ is the same for the child, and $\lambda^p$ measures the parent's degree of altruism. Given single-sided altruism, the child household cares only about

$$\ln(c_1^d) + \rho \cdot \ln(c_2^d) + \rho^2 \cdot \ln(c_3^d).$$

Both parent and child have scope for action; either can behave strategically.

An algorithm for generating an equilibrium is as follows. Think about a child facing (24'). In terms of transfers received, the child clearly prefers an inter vivos gift to a bequest of the same present value, the preference being strict if the child household's first liquidity constraint binds. The parent may seem indifferent between a gift and bequest; in our formulation, it is never liquidity constrained in period 2. Setting the parent's bequest to 0 for the moment, perform the maximization in the child's problem conditional on gift $g^p$ from the parent. Call the utility-maximizing choices for the child $\bar{c}_1^d(g^p)$, $\bar{c}_2^d(g^p)$, $\bar{c}_3^d(g^p)$, and $\bar{H}^d(g^p)$. The corresponding criterion value in (24') is $U^d(g^p, 0, 0, 0; \mu)$. It is not difficult to see that the last is concave in $(g^p, b^p)$. Turning to the parent, assume it deduces the child's $U^d(\cdot)$ as above and then itself solves

$$\max_{c_1^p, c_2^p, c_3^p, H^p, g^p} \{\ln(c_1^p) + \rho \cdot \ln(c_2^p) + \rho^2 \cdot \ln(c_3^p) + \lambda^p \cdot U^d(g^p, 0, 0, 0; \mu)\},$$

$$\text{subject to: } c_1 + \frac{c_2}{1+r} + \frac{c_3}{(1+r)^2} + \frac{g^p}{1+r} + H^p$$

$$\leq w \cdot h^1(\mu, H^p) + \frac{w \cdot h^2(\mu, H^p)}{1+r},$$

$$c_1 \geq 0, \quad c_2 \geq 0, \quad c_3 \geq 0, \quad H^p \geq 0, \quad g^p \geq 0, \tag{28}$$

$$w \cdot h^1(\mu, H^p) - c_1 - H^p \geq 0,$$

$$[w \cdot h^1(\mu, H^p) - c_1 - H^p] \cdot (1+r) + [w \cdot h^2(\mu, H^p) - c_2] - g^p \geq 0.$$

Call the (unique) maximizing choices $\bar{c}_1^p$, $\bar{c}_2^p$, $\bar{c}_3^p$, $\bar{g}^p$, and $\bar{H}^p$, and call the corresponding total utility of the parent $\bar{V}$.

The steps so far determine a Nash equilibrium: if the parent household can irrevocably commit to gift $\bar{g}^p$ and bequest 0, the child household will want to select $\bar{c}_1^p(\bar{g}^p)$ and $\bar{H}^d(\bar{g}^p)$; the parent then achieves felicity $\bar{V}$, the highest it can obtain under any circumstances. The condition for efficient human capital investment, (27), will hold if $\bar{g}^d$ is high enough to lift the child's liquidity constraint.

A problem is that this equilibrium may not be sustainable without a technology for guaranteeing the parent's commitment (this issue arises in Bernheim and Stark (1988)). The child and parent have conflicting interests (i.e., the child cares only about itself, while the parent cares about both itself and its child), and although the child is only a beneficiary, it has enough decision possibilities to behave strategically. The Samaritan's dilemma can reappear, this time with the parent being the Samaritan. If, for example, the parent transfers $\bar{g}^p$ in period 2, the child may consume the total sum immediately – presenting itself to the parent in period 3 with no saving and no human capital. At that point, from the parent's perspective $b^p = 0$ may no longer be optimal, and there is nothing to gain by preaching to the child, "I told you that $\overline{g}^p$ was my total transfer – you will get nothing more from me". The child knows the parent's utility function and can see that, words aside, the parent's self-interest now requires a positive bequest – possibly quite large.

As in Bernheim and Stark (1988) the parent might seek to limit the child's power by raising its own consumption in youth and middle age, $c_1^p$ and $c_2^p$, above levels which would otherwise be in its best interest. Or, the parent might be able to obtain total utility $\overline{V}$ with more sophisticated play. Steps for a parent trying to do the latter are: (i) compute $\overline{c}_i^p$, $\overline{H}^p$, and $\overline{g}^p$ as above; (ii) solve for the $\overline{c}_i^d(\overline{g}^p)$ and $\overline{H}^d(g^p)$ which maximize the descendant's problem conditional on $\overline{g}^p$ and nonstrategic play (on the part of the child); (iii) instead of handing $\overline{g}^p$ over in period 2, purchase human capital $\overline{H}^d(\overline{g}^p)$ oneself for the child, make a financial gift in period 2 of only

$$\overline{c}_1^d(\overline{g}^p) - w \cdot h^1(\mu, \overline{H}^d(\overline{g}^p))$$

and hold the rest of one's intended total transfer $\overline{g}^p$ for a bequest in period 3. By exercising direct control in this way, the parent may be able to fashion the original Nash consumption and human capital choices into a subgame perfect equilibrium. Specifically, if the parent's desired aggregate transfer $\overline{g}^p$ is large enough to pay for all of $H_1^d(\overline{g}^p)$ and part of $\overline{c}_1^p(\overline{g}^p)$, steps (i)–(iii) will work.

If $\overline{g}^p$ is not as large as $\overline{H}^d(\overline{g}^p)$, the parent and child may jointly purchase the child's human capital. Then difficulties may emerge: as the parent buys units of $H^d$, the child may withdraw some of its own funds, using them for current consumption. Conceivably the child's second-period-of-life earnings fall so low that it can extract a financial bequest $b^p$.[24]

A number of implications follow. First, we can see that intergenerational transfers within family lines can take several forms – paying for schooling, lifetime gifts, and bequests at death – and that parents will not generally be indifferent among them. On the contrary, a parent will tend to place highest priority on purchases of human capital for its descendants. If its desired total transfer is not exhausted, it will turn next to an inter vivos gift. If it has purchased enough human capital to to satisfy condition (27), and made a financial gift large enough to lift the child's first-period-of-life liquidity constraint, any residual in the total transfer will serve as a bequest. The parent will want to be careful not to part with the last sum prior to its death. Studies such as Tomes (1981) provide some empirical support for this sequence.

---

[24] Another option is for the parent to purchase the full amount of $H^d$ satisfying (27), limiting the child's scope for strategic behavior. If the requisite expenditure exceeds $\overline{H}^d(\overline{g}^p)$, the parent will not be able to secure $\overline{V}$ – but this play conceivably still gives the parent's best payoff among subgame perfect outcomes.

Second, the simpler model of Section 2 implied that intergenerational transfers will heavily depend on parent–child earning comparisons: a parent with very high earnings relative to its child will tend to leave a large bequest, while a child with relatively great earnings may get no inheritance at all. Further, bequests would be "luxury goods", rising more than proportionately with parent resources ceteris paribus. In the more sophisticated model of this section, even a child with a very high relative earning potential may receive a sizable transfer in the form of education and an inter vivos gift – if he/she faces stringent liquidity constraints early in life (recall Section 2.4). The luxury-good character of transfers may be evident only for altruistic bequests at death.

Third, since human capital purchases and gifts have priority, they should be the most prevalent. Only the most prosperous (relative to their children) parents, and the most altruistic, should go as far as to make bequests.

Fourth, consider a family line in which the parent makes a lifetime transfer but not a bequest – in fact desiring $b^p < 0$. According to the analysis above, this would be indicative of a binding liquidity constraint on the child's household in its youth. The parent then has an operative transfer link to the young descendant household but inoperative links thereafter; within the child household, the Euler relation does not hold with equality between youth and middle age. In terms of neutrality, the first-period-of-life child household and the middle and old aged parent are connected – so that redistributions of resources among the three would leave consumption and welfare unchanged. No such connections hold between the parent and middle aged child or between the young and middle aged child, on the other hand, so that Ricardian neutrality on a dynastic time scale fails (see, for instance, Altig and Davis, 1989; Drazen, 1978).

### 3.4. Conclusion

One might expect that altruistic links would promote harmony, or at least unity of purpose, within family lines. Yet, beyond our simplest models that does not necessarily seem correct. With two-sided altruism, parents may act strategically to extract more help from their children than the latter wish to provide. This can lead to Pareto inefficient outcomes. With one-sided altruism and multi-year household overlaps, children may be the ones to act strategically. Parents may respond by withholding their transfers until the end of their lives and by making gifts in kind rather than in the fungible form (i.e., money) which economists would usually advocate as the most useful for recipients.

Section 1's simple formulations can be extended to an enduring economy with endogenous factor prices. Heterogeneity of earning abilities seems realistic and is seen to play an important role in the modeling. The prevalence of binding nonnegativity constraints on interfamily transfers is endogenously determined. Although life-cycle and bequest-motivated theories of saving are sometimes posed as alternatives, they are seen not to be mutually exclusive and may in fact be complementary: altruism can provide an explanation for very high wealth accumulation in the upper segments of the distribution of earnings, and the life-cycle model may explain other saving.


## 4. Transactions cost approach

We interpret a second class of models as falling under the "transactions cost approach" (e.g., Pollak, 1985). The idea is that two or more households, generally in the same family line, sometimes interact outside of conventional market channels, seeking mutual advantage at low cost. As the central core of theory is less settled in this case, we organize our presentation in terms of examples from the literature, and our treatment is briefer.


### 4.1. Production

There may be benefits to be gained from two or more households combining their inputs in home production. If the gains are specific to particular households (say, to relatives), the households may work together or exchange time or services with one another without the intermediation of markets.

Joint production of housing services through shared living arrangements is one example (e.g., Kotlikoff and Morris, 1988; Schwartz et al., 1984; Rosenzweig and Wolpin, 1993). Suppose a parent and grown child have financial resources $y^p$ and $y^d$, respectively, to spend on food and shelter. Home production transforms these resources to a single consumption index for each household, $c^p$ and $c^d$, measured in the same units as $y$. The parent household's utility depends on $c^p$ and on its level of privacy; the child household's utility depends on $c^d$ and on its privacy. In our simple example there is no altruism. If the parent and child live separately, each has a high privacy level, say, one, but $(c^p, c^d)$ possibilities are restricted to the area under the lines ending at the endowment point $E$ in Fig. 4. If the parent and child live together, privacy levels fall, say to $x$, but economies of scale move the consumption frontier for $c^p$ and $c^d$ to curve $AB$ (in the words of Rosenzweig and Wolpin (1993: p. 85), "To the extent that households contain public goods that can be jointly consumed – television, plumbing facilities, a kitchen – providing an existing room or bed is cheaper than paying the rent for another residence"). Given the value of privacy, there may be no point on $AB$ providing each party at least as much utility as at $E$. Indeed, if the parties were unrelated, $x$ might be so low as to assure this. Fig. 5 graphs utility for the parent, $u^p$, and child, $u^d$; $A$, $B$, and $E$ from Fig. 4 map to $A'$, $B'$, and $E'$. If $E'$ is northeast of the $A'B'$ frontier, the model predicts separate living arrangements.

With a parent and child, natural companionability may lead to a fairly high $x$. Then $E'$ may be below $A'B'$ – implying that some $(c^p, c^d)$ allocations with shared living

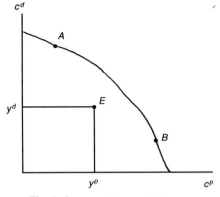

Fig. 4. Consumption possibilities.

benefit both parties.[25] This is the illustrated case. With joint tenancy, Kotlikoff and Morris (1988) assume that Nash bargaining leads to an outcome such as $C'$. Each party ends up better off than at $E'$. Note that altruistic "transfers" are not taking place. Rather, each party attains its endowment utility plus a portion of the surplus from the advantages of shared housing. The "interaction of households" takes the form of a (nonmarket) business arrangement: each supplies inputs of money and time, and both draw an output of housing services.[26]

Bernheim et al. (1985) (see also Cox, 1987) present a second example – if we think of their model as follows. A parent has resources of time and money and, through home production, generates consumption $c^p$. Similarly, the parent's grown child has resources and generates $c^d$. If the two produce separately, the outcome in consumption space is $E$ (see Fig. 6). For simplicity, assume that each party cares only about itself: the parent's utility depends only on $c^p$, and the child's only on $c^d$.

Let there be advantages to combined production: if the parent wants personal services as a portion of $c^p$, suppose the child can provide them better than alternative suppliers – perhaps because the parent enjoys the child's companionship during the provision process. Then if the parent purchases attentions from the child instead of through impersonal markets, the pair may be able to attain consumption frontier $AB$.

We have a bilateral monopoly situation: the parent cannot (by assumption) find a close substitute for the child's services, and the child cannot find a customer willing to pay as much as the parent. To develop an equilibrium, Bernheim et al. (1985) impose a time sequencing on actions: the child provides services, and the parent pays later (not having had a chance to precommit), perhaps with a bequest. Cox (1987) lets the

---

[25] In the literature, privacy seems to be a normal or luxury good: low income relatives are more likely to live together.

[26] Returning to the issues of Section 2.3, there will be no policy neutrality: a government program which redistributes initial resources will move the threat point $E'$, causing the bargaining outcome to change as well.

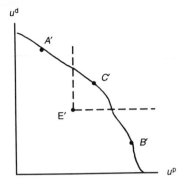

Fig. 5. Utility possibilities.

parent purchase services from the child, paying at the same time the child works – but he allows the parent to make a take-it-or-leave-it offer (thus extracting all of the exchange's surplus). The sequential framework is not interesting without parental altruism. In Cox's case, we would move to $F$ in Fig. 6; the child is indifferent between $E$ and $F$; the parent prefers $F$. Funds will pass from the parent to the child for the purchase of the latter's services. The monetary flows stem from transactions not transfers.

An alternative (see Cox, 1987: p. 517) assumes a Nash bargaining process – as well as simultaneous actions (the child supplying attentions and the parent providing payment). Let $E$ be the threat point – each party refusing to participate unless it can do at least as well as under autarky. Bargaining leads to an outcome to the northeast of $E$, such as $G$. Again, we have a (nonmarket) transaction. The new feature is that instead of the parent usurping all of the gains from joint production, each party captures a share.

Bernheim et al. (1985) find empirical support for the transactions model: their data shows a positive correlation between the size of a parent's potential estate and the quantity of services provided by its offspring (services being measured by numbers of visits and telephone calls). Tomes (1981), on the other hand, using data from interviews of surviving relatives, finds a negative relation between inheritances received and frequency of visits with the decendent. Cox (1987) has data on inter vivos monetary flows between households (see Section 2.4). In regression analysis, a recipient's flow is positively related to his income. That seems to be evidence against the altruistic model, but it supports, or at least fails to contradict, an exchange formulation.

## 4.2. Insurance and credit

Adverse selection and moral hazard are potential troubles for insurance. In view of this, instead of relying on markets, families might turn to insuring their own members. A potential cost is that the pool for sharing risk is then quite small – presumably a

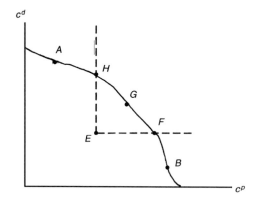

Fig. 6. Parent–child consumption possibilities in Bernheim et al. (1985).

handful of relatives. A benefit is that if participation is mandatory and outsiders are excluded, adverse selection may be controlled. Further, families presumably have good information about their members, providing restraints on moral hazard. One modeling difficulty lies in understanding how families can enforce contracts.

Kotlikoff and Spivak (1981) examine the ability of families to provide their members with substitutes for market annuities (recall Section 2.2) – in other words, insurance against outliving one's resources. For example, a husband and wife can pool their resources, with one inheriting everything when the other dies; the one who lives the longest is aided by the other's estate. Adding a third adult, such as a grown child, broadens the risk sharing. Kotlikoff and Spivak's calculations suggest that a complete absence of annuities leads to a utility loss equivalent to 25–35% of lifetime resources; self-provision by a husband and wife team can cut this 40–50%; adding a child to the insurance pool cuts the original loss by over 70%.

Family provision of annuity protection in the last case might take the following form: the parties agree, perhaps implicitly, that the parents will begin retirement with a substantial amount of wealth; if the parents die quickly, the child will inherit the sum; but if either parent lives beyond some specified age, the sum will be exhausted and the child will step forward with support. Observed bequests might therefore be, in effect, payments from parents dying early made in return for old age support promised for some threshold date. However, there may be problems with enforcement: parents may surreptitiously deplete their wealth, or children may refuse to make promised payments. (See the related discussion in Kotlikoff and Spivak, Section 3.) These difficulties will disappear if parents are altruistic and desire to leave a large estate: they can then retire with more than enough funds to support themselves; bequeath the principal when they die, gaining the altruistic pleasure of making a bequest; and reduce the size of their estate if they live a long time (e.g., Friedman and Warshawsky, 1990). If the parent household controls everything in this case, cheating or strategic behavior is impossible.

Lucas and Stark (1985), Stark and Taylor (1991) and Rosenzweig (1988a,b) consider a different type of insurance: adult children move to different regions but make remittances back to their parents or siblings. The possible benefits are clear, particularly in agriculture: drought may strike one region but spare another, and siblings in the lucky area can provide financial assistance to other family members.

Lucas and Stark (1985) study remittances from migrants in rural Botswana. They find evidence consistent with coinsurance: remittances seem to be larger when recipients are drought striken. Also, parents who have bequeathable wealth are likely to receive larger remittances, and there seem to be some indications of altruism. Finally, more educated migrants seem to make higher remittances – acting as if they were repaying loans. Rosenzweig (1988a,b) reports similar empirical results: he studies rural Indian villages in which sons often work on their father's land but daughters move after marriage. The pattern of marriages suggests intentional spacial diversification, and transfers between households located in different villages but linked through marriage are about 10% as large as farm profits. Households with smaller inherited wealth seem to work harder at establishing these connections. Transfers based on kinship seem preferred to borrowing in financial markets as a way of smoothing consumption, although smaller in absolute terms. (It is also the case that the overall amount of consumption smoothing attained via transfers may be relatively small.)

How are such arrangements enforced? One possibility is that relatives value each others' affections, and they fear that default on a family-line agreement would automatically jeopardize these ties. This fear could ensure that all sides obey an agreement, facilitating implicit contracts which would otherwise be impractical. Another possibility is that an altruistic parent can coordinate risk sharing among its offspring. Consider a father with two sons, $A$ and $B$, in a country with two regions, east and west. In either region a man can derive an agricultural payoff of 2 in good weather and 1 in bad. There is a 50:50 chance of good weather in each region, and outcomes in the two are perfectly negatively correlated. The parent has wealth 1, all of which he desires to bequeath. Left to themselves the sons might settle in the same region, say the one in which they grew up. Family-line resources would end up 3 or 5, with equal ex ante probabilities. If, however, the father told son $A$ to move away, promising to bring his payoff exactly to 2 no matter what, the remaining estate going to $B$, family-line resources could be 4 with probability one. Expected utility would then be higher for each son and for the (altruistic) father. A third possibility is strong two-sided altruism: a fortunate household makes transfers to others in its family line out of empathy; in the future, luck may shift, and the same household may receive help.

In the third instance above, generosity leads to transfers – there is no sense of quid pro quo – and the analysis of Sections 2–3 applies. The second also depends on altruism, having the spirit of Becker's famous "Rotten Kid Theorem". The first could have far-reaching, novel consequences.

Section 3.3 examined cases in which young households might be liquidity constrained – facing a higher marginal utility of consumption early in adulthood than later: (i) earnings tend to rise with experience, households with convex preference orderings prefer level consumption throughout their lives, yet bankruptcy laws make financial institutions reluctant to extend loans without collateral; and (ii) education tends to raise one's wages and hence is most valuable if obtained early in life (when many working years remain), yet markets may be reluctant to offer loans for the purchase of schooling because of the absence of tangible collateral. Businessmen may have trouble securing loans as well: the formal banking sector may be underdeveloped, or problems of adverse selection and moral hazard may make credit prohibitively expensive – especially for small loans. In any of these cases, interfamily exchange may provide benefits and may increase overall efficiency. As above, fear of losing familial affections may enforce loan repayments even when collateral is absent; and/or relatives may, for noneconomic reasons, have good information about one anothers' work habits, reliability, and business success – reducing potential problems of adverse selection and moral hazard.

Consider the following two-period model: at time $t$, a parent has financial savings $s > 0$ and its child could profit from an additional period of schooling. In fact, suppose the child's educational opportunities yield a return surpassing the market rate of interest. Without tangible collateral, the child cannot obtain a market loan. Consumption takes place at time $t + 1$. We can use Fig. 6 again to illustrate the possible outcomes. With no parent-to-child loan, the child cannot finance time-$t$ schooling, and consumption ends up at $E$. With a loan from the parent at $t$, repaid at $t + 1$, consumption on the frontier $AB$ becomes feasible. If the parent extends a loan at the market interest rate – repayment being enforced by the child's fear of losing familial ties – period $(t + 1)$ consumption takes place at $H$. If the parent extracts an interest payment above the market level, an outcome between $H$ and $F$ results. In any case, economic efficiency rises, and the interfamily transactions represent exchange rather than transfers.[27]

## 4.3. Paternalistic preferences and the demonstration effect

The treatment of altruism in Sections 2–3 took the simple form of a parent caring about its child's total consumption level. We skipped over (but see footnote 4) the fact that a child has a vector of consumption goods and that the child may weigh the vector's components in a manner different from its parent. This could lead the parent willingly to pay to influence the child's behavior.

To take an example, suppose a parent has utility $u^p$ depending on its own consumption, $c^p$, and on its grown child's education, $H^d$; i.e., $u^p = u^p(c^p, H^d)$. The parent need not be altruistic at all – it may care about $H^d$ only to the extent that a well-educated child reflects (in society) well on the intelligence, nurturing, and generosity of the

---

[27] See the "implicit contracts" in Ehrlich and Lui (1991), for example.

child's parent (see Pollak, 1988). The child may care only about the consumption its earnings, say, $e(H^d)$, net of schooling costs, $H^d$, make possible:

$$u^d = u^d(c^d) = u^d(e(H^d) - H^d).$$

Without parental intervention, given perfect capital markets the child would choose the economically efficient level of $H^d$. The parent, however, might be willing to subsidize an even higher $H^d$, for the sake of its own social aggrandizement. The subsidy would not be a transfer: the parent would pay the subsidy to obtain a larger $H^d$ than otherwise. (Of course, we again have a bilateral monopoly situation, so a variety of outcomes are possible.)

More generally, a parent might pay subsidies designed to modify its children's behavior and might make altruistic transfers as well. The transfers fall under the analysis of Sections 2–3, but the subsidies do not.

Recent work by Cox and Stark (1993) (see also Bergstrom and Stark, 1993) considers a different process of exchange. Consider the following setup: in stage 1, a household passes its youth and its parent lives through old age; in stage 2, the household passes its old age and its child lives through the first-period of adulthood. The household in question may care only about its own consumption. Nevertheless, it may make a "transfer" to its elderly parent in stage 1 in order to inculcate a sense of responsibility to do likewise in its child. In other words, a household may make a "transfer" to its parent solely to teach its child to make a "transfer" to it later. The authors call this the "demonstration effect."

Cox and Stark examine data from the 1987 *National Survey of Families and Households*. They find evidence that a household which took in its parents is more likely to itself be taken in by its children. When the model applies, "transfers" of time, money, and care constitute (oblique) exchanges rather than gifts.

## 5. Conclusion

In summary, relatives may find advantages to engaging in joint production or purchasing services from one another outside of markets. One implication certainly is that not all intra-household interactions need involve altruism. A second is that we cannot assume that measured monetary flows passing among relatives necessarily constitute "transfers" – as opposed to payments for goods and services or for subsequent repayment with interest. A third is that transactions-cost formulations may be most applicable where participant incomes and sums transacted are low. Finally, although this chapter analyzes altruism and exchange separately, in practice the two may often accompany one another – with altruism reducing enforcement difficulties in interfamily exchanges.

# References

Abel, A. (1985), "Precautionary saving and accidental bequests", American Economic Review 75: 777–791.

Aiyagari, S.R. (1994), "Uninsured idiosyncratic risk and aggregate saving", Quarterly Journal of Economics 109: 659–684.

Altig, D. and S.J. Davis (1989), "Government debt, redistributive fiscal policies and the interaction between borrowing constraints and intergenerational altruism", Journal of Monetary Economics 24: 3–30.

Altonji, J.G. and A. Siow (1987), "Testing the response of consumption to income change with (noisy) panel data", Quarterly Journal of Economics 102: 293–328.

Altonji, J.G., F. Hayashi and L.J. Kotlikoff (1992), "Is the extended family altruisitically linked? Direct tests using micro data", American Economic Review 82: 1177–1198.

Atkinson, A.B. (1971), "Capital taxes, the redistribution of wealth and individual savings", Review of Economic Studies 38: 209–228.

Auerbach, A. and L. Kotlikoff (1987), Dynamic fiscal policy (Cambridge University Press, Cambridge).

Avery, R.B. and A.B. Kennickell (1991), "Household saving in the U.S.", Review of Income and Wealth 37: 409–432.

Barro, R.J. (1974), "Are government bonds net worth?", Journal of Political Economy 82: 1095–1117.

Becker, G.S. (1967), "Human capital and the personal distribution of income: an analytical approach", Woytinsky Lecture (University of Michigan, Ann Arbor, MI).

Becker, G.S. (1974), "A theory of social interactions", Journal of Political Economy 82: 1063–1093.

Becker, G.S. (1991), A treatise on the family (Harvard University Press, Cambridge, MA).

Becker, G.S. and N. Tomes (1976), "Child endowments and the quantity and quality of children", Journal of Political Economy 84: S143–S162.

Becker, G.S. and N. Tomes (1979), "An equilibrium theory of the distribution of income and intergenerational mobility", Journal of Political Economy 87: 1153–1189.

Bergstrom, T.C. and O. Stark (1993), "How altruism can prevail in an evolutionary environment", American Economic Review 83: 149–155.

Bernheim, B.D. (1987), "Ricardian equivalence: an evaluation of theory and evidence", NBER Macroeconomics Annual 2: 263–303.

Bernheim, B.D. (1991), "How strong are bequest motives? evidence based on estimates of the demand for life insurance and annuities", Journal of Political Economy 99: 899–927.

Bernheim, B.D. and K. Bagwell (1988), "Is everything neutral?", Journal of Political Economy 96: 308–338.

Bernheim, B.D. and O. Stark (1988), "Altruism within the family reconsidered: do nice guys finish last?", American Economic Review 78: 1034–1045.

Bernheim, B.D., A. Shleifer and L.H. Summers (1985), "The strategic bequest motive", Journal of Political Economy 93: 1045–1076.

Blanchard, O.J. and S. Fischer (1989), Lectures on macroeconomics (MIT Press, Cambridge, MA).

Blinder, A.B. (1974), Toward an economic theory of income distribution (MIT Press Cambridge, MA).

Bruce, N. and M. Waldman (1990), "The rotten-kid theorem meets the Samaritan's dilemma", Quarterly Journal of Economics 105: 155–167.

Buchanan, J.M. (1975), "The Samaritan's dilemma", in: E.S. Phelps, ed., Altruism, morality and economic theory (Russell Sage Foundation, New York).

Campbell, J.Y. and N.G. Mankiw (1990), "Permanent income, current income and consumption", Journal of Business and Economic Statistics 8: 265–280.

Carroll, C.D. and L.H. Summers (1991), "Consumption growth parallels income growth: some new evidence", in: B.D. Bernheim and J.B. Shoven, eds., National saving and economic performance (University of Chicago Press, Chicago, IL).

Cox, D. (1987), "Motives for private income transfers", Journal of Political Economy 95: 508–546.

Cox, D. (1990), "Intergenerational transfers and liquidity constraints", Quarterly Journal of Economics 105: 187–218.

Cox, D. and G. Jakubson (1996), "The connection between public transfers and private interfamily transfers", Journal of Public Economics, in press.

Cox, D. and F. Raines (1985), "Interfamily transfers and income redistribution", in: M. David and T. Smeeding, eds., Horizontal equity, uncertainty and measures of well-being (University of Chicago Press for NBER, Chicago, IL).

Cox, D. and O. Stark (1993), "Intergenerational transfers and the demonstration effect", Working paper.

Davies, J.B. (1981), "Uncertain lifetime, consumption, and dissaving in retirement", Journal of Political Economy 89: 561–577.

Deaton, A. (1991), Saving and liquidity constraints", Econometrica 59: 1221–1248.

Diamond, P.A. (1965), "National debt in a neoclassical growth model", American Economic Review 55: 1126–1150.

Drazen, A. (1978), "Government debt, human capital and bequests in a life-cycle model", Journal of Political Economy 86: 505–516.

Eckstein, Z., M.S. Eichenbaum and D. Peled (1985), "The distribution of wealth and welfare in the presence of incomplete annuities markets", Quarterly Journal of Economics 100: 789–806.

Ehrlich, I. and F.T. Lui (1991), "Intergenerational trade, longevity and economic growth", Journal of Political Economy 99: 1029–1059.

Evans, M.K. (1969), Macroeconomic activity (Harper and Row, New York).

Feldstein, M. (1988), "The effects of fiscal policies when incomes are uncertain: a contradiction of Ricardian equivalence", American Economic Review 78: 14–23.

Friedman, B.M. and M.J. Warshawsky (1990), "The cost of annuities: implications for saving behavior and bequests", Quarterly Journal of Economics 105: 135–154.

Galor, O. and J. Zeira (1993) Distribution and mcroeconomics'', Review of Economic Studies 60: 35–52.

Hall, R.E. and F.S. Mishkin (1982), "The sensitivity of consumption to transitory income: estimates from panel data on households", Econometrica 50: 461–482.

Hori, H. and S. Kanaya (1989), "Utility functional with nonpaternalistic intergenerational altruism", Journal of Economic Theory 49: 241–265.

Hubbard, R.G. and K.L. Judd (1987), "Social security and individual welfare", American Economic Review 77: 630–646.

Hubbard, R.G., J. Skinner and S.P. Zeldes (1994), "The importance of precautionary motives in explaining individual and aggregate saving", Carnegie-Rochester Conference Series on Public Policy 40: 59–125.

Hurd, M.D. (1987), "Savings of the elderly and desired bequests", American Economic Review 77: 298–312.

Hurd, M.D. (1989), "Mortality risk and bequests", Econometrica 57: 779–814.

Ioannides, Y.M. (1986), "Heritability of ability, intergenerational transfers and the distribution of wealth", International Economic Review 27: 611–624.

Jappelli, T. (1990), "Who is credit constrained in the U.S. economy", Quarterly Journal of Economics 105: 219–234.

Kimball, M.S. (1987), "Making sense of two-sided altruism", Journal of Monetary Economics 20: 301–326.

Kotlikoff, L.J. (1988), "Intergenerational transfers and savings", Journal of Economic Perspectives 2: 41–58.

Kotlikoff, L.J. (1989), What determines savings? (MIT Press, Cambridge, MA).

Kotlikoff, L.J. and J. Morris (1988), "Why don't the elderly live with their children?", Working paper no. 2734 (NBER, Camdridge, MA).

Kotlikoff, L.J. and A. Spivak (1981), "The family as an incomplete annuities market", Journal of Political Economy 89: 372–391.

Kotlikoff, L.J. and L.H. Summers (1981), "The role of intergenerational transfers in aggregate capital accumulation", Journal of Political Economy 89: 706–732.

Kotlikoff, L.J., A. Razin and R.W. Rosenthal (1990), "A strategic altruism model in which Ricardian equivalence does not hold", Economic Journal 100: 1261–1268.

Kotlikoff, L.J., J. Shoven and A. Spivak (1986), "The effect of annuity insurance on savings and inequality", Journal of Labor Economics 4: S183–S207.

Kurz, M. (1984), "Capital accumulation and the characteristics of private intergenerational transfers", Economica 51: 1–22.

Laitner, J. (1979a), "Household bequest behavior and the national distribution of wealth", Review of Economic Studies 46: 467–483.

Laitner, J. (1979b), "Bequests, golden-age capital accumulation and government debt", Economica 46: 403–414.

Laitner, J. (1980), "Intergenerational preference differences and optimal national saving", Journal of Economic Theory 22: 56–66.

Laitner, J. (1988), "Bequests, gifts and social security", Review of Economic Studies 55: 275–299.

Laitner, J. (1991), "Modeling marital connections among family lines", Journal of Political Economy 99: 1123–1141.

Laitner, J. (1992), "Random earnings differences, lifetime liquidity constraints and altruistic intergenerational transfers", Journal of Economic Theory 58: 135–170.

Laitner, J. (1993), "Long run growth and human capital", Canadian Journal of Economics 26: 796–814.

Laitner, J. and F.T. Juster (1993), "New evidence on altruism: a study of TIAA-CREF retirees", Discussion paper no. 86 (Institute for Empirical Macroeconomics, Federal Reserve Bank of Minneapolis, Minneapolis, MN).

Lampman, R. and T.M. Smeeding (1983), "Interfamily transfers as alternatives to government transfers to persons", Review of Income and Wealth 29: 45–66.

Lindbeck, A. and J.W. Weibull (1988), "Altruism and time consistency: the economics of fait accompli", Journal of Political Economy 96: 1165–1182.

Loury, G.C. (1981), "Intergenerational transfers and the distribution of earnings", Econometrica 49: 843–867.

Lucas, R.E.B. and O. Stark (1985), "Motivations to remit: evidence from Botswana", Journal of Political Economy 93: 901–918.

Mariger, R. (1986), Consumption behavior and the effects of government fiscal policies (Harvard University Press, Cambridge, MA).

Menchik, P.L. (1980), "Primogeniture, equal sharing and the U.S. distribution of wealth", Quarterly Journal of Economics 94: 299–316.

Menchik, P.L. (1988), "Unequal estate division: is it altruism, reverse bequests, or simply noise?", in: D. Kessler and A. Masson, eds., Modelling the accumulation and distribution of wealth (Clarendon Press, Oxford).

Menchik, P.L. and M. David (1983), "Income distribution, lifetime savings and bequests", American Economic Review 73: 672–690.

Modigliani, F. (1986), "Life cycle, individual thrift and the wealth of nations", American Economic Review 76: 297–313.

Modigliani, F. (1988), "The role of intergenerational transfers and life cycle saving in the accumulation of wealth", Journal of Economic Perspectives 2: 15–40.

Modigliani, F. and R. Brumberg (1954), "Utility analysis and the consumption function: an interpretation of cross-section data", in: K.K. Kurihara, ed., Post Keynesian economics (Rutgers University Press, New Brunswick, NJ).

Phelps, E.S. and R.A. Pollak (1968), "Second-best national savings and game equilibrium growth", Review of Economic Studies 35: 185–200.

Pollak, R.A. (1985), "A transaction cost approach to families and households", Journal of Economic Literature 23: 581–608.

Pollak, R.A. (1988), "Tied transfers and paternalistic preferences", American Economic Review 78: 240–244.

Ramsey, F.P. (1928), "A mathematical theory of saving", Economic Journal 38: 543–559.

Rosenzweig, M. (1988a), "Risk, private information and the family", American Economic Review 78: 245–250.

Rosenzweig, M. (1988b), "Risk, implicit contracts and the family in rural areas of low-income countries", Economic Journal 98: 1148–1170.

Rosenzweig, M. and K.I. Wolpin (1993), "Intergenerational support and the life-cycle incomes of young men and their parents: human capital investments, coresidence and intergenerational financial transfers", Journal of Labor Economics 11: 84–112.

Runkle, D.E. (1991), "Liquidity constraints and the permanent-income hypothesis", Journal of Monetary Economics 27: 73–98.

Samuelson, P.A. (1958), "An exact consumption-loan model of interest with and without the social contrivance of money", Journal of Political Economy 66: 467–482.

Schwartz, S., S. Danziger and E. Smolensky (1984), "The choice of living arrangements by the elderly", in: H.J. Aaron and G. Burtless, eds., Retirement and economic behavior (Brookings Institution, Washington, DC).

Selten, R. (1975), "Reexamination of the perfectness concept for equilibrium points in extensive games", International Journal of Game Theory 4: 25–55.

Solon, G.R. (1992), "Intergenerational income mobility in the United States", American Economic Review 82: 393–408.

Stark, O. (1989), "Altruism and the quality of life", American Economic Review 79: 86–90.

Stark, O. and J.E. Taylor (1991), "Migration incentives, migration types: the role of relative deprivation", Economic Journal 101: 1163–1178.

Stokey, N.L. and R.E. Lucas (1989), Recursive methods in economic dynamics (Harvard University Press, Cambridge, MA).

Tobin, J. (1967), "Life cycle saving and balanced growth", in: W. Fellner, ed., Ten economic studies in the tradition of Irving Fisher (Wiley, New York).

Tomes, N. (1981), "The family, inheritance and the intergenerational transmission of inequality", Journal of Political Economy 89: 928–958.

Weil, P. (1987), "Love thy children: reflections on the Barro debt neutrality theorem", Journal of Monetary Economics 91: 377–391.

Williamson, O.E. (1979), "Transactions–cost economics: the governance of contractual relations'', Journal of Law and Economics 22: 233–262.

Yaari, M.E. (1965), "Uncertain lifetime, life insurance and the theory of the consumer", Review of Economic Studies 32: 137–150.

Zeldes, S. (1989), "Consumption and liquidity constraints: an empirical investigation", Journal of Political Economy 97: 305–346.

Zimmerman, D.J. (1992), "Regression toward mediocrity in economic stature", American Economic Review 82: 409–429.

# PART II

# FERTILITY

*Chapter 6*

# THE COST OF CHILDREN AND THE USE OF DEMOGRAPHIC VARIABLES IN CONSUMER DEMAND

BERNARD M.S. VAN PRAAG

*University of Amsterdam*

and

MARCEL F. WARNAAR*

*National Institute for Family Finance Information, Amsterdam*

## Contents

*The authors are grateful for the hospitality of the Netherlands Institute for the Advancement of Science (NIAD), Wassenaar, when writing this paper.

*Handbook of Population and Family Economics. Edited by M.R. Rosenzweig and O. Stark*
*© Elsevier Science B.V., 1997*

# 1. Introduction

An issue in family economics which is perhaps more debated among noneconomists than among economists themselves is the so-called *cost of children*. As children live in a household there are a lot of joint costs, e.g., for housing, heating, etc. and therefore it is not so easy to say which part of household cost should be attributed to the children. When looking at orphanages or boarding schools we see that in such institutes the cost for feeding and maintenance of orphans and pupils may be determined by accounting methods. A similar method may be applied in the case of slavery, where it was more or less an economic decision whether children should be bred. In the slavery context (Fogel and Engerman, 1974), there was conceptually not much difference with the decision framework used in cattle-breeding. These methods are considered in Section 2 of this chapter.

It would be tempting to utilize these estimates within the family context. However, before doing so we have to ask why we need cost of children estimates. The primary answer is political. In modern (and not so modern) societies it is felt that families with more children need more money to reach a specific welfare level than families with fewer children. Hence, it is thought reasonable that poor families get child support from society. This is realized either through social organizations as the church or more frequently nowadays through family allowances, tax deductions and price subsidies which are family size dependent. That there are strong political forces in favor of those facilities is obvious. Most households have children, will get children or have had children to be cared for, and even the childless singles frequently understand that any society needs young people to replace the old. Given the fact that in most societies it is accepted that households with children should get some accommodation, the question arises how much.

There are endless difficulties here. The first question which arises is what we will call the absolute/relative issue. Sometimes a specific amount per child is specified, say, $1000 for the first child. However, for the poor family this may be adequate, while for the rich family it will be only a tiny fraction of real outlays for the child. This raises the question whether costs are dependent on the family's welfare level, e.g., reflected by household income, and whether it would be socially and politically acceptable that rich families get more for their children than poor families.

The latter is realized when income tax deductions are given, which are percentages of income rather than absolute amounts. Politicians are frequently advocating the second approach where the allowances are set at a level which reflects or is linked to the cost of children as perceived at the subsistence level. This approach raises the question: what is the subsistence level? (See also Section 3.)

Economists are inclined to the relative approach with some refinement, i.e., that the costs of children are not the same at all welfare levels. This is the approach we shall accept as well.

Looking at the household according to the Becker (1981) approach as a production unit with inputs and outputs, the "household costs", i.e., the minimum cost to realize a specific welfare level, are not easily decomposed and attributed to specific household members. We may take a simple per capita average, specify cost shares or we may try to identify the marginal household cost of any additional member. In this survey we are inclined to the marginal approach.

Continuing Becker's metaphor we have to stress that part of the household cost is nonmarket costs. The time-inputs of the parents should have to be evaluated as well as monetary cost components. This is mostly neglected although it gets more importance nowadays in societies where there is a mix between one-earner and two-earner families (see Homan, 1988). Finally it should be mentioned that time spent on child care may reduce the formation of human capital for parents, causing, e.g., a lower female wage when re-entering the labor market.

A child does not only generate household costs but revenues as well. In many underdeveloped economies, in peasant societies with child labor, in rural households, shopkeepers-families and (small) family firms and industries, children are quite wanted as a source of income either in paid child labor or in the family firm or farm as cheap labor. Moreover they will constitute an income source for the parents in the future, when the old may need the support of the young. A second point is the immaterial revenue derived from children. For many couples, children are either an outright joy or at least one of the principal factors which makes their life get sense. In many cultures children are a blessing and childlessness a curse.

These observations demonstrate that outlays on children (in money or in kind) may not be the correct basis on which to base allowances. There is a calculus of cost *and* revenue behind it and in some sense we are only really interested in the *balance*. If that balance is strongly negative for households, we will observe a low fertility, many abortions, infant mortality and even infanticide. In such cases a state may want to subsidize child-rearing in order to maintain the society and the state in the future.

If, however, the balance is positive, there is not much reason to compensate families, unless because polity wants to increase the birth rate still further and/or as a way of a politically desirable income redistribution. There is a tendency observed in some countries that children become a rich man's good, which would suggest that income-dependent family allowances may even increase household income inequality.

A final point which is quite basic is whether children are a product of a parental decision process (*endogenous fertility*) or that they are "just coming like the seasons" (see Nerlove et al., 1987). The answer is not clear-cut. Although even before the modern anticonception techniques were available family planning was practiced, the remarkable fall of the birth rate in the 1970s was caused in large part by the availability on a large scale of means of anticonception and for another part by the development of the economic organization, where the small family firm lost its importance, and for still another part by the fact that good old-age social security programs were started.

It is our view that family planning was much less successful and also much less applied until the 1960s than after that decade. There is a good deal of socio-ethical justification to compensate for family size differences if such differences are coming randomly on families. However, if the number of children is the outcome of a rational planning process, then we do not see much reason for the existence of welfare differences between the small and the big family nor any reason for state income compensation, except from a general population perspective. This point is first observed by Pollak and Wales (1979) and Pollak (1991). It is really fundamental for the whole look on cost of children definitions and compensation policies.

The final conclusion of this viewpoint would be that there will be no welfare differences between households of equal income, their only difference being their number of children. Any differences which are felt are due to random factors, incorrect anticipation of the future cost and revenues caused by children and preference changes after the children have been born. In this chapter we shall not go further into the endogenous fertility issue. If fertility is completely endogenous there is no reason for family equivalence scales, although clearly spending patterns of households with different composition will be different.

A final point to note is that endogenous fertility is connected with a lot of other decision processes in the household, e.g., labor supply and investment decisions. These processes are in their turn linked to perceived costs of children. The effects of the cost of children on these processes lie beyond the scope of this chapter. For an overview of literature on this issue we refer to Browning (1992).

In Section 2 we introduce some basic notions. From Section 3 on, we consider tools suggested by economists to approximate the cost of children, where roughly speaking the methodology will become more and more sophisticated. In Section 4 we look at partial approaches, in Sections 5, 6 and 7 we look at the approach based on complete demand systems. In Section 8 we look at a very different approach, utilizing subjective perceptions of need. In Section 9 conclusions are drawn.


## 2. Basic notions

First let us introduce some economic basic assumptions and notions. Quantities of commodities are denoted by $x_1, \ldots, x_n$ and the commodity vector by $x \in \mathbb{R}^n$. The corresponding prices are $p_1, \ldots, p_n$, shortly denoted by the price vector $p \in \mathbb{R}^n$.

We define $C(u, p, z)$ as the household cost function or expenditure function, that is, the minimum amount of money needed by a household of demographic type $z$ at prices $p$ to reach a specific welfare or utility level $u$.

Let us moreover assume that households of the same type have identical preferences, which implies identical household cost functions. Finally, we assume that the demographic type $z$ cannot be chosen but that it is determined by exogenous factors.

The cost difference between two demographic types $z_1$ and $z_2$ is then $C(u, p, z_1) -$ $C(u, p, z_2)$. More specifically if $z_0$ stands for a childless couple, $z_1$ for a couple with one child, etc., then

$$C(u, p, z_1) - C(u, p, z_0) \tag{2.1}$$

can be identified as the cost of the first child, and so on. In a similar way a demographic equivalence scale may be defined. Let $z_r$ stand for a reference household type, then the ratio

$$I(u, p, z) = C(u, p, z)/C(u, p, z_r) \tag{2.2}$$

is the equivalence scale with respect to the reference household $z_r$.

The central issue of this survey is how we get meaningful estimates of Eqs. (2.1) and (2.2). We shall see that this is far from easy.

The first point which transpires is that under general circumstances we are unable to speak over the cost of an additional child or the equivalence scale. Both depend on the price structure and the utility level we are looking at. Only under restricting assumptions it is possible to say that Eq. (2.1) or Eq. (2.2) do not depend on the welfare level $u$ or the price vector $p$.

## 3. Naive estimates

In this field there are roughly two branches. The first and oldest is that of the rather straightforward calculation of normative budgets. This way is theoretically not sophisticated and even incorrect. However, it is easy to explain to laymen: it has some intuitive plausibility. This method is used a great deal in practice. The second branch is much more "scientific" and hence sophisticated. It is not much used in practice. We start in this section with the first method.

Such methods are based on *normative budgets*. As explained before, each level of expenditure corresponds to one level of well-being $u$. Now the norm may be laid at a subsistence level, or a modest-but-adequate level (Bradshaw and Parker, 1991) or at any other level. Mostly a level of subsistence is defined by letting nutritional experts define a satisfactory diet in terms of calories and so on. This diet is then evaluated at current prices. This is supplemented (equally arbitrarily) by adding normative amounts for clothing, heating, etc. adding up to a specific subsistence level for a household. Another way is to estimate the ratio of food to total expenditures, the food ratio, and to blow up the food cost to the normative budget level. For instance, if the average food share in the population is 1/3 and the subsistence diet for a specific household type is worth $7000, the total subsistence cost level is $21 000 for the specific household. Comparing various household types the marginal increases are the cost of additional children. For examples, see Orshansky (1965) and Townsend (1979).

A second possibility (Bradshaw and Parker, 1991) is to focus on a specific income bracket, say the 50–60% decile, and to take the average expenditure pattern in these deciles differentiated by family size.

In this approach there are two choices to be made. First what is the reference level of well-being? Second, how do we identify families of different household size as being at the same level of welfare?

It is obvious that both questions are settled in an ad hoc and arbitrary way without any scientific basis. This does not imply that these figures are completely of no value. They give the message that households of such and such type with a specific income, say of $20 000 spend *on average* a specific amount on food, shelter, etc. This is very interesting information for similar households who like to know what the average budget is. However, this approach is unable to provide *"the"* cost of children or *"the"* family equivalence scales. A third possibility which is still more naive is just to fix ratios which are considered intuitively plausible. A primary example is the so-called Oxford-scale later on adopted by the OECD and EUROSTAT. This additive scale puts the first adult at one, other adults at 0.7 and children (below 18) at 0.5. Other examples are for example given in Whiteford (1985) and Blokland (1976). In Appendix A we give an overview of various used and estimated scales in the literature.

In economic literature, as is well known, there is something of a "high-church" theory and "low-church" practice. In economic literature the above-described methods are hardly mentioned, because they are scientifically not interesting or considered as naive, arbitrary, etc. This should not obscure the fact however that these "noninteresting" methods are nearly the only ones used in practice. For instance the OECD scale is officially adopted by various national statistical offices, like those of Denmark, Germany, France and the UK.

Such naive scales may be very differentiated. Until recently, in former Yugoslavia there was a more or less official equivalence scale,[1] which differentiates between gender, age and various job types; for instance a miner is 1.5 consumer units, while a professor counts for 0.9 (see Appendix A).

As said already, the role of children in households is ambiguous. On the one hand they require their share of the household income; hence the average consumption level in the household is reduced. On the other hand they may be additional income earners too.[2] This is especially relevant in underdeveloped countries. For instance, Mueller (1976) in a volume *Population and Development* (edited by R.G. Ridner) made quite extensive calculations on the value profile of individuals over lifetime. This was done

---

[1] This Yugoslavian scale was brought to our attention by dr. Alexandra Posarac, Belgrade. According to Eastern European colleagues, such difference scales have been in use for various purposes in the ex-communist countries.

[2] We remind the reader that we do not deal with endogenous fertility behavior in this issue.

by specifying a consumption profile $C$(age) and a production profile $P$(age) both for men and women. Both were specified in relative terms with respect to the peak consumption and production of a male set at one from 15 to 55. The consumption profile is mainly based on food consumption in rural societies and it is assumed that in total consumer expenditures food figures predominantly. Productivity per day and time input are measured by observation in the field. For example Mueller cites a study done in Korea (1930) described by Lee (1936). For 1249 farms efficiency was measured by the area covered per hour in various agricultural activities, where it was found that weeding in a paddy field yielded 34 budo (an area measure) for a male, but only 17 for a female and 14 for a male juvenile between 12 and 18 years. In this way Mueller calculates consumption $C$- and production $P$-profiles over time. In this way it is possible to say that for the period that $C > P$ the individual is on balance a cost, and when $P > C$ he is a productive asset. Then she comes to a most spectacular table in which she gives her main results from which it is derived that males present a cost until 15 years, while females are a negative asset all their life as their productive contribution to the household income (at market prices and in kind) is rather small. This result is partly explained by Mueller, as she says (pp. 127–128): "Needless to say, women perform household chores and may be just as useful as men". Although this accounting method is highly ingenious, its value is limited. With respect to consumption it rests on observations of food subsistence levels, while productivity can be measured more convincingly in this farm context. In the same way Cain (1977) calculated the cost of male children in Bangladesh.

That such methods may be operationalized and would have any value for developed economies is rather doubtful. First with a rather broad variety in life styles and in levels of welfare it is impossible to explain consumption or rather consumption expenditure levels only by age and gender. Given the variety in incomes and earning capacities also the estimation of production profiles seems impossible. Espenshade (1972) also reports on various studies of this type. We also mention Engel (1883) who did the seminal work and Dublin and Lotka (1930).

Next to monetary spendings on children, there are the opportunity costs which are mainly incurred by the housewife in terms of earnings foregone. These opportunity costs can be divided into two parts, following Lindert (1978). First, the earnings lost by not (or less) working during the period of raising a child. A rather straightforward way to account for these costs is taken by Calhoun and Espenshade (1988). They compare the number of hours worked in a paid job for females with various child-bearing patterns. They conclude that white American women in 1980 lost between 1500 and 3000 h per birth, while black women lost only 600 to 1000 h per birth. Evaluating those hours lost by appropriate wages they found that American white women lost about $25 000 per birth and black females about $5000 per birth. See also Espenshade and Calhoun (1986).

The second part of the opportunity costs is the lower wage rate women get when they return to the labor market when the children have grown up. Actually these figures must be interpreted cautiously. Although they do point to a significant loss in money income, we should not forget that this is in most cases "part of the game" of becoming a mother. Working hours outside home are replaced by working for your own child. Actually these hours have a double function: investment from the perspective of the child, caring from the perspective of the mother. Caring may be seen as the satisfaction of a want, although we realize that ex post it is frequently not evaluated that way but rather as a burden. Using the concept of "full income" (Becker, 1981; Gronau, 1991) opportunity costs of the first kind can become nonexistent.

There are signs that opportunity costs of having children are declining in the western world in the last few years. With increasing numbers of women entering the labor market and staying there when having children, it seems that the time spent on children is not so much substituting time spent on market labor, but rather the time spent on leisure. Espenshade and Calhoun (1986) argue that opportunity costs only account for 20% of the total cost of a child.

Finally, we mention the cliometric study by Fogel (1974) on slavery. He estimates consumption and productivity profiles like Mueller as a function of gender and age from historical figures from plantations and the New Orleans slave market.

The methods described above may be termed naive approaches. They look at various costs of consumption which may be attributed to the having of children. They are evaluated and added.

## 4. Traditional approaches

Two approaches with a very long history and some plausibility are the so-called adult-good method and the Engel method. A detailed comparison and evaluation of both methods is given by Deaton and Muellbauer (1986) and an application by Deaton et al. (1989).

The adult-good method has originally been proposed by Rothbarth (1943) and later on by Nicholson (1947, 1976) and by Henderson (1949, 1950). See also Gronau (1991). The basic question is how to compare the welfare levels $u_0, u_1, u_2, \ldots$ of households with zero, one or two children, etc. One needs observable proxies for these welfare levels. The idea proposed by Rothbarth is to single out some spending categories, the consumption of which is exclusively attributable to the adult couple in the household. The traditional categories are adult clothing, tobacco and alcoholic beverages. The intuitive idea is that if the childless household spends an amount $x_A$ on adult goods before the birth of the child and again $x_A$ after child birth, then the household would be at the same welfare level in both situations.

Let us assume the household demand functions for adult goods to be $g_A(x^*, z)$ where $x^*$ stands for total expenditures and $z$ for the demographic type, then the Rothbarth recipe is as follows. Households of type $z_1$ are fully compensated if

$$g_A(x_1, z_1) = g_A(x_0, z_0). \tag{4.1}$$

The amount $x_1 - x_0$ is the income amount needed to maintain the consumption of adult goods at the same level as in the $z_0$ situation. It is identified as "the cost of additional children" or more generally as the cost attributed to moving from $z_0$ to $z_1$.

Although this approach looks rather plausible to some noneconomists, it is an approach which is based on some very dubious assumptions. The first problem is that the parental utility function is identified with the household's utility function. Second it implies that parents do not derive utility through their children's consumption which may be a substitute for part of the adult good consumption. For instance, looking at your children playing may be a substitute for satisfying the need for alcoholic beverages. Obviously it may be also the other way round. It follows, that even if there would exist exclusive adult goods, then it is by no means clear that the consumption level of these goods represents parental utility. A second point is then the near-impossibility to identify the adult goods and to measure the expenditures on them.

Deaton and Muellbauer (1986) argue that compensation according to Rothbarth would imply an under-compensation. They argue that there is a difference between pure adult goods and nonpure adult goods in the sense that for the latter you need more when the family has children than when the couple is childless; they say, quoting Gorman (1976): "A penny bun costs three pence when you have a wife and a child". It follows that pure adult goods would become relatively less expensive, if your number of children increases. Assuming that adult goods are normal goods, it follows that in order to keep the utility level constant one would tend to consume more of adult goods when having children than when you are childless. However, as Deaton and Muellbauer state as well: "It is far from established that the effects of children work this way".

That consumption patterns of adult goods and other goods shift with changes in the demographic composition of the household is obvious. Gronau (1991) looks for the marginal propensity to consume adult clothing (MPC) with respect to income. He finds that the MPC falls from 0.764 to $0.764 - 0.177 = 0.587$ for one child and so on. It is not clear, however, what this finding implies for the cost of children.

The Engel method, originally proposed by Ernst Engel, is another variation on this same theme. Let the food ratio, i.e., expenditure on food divided by total expenditure, stand as a proxy for the welfare level of the household. Let the food share be denoted by $\varphi$ then $\varphi = \varphi(x, z)$. It is an empirically established fact, Engel's law, that the food share falls monotonically with rising income. Hence it is possible to solve the equation $\varphi = \varphi_y(x, z)$ for $x$ yielding a unique solution for $X_\varphi(z)$. Setting $\varphi$ constant at 30%, 25%, etc., we can find the expenditure level $X_{0.30}(z)$, $X_{0.25}(z)$,... needed to reach a specific food share $\varphi$. More or less the same objections may be raised towards this method as towards the adult good method. First it is not clear why the food share would represent the utility level in the sense that families of different compositions would enjoy equal welfare when they have an equal food share. Second it is technically very difficult to define and delineate the expenditure category "food". Does it contain nonalcoholic beverages, alcoholic beverages, meals in restaurants, etc.? As is shown, e.g., by Van

Imhoff and Odink (1992), the outcomes depend very much on the specific definition of food.

As the budget share of any other commodity group than food is first rising and then falling with rising income, another expenditure group can not be used as welfare proxy.

Deaton and Muellbauer (1986) argue that the food share method would lead to overcompensation. This is indeed likely as food spending is the category that varies the most with household size. There are a lot of categories, e.g., heating and housing where one may get a considerable economy of scale effect. Finally, just as with Rothbarth's method it is not clear that food (especially luxury food) is not a substitute for having children and deriving utility from them.

## 5. Equivalence scales and neo-classical demand systems

The basic ingredient in this section is the household cost function or expenditure function $C(p, u)$, standing for the minimum expenditure level to reach a utility level $u$ given prices $p$. It is well known (Shepherd's Lemma) that for a cost minimizing consumer holds:

$$\partial \ln C(p, u)/\partial \ln p_i = w_i, \tag{5.1}$$

where $w_i$ stands for the budget share of the $i$th commodity. Assuming a functional specification for $C(p, u, a)$ where $a$ stands for an unknown parameter vector, we may observe the budget shares $w_i$ per household and this supplies information on the unknown parameters $a$.

Let us assume for the moment we know $C(p, u)$. Then we may derive price indices as

$$P(p, p_r, u) = C(p, u)/C(p_r, u), \tag{5.2}$$

where $p_r$ stands for the reference price level.

In a similar way we may define demographic cost indexes by adding a demographic vector $z$ and looking at the ratio

$$I(p, u, z, z_r) = C(p, u; z)/C(p, u; z_r). \tag{5.3}$$

When doing this we have to remember that a reasonable cost function has to satisfy a number of restrictions. We come back to that later on, but we mention already that if we add a vector $z$, $z$ cannot be introduced in an arbitrary way.

But first let us consider a fundamental problem. In general $P$ and $I$ will depend on the utility level $u$. It follows that indexes will vary with the utility level and this is clearly undesirable as $u$ cannot be observed. Only in the case that $C$ may be factorized as

$$C(p, u) = f(p)g(u) \tag{5.4}$$

it is obvious that the price index is $P(p, p_r) = f(p)/f(p_r)$.

The price to be paid is considerable as it implies that budget shares are constant, irrespective of the level of $u$. That is, rich and poor people have the same spending pattern. Indifference curves are isomorphic; if one has one curve, one may find all others by multiplying the first curve geometrically out of the origin. If the cost function may be factorized in a price and a utility component we call the cost function *homothetic*.

In a similar way we would like to have demographic cost indices that are independent of the utility level $u$. Lewbel (1991) calls this the Independent of Base (IB)-property, while Blackorby and Donaldson (1991) call this the Equivalence Scale Exactness (ESE)-property. It is easy to see that IB is only true if $C(p, u, z)$ may be factorized into two factors, such that in one figures $u$ and in the other $z$. That is IB holds if and only if

$$C(p, u, z) = f(p, u)g(p, z). \tag{5.5}$$

Notice that this situation does not imply homotheticity. The cost index becomes

$$I(p, z) = g(p, z)/g(p, z_r). \tag{5.6}$$

We see that the index depends on demographics *and* on prices. This is intuitively plausible. Suppose the relative prices of toys and baby clothing rise steeply, then this must have different effects on childless couples than on families with small children. However, let us assume that $g(p, z)$ does not depend on $p$ either. In that case we get

$$g(p, z)/g(p, z_r) = m(z) \tag{5.7}$$

and hence

$$C(p, u, z) \equiv m(z)C(p, u, z_r). \tag{5.8}$$

In that case it implies that there is a general family equivalence index $m(z)$. It is this type of demographic index which Prais and Houthakker (1955) called the *family equivalence index*. This is also known as *Engel-type of scaling*. Notice that in cross-section analysis where we may mostly assume no price-variation over households, the equivalence index found will be seemingly of the type $m(z)$. This does not follow from the fact that $p$ does not figure in $I$, but from the empirical fact that there is no price variation in the sample. However, as soon as there is price variation either in time or due to regional differences, this price effect will come out.

The most famous way of including demographic variation up to now is the way which Barten (1964) introduced, viz. by means of commodity-specific indices. Consider, e.g., the quantity of food, $x_1$, to be bought by a household. If the household utility function is $U(x_1, x_2)$, where $x_2$ stands for "other goods", the same quantity of food will give less satisfaction to a large household than to a small one. It follows that $x_1$ for the reference household is equivalent to $x_1 m_1(z)$ for the household of type $z$, where $m_1(z) > 1$ for a household "larger" than the reference household.

Alternatively, this can be written as follows. Let $m(z)$ stand for the vector $(m_1(z), m_2(z), ..., m_n(z))$. As the consumer problem reads

$$\max\ U(x/m(z)),$$

$$\text{sub } p'x = y,$$

(5.9)

we may define the family-equivalent consumption vector $\tilde{x} = x/m(z)$ and write the problem as

$$\max\ U(\tilde{x}),$$

$$\text{sub } \tilde{p}'\tilde{x} = y,$$

(5.10)

where $\tilde{p}_i = p_i^* m_i$ are demographically corrected prices to reflect the fact that a bun of one penny costs three for a family of three. This type of scaling is called *Barten-type of scaling*.

In other words, demographic effects are translated into price changes. Each family faces its own individual prices, where some commodities become relatively more expensive or cheaper if their family composition changes.

Prais and Houthakker (1955) specify Engel curves $f_i(\cdot)$ directly, without invoking a utility function as

$$x_i/m_i(z) = f_i(y/m_0(z)).$$

(5.11)

Here, next to commodity-specific scales $m_i(z)$ a general income scale $m_0(z)$ is introduced. Prais and Houthakker postulate these equations without basing it on a formal utility maximizing model. Their specifications are ad hoc and not consistent with utility-maximization. Muellbauer (1974) explains that in general it is impossible to estimate all these effects. This is due to the adding-up effect. As expenditures $p_i x_i$ add up to income $y$, we have the identity

$$\sum_i p_i x_i = \sum_i p_i m_i(z) f_i(y/m_0(z)) = y. \tag{5.12}$$

First, the equivalence scale $m_0(z)$ is superfluous (see also Deaton and Muellbauer, 1980: p. 198). The cost function with Barten-scaling reads $C(p, u, z) = c(p^*m, u, z_r)$. It follows that $m_0(p, u, z)$ is implicitly defined by the specific scales as

$$m_0(p, u, z) = C(p^*m, u, z_r)/C(p, u, z_r). \tag{5.13}$$

A problem in practice is how to identify the $n$ specific scales if commodity spending adds up to known total expenditure or alternatively budget shares add up to one. It is obvious that only $n - 1$ demands may be estimated independently and that the $n$th demand is just a residual. So we can identify $n - 1$ specific scales, but lack both the $n$th specific scale and the overall scale $m_0$. These two scales cannot be identified by the (one) implicit restriction between them.

Actually the same problem is already there in ordinary demand analysis, as some parameters cannot be estimated due to the adding up criterion. McClements (1977) utilizes a modification of this method, first given by Singh and Nagar (1973) to estimate $m_1,...,m_n, m_0$, where he assumes quadratic Engel curves. Although McClements' results have some status in Great-Britain, there is still doubt about whether these figures are identified. There has been a heated discussion (see Muellbauer, 1979); Bardsley and McRae, 1982; McClements, 1979, 1988) about this issue, but the outcome seems to be negative.

Things become brighter if some commodity scales are fixed a priori. The most plausible way is to fix some adult good scalar at one, say $m_n = 1$. In this way the model may be identified.

Lewbel (1991) in a recent article looks under which conditions it is possible to combine Barten-scaling with the highly desirable IB property. He finds that this would be possible either if $C$ is homothetic, i.e., $C(p, u, z) = f(p, z)g(u)$ or when the Barten-scales satisfy loglinear constraints of the type $\beta \ln m = 0$. Lewbel (1985) and Pollak and Wales (1981) approach the effect of demography on demand in a more general way. Lewbel assumes that the utility depends from total expenditures $y$, prices $p$ and demographic characteristics $z$, and so he writes the indirect utility function $V = V(y, p, z)$. Now he assumes that each household type considers "adjusted" prices and income, say, $p^*$ and $y^*$ and hence its preferences are described by $V^*(y^*, p^*)$. Lewbel stipulates relationships $y^* = f(y, p, z)$ and $p^* = h(p, z)$ which depict how the "real" expenditure level is related to the nominal amount $y$, prices $p$ and household type $z$ and similarly how "real" prices are influenced by $z$.

These functions are called "modifying" functions; $f(\cdot)$ is the income modifier and $h(\cdot)$ the price modifier.

If $V^*(y^*, p^*)$ is an indirect utility function, $C^*(u, p^*) = y^*$ is a cost function. If we substitute $y^* = f(y, p, z)$ and $p^* = h(p, z)$ it follows that $C^*$ may be written

$$C^*(V^*(y^*, p^*), p^*) = C(u, p, z).\tag{5.14}$$

The question is then what are necessary conditions for $f(\cdot)$ and $h(\cdot)$, such that $C$ is a "legitimate" cost function, where a cost function is called legitimate by Lewbel if it is homogeneous of degree one in price, increasing in $u$, at least increasing in one price and concave in prices.

More down-to-earth Pollak and Wales (1981) consider and compare five different methods[3] to incorporate demographic effects on demand systems.

The five methods are:

(1) demographic translating[4]:

$$x_i(p, y) = d_i + \bar{x}_i(p, y - \sum p_j a_j);\tag{5.15}$$

(2) demographic scaling:

$$x_i(p, y) = m\bar{x}_i(p_1 m_1, p_2 m_2, \ldots, p_n m_n, y);\tag{5.16}$$

(3) Gorman specification (see Gorman, 1976):

$$x_i(p, y) = d_i + m_i \bar{x}_i(p_1 m_1, p_2 m_2, \ldots, p_n m_n, y - \sum p_j d_j);\tag{5.17}$$

(4) reverse Gorman specification:

$$x_i(p, y) = m_i(d_i + \bar{x}_i(p_1 m_1, p_2 m_2, \ldots, p_n m_n, y - \sum p_j m_j d_j));\tag{5.18}$$

(5) modified[5] Prais–Houthakker procedure (see Prais and Houthakker, 1955):

$$x_i(p, y) = s_i \bar{x}_i(p, y/s_0);\tag{5.19}$$

where $x_i$ is the new demand equation, $\bar{x}_i$ the original demand equation, $m_i$, $d_i$ and $s_i$ are functions of demographic variables $z$:

$$d_i = d_i(z),\tag{5.20}$$

$$m_i = m_i(z),\tag{5.21}$$

---

[3] Gorman (1976) considers "general linear technologies" which are more general than these five methods. The first four methods are examples of "modifying" functions, the fifth only under restrictions (see Lewbel (1986).

[4] Note that this is not a form of Barten-scaling.

[5] The modification consists of the fact that Prais and Houthakker did not include prices in their specification.

$$s_i = s_i(z). \tag{5.22}$$

The demographic parameters $d$ and $m$ are modelled as linear (or quadratic) functions of demographic variables $z$, e.g.

$$\delta_i(z) = \sum_{r=1}^{R} \delta_{ir} z_r. \tag{5.23}$$

Although all specifications look plausible Pollak and Wales try to make a choice by fitting the various modes to data. They prefer scaling (2) and the modified Prais–Houthakker method to the others, but their econometric evidence is inconclusive, as they stress themselves. However, they are themselves careful – and we support that – not to attach too much absolute value to their results.

## 6. Implementing the complete demand system approach

It is worthwhile considering some empirical work in the complete demand system approach. We notice the work of Muellbauer and Pashardes (1982), the work by Ray (1983, 1986) and the impressive and numerous contributions of Jorgenson and his group, especially Jorgenson et al. (1981) and Jorgenson and Slesnick (1983).

All these authors base themselves on a particular specification of a household cost function $C(u, p, z; \theta)$. As for the cost-minimizing consumer, Shepherd's Lemma says that the budget ratio of the $i$th commodity equals

$$w_i(u, p, z; \theta) = \partial \ln C / \partial \ln p. \tag{6.1}$$

So, we can find an explicit form of the budget shares $w_i$ and from there on we can estimate the parameters $\theta$. Basically this can be done on a cross-section of households where $z$ is varying and $p$ constant and on a time-series where prices vary and $z$ is constant. More fruitful is the combination of a cross-section and time-series, such that both $z$ and $p$ vary.

Although Barten (1964) was the pioneer in this field, there are some problems with the Rotterdam-demand system (see also Theil, 1965; Barten, 1966) which we shall not elaborate (see Phlips (1974) working on unpublished ideas by McFadden). Three of the theoretically consistent demand systems which are presently in use are:
- The Linear Expenditure System (LES) proposed by Stone (1954)
- The Almost Ideal Demand System (AIDS) due to Deaton and Muellbauer (1980b)
- The Translog System due to Christensen et al. (1975)

Ray (1983) considers the LES system and some modifications of it. He poses a general income scale $m_{0h}(z, p, u)$ such that

$$C_h(z, p, u) = m_{0h}(z, p, u)C_r(u, p), \tag{6.2}$$

where $C_r$ stands for the cost function of the reference household and $C_h$ for that of household $h$ of demographic type $z$. The variable $z$ is defined as the number of children. Then he specifies

$$m_0(z, p, u) = \overline{m}_0(z)\phi(z, p, u), \tag{6.3}$$

where $\overline{m}_0$ is the basic family component, while $f$ gives "corrections" for $p$ and $u$.
Then Ray defines

$$\overline{m}_0 = 1 + \rho z, \tag{6.4}$$

$$\varphi(z, p, u) = \varphi(z, p) = \prod_k p_k^{\delta_{kz}}, \tag{6.5}$$

with $\Sigma_k d_k = 0$ to ensure first-degree homogeneity of $C$ in prices.
The cost function itself is specified as

$$C_r(p, u) = \sum_i \sum_j \gamma_{ij} \sqrt{p_i p_j} + u \prod p_k^{\beta_k} \tag{6.6}$$

with $\Sigma\beta_k = 1$ (see also Blundell and Ray, 1982).
Moreover he looks at alternative specifications of $m$ where $m_0$ and $\phi$ are made dependent on $z_1$ and $z_2$, the numbers of children under five and above five respectively. Ray's final results are that $\rho$ is 12%, i.e., that the cost of a child is about 12% of a childless adult couple, and that the cost is significantly and positively related to the price of food. Notice that these costs are not expressed in absolute amounts but in percentages. In Ray (1986) a similar exercise is performed utilizing the cost function of the Almost Ideal Demand System (Deaton and Muellbauer, 1980b). It yields comparable results, except that in the latter case, if we suppose no specific effects, i.e., all $\delta_k = 0$, the general scale indicates that the first child adds about 21% to household costs. We notice that the specific effects are not introduced in the Barten way. Nevertheless, we surmise that their nonsignificance has to do with the identification problem mentioned above. The way in which the general scale is introduced is ingenious and the results are credible. Alessie and Kapteyn (1991) introduce habit formation and interdependent preferences in the AID-system.
A special place must be reserved for the prolific and influential work of Jorgenson and his colleagues (e.g., Slesnick and Lewbel). We follow here Jorgenson and Slesnick (1983). They start from the translog indirect utility function (see Christensen et al., 1975). However, as they employ time-series data and summary statistics they impose the condition of exact aggregation.

Let the individual demand function for a good of household $k$ be $f_k(p, y_k, z_k)$ where $y_k$ stands for income and $z_k$ for a household attribute vector, e.g., demographics), then exact aggregation implies that demand functions are linear in expenditures and attributes, i.e.

$$f_k(p, y_k, z_k) = h_1(p)y_k + h_2(p)z_k + c_k(p). \tag{6.7}$$

Actually this can be weakened by taking functions of attributes, e.g., set

$$f_k(p, y_k, z_k) = h_1(p) \ln y_k + h_2(p)z_k + c_k(p). \tag{6.8}$$

It follows that if average aggregate demand of household $k$ has a share $\pi_k$ in the population and that average demand equals

$$\sum_k p_k f_k = h_1(p)\sum_k p_k z_k + h_2(p)\sum_k p_k z_k + \sum_k p_k c_k(p). \tag{6.9}$$

The attractive point is that average aggregate demand may be predicted on the basis of population moments, e.g., the average of income or log-income and other household attributes. Obviously this is so attractive because you do not have to know the (joint) distribution of household attributes including total expenditures but only the population moments. It is clearly also a strong restriction on preferences which can only be empirically justified by its handiness in practical work.

This aggregation definition implies also similar linearity for the budget shares. It follows that the budget shares have to be of the form

$$w_k = (a_p + B_{pp} \ln p/y_k + B_{pz}z_k)/D(p), \tag{6.10}$$

where $\ln p$ is a vector of log prices and $w_k$ stands for the vector of budget shares. Clearly usual consumer theory prescribes homogeneity in prices, adding up, symmetry and nonnegativity which imply a number of restrictions on the vector $a_p$ and the matrices $B_{pp}$ and $B_{pz}$. The common denominator $D(p)$ is of the form $D = ((1 + B_{yp} \ln p)$.

Specific equivalence scales are introduced in the Barten mode by defining effective commodity prices $p_1 m_1(z_k), \ldots, p_N m_N(z_k)$. However due to the aggregation restrictions the $m(z_k)$ are already implicitly defined as

$$\ln m(z_k) = B_{pp}^{-1} B_{pz} z_k. \tag{6.11}$$

Now the variables to be explained are budget shares per individual household in a cross-section (1972). In order to catch the price effects as well, the observations are extended by aggregate budget shares $w_{58}, \ldots, w_{72}$ taken from a time-series over the period 1958–1972, aggregate expenditure $y = \Sigma y_k$ and the average budget share $w = \Sigma y_k/y^*w_k$.

## 7. The critique by Pollak and Wales (1979)

In 1979, Pollak and Wales raised a rather fundamental[6] critique on the approach via complete demand systems. As we saw in the previous section the complete demand approaches postulates an indirect utility function $V(p, y; z)$ where $z$ stands for the demographic composition. Then the equivalence scale between household types $z_1$ and $z_2$ is found by solving $V(p, y_1; z_1) = V(p, y_2; z_2)$. This method may also be applied on the inverse functions, i.e., the household cost functions. However, Pollak and Wales point to a flaw in this reasoning.

The point is that observations of demand behavior do tell us about utility differences between various (price, income)-combinations for a given household type $z$, but these observations do not tell us anything about utility differences between (price, income, $z$)-combinations. The reason is that differences in buying behavior as a reaction on changes in (price, income) reveal utility differences. The household composition however is fixed under varying (price, income)-combinations. Buying behavior is *conditional* on $z$. Of course things would be different if we could assume that the observed consumers would deal with $z$ *as if it were a commodity*. That is, the demand for children at any moment would depend on $p$, $y$ and the shadow price of children. In that case we would be able to observe indifference curves in the $(x, z)$-space. This would enable us to calculate the shadow price of children. However, in real life households cannot reduce or increase the number of children at will as a reaction on price or income changes. Therefore, we have to conclude that the observation of demand for commodities with household size fixed per household does not inform us on the shadow price of children. It only provides information on how *demand for goods* changes with varying household compositions.

Let us consider it now from another angle. Let us assume that our observations indicate that two-person households and four-person households have the same demand curves $X(p, y)$ and hence the same indifference curves. Would that indicate that the two types would enjoy equal welfare at each $(p, y)$ combination and hence that the cost of reaching a specific welfare level at given prices would be the same for both household types? Again we are ignorant. The reason is that both households may buy the same commodity bundle at given $(p, y)$ and hence see it as their choice, but they may derive different welfare levels of it. A simple example of this would be the utility function

---

[6] Of course, another critique on the use complete demand systems is possible, e.g. the aggregation of various goods into one category, leading to heterogeneous spending categories and probable under-reporting of spendings on alcohol and tobacco. We feel that the most fundamental critique is raised by Pollak and Wales.

$$U(x, z) = u(x) + g(z). \tag{7.1}$$

Maximization of the utility function with respect to $x$ under a fixed budget constraint would yield the same demand *irrespective* of $z$. Nevertheless, if $g(z)$ is not constant in $z$, different household types would derive different utility levels.

In short, household cost variations due to household type differences *cannot* be derived from observing demand for commodities. The same holds if we assume

$$U(x, z) = \phi(u(x, z); vz), \tag{7.2}$$

where $\phi$ is increasing in $u$. In that case maximization in $x$ is tantamount to maximizing $u(x, z)$ with respect to $x$. We will find household-type-dependent demand curves, but equal $u$ does not imply equal $U$. Only under *the condition* (or hypothesis) that

$$U(x, z) = f(u(x, z)) \tag{7.3}$$

will equal indifference curves imply equal utility. It is only under this hypothesis that the methods based on complete demand systems make sense. However, in the framework of ordinary demand analysis this hypothesis is untestable. The function $\phi$ specifies in fact a monotone $z$-dependent transformation of $u$. However, one of the main results of classical demand analysis, as Pareto pointed out, is that $u(x, z)$ can only be identified up to a monotone transformation. Hence from consumer demand figures we cannot find $\phi(., z)$. The upshot of this reasoning is that the results, described in the previous section are invalidated as well. They have only meaning if you accept the hypothesis that utility is not conditioned by $z$. If you do not assume that, it is hard to make any meaning out of the scales derived in Section 6.

Pollak and Wales (1979) and Pollak (1991) go even further in their negation of conventional wisdom. They pose the question whether it is reasonable to assume that households of different composition would be at a different level, when they have the same income, say, $20 000. They distinguish between two regimes, viz., the old-fashioned situation where children are God's will and the modern situation where anticonception techniques are freely available. In the first situation they see a case for differences to be compensated. In the modern situation the fact that couple A has two children and couple B three children under ceteris paribus conditions reflects the fact that given $(p, y)$ A prefers two children and B three children. As B was free to be in A's position, we cannot say that B is worse off than A. The same holds for A. Consequently A and B enjoy equal welfare and there is no reason to compensate B for having more children than A or vice versa.

This logic presupposes that children are available at will, which is certainly not true for each couple. One could even imagine that a couple which stays childless unwantedly, reaches a lower welfare level and *should therefore be monetarily compensated.*

However, this logic also overlooks the fact that the decision to take children implies a long-term decision. Obviously couples plan their children with a specific anticipated cost pattern in mind. It may well be that at the time of conception they underestimate what a grown-up child would cost or that household income and prices have not evolved according to the anticipated pattern.

Then due to anticipation errors different household types may value their welfare level differently although they have the same income and face the same prices. This would indicate that even if we support Pollak and Wales' logic in theory, there may be a case for household equivalence scales. Let us assume, as is mostly done, that more children cost more, then a family equivalence scale would be increasing in family size. Then, we may assume a rather flat scale in the modern regime and a rather steep scale in such countries where anti-conception technology is not easily available. This would be the case for poor countries and/or where education is low and/or where culture or religion is against anti-conception.

In the next section we look at a completely different approach to estimate family equivalence scales, which seems more promising than the methods considered before.

## 8. Subjective scales: the Leyden approach

In the previous section we looked at various scales. The basic problem is to construct a welfare measure $U(y, z)$ which depends on income (or expenditure level) and to compare households of different size, say $z_1$ and $z_2$ and incomes $y_1$ and $y_2$. If two households are at the same welfare level, i.e., $U(y_1, z_1) = U(y_2, z_2)$ then $y_1$ and $y_2$ are equivalent incomes for household type $z_1$ and $z_2$ respectively. The reasoning is sound. The only problem we encountered is that the construction of $U$ as a welfare proxy lacked credibility. On the other hand the demand based approach failed as well, as interhousehold-comparative utility functions could not be constructed from demand behavior data.

In this section we describe a method, initiated by Van Praag (1971) and further developed by Van Praag and Kapteyn (1973), Kapteyn and Van Praag (1976) and Van Praag and Van der Sar (1988) (see also Hagenaars, 1986). As the approach was mainly developed in Leyden, it is also called the Leyden approach. We will call the scales resulting from this approach *subjective scales*, as they are based on subjective reporting of one's own welfare.

In Van Praag (1971) it was suggested that household's (or individual's) welfare as far as derived from income could be measured directly by asking people whether they felt that their own income given their own circumstances could be called *bad, insufficient, sufficient, good*, etc. The research instrument was the so-called Income Evaluation Question (IEQ). It runs as follows:

*Please try to indicate what you consider to be an appropriate amount for each of the following cases. Under our/my conditions I would call a net income per week/ month/annum of*

> about.............. *very bad*
> about.............. *bad*
> about.............. *insufficient*
> about.............. *sufficient*
> about.............. *good*
> about.............. *very good*

*Please underline the period you refer to.*

Notice that six money amounts have to be given, which respond to six verbal labels. The amounts are denoted by $c_1, ..., c_6$ respectively. The respondent is not asked to specify an amount for an "average" household or for a representative household "like your own", but he is pinned down just on his *own* household. Evidently this is not in which we are primarily interested, but at least we know what the reference household of the individual respondent is. Without doing so, every individual would refer to a different "average" household, the characteristics (e.g., income) of which we do not know.

Now, obviously, individuals will quote different answers. Some people are rich and some people are poor. Some people have to support a large household and some a small household. However, when respondent A calls $20 000 per annum a good income while B mentions $30 000, then we shall assume that $20 000 for A is equivalent to $30 000 for B. They assign to it the same evaluative label (see also Van Praag, 1991, 1994a,b; Van der Sar and Van Praag, 1993).

Looking at the variation in the answers it seems obvious to look for some structural explanations. The most obvious explanation is by the following regression equation:

$$\ln(c_i) = \beta_{0i} + \beta_{1i} \ln(fs) + \beta_{2i} \ln(y_c) + \varepsilon_i, \tag{8.1}$$

where $y_c$ stands for current after-tax household income and $fs$ for family size. Estimation of this regression equation has been performed many times (see e.g., Van Praag and Van der Sar, 1988, or Hagenaars, 1986) on samples from the Netherlands and elsewhere. We give here a result for the Netherlands of 1991, based on about 12 000 households.

$$\ln(c_i) = 4.09 + 0.07 \ln(fs) + 0.59 \ln(y_c), \tag{8.2}$$
$$\underset{(84.1)}{} \quad \underset{(20.2)}{} \quad \underset{(124.6)}{}$$

$R^2 = 0.64$   (*t*-values in parentheses).

The value $\beta_{2i}$ has been called the preference drift effect. It reflects how needs drift with rising income. Now since there are many individual estimates of what is $c_i$ (e.g., "good") it is less clear which real income level $y_i$ is "good". That is found by looking at which current income level the own income of the household would be called good by that household. It is found by solving

$$\ln(y_c) = b_{0i} + b_{1i} \ln(fs) + b_{2i} \ln(y_c).$$ (8.3)

The result is

$$\ln(y_i^*) = (b_{0i} + b_{1i} \ln(fs))/(1 - b_{2i}).$$ (8.4)

But then it follows also how the income, evaluated by "good" or more generally by $i$ varies with family size. Its elasticity with respect to family size is

$$\frac{\partial \ln y_i^*}{\partial \ln fs} = \frac{b_{1i}}{1 - b_{2i}}.$$ (8.5)

Setting the reference level at $fs_0$ we find

$$\frac{y_i^*(fs)}{y_i^*(fs_0)} = (fs / fs_0)^{b_{1i}/(1-b_{2i})}$$ (8.6)

as the family equivalence scale for level $i$. For the example above the exponential value would be $0.07/0.41 = 0.17$. In Goedhart et al. (1977) a question similar to the IEQ has been used, which asks only for the minimum income level $y_{min}$ a household would need "to make ends meet". A similar relation was found between $y_{min}$ and $(y, fs)$, yielding a similar equivalence scale.

It is empirically found (see Van Praag and Van der Sar, 1988) that $\beta_{1i}$ falls with increasing $i$ (i.e., at higher welfare levels) but that $\beta_{2i}$ rises. As a result the exponential stays rather constant. There seems to be variation over countries. Podgorski (1991) reports a value of about 0.50 for Poland. In work for EUROSTAT (Van Praag and Flik, 1992), values for Greece and Portugal tended also to 0.50. Smeeding et al. (1990), who make similar calculations on Gallup-poll queries and Van Praag et al. (1987) found for the USA about 0.33 (see also Buhmann et al., 1987). These differences are in line with our hypothesis inspired by Pollak and Wales that the family size elasticity would be higher for less developed countries.

It is not difficult to imagine generalizations of the approach. A first thing is to differentiate children according to age and households according to one- and two-breadwinner families. Other factors may be education, climate and age of the parents, etc. Frequently such factors are introduced by means of dummy variables. Also different functional specifications may be tried. Results in this respect have been reported (see e.g., Van Praag and Flik, 1992; Van Praag et al., 1992). Kapteyn and his group try to model longitudinal effects on panel data (see e.g., Melenberg, 1992).

There are big advantages to this methodology compared to the previous ones. First, it is intuitively very plausible, second the data are cheap and easy to collect. Third, the outcomes are consistent over time and countries. Fourth, it is easy to generalize this type of scale to a multi-dimensional scale, which takes into account regional differences and sociological differences as well. Finally, as these scales are based on directly stated opinions, they approximate feelings on welfare better in our view than the scales found by arbitrary experts' judgements or rather roundabout methods.

A disadvantage, which is shared however by all other scales, is that it is empirically difficult to cover single-parent families. By lack of data it is frequently impossible to find specific scales for single-parent families. Such scales would be especially helpful for social insurance and in establishing the alimony in divorce cases. However, the results indicate that families with two working parents need more per child and that holds even more for the single-parent family.

The scales which come out of this approach are practically always flatter than the OECD scales or other official scales. Our opinion is that "official" scales as the OECD scale are mostly too steep. If scales are used to compare incomes over household types, incomes are made equivalent by dividing by the scales. If scales are too steep, it follows that welfare of large families is underestimated in comparison to that of small families. In the domain of poverty research this is very crucial. Official scales tend to give a biased reflection of the poor population, as singles and small households are under-represented.

The untested hypothesis underlying this line of research is that verbal labels like "good", "bad", etc. have the same emotional meaning to respondents. Although this will not be exactly true, it is the main assumption on which mutual understanding in a language community is based. Up to the moment there is no other instrument available to establish a better communication. We also refer to Van Praag (1991) where the translation issue is discussed and more empirical evidence is given.

In papers before 1988 the analysis was placed in a cardinal utility framework. Translating verbal labels into equally interspaced points on the $(0, 1)$-interval, it was found that $U(y)$, the relation between income levels and these numerical values is well approximated by a lognormal distribution function $\Lambda(y; \mu, \sigma)$ where $\mu$ and $\sigma$ are the average and standard-deviation of the log-responses (Van Praag, 1971, 1993). However, as shown before, we do not need this cardinal framework to derive subjective family equivalence scales.

## 9. Summary and conclusion

In this chapter we considered various methods to get a grip on the elusive concept of the cost of children. We discovered that the seemingly simple concept is not easy to define at all. In short, except at starvation level there does not seem to be a specific cost level which can be identified as the costs.

Traditional estimates start out on defining material needs at a minimum level, which are priced and add up to cost. However the choice of these inputs, especially for nonfood, is arbitrary. The imputation of joint costs and scale effects is an unsolved problem.

The more sophisticated method based on food shares tends to overestimate the cost ratios, because it does not account for fixed costs. The "adult goods" method tends to underestimate for similar reasons. The scales based on demand behavior, estimated on complete-demand systems, seem more hopeful, but Pollak and Wales forcefully argue that demand behavior does not give a valuable result either.

Subjective estimators seem to overcome these difficulties. They are not based on any economic modelling but just on the registration of opinions, where it is postulated that verbal labels have a common meaning for all respondents.

A final point which may be raised is whether the IEQ or questions of that type cover the broadest welfare concept. It is clear that many people derive immaterial welfare from having children. They are ready to trade income for kids. If we embrace that broadest welfare concept, the IEQ-based equivalence scales are incorrect as well, as they focus on a welfare concept which is only based on "what money can buy".

In the future, estimation may become even more difficult as the definition of households tends to become unclear. At the moment it is currently legitimate to distinguish between one- and two-earner households and one- and two-parent households. However, at the moment there is no convincing material available in the literature.

## Appendix A: Official Yugoslav equivalence scale

| Age and occupation | Scale | |
| --- | --- | --- |
| | Male | Female |
| Up to 1 year | 0.30 | 0.30 |
| 2–3 years | 0.40 | 0.40 |
| 4–6 years | 0.50 | 0.50 |
| 7–10 years | 0.75 | 0.70 |
| 11–12 years | 0.83 | 0.80 |
| 13–15 years | 1.00 | 0.82 |
| 16–19 years | 1.20 | 0.83 |
| 20–60 years: | | |
| farmers, fishermen, etc. | 1.25 | 1.00 |
| miners, smelters, woodcutters, shipyard workers, blacksmiths, etc. | 1.50 | 1.00 |
| mechanics, installers, electricians, engine-drivers, technicians, truck-drivers, etc. | 1.00 | 0.83 |

| Age and occupation | Scale | |
| --- | --- | --- |
| | Male | Female |
| officials, clerks, civil-servants, retailers, managers, medical doctors, nurses, engineers, teachers, professors, students, housewives, pensioners, unable to work, etc. | 0.90 | 0.80 |
| 60 years and more: | | |
| farmers, fishermen, forest workers, shipyard workers, blacksmiths, mechanics, installers, electricians, engine drivers, technicians, truck-drivers, etc. | 1.00 | 0.80 |
| officials, clerks, civil-servants, retailers, managers, medical doctors, nurses, engineers, teachers, professors, students, housewives, pensioners, etc. | 0.84 | 0.72 |
| unable to work | 0.70 | 0.65 |

## Appendix B: Overview of various equivalence scales

On the following pages, we give an overview of various used or estimated equivalence scales. First, we give the names of the authors, specification and place and time of the use of the equivalence scale. Second, we give the scales themselves. A childless couple is taken as base. We give the scales for singles (S), couples (C) having a specific number of children (S + 1, C + 3). Where equivalence scales were also split for various ages of the children, the scales in the table were calculated for children of 0, of 3 and 0 and of 6, 3 and 0 respectively. Some scales were not given by the original authors but could be calculated by adding the costs of an additional child. Large parts of this table were taken from Blokland (1976: p. 131) and Whiteford (1985: pp. 106–107).

| No. | Author | Specification | Place | Time |
| --- | --- | --- | --- | --- |
| *Budgetary methods* | | | | |
| 1 | König | | Germany | 1882 |
| 2 | Engel | | Belgium | 1895 |
| 3 | Atwater | | USA | 1895–1896 |
| 4 | Wold | | Germany Austria | 1907–1908 |
| 5 | Bowley et al. | Food | UK | 1915 |
| 6 | | Housing | UK | 1915 |
| 7 | Mun. Bureau of Labor Research | Food | Japan | 1919–1920 |
| 8 | | Clothing | Japan | 1919–1920 |
| 9 | Sydenstricker and King | Food | UK | 1921 |
| 10 | | Total | UK | 1921 |

| No. | Author | Specification | Place | Time |
|-----|--------|---------------|-------|------|
| 11 | Henderson | Head working | USA | 1954 |
| 12 | | Head not working | USA | 1954 |
| 13 | Piachaud | | UK | 1979–1980 |
| 14 | Lovering | | Australia | 1983 |
| 15 | Rowntree | Head working | UK | 1936 |
| 16 | | Head not working | UK | 1936 |
| 17 | Orshansky | | USA | 1965 |
| 18 | Beveridge | | UK | 1942 |
| 19 | Official Yugoslav Equivalence Scale | Yugoslavia | | |
| 20 | Lindert | Low consumption | Mixture of | |
| 21 | | Medium consumption | various scales | |
| | | | | |
| *Proportional methods* | | | | |
| 22 | Seneca and Taussig | Low income, food | USA | 1960 |
| 23 | | High income, food | USA | 1960 |
| 24 | | Low income, necessities | USA | 1960 |
| 25 | | High income, necessities | USA | 1960 |
| 26 | BLS | Food | USA | 1960–1961 |
| 27 | | Savings | USA | 1935–1944 |
| 28 | Nicholson | Food | UK | 1953–1959 |
| 29 | Love and Oja | | Canada | 1959 |
| 30 | Love and Oja | | Canada | 1969 |
| 31 | SWPS/ABS | Overall basic | Australia | 1974–1975 |
| 32 | | Overall detailed | Australia | 1974–1975 |
| 33 | | Head working | Australia | 1974–1975 |
| 34 | Habib and Tawil | Food | Israel | 1968–1969 |
| 35 | | Food/clothing | Israel | 1968–1969 |
| 36 | | Food/clothing/housing | Israel | 1968–1969 |
| 37 | | Low income | Israel | 1968–1969 |
| 38 | | High income | Israel | 1968–1969 |
| 39 | Podder | | Australia | 1966–1968 |
| 40 | Prais and Houthakker | | UK | 1937–1939 |
| 41 | Bureau van Statistiek (Amsterdam Scale) | | Neth. | 1917 |
| 42 | Nicholson | Food | UK | 1965 |
| 43 | Blokland | Food | Neth. | 1935–1936 |
| | | | | |
| *Consumption theory* | | | | |
| 44 | McClements | | UK | 1971–1972 |
| 45 | Blundell and Lewbel | | UK | 1970 |
| 46 | Nicholson | | UK | 1949 |
| 47 | Nicholson | | UK | 1976 |
| 48 | Cramer | | UK | 1953–1954 |
| 49 | A.M. Henderson | | UK | 1937–1938 |
| 50 | Rothbarth | | UK | 1943 |
| 51 | Garganas | | UK | 1971 |
| 52 | Bosch-Domenich | | Spain | 1980–1981 |
| 53 | Muellbauer | Overall | UK | 1975 |
| 54 | | Low income | UK | 1975 |

| No. | Author | Specification | Place | Time |
|---|---|---|---|---|
| 55 | | High income | UK | 1975 |
| 56 | Lazear and Michael | | USA | 1960–1961 |
| 57 | Kakwani | Low income | Australia | 1966–1968 |
| 58 | | High income | Australia | 1966–1968 |
| 59 | ABS/SWBS | Basic scales | Australia | 1974–1975 |
| 60 | | Head working | Australia | 1974–1975 |
| 61 | | Head not working | Australia | 1974–1975 |
| 62 | Van der Gaag and Smolensky | | USA | 1960–1961 |
| 63 | Deaton and Muellbauer | Engel method | Sri Lanka | 1969–1970 |
| 64 | | Engel method | Indonesia | 1978 |
| 65 | | Rothbarth method | Sri Lanka | 1969–1970 |
| 66 | | Rothbarth method | Indonesia | 1978 |
| 67 | Paul | | India | 1970–1971 |
| 68 | Gronau | White families | USA | 1972–1973 |
| 69 | Jorgenson and Slesnick | Urban white families | USA | 1972–1973 |

*Subjective scales*

| No. | Author | Specification | Place | Time |
|---|---|---|---|---|
| 70 | Goedhart et al. | | Neth. | 1975 |
| 71 | Kapteyn and Van Praag | Young family | Neth. | 1971 |
| 72 | | Older family | Neth. | 1971 |

*Other scales*

| No. | Author | Specification | Place | Time |
|---|---|---|---|---|
| 73 | Townsend | Head working | UK | 1968–1969 |
| 74 | | Head not working | UK | 1968–1969 |
| 75 | root (family size) | | | |
| 76 | OECD/Oxford scale | | | |

Overview of various equivalence scales (*continued*)

Household type

| | S | S+1 | S+2 | S+3 | C | C+1 | C+2 | C+3 |
|---|---|---|---|---|---|---|---|---|
| *Budgetary methods* | | | | | | | | |
| 1 | 0.56 | 0.67 | 0.89 | 1.17 | 1.00 | 1.11 | 1.33 | 1.61 |
| 2 | 0.54 | 0.69 | 0.89 | 1.14 | 1.00 | 1.15 | 1.35 | 1.60 |
| 3 | 0.56 | 0.72 | 0.94 | 1.22 | 1.00 | 1.17 | 1.39 | 1.67 |
| 4 | 0.56 | 0.62 | 0.69 | 0.83 | 1.00 | 1.07 | 1.13 | 1.28 |
| 5 | 0.56 | 0.74 | 0.92 | 1.20 | 1.00 | 1.18 | 1.37 | 1.65 |
| 6 | 0.50 | 0.63 | 0.75 | 1.00 | 1.00 | 1.13 | 1.25 | 1.50 |
| 7 | 0.56 | 0.72 | 0.94 | 1.22 | 1.00 | 1.17 | 1.39 | 1.67 |
| 8 | 0.63 | 0.78 | 0.94 | 1.09 | 1.00 | 1.16 | 1.31 | 1.47 |
| 9 | 0.54 | 0.68 | 0.89 | 1.13 | 1.00 | 1.20 | 1.40 | 1.65 |
| 10 | 0.56 | 0.68 | 0.86 | 1.07 | 1.00 | 1.12 | 1.30 | 1.51 |
| 11 | 0.76 | 0.91 | 1.14 | 1.44 | 1.00 | 1.15 | 1.37 | 1.68 |
| 12 | 0.68 | 0.86 | 1.11 | 1.45 | 1.00 | 1.17 | 1.42 | 1.76 |
| 13 | 0.62 | 0.84 | 1.11 | 1.44 | 1.00 | 1.23 | 1.50 | 1.82 |

| | Household type | | | | | | | |
| | S | S+1 | S+2 | S+3 | C | C+1 | C+2 | C+3 |
|---|---|---|---|---|---|---|---|---|
| 14 | 0.60 | 0.78 | 0.93 | 1.12 | 1.00 | 1.12 | 1.28 | 1.47 |
| 15 | 0.81 | 1.01 | 1.11 | 1.18 | 1.00 | 1.20 | 1.30 | 1.37 |
| 16 | 0.63 | 0.90 | 1.03 | 1.09 | 1.00 | 1.27 | 1.40 | 1.46 |
| 17 | 0.69 | 0.85 | 1.17 | 1.41 | 1.00 | 1.15 | 1.48 | 1.72 |
| 18 | 0.59 | 0.83 | 1.07 | 1.31 | 1.00 | 1.24 | 1.48 | 1.72 |
| 19 | 0.56 | 0.72 | 0.94 | 1.22 | 1.00 | 1.17 | 1.39 | 1.67 |
| 20 | 0.56 | 0.62 | 0.69 | 0.83 | 1.00 | 1.07 | 1.13 | 1.28 |
| 21 | 0.56 | 0.73 | 0.91 | 1.20 | 1.00 | 1.18 | 1.36 | 1.64 |
| *Proportional methods* | | | | | | | | |
| 22 | | | | | 1.00 | 1.01 | 1.30 | 1.64 |
| 23 | | | | | 1.00 | 1.29 | 1.48 | 1.56 |
| 24 | | | | | 1.00 | 1.07 | 1.41 | 1.62 |
| 25 | | | | | 1.00 | 1.26 | 1.39 | 1.49 |
| 26 | 0.60 | 0.97 | 1.27 | 1.54 | 1.00 | 1.37 | 1.67 | 1.94 |
| 27 | 0.70 | 0.98 | 1.27 | 1.64 | 1.00 | 1.28 | 1.57 | 1.73 |
| 28 | 0.59 | 0.90 | 1.14 | 1.34 | 1.00 | 1.31 | 1.55 | 1.73 |
| 29 | 0.60 | 1.00 | 1.20 | 1.40 | 1.00 | 1.20 | 1.40 | 1.60 |
| 30 | 0.69 | 1.00 | 1.28 | 1.52 | 1.00 | 1.28 | 1.52 | 1.70 |
| 31 | 0.59 | 1.00 | 1.18 | 1.35 | 1.00 | 1.18 | 1.35 | 1.53 |
| 32 | 0.58 | 1.05 | 1.14 | 1.30 | 1.00 | 1.15 | 1.28 | 1.51 |
| 33 | 0.69 | 1.10 | 1.22 | 1.40 | 1.00 | 1.14 | 1.33 | 1.67 |
| 34 | 0.58 | 1.00 | 1.38 | 1.72 | 1.00 | 1.38 | 1.72 | 2.05 |
| 35 | 0.52 | 1.00 | 1.47 | 1.93 | 1.00 | 1.47 | 1.93 | 2.38 |
| 36 | 0.73 | 1.00 | 1.20 | 1.37 | 1.00 | 1.20 | 1.37 | 1.52 |
| 37 | 0.77 | 1.00 | 1.24 | 1.47 | 1.00 | 1.24 | 1.47 | 1.71 |
| 38 | 0.86 | 1.00 | 1.24 | 1.24 | 1.00 | 1.24 | 1.24 | 1.34 |
| 39 | 0.49 | 0.74 | 0.97 | 1.17 | 1.00 | 1.25 | 1.48 | 1.68 |
| 40 | 0.53 | 0.72 | 0.99 | 1.30 | 1.00 | 1.19 | 1.46 | 1.77 |
| 41 | 0.53 | 0.95 | 1.24 | 1.48 | 1.00 | 1.42 | 1.71 | 1.95 |
| 42 | 0.54 | 0.85 | 0.99 | 1.19 | 1.00 | 1.31 | 1.55 | 1.75 |
| 43 | 0.50 | 0.73 | 0.94 | 1.15 | 1.00 | 1.23 | 1.44 | 1.65 |
| *Consumption theory* | | | | | | | | |
| 44 | 0.53 | 0.62 | 0.80 | 1.01 | 1.00 | 1.09 | 1.27 | 1.48 |
| 45 | | | | | 1.00 | 1.09 | 1.23 | 1.33 |
| 46 | | | | | 1.00 | 1.25 | 1.40 | |
| 47 | 0.64 | 0.77 | 0.89 | 1.00 | 1.00 | 1.13 | 1.25 | 1.36 |
| 48 | | | | | 1.00 | 1.12 | | |
| 49 | | | | | 1.00 | 1.17 | 1.25 | |
| 50 | | | | | 1.00 | 1.15 | 1.20 | |
| 51 | | | | | 1.00 | 1.15 | 1.21 | 1.33 |
| 52 | 0.59 | 0.87 | 1.02 | 1.08 | 1.00 | 1.24 | 1.37 | 1.42 |
| 53 | | | | | 1.00 | 1.15 | 1.30 | 1.44 |
| 54 | | | | | 1.00 | 1.16 | 1.42 | |
| 55 | | | | | 1.00 | 1.00 | 1.11 | |

| | S | S+1 | S+2 | S+3 | C | C+1 | C+2 | C+3 |
|---|---|---|---|---|---|---|---|---|
| | Household type | | | | | | | |
| 56 | 0.94 | 1.15 | 1.33 | 1.53 | 1.00 | 1.21 | 1.39 | 1.59 |
| 57 | 0.60 | 0.81 | 0.98 | 1.08 | 1.00 | 1.21 | 1.38 | 1.48 |
| 58 | 0.61 | 0.81 | 0.98 | 1.07 | 1.00 | 1.20 | 1.37 | 1.46 |
| 59 | 0.67 | 0.92 | 1.07 | 1.05 | 1.00 | 1.11 | 1.20 | 1.31 |
| 60 | 0.71 | 0.82 | 0.86 | 1.04 | 1.00 | 1.11 | 1.17 | 1.33 |
| 61 | 0.59 | 0.87 | 0.86 | 1.17 | 1.00 | 1.13 | 1.20 | 1.38 |
| 62 | 0.74 | 1.09 | | | 1.00 | 1.24 | 1.28 | 1.40 |
| 63 | | | | | 1.00 | 1.41 | 1.77 | |
| 64 | | | | | 1.00 | 1.45 | 1.86 | |
| 65 | | | | | 1.00 | 1.12 | 1.21 | |
| 66 | | | | | 1.00 | 1.10 | 1.16 | |
| 67 | 0.50 | 0.47 | 0.67 | 0.94 | 1.00 | 0.97 | 1.17 | 1.44 |
| 68 | | | | | 1.00 | 1.18 | 1.32 | 1.45 |
| 69 | 0.30 | | | | 1.00 | 1.29 | 1.72 | 1.84 |
| *Subjective scales* | | | | | | | | |
| 70 | 0.81 | 1.00 | 1.13 | 1.24 | 1.00 | 1.13 | 1.24 | 1.32 |
| 71 | | | | | 1.00 | 1.19 | 1.28 | 1.36 |
| 72 | | | | | 1.00 | 1.14 | 1.21 | 1.27 |
| *Other scales* | | | | | | | | |
| 73 | 0.71 | 0.88 | 1.04 | 1.29 | 1.00 | 1.17 | 1.33 | 1.58 |
| 74 | 0.65 | 0.86 | 1.05 | 1.36 | 1.00 | 1.20 | 1.41 | 1.71 |
| 75 | 0.71 | 1.00 | 1.22 | 1.41 | 1.00 | 1.22 | 1.41 | 1.58 |
| 76 | 0.59 | 0.88 | 1.18 | 1.47 | 1.00 | 1.29 | 1.59 | 1.88 |

## References

Alessie, R. and A. Kapteyn (1991), "Habit formation, interdependent preferences and demographic effects in the almost ideal demand system", The Economic Journal 101: 404–419.

Atwater (1896), American food materials, Bulletin 28 (US Department of Agriculture, Washington, DC).

Australian Bureau of Statistics (1981), Equivalence scales: the estimation of equivalence scales for Australia from the 1974/75 and 1975/76 household expenditure surveys (ABS, Belconnen, ACT).

Bardsley, P. and I. McRae (1982), "A test of McClements' method for the estimation of equivalence scales", Journal of Public Economics 17: 119–122.

Barten, A.P. (1964), "Family composition, prices and expenditure patterns", in: P. Hart, G. Mills and J.K. Whitaker, eds., Econometric analysis for national economic planning (Butterworths, London).

Barten, A.P. (1966), Theorie en empirie van een volledig stelsel van vraagvergelijkingen, Ph.D. dissertation (Erasmus University, Rotterdam).

Becker, G.S. (1981), A treatise on the family (Harvard University Press, Cambridge, MA).

Blackorby, C. and D. Donaldson (1991), "Adult-equivalence scales and the economic implementation of interpersonal comparisons of well-being", Discussion paper no. 91-08 (University of British Columbia, Vancouver, BC).

Blokland, J. (1976), Continuous consumer equivalence scales (Martinus Nijhoff, The Hague).

Blundell, R.W. and A. Lewbel (1991), "The information content of equivalence scales", Journal of Econometrics 50: 49–68.

Blundell, R.W. and R. Ray (1982), "A non-separable generalization of the linear expenditure system allowing non-linear Engel curves", Economics Letters 9: 349–354.

Bosch-Domenich, A. (1991), "Economies of scale, location, age, and sex discrimination in household demand", European Economic Review 35: 1589–1595.

Bowley, A.L. and A.R. Barnett-Hurst (1915), Livelihood and poverty (London).

Bradshaw, J. and H. Parker (1991), Summary budget for three families, Working paper no. 12 (Family Budget Unit, York).

Browning, M. (1992), "Children and household economic behaviour," Journal of Economic Literature 30: 1434–1475.

Buhmann, B, L. Rainwater, G. Schmaus and T.M. Smeeding (1988), "Equivalence scales, well-being, inequality, and poverty: sensitivity estimates across ten countries using the Luxembourg income study (LIS) database", Review of Income and Wealth 34: 115–142.

Cain, M. (1977), "The economic activities of children in a village in Bangladesh", Population and Development Review 3: 201–227.

Calhoun, C.A. and T.J. Espenshade (1988), "Childbearing and wives' foregone earnings", Population Studies 42: 5–37.

Christensen, L.R., D.W. Jorgenson and L.J. Lau (1975), "Transcendental logarithmic utility functions", American Economic Review 65: 367–383.

Cramer, J.C. (1979), "Employment trends of young mothers and the opportunity costs of babies in the United States", Demography 16: 177–197.

Deaton, A.S. and J. Muellbauer (1980a), Economics and consumer behavior (Cambridge University Press, Cambridge).

Deaton, A.S. and J. Muellbauer (1980b), "An almost ideal demand system", American Economic Review 70: 312–326.

Deaton, A.S. and J. Muellbauer (1986), "On measuring child costs: with applications to poor countries", Journal of Political Economy 94: 720–745.

Dublin, L.I. and A.J. Lotka (1930), The money value of man (Ronald Press, New York).

Engel, E. (1883), "Der Kostenwerth des Menschen", in: Volkswirtschaftliche Frage, Vol. 27/28.

Engel, E. (1895), "Die Lebenskosten Belgischer Arbeiterfamilien früher und jetzt – ermittelt aus Familienhaushaltrechnungen", Bulletin de l'Institut International de Statistique 9: 1–149.

Espenshade, T.J. (1972), "The price of children and socio-economic theory of fertility", Population Studies 26: 207–221.

Espenshade, T.J. and C.A. Calhoun (1986), "The dollars and cents of parenthood", Journal of Policy Analysis and Management 6: 813–817.

Fogel, R.W. and S.L. Engerman (1974), Time on the cross (Little Brown, Boston, MA).

Garganas, N. (1977), "Family composition, expenditure patterns and equivalence scales for children" in: G.C. Fiegehen, P.S. Lansley and A.D. Smith, eds., Poverty and progress in Britain 1953–1973 (Cambridge University Press, Cambridge).

Goedhart, Th., V. Halberstadt, A. Kapteyn and B.M.S. Van Praag (1977), "The poverty line: concept and measurement", Journal of Human Resources 12, 503–520.

Gorman, W.M. (1976), "Tricks with utility functions," in: M. Artis and R. Nobay, eds., Essays of economic analysis (Cambridge University Press, Cambridge).

Gronau, R. (1991), "The intra family allocation of goods – how to separate the adult from the child", Journal of Labor Economics 9: 207–235.

Habib, J. and Y. Tawil (1974), Equivalence scales for family size: findings from Israeli data (The National Insurance Institute, Bureau of Research and Planning, Jerusalem).

Hagenaars, A.J.M. (1986), The perception of poverty (Elsevier, Amsterdam).

Henderson, A.M. (1949, 1950), "The cost of children", Population Studies 3/4: 130–150, 267–298.

Henderson, R.F. (1975), Commission of inquiry into poverty, first main report (Australian Government Publishing Service, Canberra).

Homan, M.E. (1988), The allocation of time and money in one-earner and two-earner families; an economic analysis, Ph.D. dissertation (Erasmus University, Rotterdam).

Jorgenson, D.W. and D.T. Slesnick (1983), "Individual and social cost-of-living indexes," in: W.E. Diewert and C. Montmarquette, eds., Price level measurement (North-Holland, Ottawa).

Jorgenson, D.W. and D.T. Slesnick (1987), "Aggregate consumer behavior and household equivalence scales", Journal of Business and Economic Statistics 5: 219–232.

Jorgenson, D.W and L.J. Lau and T.M. Stoker (1981), "Aggregate consumer behavior and individual welfare", in: D. Currie, R. Nobay and D. Peel, eds., Macro-economic analysis (Croom-Helm, London).

Kakwani, N. (1980), Income inequality and poverty: methods of estimation and policy applications (Oxford University Press, Oxford).

Kapteyn, A. and B.M.S. Van Praag (1976), "A new approach to the construction of family equivalence scales", European Economic Review 7: 313–335.

König, J. (1882), Prozentische Zusammensetzung und Nahrgeldwert der menschlichen Nahrungsmittel.

Lazear, E.P. and R.T. Michael (1980), "Family size and the distribution of real per capita income", American Economic Review 70: 91–107.

Lewbel, A. (1985), "A unified approach to incorporating demographic or other effects into demand systems", Review of Economic Studies 52: 1–18.

Lewbel, A. (1986), Additive separability and equivalent scales, Econometrica 54: 219–222.

Lewbel, A. (1991), "Cost of characteristics indices and household equivalence scales", European Economic Review 35: 1277–1293.

Lindert, P.H. (1978), Fertility and scarcity in America (Princeton, NJ).

Love, R. and G. Oja (1977), "Low income in Canada", Review of Income and Health 23: 39–61.

Lovering, K. (1984), Cost of children in Australia (Institute of Family Studies, Melbourne).

McClements, L.D. (1977), "Equivalence scales for children", Journal of Public Economics 8: 191–210.

McClements, L.D. (1979), "Muellbauer on equivalence scales", Journal of Public Economics 12: 233–242.

McClements, L.D. (1988), "A comment on the Bardsley and McRae test for a method of estimating equivalence scales", Journal of Public Economics 37: 261–263.

Melenberg, B. (1992), "Micro-econometric models of consumer behavior and welfare", Working paper (Catholic University Brabant, Tilburg).

Muellbauer, J. (1974), "Household composition, Engel curves and welfare comparisons between households", European Economic Review 5: 103–122.

Muellbauer, J. (1977), "Testing the Barten model of household composition effects and the costs of children", The Economic Journal 87: 460–487.

Muellbauer, J. (1979), "McClements on equivalence scales for children", Journal of Public Economics 12: 221–231.

Muellbauer, J. and P. Pashardes (1982), "Tests of dynamic specification and homogeneity in demand systems", Discussion paper no. 125 (Birkbeck College, London).

Mueller, E. (1976), "The economic value of children in peasant agriculture", in: R.G. Ridker, ed., Population and development (Johns Hopkins University Press, Baltimore, MD).

Municipal Bureau of Labor Research Osaka (1921), Cost of living among laborers in Osaka, Japan, Report of Labor Research, 10.

Nerlove, M., A. Razin and E. Sadka (1987), Household and economy: welfare economics of endogenous fertility (Academic Press, Cambridge).

Nicholson, J.L. (1947), "Variations in working class family expenditure", Journal of the Royal Statistical Society 112: 359–411.

Nicholson, J.L. (1976), "Appraisal of different methods of estimating equivalence scales and their results", Review of Economics and Health 2: 1–12.

Orshansky, M. (1965), "Counting the poor: another look at the poverty profile", Social Security Bulletin 28: 3–29.

Paul, S. (1985), "On the estimation of continuous equivalent adult scales", Indian Economic Review 20: 117–142.

Phlips, L (1974), Applied consumption analysis (North-Holland, Amsterdam).

Piachaud, D. (1979), The cost of a child, Poverty pamphlet no. 43 (Child Poverty Action Group, London).

Podder, N. (1971), "The estimation of an equivalent income scale", Australian Economic Papers.

Podgorski, J. (1991), "Subjective poverty lines in Poland: an application of the Leyden poverty line definition", Working paper (Central School of Planning and Statistics, Warsaw).

Pollak, R.A. (1991), "Welfare comparisons and situation comparisons", Journal of Econometrics 50: 31–48.

Pollak, R.A. and T.J. Wales (1979), "Welfare comparisons and equivalence scales", American Economic Review 69: 216–221.

Pollak, R.A. and T.J. Wales (1981), "Demographic variables in demand analysis", Econometrica 49: 1533–1551.

Prais, S.J. and H.S. Houthakker (1955), The analysis of family budgets (Cambridge University Press, Cambridge).

Ray, R.J. (1983), "Measuring the cost of children", Journal of Public Economics 22: 89–102.

Ray, R.J. (1986), "Demographic variables and equivalence scales in a flexible demand system: the case of AIDS", Applied Economics 18, 265–278.

Rothbarth, E. (1943), "Note on a method of determining equivalent income for families of different composition", Appendix 4, in: C. Madge, ed., War-time patterns of saving and spending (Cambridge University Press, Cambridge).

Rowntree, B.S. (1942), Poverty and progress (Longman, London).

Seneca, J.J. and M.K. Taussig (1971), "Family equivalence scales and personal income tax exemptions for children", Review of Economics and Statistics 53: 253–262.

Singh, B. and A.L. Nagar (1973), "Determination of consumer unit scales", Econometrica 41: 347–355.

Smeeding, T.M., M. O'Higgins and L. Rainwater (1990), Poverty, inequality and income distribution in comparative perspective: the Luxembourg income study (LIS) (Harvester Whitesheaf, New York).

Social Welfare Policy Secretariat (1981), Report on poverty measurement (Australian Government Publishing Service, Canberra).

Stone, L (1954), "Linear expenditure systems and demand analysis: an application to the pattern of British demand", The Economic Journal 64, 511–527.

Sydenstricker, E. and W. King (1921), "The measurement of the relative economic status of families", Quarterly Publication of the American Statistical Association 17: 842–857.

Theil, H. (1965), "The information approach to demand analysis", Econometrica 33: 67–87.

Townsend, P. (1979), Poverty in the United Kingdom (Penguin, Harmondsworth, UK).

Van der Gaag, J. and E. Smolensky (1982), "True household equivalence scales and characteristics of the poor in the United States", Review of Income and Wealth 28: 17–28.

Van der Sar, N.L. and B.M.S. van Praag (1993), "The evaluation question approach: a measurement method of attitudes", Journal of Economic Psychology 14.

Van Imhoff, E. and J.G. Odink (1992), "Household equivalence scales, the Engel method and the definition of goods", Working paper (University of Amsterdam, Amsterdam).

Van Praag, B.M.S. (1971), "The welfare function of income in Belgium: an empirical investigation", European Economic Review 2, 337–369.

Van Praag, B.M.S. (1991), "Ordinal and capital utility: an integration of the two dimensions of the welfare concept", Journal of Econometrics 50: 69–89.

Van Praag, B.M.S. (1993), "Ordinal and cardinal Utility: an integration of the two dimensions of the welfare concept", in: R. Blundell, I. Preston and I. Walker, eds., The measurement of household welfare (Cambridge University Press, Cambridge).

Van Praag, B.M.S. (1994a), "The relativity of the welfare concept", in: M. Nussbaum and A. Sen, eds., The quality of life (Clarendon Press, Oxford).

Van Praag, B.M.S. (1994b), "Ordinal and cardinal utility", in: R. Blundell, I. Preston and I. Walker, eds., The measurement of household welfare (Cambridge University Press, Cambridge).

Van Praag, B.M.S. and R.J. Flik (1992), "Subjective poverty", Final report for the third poverty project on behalf of EUROSTAT, RIPE, Rotterdam.

Van Praag, B.M.S. and A. Kapteyn, (1973), "Further evidence on the individual welfare function of income: an empirical investigation in the Netherlands", European Economic Review 4: 33–62.

Van Praag, B.M.S. and N.L. Van der Sar (1988), "Household cost functions and equivalence scales", Journal of Human Resources 23, 193–210.

Van Praag, B.M.S, S. Dubnoff and N.L. Van der Sar (1987), "On the measurement and explanation of standards with respect to income, age and education" (Erasmus University, Rotterdam).

Van Praag, B.M.S., R.J. Flik and P.J.A. Stam (1992), "Poverty line concepts: an application to Czechoslovakia", Working paper (Econometric Institute, Erasmus University, Rotterdam).

Whiteford, P. (1985), "A family's needs: equivalence scales, poverty and social security", Research paper no. 27 (Development Division, Australian Department of Social Security, Canberra).

Chapter 7

# THE ECONOMICS OF FERTILITY IN DEVELOPED COUNTRIES

V. JOSEPH HOTZ

*University of Chicago*

JACOB ALEX KLERMAN*

*RAND, Santa Monica*

ROBERT J. WILLIS

*University of Michigan*

## Contents

*Hotz has been supported by NICHD Grant No. R01 HD-31590. Klerman has been supported by RAND and National Institute for Child Health and Human Development Grants No. R01 HD-31203 and P50 HD-12639.

*Handbook of Population and Family Economics. Edited by M.R. Rosenzweig and O. Stark*
© *Elsevier Science B.V., 1997*

# 1. Introduction

In this chapter we survey the intellectual development and empirical implications of the literature on the economics of fertility as it applies to fertility behavior in developed economies. The now commonly held view that fertility behavior can be analyzed within the choice-theoretic framework of neoclassical economics originated in the pioneering paper by Becker (1960).[1] Therein, Becker attempted to reconcile "the neo-Malthusian proposition that increases in income tend to stimulate fertility", with "the facts that income growth has been accompanied by secular decline of fertility and that family income is inversely associated with cross-section differentials in the industrialized countries".[2] Becker sought to address this apparent puzzle by applying
the theory of the consumer to show that these secular changes and cross-sectional differences in the completed family sizes of households in developed countries were the result of variations in family incomes and the "prices", or opportunity costs of children.

In surveying the literature which followed Becker's pioneering work, we have two primary objectives. First, we seek to review the important theoretical developments, or model features, spawned by the attempts to explain household fertility behavior within a neoclassical framework. In the process we characterize how the development of the theory of the allocation of time, the concepts of household production theory, and human capital investment theory, among others, helped improve our understanding of the fertility decisions of households in developed societies.

Second, we attempt to characterize the implications that these models provide for empirical assessments of the determinants of fertility behavior. As is true in many other subfields of economics, strategies for identifying the effects of relationships implied by neoclassical economic models of consumer choice, even those as straightforward as the effect of a price change on a household's demand for a good, are often controversial. Assessing the validity of implications of economic models of fertility is no exception to this pattern. Below, we characterize the identification problems as they arise in this context, and we highlight several studies which, in our view, follow exemplary strategies for obtaining estimates of causal relationships, especially with respect to their credibility.

The balance of the chapter proceeds in four sections. The next section lays out some stylized facts. It provides a brief description of the key trends in fertility for developed economies. We consider those dimensions of fertility which have been emphasized in the static and dynamic theoretical and empirical literature considered in

---

[1] Another influential, slightly earlier model of fertility was presented by Leibenstein (1957). In it, Leibenstein stressed the importance intergenerational transfers such as old age security as a motivation for fertility in developing countries.

[2] Willis (1973).

the remainder of the chapter. While our depiction relies primarily on data for the US, many of these trends appear to hold in all countries which are characterized by market-based economies and relatively high standards of living.

The third section, following much of the extant literature, takes a static perspective to the modeling. Applying the neoclassical theory of consumer choice to household fertility, the section applies several developments of the neoclassical framework to the salient features of fertility. We begin by considering standard price effects and consider generalizations to include marital status and the use of "costly" methods (contraception and abortion) to control a woman's fertility. Adopting the conventions of the literature, we then consider pure income effects (identified with male earnings and the literature on quantity–quality) and the effects of changes in the value of women's time (incorporating both income and substitution/price effects).

In Section 4, we review the literature on dynamic models of fertility behavior over the parents' life cycle. We outline the ways in which these models extend the static models and examine what implications they provide for dimensions of fertility behavior which cannot be addressed with the earlier models, namely, the timing of first births, spacing of children, and contraceptive behavior.

After this review of the theoretical models of fertility, we discuss, in Section 5, the broad issues in estimating the implications of the theory for observed fertility behavior. We discuss various solutions to the fundamental identification problems which arise in assessing the impact of prices and income on both lifetime and life-cycle fertility behavior. Throughout this discussion we use several key empirical studies in the literature which we think best illustrate both the strengths and weaknesses of the various strategies for identifying price and income effects on household-level fertility behavior. We devote special attention to the empirical strategies (econometric approaches) used to analyze fertility behavior within a life-cycle (or dynamic) context in the estimation of dynamic models. We review the analysis of aggregate time-series data, hazard models, and estimable structural models derived from the optimal solutions to the intertemporal dynamic programming problems faced by parents.

The paper concludes with a short summary.

## 2. Fertility in the US: data, trends and the stylized facts

In this section we provide an overview of the important trends and patterns in fertility and fertility-related behavior over the twentieth century for developed countries. More precisely, we focus on the trends for the United States, although we note where the US experience differs from that of other developed economies. While not intended to be a comprehensive discussion, we attempt to develop what we see as the key "stylized" facts that existing neoclassical economic models have attempted to explain and/or must confront in the future.

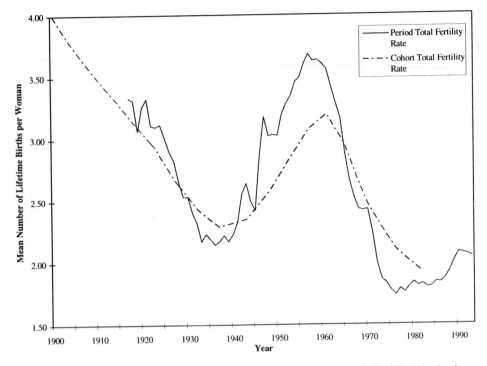

Fig. 1. Period and cohort total fertility rates in the US, 1900–1993. *Source*: NCHS, *Vital Statistics for the US*, selected years.

## 2.1. Completed family size

Given the focus of static economic models of fertility on explaining differences in the lifetime fertility of families, we begin by examining the trends in the total number of children born to women (and their mates) over their lifetimes. Fig. 1 displays annual measures of total fertility rates (TFRs) for the US over the twentieth century. TFRs are the sum of age-specific birth rates over those ages (15–44) during which women are fertile; the figure contains both *period* and *cohort* TFRs. The period TFRs displayed in Fig. 1 measure the total lifetime number of births that would be predicted if a representative woman realized the age-specific fertility rates that prevailed in particular years.[3] Cohort TFRs measure the average number of children born to women of a par-

---

[3] The *period total fertility rate* for year $t$ is given by

$$TFR_t = \sum_{a=15}^{44} BR_{t,a} \times 1000.$$

ticular birth cohort[4] and each birth cohort's TFR is displayed in the year in which that cohort attained its mean age of fertility.[5]

Regardless of the measure used, it is clear that the US has experienced a substantial decline in the lifetime fertility of women and their mates from the beginning to the end of the twentieth century. At the turn of the century, the typical woman bore four children over her lifetime (based on cohort TFRs) while women who reached the age of 45 in recent years bore, on average, only 1.9 children; at the latter level of lifetime fertility, the US population would not even replace itself from one generation to the next if it did not experience net in-migration. As noted in the Introduction, the negative association between economic development and completed family size was one of the empirical puzzles which Becker sought to reconcile with a neoclassical economic model of consumer choice. While the exact timing of the decline and the fluctuations around the long-run trend vary, all other developed countries experienced this same sort of long-run decline as their per capita incomes and standard of living rose.[6] Since the 1960s, the total fertility rates of almost all developed countries have converged to total fertility rates just below rates at which a country's population would be replaced by births.

The long-run decline in the lifetime fertility of American women was temporarily interrupted by the post-war baby boom when the women, whose fertility fueled the boom, experienced total lifetime fertility of 3.2 births. While explaining the post-war baby boom and subsequent baby bust in the US has been the focus of much numerous economic studies,[7] it is important to note that the magnitude of this "boom and bust" cycle in US fertility is unprecedented; no other developed country experienced the fertility increase after World War II that the US did.[8]

We next examine what has happened to other aspects of fertility behavior over the twentieth century which contribute to the trends in period TFRs. In particular, we ex-

---

[4] The *total fertility rate* for women in birth cohort $c$ (i.e., women born in year $c$) is given by

$$TFR_C = \sum_{i=14}^{44} BR_{c+i,a+i} \times 1000,$$

where the age-specific fertility rate, $FR_{t,a} =$ (Number of births in year $t$ to women of age $a$/Population of women of age $a$ in year $t$) $\times$ 1000.

[5] The *mean age of fertility* for the $c$th birth cohort is given by

$$A_c = \sum_{a=15}^{44} \frac{a \cdot FR_{c+a,a}}{\sum_a FR_{c+a,a}}.$$

[6] For example, the period TFR in Sweden was 4.0 in 1905 and declined to 1.6 by the mid-1980s. See Walker (1995).

[7] Many of these studies are reviewed in Macunovich (1994).

[8] For example, the peak in Sweden's post-war period TFR was 2.5 which occurred in 1964. See Walker (1995).

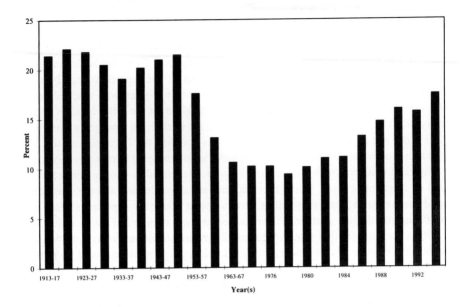

Fig. 2. Percent of women in US who are childless by age 40–44: 1913–1994. *Source*: NCHS, *Vital Statistics for the US*, selected years.

amine the trends in childlessness, the age at first birth and the incidence and tempo of childbearing after the first. Below, we treat each in turn.

## 2.2. Childlessness

While the vast majority of women in developed countries become mothers, a sizable fraction of them bear no children and, as can be seen in Fig. 2, the incidence of childlessness has fluctuated a great deal over the twentieth century. For example, over the last 20 years, the incidence of childlessness in the US has almost doubled, going from 9% of women who reached age 40–44 in 1978 to 18% for comparably aged women in 1994. (We note that while childlessness has increased among white women in the US, it has declined among non-white women, more or less continuously, since the mid-1940s.[9]) Some of this increase reflects the decline in the fraction of women who are married over this same period.[10] But the incidence of childlessness has risen among

[9] See Chen and Morgan (1991).

[10] For example, the percentage of women in the US who were ever married by ages 30–34 declined from 86.1% in 1970 to 72.8% in 1988. See Olsen (1994).

married women as well.[11] While this recent increase in childlessness in the US has drawn a great deal of attention by demographers,[12] Fig. 2 makes clear that the current rates of childlessness are not unprecedented. Cohorts who reached maturity early in the century had extremely high rates of non-marriage and, of those who married, many remained childless. In fact, what Fig. 2 suggests is that the nearly universal marriage and motherhood of cohorts of women who participated in the baby boom was atypical.[13]

### 2.3. The mother's age at first birth and the pacing of subsequent births

Trends in a country's fertility rates depend, in part, on women's timing of childbearing over their reproductive careers. In addition to changes in the total number of births to women, the measured fertility rates over the post-war baby boom and bust cycle for the US also reflected changes in the life-cycle timing of childbearing by women who were of childbearing age during this era. To see this, compare the trends in cohort and period fertility rates after 1940 that are displayed in Fig. 1. Recall that the period TFR in a particular year is a synthetic characterization of what completed fertility would be if a woman who bore children at the age-specific rates that prevailed in that year; in contrast, cohort TFRs represent the total childbearing of women in the same birth cohort. As one can see, during the baby boom, period TFRs exceeded the cohort rates and, over the subsequent baby bust, the cohort rates were higher. These discrepancies reflect changes in the timing of births by women who were of childbearing age over this period. As shown in Fig. 3, fertility rates for younger women rose and fell over the course of the baby boom and bust. In essence, the baby boom was fueled by women shifting their childbearing to earlier ages and the subsequent bust was largely the result of the tendency for childbearing to be delayed. Thus, explaining the baby boom and bust rests heavily on explaining why there was a shift in timing of births as much as explaining what caused the completed fertility of women to change.

A common way of characterizing the timing of births is in terms of the probability of a woman's first birth at different ages and spacing between subsequent birth parities. In Fig. 4, we present the trends in first birth probabilities at ages 20 and 35, separately for white and non-white women in the US Among whites, there is clear evidence that childbearing shifted to later ages; first birth probabilities, as of age 20, have declined since the early 1960s while the probability of having a first birth at age 35 has increased. Among non-white women, first birth probabilities at age 20 have declined since 1970 – although at a slower rate than was the case for whites – and

---

[11] See Morgan and Chen (1992).

[12] See, for example, Bloom (1982), Rindfuss et al. (1988), Chen and Morgan (1991).

[13] See Goldin (1992) for an interesting historical analysis of the relationship between childless and educational attainment during the twentieth century among women in the US.

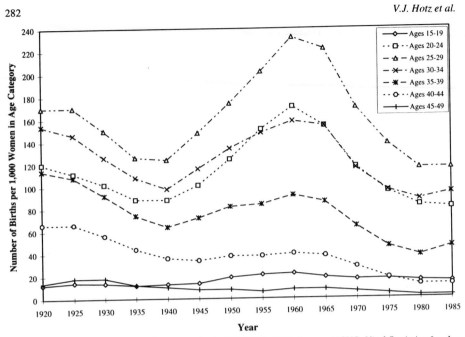

Fig. 3. Age-specific fertility rates for women in the US: 1920–1985. *Source*: NCHS, *Vital Statistics for the United States*, selected years.

have increased at age 35 at a rate substantially higher than whites. Beginning in the late 1980s, the first birth probabilities for 20-year-olds began to rise among whites and non-white women in the US. While not pictured here, a similar trend was observed among teenage women.[14] Finally, we note that the recent trend toward women delaying their childbearing is not unique to the US; women residing in other developed countries, such as Sweden, increasingly have tended to delay their childbearing until they are older.[15]

There have also been decided trends in the spacing of births as well. In Figs. 5 and 6, we display the probability of second and third births, respectively, *conditional* on reaching the beginning of each subsequent interval without having had a birth of the next parity, i.e., the hazard rate associated with the parents' decision to progress to the next parity. Each figure displays these probabilities for three different *parity-cohorts*, representing different years at which the first (or second) birth occurred. Both figures indicate that the spacing of intervals between first and second and second and third births has *lengthened* over time (i.e., for more recent parity-cohorts). What is especially noticeable is that probability of short interbirth intervals (e.g., those at intervals

[14] This recent trend toward higher rates of motherhood among teenagers has fueled much of the recent social concern about the teenage childbearing "problem" in the US.

[15] See Walker (1995).

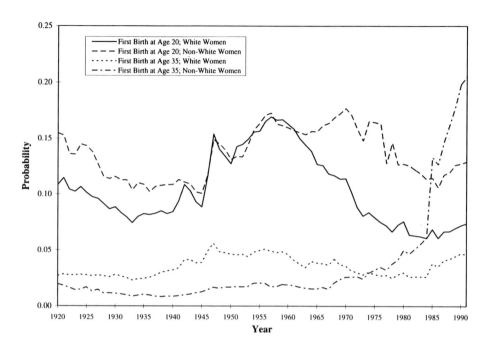

Fig. 4. First birth probabilities in US by race and for various ages: 1917–1991. *Source*: NCHS, *Vital Statistics for the United States*, selected years.

of 12–17 and 18–23 months) declined rapidly over time. Consistent with the decline in completed fertility since the peak of the baby boom, the hazard rates for both second and third births have declined at all durations over time. By five years after the first birth, these conditional probabilities imply that 80%, 72% and 63% of women who had a first birth would have had second births in the three succeeding parity-cohorts (1950–1959, 1965–1969, 1975–1989, respectively).[16] The corresponding percentages for having a third birth within five years after the second birth are 64%, 45% and 35%, respectively.

## 2.4. Marital and nonmarital childbearing

At the beginning of the 1960, marriage was a virtual pre-condition for childbearing in most developed societies in that less than 10% of all births occurred out-of-wedlock in

---

[16] These calculations are taken from Morgan (1995).

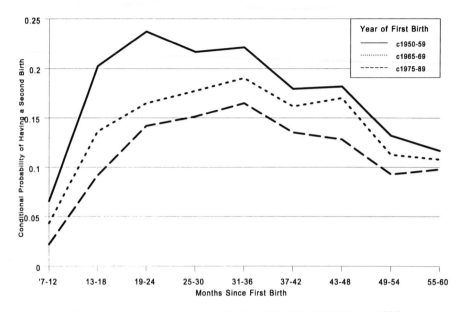

Fig. 5. Trends in the timing of second births in US; 1950–1989 (Morgan, 1995).

the countries of Western Europe and in the US.[17] During the next 35 years, this fraction steadily increased in these countries. In Panel A of Table 1 we display the trends in out-of-wedlock childbearing in the US from 1963 to 1992. In 1963, less than 6% of births were out-of-wedlock; by 1992, out-of-wedlock births accounted for 30% of all births. Among whites, the ratio of out-of-wedlock births was 3% in 1963 and it rose to 23% in 1992, a 642% increase over this 30-year period. Among blacks, who have historically had higher rates of out-of-wedlock childbearing, out-of-wedlock births rose from 45% of all births in 1973 to 68% in 1992. As recorded in Panel A of Table 1, the proportions of births occurring out-of-wedlock have become exceptionally high among teenagers in the US. Among all races, the percentage of births occurring out-of-wedlock among women, age 15–19, increased from 17% in 1963 to 70% in 1992. These rates are even higher among black teenage women, where 93% of this demographic group's births occurred out of wedlock in 1992.

The trends for Western Europe in nonmarital fertility since 1960 mirror those for the US. By the late 1980s, the fraction of births born to unmarried women had also increased throughout Western Europe, albeit at radically different rates in different countries. In the Netherlands, to take one extreme, out-of-wedlock childbearing was virtually unknown until the mid-1970s, then began to increase substantially, but as late

---

[17] See Ermisch (1991) for data on trends in Western Europe and DaVanzo and Rahman (1993) for those in the US.

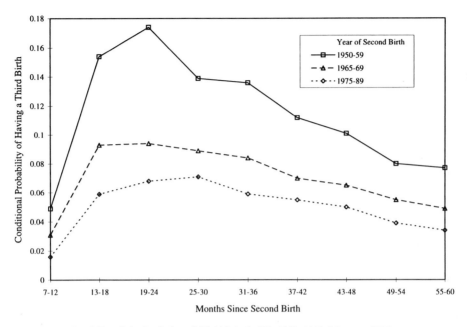

Fig. 6. Trends in the timing of third births in US; 1950–1989 (Morgan, 1995).

as 1988 only 8% of births were nonmarital, a rate similar to that of West Germany. At the other extreme, rates of out-of-wedlock childbearing had increased to over 50% in Sweden and nearly as high elsewhere in Scandinavia. Moreover, the growth of non-marital fertility began accelerating elsewhere in Europe in the mid-1970s, reaching a level of more than 25% by 1988 in England and France, similar to levels in the US at that time.

The increasing proportion of births occurring out of wedlock in advanced countries reflects three important changes over the last three decades. First, the rate of childbearing among unmarried women has increased. In the US, for example, the birth rate of unmarried women, age 15–44, went from 23 to 45 births per 1000 women over the period 1963 to 1992. While the rates of childbearing among unmarried women were higher and increased among black women, the rate of childbearing among white women actually increased more rapidly over this period, going from 11 to 35 births per 1000 women over this 30-year interval. Second, the rate of childbearing among married women has declined over this period. In 1963, the height of the baby boom in the US, the rate of childbearing among women of all races who were married was 146 births per 1000 women; the corresponding rate was 90 births per 1000 women in 1992. Third, the proportion of women of childbearing ages who were married de-clined over the last three decades. Olsen (1994) notes that from 1960 to 1988, the percentage of women, age 14–44, who were married went from 72% in 1960 to

Table 1
US trends in nonmarital childbearing by race and age: 1963–1992

| Ages | Ratio of births to unmarried women to all births | | | | | | | Births per 1000 unmarried women | | | | | | | Births per 1000 married women | | | | | | |
|---|---|---|---|---|---|---|---|---|---|---|---|---|---|---|---|---|---|---|---|---|---|
| | 1963 | 1968 | 1973 | 1978 | 1983 | 1988 | 1992 | 1963 | 1968 | 1973 | 1978 | 1983 | 1988 | 1992 | 1963 | 1968 | 1973 | 1978 | 1983 | 1988 | 1992 |
| *All races:* | | | | | | | | | | | | | | | | | | | | | |
| 15–19 | 0.17 | 0.27 | 0.34 | 0.44 | 0.53 | 0.65 | 0.70 | 15 | 20 | 23 | 25 | 30 | 36 | 45 | 487 | 436 | 340 | 323 | 348 | 371 | 410 |
| 20–24 | 0.06 | 0.08 | 0.11 | 0.16 | 0.23 | 0.33 | 0.41 | 40 | 37 | 32 | 35 | 42 | 56 | 69 | 321 | 243 | 181 | 188 | 203 | 209 | 213 |
| 25–29 | 0.03 | 0.04 | 0.05 | 0.07 | 0.11 | 0.16 | 0.20 | 49 | 38 | 30 | 29 | 36 | 49 | 57 | 206 | 157 | 131 | 137 | 146 | 154 | 160 |
| 30–34 | 0.03 | 0.04 | 0.05 | 0.06 | 0.09 | 0.12 | 0.14 | 33 | 28 | 20 | 17 | 22 | 32 | 38 | 114 | 80 | 61 | 68 | 79 | 91 | 97 |
| 35–39 | 0.03 | 0.05 | 0.06 | 0.07 | 0.10 | 0.13 | 0.15 | 16 | 15 | 11 | 8 | 10 | 15 | 19 | 57 | 38 | 24 | 21 | 25 | 32 | 37 |
| 40–44 | 0.04 | 0.05 | 0.08 | 0.10 | 0.13 | 0.16 | 0.18 | 4 | 4 | 3 | 2 | 3 | 3 | 4 | 16 | 11 | 6 | 5 | 4 | 6 | 6 |
| 15–44 | 0.06 | 0.10 | 0.13 | 0.16 | 0.20 | 0.26 | 0.30 | 23 | 24 | 24 | 26 | 30 | 39 | 45 | 146 | 117 | 95 | 94 | 94 | 91 | 90 |
| *Whites:* | | | | | | | | | | | | | | | | | | | | | |
| 15–19 | 0.09 | 0.16 | 0.19 | 0.29 | 0.39 | 0.54 | 0.60 | 7 | 10 | 11 | 14 | 19 | 25 | 33 | 473 | 422 | 328 | 318 | 339 | 356 | 393 |
| 20–24 | 0.03 | 0.05 | 0.05 | 0.08 | 0.14 | 0.23 | 0.32 | 21 | 23 | 16 | 18 | 27 | 39 | 53 | 319 | 240 | 179 | 184 | 199 | 206 | 207 |
| 25–29 | 0.01 | 0.02 | 0.02 | 0.03 | 0.07 | 0.10 | 0.14 | 23 | 22 | 16 | 15 | 24 | 36 | 45 | 204 | 158 | 132 | 137 | 146 | 154 | 159 |
| 30–34 | 0.01 | 0.02 | 0.02 | 0.03 | 0.05 | 0.08 | 0.10 | 15 | 15 | 11 | 9 | 16 | 24 | 32 | 113 | 79 | 61 | 67 | 79 | 91 | 96 |
| 35–39 | 0.02 | 0.02 | 0.03 | 0.04 | 0.07 | 0.09 | 0.11 | 5 | 5 | 6 | 5 | 8 | 12 | 16 | 35 | 23 | 23 | 20 | 24 | 31 | 36 |
| 40–44 | 0.02 | 0.03 | 0.04 | 0.06 | 0.07 | 0.13 | 0.15 | 5 | 5 | 2 | 1 | 2 | 3 | 4 | 35 | 23 | 6 | 4 | 4 | 5 | 6 |
| 15–44 | 0.03 | 0.05 | 0.06 | 0.09 | 0.13 | 0.18 | 0.23 | 11 | 13 | 12 | 14 | 20 | 27 | 35 | 143 | 115 | 94 | 93 | 93 | 90 | 90 |
| *Blacks:* | | | | | | | | | | | | | | | | | | | | | |
| 15–19 | | | 0.71 | 0.83 | 0.89 | 0.91 | 0.93 | | | 95 | 88 | 86 | 96 | 106 | | | 454 | 353 | 476 | 561 | 595 |
| 20–24 | | | 0.39 | 0.53 | 0.61 | 0.69 | 0.75 | | | 116 | 111 | 107 | 134 | 144 | | | 192 | 212 | 227 | 227 | 248 |
| 25–29 | | | 0.26 | 0.32 | 0.41 | 0.49 | 0.55 | | | 85 | 80 | 80 | 97 | 98 | | | 113 | 124 | 127 | 132 | 144 |
| 30–34 | | | 0.23 | 0.26 | 0.33 | 0.41 | 0.47 | | | 58 | 44 | 44 | 57 | 58 | | | 58 | 66 | 70 | 74 | 83 |
| 35–39 | | | 0.23 | 0.26 | 0.31 | 0.38 | 0.45 | | | 28 | 19 | 19 | 24 | 26 | | | 30 | 28 | 27 | 29 | 34 |
| 40–44 | | | 0.23 | 0.28 | 0.32 | 0.37 | 0.42 | | | 8 | 6 | 5 | 5 | 5 | | | 10 | 7 | 6 | 6 | 7 |
| 15–44 | | | 0.45 | 0.53 | 0.58 | 0.63 | 0.68 | | | 89 | 81 | 77 | 87 | 87 | | | 98 | 94 | 88 | 83 | 86 |

*Source:* NCHS, Vital Statistics and Health Statistics, "Births to Unmarried Mothers: United States, 1980–92", Series 21, No. 53, June 1995 and NCHS, *Vital Statistics for the US,* Vol. 1 – Natality, 1995.

54% in 1988. Among women, age 20–24 – the age category which had the highest rates of childbearing at the peak of the baby boom – marriage rates fell from 69.5% in 1960 to 35.7% in 1988.[18] (We note that these declines in marriage rates in the US reflect both an increasing tendency to delay the entry into marriage as well as increasing rates of divorce.[19]) While the causal links between marriage and fertility cannot be inferred from these trends, it is clear that the close tie between marriage and childbearing no longer reflects the contemporary scene in the developed countries of the world.

### 2.5. Contraceptive practices

Since the beginning of the 1960s, the world has experienced a "revolution" in the technology of methods available to control fertility. At the outset of this decade, the Pill and the Intrauterine Device (IUD) were introduced in most developed economies, as well as developing countries, and both methods, especially the Pill, experienced a high rate of adoption by women of childbearing ages. By the mid-1960s, over one-third of all married women in the US, age 15–44, reported using either the Pill or an IUD.[20] Over the subsequent three decades, the rates of utilization for both methods have declined, especially that for the IUD, and other methods of contraception have increased.

In Table 2, we provide a more detailed picture of the changing pattern of contraceptive utilization of the various contraceptive methods used by women of childbearing ages in the US from 1982 to 1990. Therein, we display how these utilization rates varied across a variety of different socioeconomic characteristics of women in the US There have been several important trends, or lack of them, over the last 15 years. First, there has been remarkably little change over time in the proportion of women of childbearing age who use some form of contraception while engaged in sexual activity. The only exception to this pattern is among never married women, where the percentage using some form of contraception has increased from 1982 to 1990 by eight percentage points. Second, there has been a precipitous increase in the use of condoms. This is especially true among those who are young and unmarried, where rates of condom utilization have doubled since 1982. This increase in the rates of condom use for these groups appears to reflect the desire for increased protection against contracting the HIV virus.[21] Third, there has been a slight increase, over the last 12 years,

---

[18] See Olsen (1994) for more on the relationship between trends in marriage and fertility in the US.

[19] See DaVanzo and Rahman (1993) and Weiss (this volume) for a more complete discussion of trends in marriage and divorce in the US.

[20] The early trends in contraceptive utilization are discussed in Ryder and Westoff (1973).

[21] See Ahituv et al. (1996).

Table 2

Incidence and utilization patterns for various contraceptive methods for women, age 15–44, in US: 1982, 1988 and 1990

| | % of women using any method | | | % of women using particular method, given using some method | | | | | |
|---|---|---|---|---|---|---|---|---|---|
| | | | | Female sterilization | | | Male sterilization | | |
| | 1982 | 1988 | 1990 | 1982 | 1988 | 1990 | 1982 | 1988 | 1990 |
| *Age* | | | | | | | | | |
| 15–24 | 40.8 | 45.7 | 43.9 | 3.2 | 3.1 | 4.2 | 2.7 | 1.0 | 0.9 |
| 25–34 | 66.7 | 66.3 | 63.2 | 22.1 | 24.8 | 25.2 | 10.1 | 10.0 | 9.1 |
| 35–44 | 61.6 | 68.3 | 68.9 | 43.5 | 47.7 | 47.9 | 19.9 | 20.8 | 22.9 |
| *Race* | | | | | | | | | |
| Hispanic | | 50.4 | 52.2 | | 31.7 | 33.1 | | 4.3 | 6.4 |
| White, non-Hispanic | 52.0 | 62.9 | 60.5 | 22.1 | 25.6 | 27.3 | 12.2 | 14.3 | 15.5 |
| Black, non-Hispanic | 56.7 | 56.8 | 58.7 | 30.0 | 37.8 | 41.0 | 1.4 | 0.9 | 1.3 |
| *Marital status* | | | | | | | | | |
| Currently married | 69.7 | 74.3 | 70.7 | 26.9 | 31.4 | 33.5 | 15.5 | 17.3 | 19.2 |
| Divorced, separated, widowed | 55.5 | 57.6 | 57.3 | 39.2 | 50.7 | 52.1 | 3.4 | 3.6 | 2.8 |
| Never married | 35.3 | 41.9 | 43.0 | 3.7 | 6.4 | 9.6 | 1.8 | 1.8 | 1.1 |
| *Woman's educational attainment* | | | | | | | | | |
| 0–11 | | 60.2 | 60.6 | | 51.9 | 58.0 | | 6.9 | 6.8 |
| 12 | | 67.5 | 66.3 | | 34.3 | 38.4 | | 15.0 | 15.7 |
| 13 and over | | 65.8 | 63.1 | | 20.7 | 22.3 | | 12.6 | 13.7 |
| *Income (% of poverty level)* | | | | | | | | | |
| 0–149 | | 60.2 | 59.4 | | 42.8 | 47.2 | | 5.2 | 6.2 |
| 150–299 | | 67.1 | 66.2 | | 34.5 | 38.5 | | 13.1 | 11.8 |
| 300 and over | | 67.0 | 64.0 | | 23.5 | 25.1 | | 15.1 | 16.5 |

*Source*: National Surveys of Family Growth, 1982, 1988, 1990.

in the proportion of women who have elected to become surgically sterilized and, thus, cease their childbearing completely. It is interesting to note that while sterilization has increased among married women by 24% over this period, it has increased more among divorced, separated or widowed women (33%) and among those who have never married (159%).

Over the last 20 years, the US and other developed countries have seen important changes in the incidence of another method for preventing births, namely induced abortions. Abortions first became legal in the US in 1967 when the State of Colorado enacted legislation which legalized the right of women to abort their fetuses during the early stages of their pregnancies. Abortions during the first trimester of a pregnancy became legal in all of the US as a result of the highly controversial Supreme Court

| Pill | | | IUD | | | Diaphragm | | | Condom | | | Other methods | | |
|------|------|------|------|------|------|------|------|------|------|------|------|------|------|------|
| 1982 | 1988 | 1990 | 1982 | 1988 | 1990 | 1982 | 1988 | 1990 | 1982 | 1988 | 1990 | 1982 | 1988 | 1990 |
| 57.6 | 63.6 | 53.8 | 3.4 | 0.2 | 0.4 | 9.0 | 2.4 | 0.3 | 13.5 | 23.5 | 34.3 | 10.6 | 6.3 | 6.1 |
| 24.7 | 32.9 | 35.4 | 9.7 | 2.1 | 0.7 | 10.3 | 7.2 | 3.5 | 11.4 | 13.8 | 17.4 | 10.7 | 9.1 | 8.8 |
| 3.7 | 4.3 | 6.7 | 6.9 | 3.2 | 2.6 | 4.0 | 6.0 | 3.5 | 11.3 | 11.2 | 9.8 | 10.8 | 6.9 | 6.7 |
| | 33.4 | 31.4 | | 5.0 | 1.9 | | 2.4 | 1.5 | | 13.6 | 17.1 | | 9.6 | 8.8 |
| 26.7 | 29.5 | 28.5 | 6.9 | 1.5 | 1.3 | 8.8 | 6.6 | 3.9 | 12.7 | 16.2 | 17.0 | 10.7 | 7.3 | 7.4 |
| 38.0 | 38.1 | 28.5 | 9.1 | 3.2 | 1.4 | 3.5 | 2.0 | 1.6 | 6.2 | 10.1 | 19.4 | 11.7 | 8.0 | 6.8 |
| 19.3 | 20.4 | 20.6 | 6.9 | 2.0 | 1.4 | 6.5 | 6.2 | 4.1 | 14.1 | 14.3 | 14.0 | 10.8 | 8.4 | 7.3 |
| 28.4 | 25.3 | 22.4 | 11.5 | 3.6 | 2.5 | 6.7 | 5.3 | 0.9 | 1.5 | 5.0 | 9.7 | 9.2 | 5.7 | 9.6 |
| 53.0 | 59.0 | 50.5 | 5.4 | 1.3 | 0.8 | 13.4 | 4.9 | 0.6 | 11.6 | 19.6 | 30.1 | 11.1 | 7.0 | 7.3 |
| | 22.6 | 18.4 | | 3.8 | 1.7 | | 1.3 | 0.2 | | 6.4 | 11.7 | | 7.2 | 3.3 |
| | 29.4 | 26.8 | | 1.7 | 1.1 | | 2.8 | 1.7 | | 10.7 | 11.0 | | 6.1 | 5.3 |
| | 28.7 | 28.0 | | 2.2 | 1.7 | | 10.0 | 4.6 | | 16.4 | 19.3 | | 9.5 | 10.4 |
| | 31.3 | 24.8 | | 3.3 | 1.1 | | 2.3 | 0.6 | | 10.2 | 14.9 | | 5.0 | 5.3 |
| | 26.6 | 26.6 | | 2.4 | 2.5 | | 5.0 | 1.9 | | 11.4 | 12.9 | | 7.0 | 5.8 |
| | 27.8 | 27.3 | | 1.7 | 1.0 | | 8.0 | 4.2 | | 14.5 | 16.8 | | 9.3 | 9.2 |

decision in the case of Roe v. Wade in 1973.[22] We present, in Table 3, statistics on annual abortion rates in the US subsequent to this decision. The proportion of pregnancies which ended in abortions increased after the Roe v. Wade decision, peaking in 1981 when 30% of pregnancies were terminated by an abortion. Since the early 1980s abortion rates have leveled off and fallen slightly in the US. We also provide, in Table 3, abortion rates for a number of developed countries in selective years. While rates of abortion have been relatively high in countries in Eastern and Central Europe – coun-

---

[22] See Merz et al. (1995, 1996) for more on the judicial and legislative history of abortions in the US.

Table 3

Proportion of abortions to pregnancies ending in abortion or live birth; rate of abortions per 1000 women aged 15–44; and number of reported abortions (in thousands):United States, selected years 1973–1992 and other countries (year in parentheses).

| Country, year | Proportion | Rate | Abortions |
|---|---|---|---|
| *United States* | | | |
| 1973 | 0.193 | 16.3 | 744.6 |
| 1975 | 0.249 | 21.7 | 1034.2 |
| 1977 | 0.286 | 26.4 | 1316.7 |
| 1979 | 0.296 | 28.8 | 1497.7 |
| 1981 | 0.301 | 29.3 | 1577.3 |
| 1983 | (0.304) | (28.5) | (1575.0) |
| 1985 | 0.297 | 28.0 | 1588.6 |
| 1988 | 0.286 | 27.3 | 1590.8 |
| 1991 | 0.274 | 26.3 | 1556.5 |
| 1992 | 0.275 | 25.9 | 1528.9 |
| | | | |
| *Eastern and Central Europe* | | | |
| Soviet Union (1987)[a] | 0.549 | 111.9 | 6818000 |
| Czechoslovakia (1987) | 0.422 | 46.7 | 156600 |
| Hungary (1987) | 0.402 | 38.2 | 84500 |
| German Dem. Rep. (1984) | 0.297 | 26.6 | 96200 |
| | | | |
| *Selected other countries* | | | |
| Australia (1988) | 0.204 | 16.6 | 63200 |
| Belgium (1985) | 0.122 | 7.5 | 15900 |
| Canada (1985) | 0.166 | 12.1 | 74800 |
| Denmark (1987) | 0.270 | 18.3 | 20800 |
| England and Wales (1987) | 0.186 | 14.2 | 156200 |
| France (1987)[a] | 0.173 | 13.3 | 161000 |
| German Fed. Rep. (1986)[a] | 0.128 | 7.0 | 88500 |
| Italy (1987)[a] | 0.257 | 15.3 | 191500 |
| Japan (1987)[a] | 0.270 | 18.6 | 497800 |
| Netherlands (1986) | 0.090 | 5.3 | 18300 |
| New Zealand (1987) | 0.136 | 11.4 | 8800 |
| Singapore (1987) | 0.327 | 30.1 | 21200 |
| Sweden (1987) | 0.249 | 19.8 | 34700 |

[a]Based on statistics that are incomplete.

*Sources*: US data: Henshaw and Van Vort (1994). US data in parentheses are estimated by interpolating the numbers of abortions. International data: Henshaw (1990: Table 3, p. 86).

tries which were members of the former Communist bloc – abortion rates in other developed countries have tended to be lower than those in the US.

These trends in contraceptive practices among women in the US, including abortions, reflect, in part, the constellation of factors which have changed the incentives to bear children by men and women of childbearing ages in the US. We return to discuss

Table 4
Labor force participation rates for wives, husband present, by age of own youngest child in US: 1975–1994

| Presence and age of child | 1975 | 1980 | 1985 | 1990 | 1994 |
|---|---|---|---|---|---|
| All wives | 44.4 | 50.2 | 54.2 | 58.2 | 60.6 |
| No children under age 18 | 43.8 | 46.0 | 48.2 | 51.1 | 53.2 |
| With children under age 18 | 44.9 | 54.3 | 60.8 | 66.3 | 69.0 |
| Under 6, total | 36.7 | 45.3 | 53.4 | 58.9 | 61.7 |
| Under 3 | 32.7 | 41.5 | 50.5 | 55.5 | 59.7 |
| 1 year or under | 30.8 | 39.0 | 49.4 | 53.9 | 58.8 |
| 2 years | 37.1 | 48.1 | 54.0 | 60.9 | 64.5 |
| 3–5 years | 42.2 | 51.7 | 58.4 | 64.1 | 64.6 |
| 3 years | 41.2 | 51.5 | 55.1 | 63.1 | 62.9 |
| 4 years | 41.2 | 51.4 | 59.7 | 65.1 | 63.9 |
| 5 years | 44.4 | 52.4 | 62.1 | 64.5 | 67.1 |
| 6–13 years | 51.8 | 62.6 | 68.2 | 73.0 | 75.5 |
| 14–17 years | 53.5 | 60.5 | 67.0 | 75.1 | 77.2 |

*Source*: Current Population Surveys, 1975, 1980, 1985, 1990, 1994.

what hypotheses from economic models of fertility might be used to explain these patterns.

## 2.6. Relationship between fertility and female labor force participation

One of the important social trends in developed countries has been the rise, over time, in labor force participation of women in both developed and developing countries.[23] The relationship between this trend, and its causes, and that of fertility has been an important focus of the economic models of fertility to be discussed below. One of the most noticeable trends, at least in the US, has been the precipitous rise in the labor force participation rates of mothers with young children. These trends are displayed in Table 4. While the labor force participation rates of all wives increased by 36% over the last 20 years, the rates increased by 83% for women with children under the age of three and by 91% for women with children one year old or younger. As of 1994, there is virtually no difference in the labor force participation rates of married women with children of different ages. It appears that it is no longer the case that mothers with young children curb their labor force participation to the same extent that women did even 20 years ago. There are a number of possible explanations for this reduction in the negative association between the presence of young children and the mother's attachment to the labor force. These include the increase in the availability of market

[23] See Heckman and Killingsworth (1996).

substitutes (i.e., child care) for the mother's time and the fact that more recent cohorts of women have higher levels of educational attainment which may increase the opportunity cost of remaining out of the labor force to care for their children.[24] Below, we offer some possible explanations for the breaking of this association, based on the economic models of fertility and women's time allocation decisions.

## 3. Static models of fertility behavior

In one sense, the economic approach to explaining fertility behavior is nothing more than an application of neoclassical models of consumer demand. Such models view parents as consumers who choose that quantity, or number, of children which maximizes their utility subject to the price of children and the budget constraint they face. In this simple setting, we assume that the relevant unit of time for these choices is the parents' lifetime. We use the term "static" to characterize this one period lifetime perspective. In this section, we ignore such issues as the possibility that the constraints that parents face, in terms of prices and budget constraints, may vary over the parents' life cycle, the potential uncertainty that parents may have at any point in time about these constraints in future periods, or the apparent fact that fertility outcomes unfold over time as well. Admitting these possibilities and addressing their implications will be considered when we consider dynamic models of fertility behavior below. Finally, we assume that, aside from their budget constraint, there are no obstacles to the ability of parents to choose their family size.

More formally, we assume that parents maximize a utility function,

$$U = U(n,s),$$
(1)

which depends on the outcome of interest, the number of children, which is denoted by $n$, and a good, $s$, which characterizes all other consumption. (We assume that that utility function has all the conventional properties, i.e., increasing and concave in both arguments.) In this simplified model, parents are assumed to choose $n$ and $s$ so as to maximize Eq. (1) subject to the following (conventional) budget constraint:

$$I = \pi_s s + p_n n,$$
(2)

where $I$ is the household's income, $p_n$ is the per unit "price" of children, and $\pi_s$, is the per unit price of the composite commodity. Taking the price of the composite good as numeraire, this simple model yields a relatively simplistic, but standard, demand-for-children function,

----

[24] See Leibowitz and Klerman (1995).

$$n = N(p_n, I),\tag{3}$$

which depends upon the price of children and parental income. The effect of changes in the price of children on completed fertility are characterized by the standard income and substitution effects of consumer theory and changes in parental income give rise to income effects with respect to the "purchase" of children.

Given data on households who are subjected to exogenous variations in this price and parental income and a parametric specification of Eq. (3), estimation of $\partial n / \partial p_n$ and $\partial n / \partial I$ would constitute the focus of an econometric investigation of the economic model. Without substantial deviation from this simple model, one can envision investigations of the price responsiveness of the demand for children due to exogenous changes in the cost of rearing children or changes in governmental policies which affect the cost of children (e.g., changes in tax deductions for dependents or public assistance benefits). The simple neoclassical approach to fertility yields unambiguous predictions about price effects, assuming that children are not Giffen goods. The empirical challenge is to find proxies for the price of children. As is well known, neoclassical theory does not yield unambiguous predictions about income effects, although there has been a presumption in the literature that they are positive, i.e., children are not inferior goods. Nonetheless, determining the direction and magnitudes of the effect of income on the demand for children is an important objective for econometric studies of fertility. Again, the essential question is how does one obtain exogenous variation in income facing households with which to identify such income effects. In our discussion below of the estimation of the empirical implications of static models of fertility, we discuss these challenges in some detail and describe what one might call "best practice" examples in the empirical literature for economic models of fertility behavior.

While a generic model of consumer choice generates a limited set of potentially testable predictions, such a model fails to capture the special features of fertility choices. As noted in the Introduction, the challenge of adapting neoclassical economic models to fertility behavior has given impetus a number of important extensions of this simple model. These extensions not only attempt to address the distinctive aspects of this set of behavior but also represent important adaptations of the application of economics to human behavior. In the following sections, we describe several of the key adaptations of the model of consumer demand which have a prominent role in the intellectual development of the static theory of fertility behavior.

We begin by examining two important contributions to the early literature on the economics of fertility. The first, the quality–quantity model of fertility, acknowledged that parents not only demanded numbers of children but also children with certain qualities. The second contribution was to acknowledge the important of parental time, especially the mother's in the rearing development of children. Elements of these two model features are found in Becker (1960) and Mincer (1963) and are synthesized within the Becker (1965) household production framework by Willis

(1973), with some further implications of the quality–quantity model developed in Becker and Lewis (1973).[25] We then survey a recent line of research which addresses the relationship between fertility and marriage. The initial models of fertility presumed that childbearing took place within marriage. As is clear from the trends noted in Section 2, this is an increasingly less accurate description of childbearing within developed countries. We discuss recent models which attempt to provide an explanation for why the link between fertility and marriage may be changing over time.

### 3.1. The quality–quantity model

Recall from the Introduction that Becker's seminal paper on applying neoclassical economic theory to fertility began with the puzzle that fertility tends to be negatively related to income both in time series and cross section. Becker (1960) rejected explanations for this relationship which assert that children are inferior goods or that high income families, who spend more on their children, have lower fertility because they face higher prices of children. Instead, he argued that the puzzle could be resolved within a model of stable preferences in which children are a superior good by recognizing that the demand for children involves, in addition to the quantitative dimension represented by the number of children, a qualitative dimension associated with the choice of expenditures per child. Adapting a model introduced by Theil (1952) and Houthakker (1952) for the study of consumer budget data, Becker proposed a simple model of fertility behavior in which parents had preferences both for the number of children and the quality per child. This static, lifetime model is an adaptation of the simple model oulined above.

In particular, a newly married couple is considered to act as a unitary household with a single decision maker with preferences given by the utility function

$$U = U(n, q, s), \tag{4}$$

where $n$ continues to denote the number of children, $s$ the parents' standard of living,

---

[25] These two papers were published in March/April of 1973 and 1974 as part of two special issues of the *Journal of Political Economy* which were reprinted in T.W. Schultz (1974). Willis (1987) suggests that this collection of papers marks the emergence of the economics of the family as a distinct subfield in economics. In addition to the Willis and Becker–Lewis papers, the collection includes other papers on the economics of fertility (Ben-Porath, 1973; DeTray, 1973; Hashimoto, 1973; Michael, 1973), investment in children (Leibowitz, 1974), investment in human capital by women (Mincer and Polachek, 1974), the economic analysis of child care (Heckman, 1974b), and the theory of marriage (Becker, 1973, 1974). In this paper, we reference papers in this collection by their *Journal of Political Economy* citation but sometimes refer to the collection itself as the "Schultz volume".

and $q$ is the quality per child.[26] In place of Eq. (2), the household's lifetime budget is now given by

$$I = \pi_c nq + \pi_s s,$$ (5)

where $I$ continues to denote total family lifetime income, $\pi_c$ is a price index of goods and services devoted to children and $\pi_s$ is a price index of goods and services consumed by adults. The unusual feature of this problem is that the budget constraint is nonlinear because quantity and quality enter multiplicatively. It is this quality–quantity interaction that leads to certain distinction features of the demand for children that we will describe shortly and to which we will return at several later points in this paper.

One immediate implication of the model of Eqs. (4) and (5) that was stressed by Becker (1960) is that the income elasticities of demand for $n$, $q$ and $s$ must satisfy the relationship

$$\alpha(\varepsilon_n + \varepsilon_q) + (1 - \alpha)\varepsilon_s = 1,$$ (6)

where $\alpha$ is the share of family income devoted to children and the $\varepsilon$'s denote income elasticities. If children are normal goods in the sense that total expenditures on children are an increasing function of income, then the *sum* of the income elasticities of the number and quality of children must be positive (i.e., $\varepsilon_n + \varepsilon_q > 0$), but it is still possible that the income elasticity of demand for the number of children is negative (i.e., $\varepsilon_n < 0$) if the income elasticity of quality is large enough. Although he was unable to cite estimates of the demand for other goods in which the income elasticity of demand for quantity was negative, Becker did cite studies showing that quality elasticities tended to be larger than quantity elasticities. He ended up arguing that income is likely to have a small positive effect on fertility, but believed that a negative correlation between birth control knowledge and income might change the overall sign of the income–fertility relationship to negative.[27]

The quality–quantity model did not receive much attention again until the two above mentioned papers by Willis (1973) and Becker and Lewis (1973). These papers provide a formal analysis of the model in which the implications of the nonlinearity in the budget constraint in Eq. (5) are explored. Maximizing household utility in Eq. (4)

---

[26] The term "unitary model of the household" was introduced by Chiappori et al. (1993) to distinguish traditional theories of household behavior in which all members of the household act as if they were a single decision maker from newer "collective" theories in which the separate interests of individuals within a household are considered. Later in this chapter, we consider some implications of the collective approach for fertility behavior. (See also the chapters by Bergstrom and Weiss in this volume for further discussion of this point.)

[27] Becker (1960) attempted to show empirically that a positive relationship between income and fertility exists when birth control knowledge is held constant, but the data used in the empirical analysis (e.g., data from subscribers of *Consumer Reports*) would not meet current standards for data quality.

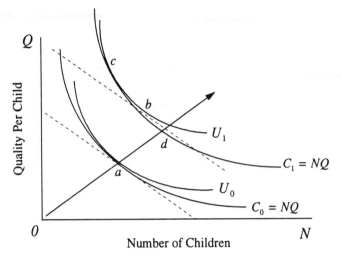

Fig. 7. Interaction of the demand for quality and quantity of children.

subject to the family budget constraint in Eq. (5) yields the following first-order conditions:

$$MU_n = \lambda q \pi_c = \lambda p_n, \quad MU_q = \lambda n \pi_c = \lambda p_q, \tag{7}$$

where the $MU$'s are marginal utilities and the $p$'s are marginal costs or shadow prices of the number of children and quality per child, respectively, and $\lambda$ is the marginal utility of income. These conditions imply that the shadow price of the number of children is an increasing function of child quality and, similarly, that the shadow price of child quality is an increasing function of the number of children. Additionally, since $n$ and $q$ are chosen by the household, the shadow prices are endogenous. It is ironic that the same model Becker (1960) used to demonstrate why rich and poor households really face the same prices of children despite evidence that the rich spend more per child is used by Becker and Lewis (1973) to show that the shadow price of the number of children is higher under these circumstances.

The household's optimal choice of number and quality of children is illustrated by the indifference curve diagram in Fig. 7. Equilibrium occurs at point *a*. At this point, the indifference curve $U_0$ is tangent to the budget constraint, $c_0 = nq = (I - \pi_s s(\pi_c, \pi_s, I))/\pi_c$, where $c_0$ is the household's real expenditure on children and $s(\pi_c, \pi_s, I)$ is the demand function for parents' standard of living. The assumption that this tangency point corresponds to maximum utility implies that the indifference curve must be more concave than the budget constraint, $c_0 = nq$, which is a rectangular hyperbola. Thus, quality and quantity cannot be too closely substitutable in consumer preferences if second-order conditions for utility maximization are to be satisfied.

The nonlinearity of this budget constraint causes a quality–quantity interaction as income increases that results in an induced substitution effect against the number of children and in favor of quality per child if the income elasticity of demand for quality exceeds the income elasticity of demand for number of children, an assumption that both Becker and Lewis (1973) and Willis (1973) believed to be empirically plausible. To see this, note that Eq. (6) implies that the marginal rate of substitution between the quantity and quality of children is $MU_n/MU_q = p_n/p_q = q/n$ so that the relative cost of the number of children tends to increase as the ratio of quality to quantity increases, as it will if $\varepsilon_n > \varepsilon_q$.

This quality–quantity interaction is illustrated diagrammatically in Fig. 7. If the income elasticities for quality and quantity were equal, the income-expansion path would be given by ray $Oad$ and the ratio of quality to quantity and the marginal rate of substitution between quality and quantity both remain constant. If $\varepsilon_n > \varepsilon_q$, the total effect of an increase in income that raises total expenditures on children from $c_0$ to $c_1$ is to move optimal consumption from point $a$ to point $c$. This total effect may be decomposed into a "pure income effect", holding $p_n/p_q$ constant, from point $a$ to point $b$, and an "induced substitution effect" from point $b$ to point $c$. As drawn in Fig. 7, the total effect of an increase in income leaves the number of children unchanged because the pure income effect, which tends to increase desired fertility, is offset by a substitution effect against fertility induced by the increased expense per child associated with higher desired quality.

The budget in Eq. (6) was generalized by Becker and Lewis (1973) to incorporate costs of the number of children that are not dependent on quality and costs of quality that are not dependent on the number of children. This generalized budget may be written

$$I = \pi_n n + \pi_q q + \pi_c nq + \pi_s s, \tag{8}$$

where $\pi_n$ and $\pi_q$, represent these independent cost components so that the marginal costs of numbers and quality become, respectively, $p_n = \pi_n + \pi_c q$ and $p_n = \pi_n + \pi_c n$. As an application, they consider a case in which $\pi_q = 0$ and $\pi_n$ represents the opportunity cost of fertility control. The introduction of a new contraceptive method such as the oral contraceptive pill, which does not interfere with sexual pleasure, will reduce the cost of averting births and, therefore, *increase* the marginal cost of a birth without affecting the marginal cost of child quality.[28] The increase in $p_n$ leads to a substitution effect against fertility which increases $q/n$, thereby inducing a further substitution effect against fertility and in favor of quality. Their analysis suggests that the elasticity

---

[28] See Michael (1973), Michael and Willis (1975) and Heckman and Willis (1975) for economic analyses of the relationship between contraception and fertility behavior.

of demand for number of children is likely to be more negative with respect to variables such as contraception or maternity costs, which affect $\pi_n$, than it is with respect to variables such as the female wage which, as we shall show shortly, affect $\pi_c$. A parallel analysis suggests that a decrease in $\pi_q$ due to, say, an increase in parents' education, may have a negative effect on fertility because the direct substitution effect which increases $q$ causes an increase in $p_n$. Other examples of factors affecting $\pi_q$ might include the quality of a neighborhood, school quality and cultural factors.

The simple analytics of child quality described above proceeded without an explicit discussion of what is meant by child quality. There are several alternative concepts of child quality in the literature. In Becker (1960), children are treated as a durable consumption good and child quality is indexed by expenditures per child in much the same way that quality might be judged by price in markets for automobiles in a world of well-informed consumers.[29] The linkage between expenditures per unit and quality that is implicit in this approach was made explicit in the "new consumer theory" of Lancaster (1966) in which, for example, an automobile is viewed as a bundle of "characteristics" such as power, comfort, safety, and so forth which enter the consumer's utility function.[30] With the exception of studies of the effect of sex preference on fertility,[31] the characteristics approach has not been widely used in economic models of fertility. The dominant view of child quality in the literature on fertility behavior and family economics is based on the theory of human capital form, envisioned as a model of human development.[32]

## 3.2. Time allocation and the demand for children

A second major reason for a negative relationship between income and fertility, in

---

[29] For a variety of reasons, it is extremely difficult to disentangle expenditures on children from expenditures on other persons within a household. A number of indirect approaches have been suggested to estimate the "cost of children" based upon equivalency scales which depend upon how observed household consumption patterns (e.g., proportion of income spent on food) vary as income and household consumption vary. See Browning (1992) for a survey of this literature. This literature is not helpful in understanding fertility behavior because (a) estimates of child costs are derived under the assumption that variations in household composition, including the number of children, are exogenous and (b) total expenditures on children are not decomposed into an endogenous part reflecting child quality and an exogenous part measuring the price index of children faced by the household.

[30] When goods are traded, implicit prices for these characteristics may be established in "hedonic markets" (Rosen, 1974). Since children are not traded, at least openly, this feature of hedonic theories is of little use in attempting to measure the costs of children of given characteristics.

[31] See Ben-Porath and Welch (1976) and Sah (1991).

[32] This appeal to human capital theory as a way of characterizing child quality was first explicitly introduced by Leibowitz (1974) and is formally developed in the seminal paper by Becker and Tomes (1976). In that paper, parents, who care about the lifetime economic well-being of their children, influence their children's well-being either through the direct transfer of money or by investing in the child's human capital.

addition to quality–quantity interaction, is the hypothesis that higher income is associated with a higher cost of female time, either because of increased female wage rates
or because higher household income raises the value of female time in nonmarket activities. Given the assumption that childrearing is a relatively time intensive activity,
especially for mothers, the opportunity cost of children tends to increase relative to
sources of satisfaction not related to children, leading to a substitution effect against
children. As noted earlier, the cost of time hypothesis was first advanced by Mincer
(1963) and, following Becker's (1965) development of the household production
model, the relationship between fertility and female labor supply has become a standard feature of models of household behavior.

A simple framework for analyzing the interplay between time allocation, labor
supply and fertility behavior was introduced by Willis (1973). He assumes that household decisions are made jointly by a married couple who derive utility from adult
standard of living and from the number and quality of children as given by the utility
function in Eq. (4). Following Becker (1965), it is assumed that these basic commodities, satisfaction from children and adult standard of living, cannot be purchased directly in the market. Rather, the household uses the nonmarket time of household
members and purchased goods as inputs into household production processes whose
outputs enter into the utility function. The analysis takes place within a static, lifetime
framework in which choices concerning the number of children, the fraction of wife's
time supplied to the labor market and so forth are assumed to be made at the beginning of marriage and are not subject to revision. Extension of the model to a dynamic
life-cycle context are treated later in the paper.

Several simplifying assumptions are made which allow the model to be analyzed
using the simple two-good, two-factor general equilibrium model familiar to students
of international trade theory. First, it is assumed that only the wife participates in the
production of household commodities while the husband is fully specialized in market
work and his income, $H$, is treated as exogenous. Total family income is $I = H + wL$
where $w$ is the wife's real wage and $L$ is her labor supply. Second, satisfaction from
children is measured by "child services", $c = nq$, and the determination of the division
of $c$ between the number and quality of children is left aside for the moment. Third,
household production takes place according to constant returns production functions,
$s = g(t_s, x_s)$ and $c = f(t_c, x_c)$, where $t_s$ and $t_c$ are the wife's time inputs $x_s$ and $x_s$ are purchased goods devoted, respectively, to the production of adult standard of living and
child services. A key assumption of the model is that the production technology for
children is time intensive relative to the technology for parents' standard of living. The
total time of the wife, $T$, is allocated between home and market work; that is $T = t_c + t_s$
$+ L$. Similarly, purchases of market goods are constrained by total household income
so that $I = H + wL = x_c + x_s$.

The solution of this model is illustrated diagrammatically in Fig. 8. Household production is depicted in Panel A with an Edgeworth Box diagram in which the horizontal dimension of the box measures the total amount of wife's time that is devoted to

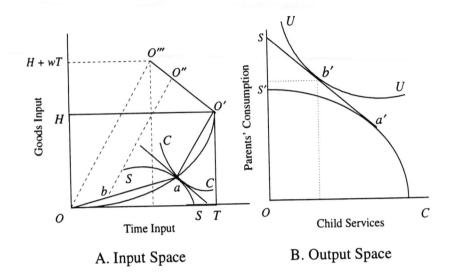

Fig. 8. Time allocation and fertility decisions.

household production (i.e., $t_c + t_s = T - L$) and the vertical dimension measures the total expenditure on goods (i.e., $x_c + x_s = T + wL$). When the wife does no work, the diagonal corners of the Edgeworth box are $OO'$; as the fraction of the wife's lifetime which is devoted to market work increases, the northeast corner of the box moves to points such as or $O'''$ where the slope of the line $O'O'''$ is determined by the wife's market wage, $w$.

Assuming that the wife does no market work, all possible efficient allocations of time and goods occur along the contract curve, $OO'$. Within the box, isoquants corresponding to increasing outputs of child services such as $CC$ emanate from the origin at $O$ while isoquants for parents standard of living such as $SS$ originate at $O'$. The assumption that children are relatively time intensive implies that the contract curve lies below the diagonal of the box. The (absolute value of the) common slope at the tangency between $CC$ and $SS$ at point $a$ is equal to the shadow price of the wife's time, $\hat{w}$, given by the ratio of the marginal products of time and goods in each activity (i.e., $\hat{w} = f_t/f_x = g_t/g_x$). As drawn, the shadow price of time at point $a$ is equal to the value to wife's market wage given by the slope of $OO'''$. The corresponding outputs of $c$ and $s$ are indicated at point $a'$ on the production possibility frontier in Panel B of Fig. 8.

If the output of child services is increased by moving along the contract curve to the northeast of point $a$ in Panel A, the shadow price of time increases because ratio of goods to time in the production of both $c$ and $s$ must increase, as is seen geometrically by the fact that rays to the origin from both origins become steeper as points to the northeast of $a$ are selected. Given that children are relatively time intensive, an increase in the price of the time input leads to an increase in the relative cost of the time intensive output. Thus, the relative shadow price of children, $\pi_c/\pi_s$, which is equal to the (absolute value of the) slope of the production possibility frontier in Panel B, tends to increase as the output of children rises above the level indicated at point $a'$. Conversely, as the output of $s$ is increased and input allocations occur to the southwest of point $a$, the shadow price of the wife's time falls below the market wage, implying that it is inefficient for her spend all of her time in household production. As the wife enters the labor market, thereby increasing household money income and decreasing the supply of nonmarket time, the shadow price of her time can be increased to equality with her market wage and household output can be increased beyond the boundaries of the production frontier associated with full-time housework. For example, the time intensities of $c$ and $s$ production at point $b$ along the contract curve $OO'$, which is associated with a positive amount of market labor by the wife, are the same as the intensities at point $a$ along the contract curve $OO'$, but the output of $c$ is smaller and of $s$ is larger at point $b$. Given constant returns technology, the ratios of the marginal products of inputs remain constant if factor intensities remain constant. In addition, constancy of the shadow prices of inputs implies that the relative marginal cost of outputs remains constant. Hence, point $b'$ on the production frontier in Panel B, which corresponds to point $b$ in Panel A, must lie along the tangent at point $a'$ on bowed-out production possibility curve that constrains the household when the wife does not participate in the labor market.[33] The fact that points such as $b'$ along $a'b'$ lie outside that frontier illustrates the efficiency gain to the household of adjusting the total supplies of time and goods through variations in the wife's labor supply. Since the wife cannot supply negative amounts of labor, these adjustments are not possible for outputs of child services greater than the output at point $a'$ so that the household is constrained over this range by the bowed-out frontier.[34]

The household's fertility decision is determined by maximization of its utility subject to the production possibility frontier. In Panel B of Fig. 8, this optimum is shown at the tangency between the household's indifference curve and the linear segment of the production frontier at point $b'$. The associated allocations indicated by point $b$ in Panel A show that the wife is supplying a positive of amount of market labor and the shadow price of her time is equal to her market wage (i.e., $w = \hat{w}$) corresponding to an Edgeworth box whose northeast corner is at point $O''$. If the household had a stronger preference for children relative to adult commodities such that its optimal choice oc-

---

[33] The straight line segment $a'b'$ is the envelope of production frontiers defined by Edgeworth boxes associated with different positive values of wife's labor supply. For example, the frontier determined by the Edgeworth box whose corner is at point $O''$ in Panel A of Fig. 8 is tangent to $a'b'$ at point $b'$.

[34] The analysis would be modified if purchased child care is introduced into the model. See Heckman (1974b) for an early analysis of child care and see Gustafsson and Stafford (1992) for a recent application to subsidized day care in Sweden. Macunovich (1994) points out that the relationship between a given woman's wage rate and the shadow price of children is broken if, at the margin, the cost of child services is determined by the market cost of child care rather than by the mother's wage rate.

curs on the production frontier to the right of point $a'$, the wife would do no market work and the shadow price of time would exceed the market wage.

More generally, imagine a large population made up of households with identical resources but heterogeneous preferences for children such that some households choose every point along the production frontier $Ca'S$ in Panel B. In this population, we would observe some fraction of the population made up of high fertility women who never work during their marriage consisting of households who choose points to the right of point $a'$ on the production frontier in Panel B and who choose an Edgeworth box whose northeast corner is at point $O'$ in Panel A. We would also observe some fraction of the population consisting of childless women who devote a substantial fraction of their married lives to market work consisting of households whose optimal choice of fertility is a corner solution at point $S$ in Panel B with a corresponding choice of market labor implied by the Edgeworth box whose corner is at $O'''$ in Panel B. Note that even these childless women may devote a considerable fraction of their married lives to nonmarket work.[35] Finally, we would observe some fraction of the population made up of households in which wives combine motherhood and market work such as, for example, households whose preferences are depicted in Panel B. In this group, there would tend to be a negative correlation between completed fertility and fraction of married life devoted to market work. We return to this point in our discussion of empirical models of completed fertility below.

The major empirical hypotheses of this static model are developed from comparative static analysis of the effects of exogenous variations in husband's income and female wage rates on fertility choices and related labor supply decisions by the wife. These results are presented diagrammatically in Fig. 9 for an increase in the wife's market wage, $w$, and for an increase in the husband's income, $H$, in Fig. 10. (See Willis (1973) for mathematical derivations.)

An increase in $w$ causes the point at which it is efficient for the wife to enter the labor market to shift from point $a$ to point $c$ on the production frontier in Fig. 9 so that the linear portion of the new frontier, corresponding to $L > 0$, is both outside of and steeper than the linear portion of the old frontier, implying that the increase in $w$ increases the household's real income and increases the opportunity cost of children. Given a household with preferences indicated by the indifference curves in the diagram, the increase in $w$ causes the household to move its optimal choice from point $b$ to point $d$. The total effect of the increase in $w$ on $c$ is ambiguous because the substitution effect against $c$ be more than offset by a positive income effect in favor of $c$. Even if the income effect dominates so that $c = nq$ increases, it is possible that fertility decreases while child quality increases. Indeed, Willis (1973) argues that this may be

---

[35] To keep the diagrams in two dimensions, the model has ignored the contributions of husbands to household production. Evidence on household time allocation from a broad sample of countries suggests that this is not a very unrealistic simplifying assumption. See Juster and Stafford (1991).

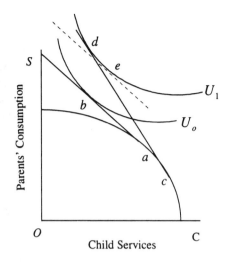

Fig. 9. Effect of an increase in the female wage.

the probable outcome because it seems unlikely that child quality would decrease while parents' standard of living increases sharply.[36]

Although the income effect associated with increasing female wages may push women away from childlessness toward married lives in which they combine motherhood and work, this effect may be offset by increasing returns to human capital investments in labor market careers caused by the fact that the returns to a given investment in human capital are proportional to its rate of utilization. To the extent that rising female wages lead women to devote a larger fraction of their lives to market work, there is a larger return to investments for women in market-related skills and reinforcing effects on their incentive to supply market labor and on the shadow price of time.[37] As shown by Willis (1973), investment in wife's human capital leads to a non-convex production possibility frontier which decreases the likelihood that a mix

[36] We note that the weight of the income effect relative to the substitution effect caused by an increase in the wife's wage is smallest in the neighborhood of point *a* in Fig. 10 where women have high fertility and spend a small fraction of married life in the labor force and largest in the vicinity of point *S* where women are childless and spend a relatively large fraction of their lives in the labor force. This suggests that a general increase in the price of female time might help to explain the decline in the variance of cohort TFR in the US since the mid-1930s first noted by Ryder (1986). Specifically, the substitution effects against fertility are not offset by income effects for households with strong tastes for children while only income effects are possible for childless households. Thus, increases in the female wage might tend to attract increasing numbers of women into the labor force and reduce fertility at high parities while, at the same time, it reduces the incidence of childlessness among women who have the lowest levels of fertility.

[37] The enormous literature on investments in human capital by women originates with Mincer and Polachek (1974) and the emphasis of the effects of increasing returns on the sexual division of labor is found in Becker (1981).

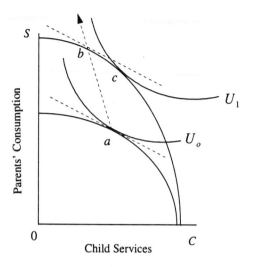

Fig. 10. Effect of an increase in the husband's income.

of motherhood and market work will dominate corner solutions involving either high fertility and specialization in home work or childlessness and an emphasis on the wife's labor market career.[38]

Finally, we note that Pollak and Wachter (1975) express concern about the robustness of the predictions concerning price and income effects that have been generated in the household production or time allocation literature, of which the Willis model is a special case. In particular, Pollak and Wachter point out that the close correspondence between market prices and shadow prices (i.e., the $\pi$'s) is lost when assumptions of constant returns to scale and exclude joint production are relaxed. However, Sanderson (1980) shows that the property of a positive relationship between the

---

[38] Increases in husbands' income may also lead to reduced variance in cohort total fertility discussed in the previous footnote. Given that children are relatively time-intensive, an increase in husband's income tends to have an asymmetric effect on the household's production frontier, increasing the potential output of adult commodities by more than it increases the potential for child-related commodities, when the wife's supply of time is held constant. This is illustrated in Fig. 10. If the household's preferences for children are relatively weak and the wife supplies a positive amount of market labor when husband's income is low, an increase in income will cause her to reduce her supply of labor. As long as she continues work at a constant wage, her price of time remains constant and, consequently, the opportunity cost of children also remains constant. Thus, in this case, the increase in $H$ leads to a pure income effect which presumably increases the demand for $c$, and, because of quality–quantity interactions, has an ambiguous effect on the demand for number of children. For households with the same initial resources and a demand for $c$ which is sufficiently strong that the wife does not work, the income effect resulting from an increase in $H$ tends to be offset by a substitution effect against children, as illustrated by the movement from point $a$ to point $c$ in Fig. 10. Because of this negative substitution effect, it is more likely that increases in husband's income will reduce fertility among households with relatively strong preferences for children.

shadow price of children and the wife's wage rate carries over to more general models when it is assumed that children are *marginally* more intensive than alternative household production activities.

### 3.3. Marriage, fertility and out-of-wedlock childbearing

As documented in Section 2, the incidence of nonmarital fertility has grown since World War II in almost all developed countries. This fact, coupled with greatly increased divorce rates and an increased proportion of children living in female-headed households, has provoked considerable alarm about the demise of the traditional family and concern about its potentially harmful effects on the well-being of women and children. While there have been a number of recent studies which attempt to describe the socioeconomic correlates of out-of-wedlock childbearing or attempt to determine empirically whether potential harmful effects are real,[39] only recently have there been attempts to develop a coherent theoretical framework for understanding the causes and consequences of out-of-wedlock childbearing. On the one hand, economic theories of fertility of the sort that we have described so far treat fertility as a "household decision", made jointly by a husband and wife who can be treated as a unitary decision maker. On the other hand, economic theories of marriage[40] note that childbearing is a leading reason for marriage but do not explicitly incorporate fertility decisions into the analysis.

A recent attempt to integrate economic theories of fertility and marriage in order to understand the growth of out-of-wedlock childbearing is presented in Willis (1995). In order to understand the interaction between marital decisions and fertility decisions, he considers a very simple model in which women and men are treated as separate decision makers. The model represents a blend of Becker's theory of marriage (Becker, 1981) and Weiss and Willis' (1985) theory of children as a collective good.[41] Under certain circumstances, the model produces results similar to those emphasized by William J. Wilson's theory of out-of-wedlock childbearing among the underclass (Wilson, 1987). Specifically, if women's resources are sufficiently great, both absolutely and relative to men's, and women are also more numerous, there may be equilibria in which men, drawn from the lower tail of the income distribution, father as many children as possible and women, also low income, voluntarily bear and rear these children out of wedlock using only their own resources or AFDC transfers. In such an equilibrium, expenditures on children are lower than in an alternative "traditional" equilibrium in which all available men marry and father children, the

---

[39] DaVanzo and Rahman (1993) provide citations to many of these studies.

[40] See Becker (1973, 1974, 1981).

[41] See Weiss (this volume) and Bergstrom (this volume) for more detailed discussion of models of marriage and household behavior in which the interests of male and female partners are considered separately.

mother and father share in the costs of childrearing, and unmarried women remain childless. "Underclass equilibria" of the latter type occur when men are relatively scarce and women's incomes are both absolutely and relatively higher.

Following Weiss and Willis (1985), assume that children are collective goods from the point of view of the parents in the sense that both parents value their children's welfare. Given that children are collective goods, there are potential gains to both parents from coordinating the allocation of their resources to their children and, arguably, this coordination is best accomplished within the context of marriage because repeated interaction between the parents reduces tendencies for free riding. Moreover, the efficient allocation of resources within marriage also benefits the children because, by sharing in their costs, both parents face lower prices of child quality. Conversely, if one parent has custody and the other parent can only influence the children's welfare by transferring money to the custodian, Weiss and Willis (1985) show that the couple will reach a Stackelberg equilibrium in which (a) the expenditure on child quality will be lower than it would be within marriage, (b) the allocation of the couple's joint resources is not Pareto optimal so that both parents could be made better off by increasing expenditures on children, and (c) the amount of money the non-custodial parent is willing to transfer to the custodian decreases as the custodian's income increases and, if the custodian's income is sufficiently high, the non-custodial parent will voluntarily contribute nothing toward the upbringing of his or her child. In a world with one woman and one man, this implies that Eve would never choose to become a single mother, nor would Adam choose to be a single father, because both parties can be made better off through marriage.

Despite these gains to marriage, Willis (1995) argues that out-of-wedlock childbearing and single parenthood may arise as an equilibrium outcome in a competitive marriage market if: (a) most women have incomes exceeding a threshold $\bar{I}$ such that they are willing to bear and rear children using only their own resources;[42] (b) men in the lower portion of the income distribution have relatively low incomes so that the gains to coordinating parental resources are relatively small; and (c) women are more numerous than men in the marriage market. Conversely, when these conditions fail to hold, he argues that there will be a "traditional equilibrium" in which all childbearing takes place within marriage and unmarried persons remain childless.

To summarize the argument, first consider a traditional marriage market equilibrium in a world in which there are equal numbers of men and women. Within each sex, assume that persons have identical preferences but vary in income. Given the

---

[42] For simplicity, assume the couple's utility functions satisfy the conditions for transferable utility such that the efficient quantity of a public good is independent of the distribution of income (Bergstrom and Cornes, 1983). In this case there is a given threshold level of income, $\bar{I}$, such that a married couple would desire to have children if their joint resources exceed this threshold (i.e., $I_m + I_f > \bar{I}$) and, similarly, such that a single mother would desire to have children if her income exceeds the same threshold (i.e., $I_f > \bar{I}$) where $I_m$ and $I_f$ refer to male and female incomes.

existence of a household public good such as children, Lam (1988) proves that the equilibrium assignment in a Beckerian marriage market involves positive assortative mating. That is, assuming that their joint income exceeds $\bar{I}$, the highest income man will marry and have a child with the highest income woman, the next highest income couple will marry and bear a child and so on until a point is reached at which joint incomes of highest income unmarried man and highest income unmarried woman are less than or equal to $\bar{I}$. In the absence of other reasons to marry, assume that all persons with incomes below this level remain unmarried and childless.

A traditional equilibrium would also hold if there is a numerical excess supply of men even if the lowest income man has an income that exceeds $\bar{I}$. In this case, all women would marry and bear children with men drawn from the upper portion of the income distribution. The remaining men in the lower tail of the income distribution will remain unmarried and childless because no such man can make any married woman better off by leaving her marriage to bear his child. A traditional equilibrium will also occur if women are in excess supply but they have incomes that are much too low to support a child on their own. In this case, a married man might wish to father children by unmarried women but he will not be able to do so without incurring costs that outweigh the benefit of maintaining a traditional marriage.

If women have incomes that are sufficiently high, however, they will desire to have children even if they must rear children entirely with their own resources where resources are interpreted to include either the woman's own labor income or AFDC transfers she is eligible to receive. From a man's point of view, this means that he may enjoy the benefits of fatherhood (or the joy of sex) at zero economic cost to himself if he decides to father children by a woman who is willing to bear all the costs of rearing them. As we have seen, both the father and the mother could always attain a still greater level of utility within marriage by making a higher expenditure on their children financed with some of the father's income. However, it is possible that a man might find it advantageous to forgo this gain if he could father children at zero cost by enough different women. Because their incomes exceed $\bar{I}$, women gain by becoming mothers rather than by remaining childless.

If women outnumber men, there may exist an "underclass equilibrium" under these circumstances such that, while high income men and women continue to bear children within marriage, some fraction of men drawn from the lower part of the income distribution father children out-of-wedlock by women who also have low incomes. Suppose, for example, that each man would prefer to forgo marriage if he could father children out-of-wedlock by two different partners and assume that the overall sex ratio is 110 males per 100 females in a large population. Marriage will still tend to take place among couples in the upper end of the income distribution because there are too few available female partners to entice males to eschew marriage. However, as the number of marriages increases, the ratio of unmarried females to unmarried males tends to increase without bound. A little arithmetic shows that each unmarried male can have two partners when 90% of men marry and 10% of men father children by the

18% of women who fail to find a marriage partner. Although these women would prefer to become married, given their low incomes they are unable to offer more utility to any married man than he obtains in partnership with a higher income woman. Similarly, no married man would find it advantageous to exchange places with a lower income unmarried man with two partners because the gains to the efficient coordination of joint resources is higher for him precisely because he has more resources.

This analysis has a variety of empirical implications, although few have yet been explored systematically. One is that a reduction in the number of partners that a man requires in order to be willing to forgo marriage may have a large effect on the fraction of births born out of wedlock. For instance, if the required number of partners per unmarried man falls from 2 to 1.2, the equilibrium fraction of men who will father children out-of-wedlock increases from 10% to 50% and the fraction of nonmarital births increases from 18% to 58%. What would cause such a shift? One cause would be a growth in the resources of women, particularly growth in the lower portions of the income distribution due to increased labor market opportunities or AFDC. Another would be a decline in the income of men in the lower portions of the income distribution. Still another would be an increase in the ratio of females to males in the marriage market caused by differential mortality or incarceration. Such factors have been emphasized by Wilson (1987) in his analysis of the high prevalence of out-of-wedlock childbearing among underclass blacks. Rapid growth of the fraction of nonmarital births among non-blacks during the past two decades coincides with growing female labor force attachment and some reduction in the male–female wage ratio that partly reflects gains for women and partly reduced earnings of men in the lower half of the wage distribution. These co-movements appear to be broadly consistent with the theory, but formal tests of the theory's capacity to explain the trends await future research. Yet another implication is that stronger enforcement of child support laws (i.e., identification of paternity, establishment of child support awards, collection of obligations) would tend to reduce the attractiveness of nonmarital childbearing by eliminating the capacity of men and women to make a private deal in which the man fathers a child but takes no financial responsibility for it.

Finally, the empirical implications of the economic model of out-of-wedlock childbearing can be enriched by bringing in some of the factors that were assumed away in the interest of simplicity. For example, it would be useful to attempt to extend the theory of out-of-wedlock childbearing presented here to include the effect of the growth of divorce and remarriage on fertility decisions using more dynamic models along the lines of those described later in this paper. Another useful extension is to incorporate the desire for sexual pleasure and imperfect fertility control into the model. In an interesting and provocative paper, Akerlof et al. (1994) argue that the growing capacity of women to control their reproduction through abortion has the paradoxical effect of increasing the likelihood of nonmarital childbearing and Kane and Staiger (1995) present empirical evidence that improved access to abortion clinics tends to increase out-of-wedlock births.

## 4. Life-cycle models of fertility

In this section, we describe the essential features of the dynamic, or life-cycle, models of fertility that have been developed in the literature. As has been noted in the study of labor supply behavior within labor economics, developing models which are explicitly dynamic and embedded within a life-cycle setting is important for several reasons. Introducing decision making within a life-cycle framework makes explicit the existence of additional margins over which parents may choose to substitute their fertility, namely, childbearing at different ages over the life cycle. As such, changes in prices and income over the life cycle may result in changes in the *timing* of fertility demand, even if they do not cause *lifetime* fertility to change. The life-cycle context is also the appropriate setting within which to consider the consequences of the stochastic nature of human reproduction, including the choice of contraceptive practices and responses of parents to the realizations of this stochastic process. Finally, the dynamic setting provides a more appropriate context within which to examine the relationships between women's labor supply, investment in human capital and childbearing decisions that were alluded to in Section 3.2.

In what follows, we provide an overview of the structure of the nascent literature on dynamic models of fertility. We begin by outlining a taxonomy of the model "features" which have been incorporated into the theoretical literature to date, indicating how they correspond to those contained in the static models considered above. We then briefly discuss the mathematical structure of the solution to the parents' optimal childbearing (or contraceptive method) decisions over their life cycle. As that discussion makes clear, these solutions do not lead to straightforward and robust implications about what life-cycle patterns of fertility behavior should be observed and how they vary as prices and income vary.[43] Finally, we summarize the implications that these models have for the dimensions of intertemporal fertility behavior whose empirical trends we surveyed earlier: namely, trends in the timing of first births, the spacing between births, total childbearing, contraceptive practices and contraceptive failures; and "unwanted" children in the US and other developed countries during the twentieth century.

### 4.1. Features of life-cycle models of fertility and the optimal solution

Existing economic theories of fertility in a life-cycle setting blend features of static models of fertility with those from at least four different strands of dynamic models of behavior: (i) models of optimal life-cycle consumption,[44] (ii) models of life-cycle la-

---

[43] As we shall discuss in Section 5, the solutions to these programs do not lend themselves to simple econometric specifications, either.

[44] See Friedman (1957).

bor supply decisions,[45] (iii) models of human capital investment and accumulation,[46] and (iv) stochastic models of human reproduction.[47] While no one model incorporates all of these strands, it is pedagogically useful to characterize the features of a comprehensive model in order to delineate those model elements which have been considered in the existing literature.[48] We consider a prototypical household which, at the outset, consists of a woman and her spouse[49] who are assumed to act in unison to make fertility and time and resource allocation decisions over a finite lifetime.[50] We characterize their lifetime in discrete time units, $t$, that index the "age" of the household unit and their lifetime runs from zero to $T$. In our comprehensive model, we assume that the couple make their choices so as to maximize a well-defined *set of preferences*, subject to *time* and *(financial) budget constraints*, to technological constraints which govern the *(re)production* and *rearing of children* and to constraints on the *production* of the woman's *stock of human capital* which determines the value of her time in the labor market at each age. The couple will make these decisions either in a *certain* (perfect foresight) or an *uncertain* setting, where the uncertainty they may face can arise either from the stochastic nature of the reproductive process or of the future income, prices or wage rates they may face. We now briefly describe the specifications of these model features which have been considered in the literature.

### 4.1.1. Preference structures and the production of child services

Following the structure of preferences considered in static models, the most general specification of lifetime parental preferences considered in the literature takes the following form:

$$U = \sum_{t=0}^{T} \beta^t u(c_t, \ell_t, s_t), \tag{9}$$

where $\ell_t$ is the amount of time the mother consumes in leisure activities at age $t$, $s_t$ is

[45] See MaCurdy (1980) and Heckman and MaCurdy (1980).

[46] Ben-Porath (1967).

[47] See Perrin and Sheps (1964).

[48] While hardly exhaustive, the following studies develop life cycle models of fertility behavior from an economic, or rational choice, perspective: Heckman and Willis (1976), Razin (1980), Hotz (1980), Cigno (1983), Happel et al. (1984), Vijverberg (1984), Moffitt (1984a), Hotz and Miller (1986), David and Mroz (1986), Newman (1988), Cigno and Ermisch (1989), Montgomery (1989), Cigno (1991), Hotz and Miller (1993), Rosenzweig and Wolpin (1993), and Walker (1995). Some of these models are surveyed in Montgomery and Trussell (1986).

[49] To date, no dynamic models have been developed which incorporate marriage decisions within a life cycle fertility model.

[50] Hotz and Miller (1986) actually develop a model in which, for analytic convenience, couples are assumed to be infinitely-lived.

parental consumption, $\beta$ is the couple's rate of time preference ($0 \le \beta \le 1$), and $c_t$, the flow of child services parents receive at age $t$ from their stock of children, is governed by the following production process:

$$c_t = (b_0, b_1, \ldots, b_{t-1}, t_{ct}, x_{ct}),$$ (10)

where $b_\tau = 1$ if the parents gave birth to a child when they were age $\tau$ ($\tau = 0, \ldots, t-1$) and $b_\tau = 0$ otherwise; and $t_{ct}$ and $x_{ct}$ denote, respectively, the mother's time and a vector of market inputs used in the production of child services. The latter inputs may include non-parental child-care services.[51] Assuming that children do not die before their parents do,[52] it follows that the couple's stock of children at age $t$ is given by

$$n_t = \sum_{\tau=0}^{t-1} b_\tau .$$

The life-cycle models of fertility found in the literature are based on several specializations of this general specification of preferences. The simplest specification in the literature, considered by Happel et al. (1984), assumes that $U$ in Eq. (9) does not depend on $\ell_t$ at any age and does not depend on $c_t$ except at age $T$, when child services are assumed to be proportional to $n_T$, the couple's completed family size (i.e., $c_T = n_T$). The latter specification closely mimics the specification of static models in that parental utility is not affected by the timing of births; all they care about is their completed family size. In many of the life-cycle models developed to date, child services, $c_t(\cdot)$, vary with the parents' age but are restricted to be proportional to the accumulated number of children, $n_t$.[53] The exceptions are the papers by Moffitt (1984b), Vijverberg (1984), Hotz and Miller (1986, 1993), which consider more general forms of $c_t(\cdot)$. For example, both Moffitt (1984b) and Hotz and Miller (1986) evaluate specifications of Eq. (10) in which parental time inputs, $t_{ct}$, and market inputs, $x_{ct}$, vary as a function of the ages of children, with young children "requiring" more maternal time and older children more market inputs.[54]

---

[51] Moffitt (1984b) explicitly considers the substitution possibilities between parental time and market-based child care inputs.

[52] Wolpin (1984) and Newman (1988) consider models in which the survival of children is governed by a stochastic mortality process.

[53] This is true of Wolpin (1984).

[54] Hotz and Miller (1993) also allow children to have an age-dependent effect on $c_t$, over and above the impact that children of different ages have via age-varying requirements of parental time and market inputs in the production of $c_t$.

### 4.1.2. Maternal time constraints

To the extent that the allocation of maternal time is explicitly incorporated, existing life-cycle models include period-by-period constraints on the mother's time of the form

$$\ell_t + h_t + t_{ct} = 1, \tag{11}$$

where we normalize the per-period amount of time available to the mother to one and where $h_t$ is the (normalized) amount of time she spends in the labor market. None of the existing life-cycle models consider the time allocation decisions of fathers; they are assumed only to provide for the rearing of children through the income they generate.

### 4.1.3. The production of children and control of fertility

The static models of fertility discussed in Section 3 presumed that parents could control their fertility perfectly and costlessly. Several of the life-cycle models in the literature maintain this assumption, allowing parents complete and costless control over their ability to have or not have a birth at each age.[55] However, controlling a woman's fertility is not likely to be either perfect or without costs, be they monetary or psychic. In fact, producing (or avoiding) births is an uncertain process which is intimately linked with the sexual activity and gratification of women and their mates. Modeling human reproduction as a stochastic process has a long tradition in population biology and formal demography.[56] In this literature, a couple's childbearing behavior is viewed as realizations of a stochastic process governing conception and pregnancy resolution events which are largely beyond the control of parents. Thus, in contrast to the emphasis on the demand for fertility found in the early, largely static, economic models, the demographic and biological literature has stressed the "supply" side of human fertility.

The models in the economics literature which allow for stochastic reproduction in their modeling of life-cycle fertility[57] assume that a couple's fertility is stochastic but controllable, in part, by the contraceptive strategies they choose. As such, we can view the couple's fertility as being governed by their "reproduction" function, which takes the form

---

[55] This is true of the models by Hotz (1980), Wolpin (1984), Moffitt (1984b), Happel et al. (1984), Vijverberg (1984), and Cigno and Ermisch (1989).

[56] See Perrin and Sheps (1964) and Sheps and Menken (1973).

[57] The initial papers to address this issue were Michael and Willis (1976) and Heckman and Willis (1976). The models developed by Rosenzweig and Schultz (1985, 1989), Hotz and Miller (1986, 1993), Newman (1988), and Montgomery (1989) also incorporate the stochastic nature of reproduction into choice-based, life-cycle models of fertility.

$$b_t = R(e_t, \phi_t),\tag{12}$$

where $e_t$ denotes a $K$-dimensional vector of whose typical element, $e_k$, denotes whether or not the $k$th contraceptive method is used, $k = 1,...,K$, and $\phi_t$ denotes the stochastic component governing the likelihood that a birth is produced with an unprotected sexual act. It follows that $b_t$ is a random variable and the parents' *birth probability function* is given by

$$p_{bt}(e_t, \mu, \sigma_\phi^2) \equiv \Pr(b_t = 1 \mid t, e_t, \mu, \sigma_\phi^2) = E_\phi\big(R(e_t, \phi_t)\big),\tag{13}$$

where $E_\phi(\cdot)$ denotes the expectations operator over the random variable $\phi_t$, and $\mu$ and $\sigma_\phi^2$ are the mean and variance, respectively, of $\phi_t$. The couple's $\mu$ can be interpreted as a couple's *fecundity*; More fecund couples have a higher probability of conception conditional on any method used, i.e., $\partial p_{bt}(e_t, \mu, \sigma_\phi^2)/\partial\mu \geq 0$, holding constant any particular contraceptive method used, $e_k$ say.[58] In addition to the pill, condoms, etc., three contraceptive methods are of particular analytic interest: (i) the use of no protection (which we indicate by $e_{1t}$); (ii) permanent sterilization, which precludes any (further) births; and (iii) an induced abortion (which we indicate by $e_{Kt}$) which, for our purposes, can be thought of as an *ex post* contraceptive method.

Most models presume that fertility control through the use of contraceptive methods, other than unprotected sex ($e_{1t} = 1$), is costly – either in out-of-pocket costs, time costs in their execution (e.g., physician visits to obtain prescriptions), or psychic costs associated with the displeasure or inconvenience of their use (e.g., using a condom which reduces the pleasure of sexual intercourse).[59] These costs can be incorporated into the model by including $e_t$ as an argument in the parents' utility function in Eq. (9), where $U(\cdot)$ is presumed to be decreasing in $e_t$, and by including the out-of-pocket costs in the parental budget constraint which is to be described below.

Finally, we note that models in which the birth process is stochastic, as in Eq. (12), transform the parents' intertemporal optimization problem into one of decision making under uncertainty. The implications of this point for strategic behavior on the part of parents are discussed below.

### 4.1.4. The household's budget constraint

The budget constraints facing parents in the existing life-cycle models of fertility vary depending upon what is assumed about their ability to save and/or their access to capital markets. All existing models assume that capital markets are either *perfect* –

---

[58] See Sheps and Menken (1973) and Rosenzweig and Schultz (1985, 1989).

[59] The Hotz and Miller (1986, 1993) model allows for stochastic births and contraceptive protection, but assumes that such protection is costless to the parents. The other models which incorporate stochastic reproduction explicitly acknowledge the costs of such protection.

i.e., parents are able to borrow and lend across time periods at a real interest rate, $r_t$ – or *perfectly-imperfect*, in which case no borrowing or saving is possible.

In models which maintain the perfect capital markets (PCM) assumption,[60] the parents face an overall, lifetime budget constraint in which assets, $A_t$, can be borrowed or lent over time. For simplicity, assume that parents start with no assets, i.e., $A_0 = 0$, and leave no bequests, i.e., $A_T = 0$. Then defining *savings* at age $t$ to be $S_t (\equiv A_t - A_{t-1})$, the parents' age $t$ budget constraint is given by

$$S_t = Y_{ht} + w_t h_t - s_t - \mathbf{p}'_{ct}\mathbf{x}_{ct} - \mathbf{p}'_{et}\mathbf{e}_t - \pi_n n_t, \tag{14}$$

where $Y_{ht}$ denotes husband's income at age $t$, $w_t$ is the wife's market wage rate, $\mathbf{p}_{ct}$ and $\mathbf{p}_{et}$ are vectors of prices for market inputs to the production of child services and the out-of-pocket costs of contraceptives, respectively, and, as before, $\pi_n$ denotes the per-unit, non-quality cost of children. A key feature of the PCM assumption is that savings in any period can either be positive or negative, i.e., parents are allowed to borrow against the future or *dissave*. In the case of perfectly, imperfect capital markets (PICM), parents cannot save, i.e., $S_t = 0$ for all $t$, and parental consumption is constrained by the following *period by period* constraint:[61]

$$Y_{ht} + w_t h_t = s_t + \mathbf{p}'_{ct}\mathbf{x}_{ct} + \mathbf{p}'_{et}\mathbf{e}_t + \pi_n n_t. \tag{15}$$

While not adopted in any of the models in the existing literature, we note that there is a third alternative for specifying the parents' budget constraint, namely the possibility of *less than perfect capital markets* (LPCM) in which parents can save for but not borrow against the future. This assumption amounts to imposing the side constraint on Eq. (14) that $S_t \geq 0$ for all $t$. Despite its realism, the LPCM assumption has not been widely used in formal models of life-cycle behavior because of its mathematical intractability. Nonetheless, we speculate below as to what implications it might have for fertility behavior over the life cycle.

Finally, we note that considering parental decision making within the life-cycle context puts the possibility that they face uncertainty about future income and prices into sharper relief. Most of the existing literature on life-cycle fertility does not incorporate this form of uncertainty. The one exception is the model of Hotz and Miller (1986, 1993) in which future realizations of husband's income, $Y_{ht}$, and the wife's wage rate, $w_t$, are treated as stochastic.

---

[60] The models of Happel et al. (1984), Moffitt (1984b), Vijverberg (1984), and Walker (1995) maintain this assumption about capital markets.

[61] The models of Heckman and Willis (1976), Wolpin (1984), Hotz and Miller (1986, 1993), and Newman (1988) adopt this assumption about the nature of capital markets available to parents.

### 4.1.5. Maternal investments in human capital

The final feature of life-cycle fertility models considered in the literature concerns the treatment of the mother's wages. In most of the models in which the allocation of maternal time is treated as endogenous, the mother's wages over her life cycle are treated as exogenously determined. Several papers, however, do introduce the possibility that the mother's participation in the labor force not only generate income for the family but also may enhance her future labor market skills, and thus her future wage rate possibilities.[62] Adding this feature also introduces a potentially important source of intertemporal variation in the opportunity cost of maternal time in the production and care of children and, thus, in the timing of births over the life cycle. We return to this point below.

The life-cycle fertility models which introduce human capital investment generally adopt a "learning-by-doing" human capital production process in which maternal wage rates are determined, in part, by the mother's past labor supply and her current work effort. More formally, this production function is given by

$$w_t = H(w_{t-1}, h_t) - \delta_1 w_{t-1} - \delta_2 w_{t-1} 1[h_t = 0], \tag{16}$$

where $H(\cdot, \cdot)$ is the human capital production function, $\delta_1$ and $\delta_2$ are rates of depreciation ($0 \le \delta_i \le 1$, $i = 1, 2$), and $1[\cdot]$ is the indicator function. The depreciation component of the mother's human capital accumulation given in Eq. (16) allows for the possibility that the woman's skills – and, thus, her subsequent wage rates – depreciate either because of age-related atrophy or because they are not utilized in the labor market.[63]

### 4.1.6. The structure of the solution to the parents' intertemporal optimization problem

While differing according to the particular model features incorporated, the life-cycle models in the literature all entail parents sequentially making choices over: (i) childbearing, or contraceptive methods, (ii) parental consumption and (iii) the allocation of the mother's time across labor market and childrearing activities so as to maximize Eq. (9) subject to the constraints implied by the relationships in Eqs. (10)–(12) (if reproduction is stochastic), Eq. (14) or (15) and, possibly Eq. (16). The parents' optimization problem can be solved using techniques in the dynamic programming literature.[64] The structure of the solution differs somewhat depending upon whether the

---

[62] The models of Cigno (1983), Happel et al. (1984), Moffitt (1984b), Cigno and Ermisch (1989) and Walker (1995) incorporate the possibility of maternal human capital investment.

[63] The latter type of human capital depreciation is considered by Hotz et al. (1996).

[64] See, for example, Bellman (1957).

model includes uncertainty with respect to future birth, income or price realizations (the "uncertainty" case) or not (the "perfect foresight" case).

For pedagogic purposes, consider the perfect foresight case. With no uncertainty, the solution to the parents' dynamic programming problem maps parental choice variables at each age to the life-cycle sequences of prices (including wages and interest rates), incomes (or initial assets) and the dimensions of the "technologies" which characterize the production of children, their rearing and human capital. That is, the optimal solution for the parents' decision to have a birth at age $t$ would be given by the following mapping:

$$b_t = b_t\left(\{p_{c\tau}\}_{\tau=0}^T, \{p_{e\tau}\}_{\tau=0}^T, \{w_\tau\}_{\tau=0}^T, \{r_\tau\}_{\tau=0}^T, A_0; \theta\right) \tag{17}$$

under the PCM assumption and

$$b_t = b_t\left(\{p_{c\tau}\}_{\tau=0}^T, \{p_{e\tau}\}_{\tau=0}^T, \{w_\tau\}_{\tau=0}^T, \{r_\tau\}_{\tau=0}^T, \{Y_{h\tau}\}_{\tau=0}^T; \theta\right) \tag{18}$$

under the PICM assumption, where, $\{z_\tau\}_{\tau=0}^t$ denotes the sequences of variables, $z_\tau$, and $\theta$ denotes a vector of the exogenous parental attributes which shape their preferences and which characterize the technologies and/or endowments governing the production functions given above. The mappings in Eqs. (17) and (18) constitute the analogue to fertility demand equations in the static context.

Several general observations can be made about the structure of the above mappings. First, they make clear that the life-cycle setting entails several alternative types of price effects (and income effects under the PICM assumption). As has been noted in the literature on life-cycle labor supply models,[65] changes in prices (or income) at any age (i.e., transitory price changes) will, in general, affect whether the couple want to have a birth at age $t$. More to the point, the effect of such price changes on contemporaneous fertility – which will generally entail income and substitution effects – may be to shift the *timing* of births over the life-cycle rather than have much, if any, effect on the number of births accumulated. (A similar conclusion applies to transitory changes in parental income.) As noted in the introduction to this section, one of the consequences of extending models of fertility to the life-cycle context is the expansion of the margins over which fertility can be shifted in response to changes. Note that this point about the potential importance of intertemporal substitution of fertility holds whether prices or incomes change over any segment of the parents' life cycle.[66]

---

[65] See MaCurdy (1980) and Heckman and MaCurdy (1980).

[66] For example, Walker (1995) notes that changes in the "slope" of price and/or wage profiles which hold parental wealth constant – what MaCurdy (1980) refers to as "evolutionary" price changes – may change the life-cycle timing of births but not have any effect on a couple's completed family size.

Second, while the mappings in Eqs. (17) and (18) express births at a given age as a function of sequences of prices, it is important to keep in mind that none of these individual prices correspond to the "price of children" concept, be it $\pi_c$ or $\pi_n$, developed under the static theory of fertility. This is because children are "durable" goods so that the "user cost" of children is a function of the sequences of prices given in Eqs. (17) and (18).[67]

Finally, while the above mappings characterize the general solutions to the parents' fertility choices, at least in the perfect foresight case, they typically cannot be expressed as closed form or particularly manageable functions. Moreover, when one extends these models to include stochastic elements, i.e., moves to the uncertainty case, these problems become even more complex. For example, the analogues to Eqs. (17) and (18) in the uncertainty setting are not, in general, obtained by simply substituting expected values in place of future prices and incomes.[68] In either the certainty or uncertainty setting, the solutions are derived via backward recursion methods and result in complex functions of future prices and incomes in the perfect foresight case or, in the case of uncertainty, of expected values of functions which involve their stochastic analogues. This problem arises, in large part, because of the discrete nature of many of the choice variables (e.g., births or contraceptive methods are characterized as discrete events) and/or the "corner" solutions which characterize the mother's labor supply decisions over her life-cycle. This feature of solutions to the parents' life-cycle choice complicates the task of devising econometric specifications of the life-cycle models developed in the existing literature.[69] It also has limited the ability to obtain unambiguous comparative dynamic predictions from these models. Nonetheless, several of the models developed in the literature do appear to give some general predictions about how several dimensions of life-cycle fertility respond to variations in prices and income and the alternative specifications of the model features described above. In the next several sections, we briefly discuss these implications.

## 4.2. The optimal timing of first births

As we noted in Section 2, the age at which women in developed countries begin their childbearing has varied substantially over the twentieth century and differs across ethnic groups. Recall that since the 1960s first births have shifted to later ages in the US and that this decline has been much more pronounced for white women compared to non-whites (see Fig. 4). The life-cycle models developed to date have suggested several factors which account for when, in the life cycle, it is optimal for couples to

---

[67] See Walker (1995) for a discussion of this point.

[68] Thus, the specifications of dynamic fertility demand and labor supply functions in Ward and Butz (1980), which are based on this approach, have no theoretical basis.

[69] As discussed below, Wolpin (1984) and Hotz and Miller (1993) do develop models which are consistent with the economic structure and, at the same time, are estimable.

begin their childbearing. What determines the optimal age at which to begin childbearing in these models primarily hinges on: (i) what one assumes about how parents value their offspring; (ii) the structure of capital markets; and (iii) how the maternal time costs of mothers vary over her life cycle. Birth timing may also be affected by contraceptive strategies to avoid having too many births.

Consider, for example, the model by Happel et al. (1984). Recall that these authors assume that parental preferences depend only on completed family size; their flow of utility from children does not depend upon how much of their life cycles they share with their children. With little loss of generality, they assume that the couple only has one child; the only choice is when to have it. Consider the case where capital markets are perfect, i.e., the PCM assumption holds. Then the timing of childbearing over the parents life cycle depends on the "costs" that childbearing imposes on parental consumption due to the loss of income that results from the mother's labor force withdrawal to care for newborns. This loss in income depends on the rate at which earnings depreciate due to absence from the labor force (the value of $\delta_2$ in Eq. (16)) and the initial level of earnings at the start of a couple's life cycle ($w_0$). If mothers start with little or no earning power ($w_0$ at or near 0) and skills depreciate with absence from the market ($\delta_2 > 0$), then it is optimal for women to have their children early to minimize the loss in their total lifetime earnings. If a mother has positive initial earnings ($w_0 > 0$) and $\delta_2 > 0$, then she is better off to postpone her childbearing, minimizing the loss of lifetime earnings that result from the time she takes to rear her children. If woman's skill does not depreciate with an absence from the market then under the PCM assumption, women are indifferent as to whether they have their children early or late as the loss of lifetime earnings to have a child is the same at whatever age they start their childbearing.

If capital markets are perfectly-imperfect (PICM holds), the time path of the father's income – which played no role in the optimal timing of births under the PCM assumption – now matters. In particular, Happel et al. (1984) show if the mother's skills do not deteriorate during her absence from the market ($\delta_2 = 0$), the optimal time to have births is when the husband's income is highest, i.e., when the marginal utility of income for parental consumption is the lowest. Assuming that husband's earnings rise, this implies that the couple postpones its childbearing; in essence, children are postponed until the parents minimize the impact on their own consumption and "can afford" children. Finally, if women's skills do depreciate ($\delta_2 > 0$), then the timing of childbearing depends upon the relative importance of giving up parental consumption (i.e., the marginal utility of income in terms of parental consumption) and the marginal loss of income due to this depreciation.

While Happel et al. do not consider the case in which savings are possible but borrowing against future income is not (i.e., the LPCM assumption), one might speculate that such restriction on capital markets would still imply that childbearing would be postponed until the couple had achieved a "nest egg" to finance having the wife leave the labor market to have children. Such predictions seem to be consistent with anecdotal evidence that in the early part of this century, many couples in the US, especially those in which the women were not highly skilled (i.e., $\delta_2 \approx 0$), postponed their child-bearing until they had saved enough to have their children.

Recall that Happel et al. (1984) assume that the utility parents derive from children only depends on the total number they bear. Most of the other life-cycle models of fertility relax this restriction and have parents derive utility from children as soon as they are born, i.e., $c_t$ enters $U$ in Eq. (9) for ages $t < T$. Allowing for children to generate parental utility as soon as they are born provides another impetus for children to be born early, rather than, late in the life cycle. Nonetheless, Moffitt (1984b) shows that it still may be optimal for parents to postpone their first births. Moffitt's model, which is not dissimilar to that of Happel et al., assumes that: (i) parents receive utility from child services and the leisure time of mothers; (ii) capital markets are assumed to be perfect; (iii) children require maternal time inputs; and (iv) working in the labor force can increase a mother's future wages. Moffitt (1984b) shows that couples may choose to postpone their childbearing either because of the opportunity cost of human capital accumulation early in their life cycle exceeds the value of children or, even in the absence of the human capital investment motive, the couple's marginal utility of the first unit of the mother's time in leisure activities exceeds that of the utility achieved from having a child.

Finally, the existing theories of life-cycle fertility suggest another motive for postponing the age at first birth. This motive arises when human reproduction is assumed to be stochastic, as in Eq. (12). As first noted by Heckman and Willis (1975), imperfect fertility control and the potential for contraceptive failure may lead couples to contracept early in their life cycles, even though they would choose not to if contraception were perfectly effective and costless.[70] In this case, couples may find it optimal to engage in a "precautionary" contraception strategy early in their life cycles so as to reduce their risk of having more births than they would have chosen to have if their fertility were perfectly and costlessly controllable.

## 4.3. The optimal spacing of births

A good deal of attention has been paid in the life-cycle models of fertility to their predictions concerning the spacing of births. This attention is due, in part, to the inherent interest in obtaining predictions about the spacing of births. The ability to develop dynamic models which generate spacing between births is also an important "litmus" test of the model itself. As noted by Newman (1988), "there is a tendency in dynamic programming models for the optimal solution to involve building up a stock

---

[70] Couples always can avoid births by abstaining from sexual intercourse. In addition, couples may have access to abortions or sterilization, each of which is a "perfect" form of fertility control. However, either or both methods may be viewed as too "costly" for parents to use, especially young couples.

either at the beginning or end of the period. Since this [prediction] runs counter to observations of fertility over the childbearing period, a dynamic model must be able to generate a spacing pattern where the births do not occur all at once".[71] Since biological constraints would prevent most couples from having all desired births at once, Newman's point should be reformulated as a question that asks why, once the first birth occurs, couples do not choose to have all subsequent births as quickly as possible. In what follows, we briefly discuss several different mechanisms within existing models which tend to generate spacing between births and discusses what predictions these mechanisms generate about what leads to longer versus shorter birth intervals.

As is suggested by the discussion in the previous two sections, life-cycle models of behavior imply that intertemporal variation in the timing of "consumption" of any commodity, including durable goods like children, tend to result from life-cycle variation in income, in the absence of perfect capital markets, and/or in the prices or costs associated with these goods. Consider, first, the role of life-cycle variation in income when capital markets are perfectly-imperfect (i.e., under the PICM assumption). In this setting, as discussed in Heckman and Willis (1975), Wolpin (1984), and Newman (1988), variations in the life-cycle profile of household income shapes the timing and spacing of births. As the quote by Newman (1988) suggests, models in which parents derive service flows from children, once they are born, tend, all else equal, to generate early childbearing and no (or minimal) spacing between births. But, in the absence of capital markets, spacing arises as a resolution of the tension between the desire to have children early (given discounting and a finite fertile stage) and the economic incentive to have children later when income is high. Thus, for example, rising income profiles, with an inability to save or dissave, gives rise to the incentive to space births, especially to the extent that, once born, children incur "maintenance" costs for some portion of their lives. Thus, the models of Heckman and Willis (1975), Wolpin (1984), and Newman (1988) all predict that the more rapid the rise in household (or father's) income, ceteris paribus, the more likely it is that parents will contracept in order to space their births.[72]

Another way spacing is generated within life-cycle models of fertility is due to price variation. In general, if the prices associated with rearing children vary over the parents' life cycle, spacing may also be generated. The models of Moffitt (1984b) and Hotz and Miller (1986) generate such life-cycle variation through the costs of maternal time in the care of children by imposing a technological restriction on the production function for child care services in Eq. (10). In their models, they incorporate the assumption, used by Willis (1973) in his static model of fertility, that the production of child services for young children are intensive in the mothers time. Put another way, $t_{ct}$

---

[71] Newman (1988: p. 50).

[72] While allowing parents access to capital markets mitigates one of the incentives to postpone and/or space births, it does not preclude it. As Heckman and Willis (1975) note, it still may be optimal for parents to space births, even in the presence of capital markets, if the market rate of interest, $r$, exceeds the parents' rate of time preference $\beta$.

is assumed to be higher when children are young. To the extent that caring for young children is so intensive that it requires the mother to withdraw from the labor force, the shadow price of the mother's time rise, exceeding her market wage, as in the Willis (1973) model. In the face of the temporary price rise, postponing the next birth, until this "price" declines, generates the incentive to space births.

## 4.4. Contraceptive choice and the efficacy of contraceptive methods

An important feature found in many of the life-cycle models of fertility is the explicit incorporation of stochastic reproduction. Such models have focused the attention on the contraceptive strategies that parents follow over their life cycles in an attempt to control their reproduction. Incorporating the strategic dimension of contraceptive practices has generated several new insights on issues related to the failure rates of contraceptive methods.

Much of the family planning literature has taken the perspective that various methods have inherent rates of failure to prevent births.[73] While it is true that methods differ in the technology by which births are prevented and may produce different failure rates in practice, it is not true that the failure rate of any given method is independent of choices made by a woman and/or her partner about trade-offs between, say, activities that bring sexual pleasure and ways of using a given method to minimize the probability of pregnancy. Beginning with Michael and Willis (1975) and Heckman and Willis (1975), forward looking economic models of fertility have treated contraception as imperfect and costly and have assumed that couples choose methods and use them in ways that reflect a balance between the "costs" of contraception and the benefit of preventing a birth temporarily or permanently. For instance, Michael and Willis (1975) suggest that a couple who wish to terminate their childbearing is more likely to incur the fixed costs of learning about and paying for a contraceptive such as the Pill which is highly effective and has a low marginal cost because it does not interfere with sexual pleasure than is a similar couple that is just attempting to space births. Similarly, a teenager who engages in sex sporadically may not be willing to invest in contraceptive methods with high fixed costs and low marginal costs while a more sexually active teenager might make such investments. The point that contraceptive efficacy is a matter of choice is also featured in the more recent work of Rosenzweig and Schultz (1985, 1989) and Hotz and Miller (1993). For example, Rosenzweig and Schultz (1989) note that an optimizing model suggests that there is likely to be a systematic relationship between the efficacy of methods with the levels of educational attainment of the couple. In particular, they show that more educated parents can use less "costly" methods, i.e., ones which allow for greater "pleasure" during sexual intercourse, and still achieve high levels of production because of their greater ability to produce "protection".

---

[73] See Trussell and Kost (1987) for a survey of the contraceptive effectiveness literature.

## 5. Empirical implications of models of fertility: identification issues, econometric approaches and empirical examples

The previous two sections outlined several of the unique intellectual contributions of static and dynamic economic models of parental fertility decisions. These models all imply that parents' demand for children depend on the price(s) of children, the prices of other goods and services, including child quality, the mother's market wage rate(s) and levels of household income. However, as our discussion of these models made clear, the exact nature of these relationships and, thus, the predictions of how variation in prices, wages and income will affect parental demands depend on which model features one considers. As such, determination of the appropriateness of the predictions of these theories is an empirical question. Furthermore, even when the comparative static or dynamic predictions are clear, the magnitudes of the effects are often of considerable intrinsic interest.

In this section, we discuss the issues involved in estimating the sign and magnitude of the price and income effects implied by these theories. Our discussion begins with a detailed discussion of the issues involved in estimating reduced-form price and income effects for the demand for children. There many of the issues are closely related to parallel issues in the larger labor supply literature. We then turn to the issues which are raised in estimating the parameters of quantity–quality models.

### 5.1. Strategies for identifying price and income effects for parental fertility choices

All of the models of fertility discussed in the previous two sections imply that the demand for children depends on various types of "prices" – including prices of children, their quality, the price of mothers' time, the prices of contraceptive practices, etc. – and household income. In this section, we consider the issues associated with obtaining unbiased (or consistent) estimates of the "reduced-form" effects of "exogenous" changes in various prices which are related to children and their production and in household income on the number of children demanded (and borne) by parents over their lifetimes or over some specified period of their life cycles. To illustrate the estimation issues, we focus on the implications of static models for a couple's demand for children. All of the models outlined in Section 3 imply a mapping between the number of children born and a set of prices (the $\pi$'s) and family income ($I$). Let this mapping be denoted by

$$n = N(\pi_n, w, \pi_e, I; \pi_o, \theta),  \tag{19}$$

where $\pi_n$, $w$, $\pi_e$, and $I$ have been defined above and $\pi_o$ denotes a vector of all other prices which, either directly or indirectly, affect parents' demand for children and $\theta$ denotes a vector of other household-specific attributes which affect $n$, including traits which characterize parental preferences, technologies which influence the production of children and services related to children, and endowments of fixed-factors – such as parental fecundity – which affect these production processes.

Much of the empirical literature on fertility, either consciously or de facto, has sought to obtain estimates of the own-price effect of fertility, $\partial n/\partial \pi_n$, the effect of exogenous variation in the mother's market wage (or market-based opportunity cost of her time) on fertility, $\partial n/\partial w$, and of the effect of changes in the "price" of contraceptive methods on fertility, $\partial n/\partial \pi_e$. Furthermore, as we have already noted, explaining the sign and magnitude of the effect of exogenous changes in family income on fertility, $\partial n/\partial I$, was one of the primary motivations for the early applications of neoclassical economic models to fertility. Obtaining estimates of such effects is of interest for several reasons. First, such effects address questions of how fertility behavior responds to exogenous variations in the constraints which parents face when making the fertility decisions. Second, knowledge of such effects may provide good approximations to the consequences of policy interventions, especially in contexts in which the intervention is a marginal change and in which one otherwise expects the preferences and technologies facing households to remain constant. Third, such estimates provide important benchmarks against which to compare estimates of the "structural" relationships suggested by the theoretical models discussed in Sections 3 and 4. In the final analysis, such structural models must accord with those which purport to characterize the mechanisms by variations in prices and income affect behavior. A fourth reason, related to the third, is that the identification of reduced-form price and income effects is typically less demanding than is the identification of more structural effects.

Nonetheless, estimating the sign and magnitude of the effects corresponding to this theory is a non-trivial challenge. The major issue is the standard problem of econometric identification. Our economic theory has predictions about the effect of an exogenous change in prices or income holding all else constant. The variation in income and prices recorded in the data does not necessarily reflect such exogenous variation. Thus, simple regressions of fertility on observed income and prices will not recover the concepts corresponding to the economic theory of fertility. The challenge is to extract estimates of the effect of such exogenous variation in prices and income from observational data.

In considering approaches to estimation, it is useful to consider two particular reasons why the variation recorded in the data may not correspond to the exogenous variation considered in the economic theory of fertility – one at the individual level, the other at the market level. At the individual level, fertility regressions are subject to the standard unobserved individual characteristics concern of the labor supply literature. Cross-sectional data on households record variation in observed fertility, income, and some prices (in particular women's wages and the cost of child care). While some of this variation in prices undoubtedly reflects exogenous variation (e.g., in the demand for labor), it seems likely that much of the observed correlation is due to a correlation between the woman's wage or the husband's income and the household's preferences for children.

In particular, consider a simple linear approximation to the general demand for children equation given above (ignoring any issues related to the limited dependent variable nature of the number of children):

$$n = N(\pi_n, w, \pi_e, I; \pi_o, \theta).$$                                                         (20)

Note that human capital accumulation considerations imply that $w$ and $I$ reflect earlier choices of the household. Similarly, quantity–quality theory implies that many components of the cost of children (e.g., type of child care) also reflect household choices. Denoting this vector of household choices generically by $X$, the equivalent reduced-form demand functions would be

$$X = \gamma_0 + \gamma_n \pi_n + \gamma_w w + \gamma_e \pi_e + \gamma_I I + \gamma'_\pi \pi_o \gamma'_\theta \theta.$$          (21)

Thus, in general, any omitted (or imperfectly measured) prices or any taste variation (i.e., in $\theta$) will induce simultaneous equations bias and inconsistent estimates of the parameters of interest.

In particular the standard theory of human capital accumulation[74] suggests that such simultaneous equations bias is likely. Fertility decisions are among the most central life-style decisions for women and couples. Since child rearing has historically been intensive in women's time, and in particular negatively correlated with women's labor force participation, women with preferences for larger numbers of children are likely to spend more time not working.[75] Less time working implies less time to earn returns on accumulated human capital, and thus a smaller optimal investment. This relation between expected labor supply and the optimal human capital investment is reinforced if time out of the labor force for childrearing may require the forfeiting of firm-specific human capital and the depreciation of general human capital. Thus, unobserved variation in preferences for the number of children will induce a spurious negative correlation between observed wages and fertility.

A similar critique applies when considering variation in the price of children. The theory suggests that exogenous variation in the cost of raising children should lower fertility. Below, we discuss the literature on estimating the structural effects implied by quantity–quality models. Here, we consider more reduced-form approaches relating the "price of children" to the quantity dimension of fertility. One large component of the cost of children is child care. There is considerable variation in the price of an hour of child care. Some of that price variation is undoubtedly due to variation in the price of a constant quality child care, but much of it is induced by variation in the

---

[74] See, for example, Mincer (1963).
[75] See Rosenzweig and Schultz (1985).

quality of the child care provided. In the previous section, we discussed the theoretical literature which has developed to explain the lack of a strong positive effect of family income on the number of children.[76] Nevertheless, since the quality of child care is clearly a normal good – unless the included regressors perfectly control for the appropriate lifetime income concept – there will be a spurious correlation between observed prices paid for child care and the omitted components of the appropriate income concept. Therefore, using observed variation in the price of children (e.g., the cost per hour of child care) will induce omitted variable bias in the estimated effect of exogenous changes in the price of children on the demand for (the quantity of) children.[77]

This critique suggests using household data which spans multiple markets. Differences across markets in the characteristics of those supplying labor, endowments of natural resources, and available technology will induce exogenous variation in equilibrium prices of quality adjusted labor. Furthermore for some prices (e.g., welfare benefits, abortion regulations, tax policies), only inter-market variation exists (either across governmental jurisdictions or in different time periods).

While such multiple-market data provides variation in prices, there is reason to believe that such aggregate price variation may also be endogenous. For market prices (e.g., male and female wages and the price of child care), such endogeneity might arise from standard market equilibrium considerations. Market clearing prices equalize market supply for the good (the sum over the individual supplies) and market demand for the good (the sum over the individual demanders). Adopting linear approximations, we have:

$$X^S = a_0^S + a_\pi^S \pi + a_Z^S Z^S + a_\theta^S \theta,$$
$$X^D = a_0^D + a_\pi^D \pi + a_Z^D Z^D + a_\theta^D \tau, \tag{22}$$

where $Z^S$ and $Z^D$ summarize the characteristics of the individual supplies of the good (labor, child care) and those demanding it (households), $\theta$ represents the sum of taste

---

[76] See Becker and Lewis (1973) and Willis (1973).

[77] This discussion of variation in women's wages and child care prices is in addition to the standard problem that the observed prices are a censored sample of all prices (Heckman and Killingsworth, 1986). In most standard datasets, wages are recorded only for workers. Similarly, child care prices are recorded only for those who purchase child care. Thus, estimating models of the effect of women's wages or child care costs on fertility will usually require imputing a wage or price for those women for whom no wage/price is recorded in the data. Since the standard theory of labor supply suggests that women with lower market wages (relative to their reservation wages) are less likely to work and that women facing higher child care costs are less likely to purchase market child care, simply using average observed wages/prices is not in general appropriate. On average women facing higher child care costs are less likely to purchase market child care. See Heckman (1974a), Heckman and MaCurdy (1984), and Heckman and Killingsworth (1986) for surveys of the problem of selection bias in the estimation of female wage functions. For a discussion of the implications of this problem for analyzing the demand for children, see Schultz (this volume).

parameters over the households supplying the good and $\tau$ represents the sum of the technology-specific factors shifting the demand for the good. The reduced-form for market clearing prices, therefore, is a function of the individual taste parameters. In as much as tastes (or more generally anything which enters the individual household supply functions) are not distributed independently across markets (e.g., geographically or through time), market prices are potentially subject to the same simultaneous equations bias as are individual level regressions (Rosenzweig and Evenson, 1977; Schultz, 1985).[78] In particular, if in some markets women have stronger preferences for children, we would expect to see more fertility, smaller investments in human capital, and less work, and therefore higher prices for female labor (after adjusting for differences in measured human capital and experience).

A similar critique applies to public policies. Government policies (e.g., welfare payments, regulations on abortion) can be viewed as inducing price variation. That variation exists only at the market level (either across places or through time). But, at least in a democracy, public polices should be expected to respond to the distribution of tastes in the population – in particular, among voters.[79]

Similarly, while there have been major time-series changes in government policies, there have also clearly been major time-series changes in social mores with respect to fertility behavior. Some of these changes may be due to the variables included in our models, but it seems likely that the preferences of succeeding cohorts also differ. This preference variation would also be reflected in changes in elected governments through time. Thus, variation in governmental policies across states or through time are not necessarily exogenous.

The empirical literature uses three approaches to control for the potential endogeneity of the variation in prices and income: *social experiments*, *instrumental variables*, and *fixed effects* methods. We discuss each of these approaches in turn. For each approach, we begin with a general methodological discussion. We then present in detail at least one "best practice" paper applying each approach to the empirical study of fertility.

---

[78] This critique raises questions about the empirical results in the much cited work by Butz and Ward (1979) and Ward and Butz (1980). They attempt to estimate Willis's (1973) model of the effects of variation in male and female wages; in particular that as female labor force participation rates rise the negative substitution effect of pro-cyclical wages might overcome the positive income effect of male wages. Their empirical results are consistent with this theory and appear to predict fertility changes through 1980 quite closely. Their treatment of the endogeneity of male and female wages, however, is not convincing. Noting that current wages are endogenous, they instrument current wages with lagged wages. Given strong serial correlation in wages, it is not clear why lagged wages are a valid exclusion restriction, if current wages are not. See also Macunovich (1995) who shows that the Butz and Ward model does not predict well out of sample.

[79] See Ellwood and Bane (1985) for this line of argument.

### 5.1.1. Random assignment/social experiments

Treatments in social experiments can often be viewed as varying prices (or income). By construction in properly conducted social experiments, the random assignment of participants to different treatment of control groups provides exogenous variation in prices (or income). Thus random assignment guarantees that the variation in prices is independent of any taste variation or unobserved prices. Comparing subsequent fertility of those randomly assigned to different treatments (including the control group) will thus provide consistent estimates of the relative effects of the different treatments on fertility.[80]

Such use of social experiments to identify the effect of exogenous variation of prices on fertility is subject to the standard critiques of experiments in the social sciences.[81] The experiments are not always properly conducted. General equilibrium effects (or the effects on attitudes) of wide implementation are not estimated. The effect is only estimated for the subset of the population who chose to participate. Finally, the duration of the experiment is quite limited, so only the effects of short-term variation in prices can be estimated.

Maynard and Rangarajan (1994) exploit the random assignment in the Teenage Parent Demonstration to evaluate the ability of enhanced case management to prevent repeat pregnancies among welfare dependent teenage mothers. From late-1987 to mid-1991, 5297 first-time teenage mothers receiving welfare in Chicago, Illinois and Newark and Camden, New Jersey were randomly assigned either to an "enhanced services" program or to the regular AFDC program. The enhanced services were similar to those later mandated by the Family Support Act of 1988. Groups of 50 to 60 young women were assigned to a case manager. These case managers counseled the young mothers as to "what types of education and training to pursue and found appropriate programs; they coaxed and pressured them to stick to their plans; and they counseled them when crises arose". The young women were required to attend workshops to "promote personal and parenting skills; increase awareness of contraceptive methods and sexually transmitted diseases (STDs); and prepare them for later education, training, and employment". Finally, the program provided child care and transportation services to allow the women to attend school, training, or work.

Maynard and Rangarajan evaluated the program by building logistic regression models of the probability of use of any contraceptive, use of an effective contraceptive, ever subsequently pregnant, and the outcome of the most recent repeat pregnancy (live birth, abortion, or miscarriage/still birth) as of two years after the beginning of the program. The logistic regression models include controls for heterogeneity of the women (age, race-ethnicity, family background, living situation, family size, reading

---

[80] Burtless (1995) makes this argument.

[81] See Heckman and Smith (1995) and Burtless (1995).

level, educational status, contraceptive use at baseline), site, and a dummy for whether the young woman was eligible for enhanced services (whether she actually participated in the "enhanced services" offered is potentially endogenous). The randomization ensures that program eligibility was independent of background characteristics. The included regressors control for random variation in the characteristics of women assigned to enhanced services, and thus increases the precision of the estimates.

Pooling over all of the sites, the results show little effect of case management/enhanced services in reducing subsequent fertility. Use of any contraceptive method or a more effective method are unchanged (at $P$-value of 0.10), use of a less effective contraceptive method declines marginally (significant at $P$-value of 0.10, but not of 0.05). There is no effect on the probability of a repeat pregnancy (even at $P$-value of 0.10). Against expectations, the point estimate is positive. Conditional on pregnancy, there is weak evidence that women participating in the program were more likely to give birth, rather than to abort. Rough tabulations from the reported results suggest that about 41% of the women in the experimental group had a subsequent birth, but only 36% of women in the control group did; a difference of five percentage points.

These results are disappointing to those who had hoped that enhanced counseling and services to young welfare mothers would lower their probability of a repeat birth. Such a result would have been plausible under two economic theories. First, it would follow if these women became pregnant due to lack of knowledge of or access to contraceptives. The program lowered the cost of acquiring the knowledge and the access. Second, it would follow if the substitution effects of higher women's wages dominate the income effects. Then, if the program improved earnings opportunities, fertility would decline. One interpretation of the positive effect of the program on fertility is that, in this welfare population, the program raised earnings opportunities, but the income effect dominated the substitution effect. The weak statistical significance of the results does not, however, provide strong support for that interpretation.

### 5.1.2. Instrumental variables

The standard econometric approach to the endogeneity of regressors is instrumental variables. Ordinary least squares (OLS) is potentially inconsistent because the endogenous variables (e.g., women's and men's earnings opportunities, government policies) are potentially correlated with the unmodeled components of tastes. Formally, in the linear regression model for fertility in terms of observed covariates, $X$, i.e.,

$$n = X\beta + \varepsilon, \tag{23}$$

OLS will be consistent if $X$ is uncorrelated with the unobservables, $\varepsilon$. We argued earlier that unobserved preference variation is likely to be correlated with observed income of men and women and with government policies, so that OLS will in general be inconsistent.

The instrumental variables (IV) estimator posits a set of variables $Z$ which are correlated with $n$, but uncorrelated with $\varepsilon$. Given the existence of (a sufficient number of) such variables, the IV estimator is consistent: The challenge is to identify a sufficient number of identifying instruments (elements of $Z$ not in $X$). For most government policies, or distance to abortion clinics, it is difficult to conceive of plausible identifying instruments

For labor market variables, our simple supply and demand model for labor suggests a potential source of identifying instruments. In that model, anything which exogenously shifts the labor demand curve without directly shifting the labor supply curve could serve as an identifying instrument. Two candidates for such labor demand shifters are relative world prices for output and changes in production technology. Changes over time in prices and technology will induce time-series variation in market clearing earnings opportunities for men and women. As long as there is some geographic specificity to different industries (either because of natural resource endowments or because of immobile capital investments), such changes will also induce variation across regions. Such world prices and technological proxies (and their interactions with measures of natural resource endowments or immobile capital) are plausibly correlated with wages and thus with fertility (as long as wages affect fertility), but are plausibly uncorrelated with variation in tastes (across time or place).

Schultz (1985) provides a convincing example of this approach. For Sweden from 1860 to 1910, he specifies major changes in world prices (grain and butter) and technological changes (improved breeds of livestock, refrigerated transport) which shifted the demand curves for male and female labor. He notes that some Swedish industries were intensive in male labor (grain and root crops, forestry and saw mills), while other industries were intensive in female labor (dairying and milk processing, textiles and food processing). He estimates the effects of male and female labor market opportunities on fertility using time-series data on fertility for the 28 Swedish counties. Output market prices, the industrial distribution of employment (measured in the middle of the period, 1896 and 1910) and the percentage of the population urban are used as instruments to identify the male wage rate and the female-to-male wage rate. He concludes that the observed 10% increase in the female-to-male wage ratio explains a quarter of the decline in fertility. The doubling of real male wages had no effect on completed family size, but it did induce earlier marriage and a shift of fertility from women over age 30 to women under age 30.

Black et al. (1996) apply a similar approach to fertility in Kentucky. Their approach exploits wide variation in the world price of energy (induced by OPEC and the oil embargoes) and for different types of coal (induced by the Clean Air Act) and the variation in the endowments of Kentucky counties in different types of coal. They use the world prices for energy and different types of coal interacted with county coal reserves as instruments for male and female wages. Coal prices have strong effects on male wages, but weaker effects on female wages. They find a strong positive effect of higher male wages on fertility.

There are two interpretation problems with the Black et al. (1996) results. First, since they are using year-to-year variation in market prices and technology over a relatively short period of time (under two decades), there is ambiguity as to whether these effects are due to timing or whether they will lead to differences in completed family size. This seems to be a generic problem with using time-series variation in the modern period to explore the effects of economic conditions on completed fertility. It is, however, attractive for the study of the timing of fertility with respect to transitory shock to labor market opportunities. This interpretation, however, suggests the importance of incorporating the effects of, not only current labor market opportunities, but also past and future labor market opportunities. (See the discussion of estimating dynamic economic models of fertility below.)

Second, there appears to be considerable in-migration in response to coal booms. Such labor mobility is, however, problematic. In the extreme, if labor is perfectly mobile, there will be no cross-sectional variation in earnings opportunities. Black et al. (1996) do find wage variation, though it is difficult to know how much of it is a compensating differential for the conditions of coal mining.) In the less extreme case, migration may be correlated with unobserved taste variation for fertility. If so, then fertility rates by place of occurrence will be correlated with exogenous shifts in world prices and technology. In that case, these variables are not valid instruments.

### 5.1.3. Fixed effects

A third possible approach to the potential endogeneity of the prices, wages, and income in observed data is group fixed effects. In the more recent applied literature in economics, this approach is often referred to as the *difference-of-differences* (DoD) method.[82] In contrast to the instrumental variables approach which requires exclusion restrictions, fixed-effects methods attempt to include regressors to approximately control for the omitted variables inducing the endogeneity bias. If the unobserved taste variation for a group of people is (approximately) constant through time for a given geographic area, then fixed effects for that region will control for the omitted variables, and fixed-effects regressions on grouped data would consistently estimate the exogenous effects of interest.

Plausibly there are also nationwide secular trends in preferences (at least across cohorts). Assuming that the two effects are additive, we have the standard double

---

[82] Some authors argue that this method is applicable because of the fact that variation is generated by so-called *natural experiments* in which the variation is generated as a result of largely exogenous events or changes in policies.

fixed-effects DoD[83] approach to the estimation of price effects in the fertility literature:

$$n_{st} = \alpha\pi_{st} + X_{st}\beta + \gamma_s + \gamma_t + \varepsilon_{st}, \tag{24}$$

i.e., it regresses fertility in a state (or more generally some geographical unit), $s$, and time-period, $t$, on the price of interest, $\pi$, other covariates which vary across state and year, $X$, fixed effects for the state, $\gamma_s$, and years $\gamma_t$, where $\varepsilon_{st}$ is an idiosyncratic stochastic error. The included dummy variables directly control for the first-order sources of endogeneity, time-invariant state-specific variation and national secular trends. The included regressors are assumed to control for all other within state variation not controlled for by the common national year dummies; the remaining variation is assumed to be due to the price/policy of interest.

In as much as correlation between the prices/policies and the state and year effects is important, this double fixed-effects strategy will yield improved estimates compared to OLS. In as much as the changes in prices/policies within states – not correlated with the year effects – is correlated with the regression residual, the double fixed effects will not be a sufficient control and the estimates will be inconsistent. Exploring both of these issues has been a major focus of this line of research.[84]

Two papers on the determinants of abortion demonstrate the application of this fixed-effects approach. The economic theory of fertility suggests a derived demand for abortion as a method of contraception. Increased demand for children should lower the demand for abortions. Increased cost of abortion should lower the demand for abortion. Much of the literature on the determinants of abortion has focused on two government policies that make abortions more expensive: whether a state's Medicaid program treats abortion like any other medical procedure; and whether doctors require parental notification or consent before performing an abortion on a non-adult.

For both of these policies there is considerable variation in policy. In response to a sequence of Supreme Court decisions, most states changed their policy from funding

---

[83] This regression approach derives its name "difference-of-differences" from the equivalent operation on means in the evaluation literature. Consider the case where one group of, the "control states", never (or always) had the policy in place and another group of states, "the experimental states", did not have the policy in place in time 0, but did have it in place in time 1. Then, denoting the mean fertility rate in the four cells by $m$ (with an appropriate subscript), the difference-of-difference estimator for the effect of the binary policy is

$$\alpha = (m_{e1} - m_{e0}) - (m_{c1} - m_{c0}).$$

The first term is the change, in fertility in the experimental states when the policy is imposed. This difference controls for time-invariant state-specific effects. The second term is the change in fertility in the control states. The difference controls for national secular change. The "difference-in-differences" thus controls for both effects. The previous equation is the regression generalization.

[84] Meyer (1995) provides a discussion of the methodological issues in a general context.

to not funding abortions and from not requiring parental involvement in abortions to minors to requiring such involvement. The timing of these changes varied widely across the states and some states never changed their policies. The empirical literature exploits this variation, while attempting to control for the potential endogeneity of government policy.

Blank et al. (1994) estimate these policy effects using time-series of cross-section data on state abortion rates for 1974–1988. Their main data source is the Alan Guttmacher Institute's (AGI) survey of abortion providers. As a survey of providers, it records the total number of abortions by state of occurrence, but includes no demographic information. Using Census Bureau population estimates, they estimate linear regression models for the log of the abortion rate (abortions per woman aged 15–44). Their model includes policy variables (Medicaid funding, parental involvement, AFDC payment levels), political climate variables, the number of abortion providers in the state, and demographic variables (marriage rate, summary measures of age distribution of women, race of women, urban), and economic conditions (female labor force participation rate, log per capita income, unemployment rate). Because of concerns about the endogeneity of the number of abortion providers, they instrument for it using the number of hospitals and the number of physicians in the state as identifying variables (most of their results are robust to whether or not they instrument).

The estimated results are sensitive to the inclusion of double fixed-effects. Without the fixed effects, enforced parental involvement laws significantly lower abortions (at the 0.01 level), but the effect of Medicaid funding restrictions is insignificant (even at the 0.05 level, though the point estimate is negative). Adding fixed effects for state and year causes the parental involvement effect to turn positive (the "wrong sign") and insignificant. The Medicaid funding effect, however, triples in magnitude and becomes significant at the 0.01 level of significance.

Their specification includes a strong specification test of whether the estimated effect of Medicaid funding is causal or due to omitted taste variables which vary within a state over time and not perfectly correlated with the national time effects. The extensive litigation of the Medicaid funding issue implies that there were many states which had laws (or administrative actions) forbidding the reimbursement of abortions by Medicaid, but which nevertheless paid for abortions pending the final judicial decision. While the legislative decisions are likely to have some correlation to shifts in within-state public sentiment, the timing of the judicial decisions is likely to have a much weaker correlation.

To use this information, in addition, to the variable for not funding abortions through Medicaid, they include a variable describing whether there is an unenforced Medicaid funding restriction. In the fixed-effects model, the unenforced restriction dummy is negative, significant (at the 0.05 level), and nearly half the magnitude of the effect of funding itself. This result suggests both that changes in attitudes towards abortion shift both abortion rates and state policies (whether or not they are enforced) and that the double fixed-effects strategy alone is not sufficient to eliminate all of the endogeneity of state policies.

Joyce and Kaestner (1995) consider the effect of parental involvement laws in more detail. They note that the parental involvement laws only affect minors. Therefore, with data which records the number of abortions to adults and minors separately, they can apply a triple fixed-effects or difference-of-differences approach to the abortion ratio, $r$, the fraction of pregnancies (computed as abortions plus live births) which are aborted[85]:

$$r_{stg} = \alpha \pi_{stg} + \gamma_{sg} + \gamma_{tg} + \gamma_{st} + X_{stg}\beta + \varepsilon_{stg}. \tag{25}$$

The policy effect, $\pi$, is set to one only in state–year combinations in which there was an enforced parental involvement law and then only for minors. This additional level of data allows them to include demographic group-specific (i.e., adults vs. minors) for state and year, and to include dummy variables for each state–year combination. Thus, rather than relying on observed covariates (state economic and political conditions) to control for within state variation, they can take a non-parametric approach, including a dummy variable for each state–year combination.

Since the AGI data do not separately tabulate abortions by demographic group, Joyce and Kaestner analyze data from three states: Tennessee, South Carolina, and Virginia. These three states require that all abortions be reported to the state health department. For these three states the data appears to be of high quality and relatively complete, and the states appear to have good reciprocal reporting arrangements with neighboring states such that out-of-state abortions are also recorded.[86]

Joyce and Kaestner use these data to explore the effect of the enforcement of parental involvement laws on the abortion ratio. Including double fixed effects and using Virginia as a control, they find a significant effect. Parental involvement laws lower the abortion rate. In the triple fixed effects, however, the point estimate remains negative, but falls to a quarter of its earlier value and is not statistically significant. Additional analyses show some evidence (the associated *P*-value is 0.05) of an effect on the abortion rates of both white and black 16-year-olds (about 5%), but not for any other age group.

## 5.2. Identifying the key implications of the quantity–quality models of fertility: the use of twins

Until now, we have focused on the identification of the reduced-form effects of prices and income on fertility that are suggested by the static models discussed in Section 3. While

---

[85] By modeling the abortion ratio, rather than the abortion rate (abortions per woman, as in Blank et al. (1994)), they miss any effect of parental involvement laws on contraceptive practice (or coital frequency).

[86] Most states do not have any such reporting requirement. Among those that do, much of the data appears to be of poor quality. The counts of abortions are considerably below the AGI estimates.

informative and of substantive interest, identifying such effects does not enable one to distinguish the unique predictions generated by the quantity–quality model of fertility. That model implied a fundamental interaction between the shadow price of the quantity of children with that for the quality of children. In particular, the key feature of the quantity–quality model is the fact that $\pi_c$, the shadow price of a one unit increase in child quality for one child, is not equal to zero. As discussed in Section 3.1, $\pi_c \neq 0$ implies that the price of children depends on the quality parents choose to provide their children and that the price of parents' increasing the quality of their children depends on the number of children. Moreover, it is this feature of the quantity–quality model which gives rise to the possibility that household income and numbers of children will be negatively correlated.

In an influential paper, Rosenzweig and Wolpin (1980a) – see also Rosenzweig and Wolpin (1980b) – consider the conditions required to identify (or test) this implication of the quantity–quality theory. They show that distinguishing the presence of a nonzero $\pi_c$ requires independent variation in $\pi_n$ or $\pi_q$ as well as restrictions on the cofactors of the system of demand equations for fertility ($n$), child quality ($q$) and parental consumption goods ($s$). As we have argued above, the ability to identify the effect of exogenous variation in $\pi_n$ (or, for that matter, in $\pi_q$) is inherently difficult to obtain. However, Rosenzweig and Wolpin show that knowledge of the effect of an exogenous change in $n$ on $q$, i.e., $\partial q / \partial \overline{n}$, is equal to

$$\frac{\partial q}{\partial \overline{n}} = \left(\frac{\partial q}{\partial \pi_n}\right)_{\overline{u}} \left(\frac{\partial n}{\partial \pi_n}\right)_{\overline{u}}^{-1}, \tag{26}$$

where $(\partial q / \partial \pi_n)_{\overline{u}}$ is the compensated cross-price effect of $\pi_n$ on $q$ and $(\partial q / \partial \pi_n)_{\overline{u}}$ is the own-price of $\pi_n$ on $n$. Rosenzweig and Wolpin exploit the natural experiment generated by the occurrence of twins at a couple's first birth event to identify Eq. (26), the exogenous impact of a fertility change on the quality of children.

As noted above, identification of $\partial q / \partial \overline{n}$ is not sufficient to test for the quantity–quality implication that $\pi_c \neq 0$. Additional restrictions on the structure of the parental utility function is required. In their empirical application, where $q$ denotes the amount of education chosen by parents, the authors find that $(\partial q / \partial \pi_n)_{\overline{u}}$ is sufficiently negative that for plausible restrictions on parental preferences, the quantity–quality model would be rejected by their data.

More generally, the use of the exogenous variation in fertility generated by the use of the occurrence of twins to identify the exogenous impact of fertility on parental demand for other goods on quality[87] represents a creative use of randomly-occurring

---

[87] In Rosenzweig and Wolpin (1980b), they utilize the twins-as-a-natural-experiment to identify the exogenous impact of fertility on the mother's labor supply decision. In a related but distinct approach, Rosenzweig and Schultz (1985) show that one can exploit the exclusion-of-prices restrictions from the reproduction function in Eq. (9) that are implied by optimizing behavior on the part of parents to identify the exogenous impact of fertility on the labor supply and contraceptive choices of parents. See Schultz (this volume) for a discussion of this model.

biological phenomena to identify structural relationships. More recently, this type of strategy has been followed to identify the effects of early childbearing on the subsequent choices of young mothers using the random occurrences of twins [88] and the random occurrences of miscarriages.[89]

## 5.3. Econometric approaches to life-cycle models of fertility

Two considerations suggest exploring explicitly dynamic econometric approaches: the inherent multi-period nature of the data and our intrinsic interest in the dynamic characteristics of fertility discussed in the previous section. Corresponding to each of these considerations there is a simple, natural, basically static econometric approach which is incomplete. We begin this section by discussing more thoroughly each of these considerations and the corresponding natural approaches. We then discuss in detail two other, more explicitly dynamic – econometric approaches: systems of *hazard models* and *estimable dynamic programming* models.

### 5.3.1. Applying the econometric approaches of static models to life-cycle fertility behavior

The first consideration pushing analysis towards an explicitly dynamic econometric approach is the inherently multi-period nature of the data. Our static theory is a one-period formulation of the choice of completed family size. The direct empirical implementation of such models would analyze completed family size for women of an appropriate age, where the end of childbearing is by convention usually set at 44.[90] This approach has the twin problems that the standard data does not come in that form[91] and that doing so would imply analyzing data for which most fertility occurred two decades earlier (in the woman's mid-twenties).

Instead, the standard approach in the static empirical literature has been to apply the static models directly to age-specific fertility rates. Current period fertility is regressed on current period covariates. As is noted in the labor supply literature,[92] such a specification is in error. Even in a perfect certainty framework, current period choices are a function of all current and future prices. Once that premise is granted the identification issues of the previous section become much more difficult. We now re-

---

[88] See Bronars and Grogger (1993).

[89] See Hotz et al. (1995).

[90] See Newman and McCulloch (1984).

[91] The birth certificate data only record births (so that it is a non-trivial problem to recover completed family size), the June CPS is usually asked only of women of childbearing (age 15–44), and by age 44 many children born to young mothers have often already left the household (so we cannot simply use the survey's own household rosters).

[92] See Heckman and MaCurdy (1980).

quire identifying information, not merely for the single current period price, but also information that separately identifies all possible past, current, and future prices. For standard instrumental variables approaches, what we argued above was a hard problem becomes nearly insurmountable. One role for a dynamic econometric approach is to use econometric theory to suggest more structure for the problem. Such a priori information would constrain the way in which the vector of prices enters current period decisions. Such cross-age restrictions lower the required amount of separate identifying information.[93]

The issues are particularly salient because one natural interpretation of age-specific regressions suggests a crucial role for past prices. It seems likely that some of the observed variation in age-specific fertility with respect to variation in prices is not variation in completed family size, but variation in the timing of fertility. In as much as this is correct, current period price effects should have the opposite sign from previous (and future) period price effects. A dynamic econometric model should help us to impose such structure.

For fixed-effect approaches, this critique raises a fundamental issue of interpretation. Fixed-effect approaches are usually applied across calendar years to an age-specific fertility rate. Such regressions should be interpreted as identifying the effect of a deviation from the mean level of the covariate over time. Thus, for example estimated income effects should be interpreted as the effect of transitory variations in income.[94] They do not identify the concept of interest in the static model – a lifetime shift in income. To identify the static income effects, we would need time-series of cross-sections on cohorts, i.e., lifetime fertility.[95]

### 5.3.2. Hazard models as a reduced-form approach to dynamic models

The second consideration pushing analysis towards an explicitly dynamic econometric approach is our interest in the inherently dynamic characteristics of the fertility process. From both theoretical and policy perspectives, the age at first birth, the spacing between births, and the joint timing of fertility with other life-cycle choices are inherently interesting. These characteristics simply do not appear in the static formulation.

The standard empirical approach to modeling these dynamic characteristics of the birth process has been ad hoc. It applies standard single equation limited dependent variable approaches to the data.[96] Age at first birth is regressed on covariates; interbirth timing is regressed on covariates. The summary measures presented in the second section of this paper are in that spirit. As we noted there, however, the fertility

---

[93] See Wolpin (1984) for more on this argument.

[94] See Silver (1965), Wilkinson (1973), Jackson and Klerman (1996), and Black et al. (1996) for examples of this line of research.

[95] See Schultz (1989) and Rosenzweig (1995).

[96] See Newman (1981) and Newman and McCulloch (1984) for references to the earlier literature.

decision is inherently discrete and there is considerable heterogeneity in completed family size. Thus, any single equation approach inherently runs into the problem of how to treat the women who never have the event. For example, how should we treat women who never have a birth in regressions on age at first birth? or women who have never had a birth up to the interview date? or women who never/up to the interview data had a subsequent birth in regressions on inter-birth timing? One approach to this problem is standard hazard modeling (Lancaster, 1990). In that approach, instead of directly modeling the timing of the event, we model the probability of the occurrence of the event in each period (Newman and McCulloch, 1984). Taking the probability of the event in period $d$, conditional on it not having occurred through period $d - 1$ as $h(d)$, the probability of an event occurring in period $d$ is simply

$$f(d) = h(d)\prod_{k=1}^{d-1}\{1 - h(k)\}$$

and the probability that the event does not occur through $d$ periods is simply

$$f(d) = \prod_{k=1}^{d}\{1 - h(k)\},$$

where in both expressions, we can allow $h(k)$ to depend on time-varying covariates.

This hazard approach provides a natural way to model incomplete histories, non-occurrence of the event (a subsequent birth) and a natural set of covariates (current period values). It, however, does not solve several other problems. First, it provides little insight into how to summarize the information in past and future covariates. Second, it does not solve the dynamic selection problem. To be in the sample of individuals on which we estimate the time between the first and second birth, one must have had a first birth. This is a selected sample. This simple hazard model provides no insight into the effects of that selection. Finally, this model has the unfortunate characteristic of mixing the parameters for the speed with which the event occurs with the parameters for whether or not the event occurs. No such restriction follows from economic theory. It is not hard to imagine some values of covariates inducing those women who will desire a subsequent birth to do it more quickly, but inducing fewer women to desire the subsequent birth. This simple hazard model fails to allow for this possibility.

One such dynamic econometric strategy is to apply systems of hazard models. As is implied by the name, life-cycle fertility is naturally analyzed using the standard birth process of the stochastic processes literature.[97] In that approach, completed fertility is viewed as the result of separate processes governing the transition to each parity. In its

---

[97] See Karlin and Taylor (1975) and Sheps and Menken (1973).

most general form, the model simply posits that current period fertility is a function of age, time since last birth, the woman's time-invariant characteristics and all the time-path of all time-varying covariates. Thus, we have a system of hazard models (one for each parity), linked by woman-specific common covariates, some of which are observed by the econometrician and some of which are not.

Newman and McCulloch (1984), Heckman and Singer (1984), Heckman and Walker (1987, 1991) develop a refinement of this systems of hazards approach, the model suggests some natural simplifications of this general (and inestimable) specification. In these papers, the feasible formulation, the current period hazard is modeled as a linear index function, i.e.,

$$I_{ijt} = \alpha_j(a) + \delta_j(d) + X\beta_j + \rho_j\mu_i, \tag{27}$$

where the function includes, respectively, a general function of the age of the woman, a general function of the duration since the last birth, a linear vector of covariates, and a random effect, $\mu_i$. Each of the parameters – including the factor loading on the random effect, $\rho_j$ – can be allowed to vary with parity. Newman and McCulloch (1984) take the random effect to be person-specific and time-invariant. In that case, given an assumed functional form for its distribution it can be integrated out as a random effect.[98]

This system of hazards formulation suggests natural restrictions on how the covariates enter the model. As in the static models, such models are usually implemented including only current period covariates in the current period hazard. The model summarizes the values of past covariates through its dependence on parity, time since last birth, and the dynamic selection of the time-invariant random effect. It thus easily imposes some of the ideas of the previous sections. Strongly peaked preferences for a given number of children (as in our first dynamic theoretical models) will be fit through non-defective hazards for parities below the desired fertility size and essentially zero hazards thereafter. See, for example, Heckman and Walker (1991) who use this characteristic of the model to focus on the decision to have a third child in Sweden. Similarly, the parity specific hazards provide a natural way to allow time-varying covariates to affect the timing of the transition to each parity separately from how they affect completed family size.

Heckman and Walker (1991) show that, under most conditions, if there is persistent heterogeneity across parities. estimates of the parameters of the hazards obtained by estimating the model separately will be biased. They note that "the study of unobservable in multi-state duration models is still in its infancy." Whether their permanent-transitory structure is the appropriate one is an open question. If we begin the process

---

[98] Heckman and Singer (1984) use non-parametric maximum likelihood estimator in the presence of such a mixing distribution.

with exposure to regular non-contracepting sexual relations, this is a natural characterization of the demographic concept of fecundity. In their work on the Hutterites, a non-contracepting (natural fertility) population (Heckman and Walker, 1987), they find that such woman-specific time-invariant effects are quite important in explaining the joint timing of births. In their work on Sweden, Heckman and Walker (1991) find no evidence of such individual specific heterogeneity. The motivation used by Newman and McCulloch (1984) in their study of birth intervals may suggest part of the reason. Dynamic theories of fertility suggest that woman-specific (approximately) time-invariant population heterogeneity in the unobserved component of preferences and prices will not always have similar effects on inter-birth timing as it has on first birth timing; such differences in effects would arise if the timing of the first birth was determined by different factors than was the spacing of subsequent births. If this were the case, then future analysts may wish to generalize the specification of the heterogeneity to detach the interval until the first birth from subsequent inter-birth intervals in a manner consistent with the general formulation in Heckman and Singer (1985). Such an approach, however, is unlikely to be promising in many developed countries because for the modal family size of two, there is only one inter-birth interval, making estimation of the correlation in unobservable between inter-birth intervals impossible. This is especially true in Sweden – the source of the data in Heckman and Walker (1991) – where third births are not common and fourth births are rare.

Heckman and Walker (1987) generalize this model to include previous durations as covariates and to allow for specific stopping behavior. In particular, they model the probability of no birth within $d$ periods of the $j$th birth (the survivor function) as

$$S_j(d) = P^{j-1} + (1 - P^{j-1}) \prod_{k=1}^{d} \{1 - h(k)\},$$

i.e., the probability of parity-specific stopping behavior after the $(j-1)$th birth, $P$, plus the probability that that there is not parity-specific stopping behavior, but that the birth has not occurred yet. Since the fertility process only runs for finite time – it is conventionally truncated at age 45 – some of the $1-P$ women who do not exhibit parity-specific stopping behavior will nevertheless never have the $j$th birth. According to the specification of the model, they might have done so under some time-path of the covariates.

### 5.3.3. Estimating structural models of life-cycle fertility using dynamic stochastic discrete choice models

Estimable stochastic dynamic programs are an alternative explicitly dynamic approach.[99] This approach attempts to impose more directly the insights of economic theory both to summarize the effect of non-contemporaneous prices and to estimate deeper structural parameters. Wolpin's (1984) approach builds directly from an explicit optimization problem, where he deliberately adopts a sufficiently simple formulation to allow numerical computation of the exact optimal life-cycle profiles.

He begins with an additively separable life-cycle utility function. In each period, $t$, the woman's/household's problem is

$$\max \mathrm{E}_t \sum_{k=0}^{\tau-t} \delta^k U_{t+k}(M_{t+k}, X_{t+k}), \tag{28}$$

where $M$ is the stock of children and $X$ is other consumption, subject to a period-by-period budget constraint (i.e., no borrowing or saving),

$$Y_t = X_t + cn_t, \tag{29}$$

where $Y$ is income, $X$ is consumption (with a price normalized to unity) and $c$ is the price of a child in its first year of life (denoted by the dummy variable $n$; after the first period children are assumed to be free).[100] For given values of the parameters, this model can be solved numerically by the principle of optimality.[101] In particular, the model has only a single control variable ($n$, whether or not to have a child in this period) and a single state variable ($M$, the stock of children at the beginning of the period). The optimal policy is computed by backwards recursion, comparing the utility of each choice.

To simplify the computation of the optimal policy, Wolpin assumes that the utility function is quadratic in the stock of children and other consumption:

$$U_t(M_t, X_t) = (\alpha_1 + \xi_t)M_t - \alpha_2 M_t^2 + \beta_1 X_t - \beta_2 X_t^2 + \gamma M_t X_t. \tag{30}$$

The second term, $\xi$, induces the stochastic element into the model. This component is assumed to be an i.i.d. preference shock that is observed by the decision-maker, but not by the econometrician. Assuming that $\xi$ is normally distributed induces a probit

---

[99] For a general overview of the literature on estimable dynamic programs, see Eckstein and Wolpin (1989). Papers applying a dynamic programming approach to the theory of fertility include Heckman and Willis (1976), Wolpin (1984), Rosenzweig and Schultz (1985), Newman (1988), Montgomery (1988), Hotz and Miller (1988a,b, 1993), David and Mroz (1989), and Ahn (1995).

[100] Consistent with the developed country context of this review, we have suppressed the child mortality terms which are a substantive focus of Wolpin's paper. Note also that the model Wolpin estimates adds to this budget constraint dummy costs for births in the first two periods and an additional quadratic set of cost terms in the age of the woman.

[101] See Bellman (1957).

form for the choice probabilities. The non-stochastic part of the probit is given by the difference in the expected utility of choosing to have or not have a child in this period. Since for given values of the parameters, these two components can be computed (by backwards recursion), the structural parameters of the economic choice problem – those appearing in the utility function and in the budget constraint – can be estimated by maximizing the implied likelihood.

This formulation is attractive because the restrictions on how current, past, and future prices enter the model are explicitly stated in terms of the underlying economic theory. The major problem appears to be computational. Wolpin deliberately formulates his decision problem in nearly the simplest possible form. There is only one state variable, the number of children. The utility function is quadratic. In particular, this specification rules out human capital accumulation, both saving and borrowing, differential utility or cost of children by their age, and heterogeneity in preferences or in fecundity. These restrictions are not intrinsic to the method, but including any of them will require significantly greater computational effort. However, with computing power for a given price doubling every eighteen months (Moore's Law), these purely computational considerations are likely to recede in importance. As they recede, the direct relation between the economic choice problem facing the household and the econometric parameters should make this approach more widely used.[102]

Hotz and Miller (1993) propose and implement an alternative, much less computationally intensive, approach to the estimation of the structural parameters of the utility function in dynamic models. Wolpin's approach is computationally intensive because he requires backwards recursion to compute the probability of each choice. Hotz and Miller show that, under certain conditions (including no unobserved heterogeneity), the future choice probabilities can be replaced by non-parametric estimates of those probabilities, where the non-parametric estimates are based on observed individuals with the same (or similar) state variables. The resulting Conditional Choice Probability (CCP) estimator is no more difficult to estimate than a standard multinomial logit model.

Their empirical application exploits this computational simplicity to estimate a much richer model than in the earlier dynamic programming literature. Rather than Wolpin's assumption of perfect fertility control, they allow for imperfect contraception and also sterilization. They also allow the utility and cost of children to vary with the age of the children (in years) which induces a desire for spacing. They then estimate the model and explore its implications by simulation of the comparative dynamics. The implied contraceptive choice decision rules imply that, ceteris paribus, "the more children a couple has, especially past two, the more likely they are to use more effec-

---

[102] See Ahn (1995) which focuses its substantive interest on the relative value of children by sex, using Korean data. That model allows the utility of children to vary with their age and sex. Note also that Ahn adopts Rust's (1987) specification of the choice probabilities as extreme value. Because a closed form exists for the expected value of an extreme value choice, this considerably simplifies the computational problem.

tive contraceptive control and that parents do alter their contraceptive strategies to space births and to diminish the chances of pregnancy at later stages of their life cycles as their children grow older."

## 6. Conclusion

Following Becker's insights that the standard tools of economic theory could be usefully applied to private household choices, a large theoretical and empirical literature has emerged. This chapter has reviewed that theory and the econometric issues in estimating models based on the theory. As is true in much of applied economics, the theory and econometric methods are much better developed than the empirical literature. The crucial challenge is to find plausibly exogenous variation in proxies for the price and income concepts appearing in the theories. Our discussion has provided a taxonomy of possible identifying information and gives us considerable hope that additional progress can be made in advancing our empirical understanding of fertility behavior.

## References

Ahituv, A., V.J. Hotz and T. Philipson (1996), "The responsiveness of the demand for condoms to the local prevalence of AIDS", Journal of Human Resources, in press.

Ahn, N. (1995), "Measuring the value of children by sex and age using a dynamic programming model", Review of Economic Studies 62: 361–379.

Akerlof, G., J. Yellen and M. Katz (1994), "An analysis of out-of-wedlock childbearing in the United States", Unpublished paper (University of California, Berkeley, CA).

Becker, G. (1960), "An economic analysis of fertility", in: Demographic and economic change in developed countries, Universities-National Bureau of Economic Research Conference Series 11 (NBER, Princeton, NJ) pp. 209–231.

Becker, G. (1965), "A theory of the allocation of time", Economic Journal 75: 493–517.

Becker, G. (1973), "A theory of marriage, Part I", Journal of Political Economy 81: 813–846.

Becker, G. (1974a), "A theory of marriage, Part II", Journal of Political Economy 82: S11–S26.

Becker, G. (1974b), "A theory of social interaction", Journal of Political Economy 82: 1063–1093.

Becker, G. (1981), A treatise on the family (Harvard University Press, Cambridge, MA).

Becker, G. and H.G. Lewis (1973), "On the interaction between quantity and quality of children", Journal of Political Economy 81: S279–S288.

Becker, G. and N. Tomes (1976), "Child endowments and the quantity and quality of children", Journal of Political Economy 84: S143–S162.

Bellman, R. (1957), Dynamic programming (Princeton University Press, Princeton, NJ).

Ben-Porath, Y. (1967), "The production of human capital and the life cycle of earnings", Journal of Political Economy 74: 352–365.

Ben-Porath, Y. (1973), "Economic analysis of fertility in Israel", Journal of Political Economy 81: S202–S233.

Ben-Porath, Y. and F. Welch (1976), "Do sex preferences really matter?", Quarterly Journal of Economics 90: 285–307.

Bergstrom, T. and R. Cornes (1983), "Independence of allocative efficiency from distribution in the theory of public goods", Econometrica 51: 1753–1765.

Black, D., S. Sanders and K. Daniel (1996), "How much does local economic growth help the poor? Evidence from the Appalachian coal boom and bust", Unpublished manuscript (Carnegie Mellon University, Pittsburg, PA).

Blank, R., C. George and R. London (1994), "State abortion rates: the impact of policy, provider availability, political climate, demography and economics", Working paper no. 4583 (NBER, Cambridge, MA).

Bloom, D. (1982), "What's happening to the age at first birth in the United States? A study of recent cohorts", Demography 19: 351–370.

Bronars, S. and J. Grogger (1995), "The economic consequences of unwed motherhood: using twin births as a natural experiment", American Economic Review 84: 1141–1156.

Browning, M. (1992), "Children and household economic behavior", Journal of Economic Literature 30: 1434–1475.

Burtless, G. (1995), "The case for randomized field trials in economic and policy research", Journal of Economic Perspectives 9: 63–84.

Butz, W.P. and M.P. Ward (1979), "The emergence of countercyclical US fertility", American Economic Review 69: 318–28.

Chen, R. and S.P. Morgan (1991), "Recent trends in the timing of first births in the United States", Demography 28: 513–533.

Chiappori, P.-A., L. Haddad, J. Hoddinot and R. Kanbur (1993), "Unitary versus collective models of the household: time to shift the burden of proof", Unpublished paper presented at the American Economics Association Meetings, Anaheim, CA.

Cigno, A. (1983), "Human capital and the time-profile of human fertility", Economics Letters 13: 385–392.

Cigno, A. (1991), Economics of the family (Clarendon Press, Oxford).

Cigno, A. and J. Ermisch (1989), "A microeconomic analysis of the timing of births", European Economic Review 33: 737–760.

DaVanzo, J. and M.O. Rahman (1993), "American families: trends and correlates", Population Index 59: 350–386.

David, P. and T. Mroz (1986), "A sequential econometric model of birth-spacing behavior among rural French villagers, 1749–1789", Unpublished manuscript (University of North Carolina, Chapel Hill, NC).

David, P., T. Mroz and K. Wachter (1985), "Rational strategies of birth-spacing and fertility regulation in rural France during the ancien regime", Unpublished manuscript (Stanford University, Stanford, CA).

DeTray, D. (1973), "Child quality and the demand for children", Journal of Political Economy 81: S70–S96.

Eckstein, Z. and K. Wolpin (1989), "The specification and estimation of dynamic stochastic discrete choice models: a survey", Journal of Human Resources 24: 562–598.

Ellwood, D. and M.J. Bane (1985), "The impact of AFDC on family structure and living arrangements", in: Research in labor economics, Vol. 7 (JAI Press, Greenwich, CT).

Ermish, J. (1991), Lone parenthood: an economic analysis (Cambridge University Press, Cambridge).

Friedman, M. (1957), A theory of the consumption function (Princeton University Press, Princeton, NJ).

Goldin, C. (1992), "The meaning of college in the lives of American women: the past 100 years", Working paper no. 4099 (NBER, Cambridge, MA).

Gustafsson, S. and F. Stafford (1992), "Child care subsidies and labor supply in Sweden", Journal of Human Resources 27: 204–230.

Happel, S., J. Hill and S. Low (1984), "An economic analysis of the timing of childbirth", Population Studies 38: 299–311.

Hashimoto, M. (1974), "Economics of postwar fertility in Japan: differentials and trends" Journal of Political Economy 82: S170–S194.

Heckman, J. (1974a), "Shadow prices, market wages and labor supply", Econometrica 42: 679–694.

Heckman, J. (1974b), "Effects of child-care programs on women's work effort", Journal of Political Economy 82: S136–S163.

Heckman, J. and M. Killingsworth (1986), "Female labor supply: a survey", in: O. Ashenfelter and R. Layard, eds., Handbook of labor economics (North-Holland, Amsterdam) pp. 103–204.

Heckman, J. and T. MaCurdy (1980), "A life-cycle model of female labour supply", Review of Economic Studies 47: 47–74.

Heckman, J. and T. MaCurdy (1984), "Labor econometrics", in: Z. Griliches and M. Intriligator, eds., Handbook in econometrics, Vol. 3 (North-Holland, Amsterdam) pp. 103–204.

Heckman, J. and B. Singer (1984), "Social science duration analysis", in: J.J. Heckman and B. Singer, eds., Longitudinal analysis of labor market data (Cambridge University Press, Cambridge).

Heckman, J. and B. Singer (1985), "A method for minimizing the impact of distributional assumptions in econometric models of duration data", Econometrica 52: 271–320.

Heckman, J. and J. Smith (1995), "Assessing the case for social experiments", Journal of Economic Perspectives 9: 85–110.

Heckman, J. and J. Walker (1985), "Economic models of fertility dynamics: a study of Swedish fertility", Research in Population Economics 7: 3–91.

Heckman, J. and J. Walker (1987), "Using goodness of fit and other criteria to choose among competing duration models: a case study of Hutterite data", in: C. Clogg, ed., Sociological methodology 1987 (American Sociological Association, Washington, DC).

Heckman, J. and J. Walker (1989), "Forecasting aggregate period-specific birth rates: the time series properties of a microdynamic neoclassical model of fertility", Journal of the American Statistical Association 84: 958–965.

Heckman, J. and R. Willis (1975), "Estimation of a stochastic model of reproduction: an econometric approach", in: N. Terleckyj, ed., Household production and consumption (Columbia University Press, New York).

Henshaw, S. (1990), "Induced abortion: a world review, 1990", Family Planning Perspectives 26: 101–106, 112.

Hotz, V.J. (1980), A life cycle model of fertility and married women's labor supply, Ph.D. Dissertation (University of Wisconsin-Madison, Madison, WI).

Hotz, V.J. and R. Miller (1988a), "An empirical analysis of life cycle fertility and female labor supply", Econometrica 56: 91–118.

Hotz, V.J. and R. Miller (1988b), "The economics of family planning", Unpublished manuscript (University of Chicago, Chicago, IL).

Hotz, V.J. and R. Miller (1993), "Conditional choice probabilities and the estimation of dynamic models", Review of Economic Studies 60: 497–530.

Hotz, V.J., J. Klerman and S. Sanders (1996), "The role of savings, human capital in the timing of fertility explaining recent trends in teenage and out-of-wedlock childbearing: a theoretical treatment", Research in progress (University of Chicago, Chicago, IL).

Hotz, V.J., S. McElroy and S. Sanders (1995), "The costs and consequences of teenage childbearing for mothers", in: R. Maynard, ed., Kids having kids: the consequences and costs of teenage childbearing in the United States, in press.

Houthakker, H. (1952), "Compensated changes in quantities and qualities consumed", Review of Economic Studies 19: 155–161.

Jackson, C. and J. Klerman (1994), "Welfare, abortion and teenage fertility", Unpublished manuscript (Rand Corporation, Santa Monica, CA).

Jackson, C. and J. Klerman (1996), "Welfare and american fertility", Unpublished manuscript (Rand Corporation, Santa Monica, CA).

Joyce, T. and R. Kaestner (1995), "The effect of parental involvement laws on pregnancy resolution", Unpublished manuscript (City University of New York, New York).

Juster, F.T. and F. Stafford (1991), "The allocation of time: empirical findings, behavioral models and problems of measurement", Journal of Economic Literature 29: 471–522.

Kane, T. and D. Staiger (1995), "Teen motherhood and abortion access", Unpublished paper (Harvard University, Cambridge, MA).

Karlin, S. and H. Taylor (1975), A first course in stochastic processes, 2nd edn. (Academic Press, New York).

Lam, D. (1988), "Marriage markets and assortative mating with household public goods", Journal of Human Resources 23: 462–487.

Lancaster, K. (1966), "A new approach to consumer theory", Journal of Political Economy 74: 132–157.

Lancaster, T. (1990), The econometric analysis of transition data (Cambridge University Press, New York).

Leibenstein, H. (1957), Economic backwardness and economic growth (Wiley, New York).

Leibowitz, A. (1974), "Home investments in children", Journal of Political Economy 81: S111–S131.

Leibowitz, A. and J. Klerman (1995), "Expalining changes in married mother's employment over time", Demography 32: 365–374.

Macunovich, D. (1994), "A review of recent developments in the economics of fertility", Unpublished manuscript (Williams College, Williamstown, MA).

Macunovich, D. (1995), "The Butz–Ward fertility model in the light of more recent data", The Journal of Human Resources XXX: 229–255.

MaCurdy, T. (1980), "An empirical model of labor supply in a life cycle setting", Journal of Political Economy 89: 1059–1085.

Maynard, R. and A. Rangarajan (1994), "Contraceptive use and repeat pregnancies among welfare dependent mothers", Family Planning Perspectives 26: 198–205.

Merz, J., C. Jackson and J. Klerman (1995), "A review of abortion policy: legality, Medicaid funding and parental involvement, 1967–1994", Working paper 95-14 (Rand Corporation, Santa Monica, CA), forthcoming in Women's Rights Law Reporter.

Merz, J., J.A. Klerman and C. Jackson (1996), "A chronicle of abortion legality, Medicaid funding and parental involvement, 1967–1994", Mimeo. (Rand Corporation, Santa Monica, CA).

Meyer, B. (1995), "Natural and quasi-natural experiments", Journal of Business and Economic Statistics 13: 151–162.

Michael, R. (1973), "Education and the derived demand for children", Journal of Political Economy 81: S128–S164.

Michael, R. and R. Willis (1975), "Contraception and fertility: household production under uncertainty", in: N.E. Terleykyj, ed., Household consumption and production (National Bureau of Economic Research, New York) pp. 27–93.

Mincer, J. (1963), "Market prices, opportunity costs and income effects", in: C. Christ et al., eds., Measurement in economics: studies in mathematical economics in honor of Yehuda Grunfeld (Stanford University Press, Stanford, CA).

Mincer, J. and S. Polacheck (1974), "Family investment in human capital: earnings of women", Journal of Political Economy 82: S76–108.

Moffitt, R. (1984a), "Profiles of fertility, labour supply and wages of married women: a complete life-cycle model", Review of Economic Studies 51: 263–278.

Moffitt, R. (1984b), "Optimal life-cycle profiles of fertility and labor supply", Research in Population Economics 5: 29–50.

Montgomery, M. (1988), "A dynamic model of contraceptive choice", Unpublished manuscript (Population Council, New York).

Montgomery, M. (1989), "Dynamic behavioural models and contraceptive choice", Journal of Biosocial Science 11: 17–40.

Montgomery, M. and J. Trussell (1986), "Models of marital status and childbearing", in: O. Ashenfelter and R. Layard, eds., Handbook of labor economics (North-Holland, Amsterdam) pp. 205–271.

Morgan, S.P. (1995), "Characteristic features of modern American fertility: a description of late twentieth century U.S. fertility trends and differentials", Unpublished manuscript (University of Pennsylvania, Philadelphia, PA).

Morgan, S.P. and R. Chen (1992), "Predicting childlessness for recent cohorts of American women", International Journal of Forecasting 8: 477–493.

Newman, J. (1981), "Economic analysis of the spacing of births", American Economic Review 73: 33–37.

Newman, J. (1988), "A stochastic dynamic model of fertility", Research in Population Economics 6: 41–68.

Newman, J. and C. McCulloch (1984), "A hazard rate approach to the timing of births", Econometrica 52: 939–961.

Olsen, R. (1994), "Fertility and the size of the U.S. labor force", Journal of Economic Literature XXXII: 60–100.

Perrin, E and M. Sheps (1964), "Human reproduction: a stochastic process", Biometrics 20: 28–45.

Pollak, R.A. and M. Wachter (1975), "The relevance of the household production function and its implications for the allocation of time", Journal of Political Economy 83: 255–277.

Razin, A. (1980), "Number, spacing and quality of children", in: J. Simon and J. Da Vanzo, eds., Research in population economics, Vol. 2 (JAI Press, Greenwich, CT).

Rindfuss, R., S.P. Morgan and G. Swicegood (1988), First births in America: the timing of parenthood (University of California Press, Berkeley, CA).

Rosen, S. (1974), "Hedonic prices and implicit markets: product differentiation in pure competition", Journal of Political Economy 82: 34–55.

Rosenzweig, M. (1995), "Welfare, marital prospects and nonmarital childbearing", Unpublished manuscript (University of Pennsylvania, Philadelphia, PA).

Rosenzweig, M. and R. Evenson (1977), "Fertility, schooling and the economic contribution of children of rural India: an econometric analysis", Econometrica 45: 1065–1080.

Rosenzweig, M. and T.P. Schultz. (1985), "The demand for and supply of births: fertility and its life cycle consequences", American Economic Review 75: 992–1015.

Rosenzweig, M. and T.P. Schultz (1989), "Schooling, information and non-market productivity: contraceptive use and its effectiveness", International Economic Review 27: 55–76.

Rosenzweig, M. and K. Wolpin (1980a), "Testing the quantity-quality fertility model: the use of twins as a natural experiment", Econometrica 48: 227–240.

Rosenzweig, M. and K. Wolpin (1980b), "Life-cycle labor supply and fertility: causal inferences from household models", Journal of Political Economy 88: 328–348.

Rosenzweig, M. and K. Wolpin (1993), "Maternal expectations and ex post rationalizations: the usefulness of survey information on the wantedness of children", Journal of Human Resources 28: 205–229.

Rust, J. (1987), "Optimal replacement of GMC bus engines: an empirical model of Harold Zurcher", Econometrica 55: 999–1034.

Ryder, N. (1986), "Observations on the history of cohort fertility in the United States", Population and Development Review 12: 617–643.

Ryder, N. and C. Westoff (1973), Reproduction in the United States, 1965 (Princeton University Press, Princeton, NJ).

Sah, R. (1991), "The effect of child mortality changes on fertility choice and parental welfare", Journal of Political Economy 99: 582–606.

Sanderson, W. (1980), "A new non-utilitarian economic model of fertility and labor force behavior", Revue Economique 31(6).

Schultz, T.P. (1985), "Changing world prices, women's wages and the fertility transition: Sweden, 1860–1910", Journal of Political Economy 93: 1126–1154.

Schultz, T.W. (1974), The economics of the family: marriage, children and human capital (NBER, Chicago, IL and London).

Sheps, M. and J. Menken (1973), Mathematical models of conception and birth (University of Chicago Press, Chicago, IL).

Silver, M. (1965), "Births, marriages and business cycles in the United States", Journal of Political Economy 73: 237–255.

Theil, H. (1952), "Qualities, prices and budget inquiries", Review of Economic Studies 19: 129–147.

Trussell, J. and K. Kost (1987), "Contraceptive failure in the United States", Studies in Family Planning 18: 237–256.

Vijverberg, W. (1984), "Discrete choices in a continuous time model: life-cycle time allocation and fertility decisions", Research in Population Economics 5: 51–85.

Walker, J. (1995), "The effect of public policies on recent Swedish fertility behavior", Journal of Population Economics 8: 223–251.

Ward, M. and W. Butz (1980), "Completed fertility and its timing", Journal of Political Economy 88: 917–941.

Weiss, Y. and R. Willis (1985), "Children as collective goods and divorce settlements", Journal of Labor Economics 3: 268–292.

Wilkinson M. (1973), "An econometric analysis of fertility in Sweden, 1870–1965", Econometrica 41: 633–642.

Willis, R. (1973), "A new approach to the economic theory of fertility behavior", Journal of Political Economy 81: S14–S64.

Willis, R. (1987), "What have we learned from the economics of the family?", American Economic Review Papers and Proceedings 77: 68–81.

Willis, R. (1995), "A theory of out-of-wedlock childbearing", Unpublished manuscript (University of Michigan, Ann Arbor, MI).

Wilson, W.J. (1987), The truly disadvantaged (University of Chicago Press, Chicago, IL).

Wolpin, K. (1984), "An estimable dynamic stochastic model of fertility and child mortality", Journal of Political Economy 92: 852–874.

# Chapter 8

# DEMAND FOR CHILDREN IN LOW INCOME COUNTRIES

T. PAUL SCHULTZ*

*Yale University*

## Contents

*I have benefited from the comments of workshop participants at the Carolina Population Center, Rand, IIASA, Gothenberg, Iowa State, Princeton, and Peking Universities, and from L. Bollinger, A. Judd, Y. Hayami, A.C. Kelley, and T.N. Srinivasan. The research assistance of Jeffrey DeSimone and Blaise Bourgeois is gratefully acknowledged and the partial support of the Institute for Policy Reform.

*Handbook of Population and Family Economics. Edited by M.R. Rosenzweig and O. Stark*
© *Elsevier Science B.V., 1997*

## 1. Introduction

The decline in average fertility in low-income countries that has occurred since 1960 can be partly understood in terms of models of household demand behavior, as can the variation across individuals in fertility at one point in time. But the origins and ramifications of these differences in fertility are far from fully understood. Much recent research on fertility has been guided by the realization that the family functions as coordinator of many demographic and economic production and consumption activities. Economic and time constraints on families are therefore thought to influence not only births, but also to affect many other forms of interdependent family behavior, including inter- and intrahousehold transfers, migration, savings and consumption behavior, and investments in human and nonhuman capital. Separating individual and family decision-making into compartments is a common practice designed to facilitate modeling a particular behavioral relationship. But it is a shortcut that can compromise the realism of analysis of family behavior and distort its implications.

In this chapter, economic models for understanding empirical regularities in fertility in low-income countries are first outlined in their simplest form. Assumptions are then relaxed or behavior is allowed to interact among several "compartments". Two alternative research strategies can be adopted for modeling more of these compartmentalized outcomes, such as fertility and parent investments in child quality. Reduced-form relationships can be estimated that may answer some overall questions on how exogenous constraints affect each family outcome, but do not decompose how one outcome depends on other jointly determined outcomes in some full model. Alternatively, a "structural model" can be specified, and additional information can be used to recover or identify the interdependencies represented in the model's structure. A recurrent theme in this chapter is the limits to our knowledge about the "full" structural model linking fertility to other family outcomes. A consequence of this view is that estimation of reduced-forms continues to perform an important analytical function for the study of the demand for children, despite its obvious limitations.

In general, the empirical patterns in fertility and family behavior discussed in this chapter have their counterparts in high-income countries, and often can be documented in both contemporary and preindustrial periods for those countries. It is, therefore, unclear that the economic models and methods used to study fertility in high- and low-income countries should be segregated as in this volume (Schultz, 1981). But the salient questions and the available data often differ between the two groups of countries, and hence the choice of models and statistical methods that receive the most attention will also differ somewhat between the studies of these two types of populations.

In many low-income countries, total fertility rates have declined by 50% or more since 1960. Regional and country-specific variation in the timing of this demographic transition is striking and calls for a coherent quantitative economic explanation. Most empirical analysis of fertility has focused on explaining cross-sectional variation

350

within a single country, first across subnational regions and then, as household surveys became more widely available, across individuals. Much less analysis of changes in fertility over time has occurred, either within (relatively closed) aggregates, such as nations, or within extended families between generations. Therefore, in Section 5.6, national data are examined to test some hypotheses regarding the demand for children that may help to account for the broad outlines of the contemporary demographic transition. The paucity of economic studies of the fertility transition may reflect more than a shortage of data. It may also signal that many observers do not think that this remarkable decline in fertility is due to the changing economic constraints facing families. Rather, they associate this decline in fertility with the provision of subsidized modern birth control through organized family planning programs. Thus, the cost effectiveness of family planning, education, and health programs as means to help people achieve a lower level of fertility are considered later in this chapter.

## 2. Regional trends in birth and death rates

Table 1 reports the size of the world's population from 1750 to 2000, as well as population by current income level and region of the developing world. All of these estimates are subject to substantial uncertainty and yet illustrate certain broad regional patterns in the demographic transition, by which is meant sustained declines in death and birth rates that lead to a showing of population growth. The difference between the crude birth rate and the crude death rate (per 1000 population) is equal to the rate of population growth, not including immigration and emigration. In the higher income countries, i.e., Europe (including Asiatic USSR), North America, Australia, New Zealand, and Japan, the population increased 2.8 times from 1750 to 1900, supported by agricultural and industrial revolutions, whereas the rest of the world's population did not quite double (80%). Conversely, in the twentieth century the population of the higher income countries will increase 1.3 times, while the population of the lower income countries will increase 3.7 times. As a consequence, the share of the world's population living in the high-income countries increased from a fifth in 1750 to a third in 1900, and will subside back to a fifth by the year 2000.

Different regions thus experienced their "population explosion" at different times, and the amplitude of the explosion has tended to be larger, though the duration shorter, for those entering later into their demographic transition. The higher income countries experienced their most rapid population growth from about 1850 to 1900, when they grew at about 1.0% per year. This population growth rate was again briefly exceeded during the baby boom of 1950–1955, but today these more developed countries are growing at less than 0.4% per year, and will probably reach zero growth, in the absence of immigration, early in the next century. Population growth in Latin America peaked in the 1960s when it approached 3.0% per year, and will have declined to 1.7% by 2000. The population of East and South-East Asia increased at its maximum

Table 1
Population of world by region with vital rates and population growth[a]

| | 1750 | 1850 | 1900 | 1950 | 1960 | 1970 | 1980 | 1990 | 2000 |
|---|---|---|---|---|---|---|---|---|---|
| 1. World population (millions) | 728 | 1171 | 1608 | 2516 | 3020 | 3698 | 4448 | 5292 | 6261 |
| Birth rates (per thousand population) | – | – | – | 37.5 | 35.2 | 31.5 | 27.6 | 26.4 | 22.9 |
| Death rate (per thousand population) | – | 6.5 | 7.8 | 19.7 | 15.4 | 12.1 | 10.4 | 9.2 | 8.2 |
| Population growth rate | 4.5 | – | – | 17.0 | 22.9 | 19.4 | 17.2 | 17.2 | 14.7 |
| 2. Higher income population[a] | 145 | 329 | 554 | 832 | 945 | 1049 | 1137 | 1207 | 1264 |
| Birth rate | – | – | – | 22.6 | 20.1 | 16.7 | 15.2 | 13.9 | 13.1 |
| Death rate | – | – | – | 10.1 | 9.0 | 9.3 | 9.6 | 9.6 | 9.7 |
| Population growth rate | 6.5 | 10.6 | 9.9 | 12.5 | 11.1 | 7.4 | 5.6 | 4.3 | 3.4 |
| 3. Lower income population[b] | 583 | 842 | 1054 | 1684 | 2075 | 2649 | 3312 | 4086 | 4997 |
| Birth rate | – | – | – | 44.6 | 41.9 | 37.1 | 31.7 | 30.0 | 25.3 |
| Death rate | – | – | – | 24.3 | 18.3 | 13.2 | 10.6 | 9.1 | 7.8 |
| Population growth rate | 4.0 | 4.9 | 6.7 | 20.3 | 23.6 | 23.9 | 21.1 | 20.9 | 17.5 |
| 4. Latin America population | 16 | 33 | 63 | 166 | 218 | 286 | 323 | 448 | 538 |
| Birth rate | – | – | – | 42.5 | 41.1 | 35.4 | 30.6 | 26.8 | 23.1 |
| Death rate | – | – | – | 15.4 | 12.1 | 9.7 | 7.9 | 7.0 | 6.5 |
| Population growth rate | 8# | 13# | 20 | 27.1 | 29.0 | 25.7 | 22.7 | 19.8 | 16.6 |

| | | | | | | | | | |
|---|---|---|---|---|---|---|---|---|---|
| **5. Southeast Asia and East Asia population[c]** | | | | | | | | | |
| Birth rate | – | – | – | 41.5 | 37.0 | 31.2 | 21.9 | 21.7 | 16.6 |
| Death rate | – | – | – | 23.5 | 16.4 | 9.83 | 7.49 | 6.97 | 6.80 |
| Population | 475 | 741 | 915 | 853 | 1017 | 1274 | 1536 | 1781 | 2045 |
| Population growth rate | 4.7 | 4.3 | 5.4 | 18.0 | 20.4 | 21.7 | 14.4 | 14.7 | 9.80 |
| **6. South and West Asia population[d]** | | | | | | | | | |
| Birth rate | – | – | – | 45.1 | 43.4 | 40.4 | 37.6 | 33.6 | 27.7 |
| Death rate | – | – | – | 25.0 | 19.8 | 16.3 | 13.0 | 10.3 | 8.15 |
| Population | – | – | – | 523 | 652 | 829 | 1047 | 1333 | 1668 |
| Population growth rate | – | – | – | 20.1 | 23.6 | 24.1 | 24.6 | 23.3 | 19.6 |
| **7. African population** | 95 | 95 | 120 | 222 | 279 | 362 | 477 | 642 | 867 |
| Birth rate | – | – | – | 49.2 | 48.7 | 46.6 | 45.3 | 43.5 | 39.5 |
| Death rate | – | – | – | 26.9 | 22.9 | 19.2 | 16.4 | 14.6 | 11.6 |
| Population growth rate | -1.1 | 4.8 | 9.4 | 22.3 | 25.8 | 27.4 | 28.9 | 28.9 | 27.9 |

–, estimates for the disaggregation between birth and death rates are not reported.

[a] Population estimates in millions. Crude birth, death and natural population growth rates in annual growth per thousand population in the 5-year period following the year reported from 1950 to 2000, for the 50-year period following the year reported in 1750, 1800, and 20-year period after 1900. Estimates for 1750, 1850, 1900 from: S. Kuznets, *Modern Economic Growth*, 1966, Table 2.2 derived by him from Carr-Saunders (1936), except where modifications drawn from J.D. Durand, 1974, *Historical Estimates of World Population: An Evaluation*. Estimates for 1950 to 1990 and projections for the year 2000 from United Nations, 1991, *World Population Prospects 1990* medium variant.

[b] Higher Income Industrially Advanced Countries includes Europe, Asiatic USSR, North America, Australia and New Zealand and Japan. Lower Income Countries includes all other countries.

[c] South East and East Asia extends from Myanmar to Mongolia excluding Japan and Asiatic USSR.

[d] Southern and Western Asia extends from Bangladesh to Turkey.

rate of 2.2% in 1970, and will plunge to 1.0% by the turn of the century. This region is of course dominated by China, which experienced a sharp decline in its fertility from 1970 to 1980, but many other countries in the region have reported similarly large fertility declines, without the imposition of the Chinese "one-child family" policy. South and West Asia had its peak population growth rate of 2.5% somewhat later, in 1980, and this rate may decline to 2.0% by the year 2000. For example, India, Pakistan, and Bangladesh have not shown much decline in population growth rates since 1960, because gradual declines in death rates have numerically counterbalanced declines in birth rates. The population of Africa is still growing at its peak rate of 2.9%, and forecasts for this continent are particularly uncertain given gaps in data and the AIDS epidemic.

Crude birth and death rates are influenced by swings in the age composition of populations. It is useful for comparative purposes, therefore, to consult measures of fertility and mortality that are independent of age composition, and although they may appear to refer to a birth cohort or a representative agent over her lifetime, they are actually derived from vital rates for a particular year or period. The "total fertility rate" is the average number of children that would be born alive to a woman during her lifetime, if during her childbearing years she were to bear children at each age at the prevailing age-specific birth rates. "Infant mortality" is the number of deaths of infants under one year old in a given year per 1000 live births. Although infant mortality has declined most dramatically, the entire schedule of age-specific mortality can also be summarized in "life expectancy" at birth, or the average number of years a newborn would live, if current age-specific mortality were maintained. Estimates and projections of these three demographic indicators are reported in Table 2 from 1950 to 2000 for the same regions of the world.

Total fertility rates in the higher income countries have fallen from 2.8 children per woman in 1950 to 1.9 in 1990. In the long run, a total fertility rate of about 2.1 is required for a population to just replace itself, in the absence of immigration or emigration. Table 2 suggests the marked decline in infant mortality and increase in life expectancy in East and South-East Asia in the 1960s was followed by the decline in total fertility rates in the 1970s. Latin America, South and West Asia, and particularly Africa achieved a more gradual decline in infant mortality, and this may help to explain the timing and pace of the subsequent fertility declines in these regions.

Antibiotics, insecticides (that curbed vector borne diseases such as malaria), vaccines, and other public health measures that spread after World War II are attributed a central role in the decline in mortality in lower income countries (Preston, 1980). The persisting high levels of child mortality and the relatively low levels of female education in Africa are mentioned as contributing to the high levels of fertility in Africa. Others have argued that special features of the African family, such as co-residence of the extended family, fostering of children, and limited responsibility of fathers for the costs of childrearing, could help to explain the high African fertility levels (Caldwell and Caldwell, 1987). The shortage of reliable household survey data containing a

Table 2
Period measures of fertility, infant mortality and life expectation at birth for world's regions[a]

|  | 1950 | 1960 | 1970 | 1980 | 1990 | 2000 |
|---|---|---|---|---|---|---|
| 1. World |  |  |  |  |  |  |
| Total fertility rate | 5.00 | 4.98 | 4.46 | 3.65 | 3.31 | 2.96 |
| Infant mortality rate | 155 | 118 | 93 | 79 | 63 | 51 |
| Life expectation | 47.5 | 53.2 | 58.6 | 60.4 | 63.9 | 67.0 |
| 2. Higher income |  |  |  |  |  |  |
| Total fertility rate | 2.84 | 2.69 | 2.20 | 1.93 | 1.88 | 1.91 |
| Infant mortality rate | 56 | 32 | 22 | 16 | 12 | 9 |
| Life expectation | 66.0 | 69.8 | 71.1 | 72.8 | 74.9 | 76.6 |
| 3. Lower income |  |  |  |  |  |  |
| Total fertility rate | 6.19 | 6.09 | 5.41 | 4.19 | 3.71 | 3.20 |
| Infant mortality rate | 180 | 136 | 105 | 89 | 70 | 57 |
| Life expectation | 42.2 | 48.5 | 55.2 | 59.4 | 63.3 | 66.5 |
| 4. Latin America |  |  |  |  |  |  |
| Total fertility rate | 5.87 | 5.96 | 4.99 | 3.93 | 3.25 | 2.81 |
| Infant mortality rate | 126 | 100 | 81 | 61 | 48 | 37 |
| Life expectation | 51.9 | 57.3 | 61.3 | 65.2 | 68.1 | 70.4 |
| 5. South East and East Asia |  |  |  |  |  |  |
| Total fertility rate | 5.78 | 5.47 | 4.59 | 2.77 | 2.47 | 2.13 |
| Infant mortality rate | 175 | 114 | 72 | 46 | 34 | 24 |
| Life expectation | 44.1 | 51.5 | 61.6 | 66.3 | 69.7 | 72.1 |
| 6. South and West Asia |  |  |  |  |  |  |
| Total fertility rate | 6.17 | 6.07 | 5.78 | 5.16 | 4.47 | 3.61 |
| Infant mortality rate | 190 | 157 | 134 | 111 | 88 | 68 |
| Life expectation | 39.6 | 45.4 | 50.2 | 55.1 | 59.9 | 64.4 |
| 7. Africa |  |  |  |  |  |  |
| Total fertility rate | 6.65 | 6.79 | 6.62 | 6.40 | 6.03 | 5.31 |
| Infant mortality rate | 188 | 165 | 137 | 116 | 94 | 77 |
| Life expectation | 37.7 | 41.8 | 45.9 | 49.6 | 54.1 | 58.1 |

[a]See notes on regional definitions to Table 1. Rates refer to the 5-year period following the year reported.
*Source*: United Nations, 1991, *World Population Prospects 1990*, medium variant.

combination of economic and demographic information has, until recently, prevented researchers from contributing much to debates of this nature about the causes for high fertility (Thomas and Muvandi, 1992). But progress in understanding the household and community constraints on the demand for children promises to also account for some of the variation in African experience as it already has in Latin America and Asia.

## 3. Micro foundations for household behavior

Household economic models of fertility originated in the writings of Becker (1960, 1965), Mincer (1963), and Leibenstein (1957), and have been restated with changing emphasis thereafter (T.W. Schultz, 1974; T.P. Schultz, 1976a, 1981). As currently employed, most household models of the demand for children share certain features. First, the traditional money income budget constraint is replaced by a time budget constraint, endogenizing the allocation of time between market labor supply and non-market activity. This is especially important for women because some of their labor market activities cannot be readily combined with child care.

Second, demographic and economic behavior depend on the household stocks of human and physical capital. Labor is particularly heterogeneous in its productive attributes and alternative uses and is valued distinctly for each family member, particularly if labor is used in rearing children. Separate labor supply equations for husband, wife, and children are a minimum accommodation to the existence of the multiperson family. Yet the family takes on a variety of extensive forms, and many models have been devised to represent this flexible institution across the world, possibly because different transactions costs can modify efficient long-term relationships that are designed to coordinate consumption, production, and reproduction in society (Goody, 1976; McElroy and Horney, 1978; Ben-Porath, 1980; Pollak, 1985; Chiappori, 1992; Gertler and Newman, 1993).

Third, labor market training, migration, marriage, children, and retirement savings may be accounted for by permanent and potentially foreseen life-cycle conditions and should be less strongly influenced by transitory developments in a person's lifetime. Since many of the same long-term opportunities, traits, expectations, and preferences are attributed a role in determining these interrelated life-cycle decisions and interdependent resource allocations, it is only reasonable to view these life-cycle outcomes as jointly and simultaneously determined.

However, estimation of household demand systems was initially based on the assumption that a block recursive stochastic structure adequately represented by time-ordered behaviors of the individual and household (Orcutt et al., 1961; Wold, 1964). Path analysis was analogously justified in the sociological study of the unfolding of life-cycle ordered events (Duncan, 1966). But this statistical approach depended on the simplifying assumption that errors are independent across demand equations. In the study of long-run household life-cycle behavior, such recursivity of errors is unlikely. To assume, for example, that the number of children a woman bears is an exogenous shock determining the schooling of her children contradicts the household demand framework, wherein both outcomes are evaluated together, even though the fertility decision formally occurs before the schooling decision and contains an unpredictable error component. Preferences of consumers and biological traits relevant to household reproduction, such as desired fertility and fecundity, are likely to be persistent. They are, therefore, impounded in statistical errors to equations accounting for many forms of demographic and economic behavior over the life cycle and tend to be serially correlated and correlated across behavioral equations. Identification of recursive structures in the household demand framework may be difficult, therefore. Even when plausibly approached as a simultaneous equation system or a multistate duration model, it may be difficult to identify convincingly the structural parameters that relate one endogenous outcome to another endogenous outcome within the same household.

There is growing agreement on suitable exogenous constraint variables and endogenous choice variables that the household determines jointly with fertility. Reduced-form equations are thus often estimated to explain several of the household economic and demographic choice outcomes in terms of a common list of conditioning exogenous variables: household endowments, skills, the local prices of inputs and outputs, wages, local public sector services, and environmental factors, such as climate and endemic diseases. An empirical body of knowledge is thus accumulating on which to generalize about the relative magnitude of specific reduced-form parameters across a variety of populations. Parameters describing household production technology may also exhibit sufficient stability in some areas such as reproduction, nutrition or health to permit the replication of estimates (Rosenzweig and Schultz, 1988). Regularities are emerging in reduced-form and structural demand and technology parameters over time and across societies.

The general household demand model clarifies various types of relationships and classifications of variables, but in its unrestricted form it offers few predictions that can be tested empirically. Nonetheless, as with many conceptual frameworks, it also focuses the analysis and structures the empirical research. Simplifying and restricting the characteristics of the consumer's utility function (i.e., preferences) or the household production relations (i.e., technology) may be justified, in which case theory can undoubtedly provide more testable predictions. It is not always possible, however, to distinguish then whether a rejection of the predictions is due to the inadequacies of the general theory or the invalid specific restrictions imposed on the framework.

## 3.1. The general household demand framework

Parents are assumed to maximize their lifetime utility, which depends on, say, six commodities: their number of children, $C$; the average education and health of their children, $E$ and $H$; the average leisure activities of the husband and wife, $L_h$, $L_w$, respectively; and another composite household commodity, $G$:

$$U = U(C, E, H, L_h, L_w, G). \tag{1}$$

Each of these arguments of the utility function may be thought of as produced in the home by constant returns to scale technology with market goods, $X$, and the non-market time, $t$, subscripted to husband and wife:

$$i = \alpha_i(X_i, t_{hi}, t_{wi}, \mu_i), \tag{2}$$

where $i = C, E, H, L_h, L_w, G$. A couple-specific trait represented by $\mu_i$ influences production possibilities and is partially known to the couple, though it is not controlled by them. For example, it might be exogenous genetic or environmental factors that affect the couple's production of births, or what shall be called simply "fecundity" (Rosenzweig and Schultz, 1983, 1985, 1987).

The allocation of each individual's time across household production activities is assumed to be mutually exclusive in Becker's (1965) original model; namely, no jointness in production is permitted. This can be relaxed with little added complexity (Rosenzweig and Schultz, 1983). Together with time supplied to the market labor force, $t_{jm}$, the alternative uses of time sum in the Becker framework to an exogenously given time budget constraint:

$$\Omega_j = t_{jm} + \sum_i t_{ji} + \sum_j L_j, \tag{3}$$

where $j = h,w$ and $i = C, E, H, L_h, L_w, G$. Market income is equal to the lifetime wage rate, $W_j$, received by each member of the family, times their market labor supply, plus income from nonhuman capital endowments of husband and wife, $V_h$ and $V_w$. For simplicity, children are assumed to acquire property only as adults.

$$Y = t_{hm}W_h + t_{wm}W_w + V_h + V_w. \tag{4}$$

If the household production functions, Eq. (2), exhibit constant returns to scale, and all family members work some time in the market, i.e., $t_{jm} > 0$, full income, $F$, can be defined (below) as an observed exogenous budget constraint (5), and the shadow prices of the household commodities (i.e., $\pi_i = $ the opportunity cost of the market goods and household member's time inputs used to produce a unit of the commodity) are then fixed by market-set prices and wages and do not depend on the bundle of commodities consumed by the household. Otherwise, these shadow prices will depend on parent preferences and returns to scale and cease to be exogenous (Pollak and Wachter, 1975). If family members withdraw entirely from the market labor force, an interior solution does not occur, and the model takes on added complexity. If children worked, and their allocation of time was an input in the production of $E$ and $H$, full income would become endogenous because it would depend on fertility. Full income is designed here to replace market income as a new exogenous resource constraint that is not affected by the family market labor supply decisions. The concept of full income, although it contains all of these ambiguities for empirical analyses of life-cycle behavior (Gronau, 1986), is nonetheless heuristically valuable:[1]

$$F = \Omega_h W_h + \Omega_w W_w + V_h + V_w. \tag{5}$$

Becker's (1965) household production framework suggests that household behavior can be interpreted as jointly allocating time between market and nonmarket production and combining market goods and nonmarket time to produce commodities that are the final source of utility to the members of the household. It also assumes that the family can be approximated as a unified optimizing consumer, an assumption that has since become standard in neoclassical studies of family labor supply (Ashenfelter and Heckman, 1974; Smith, 1980; Killingsworth, 1983).[2]

Reliance on the existence of a well-behaved nuclear family utility function is a limitation of the conceptual framework. In practice, however, the decision problem can be reframed in terms of the constraints facing an independent individual, as is standard practice in the study of the factors conditioning the establishment and dissolution of cohabiting relationships or legally/religiously contracted marriages (Becker, 1981; Boulier and Rosenzweig, 1984; Montgomery, 1986; Chiappori, 1992).

Nash-bargaining models of demand behavior of spouses within marriage draw attention to the distinctive effect of each spouse's own wealth, $V_h$ and $V_w$, as they influence a spouse's "threat-point". Individualistic approaches to family behavior direct

---

[1] The household production approach is criticized because in a (less specialized) home production environment, time is frequently employed to advance several activities at one time, such as a mother caring for her children while doing housework, or tending some own-account business pursuits. Variable returns to scale are also expected in household production. The properties of household technology that Becker postulated are required to preserve the "adding up" property of full income and maintain the exogeneity of shadow prices. But neither shadow prices nor full income are generally observed or empirically needed except to facilitate comparisons of family welfare. This is difficult to interpret anyway when family composition is allowed to vary (Gronau, 1986). Another feature ignored is the public-good aspect of some commodities. Children may be enjoyed by both parents without necessarily reducing either's pleasure. How these restrictions on technology actually distort analysis has not been demonstrated without an alternative model to Becker's which could be estimated (Schultz, 1981, 1990; Gronau, 1986; Lam, 1988).

[2] Aside from casual empiricism, which suggests individuals do not always submerge their individual interests in a consistent manner within a family, there are opportunities to test empirically whether the restrictions implied by demand theory applied to the family are consistent with observed behavior. For example, the income compensated husband's market labor supply response to his wife's wage should be symmetric (equal) to the compensated wife's labor supply response to her husband's wage (Killingsworth, 1983). Similarly, it is sometimes suggested that the wife values more highly than does her husband certain allocations of family resources, such as investments in child quality ($H$, $E$ and perhaps $L_c$). In this case, increments to her wealth (e.g., dowry) or $V_w$ should increase the demand for these qualitative attributes of children more than would equal increments to the husband's wealth, $V_h$. Indeed, for this reason, the standard household model generally only includes an aggregate nonearned-income variable. Testing for significant differences in the husband and wife wealth effects is one check on the family demand model (Schultz, 1990).

our attention to customary arrangements associated with family property rights and the origin of family assets, such as inheritances, gifts, or dowry, in order to be able to impute more accurately the ownership of these assets to specific family members. If $V_h$ and $V_w$ influence family demands in the same way empirically, then there is no empirical gain from preserving the distinction, and the family utility-maximizing model that generally pools $V_w$ and $V_h$ is the more parsimonious representation of household demand behavior (McElroy and Horney, 1978). The implied neoclassical restriction on family behavior is testable if $V_w$ and $V_h$ can be separately observed and represent comparable assets, e.g., equally liquid (Schultz, 1990; Thomas, 1990).

Reduced-form demand equations for the household produced commodities are implied by maximizing Eq. (1) subject to Eqs. (2) and (3) and can be generally written as follows:

$$i = Z_i(P, W_h, W_w, V_h, V_w, M, e_i), \tag{6}$$

where $P$ is a vector of average prices of market goods and public services available to the household, $M$ is the vector of exogenous household-specific traits, including $\mu$'s that affect household's production of $i$'s, and $e_i$ are random disturbances that embody the effects of the couple's preferences and unobserved technology plus uncorrelated errors in measurement and specification.

The reduced-form derived demand functions for market goods and time allocations of household members may be written analogously:

$$X_i = X_i(P, W_h, W_w, V_h, V_w, M, f_i), \tag{7}$$

$$T_{ij} = T_{ij}(P, W_h, W_w, V_h, V_w, M, g_{ij}), \tag{8}$$

where $f_i$ and $g_{ij}$ are also uncorrelated disturbances.

Since it is assumed that market prices, local public programs, life-cycle market wages, and family nonearned income are exogenous, the reduced-form equations (6), (7), and (8) can usually be estimated consistently by standard single-equation methods. Although the researcher is unable to observe all of the productive traits of the couple, $M$, their omission from the analysis need not bias the remaining estimates. This depends, of course, on the assumption that the unobserved productive traits of the couple, such as fecundity, are distributed independently of economic endowments, prices, and programs, or that the other elements of $M$ are uncorrelated with the $P$, $W$'s and $V$'s. The reduced-form demand equations embody the more fundamental technological parameters from the household production functions, Eq. (2), and the behavioral demand parameters from the utility function, Eq. (1).

## 3.2. A simple production–demand model of fertility

Children are assumed to be a source of satisfaction for parents, or they may also produce future services that parents value, and their children consume resources that have alternative uses. In addition, parents must have some, albeit imperfect, control over how many children they have (see, for example, Becker, 1960; Coale, 1973; Willis, 1974; Bryant, 1990). If only two goods are distinguished that yield utility for parents, children and a composite bundle of other goods, $G$, some assumptions must be made about how $C$ and $G$ are produced, beyond the linear homogenous production technology implied by Eq. (2). One empirical generalization that fits most societies is that the opportunity value of a mother's time in child bearing and rearing exceeds the value of a father's time in child rearing, i.e., $t_{wc}W_w > t_{hc}W_h$, and that the value of the mother's time input to children as a share of the total opportunity cost of producing children, called mother's "time intensity", $\alpha_{wc}$, exceeds her time intensity in the production of the other good $G$, i.e. $\alpha_{wc} > \alpha_{wg}$. If the wage or shadow value of her time increases, this will then raise the opportunity cost of children relative to other goods, and if "full" income is held constant, this will lower the demand for children. However, when the woman's wage is observed to increase, so does full income. The (negative) income-compensated price effect of an increase in a woman's wage is offset by a (positive) income effect, for children are thought to be a normal good. The observed uncompensated female wage effect may, therefore, be either positive or negative on the demand for children.

In the case of the man's wage, it is less obvious whether children are more male-time intensive than the composite good, or, in other words, whether the income-compensated price effect of the male wage on the demand for children is negative, and if negative, whether it is sufficiently large to outweigh the positive income effect. The elasticity of the demand for children with respect to the wage of the man or woman in this two-commodity case can be decomposed according to the Slutsky equation into compensated full price ($\pi_c$) and full income elasticities (Ben-Porath, 1974; Schultz, 1981):

$$\eta_{CW_j} = \eta_{C\pi_c}(\alpha_{jc} - \alpha_{jg}) + \eta_{CF}\left(\frac{W_j t_{jm}}{F}\right), \quad j = w, h. \tag{9}$$

The income elasticity ($\eta_{CF}$) is weighted by the market earnings of the individual whose wage is varying. Thus, the presumably positive income effect associated with a man's wage is weighted more heavily than for a woman's wage, to the extent that his wage exceeds hers and to the extent that he works more hours in the market labor force than she. The compensated price elasticity ($\eta_{C\pi_c}$) is weighted by the difference between that spouses time intensities in $C$ and $G$. Although the sign of the male or female wage effect on fertility is not prescribed by this theory, it is clear that the male wage will exert a more positive (or less negative) effect on fertility than the female wage.

As an empirical observation, virtually all cross-sectional studies of fertility have found fertility to be inversely related to women's wages, or to the most common proxy for wages, education (Schultz, 1976a). Thus, the child price effect associated with women's wage rates empirically exceeds in absolute value the income effect. The male wage is often associated with higher fertility in traditional agricultural societies, but is also found to be associated in some instances with lower fertility in industrially advanced, high-income societies. The extent of land ownership or value of physical assets is often associated positively with fertility, but it is moot whether these wealth variables are indeed exogenous as is generally assumed within this framework (Stys, 1957; Rosenzweig and Evenson, 1977; Schultz, 1990, 1994).

The most important implication of the household demand framework is that different sources of family income have different effects on the demand for children. The woman's wage has the most negative (or smallest positive) effect on fertility, the man's wage a less negative or possibly positive effect, and inherited wealth or natural resource income has the largest positive effect, because it does not embody any offsetting price effect to deter the demand for children (Schultz, 1981).

Willis' (1974) model of fertility advanced two additional restrictions on this more general framework: men provide no time in the rearing of children, and women's education increases woman's market wage opportunities but does not increase her home productivity. This latter assumption followed an earlier approach of Becker (1964: p. 178) and suggested that women would productively benefit from education only to the extent that they worked in the market labor force. This line of reasoning has subsequently been rejected by some researchers because it led to downward biased estimates of the returns to education for women compared to men if nonmarket productivity was enhanced by education (Schultz, 1989). Given his assumptions, Willis showed that as women allocate some of their time to the labor market (for a constant wage), education would only then raise market wages and reduce fertility, a prediction that is not confirmed in low-income country studies. More interesting, the direct effect of a man's wage is to increase fertility for it embodies only an income effect; men do not allocate time to childrearing. But this male wage effect is larger for women who participate in the labor market, because their marginal value of time does not depend on their husband's wage. For a woman working entirely within the home, additions to male income raise her marginal product at home and hence raise the price of children which are intensive users of her time. Because the woman's labor force participation is endogenous in Willis' model, empirical implications of this setup are difficult to test.[3] More important, the working assumption regarding men's time allocation and

---

[3] Assuming linear specifications for the fertility demand equations and the participation equation, a reduced-form fertility equation is expressed as a mixture model of the distinctive fertility demand equations for participating and nonparticipating wives. Only the quadratic terms on women's education and male income are signed by the restricted theory, and these higher order terms are only briefly examined by Willis based on his analysis of a 1960 US Census sample.

women's benefits from education are not particularly attractive ways to simplify the model.

Becker's (1960) idea that children are consumer durables that come in various qualities met with understandable skepticism (Blake, 1968). The price of children could rise, Becker suggested, for two possible reasons: first, the demand of parents to invest in higher quality children could increase; and second, the price of inputs to produce a constant-quality child could increase. The inverse empirical relationship between fertility and the resources a parent invests per child is known as the "quantity–quality tradeoff". Sociobiologists speculate on why a particular balance of quantity and quality occurs in various species, in addition to man (Becker, 1981).

When inputs to produce children are viewed as contributing to the production of both the number of children and their quality, and both are to some degree parental choices, the simple cost of a child is not an exogenous price to which consumers respond, but is itself a choice variable. The problems with then constructing a constant-quality child price series have proven to be insurmountable (Lindert, 1980; Espenshade, 1984). What began as an appealing empirical regularity between quantity and quality must not be interpreted as a causal relationship; both outcomes embody an element of choice and are affected by the same consumer's budget constraint (Becker and Lewis, 1974; T.W. Schultz, 1974; Becker and Tomes, 1976; Rosenzweig and Wolpin, 1980a; Cigno, 1991).

### 3.3. Quantity and quality of children

Willis (1974) assumed that child services ($S$) were produced as the product of the quantity of children ($C$) and quality ($Q$), both of which are produced by linear homogeneous household production functions (Eq. (2)) (quality could be either education, $E$, or health, $H$, in the previous notation). The full income constraint is then rewritten as follows where $\pi_i$ refers to the shadow price of the $i$th commodity, inclusive of its market and time inputs:

$$F = \pi_s CQ + \pi_g G. \tag{10}$$

The marginal cost of quantity or quality of children then depends on the other dimension of child services demanded by the couple:

$$\partial F/\partial C = \pi_s Q, \qquad \partial F/\partial Q = \pi_s C. \tag{11}$$

This specification involving an interaction between commodities in the budget constraint implies that parents view quality and quantity as substitutes (Rosenzweig and Wolpin, 1980a), and that they also do not treat quality of any one child as distinct from that of their other children. Parents are thus assumed to be "bound" to treat all of their children equally. This simplification in the Becker/Willis framework can be contrasted with earlier analyses of consumer expenditures that allowed for quantity and quality to vary independently with income (Houthakker, 1952; Theil, 1952). Casual empirical evidence is not entirely consistent with this simplified multiplicative quantity–quality model. Are first-born treated by parents in the same way as subsequent children? Psychologists are doubtful (Zajonc and Marcus, 1975; Ernst and Angst, 1983). Do parents invest the same amount in the quality of daughters as sons? Sex differences in human capital are still marked in some countries, and these appear to stem mostly from school enrollment decisions within the family (Birdsall, 1980; Behrman et al., 1982; Schultz, 1993b). It is, of course, possible to think of male and female births as different commodities in the utility function of parents, with also perhaps distinct costs and benefits. Thus, it is not innocuous to assume that parents demand uniform quality for their children.

The assumption of the quantity–quality model should be viewed as a testable restriction on the more general framework in which quality and quantity are not necessarily a source of interactive costs or substitutes for each other. It is not straightforward, however, to estimate the cross-commodity effects, because all market prices, household endowments, etc. are arguably determinants of both $Q$ and $C$, leaving no obvious exclusion restriction to account for exogenous variation in $C$ in the demand equation for $Q$ or to identify $Q$ in the $C$ equation.

Two approaches are used to measure exogenous variation in fertility to estimate behavioral adjustment of child quality. Having a twin on first birth is uncorrelated within a sample of mothers with factors determining the demand for children, e.g., endowments, prices/wages, and preferences, and yet twins are correlated with children ever born because some couples want only one child or want few births and are unable to perfectly avoid subsequent births. Twins are, therefore, a valid instrument to predict children ever born and thereby estimates without simultaneous equation bias the effect of exogenous variation in fertility on other forms of household behavior. Rosenzweig and Wolpin (1980a) rely on information on twins to predict $C$ that is used to explain the demand for $Q$, measured in a large Indian rural survey by the schooling received by children in the family. They use the same econometric approach to assess how unanticipated fertility "shocks" affect subsequent labor force participation of mothers in the United States (Rosenzweig and Wolpin, 1980b).

A second strategy for isolating the behavioral effects of unanticipated variation in fertility first obtains consistent estimates of the (biological) technology of reproduction and uses these estimates to derive residual variation in reproduction given predicted contraceptive behavior. Unpredictable failures of specific contraceptive practices, which yield unplanned births (adjusting for the heterogeneous biological/behavioral fecundity of couples), are then used to explain subsequent fertility, contraceptive choice, and child quality (Rosenzweig and Schultz, 1985, 1987, 1989; Schultz, 1992). In all of these studies, discussed further in Section 3.6, the empirical evidence supports the hypothesis that the number of children and the quality of children are substitutes, insofar as parents adjust to unanticipated increases in fertility by reducing child quality.

Another approach is to estimate directly cross-price effects. Does the provision of lower cost schooling and health services reduce fertility as well as increase the demand for the quality services? Does the provision of lower cost birth control supplies reduce fertility and raise the amount of schooling and nutrition that children receive in a community? Such estimates of cross-price effects are not compensated for their associated income effects. In the case of school and health prices on fertility, the income effect would operate so as to understate the income-compensated substitution effect. In the case of the effect of birth control prices on child quality, the income effect itself could be responsible for the observed substitution inferred from the observed uncompensated cross-price effect. The empirical patterns of cross-program price effects on the quantity of children will be discussed further in Section 5.5.

## 3.4. Empirical applications to the demand for children

To apply the general household demand framework outlined in Section 3.1, restrictions and simplifications can help to focus the empirical analysis. It is necessary for the researcher to decide first which are the more important constraints on the choice or choices studied in a particular setting and then to derive predictions that can be tested empirically. One study of district-level data from rural India illustrates how this general framework may be restricted to consider a variety of household decisions as parallel reduced-form outcomes. Rosenzweig and Evenson (1977) considered three outcomes recorded in the 1961 Indian census: surviving fertility (children aged 5–9 per woman of childbearing age), child school-enrollment rates, and child labor force participation rates. These are explained in terms of district-level agricultural wage rates for men, women and children, as well as land holdings and other aspects of the district economy, society, and climate.

To assess the likely substitutability or complementarity of household behavioral outcomes, previous empirical studies can provide some guidance. For example, as noted in Section 3.3, the number of children demanded is often assumed to be a substitute for child schooling and child leisure, while schooling and child leisure may themselves be viewed as complements, if leisure includes homework for school. Women are generally assumed to contribute time to the "production" of children and the other home commodity $(G)$, whereas children allocate their time among only schooling, labor force work, and leisure. Without good measures of exogenous wealth income, such as inheritances, from which to infer income effects, only uncompensated price and wage effects are observable. Rosenzweig and Evenson assume, therefore, that compensated substitution effects dominate income effects in the relevant Slutsky equations, leaving the sign of the compensated and uncompensated effects the same. Adult leisure is neglected, whereas child health is viewed as captured in the surviving measure of fertility they analyze, viz. child–woman ratios. These restrictions imply that the own-wage effects on the demand for children are reinforced by cross-wage effects, operating on the demand for other commodities, and that income effects do not outweigh the compensated wage effects that operate in predictable directions on the observed household demands.

With these restrictions on the general model, Rosenzweig and Evenson show that exogenously higher women's wages should then be associated with lower levels of fertility, higher child-schooling levels, and lower child labor force participation rates. Conversely, exogenously higher child wages should be associated with higher levels of fertility, lower schooling, and higher child labor force participation. More controversial restrictions are still needed to establish the signs of the effects of the size of land holdings on family size (positive), school enrollments (negative), and employment of children in the labor force (positive). An interesting feature of the data is that child labor force and schooling decisions can be analyzed separately for boys and girls, thereby shedding light on substitution possibilities among these types of family labor and intrahousehold gender-based resource allocations (see also Rosenzweig and Schultz, 1982a; Schultz, 1993b).

Wage rates for men, women and children are critical determinants of the demand for children, but they pose special problems for measurement and analysis at either the aggregate or individual levels. When observations relate to couples, and the wage rates are averages for their residential communities, the working assumption that such community wage opportunities are exogenous determinants of fertility appears defensible. Hence, these aggregated wage rate variables are admissible in reduced-form equations for individual household demand behavior. But when the units of observation are aggregates, as in the case of districts in India, inter-district variation in wages may be due to either labor demand factors or unobserved labor supply factors that could be determined jointly with fertility. Wage rates must then be treated as endogenous, at least for women and children for whom labor supply is not inelastic (cf. Schultz, 1985). Consequently, Rosenzweig and Evenson (1977) treated their child wage series as endogenous and based their estimates of the child wage effects on instrumental variables, such as rainfall, irrigation, and nonfarm employment opportunities that were thought to be exogenous and yet may influence the derived demands for child labor. However, they treat their female wage series as exogenous. Regardless, many of the behavioral patterns predicted by their restricted model are empirically confirmed in their district-level analysis of wage and farm asset variables that affect fertility, schooling, and child labor force participation (by sex). Their restricted household demand model does not imply the sign of the relationship between the husband's wage and the household's demand for numbers of children and their schooling. Regional male wages were found to be positively associated in rural India with surviving fertility and negatively associated with child schooling levels as suggested by the simpler models outlined in Section 3.2. Most of these empirical patterns are also observed in other studies of fertility in low-income agricultural populations (Schultz, 1976a; Mueller, 1984).

Wage rates of individual family members are thought to play an important role as the opportunity cost of time in explaining many forms of household economic and demographic behavior and are particularly useful in the study of fertility. Life-cycle average wages, as an exogenous constraint on lifetime choices, are not straightforward to measure at the individual level for at least two reasons: (1) current wages of an individual become endogenous over the life-cycle as they reflect prior cumulative investments in specialized skills; and (2) wages are not observed for all persons if, for example, some currently work only in the home or work as a self-employed or family worker. Both problems appear to be more serious for inferring the wage of women than the wage of men. Having and caring for children competes for the mother's time that could otherwise be invested in gaining skills and experience that are productive in market work. Current and future wages of women are thus depressed by fertility.

A standard econometric procedure to approximate the exogenous or initial life-cycle wage profile is to use instrumental variables to impute a value for the wage to each individual, and this wage is thereby uncorrelated with the individual's previous idiosyncratic time allocation, career, and fertility decisions, etc. The specification of these instrumental wage equations builds on the human capital earnings function (Mincer, 1974), except that the dependent variable is the logarithm of the wage rate, and measures of labor supply, such as weeks worked, must be excluded from the instruments because they are themselves endogenous. This instrumental variable human capital wage function is fit for men and women (and potentially for boys and girls) separately, and the imputed value is assigned as the life-cycle wage for each person in the sample. Actual labor market experience or tenure on the job are for similar reasons not legitimate instrumental variables for predicting wage rates, for they are endogenously determined by past labor supply, job search and training behavior, particularly for women. Post schooling potential experience is treated as exogenous, being essentially the difference between age and years of schooling. Some studies hold post schooling experience constant (at, say, the "overtaking point" of ten years when investment in on-the-job training is small and the wage approximates labor's current marginal product (Mincer, 1974: p. 93)) to disentangle crudely the effect of life-cycle wage levels from age, which can exert its own effect on fertility over the life-cycle and can differ between birth cohorts. Regardless, with predicted wages as explanatory variables in the household demand model, standard errors should then be adjusted (Murphy and Topel, 1985).

The wage equations should also be corrected for sample selection bias (Heckman, 1987) because they must usually be based on a relatively small and potentially unrepresentative sample of wage earners. This can be particularly serious in the case of women and children, whose wage participation rates are lower than for men. The most widely used identification restriction in sample selection models for wage earners is nonearned income or nonhuman wealth, preferably from land or inherited assets that do not reflect the individual's own labor productivity, work, and savings behavior. Nonearned income is postulated to reduce the likelihood that the individual is observed to work for wages, but has no causal correlation with the market wage rate the individual is offered.[4]

## 3.5. *Interdependencies among endogenous variables: fertility and mortality*

Studies of interregional variation in household demographic and economic behavior have analyzed jointly several household outcomes such as fertility, age at marriage, proportion legally and consensually married, female and child labor force participation rates, and finally, family market income (T.P. Schultz, 1969, 1972, 1981; Nerlove and Schultz, 1970; DaVanzo, 1971; Maurer et al., 1973). Evidence from Puerto Rico, Taiwan, Egypt, Chile, and Thailand suggests that in low-income countries increased women's education and wage rates help to account for women's increased participation in the market labor force, decreased or delayed marriage, and reduced fertility. These investigations also sought in addition to reduced-form estimates to measure how various endogenous variables ($i$'s and $t$'s) affect each other. A priori identification restrictions were exploited across structural behavioral relationships. The timing of marriage, and levels of fertility and family labor supply behavior were assumed to be jointly determined, but the choice of identifying exclusion restrictions were debatable.

Only under special conditions is it possible to estimate the consequences of a change in the level of one household demand commodity (or choice) on another; for example, as noted earlier, the effect of a decline in fertility on the average level of child schooling, or quantity on quality. Any of the reduced-form determinants of one outcome in Eq. (6) may be an important determinant in another reduced-form equation. The exception to this rule is when one of the commodities is not chosen by the household but is randomly allocated, as if by a stochastic rationing mechanism. The clearest example, already noted, is the occurrence of twins, which can then be related to other adjustments in the household's pattern of consumption and behavior. In rural India, Rosenzweig and Wolpin (1980a) show evidence that twins are associated with a decrease in the schooling levels of other children in the family. This accommodation

---

[4] In estimating wage rates for use in household demand studies, sample selection bias can be a serious problem for men (Anderson, 1984) and women (Griffin, 1986) in low-income countries. There are many econometric issues that arise with such wage correction and imputation schemes. Multiple sources of sample selection may be present, such as nonreporting among wage earners. If the researcher understands what causes the different types of selection, and each selection rule can be identified by distinct variables, the selection bias corrected estimates should be considered even if the point estimate of inverse Mill's ratio ($\lambda$) is insignificant. But reliance on functional form alone (e.g., the normal distribution of the error term in the probit selection rule) to achieve identification may not be sufficiently powerful to improve empirical results. Economic or institutional knowledge of the selection mechanisms is not only helpful but perhaps essential for dealing with this widespread econometric problem in micro research based on household surveys.

of household demand for $E$ to an exogenous fertility supply shock, i.e., twins, can be expressed as

$$\partial E/\partial \overline{C} = (\partial E/\partial \pi_c)/(\partial C/\partial \pi_c), \tag{12}$$

where the effect of an exogenous change in $C$ on $E$ is equal to the compensated cross (shadow) price effect of $\pi_c$ on $E$, divided by the compensated own-price effect on $C$ (Rosenzweig and Wolpin, 1980a).[5] Since the compensated own-price effect is negative, the negative sign observed in India for $\partial E/\partial \overline{C}$ from twins implies that exogenous variation in children and child schooling are substitutes, i.e., $(\partial E/\partial \pi_c) > 0$. Without further restrictions on the cofactors of the general demand model, it is not possible to discriminate between (i) the interaction of child quality (schooling) and quantity in the full income constraint, as hypothesized by Becker and Lewis (1974), or (ii) the conventional interpretation in consumer demand studies where child quality and quantity are viewed as substitutes by parents, i.e., an arbitrary restriction on the parents' utility function (Eq. (1)).

In a similar study of the effect of twins on mother's market labor supply behavior, Rosenzweig and Wolpin (1980b) identify the consequences of this exogenous fertility supply shock on another household demand (i.e., women's labor supply). It should be noted, however, that these "twin"-based estimates of the effects of fertility need not provide an appropriate measure of how household demands would respond to voluntary changes in fertility, because these changes in fertility embody the demands of couples adjusting to changes in prices, wages, and technology.

One major demographic development is often interpreted as having been due primarily to exogenous and unforeseen technological developments. It is the sharp decline in mortality in low-income countries in the period after World War II that had a disproportionate effect on reducing infant and child mortality. Many observers have attributed the change in level of mortality to the spread of new public health technologies that progressed independently of economic development (Stolnitz, 1975; Preston, 1980). To the extent that this decline in child mortality was unrelated to parent resources, prices, or preferences, the resulting increase in surviving children that parents experienced could be interpreted as an exogenous shift in the biological "supply" of children (Schultz, 1981). The behavioral adjustment of parents to this development may then be analogous to that measured in the twin statistical studies.

---

[5] When demand for one good exceeds supply, and existing supplies are allocated independently of preferences, prices or income, the problem of rationing arises (Tobin and Houthakker, 1950). The effect on fertility of supply shocks associated with twins which occur randomly are analogous to rationing, and twins are then expected to modify other forms of household consumption (and perhaps production) behavior in proportion to the compensated cross-substitution price effect between the rationed (shocked) and unrationed good divided by the compensated own-price effect of fertility as shown in Eq. (12).

However, it is more realistic to recognize that part of a decline in child mortality over time and variation in child mortality in the cross-section is explained by economic variables that belong in the reduced-form equations of the family demand model. When the partial effects of parent education, wages, and family planning programs on fertility are held constant by statistical means, child mortality is still generally observed to be related to fertility. But such a partial association could still reflect unobserved variables that affect both fertility and child mortality, or the reverse effect of fertility on child mortality by a "crowding" effect of a large number of siblings on a child's likely mortality. An exogenous factor must be specified that affects child mortality but does not influence parent reproductive demands in order to identify estimates of the parent fertility response to exogenous variation in child mortality. The choice of such an identification restriction should be dictated by a well-founded theory or knowledge of the technology of the relevant processes. If the identifying restriction is arbitrary, the estimates are likely to be misleading.

Household demand theory does not provide strong predictions when it comes to the nature of the response expected of parents to an exogenous change in child mortality, as in the case where public health interventions eradicate a childhood disease without requiring any change in parent behavior. Parent demand for births may be viewed as a derived demand due to the value parents attach to surviving children, i.e., those who do not succumb to the host of infectious and parasitic diseases that are particularly lethal to a malnourished infant or child in a low-income environment (Schultz, 1969). An exogenous reduction in such child mortality reduces the cost of producing a survivor, while it also reduces the number of births needed to have a survivor. If parent demand for surviving children is price inelastic, and the cost per surviving child decreases in proportion to the increase in survival rate, then price theory implies that parents will respond to an exogenous decline in child mortality by reducing the number of births they demand (Ben-Porath, 1974; O'Hara, 1975; Schultz, 1981; Sah, 1991). This result may be strengthened if the decline in mortality extends to later ages, thereby increasing the expected returns to investments in the human capital of children, and these forms of child quality are seen by parents as a substitute for a greater number of children. Incorporating the consumer's aversion to risk and the uncertainty of child mortality can further modify how parents react to changes in death rates over time. Section 5.2 reports the empirical evidence on this very important economic and demographic relationship, one that may tie together the demographic transition.

### 3.6. Estimating household production functions

Another methodological approach for measuring the responsiveness of fertility to exogenous variation in demographic variables involves explicitly estimating more of the structure of the general model, and thereby isolating variation in mortality or fertility that cannot be attributed to behavior. This residual variability can then be viewed as an exogenous unexpected "shock". First, the reduced-form demand equations, (7) and (8), are estimated for the inputs to the household production function (Eq. (2)). Individual predictions of input demands based on these estimated equations then permit the estimation of the household production functions parameters by instrumental variable techniques. These estimates are consistent, because the instruments – prices, programs, wages, and family wealth – are assumed independent of the production trait, $\mu$. Based on the estimates of the technical production parameters to Eq. (2), expected outcomes, $i^e$, are calculated, given the couple's actual input behavior. The deviation of the actual behavioral production outcome from that which is expected, $i - i^e$, is then a measure, albeit with error, of the couple-specific trait, $\mu_i$. Data on individual outcomes over time can improve the precision of the estimation of the time-persistent component of this forecast error, which $\mu_i$ is intended to represent. This measure of the exogenous variation in, say, child health, measured, for example, by deviations of a mother's actual infant mortality from expected infant mortality, can then be employed to explain subsequent fertility (Rosenzweig and Schultz, 1982b, 1983). This roundabout procedure provides another way to estimate the reproductive replacement response of parents to exogenous variation in child mortality, i.e., an exogenous shock to child health.[6]

Estimation of a household production function (Eq. (2)) for a couple's conception probability leads to analogous instrumental variable estimates of a reproduction function (Schultz, 1984; Rosenzweig and Schultz, 1985, 1987). Technically unexplained deviations in a couple's reproductive performance over time, given their contraceptive behavior, can be interpreted as a measure of exogenous fecundity or variation in the supply of births, again measured with error. This exogenous variation in "fertility supply" can then be employed to explain subsequent modifications in the couple's contraceptive behavior, the wife's market labor supply, and even her market wage rate. It is theoretically expected and empirically confirmed that couples who have a higher than expected probability of conceiving in one period are more likely to adopt a more effective method of birth control or sterilization in a subsequent period (Rosenzweig and Schultz, 1985, 1989; Schultz, 1992).

The primary conclusion drawn from these estimations of household production functions is that a priori structure must be imposed on the household demand model to get behind the reduced-form equations (6), (7), (8). To estimate the underlying household production-demand structure requires a method to remove the bias caused by

---

[6] It also provides an intuitive approximation for how couples respond to the anticipated portion of the child mortality they experience compared with the unanticipated portion. If the unanticipated variation in child mortality is measured with more error than the anticipated portion, estimates of the response to observed variables that includes this unanticipated component will tend to be biased toward zero compared to the estimates based on the anticipated portion. The response to expected child mortality may also occur throughout the lifecycle, or in other words through both ex ante "hoarding" as well as ex post "replacement" (see Section 5.2). This may be most evident when the age-at-marriage is noted to occur earlier in communities that have higher child mortality rates (for the example of Taiwan, see Schultz (1980)). Malthus' model that relied on marriage age to compensate for economic and demographic conditions may have considerable explanatory power in some low income populations.

heterogeneity in the couple-specific traits, $\mu_i$. Estimates of bias due to omitted variables is a problem at all stages of household demand and production studies. The unavoidable omission of inputs is probably more serious in the estimation of complex cumulative household production processes (such as those underlying adult health or even child health, nutrition, or education) than it is in the estimation of shorter and relatively simpler processes underlying the determination of conception and birth or even birth-weight (Strauss, 1986). Because contraceptive behavior is the predominant and observable endogenous factor determining conception rates in modern societies (Bongaarts, 1978; Bongaarts and Potter, 1983), the estimation of reproduction functions is a promising approach to integrate biological and behavioral factors in the study of fertility, a frequently stated goal of demographers (Easterlin et al., 1980; Wolfe and Behrman, 1992).

### 3.7. Endogenous preferences and time-series change

There is probably substantial individual heterogeneity in the demand for numbers of children, i.e., tastes, just as there is heterogeneity in biological supply of children, i.e., fecundity. The writings of Easterlin (1968, 1978), Tabbarah (1971), Easterlin and Crimmins (1985) and Easterlin et al. (1980) argue the desirability of endogenizing tastes for children, intertemporally and intergenerationally. Although some find this goal attractive, empirically testable implications of this line of research remain elusive (Stigler and Becker, 1977; Wolfe and Behrman, 1992). Are "taste" variables, such as "desired fertility" or "the value placed on one's children's education", exogenous or endogenous to an economic model of individual and family demands? (Wolfe and Behrman, 1992). When Easterlin's (1968) theory of intergenerational taste-formation and cohort fertility differences is used to account for cross-sectional variation in individual fertility, it receives scant empirical support (Ben-Porath, 1975). But the paucity of time-series studies of fertility based on the conventional household demand framework also leaves one to doubt whether the demand approach outlined here has much power to explain intercohort variation in fertility in high- or low-income countries (cf. Schultz, 1994).

The study by Butz and Ward (1979) is an exception, but one that illustrates how fragile the existing time-series evidence on fertility determinants is. They examine variation in US age-specific marital birth rates from 1947 to 1975. Lacking a national wage series for women in the United States, they use a Bureau of Labor Statistics series on the occupational category of personal services, which was predominantly female.[7] Recognizing that this female wage series is endogenous in a model of fertility, they identify the wage with instrumental variables that are one- and two-year lagged

---

[7] Their series on female earnings, divided by another series on hours, produced a wage rate series that did not parallel other population based series on women's productivity, earnings, or hours. A more defensible series has since been derived from the Current Population Survey by Macunovich (1991) that confirms the peculiar behavior of the Butz–Ward series.

wages. The lagged wage series are, of course, as endogenous as the current wage series, being affected by the same unobserved variables that explain evolving trends in women's careers and fertility in this period (Schultz, 1981). The issue that is unanswered by most such macroeconomic models of fertility is what underlying forces outside the influence of the household sector can explain the changing wage of women relative to men.[8] When a more representative wage series for women was constructed by Macunovich (1991), and the same model as reported by Butz and Ward was reestimated, she found little consistency between her estimates and theirs. In addition, even their own estimates were not consistent with an important prediction of the Willis (1974) model: the positive effect on fertility of the male wage should be larger among women who participate in the labor force than among those who do not. Butz and Ward's estimates suggest that the male wage effect became smaller over time as the labor force participation rate of wives increased. Although there are few satisfactory efforts to explain cycles in US birth rates, I know of no micro analyses of time-series changes in fertility in low-income countries. Later, in Section 5.6, some aggregate data are examined to determine if the secular changes in fertility levels that have occurred in the last two decades in low-income countries can be partially accounted for within the household demand framework.

There are many ways to expand further the household demand framework and add commodities or activities. Savings by the family in the form of physical capital formation for retirement is similar to the formation of human capital in children in that it extends over many years. Indeed, the Modigliani and Brumberg (1954) life-cycle savings hypothesis is well designed for study in the household demand framework. Savings over the life cycle may foster a variety of human capital investments, insurance arrangements across members of an extended family, and even transfers between generations. Economists have long speculated that families may invest in the migration of their members both to augment their income and to diversify their portfolio of human and physical capital, insuring themselves against the variation of income derived from a single livelihood, regardless of whether the variation is due to climate in agriculture or business cycles in other sectors of the economy (Rosenzweig and Stark, 1989; Stark, 1991). Little empirical analysis at the household level has sought to test the implications of these theories and to distinguish between various motives of altruism or market exchange and how they are related to fertility (Cox and Jimenez, 1992a; Hoddinott, 1992).

*3.8. Dynamic models and birth spacing*

Most economic theories of fertility address the determinants of the number of children

---

[8] A study of Sweden from 1860 to 1910 suggests part of this trend can be linked to the changing relative prices of outputs that are dependent on more or less of women's time, dairy products versus cereal grains (Schultz, 1985).

a couple demands over their lifetime. This demand for children is, however, satisfied by a supply of births, which is biologically produced and matured with much uncertainty. Sexual intercourse, lactation, birth control, and abortion interact to determine birth rates in a highly complex chain of uncertain events that are described by demographers (Bongaarts and Potter, 1983). A dynamic stochastic model of fertility decision-making therefore has much appeal (Newman, 1981, 1988; Olsen and Wolpin, 1983; Newman and McCulloch, 1984; Wolpin, 1984; Hotz and Miller, 1988). If these features of the fertility determining process are modeled as a general dynamic programming problem, complexity in other aspects of the choice problem must generally be sacrificed. It may be useful to briefly retrace the use of dynamic elements in models of fertility and refer the reader elsewhere to an introduction to the theoretical and econometric methods (Heckman and Singer, 1985; Eckstein and Wolpin, 1989; Lancaster, 1990).

The static choice framework can be supplemented by a stock-adjustment equation in which a proportion of the divergence between the actual and desired fertility rate is eliminated in each time period (Schultz, 1974, 1980; Lee, 1980a,b). As a means to model aggregate fertility rates, the approach provides a smoothing mechanism that may approximate time-series data. Partial adjustment models often specify lagged fertility as an explanatory variable for current fertility. Lagged endogenous variables are themselves endogenous in a lifetime optimizing framework, and this problem is particularly serious in the case of fertility where unobserved heterogeneity in preferences and fecundity are undoubtedly persistent. Consequently, to obtain consistent estimates of these models legitimate instruments are needed to endogenize the measure of lagged fertility. No maximizing behavior is postulated to motivate the rate at which behavior converges to the "desired" reproductive goal, but this shortcoming is evident in most economic models of asset allocation behavior.

To incorporate birth spacing explicitly into a household demand model, the interval between births can be added directly as an argument to the couple's utility function. Perhaps a longer birth interval should be interpreted as a "good", if longer birth intervals enhance the quality of the resulting child, as postulated by Razin (1980) and suggested by psychologists (Zajonc and Markus, 1975). As completed fertility in industrially advanced countries, such as the United States, declined in the last century from 5–7 children to 2–3, the intervals between births did not increase on average, but may have even decreased (Ryder, 1969). Thus, if wider birth intervals were viewed by parents, as Razin theorized, as a desirable increase in child quality, there must be some offsetting increase in the cost of having more widely spaced children. One way to explain these birth spacing patterns is to hypothesize that the technology of producing children embodies economies of scale, such that a woman rearing children at shorter intervals incurs lower costs per child (Newman, 1981). There is considerable empirical evidence to support this conjecture (Espenshade, 1984). A mother's market labor supply decreases on average by more hours with one child than it does with the arrival in close succession of a second or subsequent child. Although these data relate mostly to married women in the US, the existence of such economies of production with shorter birth intervals is a plausible hypothesis in low-income environments as well. The opportunity cost of a child associated with a mother's loss of time from the labor force increases as a woman becomes better educated. It is not surprising then to observe that better educated women both reduce their completed fertility and shorten their average birth interval in order to minimize their time out of the labor force (Ross, 1974; Newman, 1981). Regardless of whether wider birth spacing is a good proxy for child quality (and maternal health), the benefits of longer intervals are certainly not linear or perhaps not even positive after several years. Most estimates of the consequences of birth intervals in low-income countries are potentially biased, for they treat birth intervals as exogenous and analyze the inverse association between the length of the prior birth interval and the health of a child and mother as an estimate of causal effect (National Research Council, 1989). It is not yet clear whether increments to birth intervals in a relatively healthy and well-fed population are indeed important for the health of mother or child, except in extreme cases.

Several methodological approaches have been used by economists to describe covariates of the spacing of births. The hazard rate of having a birth, given no birth has yet occurred in an interval, can be generally expressed in terms of (1) systematic effects of exogenous conditioning variables, (2) a random component called heterogeneity of the population, and (3) a duration dependence of the hazard as the interval increases (Newman and McCulloch, 1984; Lancaster, 1990). The hazard framework is flexible and deals explicitly with right censoring of the data due to incomplete spells of childbearing; however, because of its nonlinear structure, it does not readily allow for the incorporation of endogenous explanatory variables. Another disadvantage of the model is that it often examines a sample conditional on the woman's being in the relevant birth interval, whereas, clearly, having the previous birth (initial condition) is also endogenous to the same type of reproductive choice process, and raises issues of sample selection bias. The risk of conception cannot be assumed to start with marriage, because marriage is endogenous to a model of reproduction and causation may be in the opposite direction. The left censoring problem can be mitigated by tracing the woman back to the age at menarche, which can be assumed exogenous, and then analyzing the onset of childbearing, or the hazard of the first birth. Indeed, the timing of this first birth may be a critical threshold for predicting the pace of subsequent childbearing in many parts of the world.

Multistate models can also jointly estimate the various transition hazards and accommodate the persistent effect of unobservables across parities for the individual, such as might be caused by fecundity or couple-specific heterogeneity (Heckman and Walker, 1991; Tarisan, 1993). Joint estimation of all birth interval hazards seeks to replicate patterns of fertility revealed in aggregate data better, and to simulate the consequences of changes in the conditioning variables over time more accurately than unrestricted reduced-forms, presumably because they embody the nonlinear structure of the valid model.

In Southeast and East Asia and in Latin America the transition to lower fertility was generally signalled by a decision to stop further childbearing after presumably reaching a target family size, because age-specific birth rate for woman older than 30 declined rapidly. This pattern of not spacing but stopping births over the life-cycle, which was also observed earlier in industrialized countries, provided a basis for demographers to measure the adoption of birth control as a function of fertility declines by parity relative to some "natural" schedule in age-specific fertility (Oken, 1991). But in Africa, birth intervals even at early parities may be increasing in some countries (e.g., Zimbabwe, Botswana, Kenya) where the education of females has been catching up to that of males and child mortality has fallen sharply. Alternative economic models are needed that can account for the adoption of such different regimes of fertility control in different regions of the developing world. This is a challenge for economists as economic-demographic household surveys become available for a growing number of African countries.

### 3.9. Birth control and family planning

Differences in costs and benefits of a child to parents by birth order provided one motivation for modeling fertility as a dynamic process in the previous section. One set of costs of rearing a certain number of children is the search-, user-, and psychic-costs associated with finding and employing a technique to avoid unwanted births. These costs and the uncertainty of birth control can also be analyzed in an economic framework (Schultz, 1971, 1988, 1992).

There is an interdisciplinary debate, however, on how to interpret the widespread adoption of birth control that often occurs with modernization. Customs and institutions, such as delayed marriage, prolonged breastfeeding, postpartum taboos on intercourse, are employed to some degree by all populations to control unwanted reproductive capacity (Dumond, 1975). Are these mechanisms merely strengthened and gradually supplemented by individual birth control practices as economic and demographic conditions motivate couples to gain greater control of their fertility? Or are fundamental cultural changes required before people are able to even consider reproduction as amenable to individual control? Is "ideational" change a prerequisite for society to control fertility? If this is the case, this process is not, as economists have argued, a marginalist adjustment to a changing balance of costs and benefits of having various numbers of children (Coale, 1973; Cleland and Wilson, 1987). A third paradigm emerged in the 1950s, as it became clear how rapidly the population of the Third World was growing. It was hypothesized that in order for people in low-income countries to reduce their fertility substantially, they must be provided with socially acceptable, convenient, and low-cost modern means of birth control. Improved technological options of birth control developed in the 1960s in the form of the pill (steroid), the intrauterine device (IUD), and sterilization seemed promising in that they operated independently of coition and could be delivered at relatively low cost. Implementing this technological "solution" to rapid population growth, according to this third school of thought, depended on subsidies, outreach, education and communications programs to accelerate the diffusion of modern birth control worldwide. Debate has flourished on whether the supply of birth control methods (i.e., family planning) would substantially lower birth rates unless peoples' preferences changed or the opportunities and relative prices facing people changed so as to curb their demand for births (Bulatao and Lee, 1983; Lapham and Simmons, 1987; Westoff et al., 1989). But it should come as no surprise that both supply and demand must be taken into account (Easterlin and Crimmins, 1985; Rosenzweig and Schultz, 1985; Schultz, 1986, 1992).

## 4. Institutional change and macroeconomics of fertility

Fertility, through its effect on the size, growth, and age composition of the population, can have consequences on the macroeconomic system, and social institutions can affect the microeconomic incentives to demand children. To the extent that the consequences of fertility extend beyond the family, an externality may be associated with fertility. For example, population growth in excess of some level, say 1% per year, may generate congestion or pollution costs and may make it difficult for markets to adjust and equilibrate wages to minimize unemployment or attract sufficient investment required to create sufficient new jobs. In such cases, there may be a social need for a compensating tax or transfer to motivate parents to take into account the costs, and possible benefits, they cause the society through their private demand for children (National Research Council, 1986).

Alternatively, institutions may be established by the public or private sector that substitute for (or complement) some critical services that children provide to parents. Credit markets may permit parents to save reliably for their consumption needs in old age. Mandatory social security systems financed by a scheme of wage deductions would appear to contribute to reducing the private demand of parents for children (Cox and Jimenez, 1992b). Children of other parents will support through their wage deductions the pensions and medical care of the elderly even if the elderly have no children themselves (Becker and Barro, 1988).

The dilemma with these issues of macro economics of fertility is that the quantitative importance of the programs, incentives, and mechanisms that are modeled have not been assessed. Are social security programs responsible for below replacement fertility in high-income countries today, or is the low desired level of fertility in these countries the reason why the public has voted for such institutionalized support mechanisms for the elderly? We can hypothesize many plausible effects of fertility on the environment that are not borne by parents, which might provide a justification for society to subsidize parents to have fewer children, and the case is more persuasive when a population is growing rapidly (National Research Council, 1986). But there is relatively little hard empirical evidence that these externalities are substantial in magnitude, or large enough to change parents' reproductive goals if they were appropriately shifted to parents through conditional taxes and transfers. There are also those who argue that population growth induces certain changes in agricultural production technology such that, in the long run, it raises output per capita and encourages development (Boserup, 1965) rather than inducing the lower wage rates that Malthus foresaw. But these positive externalities of population growth anticipated by the technological optimists (Simon, 1981) are no easier to evaluate empirically than are the negative nonlinear externalities projected by the pessimists (Meadows et al., 1972).

## 4.1. Overlapping generations model

Changes in investments in children, fertility, and savings can be related in a general equilibrium system in which prices are determined endogenously within the model. A general equilibrium approach to the macroeconomic problems of growth, investment, and consumption over time has been formulated around a microeconomic theory of exchange between overlapping generations. Samuelson (1958) first used this model to provide a rationale for money, but its application to the demographic-economic transition is more recent. This application treats the fertility decision as endogenous (Razin and Ben Zion, 1975; Eckstein and Wolpin, 1982). As capital accumulates and wage rates increase, parents substitute away from children and toward the consumption of goods, if the costs of children are linked to the wage rate or the value of time. Also, as income per capita grows, the demand for children increases. The path of fertility generated by this stylized model depends on the relative magnitude of the goods-cost and time-cost of rearing children. It is plausible that, according to these models, fertility could first increase and then decrease as the labor share of output increases with the onset of modern economic growth. Thus, Malthus' model of aggregate growth is provided with a growth path that leads, due to the time-cost of children, to a zero population growth rate while permitting the level of per capita income to secularly increase. But these overlapping generations models of growth (e.g., Becker and Barro, 1988; Becker et al., 1990; Becker, 1992) do not distinguish between the wage rate of men and women, which is the strongest empirical regularity accounted for by the microeconomic demand for children framework (Schultz, 1981).

If the cost of children to parents is an increasing function of women's wage, and nonhuman capital is more complimentary with women's labor than with men's, capital formation affects fertility and prescribes the path to the demographic transition. Galor and Weil (1993) propose such a growth model with distinct male and female labor and specific technological assumptions with endogenous fertility that connects the gender wage gap to development, demographic transition, and also allows for multiple equilibria, or a low level trap. Growth theorists are thus beginning to grapple with the mechanism by which population growth is endogenized, yet there remains no consensus on what motivates parents or society to invest differentially in the human capital of females and males (Schultz, 1993b). Developing hypotheses for what governs the increase in female-specific human capital will undoubtedly receive more study in the future.

## 4.2. Credit markets, social security, and life-cycle savings

Much of the early discussion of the probable consequences of rapid population growth assumed that increases in the size of surviving families would depress private household savings, public productive savings, and investments, as conventionally measured (Coale and Hoover, 1958). Empirical evidence is very limited on the direct association between the composition and level of savings and the size of surviving family (World Bank, 1984). The aggregate record and existing household evidence (e.g., Kelley, 1980) do not confirm that the Coale–Hoover hypothesis is important; since World War II, population growth rates and national savings rates have both increased, as, for example, in India. Here again, to evaluate the consequences of fertility one should identify the cause of the variation in fertility. Would local child health, family planning, and schooling investments that reduced fertility also raise (or lower) physical savings rates? Are children complements for bequest savings or substitutes for physical savings that provide for consumption requirements during retirement? What would be the consequences for household savings, if the increase in surviving fertility were due to exogenous eradication of endemic and epidemic childhood diseases that left parents in middle age with more living children? These are hard questions to answer. They will require unusual economic and demographic information at the household and intergenerational level. But given the centrality of the savings relationship in hypothesized models of demographic and economic development, more research can be expected on savings behavior within the demand for children framework.

## 4.3. Mobility, marriage, risk, and technical change

Rosenzweig (1992) considers the management of risk ex post by the household through the sale of buffer stocks of livestock, credit, or interhousehold transfers that involve both the marriage of daughters (Rosenzweig and Stark, 1989) and the outmigration of sons and daughters into alternative production environments. He finds evidence in his Indian sample that the adoption of high yielding varieties (hyv), which is associated with the Green Revolution, is inhibited by the existence of extended family contacts, presumably because interhousehold transfers are predicated on families monitoring each other's incomes and risks. The cost of monitoring is lower if all family members use well-understood traditional farming methods. But once hyv adoption occurs, the diminished use of interhousehold transfers within the extended family may free women of performing their traditional function through marriage markets. Families may then be encouraged to invest more in the education of women, for daughters are then free to migrate to work outside of the family where market returns to education can be earned and potentially remitted to parents. This suggests that the extended family as a traditional institution to pool risk may initially resist technical change and investing in women. When these investments are ultimately forthcoming, fertility declines, and new technology is adopted that further weakens the extended family as a provider of credit and insurance. As the "green revolution" begins to shift families from depending on the extended family to relying on the credit market and accumulation of their own buffer stocks, the family may demand more education for its females and seek fewer children for old age security (Quisumbing, 1991). Here is another set of issues that may eventually illuminate the institutional and technical constraints that modify fertility and the status of women.

## 5. Empirical evidence

Empirical studies have been cited earlier to illustrate methodological approaches to the study of fertility or justify a specific restriction on the more general demand framework. This section summarizes the empirical evidence and outlines some data and econometric problems that frequently arise in implementing the framework.

A central insight of the household production model of the demand for children is that different sources of household income imply different associated changes in the shadow price of children, and hence in the demand for children. These predictions have not been shown to be particularly sensitive to whether the family is viewed as a neoclassical integrated utility maximizing entity (Becker, 1981), or as a Nash cooperative bargaining pair who resist pooling resources to maintain their distinctive options outside of a marriage (McElroy and Horney, 1978) or their distinctive spheres of influence in a noncooperative family regime (Schultz, 1989, 1990; Lundberg and Pollak, 1993). Regardless of which model of the "family" is posited, an increase, for example, in the productive value of women's time should have a more negative effect on fertility than an increase in the value of men's time, at least as long as the bulk of child care occurs within the family and not within some alternative communal or market child care institution.

### 5.1. Fertility effects of wages and nonhuman capital

Because of the econometric complexities of estimating the shadow value of the time of women and men without selection or simultaneous equation bias, many studies rely on education as a proxy for the wage, even though it undoubtedly represents more than just the value of an individual's time (T.W. Schultz, 1974). A few studies are sufficiently detailed that they hold constant for both the wage opportunities and education of the spouses. But as a consequence, they typically assume education affects fertility linearly. Nonlinear effects of either or both education and wages are thus mixed in the jointly estimated education and wage coefficients (e.g., DeTray, 1974). Where only education is entered nonlinearly as a series of splines or unrestricted dummy variables, increasing education of women is generally associated with lower fertility, certainly after a threshold of about four years of schooling, a level which may be roughly equivalent to functional literacy (e.g., Schultz, 1976a, 1989; Anker and Knowles, 1982; Cochrane, 1983; Lavy, 1985; Okojie, 1991; Ainsworth and Nyamete, 1992; Wolfe and Behrman, 1992; Lam et al., 1993; Pitt, 1993).

Because there is generally positive assortative mating by years of education and the effects on fertility of male and female education may be in opposite directions (as in the case of female labor force participation outside of the family), controlling for husband's education in a fertility equation sometimes increases the negative partial association between female education and fertility. Nonetheless, although male education is not held constant, the tabulations of different dimensions of fertility in Table 3 by the woman's education in 38 countries where World Fertility Surveys were conducted during the 1970s illustrate the anticipated general pattern, with some informative variations. In all regions distinguished, women at age 40–49 with seven or more years of schooling have 1.6–2.9 fewer births than women with no schooling (column (1)). Total fertility rates (TFR), which reflect current birth rates summed over ages, differ by even a larger amount between women with more and less education (column (2)). The difference between the children ever born at age 40–49 (column (1)) and "desired" fertility across all ages (column (3)) might be viewed as an indicator of the emerging demand for nontraditional birth control among women in the childbearing ages. In Asia and Latin America this measure of latent demand for greater birth control is concentrated among the least educated women. This is the group that would seem most likely to benefit from a family planning outreach program because the reproductive goals of this group are changing most rapidly. But as of the 1970s, there was little evidence of much latent demand to restrict traditional fertility levels among African women, either among those with high or low educational levels. This may be because the levels of child mortality in Africa remain unusually high (Maglad, 1990; Okojie, 1991; Benefo and Schultz, 1992).

Increasing men's education, although it does not exert a uniform effect across developing countries, is widely associated with increasing fertility in Africa, particularly in rural areas (Anker and Knowles, 1982; Ainsworth, 1989; Okojie, 1991; Benefo and Schultz, 1992; Montgomery and Kouame, 1993). It is also related to earlier childbearing, if not always greater completed fertility, during the early industrialization process with the shift of populations to urban areas (Schultz, 1985). Land ownership or other physical assets are generally associated with higher fertility in low-income agricultural societies (Stys, 1957; Rosenzweig and Evenson, 1977; Chernichovsky, 1982; Anker and Knowles, 1982, Table 37; Merrick, 1978; Maglad, 1990; Schultz, 1990; Mukho-

Table 3

Measures of cumulative, recent, and desired fertility: averages for world fertility survey countries by region and respondent's education

| Regions (number of countries observed) Years of schooling completed by women | Children ever born[a] | Total fertility rate[b] | Desired family size[c] |
|---|---|---|---|
| | (1) | (2) | (3) |
| Africa (8–10) | | | |
| 0 years | 6.4 | 7.0 | 6.9 |
| 1–3 | 6.5 | 7.2 | 6.4 |
| 4–6 | 6.1 | 6.2 | 5.9 |
| 7 or more | 4.8 | 5.0 | 5.0 |
| Difference (0–7+) | −1.6 | −2.0 | −1.9 |
| Latin America (13) | | | |
| 0 years | 7.1 | 6.8 | 4.8 |
| 1–3 | 6.8 | 6.2 | 4.7 |
| 4–6 | 6.0 | 4.8 | 4.2 |
| 7 or more | 4.2 | 3.2 | 3.7 |
| Difference (0–7+) | −2.9 | −3.6 | −1.1 |
| Asia and Oceania (9–13) | | | |
| 0 years | 6.7 | 7.0 | 5.4 |
| 1–3 | 6.7 | 6.4 | 4.3 |
| 4–6 | 6.4 | 5.8 | 4.2 |
| 7 or more | 4.9 | 3.9 | 4.0 |
| Difference (0–7+) | −1.8 | −3.1 | −1.4 |

[a]Women aged 40–49 years.

[b]The average number of children that would be born alive to a woman during her lifetime, if during her childbearing years she were to bear children at each age in accord with the estimated age-specific birth rates in the five years before in the survey.

[c]Means are adjusted for the effects of age differences between educational groups.

*Source*: Summary of data collected in 38 World Fertility Surveys around 1975. United Nations (1987), Tables 112 and 115.

padhyay, 1991; Benefo and Schultz, 1992). However, no effect of wealth or nonearned income on fertility is also found in other studies, such as Anderson's (1983) in Guatemala.

As economic development proceeds, it becomes more difficult to estimate the effect of nonhuman capital wealth on the demand for children. First, the share of income arising from nonhuman capital tends to decrease as investments in human capital mount. Second, nonhuman capital becomes increasingly the product of life-cycle work and savings, and thus ceases to be exogenous to an individual's demand for children. Consequently, as societies shift from rural-agricultural to urban-centered production activities, inherited physical assets in the form of land and business capital become a relatively small source of income for most people. It is empirically more difficult, therefore, to assess the effect of nonhuman wealth on the demand for children in urbanized higher income societies (cf. Schultz, 1990).

Measurement of the opportunity value of the time of children is easier to document at the anthropological level (e.g., Nag et al., 1978) than in a large representative household survey. Occasionally it is possible to measure major regional variations in the productivity of child labor. It has been observed that fertility is higher in high child wage regions (Rosenzweig and Evenson, 1977; Lavy, 1985). It is more common, however, for child and female wages to vary together, for both women and children are in many settings supplemental sources of unskilled labor, drawn into the agricultural work force mostly during peak labor demand periods, such as during harvest. At other times in the year, their wage opportunities may be low enough that they allocate their time to work in the home or school. If this is often true, then there may not be sufficient independent regional variation in child wages and female adult wages to estimate their separate effects (and presumably of opposite sign) on fertility (Lindert, 1980). Surveys of rural areas of low-income countries suggest that many children work in the labor force, but they generally work for their parents in an unpaid capacity. Consequently, reporting a wage rate for child labor is rare, even though parents may be paid more when they hire themselves out with the assistance of their children.

There are regrettably many studies of fertility determinants that include only adult education, literacy, or a single wage or household income variable, and do not distinguish between the productivity of men and women in the household. These studies are of little use here to confirm or reject the relevance of the demand framework for fertility. It may be observed generally that rising incomes are associated with declining fertility, but the magnitude of this relationship is not likely to be similar in Kuwait and Libya as it would be in Thailand or Korea.[9] The mix of income sources received by the household tends to change with modern economic growth, and how it changes should influence the effects of income growth on fertility. To use the household demand framework to explain fertility requires that income be disaggregated according to source, including male and female productivity, nonhuman capital income, and other exogenous entitlements that might substitute for or complement investments in children, such as communal land arrangements, and social security pensions (Mueller and Short, 1983).

Studies of fertility determinants can be potentially biased as a source of evidence on the demand framework because they include among the explanatory variables other simultaneously determined household choices or behaviors. For example, controlling for female labor force participation or child schooling rate (e.g., Anker and Knowles, 1982) raises the possibility that the coefficients on other economic variables in the

---

[9] In the former countries income arises predominantly from nonhuman capital sources, i.e., oil exports, whereas in the latter countries, human capital is more important and women are today receiving a substantial share of the human capital (Schultz, 1994).

model may be subject to simultaneous equation bias, as discussed earlier. It is essential, therefore, that a parsimonious set of male and female wage–education variables and nonearned income variables be included in the core economic reduced-form equation for fertility and that the inclusion of additional control variables be justified by the theoretical framework of the study.

## 5.2. Child mortality

The positive covariation of child mortality and fertility was first interpreted as evidence of a causal relationship from the former to the latter (Schultz, 1969). This effect might come about through two reinforcing channels, however. The first involves a couple having or "hoarding" more births than "desired" because the couple formed the expectation that some of their children may die. A second involves a "replacement" response following a child death (Schultz, 1969, 1976b; Ben-Porath, 1976; Sah, 1991). Although birth and child death rates tend to be strongly positively associated in most aggregate (i.e., by administrative areas) and individual analyses of fertility determinants, extracting the causal relationships of interest from this correlation has proven more complex.

In estimating these effects, it has become clear that the likelihood of child mortality and fertility are often affected by many of the same household and community variables, some of which are probably unobserved. Moreover, having many children, presumably at short birth intervals, is likely to also strain the health of the mother and the resources of the family to care for each child, generating a "crowding" effect of high fertility on high child mortality (cf. Rosenzweig and Schultz, 1982b; Birdsall, 1988, 1991). In the last two decades, therefore, various estimation strategies for dealing with the resulting simultaneous equation bias and the discrete and sequential nature of child death and birth processes have been developed and implemented.

Using the 1973 Census sample of Colombia, Olsen (1980) estimated that the replacement response effect was about 0.3, rather than the ordinary least squares estimate of 0.5, suggesting that for every three child deaths prevented there was one fewer birth. Rosenzweig and Schultz (1982b) estimated, from the same data source using instrumental variables method, the sum of replacement and expectation response rates of between 0.14 and 0.42 for various cohorts of women between the age of 24 and 54.[10] Lee and Schultz (1982) estimated the replacement response in Korea in 1971 as between 0.35 and 0.51, using Olsen's (1980, 1988) method. Maglad (1990), using the instrumental variables method, estimated for a small sample in rural Sudan a replacement/expectation rate in 1987 of between 0.56 and 0.73. Okojie (1991) obtained

---

[10] They used information regarding the status of malaria eradication campaigns in the municipio, climate, and transportation infrastructure as variables that are significantly associated with child mortality, but they postulate that these variables are not directly responsible for elevating fertility.

significant estimates of replacement/expectation responses for Bendel state of Nigeria from a sample collected in 1985. Benefo and Schultz (1992) estimated by instrumental variables a replacement/expectation rate of about 0.2 from a national sample of Ghana collected in 1987–1989 and obtained a similar value for Côte d'Ivoire in 1985–1988. Mauskopf and Wallace (1984) estimated the replacement probability for Brazil was nearly 0.6 and found that it increased from 0.44 to 0.98 as the woman's education increased from none to five or more years. Dynamic models, discussed more extensively by Wolpin in this volume, were also formulated to deal with the timing of the child deaths and the subsequent birth histories of women in Costa Rica and Malaysia, respectively (Newman, 1981; Olsen and Wolpin, 1983; Wolpin, 1984). Finally, in a high-income environment, Rosenzweig and Schultz (1983) estimated by instrumental variables a replacement effect of about 0.2 from a 1967–1969 sample of legitimate births for the United States.

Aggregate data on fertility have also been used to estimate the response of fertility to child deaths, or $dC/dD$, with varied results. In Taiwan where the registration of child mortality and fertility is unusually complete for a low-income country, the cross-district relationship of child survival to age 15 to total fertility exceeds the compensatory level, in other words that $dC/dD > 1$. If the relationship were causal a decline in child mortality would then lead to a sufficient decline in fertility to reduce the surviving size of families, and eventually lead to a slower rate of population growth. Examining different age-specific birth rates, the response in Taiwan appears to be relatively larger among older women. To correct for bias in these estimates that might arise from time persistent unobserved variables that could affect both child mortality and fertility, fixed effects for the 361 districts are included in the pooled cross sections from 1964 to 1969. The coefficients on the two-year lagged child mortality variable remains significant for predicting age-specific birth rates for women between the ages of 25 and 49, but the magnitude decreases about one half from that estimated from the district levels without fixed effects. The magnitude of the overall response of fertility obtained from the fixed-effect estimates is still more than fully compensating for changes in child mortality.

Census data for birth cohorts of (surviving) women in Taiwan also suggest that an overcompensating relationship exists across provinces between the log of average children ever born and log of child survival rates, when time trends are admitted (Schultz, 1976b). In Section 5.6, data for low-income countries are analyzed using instrumental variable methods to identify the child mortality effect on fertility. Under the assumption that calorie availability may affect child mortality but not directly fertility, the response estimates exceed one, controlling for education, income and employment structure. Why should aggregate estimates of this relationship be substantially larger than those obtained from individual level data? One possible explanation of this difference is that *actual* child mortality is not a good indicator of the *expected* child mortality that leads parents to insure against this risk by their excess hoarding of births. The instruments that account for variation in actual child mortality may only estimate the ex post replacement response to deviations of actual from expected child mortality. If this were correct, the decline in child mortality is a more important factor in the declines in fertility than currently believed on the basis of microanalyses of household surveys. This hypothesis could also explain why in portions of Europe, such as the United Kingdom, where the decline in child mortality was limited until the end of the nineteenth century, the decline in fertility did not start until then, whereas in the low-income countries in which the recent decline in child mortality has exceeded that among adults, fertility has fallen more rapidly than demographers would have forecast.

Because of the difficulty of finding valid instrumental variables that account for the variation in child mortality, but which can be theoretically excluded from the fertility function, there is limited agreement on empirical methods for estimating this critical relationship (Pitt and Rosenzweig, 1989). Until there is a better empirically based understanding of the policy and environmental determinants of child mortality in low-income countries, estimates of the effect of child mortality on fertility will be uncertain (see Chapter 10, this volume). An alternative estimation strategy for the further analysis of the demand for children is to omit child mortality and treat the resulting fertility equation as a reduced-form that will capture the effects of household/community characteristics (including public health measures) on fertility (Schultz, 1994). Some portion of the effect of these conditioning variables on fertility, however, probably occurs through their intermediary effect of reducing child mortality. Section 5.6 presents evidence from low-income countries that the effect of women's education (or value of time) and family planning programs on fertility may be partly due to these conditioning variables operating through child mortality.

### 5.3. Sex preference of parents and fertility

One aspect of the uncertainty of childbearing is the sex of offspring (Ben-Porath and Welch, 1976, 1980). Parents can have preferences between boys and girls for at least three reasons. First, net economic productivity of boys may exceed that of girls, given their respective child rearing and human capital investment costs. For example, the private economic returns to the education of boys could exceed the returns to girls in the labor market and home, although there is little evidence of this (Schultz, 1993b). Second, the remittance rate to parents from the economic productivity of boys and girls may differ such that the old age insurance value for parents of an investment in boys exceeds that of an investment in girls. Third, the noneconomic value to parents of boys may exceed that of girls, perhaps because boys can perform customary rituals at the death of parents or maintain the family line.

Whatever the reason, it is clear that some cultures exhibit a stronger preference for sons than do other cultures. North India and China are often noted for a son preference. But even countries that have voluntarily made substantial reductions in birth rates, such as South Korea, reveal evidence that strong sex preferences for offspring remain (Park, 1983; Ahn, 1991). As long as the sex outcome of any conception is random, these asymmetric preferences of parents can have little impact on the aggregate sex ratio of births, although they change noticeably the sex ratio by family size and of the last birth (Park, 1983). Statistical tests to measure sex preference can, for example, distinguish how these preferences for sons are strongly evident among the Chinese in Malaysia but are not indicated among the Malays (Leung, 1988). The impact of such a sex preference on the level of overall fertility, however, may not necessarily be large (Schultz and DaVanzo, 1972; Ben-Porath and Welch, 1976, 1980; Cleland et al., 1983; Arnold, 1987; Leung, 1988, 1991; Srinivasan, 1992; Zhang, 1990; Davies and Zhang, 1992).

But when parental sex preference affects the survival probabilities of the fetus or infant, the sex composition of the population can, of course, be changed substantially (Rosenzweig and Schultz, 1982a). The excess in female child mortality over male child mortality in India and several other countries of South Asia, such as Pakistan, Nepal, and Bangladesh, implies that within the family in this region the allocation of nutrition and health care between boys and girls differs. When the one-child policy was pronounced in China, the male to female ratio of births increased from the standard level of 1.06 to 1.10 and 1.15 in the 1970s.[11] This pattern was also reflected in the higher female than male child mortality that occurred during the 1959–1961 famine following Mao's "Great Leap Forward" (Ashton et al., 1984; Coale, 1984; Banister, 1987).

One measure of sex preference is a comparison of the sex ratio at birth across parities. With higher parities and with the prior births being only girls, the male to female sex ratio of births increases in Korea (Ahn, 1991, 1992). This is illustrated in Table 4 for 1980–1989, a period when fetal screening for sex increased. Although this pattern of change in the sex ratio of births by parity could be explained in Korea by fetal screening for sex followed by selective abortion, these sex determination technologies were less widely available in China in the 1970s where a similar pattern was noted. The explanation in China might involve the concealment of female births to avoid parents' being limited from having additional births, or possibly infanticide, historically a widely documented practice in the West and East (Langer, 1974; Scrimshaw, 1978). More recent data from China in Table 1 indicates a new trend upward in the sex ratio at birth to 114 by 1989, as ultrasound diagnostic equipment became more widely available (Zeng et al., 1993).

As screening of fetuses to determine sex by amniocentesis becomes more widely and cheaply available and ultrasound technologies provide less invasive technologies for obtaining approximately the same information, we may observe a substantial swing in sex ratios at birth in some regions. Economists should study these emerging imbalances in the sex composition of a cohort for evidence of how the marriage market equilibrates, and what changes in household and individual behavior occur when young brides become more highly prized.

---

[11] As confirmed from analyses of The 1982 Fertility Survey that compiled retrospective pregnancy histories.

Table 4
Male-female birth ratios by birth order in Korea and China

| Country and year | Total | Birth order | | | | |
|---|---|---|---|---|---|---|
| | | 1 | 2 | 3 | 4 | 5+ |
| Korea | | | | | | |
| 1980 | 1.04 | 1.06 | 1.04 | 1.03 | 1.02 | 0.96 |
| | (888355)[a] | (351213) | (278814) | (149015) | (59370) | (49859) |
| 1985 | 1.10 | 1.06 | 1.08 | 1.33 | 1.57 | 1.54 |
| | (636621) | (328212) | (241201) | (47228) | (12778) | (7191) |
| 1989 | 1.13 | 1.05 | 1.14 | 1.90 | 2.17 | 2.14 |
| | (613240) | (328044) | (241249) | (34794) | (6551) | (2605) |
| China | | | | | | |
| 1982 | 1.07 | 1.07 | 1.07 | 1.09 | 1.12[b] | – |
| 1985 | 1.11 | 1.06 | 1.16 | 1.14 | 1.22 | – |
| 1989 | 1.14 | 1.05 | 1.21 | 1.25 | 1.32 | – |

[a]Number of births are in parentheses for Korea.
[b]Fourth order and higher orders combined in China.
*Source*: Korea from Ahn (1991: Table 6). Data from *Annual Report on the Vital Statistics* (1990), National Bureau of Statistics, Economic Planning Board of Korea, Seoul; China from Zeng et al. (1993: Table 1).

## 5.4. Technical and institutional change

One reason parents are thought to demand children is that children provide parents with a relatively secure means of support and care in their old age (Cain, 1981). Lacking alternative means for savings and investment or credit, children can provide parents with a special service to smooth their consumption at the end of their life when their productive potential is likely to be low. This hypothesis that fertility is affected by parents' desire for old age support is plausible, but difficult to test. If, with the improvement of credit markets and the increased wealth holding of parents, fertility declines, this could be construed as consistent with the hypothesis. The most radical change in institutions that would substitute for children in this regard is the introduction by the state of a mandatory social security system.

National systems of retirement pensions should, thus, devalue children, who traditionally perform this old age security function, and contribute to a decline in the demand for children. Cross-country regressions to explain total fertility rates have included national data on the coverage of the social security system and the benefit level, while controlling for income per capita and infant mortality, among other things. The benefit level was then associated with lower fertility (Hohm, 1975). Critics of this work have readily found other indexes of modernization that made the social security benefit variable statistically insignificant (Kelly et al., 1976). More compelling perhaps, the critics noted that there was no relationship between the timing of the introduction of social security systems in the various countries and the year when sustained declines in marital fertility began. One could be even more skeptical of such evidence and argue that what is needed is a forcing variable that would serve as an instrument and explain when social security is introduced in different countries, but this variable should have no independent role in modifying reproductive goals. Without such an identifying variable, it is not obvious how a time-series analysis of country aggregate data could be used to test the old age security hypothesis or assign a magnitude to the effect of social security on fertility.

Other evidence has been assembled at a lower level of aggregation. Nugent and Gillaspy (1983) analyzed child–woman ratios across municipios (counties) of Mexico between the censuses of 1970 and 1980, and showed that the relative importance of sugar cropping, which was brought under the coverage of the social security system in this decade, explained fertility declines, while income and income inequality growth contributed to a rise in fertility. Nugent (1985) cites many other studies that suggest that the fertility of those covered by social security is lower than those not covered.[12] However, this leaves the possibility that when social security is available only on certain jobs, workers who were otherwise indifferent might seek out, or be best qualified for, those certain jobs with social security. One hypothesis is then that self-selection occurs whereby persons who want fewer children have a stronger reason to seek the jobs that provide them with a retirement scheme. Self-selection bias is possible, but how might it be corrected by the analyst (Cox and Jimenez, 1992b)? True randomized social experiments, or more commonly "virtual" experiments created by administrative rules and restrictions on eligibility or access, may permit researchers to evaluate the consequences of differing program treatments on the behavior of otherwise similar people.[13] One such social experiment in South Indian tea estates provided retirement

---

[12] Studies based on individual household surveys have proposed other approaches to testing the old age security hypothesis for explaining fertility. Raut (1992) finds a negative partial association between fertility and wealth, interpreting this wealth as providing the parents with an alternative to depending on children for old age support. But the direction of the causality is unclear. He also estimates a probit equation to predict whether parents plan to rely on their children for support and finds it is less likely if the husband earns more or has more assets. Jensen (1990) hypothesizes that only parents who have provided for their own old age support will begin to contracept. He finds a relationship between relying on nonchild support and use of contraception. But both outcomes are choice variables and no causal interpretation is clear. See also the review of the literature by Nugent and Anker (1990).

[13] Fixed-effect specifications or first-differencing regional data also eliminates omitted time-invariant regional variables that might be correlated with the program variables and bias estimates of program effects (Schultz, 1974, 1980; Foster and Roy, 1992; Gertler and Molyneaux, 1993). Because the fixed-effect methods do not deal with changing unobserved regional variables that may also be correlated with program allocations, it is preferable to model explicitly the allocation of program effort across regions and over time, and then instrument program treatment levels according to insights drawn from the model (Rosenzweig and Wolpin, 1986, 1988; Pitt et al., 1993). Unfortunately, insight into the administrative allocation rules of public welfare programs, such as family planning, is typically clouded by bureaucratic systems and political arrangements of governance.

pension payments for avoiding higher order births to all women in a selected number of 18 surveyed tea estates. It was confirmed that a larger decline in fertility occurred from 1971 to 1977 among the women workers in the treatment (pension) estates than in the control estates (Ridker, 1980).

Communal land tenure institutions are often singled out as being pronatal, for to rent or inherit the right to use the community's land, you must have a child. In Mexico the Ejido system also rewarded only male heirs unless the woman was without a husband and supported her family. Studies of municipio differences in child–woman ratios suggest that this institution is associated with unexplainably higher levels of fertility across two states (DeVany and Sanchez, 1979). It is also hypothesized that communal land holding deters women from gaining title to land and thus using this title to borrow the credit needed to adopt modern agricultural technologies (Boserup, 1970; Moock, 1986). These communal property institutions limit the income and productivity gains of women in Africa more than men, because women perform most of the work in agriculture. The deteriorating productivity of women compared to men in Africa is then another factor possibly contributing to the high levels of fertility in Africa (Schultz, 1989).

A study of West Bengal in India has sought to estimate how the adoption of new agricultural technologies affect fertility, labor market participation, and child schooling. High yielding variety adoption associated with the green revolution in this irrigated rice growing region has had the effect of raising male incomes more rapidly than female wages. Although household income has risen on average, women's participation in farm labor has declined and fertility has not markedly declined (Mukhopadhyay, 1991). Here is perhaps an example where gradual modern economic growth has not induced an improvement in women's productivity and, therefore, has failed to accelerate declines in fertility. Education is only slowly improving for Bengali women, reducing gradually their child mortality and fertility.

### 5.5. Cross-program effects

The consequences of programs and policies on household behavior can be evaluated by estimating reduced-form type relationships, if program activities are allocated across regions independently of individual preferences or unobserved environmental behavioral determinants (Schultz, 1988). Program services may substitute for or complement other consumption and investment activities which are distinct from those targeted by the program. Such cross-program effects can be important if household commodities are complements or substitutes for one another. As noted above, household demand studies have confirmed that child health services, schooling services, and family planning services often appear to exert reinforcing cross-price effects on child health, child educational attainment, and decreased fertility. For example,

Rosenzweig and Schultz (1982b) report that the local availability of clinics and hospital beds and family planning expenditures per capita are associated with lower child mortality *and* lower fertility across women in urban areas of Colombia in 1973. The reinforcing effects are generally statistically significant among women from age 15 to 49. Rosenzweig and Wolpin (1982) assess cross-program effects on fertility, child mortality and schooling in rural India, and find reinforcing program effects from family planning clinics, dispensaries, hospitals, and secondary schools (see also Duraisamy and Malathy, 1981).

Rosenzweig and Wolpin (1986) also estimate the direct and cross-program effects of family planning and health clinics on anthropometric indicators of child health and nutritional status in the Philippines. In this study, however, the authors use cross-sectional information from repeated rounds of the Laguna Survey. Alternative estimates of the effects of programs on these long-run measures of child health (viz. age-standardized height and weight) can then be based on three statistical specifications of the same reduced-form equation. Community fixed-effects and child fixed-effects are introduced to eliminate possible bias due to omitted time-invariant community and individual variables. But the fixed-effect estimates are also quite unstable and imprecise, probably because the fixed-effect specification relies heavily on relatively small changes over time in the anthropometric measures of accumulated nutrition and health, and errors in measuring these variables can be substantial relative to the pertinent "signal" (Griliches and Hausman, 1986). Although the promise of longitudinal data to illuminate the behavioral effects of changes in economic constraints and program interventions is great, means must be found to exploit the panel features of such data without sacrificing the useful information contained in the cross section. The challenge of using time-series of cross sections is reflected in earlier household demographic studies based on regional data over time (Nerlove, 1965; Nerlove and Schultz, 1970; Schultz, 1974, 1980).

Three issues may be distinguished in evaluating the effectiveness of social welfare programs: (1) how the benefits from expenditures on such programs are maximized, taking into consideration how the benefits may vary with scale of the program and interactions across programs; (2) how private and public sector programs differ in their cost-effectiveness and specific features of the populations served by these different delivery systems; and (3) how equitable the program benefits are in reaching different disadvantaged segments of the population. Combining data from household surveys with regional-level data on public expenditures on various social welfare programs provides a basis for program evaluations, including family planning (Schultz, 1971, 1988).

Programs that have the same objective may be complementary, in which case they strengthen the effectiveness of each other, or they may substitute for each other, in which case their effect in combination is less than the sum of their separate effects. It is also possible that these interactions may change sign with the scale of the program. They could potentially reinforce each other when the programs are operating at a small scale, and then begin to substitute for each other as the sizes of the programs increase and the market becomes saturated.

For example, in Thailand (Schultz, 1992) public sector subsidies for birth control were channeled through both the public health ministry's clinics and through private, non-profit family planning programs. Since the objective of both programs was to reduce unwanted births, econometric estimation of program effects can be combined. Poisson regressions were estimated for the number of births that a woman had in the last five years.[14] Nonlinear effects of regional expenditures per woman of reproductive age on this five-year birth rate confirmed that both the public and private programs were reducing fertility, after controlling for the principal demand determinants such as the woman's education and household expenditures. In this case the larger public program was subject to diminishing returns to scale, as was also found in Taiwan for two competitive field worker programs (Schultz, 1971, 1974, 1988). Provision of similar services through alternative delivery systems appeared to be substitutes, and each program or type of field worker had its greatest payoff where the other program was absent.

Finally, in the evaluation of social welfare programs, such as family planning, where a clear behavioral change is sought and can be measured, it is important to understand how the program benefits are distributed across the population. If it is more costly and difficult for a less educated woman to evaluate and adopt modern family planning methods than it is for a woman with more education, then subsidies to and educational promotion of family planning services are likely to have a greater effect on birth rates among the least educated in the country. This appears to have been generally the case in Latin America and Asia, but it depends on how the demand for children changes in these groups. If only better educated women want to reduce their traditional levels of fertility and thus they were the only ones who adopt and use modern methods of birth control, the benefits of a family planning program would be concentrated among the educated elite. Family planning programs during this early stage in the demographic transition may not benefit the poor but serve the needs of only the upper classes. Extending such programs into remote rural areas where the program's services are not yet demanded may be costly and ineffective. Later in the demographic transition, the opposite can be true, when urban subsidies for birth control are ineffective, and the rural outreach activities benefit the poor (Schultz, 1988).

Estimating interaction effects between the woman's characteristics (e.g., education, age, ethnicity, region, etc.) and the intensity of the program in her region can measure the nonuniform distribution of the benefits of the family planning program. These

---

[14] If fertility is treated as a time homogeneous process, the number of births during a specific time period takes a discrete value, $0, 1, 2, \ldots$. The Poisson model is one framework for describing the number of such events observed for different persons. Overdispersion may occur when the variance of such a count variable exceeds the mean, violating an underlying assumption of the Poisson model and require special adjustments. See Maddala (1983).

interaction effects also inform the policymaker of how the "price" elasticity of demand for the family planning service varies across segments of the population. This information might encourage a program to price discriminate across markets, if markets can be administratively separated along the lines of the consumer characteristics or regions. Maximizing the program's impact on birth rates for a given public sector budget might not always be a sufficient social goal. The equitable distribution of benefits may also be taken into account in setting priorities. Programs also assist people in shifting among methods of birth control, such as from abortion to modern contraceptives. Although this consequence of the program may not affect the numbers of births, it should be considered by the policy maker. How these benefits are to be measured is unclear.

## 5.6. Inter-country comparisons of fertility

When models of individual behavior are estimated from variation in average behavior and average conditioning variables for large aggregates such as countries, the properties of the estimates depend on many tenuous aggregation assumptions (Theil, 1954).[15] There are, however, potential offsetting advantages of these aggregate data for testing hypotheses. The same relationship can be estimated on the basis of cross-sectional or time-series variation or on a pooled combination of both for the same sample of countries. It is then possible to assess whether the relationship observed across countries at various levels of development forecasts reasonably well changes occurring in countries over time.[16] As already noted, the principal empirical puzzle motivating this paper is why the timing of the decline in mortality and fertility differs across countries and over time.

A static model of the demand for lifetime fertility has been outlined and suggests at least six empirical predictions (1) increased education of women raises the cost of

---

[15] I am particularly concerned about variables that may exert a nonlinear effect on fertility, but which exhibit little variation at the aggregate level, such as age, but are subject to substantial variation at the individual level. In such cases, the estimation of the effect of a variable such as age on fertility from inter-country variation in average age could be misleading. Moreover, other demographic linkages between age composition (youthfulness of the population) and (high) fertility are expected as long as fertility patterns are affected by unobserved variables that persist over time.

[16] Omitted country-specific effects can bias cross-sectional estimates if they are correlated with included variables (Hausman and Taylor, 1981). By first-differencing the data on levels, the estimated time-series relationship is purged of any country-specific omitted factors that might influence fertility, such as culture, assuming that they do not change during the observational period. Kuznets (1971) was also careful to juxtapose evidence of relationships he derived from comparisons of countries at different levels of development with that derived from comparisons over time within countries. Deviation between the cross-sectional and time-series evidence was frequently a basis for him to reappraise the relevant theory and assumptions underlying the empirical evidence.

childbearing and reduces fertility; (2) increased education of men may increase or decrease fertility, but in either case will reduce fertility less (algebraically) than will the education of women; (3) reduced child mortality, assuming the demand for surviving children is price inelastic, is associated with a decline in the demand for births; (4) increased national income per adult that is not associated with adult education approximates the share of wealth and natural resource income in a society, and this income from nonhuman capital sources is expected to increase the demand for children, if they are a normal good. It is also widely conjectured that (5) the net cost of child rearing is greater for parents in urban than in agricultural areas and the opportunities for children to work productively in a context where they can be monitored by parents tend to be greater in an agricultural setting than in a nonagricultural one; and (6) the cost of vocational training of a child appears greater for parents in urban than in rural environments in an open developing economy.

To test these hypotheses suggested by the microeconomic model of fertility and confirmed by studies of household data, a reduced-form demand equation is estimated from national data where fertility is measured by the current total fertility rate.[17] The explanatory variables seek to measure sources of national income, because they embody different shadow-price effects for children. The productivity of women's time discourages fertility because women are primary child caregivers. On the other hand, the productivity of men's time is more neutral in its child price effects, and nonlabor income may be pronatal. Three additional explanatory variables represent other sources of variation in the relative price of children, holding constant the level and composition of national income: child mortality, rural/urban residence, and agricultural employment. It can be argued, however, that child mortality, rural/urban residence and sector of employment are endogenous, because the allocation of family resources may influence child mortality and interregional and intersectoral mobility. Here mobility is interpreted as predetermined by demands for output. Only child mortality is explained within the model and its exogeneity tested.

The priority society assigns generally to education, and, more specifically, to the education of women compared to that of men, may itself reveal the relative importance to society of women working at home and having a large number of children.

---

[17] The Total Fertility Rate (TFR) is the sum of current age-specific birth rates, and is sometimes estimated from periodic sample surveys reporting births in the last five years. It is a synthetic approximation for the average lifetime fertility of women. It would be preferable to analyze the actual cumulative lifetime fertility of various birth cohorts and relate this measure of cohort fertility to the lagged conditions prevailing when the cohort made its fertility decisions. However, such cohort data is not available for many low-income countries and thus the common practice of analyzing TFRs is adopted. There may also be some improvement in model specification if the explanatory variables were lagged a few years to reflect biological time to conception and gestation (say two years) and the adjustment of expectations (unknown). Given the smooth evolution of many of these aggregate series, there may not be much to gain from introducing lags for those few variables that contain substantial annual variation, such as GDP. Child mortality was lagged five and ten years and GDP by two and five years without changing the findings discussed here.

One way to explore the role of such cultural value systems is to select features of the culture that are arguably fixed in the near term and add them as controls in the fertility equation to assess the robustness of the partial correlations between fertility and the previously enumerated determinants of economic demands. Therefore, controls for religion are included representing the proportion of the population that is reported to be Catholic, Protestant, and Muslim, where other religions are absorbed into the overall intercept.[18]

The variables suggested by the hypotheses outlined above are often available from standardized sources beginning with 1970 data; the definitions and sources are reported in the data appendix. In several instances the choice of an empirical measure of a variable is discussed further below. More flexible functional forms were explored to improve statistical fit, and where only a linear or log linear specification is reported, higher order terms and interaction variables were considered and rejected because they were not statistically significant at the 5% level. Not only does the high level of aggregation of intercountry analysis pose problems for interpreting the evidence, there are valid concerns that the quality of some of the national data is low. Some variables must be inferred in some countries from analysis of infrequent surveys and then interpolated between benchmark years, or estimated on the basis of data from neighboring countries, e.g., child mortality in parts of Africa. If a dependent variable is measured with random error, such as fertility, it need not bias the estimates reported here. If it is an explanatory variable that is measured with error, however, standard estimates of the effect of that variable are biased toward zero in the simple two-variable case. Of course, the measurement error need not be random, and the multivariate case of even random error leaves the direction of the parameter bias in doubt. The credibility of intercountry multivariate regressions is consequently lower than similarly specified statistical studies based on micro data on households and individuals. Nonetheless, as noted earlier, something may be learned from the aggregate record if the empirical analysis is sufficiently well focused on the basis of prior microeconometric studies.

Income (GDP per adult) in constant local prices may be compared across countries in two alternative series. The purchasing power (PP) of the local currency for a broad bundle of consumer goods may be used (Kravis et al., 1982; Summers and Heston, 1991), or the nation's productivity in producing internationally tradable commodities can be inferred from foreign exchange (FX) parities (World Development Report, 1992). Since much of personal income is spent on nontradable goods, e.g., personal services and housing, the consumer purchasing power parity measure of national average income has more appeal for understanding how increasing productivity due to the accumulation of physical capital and natural resources (i.e., other than human capital) is related to household fertility choices. The results reported here are, there-

---

[18] An alternative set of controls might allow for fertility values to differ by region, which would overlap considerably with religion, but appear more ad hoc.

fore, based on the purchasing power parity equivalence, but the general conclusions are not affected if foreign exchange rates in 1980 are adopted as the basis of comparison.[19]

Information is not available in any country on the wage opportunities for all men and women. Only a handful of countries report sex-specific wages, and then these are not standardized for education, age, or other productive characteristics. Nor are the wage rates available for the entire population, but only for the labor force in wage or salary employment in specific sectors, such as larger firms in manufacturing (ILO, *Yearbook of Labour Statistics*). Unfortunately, there is no agreed-upon methodology for using available wage data to infer the level of labor productivity or shadow wage for all men or all women in a country.

An alternative approach is to treat average educational attainment for men and women as a proxy for wage rates. Until recently, macroeconomic growth models have relied on current enrollment rates to proxy stocks of educational capital embodied in the national labor force (Barro, 1991; Mankiw et al., 1992). As noted some time ago (Denison, 1962), this is not a promising solution. The amount of education per adult is a better measure of the stock of educational capital embodied in the potential work force. "Years" of schooling have been found to be highly correlated with the logarithm of the wage rate of individuals and groups. National income per adult is also expressed in logarithmic terms when it is combined with years of schooling.[20]

National product is thus represented by three variables – different levels of education (human capital) of women and of men, and the logarithm of real GDP per adult. When the human capital endowments of female and male education are held constant, the GDP variable is expected to capture the effects of physical capital and natural resource endowments per adult.[21] Child mortality to age five, the supply of calories,

---

[19] The variance of the logarithms of income per adult, the explanatory variable in the subsequent regressions, is smaller when income is compared on the basis of PP rather than FX (0.67 versus 0.96). As expected, the elasticities of fertility and child mortality with respect to income are, therefore, estimated to be larger based on the less variable PP than FX income series. The statistical significance of the partial association between fertility and the PP and FX income series is nearly identical; for example, the *t*-ratios for the income variable do not change to two decimals.

[20] Surveys and censuses are often available reporting the level of education attained by all men and women. Making plausible assumptions regarding the number of years that individuals have completed at each level of schooling in each country, it is possible to estimate the average number of years of education completed by men and women over the age of 15 in about 75 low-income countries during the 1970s and 1980s (World Bank, 1991, supplementary data base).

[21] Clearly, future work is needed to construct a directly observable measure of nonhuman capital and natural resources that explains the variation in national productivity. The reason that GDP is divided by persons over age 15 and not all persons is to avoid including indirectly in this measure the fertility choice; the proportion of the population under age 15 is largely a function of fertility in the last decade or two. Elsewhere I have used a proxy for natural resource wealth or net fuel exports as a share of GDP (Schultz, 1994).

urbanization, and labor force composition are estimates compiled by the Population Division of the United Nations, FAO, and ILO, respectively, based on periodic surveys or censuses, whereas several family planning variables are described later.[22]

### 5.6.1. Empirical findings

The analysis includes developing countries (i.e., excluding OECD countries and centrally planned European countries) for which data were available on total fertility rates (TFR) and years of education by sex, as well as (PP) income, child mortality, urbanization, and the share of male labor force in agriculture. The three years examined (1972, 1982 and 1988/1989) were selected because information on family planning activity was available in each. The data appendix lists the countries in the sample and the source of data for each variable. Regression (1) in Table 5 is based on pooling of the three cross sections, providing a sample of 217 country–year observations. In interpreting the cross-sectional estimates, the significance tests are undoubtedly overstated, because the repeated cross sections are initially treated as independent observations. Alternative assumptions regarding the structure of the errors underlying this panel of about 70 countries are incorporated into the later estimates. The six core variables alone explain two-thirds of the variance ($R^2$) in the total fertility rate. Regression (1) also allows the intercepts to shift for each period's cross section, although they are not jointly statistically significant at the 5% level, and three religion variables are included, which are highly significant. The coefficient on each of the core economic variables is statistically significant and of the expected sign. Countries which have a greater share of their population affiliated with the Protestant, Catholic or Muslim religions have, as expected, higher fertility. The joint $F$ test of the equality of all slope coefficients in the three cross sections is not rejected at the 5% level ($F(9,190) = 1.28$, $P = 0.25$).[23] In sum, one obtains a similar relationship in each separate cross section. In this 16-year period, from 1972 to 1988, there is substantial stability in the multivariate relationship across low-income countries between total fertility rates and the variables implied by the demand for children framework: women's and men's educa-

---

[22] The share of the labor force in agriculture is approximated by the share of the male labor force in agriculture because the extent to which women working in agriculture are counted in the labor force varies substantially across countries and introduces error.

[23] If the three cross sections are separately estimated, the effect of women's wage is significant in all three years but declines in value over time, as does urbanization, whereas the estimated effect of child mortality increases over time and the higher level of fertility associated with the Protestant faith increases in magnitude over time. As summarized by the Chow test, these slope coefficients are not statistically different over time at the 5% significance level.

Table 5
Cross-country regressions of the total fertility rate (TFR) and child mortality rate to age five (CMR)[a]

| | (1) | (2) | (3) | (4) | (5) |
|---|---|---|---|---|---|
| Dependent variable: | Fertility (TFR) | Child mortality (CMR) | Fertility (TFR) | Fertility (TFR) Reduced-form | Means (SD) |
| Estimation method: | OLS[c] | OLS | 2SLS[c] | OLS | |
| Explanatory variables | | | | | |
| Years of female education[b] | −0.513 | −13.2 | −0.225 | −0.551 | 3.35 |
| | (7.35) | (5.10) | (1.56)[a] | (8.37) | (2.21)[a] |
| Years of male education[b] | 0.175 | 1.42 | 0.145 | 0.179 | 5.10 |
| | (4.01) | (0.83) | (2.51) | (4.14) | (2.49) |
| Log of GDP per adult | 0.478 | −25.7 | 1.16 | 0.517 | 7.97 |
| (1988$, purchasing power parity) | (2.98) | (4.12) | (3.43) | (3.32) | (0.818) |
| Urban % of population | −0.0117 | 0.370 | −0.0175 | −0.0084 | 37.9 |
| | (2.27) | (1.80) | (2.48) | (1.61) | (21.5) |
| % of male labor force in agriculture | 0.0160 | 0.861 | −0.0025 | 0.0190 | 50.9 |
| | (3.49) | (5.05) | (0.26) | (4.43) | (25.4) |
| Catholic % of population | 0.0116 | 0.261 | 0.0050 | 0.0115 | 34.8 |
| | (5.03) | (2.89) | (1.26) | (5.08) | (36.9) |
| Protestant % of population | 0.0212 | 0.540 | 0.0103 | 0.0239 | 8.87 |
| | (3.97) | (2.60) | (1.27) | (4.62) | (13.0) |
| Muslim % of population | 0.0086 | 0.645 | −0.0044 | 0.0119 | 26.1 |
| | (2.84) | (5.71) | (0.68) | (4.21) | (36.0) |
| Year 1982 dummy | 0.023 | −9.09 | 0.256 | 0.0190 | 0.341 |
| | (0.16) | (1.55) | (1.19) | (0.13) | |
| Year 1988 dummy | 0.234 | −12.7 | 0.532 | 0.202 | 0.341 |
| | (1.43) | (1.99) | (2.19) | (1.24) | |
| Calories consumed per capita | | −0.152 | | −0.0035 | 2373 |
| per day | | (2.07) | | (1.91) | (367) |
| Calories per capita squared ×10⁻³ | | 0.0238 | | 0.00053 | 5764 |
| | | (1.60) | | (1.43) | (2474) |
| International planned parenthood fed- | | | | −0.00036 | 27.9 |
| eration (US¢/woman) | | | | (0.34) | (60.4) |
| Child mortality to age five (CMR) | 0.00460 | | 0.0251* | | 136 |
| | (2.69) | | (3.02) | . | (75.5) |
| Family planning activity | | | | | 34.6 |
| score (FPA) | | | | | (25.3) |
| Intercept | 0.454 | 5.20 | −6.90 | 5.79 | 5.35[d] |
| | (0.33) | (5.29) | (2.03) | (2.35) | (1.54) |
| $R^2$ | 0.710 | 0.814 | | 0.722 | |
| $F$ | 45.6 | 74.5 | 27.3 | 40.5 | |

*Treated as endogenous with identification as implied by calories included in col. (3). Sample size is 217.

[a]The absolute value of $t$ ratios are reported beneath coefficients in parentheses in columns (1), (2), and (4), asymptotic $t$ ratios in col. (3) and standard deviations of variables in col. (5).

[b]Years of education for female and male adults are estimated from World Bank and UNESCO figures.

[c]OLS refers to ordinary least squares and 2SLS to two-stage least squares.

[d]Sample mean and standard deviation in parentheses of the total fertility rate that is the dependent variable in columns (1), (3), and (4).

tion, non-human capital income, urbanization, agricultural employment, and child mortality.[24] But should child mortality be treated as exogenous?

Similar factors, many of which are unobserved, affect both fertility and child mortality, introducing a spurious correlation between child mortality and fertility. It is also likely that high levels of fertility contribute to raising child mortality, causing conventional simultaneous equation bias. Finally, child mortality is probably subject to more errors in measurement than the other variables examined here, which could bias the coefficient on child mortality downward. For all of these reasons, it is advisable to treat child mortality as endogenous and measured with error in a model seeking to explain fertility.

Statistical specification tests (Wu, 1973; Hausman, 1978) of whether child mortality is exogenous to the fertility model can be implemented if mortality is identified by the a priori exclusion of a variable from the fertility equation that enters significantly into the determination of child mortality. Reductions in child mortality are often explained by availability of calories at the household and group level, most notably at very low levels of calories (Strauss, 1985; Fogel, 1990). Calorie consumption per capita is, therefore, specified as a determinant of child mortality, but the effect is allowed to vary by calorie level through the inclusion of a nonlinear quadratic term in calories.[25] Calories satisfy the conditions for an instrumental variable to identify the

---

[24] According to regression (1), for a country in which men and women both have one more year of education the total fertility rate is 0.34 child lower, or 6% lower than the sample mean of 5.4 children. If only men's education tends to be higher by one year, fertility is higher by 0.18 children. If only women's education increases one year, fertility tends to decrease by 0.51 children. Doubling of GDP per adult, holding human capital constant, is associated with an increase in the total fertility rate of 0.33. A country that has one-half of its population in urban areas compared with one which has only 10%, which is roughly comparable to Latin America vis-à-vis Africa in this period, is associated with fertility being nearly one-half child (−0.47) lower in the more urbanized country, holding these other strategic variables constant. Removing one-quarter of the male labor force from agriculture is associated with fertility decreasing by 0.4 children. A decline in infant mortality from 150 to 50 per thousand live births is associated with a decline in fertility of 0.46 children. These estimates cross multiplied by the changes from 1972 to 1988 in the conditioning variables leads to the expectation that fertility in the 66 countries common to both cross sections would have declined by 1.0, whereas fertility actually fell by only 0.78 in this subsample of countries.

[25] It would also be desirable to include a measure of the within country variation in personal calorie consumption, because greater dispersion in individual consumption, given the average level, should be associated with higher child mortality. Unfortunately, I have found no indicators of the personal distribution of calories except those constructed by Fogel (1990) for eighteenth century France and England. The FAO estimates of national calorie consumption are used here, from the World Bank *World Development Reports* of 1985 and 1991, and the figures for 1972 consumption are from the 1976 Food and Agricultural Organization *Production Yearbook*. A cubic approximation for the effect of average calories on average child mortality is not an improvement on the quadratic form reported here. The association of calories with mortality between a child's first and fifth birthday is particularly notable. Although only one-fourth of child deaths occur after infancy, they may be more sensitive to availability of calories because weaning is widespread by the second year of life. See nonlinear estimates of calorie effects on health and productivity in Brazil (Thomas and Strauss, 1992), Strauss's (1985) overview of field, and Dasgupta and Ray (1987).

effect of child mortality on fertility, which are that it is correlated with mortality and may be reasonably excluded from the list of fertility determinants. The exclusion restriction is justified by biological and demographic investigations which conclude that the effects of nutrition on reproductive potential or fecundity are negligible.[26]

To describe the channels through which economic development may lower fertility by reducing child mortality, child mortality determinants are estimated in a reduced-form equation. Other studies of household and aggregate data of child mortality and anthropometric indicators of child health, such as height for age and weight for height, suggest that a mother's education is the most important factor reducing child mortality and improving child health. In addition, some studies find that households employed outside of agriculture and with higher incomes also experience improved child health outcomes (Strauss, 1985; Schultz, 1993).

In regression (2) of Table 5, the child mortality rate (CMR) to age five is the dependent variable. The coefficients on the women's education and income are significant and negative, agricultural employment is significantly related to higher child mortality, and the religion and time trend coefficients are also significant. As expected, the availability of more calories per capita in a country is associated with lower child mortality, and the nonlinear effect of calories noted in micro studies is also jointly significant in these aggregate data. The child health benefits from increased calories continue until a country reaches an average level of about 3200 calories per

---

[26] It has been hypothesized that improvements in nutrition could also increase reproductive capacity (Frisch, 1978), but most recent evaluations of the evidence conclude that chronic malnutrition has at most a minor biological role in depressing fecundity (Trussell, 1978). If calories do increase somewhat fecundity in certain low income populations (e.g., Papua New Guinea) by decreasing anovulatory cycles, shortening the interval between menses, and reducing pregnancy wastage, this omission might mask some of the underlying positive relationship expected due to fertility responding to child mortality. Thus, the estimates reported below of the fertility response to endogenous child mortality are possibly biased downward. Another over-identifying variable was also included in the later analysis of only 1988 data in Table 3: proportion of children immunized against diphtheria, pertussis and tetanus (dpt). This variable might capture the effect of a variety of allied child health programs across countries, and it is indeed negatively and significantly associated with child mortality. But its inclusion among the determinants of child mortality increases only slightly the two-stage estimate of the effect of child mortality on fertility from 0.0205 to 0.0209. The hypothesis that calories or dpt is a valid over-identification restriction conditional on the other restriction is consistent with these data. However, the dpt immunization variable is available for only 58 countries in 1988. The other estimates in the fertility equation were very stable, whether identified by only the nonlinear calorie variable or the child immunization rates. But the effect of family planning on child mortality declines by 1988, when the child immunization variable is included, suggesting family planning in the child mortality equation may be capturing the effect of other child health programs.

capita per day, or two standard deviations above the mean of the sample, 2373 calories.[27]

Variation in calorie availability per capita, given the income, education, and agricultural employment of the population, is presumably due to international differences in the unobserved prices of nutrients, which may in turn be affected by trade and agricultural policies, poverty, and famine alleviation programs, as well as the domestic composition and productivity of agriculture.[28] Calories may influence child mortality because domestic factors affect the relative price of nutrients, such as the personal distribution of income, education, and prices.

The Wu–Hausman specification test rejects the null hypothesis that child mortality is exogenous to the fertility equation, at $P < 0.01$. Regression (3) in Table 5 is therefore estimated by two-stage least squares with endogenous child mortality identified as indicated in regression (2). Most notably, the estimated effect of endogenous child mortality on fertility is five times as large as the estimate based on the rejected hypothesis that mortality is exogenous (cf. regressions (3) and (1)). The direct effect of the woman's education on fertility is decreased by half (regression (3)), but by solving out for the implied reduced-form relationship, one finds that more than half of the total effect of the women's education on fertility now operates through its indirect child mortality reducing effect (i.e., $0.59 = (-13.2) \times (0.0251)/(-0.225 + (-13.2) \times 0.0251)$. The positive effect of income on fertility, given endogenous child mortality, more than doubles in magnitude, and the religion variables are no longer jointly statistically significant in the fertility equation, but are significant in the child mortal-

---

[27] Because only four countries which contribute eight of the 217 observations have levels of calorie consumption that marginally exceed this daily per capita value of 3193, there is little reason to attach much precision to this estimate of the calorie level that would minimize child mortality. But developed market and centrally planned economies have, on average, exceeded this level for some time, and calorie shortages should, therefore, be a minor factor elevating the levels of child mortality in the high-income world. According to regression (2), a country where calories are one standard deviation above the sample mean (i.e., 2373 + 367), the expected child mortality rate is 8% lower. Had calories been a standard deviation below the sample average, as many African countries were (i.e., 2373 – 367), the regression implies child mortality rates are expected to be 13% higher, other things equal. Adjustments of caloric availability for the biological needs associated with the age and sex composition of the national population using FAO controversial standards did not change these estimates noticeably, and, therefore, calories are expressed simply in per capita terms.

[28] Several recent studies have linked the relative price of food or nutrients to the prevalence of child malnutrition and mortality in cross-sectional surveys and over time, mostly in sub-Saharan Africa (United Nations, *SCN News*, 1992; Strauss, 1985). A recent study of a variety of measures of real income, output, and terms of trade for a number of sub-Saharan African countries did not find a relationship over time between these national series and child mortality within countries, although it did find evidence that declines in income were associated with later age at first marriage and first birth, as might be expected in a Malthusian preindustrial Europe (National Research Council, 1993).

ity equation.[29] The unrestricted reduced-form equation is reported in regression (4) excluding child mortality, for comparison with the structural effects solved from regressions (2) and (3).

### 5.6.2. Family planning

Another factor that may influence fertility is birth control. One element of the cost of birth control is the monetary and psychic cost associated with using a specific method. Another cost involves deciphering a new technology of control, evaluating it against alternatives, adopting the best method, and learning to use it effectively. This second element is a search cost which is essentially fixed, as long as technology and family constraints are unchanging. But these search costs may reoccur in a dynamic setting as innovative technologies are being introduced, such as the IUD and pill in the 1960s, and subsequent improvements in injections and sterilization. A previously rejected method may also become worthy of consideration because of changes in desired levels of fertility. As the cost of birth control decreases, individuals are expected to have fewer unwanted births. It is also likely that, in addition to reducing unwanted births, such a decrease in the cost of birth control would encourage people to switch to contraception from other less satisfactory arrangements for controlling their reproductive potential, such as Malthus' delay of marriage, reduction in the frequency of intercourse, or reliance on abortion or even infanticide. This second source of welfare gain is not evaluated here.

All countries do not provide their populations with access to all forms of birth control, or necessarily provide these technological options at the same price. Educational and outreach programs are mixed in many combinations, with subsidized family planning service systems taking many forms. It has been argued that countries which support more diversified and apparently effective family planning activities (FPA) and legislate facilitating population policies had, by the 1970s, lower total fertility rates (TFR) (e.g., Mauldin and Berelson, 1978; Lapham and Mauldin, 1985). Declines in TFR since 1972 are also linked with strengthening family planning programs (Bongaarts et al., 1990). To interpret these partial correlations between TFR and FPA as a measure of the causal effectiveness of these programs, researchers have implicitly assumed that family planning programs occur independently of other fertility determinants. Since family planning activity is related to observed determinants of fertility, such as income, education and religion, it is reasonable to conjecture that family planning activity is related to unobserved determinants of fertility as well, such as omitted measures of economic constraints that are responsible for shifting parent de-

---

[29] Other conditions that might have been expected to improve child health outcomes were not statistically significant when added to regression (2) Table 5, for example, doctors, nurses or hospital beds per capita, or percentage of population with safe water supplies or sanitation facilities.

mands for children and differences in parents' preferences. It might be argued that political support for state provision of family planning services would be stronger when an increasing share of a population "demands" fewer children, and hence want nontraditional methods of birth control. The error in the equation explaining fertility would then, almost certainly, be correlated with family planning activities (FPA). The partial correlation between fertility and family planning, even controlling statistically for other observed fertility determinants, is then a biased and inconsistent estimate of the causal effect of family planning programs on fertility. Despite these limitations of correlational analysis to answer this salient policy question, agencies involved in evaluating and funding family planning continue to present such correlational evidence as confirmation of the effectiveness of such programs in achieving their objective (Mauldin and Berelson, 1978; Bongaarts et al., 1990; World Bank, 1991).

Activities of family planning programs are summarized by an index that has been frequently used to evaluate the contribution of family planning to fertility declines (e.g., Mauldin and Berelson, 1978; Ross et al., 1988: Table 18). This "effort score" (FPA) has a mean in the current sample of 34 and ranges from zero to 84, depending on the country's commitment to family planning services and population policies.[30] Although the components in the series are not identical in every year, the index has been standardized to facilitate comparisons over time. Two model specifications are estimated: the first assumes the family planning score is exogenous (regressions (1)–(3), Table 6), and the second seeks to endogenize family planning within the overall model (regressions (4)–(6), Table 6). In regression (1) of Table 6 the child mortality rate is predicted as before but with the addition of exogenous family planning activities. The total fertility rate is then estimated in regression (2), using 2SLS and treating child mortality as endogenous, as the Wu–Hausman test again rejects its exogeneity. The results confirm previous research that finds that family planning, if it is treated as exogenous, is negatively associated with total fertility rates. But here the effectiveness of FPA is smaller than others have found. Few substantial changes in the

---

[30] In 1982 and 1988 the index is based on 30 pieces of information in four groupings: policies and program organizational support, range of services provided, record keeping for improving services, supplies of birth control services (Lapham and Mauldin, 1985). The 1972 index is based on fewer series, but is offered as compatible (Mauldin and Berelson, 1978). Aside from the subjective nature of much of the information, the major limitation of the index is that it includes contraceptive supplies. A dominant source of variation in fertility in the world is use of birth control, which is the result of both the supply of such services and the demand for them. Thus the index does not represent only the "supply" price of birth control services, but the quantity used which also embodies factors affecting the "demand" for children. It is not possible to eliminate the contraceptive prevalence components in the index for 1972. See Entwisle (1989) for an analysis that decomposes this effort score into its more and less exogenous components. The household demand model can be used to assess statistically the fertility reducing effect of contraceptive use (see Schultz, 1992a).

Table 6
Cross-country regressions of the total fertility rate (TFR) and child mortality rate to age five (CMR)[a]

| | (1) Child mortality (CMR) | (2) Fertility (TFR) | (3) Fertility (TFR) Reduced-form | (4) Child mortality (CMR) | (5) Family planning activity (FPA) | (6) Fertility (TFR) |
|---|---|---|---|---|---|---|
| Dependent variable: | | | | | | |
| Estimation method: | OLS[c] | 2SLS[c] | OLS | OLS | OLS | 2SLS |
| Explanatory variables | | | | | | |
| Years of female education[b] | −11.3 | −0.161 | −0.450 | −13.0 | 4.72 | −0.238 |
| | (4.30)[a] | (1.21) | (7.46) | (4.93)[a] | (3.24) | (1.32)[a] |
| Years of male education[b] | 1.67 | 0.152 | 0.195 | 1.33 | 1.06 | 0.144 |
| | (0.99) | (2.60) | (5.03) | (0.77) | (1.11) | (2.39) |
| Log of GDP per adult | −24.7 | 1.20 | 0.567 | −25.5 | 2.28 | 1.15 |
| (1988$, purchasing power parity) | (4.03) | (3.64) | (4.03) | (4.09) | (0.66) | (3.36) |
| Urban % of population | 0.321 | −0.0194 | −0.0108 | 0.355 | −0.0869 | −0.0172 |
| | (1.58) | (2.79) | (2.33) | (1.70) | (0.75) | (2.18) |
| % of male labor force in | 0.821 | −0.0042 | 0.0168 | 0.854 | −0.0923 | −0.0022 |
| Agriculture | (4.88) | (0.47) | (4.37) | (4.98) | (0.98) | (0.22) |
| Catholic % of population | 0.196 | 0.0030 | 0.0078 | 0.264 | −0.201 | 0.0054 |
| | (2.13) | (0.80) | (3.70) | (2.90) | (4.01) | (1.01) |
| Protestant % of population | 0.422 | 0.0065 | 0.0173 | 0.545 | −0.364 | 0.0111 |
| | (2.02) | (0.03) | (3.62) | (2.62) | (3.18) | (1.04) |
| Muslim % of population | 0.602 | −0.0062 | 0.0095 | 0.644 | −0.119 | −0.0040 |
| | (5.37) | (1.01) | (3.69) | (5.68) | (1.92) | (0.57) |
| Year 1982 dummy | −8.49 | 0.278 | 0.063 | −9.61 | 3.70 | 0.252 |
| | (1.47) | (1.31) | (0.48) | (1.60) | (1.12) | (1.16) |
| Year 1988 dummy | −8.22 | 0.673 | 0.465 | −13.3 | 15.3 | 0.503 |
| | (1.13) | (2.89) | (3.13) | (2.04) | (4.24) | (1.43) |
| Calories consumed per | 0.140 | | −0.0028 | −0.154 | 0.0428 | |
| capita per day | (1.94) | | (1.69) | (2.09) | (1.05) | |
| Calories per capita | 0.0211 | | 0.00037 | 0.0243 | −0.0098 | |
| squared ×10⁻³ | (1.44) | | (1.10) | (1.63) | (1.20) | |
| International planned parenthood | | | | −0.0174 | 0.0653 | |
| federation (¢/woman) | | | | (0.41) | (2.80) | |
| Child mortality to age five (CMR) | | 0.0257* | | | | 0.0250* |
| | | (3.15) | | | | (3.01) |
| Family planning activity score | −0.343 | −0.0102 | −0.0192 | | | 0.0022* |
| (FPA) | (2.80) | (2.08) | (6.82) | | | (0.11) |
| Intercept | 511 | −6.97 | 5.23 | 523 | −36.4 | −6.91 |
| | (5.28) | (2.06) | (2.36) | (5.30) | (0.67) | (2.02) |
| $R^2$ | 0.821 | − | 0.773 | 0.814 | 0.498 | − |
| $F$ | 71.7 | 26.8 | 53.3 | 68.5 | 15.5 | 24.6 |

*Notes*: See Table 5. Sample size is 217.

other regression coefficients are evident, with and without the inclusion of family planning.[31]

In regression (1) of Table 6 family planning is associated with lower child mortality. A standard deviation increase in the family planning score, of 25 points, is associated with a 6% decrease in child mortality, or nine fewer deaths per thousand births. Half of the effect of family planning on fertility operates through its impact on child mortality, which then leads to lower fertility ($-0.343 \times 0.0257 = -0.088$).[32] It has long been hypothesized that there may be this form of synergistic reinforcing effect of family planning and maternal-child health programs on fertility (Berelson and Taylor, 1968), and the magnitude of this interaction effect has been estimated from individual data for Colombia and India (Rosenzweig and Schultz, 1982b; Rosenzweig and Wolpin, 1982). It is possible, however, that family planning programs could in some circumstances be more effective when they are oriented toward a single objective of reducing birth rates and are not integrated with programs that foster the allied objectives of improving child health. One reason the prospects of population policies that go "beyond family planning" are said to be bleak is the comparative ineffectiveness and high cost of child health and women's education initiatives (Berelson, 1969; Berelson and Freedman, 1976). The first set of estimates in Table 6 suggests that both family planning and women's education programs exert half of their total effect on

---

[31] Several studies have sought to summarize development (or social setting) and family planning into two index variables to account for fertility. They find that there is a statistically significant interaction between them (Mauldin and Berelson, 1978; Bongaarts et al., 1990). In other words, the effect of a strong family planning program is greater in advanced social settings and smaller in less advanced social settings. This synergistic relationship between family planning and development was investigated here for each dimension of development. Interaction variables are constructed between the family planning activity score variable and all of the other demand variables. None is statistically significant in explaining fertility levels except the child mortality rate. Whether child mortality ($CMR$) is assumed to be exogenous or treated as an endogenous variable, the coefficient on the interaction of child mortality and family planning ($CMR*FPA$) is statistically significant and positive, suggesting family planning has its greatest effect on fertility in an environment where child mortality is low and vice versa. In the pooled cross section (sample $n = 217$) the three variables have the following coefficients (cf. regression (2), Table 6):

$$TFR = 0.0182 \, CMR - 0.0198 \, FPA + 0.0000843(CMR \times FPA) + \ldots + R^2 = 0.77.$$
$$\quad (4.37) \qquad\quad (3.26) \qquad\quad (2.23)$$

These results indicate that programs that reduce child mortality and those that foster family planning are complements so far as they reinforce each other in achieving the goal of reducing fertility.

[32] Bongaarts (1987) has drawn attention to the anomaly that if family planning programs reduce fertility they would also increase the proportion of first births and possibly shorten birth intervals. In most populations the incidence of child mortality is higher for first births than subsequent ones, probably for biological reasons. Consequently, this birth-order composition effect of family planning could increase child mortality. But the empirical evidence presented here suggests that this birth order composition effect is swamped by the mortality reducing effects of the mix of programs and policies measured by the family planning effort score.

fertility through their intermediary role of reducing child mortality and should not be classified as ineffective population measures, until carefully costed out.

If, as discussed earlier, family planning effort is in part a government response to parent demands for fewer children, what measurable sources of variation in family planning would be independent of fertility "demands" and thereby allow a researcher to identify statistically the unbiased impact of the "supply" of family planning effort on fertility? The meaning of any estimate of the effect of endogenous family planning on fertility depends, of course, on this choice of identification restriction. Only one variable could be found: the annual allocation of centrally provided family planning funds by country and year reported by the International Planned Parenthood Federation (IPPF). These external subsidies in 1988 (FX) dollars to another country's family planning program are divided by the number of women in that country of childbearing age, 15–45, and used to help explain the family planning effort index in regression (5) Table 6. IPPF transfers represent in the sample only 28 US cents per woman per year on average, and they are zero in 18 countries (see Table 5). The estimated effect of IPPF transfers on family planning activities is positive with a $t$ of 2.80, suggesting IPPF may be a satisfactory instrument for FPA (regression 5). International transfers from other donor agencies, such as from USAID, UNFPA, World Bank, etc. (avoiding, of course, any double counting) could not be found by country over time. It may be noted in regression (5) that family planning activities are also stronger in countries with fewer Christians and Muslims, and with more highly educated women. The Wu–Hausman test rejects again the null hypothesis that child mortality is exogenous, which has been accordingly estimated as an endogenous variable in regression (6) in Table 6. But when family planning activity is treated as endogenous and identified by IPPF transfers, the Wu–Hausman $t$ statistic is only 1.34 for the family planning variable, which is only significantly different from zero for a two-tailed test at the 20% level. This specification test suggests that one cannot reject the null hypothesis that family planning is, contrary to expectation, exogenous.

When family planning is nonetheless treated as endogenous in regression (6) of Table 6 along with endogenous child mortality, the estimate of the effect of family planning is not significantly different from zero. Given the limited information available to identify the endogenous effects of family planning on fertility, there is no reason to conclude that family planning has affected fertility. If one treats the family planning variable as exogenous in regression (2), in accord with the Wu–Hausman test, a one standard deviation increase in the family planning policy variable from 34 to 59 is associated with a 5% decrease in fertility, or about 0.26 children. Family planning's effect on child mortality indirectly contributes another 0.23 child reduction in fertility. If family planning is treated as endogenous, neither of these effects on fertility are statistically significant or substantial.

In terms of the fraction of the sample variation in fertility explained, or in terms of the change in fertility associated with a standard deviation in the conditioning variable, family planning program effort is no more "important" a determinant of fertility than women's and men's education, income, urbanization, and child mortality. The dilemma with these findings is that they do not provide a strong empirical basis on which to identify the parameter of interest – the effectiveness of family planning to reduce fertility while correcting for simultaneous equation bias.[33]

### 5.6.3. Prices of contraception

Among specific forms of birth control, prices for oral contraceptives are available from the largest number of low-income countries. In 1988, 58 low-income countries report such prices (Population Crisis Committee). The sample average price for an annual supply of 13 cycles of oral contraceptives is $40.40. This is reported to be the method used by 12% of the contracepting couples in low-income countries, the third most popular method after the IUD (24%) and sterilization (45%) (United Nations, 1989). It is not known if the price of oral contraceptives is a reasonable proxy for the prices of other birth control methods in each country. Although the average price of pills may be affected by demand driven population policies, it would seem more reasonable to assume that this price variable is uncorrelated with other unobserved determinants of fertility than the previously analyzed family planning variable. Thus, the price is treated here as exogenous.

In Table 7, the price of oral contraceptives replaces the family planning index for the smaller sample of 58 countries in 1988 for which prices are available. Estimates of child immunization are also available for these countries in 1988, reflecting progress of a major international campaign to increase child survival. The percentage of children receiving dpt (diphtheria, pertussis and tetanus) vaccine by their first birthday is therefore added as a determinant of child mortality in regression (1). Regression (2) reports the two-stage least square (2SLS) estimates, based on the Wu–Hausman test that child mortality is not exogenous. Regression (3) in Table 7 is the reduced-form for fertility that omits child mortality but includes calorie consumption and dpt immunization. These reduced-form estimates are parallel to those reported in regression (4), Table 5. Increasing child immunization for dpt by 17 percentage points, or a standard deviation, is associated with a reduction in child mortality of five per thousand births. The oral contraceptive price has the expected positive effect on fertility, and it is statistically significant at the 0.05 level one-tailed test. A standard deviation increase in the annual price of oral contraceptives, from $40 per year to $80, is associated with an increase in the total fertility rate of 0.26 children, or 5%. In short, these estimates confirm that the elasticity of fertility with respect to the price of one form of widely marketed contraception is positive, but only about 0.05.

---

[33] There are clear conceptual problems in regarding as exogenous some of the data series aggregated into the family planning effort index (Lapham and Mauldin, 1985). This index appears to measure contraceptive prevalence (Entwisle, 1989), and is thus certainly endogenous to a model of fertility determination (Schultz, 1992a).

Table 7
Cross-country regressions for 1988, with child immunization for diphtheria/pertussis/tetanus (dpt) and
prices of oral contraceptives[a]

|  | | (1) | (2) | (3) | (4) |
|---|---|---|---|---|---|
| Dependent variable: | | Child mortality (CMR) | Fertility (TFR) | Fertility (TFR) | Means (SD) |
| Estimation method: | | OLS | 2SLS[c] | OLS | |
| Explanatory variables | | | | | |
| Years of female education[b] | | −12.1 | −0.249 | −5.00 | 4.53 |
|  | | (3.34) | (1.28) | (3.82) | (2.29) |
| Years of male education[b] | | 0.263 | 0.231 | 0.237 | 6.30 |
|  | | (0.11) | (2.35) | (2.79) | (2.44) |
| Log of GDP per adult | | −12.2 | 0.608 | 0.354 | 8.08 |
| (1988$, purchasing power parity) | | (1.14) | (1.21) | (0.92) | (0.794) |
| Urban % of population | | −0.012 | −0.0134 | −0.0135 | 45.6 |
|  | | (0.05) | (1.23) | (1.41) | (22.4) |
| % male labor force in agriculture | | 0.251 | 0.0087 | 0.0139 | 44.0 |
|  | | (1.02) | (0.84) | (1.57) | (26.6) |
| Catholic % of population | | 0.325 | 0.005 | 0.012 | 39.2 |
|  | | (2.54) | (0.89) | (2.64) | (38.6) |
| Protestant % of population | | 0.810 | 0.014 | 0.031 | 8.50 |
|  | | (2.50) | (0.94) | (2.67) | (12.4) |
| Muslim % of population | | 0.548 | −0.000 | 0.011 | 24.4 |
|  | | (3.25) | (0.02) | (1.87) | (35.7) |
| Calories consumed per capita per day | | −0.282 | – | −0.0054 | 2475 |
|  | | (2.29) | | (1.22) | (398) |
| Calories per capita squared $\times 10^{-3}$ | | 0.0489 | – | 0.00093 | 6281 |
|  | | (2.04) | | (1.08) | (2004) |
| % children age one immunized | | −0.282 | – | −0.0149 | 75.2 |
| for dpt (1990) | | (2.29) | | (1.69) | (17.0) |
| Price of oral contraceptives ($/year) | | −0.0663 | 0.0066 | 0.0533 | 40.4 |
|  | | (0.68) | (1.70) | (1.51) | (39.7) |
| Child mortality rate to age five (CMR) | | | 0.0207* | | 107 |
|  | | | (2.37) | | (65.9) |
| Intercept | | 661 | −2.97 | 10.2 | 4.86[d] |
|  | | (4.20) | (0.63) | (1.81) | (1.63) |
| $R^2$ | | 0.895 | – | 0.779 | |
| $F$ | | 32.0 | 11.8 | 13.2 | |

Notes: See Table 5. Sample size is 58.

## 5.6.4. Time-series changes within countries

Data are available on all variables except the "price" of contraceptives and child immunization for 66 low-income countries in 1972, 1982, and 1988, 1989, a period

during which the total fertility rates declined on average by 0.78, or 13%. The same model may, therefore, be estimated from the cross-country or within-country variation in this panel and based on a more realistic specification of the stochastic term. In shifting from cross-sectional estimates of a behavioral relationship to estimates based on time-series variation, dynamic model limitations tend to become more salient (Kuh, 1959; Nerlove, 1965; Hausman and Taylor, 1981). Assume that fertility of country $i$ at time $t$, $F_{it}$, is a linear function of a set of concurrent conditioning variables, $X_{it}$, and a family planning program variable, $P_{it}$:

$$F_{it} = \alpha_0 + \alpha_1 P_{it} + \sum_{j=2}^{n} \alpha_j X_{jit} + u_i + e_{it}, \tag{1}$$

where it is now assumed that the error has two components, one associated with the country, $u_i$, either random or persistent over time, and another independently distributed error, uncorrelated across time or countries, $e_{it}$.

If in Eq. (1) $u_i$ is fixed and correlated with the regressors $P_i$ and $X_{ji}$, then the $\alpha$'s can be consistently estimated by introducing fixed effects (FE) for countries. This is equivalent to expressing all of the variables as deviations from their average over the time of the panel ($T$) within countries, whereby the confounding of regressors with each country's fixed effect is swept out, and one obtains

$$F_{it} - F_{iT} = \alpha_1(P_{it} - P_{iT}) + \sum_{j=2}^{n} \alpha_j(X_{ijt} - X_{ijT}) + (e_{it} - e_{iT}). \tag{2}$$

It is commonly assumed that the errors, $e_{it}$, are normal and independently and identically distributed, and then the differences in errors over time are also normal and iid. If the conditioning variables do not change in the panel, such as with religion, their coefficients cannot be estimated within the fixed-effects framework. The intercept, $\alpha_0$, vanishes if there is no time trend, or if there is a time trend, it is estimated as an intercept in Eq. (2).

The fixed-effect specification draws attention to the rudimentary dynamics in the "static" fertility behavioral model represented by Eq. (1). Fertility at time $t$ is assumed to be only a function of $P$ and $X$'s at $t$, rather than depending on a more complex history of these variables which may be incorporated into expectations about the future. In the cross section one may be approximating long-run equilibrium tendencies in behavior (Kuh, 1959), but from the first differences it becomes obvious that the "dynamic" adjustment process places inordinate weight on one episode of change in the conditioning variables to explain the concurrent movement of fertility to what is presumably a new equilibrium.[34] By extending the length of time between the observations to 6–10 years, the fixed-effect approach may be more plausible, despite the inadequacies of the implied static framework. However, the task of endogenizing child mortality rates and family planning program activity is now more difficult to implement. The cautious approach adopted here is to interpret only the reduced-form specification based on fixed effects, which is less dependent on knowledge of the dynamics of the full structural model.[35]

In Table 8, Generalized Least Squares (GLS) estimates are reported that allow for random country effects. Only single-equation models that do not contain endogenous explanatory variables are reported. The Lagrange multiplier (LM) test is performed to assess whether ordinary least squares (OLS) estimates based on the pooling of the panel data are consistent, or whether the country-specific components are significant and should be incorporated into the estimation by a suitable procedure, such as GLS or FE.[36] The next to the last row in Table 8 reports this specification test indicating that the OLS estimates should be rejected in favor of either a random-effects or a time invariant model of $u_i$.

The GLS coefficients on the core variables are similar to the pooled cross-section reduced-form OLS regression (4) in Table 5, except that income and urbanization have lost their explanatory effect. Regression (2) is based on the assumption that family planning activity is exogenous, in which case the GLS estimates suggest a standard deviation increase in FPA is associated with a total 5% decline in fertility, which is about half the size implied by regression (3) in Table 6. Regression (3) in Table 8 explaining child mortality assigns different weights to women's and men's education in lowering child mortality than in the OLS pooled results reported in regression (1) Table 6. Finally, regression (4) for family planning activity differs from OLS estimates in regression (5) in Table 6.

---

[34] If one maintained this hypothesis it would also imply the desirability of measuring fertility and conditioning variables for cohorts. Rather than relying on period measures of fertility, such as the total fertility rate, cohort measures of children ever born should be analyzed in the future, with possible corrections for censoring of completed fertility by age for cohorts under age 45. Unfortunately, there are few countries for which these more suitable cohort data on fertility exist, and if one also required child mortality and education by sex and income by cohort, there might not be any low-income countries left in the working sample.

[35] Some studies of changes in TFRs (e.g., Bongaarts et al., 1990) have regressed current fertility on lagged values of fertility and reported ordinary least squares (OLS) estimates. Clearly, country-specific unobserved factors affecting fertility will persist to some degree over the period of analysis, and such serial correlation in errors embodied in fertility violates the assumptions under which OLS estimates are unbiased. Therefore, lagged fertility must be generally treated as endogenous and the model estimated by simultaneous equation methods (see above Section 3.8).

[36] Missing data from the panel are assumed to be randomly missing; in which case including single observations in the GLS estimates is possible and the entire sample of 217 country–year observations is retained for GLS, but only 198 observations are used for FE estimates (Hsiao, 1986).

Table 8
Generalized least squares estimates from the panel of 1972, 1978 and 1988 assuming random error structure

| | (1) Fertility (FPA Endogenous) (TFR) | (2) Fertility (FPA Exogenous) (TFR) | (3) Child mortality (CMR) | (4) Family planning (FPA) |
|---|---|---|---|---|
| Dependent variable: | | | | |
| Estimation method: | GLS | GLS | GLS | GLS |
| Explanatory variables | | | | |
| Years of female education[b] | −0.454 | −0.456 | −3.21 | −0.378 |
| | (6.51)[a] | (6.78) | (1.25) | (0.26) |
| Years of male education[b] | 0.180 | 0.204 | −3.40 | 3.97 |
| | (3.43) | (4.12) | (1.68) | (3.52) |
| Log of GDP per adult (1988$, purchasing power parity) | 0.118 | 0.265 | −16.8 | 6.50 |
| | (0.86) | (1.91) | (3.38) | (2.41) |
| Urban % of population | −0.0017 | −0.0049 | −0.282 | −0.139 |
| | (0.30) | (0.93) | (1.35) | (1.17) |
| % of male labor force in agriculture | 0.0210 | 0.0190 | 0.817 | 0.0540 |
| | (4.70) | (4.39) | (4.99) | (0.57) |
| % of Catholic population | 0.0127 | 0.0104 | 0.269 | −0.204 |
| | (3.86) | (3.56) | (2.02) | (2.79) |
| % of Protestant population | 0.0256 | 0.0217 | 0.561 | −0.377 |
| | (3.35) | (3.26) | (1.82) | (2.20) |
| % of Islam population | 0.0165 | 0.0134 | 0.794 | −0.216 |
| | (4.25) | (3.88) | (5.09) | (2.51) |
| Calories consumed per capita per day ($\times 10^3$) | −0.742 | −0.815 | −12.2 | −4.35 |
| | (3.89) | (4.13) | (1.80) | (1.10) |
| IPPF expenditures | −0.0113 | – | – | 0.100 |
| | (0.14) | | | (5.83) |
| Family planning activity (FPA) | – | −0.0101 | −0.212 | – |
| | | (3.67) | (2.17) | |
| 1982 year dummy | −0.0417 | 0.0078 | −12.0 | 5.61 |
| | (0.47) | (0.09) | (3.85) | (3.06) |
| 1988 year dummy | 0.0230 | 0.231 | −14.9 | 19.9 |
| | (0.21) | (1.92) | (3.42) | (8.52) |
| Constant | 4.66 | 4.23 | 278 | −17.0 |
| | (3.91) | (1.71) | (6.39) | (0.68) |
| Pseudo-$R^2$ | 0.704 | 0.753 | 0.775 | 0.458 |
| Lagrange multiplier (LM) test rejecting OLS pooled for GLS or fixed-effects model specification (confidence level) | 85.02 (0.0000) | 49.78 (0.0000) | 96.69 (0.0000) | 70.09 (0.0000) |
| Hausman test for fixed-effects model versus GLS (confidence level for rejecting null) | (0.589) | (0.029) | (0.000) | (0.686) |

*Notes*: See Table 5.

The Hausman and Taylor (1981) specification test is reported in the bottom row of Table 8 for the null hypothesis that the $X_{ji}$ and fixed $u_i$ are uncorrelated. If the null is rejected, both OLS and GLS estimates are inconsistent, and fixed-effect estimates are preferred. If family planning is endogenous and only IPPF expenditures are included (regression (1)), the GLS estimates are accepted and preferred because of their efficiency. But if FPA is exogenous (regression (2)), the GLS estimates are rejected in favor of the FE estimates. The Hausman test also rejects the GLS estimates for the child mortality equation, but accepts them for family planning activities.

Table 9
Regressions on changes within countries from 1972 to 1988 or fixed-effect estimates[a]

| | (1) | (2) | (3) | (4) | (5) | (6) |
|---|---|---|---|---|---|---|
| Dependent variable: | Fertility (FPA endoge-nous) reduced-form | Fertility (FPA exogenous) reduced-form | Child mor-tality (CMR) | Fertility (TFR) | Family planning activity (FPA) | Fertility (TFR) |
| Estimation method: | OLS[c]-FE | OLS-FE | OLS-FE | 2SLS[c]-FE | OLS-FE | 2SLS-FE |
| **Explanatory variables** | | | | | | |
| Years of female education[b] | −0.447 | −0.478 | 13.8 | −2.35 | −3.89 | −1.72 |
| | (3.91)[a] | (4.26) | (4.71) | (0.95)[a] | (1.50) | (1.09) |
| Years of male education[b] | 0.259 | 0.291 | −11.8 | 1.82 | 7.20 | 1.20 |
| | (2.75) | (2.97) | (4.40) | (0.90) | (3.35) | (0.98) |
| Log of GDP per adult (1988$, purchasing power parity) | −0.0811 | −0.0545 | 3.60 | −0.541 | 6.51 | −0.707 |
| | (0.41) | (0.28) | (0.70) | (0.60) | (1.46) | (0.81) |
| Urban % of population | −0.00215 | −0.00248 | 0.0610 | −0.0107 | −0.310 | −0.00191 |
| | (0.20) | (0.23) | (0.21) | (0.26) | (1.23) | (0.05) |
| Percent of male labor force in Agriculture | 0.0274 | 0.0278 | 0.342 | −0.0185 | 0.0654 | 0.0127 |
| | (3.95) | (4.03) | (1.89) | (0.26) | (0.42) | (0.23) |
| Calories consumed per capita per day ($\times 10^{-3}$) | −0.652 | −0.668 | −4.94 | – | −2.32 | – |
| | (2.79) | (2.87) | (0.81) | | (0.44) | |
| IPPF expenditures per woman in (1988$) | 0.0316 | – | – | – | 0.110 | – |
| | (0.27) | | | | (4.19) | |
| Child mortality to age 5 (CMR) | – | – | – | 0.135* | – | 0.108* |
| | | | | (0.77) | | (0.87) |
| Family planning activity score (FPA) | – | −0.00323 | 0.0505 | −0.0107 | – | 0.0271* |
| | | (0.89) | (0.53) | (0.62) | | (0.69) |
| 1982 intercept | −0.0866 | −0.0662 | −31.3 | 4.17 | 6.90 | 3.07 |
| | (0.62) | (0.47) | (8.48) | (0.75) | (2.18) | (0.81) |
| 1988 intercept | −0.719 | 0.310 | −48.0 | 6.50 | 22.5 | 4.36 |
| | (0.36) | (0.01) | (8.45) | (0.76) | (4.58) | (0.80) |
| $F$ (80, 129) | 25.9 | 26.1 | 99.5 | 38.3 | 13.6 | 1.17 |

*Notes*: See Table 5. Sample size is 210, but minus 72 country fixed-effects the actual degrees of freedom is only 139.
*Endogenous variable.

Given the mixed outcomes of the specification tests, Table 9 reports, with qualifications, the fixed-effect model estimates based solely on changes over time within countries. The estimated effects of female and male education and agricultural employment remain similar to those originally obtained by OLS from pooled levels, whereas the estimated effects of income and urbanization lose statistical significance and decline in magnitude as they did in the GLS random effects estimates.[37] Family planning activity, even when assumed to be exogenous, now exerts no significant effect on fertility in the fixed-effect specification, and the magnitude of the point estimate declines by two-thirds. A standard deviation increase in the family planning score of 25 is associated over time with less than a 2% decline in fertility. Only the reduced-form FE estimates in regression (1) appear to provide a plausible interpretation of fertility changes: the effort to include child mortality or family planning as endogenous does not yield convincing FE estimates of the implied dynamic structural models.

Evaluating the effects of social intervention programs, such as family planning, is rarely possible with country level data, though such data may appear useful for testing general hypotheses about the consequences of different patterns of development and suggest linkages that warrant further study at the microeconomic level. Family planning, health, and education programs often differ substantially within a national population and this variation can provide scope to estimate the behavioral impact of various mixes of program activities. Controlling for demand determinants of fertility may improve efforts to evaluate family planning programs in such a quasi-experimental setting, because the demand factors and program activities may themselves be intercorrelated and the omission of one factor will bias estimates of the effect of the other (Schultz, 1988). Studies of Bangladesh, Indonesia, Taiwan, Thailand and China have used statistical methods to estimate the effects of family planning activity on birth rates (Schultz, 1974, 1980, 1992; Foster and Roy, 1992; Gertler and Molyneaux, 1993; Schultz and Zeng, 1992; Montgomery and Casterline, 1993). The distribution of program benefits are inferred from coefficients on interaction variables, defined as the product of the program's regional inputs and each distinguished individual exogenous group identifier defined by age, ethnicity, education, and region of residence (Schultz, 1992). The failure in the analysis in this section to document from country level data the impact of family planning on fertility should not be interpreted to imply that there is no effect. Rather, information at a more disaggregated level is a more promising basis for evaluating such social programs.

---

[37] That the effect of urbanization is insignificant in the first-differenced specification is not surprising, since these changes are probably dominated by projections of trends and are probably not greatly affected by actual current rates of rural–urban migration which might contain some information relevant to the fertility demands of parents. Income effects in short periods are obviously noisy sources of signals on the lifetime constraints relevant to a couple's fertility goals and behavior.

### 5.6.5. Summary of country comparisons

Previous studies have found that both family planning and development are associated across low-income countries with lower levels of fertility. These regularities have also been noted here. What distinguishes my approach and how do these findings differ from those of earlier studies?

First, simple static theory is used to conceptualize the constraints imposed on (not chosen by) individuals that may influence their demand for children. Development may involve a different mix of changes in these constraints in each country, some associated with declines in fertility and others with increases. Unless one gets beyond the search for a single "index of development" and focuses on measuring the dimensions of modern economic growth that have theoretically distinct effects on fertility, the search for empirical regularities between development and fertility is unlikely to be informative (Kuznets, 1958). Fertility should be statistically understood in terms of these multiple theoretical constraints, allowing their independent effects to be possibly nonlinear and to interact. Procedures that collapse the diversity of development into a single index seem archaic and counterproductive but are still common to this field of study.[38]

Second, most prior studies have included education as a demand or development indicator, but none has distinguished between the education of men and women. This practice continues despite the clear prediction of the earliest economic models of fertility that the effect of female education will be more negative than the effect of male education (Schultz, 1973). Distinguishing between the effects of the adult education of women and men is absolutely essential to test the relevance of the microeconomic model of fertility. This is not to suggest that other interpretations of female education as empowering women and thereby contributing to fertility declines, or Caldwell's (1982) view that mass education provides women with the capacity for decision making in the family, are not also viable interpretations of why gender differences in education are critical for understanding the demographic transition in low-income countries.

Third, child mortality is arguably not exogenous to the economic endowments, preferences, and conditions of the family, despite the likely importance of some com-

---

[38] The United Nations (1987) proposed that an index of development be constructed as the average of four series: GNP per capita, gross school enrollment ratio, infant mortality rate, and per capita number of radios, TVs, and cars. Bongaarts et al. (1990) use this index for their portrayal of the demographic effect of family planning. As with Mauldin and Berelson (1978), and Lapham and Mauldin (1985) countries are displayed on a two-way grid of the development index and the family planning effort index. The most recent Bongaarts et al. (1990) paper concludes that the absence of family planning programs worldwide would have led to a total fertility rate for low-income countries that would be 1.2 children higher in 1980–1985, or the TFR would have been 5.4 rather than 4.2. As a comparison, the pooled cross sections (Table 6, regression (2)) suggest that if the mean level of family planning score had not been 34 but zero, the associated TFR would have been 0.3 lower $(34 \times (-0.0089))$.

munity health measures and local disease environments in determining child deaths. But the family's resources are also important, such as the educational attainment of a mother that helps to explain empirically the probability of survival for her children (Mensch et al., 1985). Consequently, either child mortality should itself be studied jointly within the same conceptual framework with fertility or a reduced-form equation for fertility should be estimated where child mortality has been implicitly solved out of this relationship. The supply of calories per capita is specified here as a determinant of child mortality, but excluded from the fertility equation. The estimated effect of endogenous child mortality on fertility based on this identification restriction appears to be several times larger than when child mortality is viewed, as in prior studies, as if it were exogenous and measured without error. According to the estimates confirmed by exogeneity specification tests, declines in the level of child mortality in developing countries are not associated with increases in population growth, because coordinated fertility declines fully offset this demographic effect of improvements in child nutrition and survival. In this time period, improvements in child health are associated with slower population growth.

Fourth, countries that have higher permanent incomes in the cross section, given their human resource base, have higher fertility. This is not unexpected from the demand model of fertility. If the level of income is due to physical capital and natural resources, such as petroleum, which may have only a modest short-run effect on the productivity of the time of men and women, then an increment in income will not be offset by an increase in the opportunity cost of the time of parents in childbearing. A higher level of GDP per adult that is not associated with higher male and female education or lower child mortality can be expected to increase demands for children.

Fifth, the effects of gender-specific education and income on fertility are strengthened only slightly when several control variables for religion are included, such as Christianity and Islam. For example, the relatively high levels of fertility in Islamic countries are explained here mostly in terms of the underlying economic constraints on the population, including past educational investments in women. One does not have to resort to ad hoc cultural variables to explain most of the variation in fertility across low-income countries.

Sixth, family planning programs are summarized by an index used in a series of influential articles buttressing the idea that family planning is responsible for much of the reduction in fertility in low-income countries. If this family planning were an experimental treatment administered randomly to different countries, it could be argued that these programs are, as implicitly claimed, exogenous to the preexisting development and demand factors in these countries. Under this working hypothesis, family planning as an exogenous conditioning variable is indeed related to lower levels of fertility in the cross section. A standard deviation increase in the family planning score from 34 to 59 is associated with a modest 5% decline in fertility. But if family planning effort is explained within the model and endogenized, the relationship between it and fertility becomes statistically insignificant. Nevertheless, when the price of oral contraceptives is treated as an exogenous price of birth control, this more defensible exogenous family planning variable accounts for a significant, though small, share of the variance in fertility, with a doubling of the price of birth control being associated with fertility being 5% higher.

Seventh, when the fertility analysis shifts from cross-sectional levels to the more difficult to explain changes over time within countries, from 1972 to 1988, it is possible to estimate with confidence only a reduced-form specification of the fertility model. Based on fixed-effect estimates where family planning is treated as exogenous, the impact of family planning on fertility is insignificant and only one-third as large as when estimated by OLS or GLS. It is notable that female and male education, agricultural employment, and caloric availability exhibit significant estimated effects on fertility of roughly the same magnitude whether estimated by OLS, GLS or fixed-effects.

Eighth, the Bucharest World Population Conference in 1974 first asked whether fertility declines are promoted by development or by organized family planning activities? This question is, of course, poorly framed, for both are certainly relevant. But the thrust of this analysis is that the level and sex composition of human capital, the decline of agricultural employment, and the basic nutrition of the population explain most of the variation in the levels of total fertility rates and much of their changes over time, whereas family planning explains relatively little of either cross-sectional or time-series variation in fertility. Some changes associated generally with modern economic growth, such as increased male education or returns to nonhuman capital, raise fertility, whereas other changes, such as improvements in female education, urbanization, declines in the share of employment in agriculture, increases in availability of food, and a resulting decline in child mortality, lower fertility. The specific mix of these sources of growth and development in any particular country will then influence whether its development is pronatal or antinatal.

The education of women is the dominant empirical factor associated with the decline in fertility in the cross section and over time. But since male education has a weaker but countervailing effect on fertility, a critical dimension of development is likely to be the investment in schooling of females *relative* to males (Lichentenberg, 1992). Growth in income alone lowers child mortality, but has little total (reduced-form) effect on fertility. Raising calorie availability at very low levels appears to be strongly related to lowering child mortality and thereby contributes to fertility declines at early stages in the development process.

In the changes over time, family planning effort does not emerge as an important determinant of fertility. Because of the complexity of the policy formation process, and the lags between changes in the constraints on individuals and dynamic adjustments in their fertility, intercountry comparisons are not well suited to provide definitive answers on the cost effectiveness of social welfare programs, such as family planning. Program evaluation studies are more promising when conducted within individual countries, in those cases where administrative regions have implemented distinctively different policy packages without regard to socioeconomic development of the regions. When individual household survey data are then combined with administrative information on program expenditures or activities by small service regions, convincing evidence may be constructed on the contribution to fertility declines by family planning programs (or lack of it), holding constant for the principal household demand factors emphasized here. Even in these cases, the first-differencing of data by region helps to purge from the analysis potentially misleading correlations between region fixed-effects and program inputs (Foster and Roy, 1992; Gertler et al., 1992). Aggregate data for countries may not provide a credible answer to the question: how much difference has organized family planning made? But models that seek to explain cross-country differences and changes within countries may still shed light on the connections between the underlying sources of modern economic growth and their consequences for the decline in child mortality, fertility, and population growth that distinguish this century.

## 6. Conclusions

Applications of microeconomics to understand the demand for children emphasize several special aspects of children. Their cost to parents is heavily affected by the opportunity cost of the time of mothers, who in most societies contribute a disproportionate share of their time to child rearing. Demand models, consequently, predict and empirical studies confirm that increases in women's wages and education have a more negative impact on fertility than do increases in men's wages and education, or, for that matter, than does nonhuman capital income, which is indeed often associated with increased fertility in low-income agricultural settings. The changing composition of income, between labor and nonhuman capital, and between male and female productivity, are as important for the decline in fertility as the overall level of national income.

Children are also important vehicles for human capital investment that parents apparently treat as a substitute for their numbers of children. Thus, when the returns to human capital investment in the education of children increase, parents are expected to provide their children with more schooling, and will also reduce their own fertility. It is not clear from theory or empirical studies whether parents are motivated to make these child investments out of altruism or in exchange for the care and resources they expect their children to provide them in old age and in other unfavorable states of the world.

Other factors in the environment of families also appear to affect the demand for children and are reasonably subsumed within the demand model as affecting the relative cost or productivity of children. A plentiful supply of land owned by farm operators is conducive to relatively high fertility because the parents recoup more of the costs of childbearing by using children to replace costly hired farm labor. In cities, the net costs of children are thought to be higher because there is less productive work there for children within the family, and the costs of food, shelter, and vocational training are greater. Fertility clearly tends to be higher in rural-agricultural than in urban-industrial areas, holding many other factors constant.

The decline in mortality is the critical factor behind the acceleration in population growth that emerged in Europe about 1700 and spreads to low-income countries in the twentieth century. Our knowledge about the precise causes for and mechanisms producing the decline in mortality either in high- or low-income countries is fragmentary. The competing hypotheses are that nutrition improved, increases in income allowed other forms of healthy consumption to increase, public and private technologies controlled infectious diseases, or the organisms causing some (primarily childhood) diseases became less often fatal and were not immediately replaced by others. Whatever the cause of the mortality decline, the response of parents has been to reduce their births. This response of parents to the decline in child mortality can be explained within an economic demand model by the diminished need to replace children not dying, by the decreased need to use children as an insurance against uncertain mortality, and by the increased expected returns the family earns on investments that take the form of longer gestating child human capital. Although the empirical and theoretical pattern is clear, there remains ambiguity on how to allocate econometrically the substantial positive covariation between child mortality rates and fertility. Part is undoubtedly due to a response of parents to exogenous change in the health environment and part to endogenous household mediated control of family health and survival.

Finally, changes in the family are associated with changes in the state. Schools replace the family as training grounds for children and are almost everywhere publicly subsidized. Old age support and health care are provided by many state insurance schemes, which reduces the incentive to rear children to perform these functions within the family. Unfortunately, it is hard to measure with any confidence the effect of these institutional changes on fertility, but intuition tells us that they could be substantial. For many low-income countries these forms of social welfare legislation are not a realistic option to lower fertility because their cost exceeds publicly available resources. However, there are an increasing number of studies that suggest programs increasing the schooling of women, improving child health and nutrition, and diffusing family planning methods have all contributed significantly to the declines in child mortality, fertility, and population growth rates in low-income developing countries. These human resource programs certainly help to explain the puzzling variations in the world's demographic and economic development which were reviewed at the outset of this chapter. Economic models of the demand for children assist in providing an integrated framework for the study of these programs and their consequences on family behavior.

## Data Appendix

Table A-1

| Variable definition | Sources |
|---|---|
| 1. Total fertility rate | United Nations, 1990, World Development Prospects and Demographic Yearbook |
| 2. Child mortality rate per 1000 births | United Nations, 1988, Mortality of Children Under Age 5, 1980 |
| 3. Years of schooling completed by adult population by sex. | World Bank, diskette Source data, 1992 UNESCO, Statistical Yearbooks |
| 4a. Real GDP per adult in US 1988 $ using foreign exchange rates (in logarithms). | World Bank, 1991, World Tables, WDR 1990, UN Statistical Yearbook and IMF International Financial Statistics Yearbook |
| 4b. Real GDP per adult in 1985 international prices (PWT5) or purchasing power parity (in logarithms) | R. Summers and A. Heston, 1991, Expanded "Set of international comparisons 1950–1988," Quarterly Journal of Economics, 104: 327–336. |
| 5. Urban population share (%) | UN Demographic Yearbook, 1991, World Tables, 1990 World Urbanization Prospects |
| 6. Religious composition as of 1980 (%). | D. Barrett, 1982, World Christian Encyclopedia. |
| 7. Calories per capita per day | Food and Agricultural Organization, 1976, FAO Production Yearbook, 1985 and 1991 WDR |
| 8. Family planning effort score | 1972 scores in B. Berelson and W.P. Mauldin, 1978, "Conditions of fertility decline in developing countries, 1965–1975", Studies in Family Planning 9: 84–148, 1982 and 1989 scores in Ross et al. (1991) Family Planning and Child Survival Programs |
| 9. International planned parenthood Federation Expenditures in US ¢ 1988 per woman age 15–45. | 1989–90, IPPF Annual Report; 1973/74, 1983/84, 1988/89 Inventory of Population Projects, UN Population Fund. |
| 10. Oral contraceptive price 13 cycles (one year) in US $ 1990 | Access to Affordable Contraception, 1991, Report on World Progress toward Population Stabilization, Population Crisis Committee, Washington, DC |

Table A-2
Countries and years in sample

| | | | |
|---|---|---|---|
| 1. Algeria | 1972, 1982, 1988 | 41. Liberia | 1972, 1982, 1988 |
| 2.* Argentina | 1988 | 42. Libya | 1972, 1982 |
| 3. Bangladesh | 1972, 1982, 1988 | 43. Madagascar | 1972, 1982, 1988 |
| 4.* Barbados | 1972 | 44. Malawi | 1972, 1982, 1988 |
| 5. Benin | 1972, 1982, 1988 | 45. Malaysia | 1972, 1982, 1988 |
| 6. Bolivia | 1972, 1982, 1988 | 46. Mali | 1972, 1982, 1988 |
| 7. Botswana | 1982, 1988 | 47. Mauritania | 1972, 1982, 1988 |
| 8. Brazil | 1972, 1982, 1988 | 48. Mauritius | 1972, 1982, 1988 |
| 9. Burkina Faso | 1972, 1982, 1988 | 49. Mexico | 1972, 1982, 1988 |

| | | | |
|---|---|---|---|
| 10. Burundi | 1972, 1982, 1988 | 50. Morocco | 1972, 1982, 1988 |
| 11. Cameroon | 1972, 1982, 1988 | 51. Myanmar | 1972, 1982, 1988 |
| 12. Central African Republic | 1982, 1988 | 52. Nepal | 1972, 1982, 1988 |
| 13. Chile | 1972, 1982, 1988 | 53. Nicaragua | 1972, 1982 |
| 14. China | 1972, 1982, 1988 | 54. Nigeria | 1972, 1982, 1988 |
| 15. Columbia | 1972, 1982, 1988 | 55. Pakistan | 1972, 1982, 1988 |
| 16. Congo | 1972, 1982, 1988 | 56. Panama | 1972, 1982, 1988 |
| 17. Costa Rica | 1972, 1982, 1988 | 57. Papua New Guinea | 1972, 1982, 1988 |
| 18. Cuba | 1972, 1982 | 58. Paraguay | 1972, 1982, 1988 |
| 19.*Cyprus | 1982 | 59. Peru | 1972, 1982, 1988 |
| 20. Dominican Republic | 1972, 1982, 1988 | 60. Philippines | 1972, 1982, 1988 |
| 21. Ecuador | 1972, 1982, 1988 | 61. Republic of Korea | 1972, 1982, 1988 |
| 22. Egypt | 1972, 1982, 1988 | 62. Rwanda | 1972, 1982, 1988 |
| 23. El Salvador | 1972, 1982, 1988 | 63. Senegal | 1972, 1982, 1988 |
| 24. Ethiopia | 1972, 1982, 1988 | 64. Singapore | 1972, 1982, 1988 |
| 25. Fiji | 1972, 1982 | 65.*South Africa | 1988 |
| 26.*Gabon | 1988 | 66. Sri Lanka | 1972, 1982, 1988 |
| 27. Ghana | 1972, 1982, 1988 | 67. Sudan | 1972, 1982, 1988 |
| 28. Guatemala | 1972, 1982, 1988 | 68. Syria | 1972, 1982, 1988 |
| 29. Guyana | 1982, 1988 | 69. Tanzania | 1972, 1982, 1988 |
| 30. Haiti | 1972, 1982, 1988 | 70. Thailand | 1972, 1982, 1988 |
| 31. Honduras | 1972, 1982, 1988 | 71. Togo | 1972, 1982, 1988 |
| 32.*Hong Kong | 1982 | 72. Trinidad and Tobago | 1972, 1982, 1988 |
| 33. India | 1972, 1982, 1988 | 73. Tunisia | 1972, 1982, 1988 |
| 34. Indonesia | 1972, 1982, 1988 | 74. Turkey | 1972, 1982, 1988 |
| 35. Iran | 1972, 1982, 1988 | 75. Uganda | 1972, 1982, 1988 |
| 35. Iraq | 1972, 1982, 1988 | 76.*Uruguay | 1988 |
| 36. Ivory Coast | 1972, 1982, 1988 | 77. Venezuela | 1972, 1982, 1988 |
| 37. Jamaica | 1972, 1982, 1988 | 78. Zaire | 1972, 1982, 1988 |
| 38. Kenya | 1972, 1982, 1988 | 79. Zambia | 1972, 1982, 1988 |
| 39. Kuwait | 1972, 1982, 1988 | 80. Zimbabwe | 1982, 1988 |
| 40. Lesotho | 1972, 1982, 1988 | | |

## References

Ahn, N. (1991), "Measuring the value of children by sex and age using a life-cycle model of fertility", Discussion paper no. 648 (Economic Growth Center, Yale University, New Haven, CT).

Ahn, N. (1992), "The effects of the one child family policy on the second and third birth in three provinces of China", Paper (Economic Growth Center, Yale University, New Haven, CT).

Ainsworth, M. (1989), "Socioeconomic determinants of fertility in Côte d'Ivoire", Living Standards Measurement Study, no. 53 (World Bank, Washington, DC).

Ainsworth, M. and A. Nyamete (1992), "Impact of women's human capital on fertility and contraceptive use in subSaharan Africa", Presented at conference on Women's Human Capital and Development, Bellagio, Italy.

Anderson, K.H. (1983), "The determinants of fertility, schooling and child survival in Guatemala", International Economic Review 24: 567–589.

Anderson, K.H. (1984), "The sensitivity of wage elasticity to selection bias and the assumption of normality", Journal of Human Resources 17: 594–605.

Anker, R. and J.C. Knowles (1982), Fertility determinants in developing countries: a case study of Kenya (Ordina Editions, Liege).

Arnold, F. (1987), "The effect of sex preferences on fertility and family planning", Population Bulletin of the United Nations 23/24: 44–55.

Ashenfelter, O. and J.J. Heckman (1974), "The estimation of income and substitution effects in a model of family labor supply", Econometrica 42: 73–85.

Ashton, B., K. Hill, A. Piazza and R. Zeitz (1984), "Famine in China 1958–1961", Population and Development Review 10: 613–646.

Banister, J. (1987), China's changing population (Stanford University Press, Stanford, CA).

Barro, R. (1991), "Economic growth in a cross section of countries", Quarterly Journal of Economics 106: 406–441.

Becker, G.S. (1960), "An economic analysis of fertility", in: Demographic and economic change in developed countries (Princeton University Press, Princeton, NJ).

Becker, G.S. (1964), Human capital (Columbia University Press, New York).

Becker, G.S. (1965), "A theory of the allocation of time", Economic Journal 75: 493–517.

Becker, G.S. (1981), A treatise on the family (Harvard University Press, Cambridge, MA).

Becker, G.S. (1992), "Fertility and the economy", Journal of Population Economics 5: 185–201.

Becker, G.S. and R.J. Barro (1988), "A reformulation of the economic theory of fertility", Quarterly Journal of Economics 103: 1–25.

Becker, G.S. and G. Lewis (1974), "Interaction between quantity and quality of children", in: T.W. Schultz, ed., Economics of the family (University of Chicago Press, Chicago, IL).

Becker, G.S. and N. Tomes (1976), "Child endowments and the quantity and quality of children", Journal of Political Economy 84: S143–S189.

Becker, G.S., K.M. Murphy and R. Tamura (1990), "Human capital, fertility and economic growth", Journal of Political Economy 98: S12–S37.

Behrman, J.R., R. Pollak and P. Taubman (1982), "Parental preferences and provision for progeny", Journal of Political Economy 90: 52–73.

Benefo, K. and T.P. Schultz (1992), "Fertility and child mortality in Cote d'Ivoire and Ghana", Processed (Economic Growth Center, Yale University, New Haven, CT).

Ben-Porath, Y. (1974), "Economic analysis of fertility in Israel", in: T.W. Schultz, ed., Economics of the family (University of Chicago Press, Chicago, IL).

Ben-Porath, Y. (1975), "First generation effects on second generation fertility", Demography 12: 397–406.

Ben-Porath, Y. (1976), "Fertility response to child mortality: micro data from Israel", Journal of Political Economy 84: S163–S178.

Ben-Porath, Y. (1980), "The F connection", Population and Development Review 6: 1–30.

Ben-Porath, Y. and F. Welch (1976), "Do sex preferences really matter?", The Quarterly Journal of Economics 90: 285–307.

Ben-Porath, Y. and F. Welch (1980), "On sex preference and family size", in: J. Simon and P. Lindert, eds., Research in Population Economics, Vol. 3 (JAI Press, Greenwich, CT).

Berelson, B. (1969), "Beyond family planning", Science 163: 533–543.

Berelson, B. and R. Freedman (1976), "The record of family planning programs", Studies in Family Planning 7: 1–40.

Berelson, B. and H.C. Taylor, Jr. (1968), "Maternity care and family planning as a world program", American Journal of Obstetrics and Gynecology 100: 885–893.

Birdsall, N. (1980), "The cost of siblings: child schooling in urban Columbia", in: J. Simon and J. DaVanzo, eds., Research in population economics, Vol. 2 (JAI Press, Greenwich, CT).

Birdsall, N. (1988), "Economic approaches to population growth", in: H. Chenery and T.N. Srinivasan, eds., Handbook of development economics, Vol. 1 (North-Holland, Amsterdam).

Birdsall, N. (1991), "Birth order effects on time allocation", in: T.P. Schultz, ed., Research in population economics, Vol. 7 (JAI Press, Greenwich, CT).

Blake, J. (1968), "Are babies consumer durables?", Population Studies 22: 185–206.

Blau, D.M. (1984), "A model of child nutrition, fertility and women's time allocation", in: T.P. Schultz, ed., Research in Population Economics, Vol. 5 (JAI Press, Greenwich, CT).

Bongaarts, J. (1978), "A framework for analyzing the proximate determinants of fertility", Population and Development Review 4: 105–132.

Bongaarts, J. (1987), "Does family planning reduce infant mortality rates", Population and Development Review 13: 323–334.

Bongaarts, J. and H. Delgado (1979), "Effects of nutritional status on fertility in rural Guatemala", in: J. Menken and H. Leridion, eds., Natural fertility (Ordina Editions, Liege).

Bongaarts, J. and R. Potter (1983), Fertility, biology and behavior (Academic Press, New York).

Bongaarts, J., P. Mauldin and J. Phillips (1990), "The demographic impact of family planning programs", Studies in Family Planning 21: 299–310.

Boserup, E. (1965), The conditions of agricultural growth: the economics of agrarian change under population pressure (Allen and Unwin, London).

Boserup, E. (1970), Women's role in economic development (Allen and Unwin, London).

Boulier, B.L. and M.R. Rosenzweig (1984), "Schooling, search and spouse selection", Journal of Political Economy 92: 712–732.

Bryant, W.K. (1990), The economic organization of the household (Cambridge University Press, Cambridge).

Bulatao, R.A. and R.D. Lee, eds. (1983), Determinants of fertility in developing countries, 2 vols. (Academic Press, New York).

Butz, W.P. and M.P. Ward (1979), "The emergence of countercyclical U.S. fertility", American Economic Review 69: 318–328.

Cain, M. (1981), "Risk and insurance: perspectives on fertility and agrarian change in India and Bangladesh", Population and Development 7: 435–474.

Caldwell, J. (1982), Theory of fertility decline (Academic Press, London).

Caldwell, J. and P. Caldwell (1987), "The cultural context of high fertility in subSaharan Africa", Population and Development Review 13: 409–437.

Chernichovsky, D. (1982), "Fertility behavior in developing countries", in J. Simon and P. Linder, eds, Research in population economics, Vol. 4 (JAI Press, Greenwich, CT).

Chiappori, P.A. (1992), "Collective labor supply", Journal of Political Economy 100: 437–467.

Cigno, A. (1991), Economics of the family (Oxford University Press, Oxford).

Cleland, J. and C. Wilson (1987), "Demand theories of the fertility decline: an iconoclastic view", Population Studies 41: 5–30.

Cleland, J., J. Verrall and M. Vaessen (1983), "Preference for the sex of children and their influence on reproductive behavior", WFS Comparative Studies, no. 27 (International Statistical Institute, Voorburg, Netherlands).

Coale, A.J. (1973), "The demographic transition reconsidered", International Population Conference (International Union for the Scientific Study of Population, Liege) pp. 53–72.

Coale, A.J. (1984), Rapid population change in China 1952–1982, Committee on Population and Demography, Report no. 27 (National Academy Press, Washington, DC).

Coale, A.J. and E. Hoover (1958), Population growth and economic development in low income countries (Princeton University Press, Princeton, NJ).

Cochrane, S.H. (1983), "Effects of education and urbanization on fertility", in: R.A. Bulatao and R.D. Lee, eds., Determinants of fertility in developing countries, Vol. II (Academic Press, New York).

Cox, D. and E. Jimenez (1992a), "Motivations for private transfers over the life-cycle", Discussion paper (Boston College, Boston, MA).

Cox, D. and E. Jimenez (1992b), "Social security and private transfers in developing countries: the case of Peru", World Bank Economic Review 6: 155–169.

Dasgupta, P. and D. Ray (1987), "Inequality as a determinant of malnutrition and unemployment: policy", Economic Journal 97: 1011–1034.

DaVanzo, J. (1971), The determinants of family formation in Chile, 1960, R-830 (Rand Corporation, Santa Monica, CA).

Davies, J.B. and J. Zhang (1992), "Sex preference, investment in children and fertility", Processed (University of Western Ontario, London, Canada).

Denison, E.F. (1962), "The sources of economic growth in the United States and the alternatives before us", Supplementary paper no. 13 (Committee for Economic Development, New York).

DeTray, D.N. (1974), "Child quality and the demand for children", in: T.W. Schultz, ed., Economics of the family (University of Chicago Press, Chicago, IL).

DeVany, A. and N. Sanchez (1979), "Land tenure structures and fertility in Mexico", Review of Economics and Statistics 61: 67–72.

Dumond, D. (1975), "The limitation of human populations", Science 187: 713–721.

Duncan, O.D. (1966), "Path analysis: sociological examples", American Journal of Sociology 72: 1–16.

Duraisamy, P. (1993), "Changes in fertility and school attendance rates of boys and girls", Journal of Quantitative Economics, in press.

Duraisamy, P. and R. Malathy (1981), "Impact of public programs on fertility and gender specific investments in human capital of children on rural India", in: T.P. Schultz, ed., Research in population economics, Vol. 7 (JAI Press, Greenwich, CT).

Easterlin, R.A. (1968), Population, labor force and long swings in economic growth (Columbia University Press, New York).

Easterlin, R.A. (1978), "The economics and sociology of fertility: a synthesis", in: C. Tilly, ed., Historical studies of changing fertility (Princeton University Press, Princeton, NJ).

Easterlin, R.A. and E.M. Crimmins (1985), The fertility revolution: a supply–demand analysis (University of Chicago Press, Chicago, IL).

Easterlin, R.A., R.A. Pollak and M.L. Wachter (1980), "Toward a more general economic model of fertility determination", in: R.A. Easterlin ed., Population and economic change in developing countries (University of Chicago Press, Chicago, IL).

Eckstein, Z. and K. Wolpin (1985), "Endogenous fertility in an overlapping generations growth model", Journal of Public Economics 27: 93–106.

Eckstein, Z. and K. Wolpin (1989), "The specification and estimation of dynamic stochastic discrete choice models", Journal of Human Resources 24: 562–598.

Entwisle, B. (1989), "Measuring components of family planning program effort", Demography 26: 53–76.

Ernst, C. and J. Angst (1983), Birth order: its influences on personality (Springer-Verlag, Berlin).

Espenshade, T. (1984), Investing in children (The Urban Institute, Washington, DC).

Fogel, R.W. (1990), "The conquest of high mortality and hunger in Europe and America", Working paper no. 16 (NBER, Cambridge, MA).

Foster, A.D. and N. Roy (1992), "The dynamics of education and fertility: evidence from a family planning experiment", Processed (University of Pennsylvania, Philadelphia, PA).

Frisch, R. (1978), "Population, food intake and fertility", Science 200: 22–30.

Galor, O. and D.N. Weil (1993), "The gender gap, fertility and growth", Working paper no. 93-16 (Brown University, Providence, RI).

Gertler, P. and J.W. Molyneaux (1993), "How economic development and family planning programs combined to reduce Indonesian fertility", Working paper no. 93-08 (Rand Corporation, Santa Monica, CA).

Gertler, P. and J. Newman (1992), "Family productivity, labor supply and welfare in a low income country", Presented at conference on Women's Human Capital and Development, Bellagio, Italy.

Gertler, P., J.W. Molyneaux and S.H. Hatmadji (1992), "Economic opportunities, program inputs and fertility decline in Indonesia", Processed (Rand Corporation, Santa Monica, CA).

Goody, J. (1976), Production and reproduction (Cambridge University Press, Cambridge).

Griffin, C. (1986), "Methods for estimating value of time in low income countries with an application to the Philippines", Mimeo. (Yale University, New Haven, CT).

Griliches, Z. and J. Hausman (1986), "Errors in variables in panel data", Journal of Econometrics 31: 93–118.

Gronau, R. (1986), "Home production – a survey", in: O.C. Ashenfelter and R. Layard, eds., Handbook of labor economics, Vol. 1 (North-Holland, Amsterdam).

Hausman, J.A. (1978), "Specification tests in econometrics", Econometrica 46: 1251–1271.

Hausman, J.A. and W.E. Taylor (1981), "Panel data and unobservable individual effects", Econometrica 49: 1377–1398.

Heckman, J.J. (1987), "Selection bias and self-selection", in: J. Eatwell, M. Milgate and P. Newman, eds., The new Palgrave (Macmillan, London).

Heckman, J.J. and B. Singer (1985), Longitudinal analysis of labor market data (Cambridge University Press, Cambridge).

Heckman, J.J. and J.R. Walker (1991), "Economic models of fertility dynamics: a study of Swedish data", in: T.P. Schultz, ed., Research in population economics, Vol. 7 (JAI Press, Greenwich, CT) pp. 3–91.

Hoddinott, J. (1992), "Rotten kids or convincing parents: are children old age security in western Kenya", Economic Development and Cultural Change 403: 545–566 .

Hohm, C.F. (1975), "Social security and fertility", Demography 12: 629–644.

Hotz, J.V. and R. Miller (1988), "An empirical analysis of life-cycle fertility and female labor supply", Econometrica 56: 91–118.

Houthakker, H.S. (1952), "Compensated changes in quantities and qualities conserved", Review of Economic Studies 19: 155–164.

Hsiao, C. (1986), Analysis of panel data (Cambridge University Press, Cambridge).

International Labour Office (various years), Yearbook of labour statistics (ILO, Geneva).

Jensen, E.R. (1990), "An econometric analysis of the old age security motive of childbearing", International Economic Review 31: 953–968.

Kelley, A.C. (1980), "Interactions of economic and demographic household behavior", in: R.A. Easterlin, ed., Population and economic change in developing countries (University of Chicago Press, Chicago, IL).

Kelly, W.R., P. Cutright and D. Hittle (1976), "Comment on Charles F. Hohm's social security and fertility", Demography 13: 581–586.

Killingsworth, M. (1983), Labor supply (Cambridge University Press, Cambridge).

Kravis, I.B., A. Heston and R. Summers (1982), World product and income (Johns Hopkins University Press, Baltimore, MD).

Kuh, E. (1959), "The validity of cross-sectionally estimated behavior equations in time-series applications", Econometrica 27: 197–214.

Kuznets, S. (1958), "Long swings in the growth of population and in related economic variables", Proceedings of the American Philosophical Society 102: 25–52.

Kuznets, S. (1971), Economic growth of nations (Harvard University Press, Cambridge, MA).

Lam, D. (1988), "Marriage markets and assertative mating with public goods", Journal of Human Resources 23: 462–487.

Lam, D., G. Sedlacek and S. Duryea (1993), "Increases in education and fertility decline in Brazil", Presented at Population Association of America Meeting, Cincinnati, OH.

Lancaster, T. (1990), The econometric analysis of transition data (Cambridge University Press, Cambridge).

Langer, W.L. (1974), "Infanticide: a historical survey", History of Childhood Quarterly 1: 353–365.

Lapham, R.J. and W.P. Mauldin (1985), "Contraceptive prevalence: the influence of organized family planning programs", Studies in Family Planning 16: 117–137.

Lapham, R.J. and G.B. Simmons (1987), Organizing for effective family planning programs (National Academy Press, Washington, DC).

Lavy, V. (1985), "Cropping pattern, mechanization, child labor and fertility behavior in rural Egypt", Economic Development and Cultural Change 33: 777–791.

Lee, R.D. (1980a), "Aiming at a moving target: period fertility and changing reproductive goals", Population Studies 34: 205–226.

Lee, R.D. (1980b), "A stock adjustment model of U.S. marital fertility", in: J. Simon and P. Lindert, eds., Research in population economics, Vol. 3 (JAI Press, Greenwich, CT).

Lee, B.S. and T.P. Schultz (1982), "Implications of child mortality reductions for fertility and population growth in Korea", Journal of Economic Development 7: 21–44.

Leibenstein, H.A. (1957), Economic backwardness and economic growth (Wiley, New York).

Lestheghe, R. and J. Surkyn (1988), "Cultural dynamics and economic theories of fertility change", Population and Development Review 14: 1–45.

Leung, S.F. (1988), "On tests for sex preference", Journal of Population Economics 1: 95–114.

Leung, S.F. (1991), "A stochastic dynamic analysis of parental sex preferences and fertility", Quarterly Journal of Economics 104: 1064–1088.

Lichtenberg, F.R. (1992), "Have international differences in educational attainment levels narrowed?", Paper presented at workshop on Historical Perspective on the International Convergence of Productivity, New York University, New York.

Lindert, P.H. (1980), "Child costs and economic development", in: R.A. Easterlin, ed., Population and economic change in developing countries (University of Chicago Press for National Bureau of Educational Research, Chicago, IL).

Lundberg, S. and R.A. Pollak (1993), "Separate spheres of bargaining and the marriage market", Journal of Political Economy 101: 988–1010.

Macunovich, D.J. (1991), "An evaluation of the Butz–Ward hypothesis of countercyclical fertility", Paper presented at Population Association of America annual meetings.

Maddala, G.S. (1983), Limited dependent and qualitative variables in econometrics (Cambridge University Press, Cambridge).

Maglad, N.E. (1990), "Fertility in rural Sudan: the effect of landholding and child mortality", Discussion paper no. 604 (Economic Growth Center, Yale University, New Haven, CT).

Mankiw, N.G., D. Romer and D.N. Weil (1992), "A contribution to the empirics of economic growth", Quarterly Journal of Economics 107: 407–437.

Mauldin, W.P. and B. Berelson (1978), "Conditions of fertility decline in developing countries, 1965–1975", Studies in Family Planning 9: 84–148.

Maurer, K., R. Ratajczak and T.P. Schultz (1973), Marriage, fertility and labor force participation of Thai women, R-829 (Rand Corporation, Santa Monica, CA).

Mauskopf, J. and T.D. Wallace (1984), "Fertility and replacement: some alternative stochastic models and results for Brazil", Demography 21: 519–536.

McElroy, M.B. and J. Horney (1978), "A Nash bargained linear expenditure system: the demand for leisure and goods", Processed (Duke University), Partially published in: International Economic Review 22: 333–350 (1981) and expanded in 1988, in: T.P. Schultz, ed., Research in population economics, Vol. 6 (JAI Press, Greenwich, CT).

McCabe, J.L. and M.R. Rosenzweig (1976), "Female labor force participation, occupational choice and fertility in developing countries", Journal of Development Economics 3: 141–60.

Meadows, D.H., D.L. Meadows, J. Randers and W.W. Behrens (1972), The limits to growth (Potomac Asst., New York).

Mensch, B., H. Lentzner and S. Preston (1985), Child mortality differential in developing countries (United Nations, New York).

Merrick, T.W. (1978), "Fertility and land availability in rural Brazil", Demography 15: 321–336.

Mincer, J. (1963), "Market prices, opportunity costs and income effects", in: C. Christ et al., eds., Measurement in economics (Stanford University Press, Stanford, CA).

Mincer, J. (1974), Schooling. experience and earnings (Columbia University Press, New York).

Modigliani, F. and R. Brumberg (1954), "Utility analysis and the consumption function: an interpretation of cross-sectional data", in: K. Kurihara, ed., Post-Keynesian economics (Rutgers University Press, New Brunswick, NJ).

Montgomery, M.R. (1986), "Female first marriage in east and southeast Asia: a Kiefer–Neumann model", Discussion paper no. 510 (Economic Growth Center, Yale University, New Haven, CT).

Montgomery, M.R. and J.B. Casterline (1993), "The diffusion of fertility control in Taiwan: evidence from pooled cross-section time-series models", Population Studies 47: 457–480.

Montgomery, M.R. and A. Kouame (1993), "Fertility and child schooling and Côte d'Ivoire: is there a tradeoff, Processed (World Bank, Washington, DC).

Moock, J.L., ed. (1986), Understanding Africa's rural households and farming systems (Westview Press, Boulder, CO).

Mueller, E. (1984), "Income aspirations and fertility in rural areas of less developed countries", in: W.A. Schutjer and C.S. Stokes, eds., Rural development and human fertility (Macmillan, New York).

Mueller, E. and K. Short (1983), "Effects of income and wealth on the demand for children", in: R.A. Bulatao and R.D. Lee, eds., Determinants of fertility in developed countries, Vol. 1 (Academic Press, New York).

Mukhopadhyay, S. (1991), "Adapting household behavior in agricultural technology in West Bengal, India", Discussion paper no. 631 (Economic Growth Center, Yale University, New Haven, CT).

Murphy, K.M. and R.H. Topel (1985), "Estimation and inference in two step econometric models", Journal of Business and Economics Statistics 3: 370–379.

Nag, M., B.N.F. White and R.C. Peet (1978), "An anthropological approach to the study of the economic value of children in Java and Napal", Current Anthropology 19: 293–306.

National Research Council (1986), Population growth and economic development: policy questions (National Academy Press, Washington, DC).

National Research Council (1989), Contraception and reproduction: health consequences for women and children in the developing world (National Academy Press, Washington, DC).

National Research Council (1993), Demographic effects of economic reversals in subSaharan Africa (National Academy Press, Washington, DC).

Nerlove, M. (1965), Estimation and identification of Cobb–Douglas production functions (Rand McNally, Chicago, IL).

Nerlove, M. and T.P. Schultz (1970), Love and life between the censuses: a model of family decision-making (Rand Corporation, Santa Monica, CA).

Newman, J. (1981), "An economic analysis of the spacing of birth: Costa Rica", Ph.D. dissertation (Yale University, New Haven, CT).

Newman, J. (1988), "A stochastic dynamic model of fertility", in: T.P. Schultz, ed., Research in population economics, Vol. 6 (JAI Press, Greenwich, CT).

Newman, J. and C.E. McCulloch (1984), "A hazard rate approach to the timing of births", Econometrica 52: 939–961.

Nugent, J. (1985), "The old age security motive for fertility", Population and Development Review 11: 75–97.

Nugent, J. and R. Anker (1990), "Old age support and fertility", Working paper no. 172 (Population and Labour Policies Programme, ILO, Geneva).

Nugent, J. and R.T. Gillaspy (1983), "Old age pensions and fertility in rural areas of less developed countries: some evidence from Mexico", Economic Development and Cultural Change 31: 809–830.

O'Hara, D.J. (1975), "Microeconomic aspects of the demographic transition", Journal of Political Economy 83: 1203–1216.

Oken, B. (1991), "How much can indirect estimation techniques really tell us about marital fertility control", Processed (Office of Population Research, Princeton University, Princeton, NJ).

Okojie, C.E.E. (1991), "Fertility response to child survival in Nigeria", in: T.P. Schultz, ed., Research in population economics, Vol. 7 (JAI Press, Greenwich, CT).

Olsen, R.J. (1980), "Estimating the effects of child mortality on the number of births", Demography 17: 429–444.

Olsen, R.J. (1988), "Cross-sectional methods for estimating the replacement of infant deaths", in: T.P. Schultz, ed., Research in population economics, Vol. 6 (JAI Press, Greenwich, CT).

Olsen, R.J. and K.I. Wolpin (1983), "The impact of exogenous child mortality on fertility", Econometrica 51: 731–749.

Orcutt, G., M. Greenberger, J. Korbel and A. Rivlin (1961), Microanalysis of socioeconomic systems (Harper and Brothers, New York).

Park, C.B. (1983), "Preference for sons, family size and sex ratio: an empirical study in Korea", Demography 20: 333–352.

Pitt, M.M. (1993), "Women's schooling, selective fertility and infant mortality in subSaharan Africa", Processed (World Bank, Washington, DC).

Pitt, M.M. and M.R. Rosenzweig (1989), "The selectivity of fertility and the determinants of human capital investments", Processed (University of Minnesota, Minneapolis, MN).

Pitt, M.M., M.R. Rosenzweig and D.M. Gibbons (1993), "The determinants and consequences of placement of government programs in Indonesia", World Bank Economic Review 7: 319–348.

Pollak, R.A. (1985), "A transaction cost approach to families and households", Journal of Economic Literature 32: 581–608.

Pollak, R.A. and M.L. Wachter (1975), "The relevance of the household production function and its implications for the allocation of time", Journal of Political Economy 83: 255–278.

Population Crisis Committee (1991), Access to affordable contraception (Washington, DC).

Preston, S.H. (1980), "Causes and consequences of mortality decline in LDCs during twentieth century", in: R.A. Easterlin, ed., Population and economic change in developing countries (University of Chicago Press, Chicago, IL).

Quisumbing, A.R. (1991), "Intergenerational transfers in Phillippine rice villages", Discussion paper no. 632 (Economic Growth Center, Yale University, New Haven, CT).

Raut, L.K. (1992), "Old age security and gender preference hypotheses", Discussion paper no. 91-25R (University of California at San Diego, CA).

Razin, A. (1980), "Number, spacing and quality of children", in: J.L. Simon and J. DaVanzo, eds., Research in population economics (JAI Press, Greenwich, CT).

Razin, A. and U. Ben-Zion (1975), "An intergenerational model of population growth", American Economic Review 65: 923–933.

Ridker, R. (1980), "The no-birth bonus scheme", Population and Development Review 6: 31–46.

Rosenzweig, M.R. (1992), "Risk pooling, risk taking and the family", Presented at conference on Women's Human Capital in Low Income Countries, Bellagio, Italy.

Rosenzweig, M.R. and R.E. Evenson (1977), "Fertility, schooling and the economic contribution of children in rural India", Econometrica 45: 1065–1079.

Rosenzweig, M.R. and T.P. Schultz (1982a), "Market opportunities, genetic endowments and intrafamily resource distribution", American Economic Review 74: 215–235.

Rosenzweig, M.R. and T.P. Schultz (1982b), "Determinants of fertility and child mortality in Colombia", Report AID/DSPE-G-0013 (Yale University, New Haven, CT).

Rosenzweig, M.R. and T.P. Schultz (1983), "Consumer demand and household production", American Economic Review 73: 38–42.

Rosenzweig, M.R. and T.P. Schultz (1985), "The demand and supply of births: fertility and its life-cycle consequences", American Economic Review 75: 992–1015.

Rosenzweig, M.R. and T.P. Schultz (1987), "Fertility and investments in human capital", Journal of Econometrics 36: 163–184.

Rosenzweig, M.R. and T.P. Schultz (1988), "The stability of household production technology", Journal of Human Resources 23: 535–549.

Rosenzweig, M.R. and T.P. Schultz (1989), "Schooling, information and nonmarket productivity", International Economic Review 30: 457–477.

Rosenzweig, M.R. and O. Stark (1989), "Consumption, investing, migration and marriage: evidence from rural India", Journal of Political Economy 97: 905–926.

Rosenzweig, M.R. and K.I. Wolpin (1980a), "Testing the quantity–quality fertility model: the use of twins as a natural experiment", Econometrica 48: 227–240.

Rosenzweig, M.R. and K.I. Wolpin (1980b), "Life-cycle labor supply and fertility", Journal of Political Economy 89: 1059–1085.

Rosenzweig, M.R. and K.I. Wolpin (1982), "Governmental interventions and household behavior in a developing country", Journal of Development Economics 10: 209–226.

Rosenzweig, M.R. and K.I. Wolpin (1986), "Evaluating the effects of optimally distributed programs", American Economics Review 76: 470–482.

Rosenzweig, M.R. and K.I. Wolpin (1988), "Migration selectivity and the effects of public programs", Journal of Public Economics 37: 265–289.

Ross, S. (1974), "The effect of economic variables on the timing and space of births", Ph.D. dissertation (Columbia University, New York).

Ross, J.A., M. Rich, J.P. Molzan and M. Pansak (1988), Family planning and child survival (Center for Population and Family Health, Columbia University, New York).

Ryder, N.B. (1969), "The emergence of a modern fertility pattern: U.S. 1917–1966", in: S.J. Behrman et al., eds., Fertility and family planning (University of Michigan Press, Ann Arbor, MI).

Sah, R.K. (1991), "The effects of child mortality on fertility choice and parental welfare", Journal of Political Economy 99: 582–606.

Samuelson, P.A. (1958), "An exact consumption loan model of interest with or without the contrivance of money", Journal of Political Economy 66: 467–482.

Schultz, T.P. (1969), "An economic model of family planning and fertility", Journal of Political Economy 77: 153–180.

Schultz, T.P. (1971), Evaluation of population policies, R-643 (Rand Corporation, Santa Monica, CA).

Schultz, T.P. (1973), "A preliminary survey of economic analyses of fertility", American Economic Review 63: 71–78.

Schultz, T.P. (1974), "Birth rate changes over space and time: a study of Taiwan", in: T.W. Schultz, ed., Economics of the family (University of Chicago Press, Chicago, IL).

Schultz, T.P. (1976a), "Determinants of fertility", in: A.J. Coale, ed., Economic factors in population growth (Macmillan, London).

Schultz, T.P. (1976b), "Interrelationships between mortality and fertility", in: R.G. Ridker, ed., Population and development (Johns Hopkins University Press, Baltimore, MD).

Schultz, T.P. (1980), "An economic interpretation of the decline in fertility in a rapidly developing country", in: R.A. Easterlin, ed., Population and economic change in developing countries (University of Chicago Press, Chicago, IL).

Schultz, T.P. (1981), Economics of population (Addison-Wesley, Reading, MA).

Schultz, T.P. (1984), "Studying the impact of household economic and community variables on child mortality", Population and Development Review (Supplement) 10: 215–235.

Schultz, T.P. (1985), "Changing world prices, women's wages and the fertility transition", Journal of Political Economy 93: 1126–1154.

Schultz, T.P. (1986), "The fertility revolution: a review essay", Population and Development Review 12.

Schultz, T.P. (1988), "Population programs: measuring their impact on fertility" Journal of Policy Modeling 10: 113–149.

Schultz, T.P. (1989), Women and development: objectives, framework, and policy interventions, WPS-200 (World Bank, Washington, DC).

Schultz, T.P. (1990), "Testing the neoclassical model of family labor supply and fertility", Journal of Human Resources 25: 599–634.

Schultz, T.P. (1992), "Assessing family planning cost-effectiveness: applicability of individual demand-program supply framework", in: J.F. Phillips and J.A. Ross, ed., Family planning programmes and fertility (Oxford University Press, New York).

Schultz, T.P. (1993a), "Mortality decline in the low income world: causes and consequences", American Economic Review, Papers and Proceedings, 82: 337–342.

Schultz, T.P. (1993b), "Investments in women's human capital and development", Editor symposium, Journal of Human Resources 28: 690–974.

Schultz, T.P. (1994), "Human capital, family planning and their effects on population growth", American Economic Review 83: 255–260.

Schultz, T.P. and J. DaVanzo (1972), "The decline of fertility and child mortality in Bangladesh", Demography 9: 415–430.

Schultz, T.P. and Y. Zeng (1992), "The association between community and individual characteristics and fertility in rural China", Processed (Economic Growth Center, Yale University, New Haven, CT).

Schultz, T.W., ed. (1974), Economics of the family (University of Chicago Press, Chicago, IL).

Scrimshaw, S.C. (1978), "Infant mortality and behavior in the regulation of family size", Population and Development Review 4: 383–403.

Simon, J.L. (1981), The ultimate resource (Princeton University Press, Princeton, NJ).

Smith, J.P., ed. (1980), Female labor supply (Princeton University Press, Princeton, NJ).

Srinivasan, T.N. (1992), "Sex preference, stopping rules and fertility", Processed (Yale University, New Haven, CT).

Stark, O. (1991), The migration of labor (Basil Blackwell, Cambridge, MA).

Stigler, G.J. and G.S. Becker (1977), "De gustibus non est disputandum", American Economic Review 67: 76–90.

Stolnitz, G.J. (1975), "International mortality trends", in: Population debate (United Nations, New York).

Strauss, J. (1985), "The impact of improved nutrition on labor productivity and human resource development: an economic perspective", in: P. Pinstrup-Anderson, ed., The political economy of food and nutrition policies (Johns Hopkins University Press, Baltimore, MD).

Strauss, J. (1986), "Does better nutrition raise farm productivity?", Journal of Political Economy 94: 297–320.

Stys, U. (1957), "The influence of economic conditions on the fertility of peasant women", Population Studies 11.

Summers, R. and A. Heston (1991), "Expanded set of international comparisons, 1950–1988", Quarterly Journal of Economics 104: 327–368.

Tabbarah, R.B. (1971), "Toward a theory of demographic development", Economic Development and Cultural Change 19: 257–276.

Tarisan, A.C. (1993), Wage and income effects on births in Sweden and the United States, Ekonomiska Studier no. 35 (Goteborg University, Goteborg, Sweden).

Theil, H. (1952/53), "Qualities, prices and budget inquiries", Review of Economic Studies 19: 129–147.

Theil, H. (1954), Linear aggregation of economic relations (North-Holland, Amsterdam).

Thomas, D. (1990), "Intrahousehold resource allocation", Journal of Human Resources 25: 635–664.

Thomas, D. and I. Muvandi (1992), "The demographic transition in Southern Africa", Discussion paper no. 668 (Economic Growth Center, Yale University, New Haven, CT).

Thomas, D. and J. Strauss (1992), "Health, wealth and wages of men and women in urban Brazil", Presented at conference on Women's Human Capital and Development, Bellagio, Italy.

Tobin, J. and H. Houthakker (1950/51), "The effects of rationing on demand elasticities", Review of Economic Studies 18: 140–153.

Trussell, J. (1978), "Menarche and fatness: reexamination of the critical body composition hypothesis", Science 200: 1506–1509.

United Nations (1987), "Fertility behavior in the context of development", Population studies, no. 100 (United Nations, New York).

United Nations (1989), "Levels and trends of contraceptive use", Population studies, no. 110 (United Nations, New York).

United Nations (1991), "World population prospects 1990", Population studies, no. 120 (Department of International Economic and Social Affairs, United Nations, New York).

Westoff, C.F., L. Moreno and N. Goldman (1989), "The demographic impact of changes in contraceptive practice in the Third World", Population and Development Review 15: 91–106.

Willis, R.J. (1974), "Economic theory of fertility behavior", in: T.W. Schultz, ed., The economics of the family (University of Chicago Press, Chicago, IL).

Wold, H.O. (1964), Econometric model buildings: essays on the causal chain approach (North-Holland, Amsterdam).

Wolfe, B.L. and J.R. Behrman (1992), "The synthesis economic fertility model", Journal of Population Economics 5: 1–16.

Wolpin, R.I. (1984), "An estimable dynamic stochastic model of fertility and child mortality", Journal of Political Economy 92: 852–874.

World Bank (1991), "Effective family planning programs" (Population, Health and Human Resources Department, Washington, DC) (Annex: World Bank and Family Planning).

World Bank Staff (various years), World Bank development report (Oxford University Press, New York).

Wu, D.M. (1973), "Alternate tests of independence between stochastic regressors and disturbances", Econometrica 41: 733–750.

Zajonc, R.B. and G.B. Markus (1975), "Birth order and intellectual development", Psychological Review 82: 74–88.

Zeng, Y., T. Ping, G. Baochang, X. Yi, L. Bohua and L. Yongping (1993), "Causes and implications of the recent increase in the reported sex ratio at birth in China", Population and Development Review 19: 283–302.

Zhang, J. (1990), "Socioeconomic determinants of fertility in China", Journal of Population Economics 3: 105–123.

# PART III

# MORTALITY AND HEALTH

Chapter 9

# NEW FINDINGS ON SECULAR TRENDS IN NUTRITION AND MORTALITY: SOME IMPLICATIONS FOR POPULATION THEORY

ROBERT WILLIAM FOGEL*

*University of Chicago*

## Contents

*Originally presented at the Nobel Jubilee Symposium on "Population, Development, and Welfare", Lund University, December 5–7, 1991. This paper draws on materials in Fogel (in progress) and on several papers (Fogel 1986b, 1991, 1992, 1993, 1994; Fogel et al., in progress). I have benefitted from the insights and criticisms of Christopher J. Acito, Dora L. Costa, and John M. Kim.

*Handbook of Population and Family Economics. Edited by M.R. Rosenzweig and O. Stark*
© *Elsevier Science B.V., 1997*

433

## 1. Introduction

The analysis of secular trends in nutrition and mortality presented in this paper stems from the integration of recently developed biomedical techniques with several standard economic techniques. The biomedical techniques include improved approaches to the estimation of survival levels of caloric consumption and of the caloric requirements of various types of labor; epidemiological studies of the connection between stature and the risk of both mortality and chronic diseases; and epidemiological studies of the connection between body mass indexes (BMI) and the risk of mortality. The economic techniques include various methods of characterizing size distributions of income and of calories, as well as methods of relating measures of nutrition to measures of income and productivity. Considerable use is made of Waaler curves and surfaces. Waaler surfaces, which combine iso-mortality curves of relative risk for height and weight with iso-BMI curves (an index of weight for height), appear to be a versatile new analytical device that is widely applicable over time and space.

The discussion that follows is divided into four parts. Section 2 briefly describes the evolution of thought on, and knowledge of, the secular decline in mortality. Section 3 deals with new evidence and new analytical techniques that have made it possible to switch attention from famines to chronic malnutrition as the principal link between the food supply and mortality. Section 4 proposes a new theory of the way that the food supply and population were brought into equilibrium between 1700 and the twentieth century. Section 5 is a brief conclusion which also suggests some implications of the theory for current population issues.

To some scholars population theory has been equated almost exclusively with the economic theory of fertility. This paper attempts to redress the balance by focusing on the problem of mortality. Hence, the implications for population theory that are explored in Sections 3 and 4 are those connected with the theory of mortality, particularly the theory of the secular decline in mortality.

## 2. The evolution of thought on, and knowledge of, the secular decline in mortality

The attempt to explain the secular decline in mortality in a systematic way did not begin until early in the twentieth century because it was uncertain before that time that such a decline was in progress. There were two reasons for the delay in recognizing the phenomenon. First, little was known about mortality rates before 1800. Hardly a dozen life tables had been constructed before 1815 by various pioneers in demography and epidemiology. This assortment of imperfect and generally localized early tables indicated life expectancies varying between 18 and 38 years at birth and exhibited no clear time trend (Dublin and Lotka, 1936: pp. 40–45; Gille, 1949: p. 34). It was the variability of mortality rates without a clear long-term trend that allowed Malthus

(1798) to believe that the periodic mortality crises were created by the pressure of population on food supplies and that once this pressure was relieved by the positive check, mortality rates declined. Such declines were temporary, however, because of the tendency of fertility rates to push population to the limits of the food supply.

Second, there was little evidence in the first four official English tables, covering the years 1831–1880, of a downward trend in mortality. Although signs of improvements in life expectancies became more marked when the fifth and sixth tables were constructed (covering the 1880s and 1890s), there were few epidemiologists or demographers who recognized that England was in the midst of a secular decline in mortality that began about the middle of the eighteenth century and that would more than double life expectancy at birth before the end of the twentieth century. Attention was focused not on the small declines in aggregate mortality, but on the continuing large differentials between urban and rural areas, between low- and high-income districts, and among different nations (Ashby, 1915; Dublin et al., 1949; Mitchison, 1977).

Early in the twentieth century it became obvious that the latest decline in British mortality rates was not just a cyclical phenomenon. During the first two decades of the century, life expectancy in Britain increased by nearly 12 years, more than twice the increase experienced during the previous 60 years. During the next decade life expectancy increased by an additional four years, bringing the gain over the previous century to a full 20 years.

Similar declines in mortality were recorded in the Scandinavian countries, France, Germany, and other European nations. It was clear that the West (including Canada and the United States) had attained a level of survival far beyond previous experience, and far beyond that which prevailed elsewhere in the world (Dublin et al., 1949; United Nations, 1953; Stolnitz, 1955, 1956; Case et al., 1962).

## 2.1. Initial efforts to explain the secular decline in mortality

The plunge in mortality during the early years of the twentieth century delivered a major blow to the Malthusian theory of population. A secular decline of the type that had occurred was not only unanticipated by Malthus, but was precluded by his theory. Improvements in mortality were supposed to be short lived, since the elimination of deaths due to one disease would be replaced by those due to some other malady: That was the proposition that dominated thought throughout most of the nineteenth century. Efforts to reconcile the Malthusian doctrine with the observed mortality decline, to modify it, or to replace it produced a large new literature.

The drive to explain the secular decline in mortality pushed research in three directions. First there was a concerted effort to develop time series of birth and death rates that extended as far back in time as possible, in order to determine just when the decline in mortality began. Second, the available data on mortality rates were analyzed in order to identify factors that might explain the decline as well as to establish patterns or "laws" that would make possible predictions of the future course of mortality. In this connection much attention was paid to data which indicated the rate of decline by specific causes, by gender, by age structure, by place, by household structure, by socioeconomic conditions, and by date of birth.

Third, a widespread effort was undertaken to determine the relationship between the food supply and mortality rates. There were several aspects to this effort. Perhaps the most important was the emergence of a science of nutrition that identified a series of diseases related to specific nutritional deficiencies and that evolved a set of standards for nutritional requirements. A notable milestone in the development of this science was the discovery of a synergy between nutrition and infection (Scrimshaw et al., 1968). Another aspect was the emergence of the field of development economics after World War II as part of the campaign to close the yawning gap in income, health, and life expectancy between the industrialized nations and the nations of the "Third World". Still another aspect was the combined effort of economic and demographic historians to study the role of mortality crises and their relationship to famines during the seventeenth and eighteenth centuries. These studies were aimed at determining to what extent the secular decline in mortality could be attributed to the elimination of these crises and whether their elimination was in turn due to the conquest of the Malthusian positive check by technological advances in agriculture, in urban and rural sanitation, and in medicine.

The work of extending vital statistics backward in time initially focused on abstracts of parish records of baptisms, marriages, and burials that had been collected by governments. In England, such abstracts had been gathered by John Rickman, the director of the first three British censuses. Although parish abstracts were incomplete and uneven in their coverage and fraught with difficulties in transforming baptisms into births and burials into deaths, a number of scholars essayed the task between the two World Wars (Brownlee, 1916; Griffith, 1926; Marshall, 1929; cf. Gonner, 1913 and Glass, 1965). An even better set of parish records existed in the Scandinavian countries, especially Sweden, where the government collection of such records began in 1737. However, in Sweden as well as in the other Scandinavian countries, useful parish records exist as far back as the mid-seventeenth century (Gille, 1949). Despite the difficulty in interpreting and correcting these parish abstracts, alternative procedures were in agreement in revealing that mortality rates began to decline by the third quarter of the eighteenth century in England, Finland, Denmark, and Iceland and by the fourth quarter in Sweden. Before Louis Henry began the task of sampling the French parish records, Duvellard's life table together with data from civil registration (which are reliable from about 1830 on) were the principal indications of a sharp increase in French life expectancy of about ten years (from 28.0 to 38.0 for both sexes combined) between c.1770 and c.1830. However, little was known about periodic fluctuations in French national mortality rates until the results derived from the sample of parish records collected by the Institut National d'Etudes Démographiques (INED) were published (Flinn, 1974; Gille, 1949; Utterstrom, 1965; Bourgeois-Pichat, 1965; Henry, 1965).

As the accumulated research made it clear that a secular decline in mortality rates had been underway, at least in Northwestern Europe since the mid-eighteenth century (the starting date in North America was more uncertain), explanations for that decline began to multiply. Among the most influential were those put forward by Griffith (1926), Thompson and Whelpton (1933), Dublin and Lotka (1936), Carr-Saunders (1964), Peller (1948), Dublin et al. (1949), United Nations (1953, 1973), Stolnitz (1955, 1956) and Dorn (1959). By and large these studies attributed the secular decline in mortality to four categories of advances: (1) public health reforms; (2) advances in medical knowledge and practices; (3) improved personal hygiene; and (4) rising income and standards of living. The 1973 U.N. study added "natural factors", such as the decline in the virulence of pathogens, as an additional explanatory category.

## 2.2. McKeown's challenge to the consensus view

A new phase in the effort to explain the secular decline in mortality was ushered in by Thomas McKeown who, in a series of papers and books published between 1955 and the mid-1980s, challenged the importance of most of the factors that had previously been advanced to explain the decline. An epidemiologist, McKeown first gained prominence for his biomedical research, including his studies of the relationship between birth weight and perinatal mortality rates in Birmingham after World War II (Gibson and McKeown, 1950, 1951; McKeown and Gibson, 1951), before turning his attention to changes in medical practices and demographic rates.

McKeown was highly skeptical of those aspects of the consensus explanation that focused primarily on changes in medical technology and public health reforms. In their place he substituted improved nutrition. McKeown did not make his case for nutrition directly but largely through a residual argument after having rejected the other principal explanations.

Focusing on the British case, McKeown pointed out that between c.1850 and 1971 the standardized death rate attributable to infectious diseases declined from 13.0 per thousand to 0.7 per thousand. About 54% of the decline was associated with airborne diseases, 28% with water- and food-borne diseases, and 18% with diseases spread by other means (McKeown, 1976: pp. 54–63). This simple classification permitted McKeown to assess the probable impact of public health measures and personal sanitation. Cleaning up the public water supply and improving sewage systems, he argued, would have had little effect on the airborne diseases. Moreover, as long as water supplies were polluted, individuals could not protect themselves against such water-borne diseases as typhoid and cholera by washing regularly. Under such circumstances "the washing of hands is about as effective as the wringing of hands" (McKeown,

1978: p. 540). In his view public health measures did not become effective until the very end of the nineteenth century. The sharp declines in food- and water-borne diseases (which he dates in England and Wales with the start of the eighth decade) were not only due to better water and sewage systems but to improvements in food hygiene, especially pasteurization. He attributed the rapid decline of infant mortality between 1900 and 1931 mainly to the development of a "safe milk supply" (McKeown, 1976: p. 122; McKeown, 1978: p. 540). McKeown argued that improvements in personal or public hygiene would not have reduced deaths from airborne diseases unless they reduced crowding, and crowding generally increased during the nineteenth century.

McKeown's skepticism about the efficacy of early medical measures was based on his study of the temporal pattern of decline in the death rates of the most lethal diseases of the nineteenth century. Tuberculosis, the leading killer in England and America during much of the nineteenth century, provided a case in point. During 1848–54 tuberculosis caused nearly one out of every six English deaths from all causes, and one out of every four due to infectious diseases. It was not until 1882 that the tubercle bacillus was identified and an effective chemotherapy for this disease was not developed until 1947. Nevertheless, the death rate of respiratory tuberculosis declined to just 43% of its 1848–54 level by 1900 and to just 10% of that level before the introduction of streptomycin in 1947. Similarly, the major decline in the death rates from bronchitis and pneumonia, whooping cough, measles, scarlet fever, and typhoid all preceded the development of effective chemotherapies. McKeown also doubted the efficacy of the lying-in hospitals which were established during the eighteenth and nineteenth centuries, noting that well into the third quarter of the last century "hospital death rates were many times greater than those for related home deliveries" (McKeown 1976: p. 105).

McKeown was also skeptical of the contention that the decline in mortality rates was due to a decline in the virulence of pathogens. He noted that scarlet fever and influenza fluctuated in their severity in short periods of time and acknowledged that these fluctuations were due to changes in the character of these diseases. He listed typhus as another disease that might have declined due to changes in the pathogens. However, the fraction of the total mortality decline attributable to these three diseases was small. On a more general plane he noted that infectious diseases that are now relatively benign in developed nations are still quite virulent in less developed countries and argued that it is quite unlikely that pathogens would have lost their virulence only in developed countries. McKeown also minimized the impact of natural selection, arguing that in the case of tuberculosis too much of the population had been exposed to the bacillus for too long a period before the decline, and the decline itself was too rapid to be consistent with natural selection.

McKeown's arguments in favor of a nutritional explanation turned on only two items. First, he cited evidence that per capita food supplies in England increased sporadically during the late eighteenth and early nineteenth centuries and then regularly during the late nineteenth and the twentieth centuries. Second, he emphasized findings of medical researchers working in the developing countries who have concluded that there was a synergistic relationship between malnutrition and infection, and that malnutrition significantly increases the likelihood that a victim will succumb to an infection. In this connection he cited a report of the World Health Organization that made malnutrition an associated cause in 57 to 67% of the deaths of children under age five in Latin America (McKeown, 1976: p. 136).

McKeown's work set off an extensive controversy. Although some investigators believed that improvements in nutrition had made a major contribution (Meeker, 1972; Higgs, 1973, 1979; Langer, 1975; Kunitz, 1986), many held that McKeown and others had greatly exaggerated the case (Lee, 1980, 1984; Winter, 1982; Perrenoud, 1984; Fridlizius, 1979, 1984; Livi-Bacci, 1983, 1991). The doubts arose partly because of major gaps in the evidence. Razzell, for example, doubted McKeown's claim that the food supply in England grew more rapidly than the population before 1840. He argued (Razzell, 1974: pp. 6–8) that at least for the eighteenth century the evidence is "much more consistent with a reversed hypothesis – that the standard of the diet was a function of a population change". The absence of a significant gap between the mortality rates of the peerage and the laboring classes in England before 1725 was particularly vexing. "If the food supply was the critical variable", Razzell wrote, mortality reductions should have been "concentrated almost exclusively amongst the poorer" classes and the mortality rates of the aristocracy should have been "unaffected". Yet between the fourth quarter of the sixteenth century and the beginning of the second quarter of the eighteenth century, the mortality rates of the aristocracy were about as high as those of the general population. Both the high mortality rates of the nobility before 1725 and the rapid fall in these rates thereafter, although there was no apparent change in the diet of the peerage, predisposed Razzell "to look at the food supply hypothesis very critically".[1]

Efforts to relate both short- and long-term variations in the mortality rates to variations in bread or wheat prices also undermined the nutritional explanation. Appleby's (1975) regressions, which related London deaths from specific diseases to bread prices over the period from 1550 to 1750, led him to conclude that there was no correlation between the supply of food and deaths due to plague, smallpox, or tuberculosis and only slight correlations between bread prices and deaths due to typhus and "ague and fever". More sophisticated analysis by Lee (1981) revealed statistically significant but usually weak relationships between short-term variations in death rates and in wheat prices. According to Schofield (1983: p. 282) short-run variations in English mortality were "overwhelmingly determined" by factors other than the food supply and the long-run trend in mortality was unaffected by the trend in food prices (cf. Walter and Schofield, 1989).

Lindert's (1983) examination of the work of Lee, Wrigley, and Schofield confirmed their conclusions on the absence of a notable relationship between food prices and

---

[1] For a suggested resolution to the peerage paradox see Fogel (1986b).

mortality rates. Nevertheless, he was discontented with results that implied that living standards "left little or no mark on mortality". The puzzle, he acknowledged, extended to his own work with Williamson, since they have not yet been able to "find a firm causal link behind the obvious correlation between income and life expectancy after 1820". He suggested that the resolution to "the mystery of independent mortality" trends might require more complex attacks on the issue. That would be the case if the "life-extending" effect of income "was hidden behind the shift toward earlier death in the growing unhealthy cities". He also suggested that diets may "have improved in ways unmeasured by income" (pp. 147–148).

Other investigators have found evidence suggesting that McKeown underestimated the impact of public health measures on the decline in mortality. Estimates of the cause of mortality rates in the three largest urban areas of France during the nineteenth century by Preston and van de Walle (1978) led them to the conclusion that water and sewage improvements played a major role in the urban mortality decline. Not only were the declines concentrated in the waterborne diseases but the rate of decline was much more rapid in the two cities that introduced vigorous sewage and pure water programs than in the one that did not. On the other hand, deaths due to tuberculosis did not decline in Paris over a 33-year period, although deaths due to other airborne diseases showed small declines. Even these declines could have been due to the clean up of the water supply.

Preston and van de Walle stressed that diarrheal and other waterborne diseases have important nutritional consequences because they "reduce appetite, reduce the absorption of essential nutrients, increase metabolic demands and often lead to dietary restrictions" (p. 218). Thus, cleaning up the water systems not only reduced deaths caused by waterborne diseases but also contributed to the reduction in deaths due to airborne diseases because the reduction in waterborne diseases improved the nutritional status of the population, especially of infants and young children. The last point was particularly important since it called attention to the need to distinguish between diet (gross nutrition) and nutritional status (net nutrition), which represents the nutrient residual available to support cellular growth after all prior claims on the nutrient intake (diet) have been satisfied.

### 2.3. Crisis mortality and famines

During the mid-1980s the debate over the McKeown thesis was overtaken by the debate over mortality crises. The systematic study of mortality crises and their possible link to famines was initiated by Meuvret in 1946. Such work was carried forward in France and numerous other countries on the basis of local studies that made extensive use of parish records. This line of research was greatly accelerated by Goubert's 1960 study of Beauvais (cf. Goubert, 1965).

By the early 1970s several scores of such studies had been published covering the period from the seventeenth through the early nineteenth centuries in England, France,

Germany, Switzerland, Spain, Italy, and the Scandinavian countries (Smith, 1977; Flinn, 1981). The accumulation of local studies provided the foundation for the view that mortality crises accounted for a large part of total mortality during the early modern era, and that the decline in mortality rates between the mid-eighteenth and mid-nineteenth centuries was explained largely by the elimination of these crises. It was recognized that in communities as small as parishes, random factors made the variance around the trend in mortality high. To guard against treating random fluctuations in deaths as mortality crises, it was commonly assumed that only a 50% increase above the trend qualified to be treated as a mortality crisis. Even with this limitation many parishes appeared to have had frequent mortality crises, and parishes which averaged a crisis every five to ten years were not uncommon (Flinn, 1981: pp. 15–16, 48–49, 63, 94).

As a result of the cumulative impact of these local studies a consensus emerged among social and economic historians regarding the causes of the decline in the high European death rates that prevailed at the beginning of the early modern era. By the early 1970s it was widely agreed that the high average mortality rates of the years preceding the vital revolution were due to periodic mortality crises which raised "normal" mortality rates by 50–100% or more. It was the elimination of these peaks rather than the lowering of the plateau of mortality in "normal" years that was principally responsible for the much lower mortality rates that prevailed at the end of the nineteenth century (Helleiner, 1967: p. 85; Wrigley, 1969: p. 165; Flinn, 1970: p. 45; cf. Helleiner, 1965). These crises, it was held, were precipitated either by acute harvest failures or by epidemics (Flinn, 1970: p. 45). Some scholars argued that even if the diseases were not nutritionally sensitive, famines played a major role because epidemics were spread by the beggars who swarmed from one place to another in search of food (Meuvret, 1965: pp. 510–511). Whatever the differences on this issue, it was widely agreed that many of the mortality crises were due to starvation brought on by harvest failure (Wrigley, 1969: pp. 66, 165–169; Flinn, 1970: pp. 45–48; Flinn, 1974).

A mechanism by which a harvest failure was transformed into a mortality crisis was proposed by Hoskins in two influential papers published in the 1960s (Hoskins, 1964, 1968). Noting that it was possible to identify harvest failures by looking at the deviations in grain prices from their normal level, Hoskins computed the annual deviations of wheat prices from a 31-year moving average of these prices. Normal harvests were defined as those with prices that were within plus or minus 10% of the trend. He found that over the 280 years from 1480 to 1759 good harvests (prices 10% or more below trends) were about 50% more frequent than deficient harvests (prices 10% or more above trend). His most important finding, however, was that good and bad harvests (as shown by prices) ran in sequences, so there were frequently three or four bad years in a row. These sequences, he argued, were not due primarily to weather cycles but to the low yield-to-seed ratios, which he put at about four or five for wheat at the beginning of the sixteenth century. Thus, one bad harvest tended to generate another because starving farmers consumed their reserve for seeds. The consequence of several bad harvests in a row was a mortality crisis.

The wide consensus did not mean that all the investigators accepted the view that crisis mortality was the main source of the high mortality rates of the seventeenth and eighteenth centuries or that famines were the source of the crises. Some scholars pointed out that there were often mortality crises even when grain prices were normal and that there were also episodes of very high grain prices that did not result in mortality crises. Flinn called attention to a major problem with the attempt to use local studies to estimate the contribution of mortality crises to the national level of mortality: Such studies did not take adequate account of the spatial dimension. Studies of areas wider than parishes, he pointed out, would involve the "averaging of more severely affected areas with less severely affected ones" (Flinn, 1981: p. 49). Nevertheless, down to the late 1970s, such caveats were largely put aside. It was only after the publication of death rates based on large representative samples of parishes for England and France that it became possible to assess the national impact of crisis mortality on total national mortality. Although the English series extends back to 1541, the French series published by INED currently extends back only to 1740 (INED, 1977; Wrigley and Schofield, 1981). However, Rebaudo (1979) and Dupâquier (1989) have recently drawn together some samples which, though smaller than the INED samples for the years after 1740, make it possible to compare England and France over the period 1675–1725.

These series confirm one of the important conclusions derived from the local studies: Mortality was far more variable before 1750 than afterward. The standard deviation of the proportionate deviations of mortality around trend declined by nearly two-thirds in England between the second half of the sixteenth century and the second half of the eighteenth century. In the French case the decline in variability was of the same magnitude, except that rate of decline was much steeper, since it occurred in less than a century.[2]

Despite the strong correlation between the decline in the variability of mortality rates and the decline in the average level of mortality, the elimination of crisis mortality made only a small contribution to the secular decline in mortality rates. Fig. 1 and Table 1 show that even during the two centuries between 1550 and 1750, which accounted for all but 12 of the 45 crisis years identified by Wrigley and Schofield (1981: p. 334), crisis mortality accounted for less than 6% of total English mortality. When crisis mortality is expressed not as a percentage of total contemporary mortality but of premature mortality (the average cdr of the period minus the death rate in 1980 standardized on the age structure of 1701–1705), the figure rises to 6.7%. In no half century after 1750 did crisis mortality account for as much as 2% of the total mortality. Even after crisis mortality is factored out, the "normal" mortality remains above 25

---

[2] See Fogel et al. (in progress) for a comparison of the English and French rates of decline in the standard deviation of deviations from trend between 1553 and 1975.

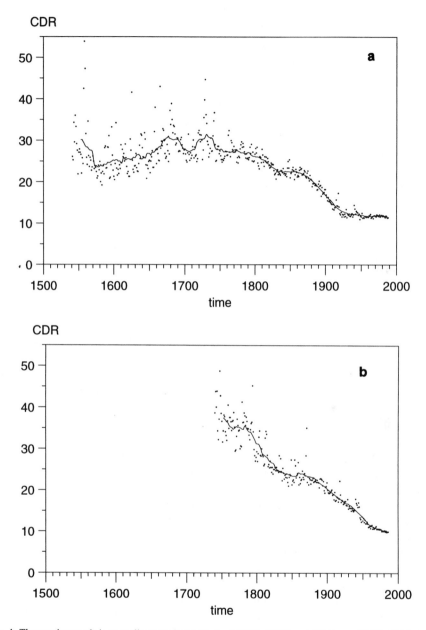

Fig. 1. The secular trends in mortality rates in (a) England (1553–1975) and (b) France (1752–1974). Each diagram shows the scatter of annual death rates around a 25-year moving average. See Fogel et al. (in progress) for sources and procedures.

Table 1
The impact of crisis mortality on the average crude death rate[a]

| Period | 1<br>Crude death rate per thousand person years | 2<br>Crisis mortality per thousand person years | 3<br>Crude death rate after factoring out crisis mortality (per thousand) | 4<br>Crisis mortality as percentage of average mortality | 5<br>Crisis mortality as percentage of "premature" mortality |
|---|---|---|---|---|---|
| *A: England, 1553–1975* | | | | | |
| 1. 1553–1750 | 27.56 | 1.38 | 26.18 | 5.00 | 6.70 |
| 2. 1751–1800 | 27.04 | 0.24 | 26.79 | 0.90 | 1.21 |
| 3. 1801–1850 | 23.90 | 0.11 | 23.79 | 0.45 | 0.63 |
| 4. 1851–1900 | 20.69 | 0.00 | 20.69 | 0.00 | 0.00 |
| 5. 1901–1950 | 13.28 | 0.18 | 13.10 | 1.36 | 2.87 |
| 6. 1951–1975 | 11.71 | 0.00 | 11.71 | 0.00 | 0.00 |
| | | | | | |
| *B: France, 1676–1975* | | | | | |
| 1. 1676–1725 | n.a. | n.a. | n.a. | 12.50 | n.a. |
| 2. 1752–1800 | 34.87 | 0.54 | 34.33 | 1.55 | 1.84 |
| 3. 1801–1850 | 26.19 | 0.61 | 25.58 | 2.33 | 2.95 |
| 4. 1851–1900 | 22.98 | 0.51 | 22.47 | 2.22 | 2.90 |
| 5. 1901–1950 | 17.10 | 0.30 | 16.80 | 1.75 | 2.54 |
| 6. 1951–1974 | 11.38 | 0.00 | 11.38 | 0.00 | 0.00 |

[a]See Fogel (1992) for the sources and methods of computation. In the English case "premature" mortality is defined as the crude death rate of a given period minus the English death rate of 1980 standardized on the English age structure of 1701–1705. In the French case the death rates of 1980 are standardized on the French age structure of 1806.

per thousand for the sixteenth, seventeenth, and eighteenth centuries. Indeed, the "normal" mortality rate of the eighteenth century (not shown in Table 1) was as high as the total mortality rate of each of the two preceding centuries, despite their many crises (see Fogel, 1992). Consequently, the escape from high mortality rates was not due primarily to the elimination of crises, but to the reduction in so-called normal mortality levels. More than 98% of the decline in mortality between the last half of the eighteenth century and the third quarter of the twentieth century was due to the reduction of "normal" mortality. If the comparison is shifted to the last half of the eighteenth century and the last half of the nineteenth century, declines in "normal" mortality account for 96% of the decline in the crude death rate.

It follows that even if every national mortality crisis identified by Wrigley and Schofield was the result of a famine, the elimination of periodic famines cannot be the principal explanation for the secular decline in mortality. This is not to deny that famines in particular localities at particular times produced great increases in local mortality rates. Too much evidence of local disasters induced by food shortages has accumulated to rule out such phenomenon. However, in light of the Wrigley and

Schofield data it now seems clear that, dramatic as they were, mortality crises, whether caused by famines or not, were too scattered in time and space to have been the principal factor in the English secular decline in mortality after 1540.

Crisis mortality played a more important role in France than in England, not only in the seventeenth and eighteenth centuries but also during the nineteenth century. Both the amplitude and the frequency of demographic crises (defined as deviations of death rates at least 10% above the moving average) were greater during 1676–1725 than afterwards. It is also true that the share of the average death rate due to crisis mortality was larger in France than in England, not only during 1676–1725 but through the end of the nineteenth century. Furthermore, as Weir's analysis (1989) indicates, French mortality crises during 1676–1725 were more closely linked to deviations in grain prices than they were in England during the same period.

Nevertheless, the principal reason for the decline in the French mortality rates of the eighteenth century was not the decline in crisis mortality, but in normal mortality. Despite the fact that French crude death rates during the last half of the eighteenth century were about 29% higher than the corresponding English rates, the differences in crisis mortality account for less than a twentieth of the average differential in the cdr's (cf. Dupâquier, 1989). Moreover, as in the English case, more than 97% of the decline in the cdr between the last half of the eighteenth century and the third quarter of the twentieth century was due to the decline in "normal" mortality.[3]

## 3. Measuring the extent and significance of chronic malnutrition

In discussing the factors that kept mortality rates high during the seventeenth and eighteenth centuries, the authors of the 1973 UN study of population noted that "although chronic food shortage has probably been more deadly to man, the effects of famines, being more spectacular, have received greater attention in the literature" (United Nations, 1973: p. 142). Similar points were made by LeBrun (1971) and Flinn (1974, 1981). But it was not until the publication of the INED data for France in 1975 (Blayo, 1975) and the Wrigley and Schofield data for England, that the limited influence of famines on mortality became apparent. In chapter 9 of the Wrigley and Schofield volume, Lee (1981) demonstrated that although there was a statistically significant lagged relationship between large proportionate deviations in grain prices and similar deviations in mortality, the net effect on mortality after five years was usually negligible. Similar results were obtained by studies of France (Weir, 1982, 1989; Richards, 1984; Galloway, 1986) and Sweden (Bengtsson and Ohlsson, 1984, 1985; Galloway, 1987; cf. Eckstein et al., 1985 and Walter and Schofield, 1989).

---

[3] Among the early doubters that famines accounted for a large share of mortality rates are Laslett (1965), Habakkuk (1974), and Flinn (1974).

By demonstrating that famines and famine mortality are a secondary issue in the escape from the high aggregate mortality of the early modern era, these studies have indirectly pushed to the top of research agendas the issue of chronic malnutrition and its relationship to the secular decline in mortality. It is clear that the new questions cannot be addressed by relating annual deviations of mortality (around trend) to annual deviations of supplies of food (from their trend). What is now at issue is how the trend in malnutrition might be related to the trend in mortality and how to identify the factors that determined each of these secular trends.

The new problems require new data and new analytical procedures. In this connection one must come to grips with the thorny issue of the distinction between diet (which represents gross nutrition) and nutritional status (which represents net nutrition: the nutrients available to sustain physical development). We do not dwell on this distinction here (see Fogel, 1986b) but only emphasize that for gross nutrition the term diet is used, and that such other terms as "malnutrition", "undernutrition", "net nutrition", and "nutritional status" are meant to designate the balance between the nutrient intake (diet) and the claims on that intake.

Malnutrition can be caused either by an inadequate diet or by claims on that diet (including work and disease) so great as to produce widespread malnutrition despite a nutrient intake that in other circumstances might be deemed adequate. There can be little doubt that the high disease rates prevalent during the early modern era would have caused malnutrition even with extraordinary diets, that is with diets high in calories, proteins and most other critical nutrients. The United States during 1820–1880 is a case in point.[4] However, recent research into agricultural output indicates that for many European nations prior to the middle of the nineteenth century, the national production of food was at such low levels that the lower classes were bound to have been malnourished under any conceivable circumstance, and that the high disease rates of the period were not merely a cause of malnutrition but undoubtedly, to a considerable degree, a consequence of exceedingly poor diets.

### 3.1. Energy cost accounting

In developed countries today, and even more so in the less developed nations of both the past and the present, the basal metabolic rate (BMR) is the principal component of the total energy requirement. The BMR, which varies with age, sex, and body weight is the amount of energy required to maintain the body while at rest: it is the amount of energy required to maintain body temperature and to sustain the functioning of the heart, liver, brain, and other organs. For adult males age 20–39 living in moderate climates, BMR normally ranges between 1350 and 2000 kcal per day depending on

---

[4] For an elaboration of the American experience see Fogel (1991) and the sources cited there.

height and weight (Quenouille et al., 1951; Davidson et al., 1979: pp. 19–25; FAO/
WHO/UNU 1985: pp. 71–72) and for reasonably well-fed persons normally represents
somewhere in the range of 45–65% of total calorie requirements (FAO/WHO/UNU,
1985, pp. 71–77). Since the BMR does not allow for the energy required to eat and
digest food, or for essential hygiene, an individual cannot survive on the calories
needed for basal metabolism. The energy required for these additional essential activities over a period of 24 h is estimated at 0.27 of BMR or 0.4 of BMR during wak-
ing hours. In other words, a survival diet is 1.27 BMR. Such a diet, it should be emphasized, contains no allowance for the energy required to earn a living, prepare food,
or any movements beyond those connected with eating and essential hygiene. It is not
sufficient to maintain long-term health but represents the short-term maintenance level
"of totally inactive dependent people" (FAO/WHO/UNU, 1985: p. 73).

Energy requirements beyond maintenance depend primarily on how individuals
spend their time beyond sleeping, eating, and essential hygiene. This residual time will
normally be divided between work and such discretionary activities as walking, community activities, games, optional household tasks, and athletics or other forms of
exercise. For a typical well-fed adult male engaged in heavy work, BMR and maintenance require about 60% of energy consumption, work 39%, and discretionary activity just 1%. For a well-fed adult male engaged in sedentary work (such as an office
clerk), a typical distribution would be: BMR and maintenance 83%, work 5%, discretionary activity 13%. For a 25-year-old adult male engaged in subsistence farming in
contemporary Asia, a typical distribution would be: BMR and maintenance 71%,
work 21%, and discretionary activity 8%. Similar distributions of energy requirements
have been developed for women as well as for children and adolescents of both sexes.
In addition, the energy requirements of a large number of specific activities (expressed
as a multiple of the BMR requirement per minute of an activity) have been worked out
(see Table 2 for some examples). In order to standardize for the age and sex distribution of a population, it is convenient to convert the per capita consumption of calories
into consumption per equivalent adult male aged 20–39 (which is referred to as a consuming unit).

Historical estimates of mean caloric consumption per capita have been derived
from several principal sources: national food balance sheets; household consumption
surveys; food allotments in hospitals, poor houses, prisons, the armed forces and other
lower-class institutions; food entitlements to widows in wills; and food allotments in
noble households, abbeys and similar wealthy institutions. National food balance
sheets estimate the national supply of food by subtracting from the national annual
production of each crop, allowances for seed and feed, losses in processing, changes
in inventories, and net exports (positive or negative) to obtain a residual of grains and
vegetables available for consumption. In the case of meats the estimates begin with
the stock of livestock, which is turned into an annual flow of meat by using estimates
of the annual slaughter ratio and live weight of each type of livestock. To estimate the
meat available for consumption it is necessary to estimate the ratio of dressed to live

Table 2

Examples of the energy requirements of common activities expressed as a multiple of the basal metabolic rate (BMR) for males and females[a]

| Activity | Males | Females |
|---|---|---|
| Sleeping | 1.0 | 1.0 (i.e. BMR × 1.0) |
| Standing quietly | 1.4 | 1.5 |
| Strolling | 2.5 | 2.4 |
| Walking at normal pace | 3.2 | 3.4 |
| Walking with 10-kg load | 3.5 | 4.0 |
| Walking uphill at normal pace | 5.7 | 4.6 |
| Sitting and sewing | 1.5 | 1.4 |
| Sitting and sharpening machete | 2.2 | – |
| Cooking | 1.8 | 1.8 |
| Tailoring | 2.5 | – |
| Carpentry | 3.5 | – |
| Common labor in building trade | 5.2 | – |
| Milking cows by hand | 2.9 | – |
| Hoeing | – | 5.3–7.5 |
| Collecting and spreading manure | 6.4 | – |
| Binding sheaves | 5.4–7.5 | 3.3–5.4 |
| Uprooting sweet potatoes | 3.5 | 3.1 |
| Weeding | 2.5–5.0 | 2.9 |
| Ploughing | 4.6–6.8 | – |
| Cleaning house | – | 2.2 |
| Child care | – | 2.2 |
| Threshing | – | 4.2 |
| Cutting grass with machete | – | 5.0 |
| Laundry work | – | 3.4 |
| Felling trees | 7.5 | – |

[a]Sources are FAO/WHO (1985: pp. 76–78, 186–191); Durnin and Passmore (1967: pp. 31, 66, 67, 72). Rates in Durnin and Passmore (1967) given in kcal/min were converted into multiples of BMR, using kcal per min of a 65 kg man and a 55 kg women of average build.

or carcass weight, as well as the distribution of dressed weight among lean meat, fat, and bones (Fogel and Engerman, 1974: II, pp. 91–99, 1992).

Household surveys are based upon interviews with families who are asked to recall their diets for a period as short as one day (the previous day) or their average diet over a period of a week, a month, a year, or an undefined period designated by their "normal diet". In recent times, such surveys may be based on a daily record of the food consumed, which is kept either by a member of the family or by a professional investigator. Institutional food allowances are based on food allotments for each class of individuals laid down as a guide for provisions purchased by the institution (as in the case of victualling allowances for military organizations and daily diet schedules adopted in abbeys, noble households, schools, workhouses, hospitals, and prisons) as well as descriptions of meals actually served and actual purchases of food for given numbers of individuals over particular time periods (Oddy, 1970; Appleby, 1979; Morell, 1983; Dyer, 1983). Food entitlements of widows and aged parents were specified in wills and contracts for maintenance between parents and children or other heirs (in anticipation of the surrender of a customary holding to an heir). Such food entitlements have been analyzed for England, France, the United States and other countries at intermittent dates between the thirteenth century and the present (Bernard, 1975; Dyer, 1983; McMahon, 1981; for studies of other countries see Hémardinquer, 1970; Fogel, 1986a).

*3.2. Estimating the levels and distributions of caloric consumption in Britain and France near the end of the Ancien Régime*

Due to the work of Toutain (1971) we have a series of estimates of average caloric consumption for France that extend back to c.1785. His estimates, which are derived from national food balance sheets, imply that the average caloric consumption in France on the eve of the French Revolution was about 1753 kcal per capita or about 2290 kcal per consuming unit. This is a very low level of energy consumption, ranking France c.1785 with such impoverished countries today as Pakistan and Rwanda (World Bank, 1987). Grantham (1993), who assembled an array of estimates made by knowledgeable contemporaries near the end of the Ancien Régime, concluded that French per capita consumption of food was the nutritional equivalent of about 3.5 hectoliters of wheat per year, which implies about 1869 kcal per day per capita, a result that tends to lend credence to Toutain's estimate for c.1785.

Work on the English caloric consumption has lagged behind that of France. Oddy (1990) and Shammas (1990), using the budgets of rural households collected by Davies for c.1790 and Eden for c.1794 (Stigler, 1954) have estimated that the mean daily caloric consumption was in the neighborhood of 2100 kcal per capita. Standardizing for age and gender and allowing for the place of these rural households in the English size distribution of income developed by Lindert and Williamson (1982; cf. Fogel, 1993) for the mid-eighteenth century, implies a national average daily caloric consumption of about 2700 kcal per consuming unit.

Recent work by agricultural historians summarized by Holderness (1989) and Allen (1994) has yielded estimates of English agricultural output at half century intervals between 1700 and 1850. The procedures used to convert these estimates into a national food balance sheet are described in Fogel et al. (in progress). Since work on the refinement of these procedures is still in progress, the estimates of average daily caloric consumption presented here are provisional and are only rough indicators of the possible course of consumption. They should be treated as illustrative, suggesting the orders of magnitude that are involved and posing provisional hypotheses aimed at stimulating future research. These estimates are as follows:

|      | kcal per capita | kcal per consuming unit |
|------|-----------------|-------------------------|
| 1700 | 2095            | 2724                    |
| 1750 | 2168            | 2816                    |
| 1800 | 2237            | 2933                    |
| 1850 | 2362            | 3076                    |

If we interpolate this series geometrically, the estimate of kcal per consuming unit in 1790 is 2909, which is about 200 kcal more than the figure obtained from the household studies.

While national food balance sheets, such as those constructed by Toutain (1971) for France over the period 1781–1952, provide mean values of per capita caloric consumption, they do not produce estimates of the size distribution of calories. However, it is necessary to estimate size distribution in order to assess the implications of a given average level of caloric consumption for morbidity and mortality rates. Size distributions are also effective tools in assessing whether particular estimates of mean caloric consumption are tenable. It is, in principle, possible to construct size distributions of calories from household consumption surveys. However, most of these surveys during the nineteenth century were focused on the lower classes. Hence, in order to make use of these surveys it is necessary to know to which centiles of either the national caloric or the national income distribution the surveyed households belong (cf. Fogel, 1987).

Three factors make it possible to estimate the size distributions of calories from the patchy evidence available to historians. First, studies covering a wide range of countries indicate that distributions of calories are well described by the log normal distribution. Second, the variation in the distribution of calories (as measured by the coefficient of variation [$s/\overline{X}$] or the Gini [$G$] ratio) is far more limited than the distribution of income. In contradistinction to income, the bottom tail of the caloric distribution is sharply restricted by the requirement for basal metabolism and the prevailing death rate. At the top end it is restricted by the human capacity to use energy and the distribution of body builds. Consequently, the extent of the inequality of caloric distributions is pretty well bound by $0.4 \geq (s/\overline{X}) \geq 0.2$ ($0.22 \geq G \geq 0.11$) (FAO 1977; US Nat. Cent. Health Stat., 1977; Lipton, 1983; Aitchison and Brown, 1966).

Third, when the mean of the distribution is known, the coefficient of variation (which together with the mean determines the distribution) can be estimated from information in either of the tails of the distribution. Fortunately, even in places and periods where little is known about ordinary people, there is a relative abundance of information about the rich. Although much remains to be learned about the ultra poor, much has already been learned about them during the past quarter century and such information is also helpful in resolving the identification problems. However, at the bottom end, it is demographic information, particularly the death rate, which rather tightly constrains the proportion of the population whose average daily

Table 3
A comparison of the probable French and English distributions of the daily consumption of
kcal per consuming unit toward the end of the eighteenth century

| Decile | A France c.1785 $\bar{X} = 2290$ $(s/\bar{X}) = 0.3$ | | B England c.1790 $\bar{X} = 2700$ $(s/\bar{X}) = 0.3$ | |
|---|---|---|---|---|
| | Daily kcal consumption | Cumulative % | Daily kcal consumption | Cumulative % |
| (1) | (2) | (3) | (4) | (5) |
| 1. Highest | 3672 | 100 | 4329 | 100 |
| 2. Ninth | 2981 | 84 | 3514 | 84 |
| 3. Eighth | 2676 | 71 | 3155 | 71 |
| 4. Seventh | 2457 | 59 | 2897 | 59 |
| 5. Sixth | 2276 | 48 | 2684 | 48 |
| 6. Fifth | 2114 | 38 | 2492 | 38 |
| 7. Fourth | 1958 | 29 | 2309 | 29 |
| 8. Third | 1798 | 21 | 2120 | 21 |
| 9. Second | 1614 | 13 | 1903 | 13 |
| 10. First | 1310 | 6 | 1545 | 6 |

*Sources and procedures*: See Fogel (1987), especially Tables 4 and 5 and note 6.


consumption of calories could have been below BMR or the baseline maintenance requirement.

Table 3 displays the caloric distribution for England and France implied by the available evidence. Several points about these distributions that lend support to Toutain's estimate for the French and the estimates derived for the English from the budget studies are worth noting. First, the average levels are not out of keeping with recent experiences in the less developed nations. Low as it is, Toutain's estimate of the French supply of calories is above the average supply of calories in 1965 estimated for such nations as Pakistan, Rwanda, and Algeria, and only slightly less (39 calories) than that of Indonesia. The English estimate is above that for 30 less developed nations in 1965, including China, Bolivia, the Philippines, and Honduras, and only slightly below (37 calories) India (World Bank, 1987).

Second, the distributional implications of the two estimates are consistent with both qualitative and quantitative descriptions of the diets of various social classes (Cole and Postgate, 1938; Drummond and Wilbraham, 1958; Pullar, 1970; Rose, 1971; Tilly, 1971, 1975; Goubert, 1973; Wilson, 1973; Hufton, 1974, 1983; Blum, 1978; Burnett, 1979; Frijhoff and Julia, 1979; Mennell, 1985). For example, Bernard's study (1975) of marriage contracts made in the Gévaudan during the third quarter of the eighteenth century revealed that the average ration provided for parents in complete pensions contained about 1674 calories. Since the average age of a male parent at the marriage of his first surviving child was about 59, the preceding figure implies a diet of about 2,146 calories per consuming unit (Fogel, 1987). That figure falls at the 47th centile of the estimated French distribution (Table 3, distribution A), which is consistent with the class of peasants described by Bernard.

The two estimates are also consistent with the death rates of each nation. The crude death rate in France c.1790 was about 36.1 per thousand while the figure for England c.1790 was about 26.7 (Weir, 1984; Wrigley and Schofield, 1981). It is plausible that much of the difference was due to the larger proportion of French than English who were literally starving (Scrimshaw, 1987). The French distribution of calories implies that 2.48% of the population had caloric consumption below basal metabolism (the minimum energy required for the functioning of the body). Table 3 implies that proportion of the English below basal metabolism was 0.66%. If a quarter of these starving individuals died each year (see Fogel, 1987), they would account for about a fifth (6.6 per 1000) of the French crude death rate, but only about a sixteenth of the English rate (1.7 per 1000) and for about half of the gap between the crude death rates of the two nations.

What, then, are the principal provisional findings about caloric consumption at the end of the eighteenth century in France and England? One is the exceedingly low level of food production, especially in France, at the start of the Industrial Revolution. Another is the exceeding low level of work capacity permitted by the food supply, even after allowing for the reduced requirements for maintenance because of small stature and reduced body mass (cf. Freudenberger and Cummins, 1976). In France the bottom 10% of the labor force lacked the energy for regular work and the next 10% had enough energy for less than 3 h of light work daily (0.52 h of heavy work). Although the English situation was somewhat better, the bottom 3% of its labor force lacked the energy for any work, but the balance of the bottom 20% had enough energy for about 6 h of light work (1.09 h of heavy work) each day.

*3.3. The implications of stature and body mass indexes for the explanation of secular trends in morbidity and mortality*

The available data on stature and on body mass tend to confirm the basic results of the analysis based on energy cost accounting: chronic malnutrition was widespread in Europe during the eighteenth and nineteenth centuries. Recent advances in biomedical knowledge make it possible to use anthropometric data for the eighteenth and nineteenth centuries to study secular trends in European nutrition, health, and risks of mortality. Extensive clinical and epidemiological studies over the past two decades have shown that height at given ages, weight at given ages, and weight-for-height (a body mass index) are effective predictors of the risk of morbidity and mortality (see the summaries in Osmani (1992), Fogel (1993); cf. Heywood (1983), Waaler (1984), Martorell (1985)).

Height and body mass indexes measure different aspects of malnutrition and health. Height is a net rather than a gross measure of nutrition. Moreover, although changes in height during the growing years are sensitive to current levels of nutrition, mean final height reflects the accumulated past nutritional experience of individuals over all of their growing years including the fetal period. Thus, it follows that when final heights are used to explain differences in adult mortality rates, they reveal the effect, not of adult levels of nutrition on adult mortality rates, but of nutritional levels during infancy, childhood, and adolescence on adult mortality rates. A weight-for-height index, on the other hand, reflects primarily the current nutritional status. It is also a net measure in the sense that a body mass index (BMI) reflects the balance between intakes and the claims on those intakes. The most widely used body mass index is weight measured in kilograms divided by height measured in meters squared (kg/m²), which is sometimes called the Quetelet index. Although height is determined by the cumulative nutritional status during an entire developmental age span, the BMI fluctuates with the current balance between nutrient intakes and energy demands. A person whose height is short relative to the modern US or West European standard is referred to as "stunted". Those with low BMIs are referred to as "wasted".

The predictive power of height and body mass indexes with respect to morbidity and mortality are indicated by Figs. 2 and 3. Fig. 2A reproduces a diagram by Waaler (1984). It shows that short Norwegian men aged 40–59 at risk between 1963 and 1979 were much more likely to die than tall men. Indeed, the risk of mortality for men with heights of 165 cm (65.0 inches) was on average 71% greater than that of men who measure 182.5 cm (71.9 inches). Fig. 2B shows that height is also an important predictor of the relative likelihood that men aged 23–49 would be rejected from the Union Army during 1861–1865 because of chronic diseases. Despite significant differences in mean heights, ethnicities, environmental circumstances, the array and severity of diseases, and time, the functional relationship between height and relative risk are strikingly similar. Both the Norwegian curve and the US all-causes curve have relative risks that reach a minimum of between 0.6 and 0.7 at a height of about 187.5 cm. Both reach a relative risk of about 2 at about 152.5 cm. The similarity of the two risk curves in Fig. 2, despite the differences in conditions and attendant circumstances, suggests that the relative risk of morbidity and mortality depends not on the deviation of height from the current mean, but from an ideal mean: the mean associated with full genetic potential.[5]

Waaler (1984) has also studied the relationship in Norway between BMI and the risk of death in a sample of 1.8 million individuals. Curves summarizing his findings are shown in Fig. 3 for both men and women. Although the observed values of the

---

[5] For a further discussion of this possibility see Fogel (1987, 1994). It is important to keep in mind that the denominators of the relative risk curves in both parts of Fig. 2 are the average mortality or morbidity rate computed over all heights. Consequently, the curves shown here will not necessarily shift merely because of a change in the overall crude death rate or the corresponding morbidity rate.

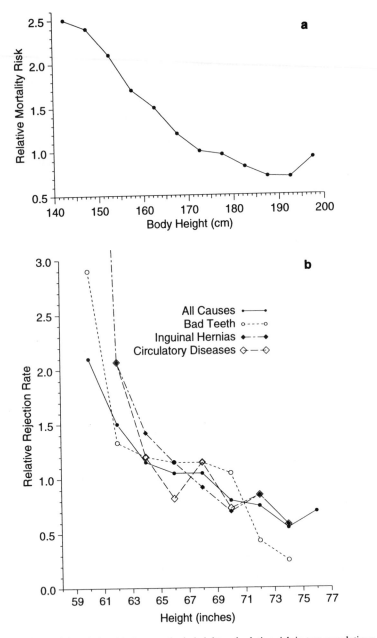

Fig. 2. Comparison of the relationship between body height and relative risk in two populations. (a) Relative mortality risk among Norwegian men aged 40–59, between 1963 and 1979. (b) Relative rejection rates for chronic conditions in a sample of 4245 men aged 23–49, examined for the Union Army.

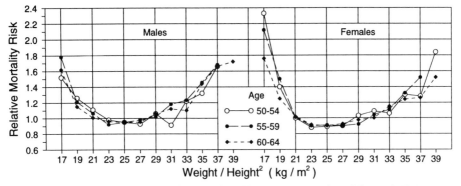

Fig. 3. Relationship between BMI and prospective risk among Norwegian adults aged 50–64 at risk (1963–1979).

BMI (kg/m²) ranged between 17 and 39, over 90% of the males had BMIs within the range 21–29. Within the range 23–27, the curve is relatively flat, with the relative risk of mortality hovering close to 1.0. However, at BMIs of less than 21 and over 29, the risk of death rises quite sharply as the BMI moves away from its mean value. It will be noticed that the BMI curves are much more symmetrical than the height curves in Fig. 2, which indicates that high BMIs are as risky as low ones.

Adult height and the BMI measure different aspects of nutritional status. Not only is stunting due to malnutrition during developmental ages, but it appears that most stunting occurs under age three, after which even badly stunted children generally move along a given height centile, that is, develop without incurring further height deficits (Billewicz and MacGregor, 1982; Tanner, 1982; Horton, 1984; Martorell, 1985). Second, no matter how badly stunted an adult might be, it is still possible to have an optimum (or good) weight for that height. Thus, for example, a Norwegian male stunted by two inches during his developmental ages could still have had a normal risk if his BMI was about 26.

The fact that even badly stunted populations may have quite normal BMIs reflects the capacity of human beings to adapt their behavior to the limitations of their food supply. Adaptation takes place in three dimensions. Small people have lower basal metabolism, because less energy is needed to maintain body temperature and sustain the function of vital organs. Small people need less food and hence, require less energy to consume their food and for vital hygiene. The third aspect of adaptation comes in the curtailment of work and discretionary activity. If a small (56 kg) man confined himself to a few hours of light work each day, he could remain in energy balance and maintain his BMI at a satisfactory level with as little as 2000 or 2100 kcal. However, a larger man (79 kg) engaged in heavy work for 8 h per day would require about 4030 kcal to maintain his energy balance at a BMI of 24 (FAO/WHO/UNU, 1985).

Although Figs. 2 and 3 are revealing, neither one singly, nor both together, are sufficient to shed light on the debate over whether moderate stunting impairs health when weight-for-height is adequate, since Fig. 1 is not controlled for weight and Fig. 2 is only partially controlled for height (Fogel, 1987, 1993). To get at the "small-but-healthy" (Seckler, 1982) issue one needs an iso-mortality surface that relates the risk of death to both height and weight simultaneously. Such a surface, presented in Fig. 4, was fitted to Waaler's data by a procedure described elsewhere (Fogel, 1993; Kim, 1996). Transecting the iso-mortality map are lines which give the locus of BMI between 16 and 34, and a curve giving the weights that minimize risk at each height.

Fig. 4 shows that even when body weight is maintained at what Fig. 2 indicates is an "ideal" level (BMI = 25), short men are at substantially greater risk of death than tall men. Thus, an adult male with a BMI of 25 who is 164 cm tall is at about 55% greater risk of death than a male at 183 cm who also has a BMI of 25. Fig. 4 also shows that the "ideal" BMI (the BMI that minimizes the risk of death) varies with height. A BMI of 25 is "ideal" for men in the neighborhood of 176 cm, but for tall men (greater than 183 cm) the ideal BMI is between 22 and 24, while for short men (under 168 cm) the "ideal" BMI is about 26.

Before using Fig. 4 to evaluate the relationship between chronic malnutrition and the secular decline in mortality rates after 1750, three issues in the interpretation of that figure need to be addressed. First, since an individual's height cannot be varied by changes in nutrition after maturity, adults can move to a more desirable BMI only by changing weight. Therefore, the $X$ axis is interpreted as a measure of the effect of the current nutritional status of mature males on adult mortality rates. Moreover, since most stunting takes place below age three (Tanner, 1982; Horton, 1984; Martorell, 1985; Steckel, 1986), the $Y$ axis is interpreted as a measure of the effect of nutritional deprivation in utero or early in childhood on the risk of mortality at middle and late ages (cf. Tanner, 1982; Steckel, 1987; Fogel et al., 1992, ch. 42 and 47).

Second, in applying Fig. 4 to the evaluation of secular trends in nutrition and mortality it is assumed that for Europeans environmental factors have been decisive in explaining the secular increase in heights, not only for population means, but also for individuals in particular families. The reasonableness of this assumption becomes evident when one considers the issue of shortness. If shortness is defined as a given number of SDs below a changing mean (i.e., short is 2SDs below the mean, whether the mean is 164 cm or 183 cm), then genetic and environmental factors may be difficult to disentangle. If, however, shortness is defined in absolute terms, say as applying to all males with heights below 168 cm, then it is quite clear that most shortness in Europe and America during the eighteenth and much of the nineteenth centuries was determined by environmental rather than genetic factors.

The point at issue can be clarified by considering the experience of the Netherlands. Shortness has virtually disappeared from that country during the past century and a half. Today, less than 2% of young adult males are below 168 cm, but in c.1855 about two-thirds were below that height. Since there has been little change in the gene pool of the Dutch during the period, it must have been changes in environmental cir-

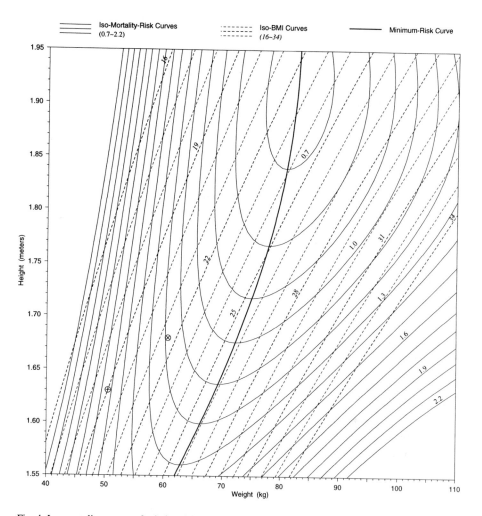

Fig. 4. Iso-mortality curves of relative risk for height and weight among Norwegian males aged 50–64. ⊕, the possible location of adult French males aged 25–34 c.1985 on the iso-mortality map. The predicted risk for French males is 1.63; ⊗, the possible location of comparable English males c.1790. The predicted risk for English males in 1.18. All risks are measured relative to the average risk of mortality (calculated over all heights and weights) among Norwegian males aged 50–64.

cumstances, nutrition, and health that eliminated about 95% of all short males from the Dutch population (Van Wieringen, 1986; Fogel, 1987). It cannot be ruled out that the remaining men shorter than 168 cm may yet be virtually eliminated from the Dutch population.

The Dutch case illustrates the general secular pattern of physical growth in the nations of Western Europe. The secular increase in mean final heights, which ranged between 10 and 20 cm (between 4 and 8 inches) over the past 200 years, cannot be attributed to natural selection or genetic drift, since these processes require much longer time spans. Nor can it be attributed to heterosis (hybrid vigor) because the populations in question have remained relatively homogeneous and because the effects of heterosis in human populations have been shown both empirically and theoretically to be quite small (Damon, 1965; Cavalli-Sforza and Bodmer, 1971; Van Wieringen, 1978; Fogel et al., 1983; Martorell, 1985; Mueller, 1986). Only the top 6% of the Dutch height distribution of c.1855 overlaps with the bottom 6% of the current distribution of final heights. Since the Dutch mean may still increase, and we do not yet know the maximum mean genetically obtainable (often referred to as the genetic potential), it may well be that even the 6% overlap between the distribution of final heights in the c.1855 generation and that of the latest generation will be cut in the next few decades, perhaps by as much as half.

Third, even if the Norwegian iso-mortality surface is applicable to European populations generally, the surface may not have been stable over time. Since height-specific and weight-specific mortality rates are measured relative to the average death rate for the population as a whole, short-term shifts in average death rates by themselves will not shift the surface. However, fundamental shifts in environment, including changes in medical technology, may change the risk surface.[6] One way of ascertaining whether there has been a change in the risk surface is by determining what part of the decline in mortality rates can be explained merely by movements along the surface (i.e. merely by changes in height and weight on the assumption that the surface has been stable since 1700).

The average final heights of men in several European countries over the period from 1700 to modern times are reported in Table 4. It will be seen that during the eighteenth century these Europeans were severely stunted by modern standards (see line 6 of Table 4). The French cohort of 18-IV is the most stunted, measuring only 163.0 cm (64.2 inches). The two next shortest cohorts are those of Norway for 18-III

---

[6] Among the major forces that change the shape of Waaler surfaces over time are shifts in the cdr per se and changes in medical technology. Even a long-term shift in the cdr level, which might be mainly attributable to improved nutrition, in itself need not necessarily alter the Waaler surface (this needs to be further investigated), since the risk levels on a Waaler surface are measured relative to the cdr of the population. Changes in medical technology are more likely to alter the Waaler surface. For instance, if rapid advances were made in treatments of diseases associated with underweight people but little progress is made in diseases associated with obesity, the relative risk level would fall for low BMIs and rise for high BMIs, tilting the Waaler surface downward on the left. In Fig. 4 in the paper, this would show up as a shift of all contour curves to the left, with the distance between contour curves widening in low-BMI regions and vice versa for high-BMI regions. Changes in lifestyles and habits would also change the Waaler surface. A population that smokes would have a different surface than a non-smoking population (low BMIs would have higher risks in a smoking population). I am indebted to John M. Kim for this footnote, which is based on work stemming from his dissertation (Kim, 1996).

Table 4
Estimated average final heights of men who reached maturity between 1750 and 1875 in six European populations, by quarter centuries (cm)

| (1) Date of maturity by century and quarter | (2) Great Britain | (3) Norway | (4) Sweden | (5) France | (6) Denmark | (7) Hungary |
|---|---|---|---|---|---|---|
| 1. 18-III | 165.9 | 163.9 | 168.1 | – | – | 168.7 |
| 2. 18-IV | 167.9 | – | 166.7 | 163.0 | 165.7 | 165.8 |
| 3. 19-I | 168.0 | – | 166.7 | 164.3 | 165.4 | 163.9 |
| 4. 19-II | 171.6 | – | 168.0 | 165.2 | 166.8 | 164.2 |
| 5. 19-III | 169.3 | 168.6 | 169.5 | 165.6 | 165.3 | – |
| 6. 20-III | 175.0 | 178.3 | 177.6 | 172.0 | 176.0 | 170.9 |

*Sources*: Fogel (1987: Table 7) for all columns except (5). Column (5): Rows 3–5 were computed from Meerton (1989) as amended by Wier (1993), with 0.9 cm added to allow for additional growth between age 20 and maturity (Gould, 1869: pp. 104–105; cf. Friedman, 1982: p. 510, n. 14). The entry to row 2 is derived from a linear extrapolation of Meerton's data for 1815–1836 back to 1788, with 0.9 cm added for additional growth between age 20 and maturity. The entry in row 6 is from Fogel (1987: Table 7).

and Hungary for 18-IV, which measured 163.9 cm (64.5 inches). Britain and Sweden were the tallest populations between 1775 and 1875, although by the end of the period, Norway nearly matched the leaders.

France was intermediate in its early growth rate, with stature increasing by about 1.10 cm per quarter century between 18-IV and 19-II. However, the French rate of increase sagged over the next half century and hovered between 165.6 and 166.7 until the turn of the twentieth century (Floud, 1983). British heights increased more rapidly (1.90 cm per quarter century) and for a longer period than the French. The cumulated increase over the first 75 years (18-III to 19-II) was 5.7 cm, more than three-fifths of the total increase in British heights between 18-III and the current generation of adults. However, British heights declined slightly with the cohort of 19-III and also remained on a plateau for about half a century (Floud et al., 1990). Swedish heights appear to have declined during the last half of the eighteenth century but then rose sharply beginning with the second quarter of the nineteenth century, initiating the marked secular increases in Swedish heights that have continued down to the present day. Indeed over the last century the three Scandinavian countries (shown in Table 4) and the Netherlands (Chamla, 1983) have had the most vigorous and sustained increases in stature in the Western World, outpacing Britain and the United States (Fogel, 1986a).

Data on body mass indexes for France and Great Britain during the late eighteenth and most of the nineteenth centuries are much more patchy than those on stature. Consequently attempts to compare British and French BMIs during this period are necessarily conjectural. It appears that c.1790 the average English BMI for males about age 30 was between 21 and 22, which is about 10% below current levels. The corresponding figure for French males c.1790 may only have been about 19, which is about 25% below current levels (Fogel et al., in progress). The conjectural nature of these figures makes the attempt to go from the anthropometric data to differential mortality rates more illustrative than substantive. However, Fig. 4 indicates the apparent location of French and English males of 18-IV on the iso-mortality map generated from Waaler's data. These points imply that the French mortality rate should have been about 38% higher than that of the English, which is quite close to the estimated ratio of mortality rates for the two countries.[7] In other words, the available data suggest that in 18-IV both France and Great Britain were characterized by the same or similar mortality risk surface (i.e., the same or similar mortality regimen) and that differences in their average mortality rates might be explained largely by differences in their distributions of height and weight-for-height.

## 4. Implications for population theory

This section of the paper explores the implications of several of the findings discussed so far for the explanation of the secular decline in mortality, for the general theory of mortality, and for the theory of long-term economic growth. Section 4.1 argues that variations in the size of individuals was a principal mechanism in equilibrating the population with the food supply, in determining the level of mortality, and in determining the level of work. Since body size was varied to bring the population and the food supply into balance, the European famines after the mid-sixteenth century were not due to acute general shortages of food. The exact nature of these famines is discussed in Section 4.2. Section 4.3 deals with the contribution of improved nutrition and health to the growth of labor productivity.

*4.1. How variations in body size brought the population and the food supply into balance and determined the level of mortality*

Today, the typical American male in his early thirties is about 177 cm tall and weighs about 78 kg (USDHHS, 1987). Such a male requires about 1794 kcal for basal metabolism and 2279 kcal for maintenance (Quenouille et al., 1951). If either the British or the French had been that large at the start of the eighteenth century, virtually all of the energy produced by their food supplies would have been required for maintenance and hardly any would have been available to sustain work. The implication of energy

---

[7] The English cdr for 11 years centered on 1790 is 26.7 and 1.38 times that number is 36.8, which is close to the French cdr derived from Weir's (1984) data for the 11 years centered on 1790.

cost accounting permitted by the recent work of agricultural historians is that to have the energy necessary to produce the national products of these two countries c.1700, the typical adult male must have been quite short and very light, weighing perhaps 25 to 40% less than his American counterpart today.

How Europeans of the past adapted their size to accommodate their food supply is shown by Table 5, which compares the average daily consumption of calories in England and Wales in 1700 and 1800 by two economic sectors: agriculture and everything else. Within each sector the estimated amount of energy required for work is also shown. Line 3 presents a measure of the efficiency of the agricultural sector in the production of dietary energy. That measure is the number of calories of food output per calorie of work input.

Column (1) of the table presents the situation in 1800, when kcal *available* for consumption were quite high by prevailing European standards (about 2933 per consuming unit daily), when adult male stature made the British the tallest national population in Europe (168 cm or 66.1 inches at maturity) and relatively heavy by the prevailing European standards, averaging about 62.1 kg (about 137 pounds) at prime working ages which implies a BMI of about 22.0. Food was abundant because in addition to a substantial domestic production Britain imported about 13% of its dietary consumption. However, as column (1) indicates, British agriculture was quite productive. English and Welsh farmers produced 21.7 calories of food output (net of seeds, feed, inventory losses, etc.) for each calorie of their work input. About 42% of this bountiful output was consumed by the families of the agriculturalists (7426/17 774 ≈ 0.42).

The balance of their dietary output, together with some food imports, were consumed by the nonagricultural sector, which constituted about 64% of the English population in 1801 (Wrigley, 1987b: p. 170). Although food consumption per capita was about 10% lower in this sector than in agriculture, most of the difference was explained by the greater caloric demands of agricultural labor.[8] Food was so abundant that even the English paupers and vagrants, who accounted for about 20% of the population c.1800 (Lindert and Williamson, 1982), had about three times as much energy for begging and other activities beyond maintenance as did their French counterparts (Fogel et al., in progress).

The food situation was tighter in 1700, when only about 2724 kcal were available daily per consuming unit. The adjustment to the lower food supply was made in three ways. First, compared to 1800 the share of dietary energy made available to the nonagricultural sector in 1700 was reduced by about a third, a reduction that was accomplished partly by constraining the share of the labor force engaged outside of agriculture. Second, the amount of energy available for work per equivalent adult worker was reduced both inside and outside of agriculture, although the reduction was somewhat greater outside of agriculture. Third, the energy required for basal metabolism

---

[8] I include the aristocracy and other members of the governing classes in the nonagricultural sector even though their wealth was mainly in land since they were not engaged in farming.

and maintenance was reduced by shrinking people. Compared with 1800, adult heights of males of 1700 were down by 5 cm, their BMI was 20 instead of 22.0, and their weights were down by about 9 kg. As a result of such constriction of the average body size of the population, the number of calories required for maintenance was reduced by 141 kcal per consuming unit daily.

The last figure may seem rather small. However, it accounts for two-thirds $(141/209 \approx 0.67)$ of the total shortfall in daily caloric consumption. That figure is large enough to sustain the proposition that variations in body size were a principal means of adjusting the population to variations in the food supply. The condition for a population to be in equilibrium with its food supply at a given level of consumption is that the labor input (measured in calories of work) is large enough to produce the requisite amount of food (also measured in calories). Moreover, a given reduction in calories required for maintenance will have a multiplied effect on the number of calories that could be made available for work. The multiplier is the inverse of the labor force participation rate. Since only about 35% of equivalent adults were in the labor force, the potential daily gain in kcal for work was, not 141 per equivalent adult worker, but 403 kcal per equivalent adult worker.

The importance of the last point is indicated by considering columns (2) and (3) of Table 5. Column (2) shows that the daily total of dietary energy used for work in 1700 was 1453 million kcal, with 819 million expended in agriculture and the balance in nonagriculture. Column (3) indicates what would have happened if all the other ad-

Table 5

A comparison of the average daily uses of dietary energy in England and Wales in 1700 and 1800 (all lines in millions of kcal, except 3)[a]

|  |  | (1) 1800 | (2) 1700 | (3) 1700 counter-factual |
|---|---|---|---|---|
| 1. | Total daily dietary energy consumed (production plus net imports) | 20481 | 12206 | 11523 |
| 2. | Energy used to produce agricultural output | 908 | 819 | 694 |
| 3. | Energy productivity in agriculture (the output/input ratio of dietary energy) | 21.7 | 16.6 | 16.6 |
| 4. | Energy consumed in the agricultural sector | 7950 | 6879 | 6879 |
| 5. | Energy consumed outside of the agricultural sector | 12531 | 5327 | 4644 |
| 6. | Energy used to produce nonagricultural output | 1582 | 634 | 0 |

[a]See Fogel et al. (in progress) for a discussion of the sources and procedures involved in the construction of this table. The numerator of the output/input ratio in line 3 excludes imported calories. The denominator includes a downward adjustment of 10% in the Atwater factor (cf. Fogel, 1994).

justments had been made but body size remained at the 1800 level, so that maintenance requirements were unchanged. The first thing to note is that energy available for food production would have declined by 15%. Assuming the same input/output ratio, the national supply of dietary energy would have declined to 11 523 million kcal, of which nearly 60% would have been consumed within the agricultural sector. The residual available for nonagriculture would hardly have covered the maintenance requirements of that sector, leaving zero energy for work in nonagriculture. In this example, the failure to have constrained body size would have reduced the energy for work by about 49% $[1 - (743/1453) \approx 0.49]$.[9]

Varying body size was a universal way that the chronically malnourished populations of Europe responded to food constraints. Such variation in height is evident in Table 4 and has been discussed in much more detail for England by Floud et al. (1990) and for Hungary by Komlos (1990). Some may want to debate whether the size mechanism was more important than variations in fertility in equating population and the food supply. That interesting question should be pursued, but here we focus on the implication of the size mechanism for the explanation of the secular decline in mortality.[10]

Fig. 5 superimposes the estimated heights and weights in France at four dates on a Waaler surface. In 1705 the food supply in France was even lower than in Britain so that it was necessary to reduce body mass even further than in Britain. Circa 1705 the French are estimated to have achieved equilibrium with their food supply at a height of about 161 cm and a BMI of about 18. Over the next 270 years the food supply expanded with sufficient rapidity so that both the height and the weight of adult males increased. However, weight appears to have increased more rapidly than height during the first 165 years. Fig. 5 indicates that it was factors associated with the gain in BMI that accounted for most of the reduction in the risk of mortality before 1870. After 1870, factors associated with the gain in height explain most of the additional mortality decline.

There is another implication of Fig. 5 that is worth making explicit. If the relative risks of mortality in Fig. 5 are standardized on the French crude death rate of c.1785, one obtains the following time series of crude death rates (per thousand):

---

[9] Other assumed distributions of the supply of food to the nonagriculture sector yield more output. If persons outside of the labour force were squeezed, some of their calories could have been diverted to production. However, even a substantial impairment of the household economy would not have closed the gap in GDP originating in the nonagricultural sector. See Fogel et al. (in progress) for further details, including a discussion of more likely adjustments, such as a drastic reduction in the size of the nonagricultural sector.

[10] For recent restatements of the Malthusian theory that focuses on fertility see Schultz (1981) and Von Tunzelman (1986); cf. United Nations (1973: ch. 3). See Easterlin (1968, 1980) on the baby-boom and cohort-size theories. The results of the European fertility project are summarized in Coale and Watkins (1986). The findings of the World Fertility Survey are reported in Cleland and Scott (1987). See Becker (1991) for an up-to-date statement of the theories of the new household economics and Goldin (1990) for an example of how these theories are applied empirically.

|         | Estimated from Fig. 5 | From registrations or samples |
|---------|-----------------------|-------------------------------|
| c.1705  | 40                    | n.a.                          |
| c.1785  | 36                    | 36                            |
| c.1870  | 26                    | 25                            |
| c.1975  | 19                    | 11                            |

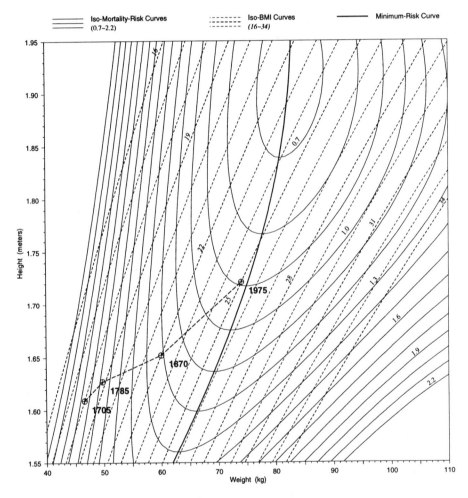

Fig. 5. Iso-mortality curves of relative risk for height and weight among Norwegian males aged 50–64, with a plot of the estimated French height and weight at four dates.

It thus appears that while factors associated with height and BMI jointly explain about 90% of the decline in French mortality rates over the period between c.1785 and c.1870, they only explain about 50% of the decline in mortality rates during the past century. Increases in body size continued to be a major factor in improving life expectancy among persons of relatively good nutritional status, but during the last century factors other than those which act through height and BMI became increasingly important.

The analysis in this section points to the misleading nature of the concept of subsistence as Malthus originally used it and as it is still widely used today. Subsistence is not located at the edge of a nutritional cliff, beyond which lies demographic disaster. The evidence outlined in the paper implies that rather than one level of subsistence, there are numerous levels at which a population and a food supply can be in equilibrium, in the sense that they can be indefinitely sustained. However, some levels will have smaller people and higher "normal" (non-crisis) mortality than others. Moreover, with a given population and technology one can alter body size and mortality by changing the allocation of labor between agriculture and other sectors. Thus, the larger the share of the labor force that is in agriculture, ceteris paribus, the larger the share of caloric production that can be devoted to baseline maintenance.[11]

Although there was a wide range of levels at which the population and the food supply could have been in equilibrium, not all of these equilibria were equally desirable. Some equilibria left those in the bottom portion of the caloric distribution with so little energy that as much as a quarter of the potential labor force was effectively excluded from production. Such equilibria also made the population highly vulnerable to periodic breakdowns in the food distribution system (famines), although chronic malnutrition was responsible for many more deaths than the famines that called attention to the plight of the lower classes. Some equilibria required 80% or more of the labor force to work in the agricultural sector. However, a fairly high degree of diversification into trade and industry was possible even at fairly low levels of average caloric production. Although England in c.1700 and France in c.1800 had similar levels of caloric consumption per consuming unit, England was able to support about 45% of its labor force in nonagricultural pursuits, while France supported about 40% of its labor force in such pursuits. The critical difference was in the relatively high output/input ratio of dietary energy in England's agricultural sector (O'Brien and Keyder, 1978; Chartres, 1985; Wrigley, 1987b; Holderness, 1989; Grantham, 1993; Allen, 1994).

One of the insights that arises from approaching economic and demographic issues from a thermodynamic perspective pertains to the measurement of trends in real

---

[11] In this connection it is worth noting that the rise of the factory reduced the pressure on the food supply by reducing the amount of dietary energy required per hour of labor. This change was due partly to the fact that jobs in light manufacturing industry were less intensive in human energy than farming and partly to the substitution of waterpower and mineral energy for dietary energy.

wages. The index constructed by Wrigley and Schofield shows that the daily real wages of English workers declined by 17% between c.1700 and c.1800, the index dropping from 495 to 413 (Wrigley and Schofield, 1981: p. 643). However, over the same period the daily work intensity of labor as measured by calories used in a day's work increased by 19% (1085/95 ≈ 1.19). Consequently, if hours of labor are quality-adjusted for the increased intensity of labor, real wages declined by 30%. This way of approaching the measurement of labor productivity has a bearing on the explanation of the sources of economic growth over the past two centuries, as shown in Section 4.3.

## 4.2. The nature of European famines

If body size was varied to bring the food supply into equilibrium with the population, why did Europe continue to have national or even continental famines into the nineteenth century? At least from the beginning of the seventeenth century, when seed yields were well in excess of four and carryover inventories of food averaged between 33 and 42% of annual consumption, famines were man-made rather than natural disasters. This hypothesis and evidence that supports it has emerged from recent efforts to assess the types of inferences that can be made validly about the supply of food from data on grain prices. Attempts to make such inferences date back beyond Gregory King, although he was the first to propose explicitly something approaching a demand curve – the famous King's Law. After King, a host of political mathematicians and economists proposed variants of King's Law to predict the shortfalls in annual grain yields from the annual deviations of grain prices around their trend (Labrousse, 1944; Hoskins, 1964, 1968; Slicher Van Bath, 1963).

The problem with this approach to the measurement of subsistence crises lies not in its logic but in the difficulty of estimating the price elasticity ($\varepsilon$). If the elasticity of the demand for grain were known, the shortfall in the supply would follow directly from the deviation in price. Efforts to estimate that parameter from King's Law or variants of it (such as the formulas of Davenant, Jevons and Bouniatian) imply values of $\varepsilon$ in the neighborhood of 0.4 (Wrigley, 1987a; Fogel, 1992). The difficulty with these estimates is that they are based on the implicit assumption that the annual supply of grains varied directly with the annual per acre yield. That assumption would be correct only if carryover inventories at the beginning of the harvest were zero. Yet carryover inventories ran between four and five months of annual consumption. When King's Law is reestimated allowing for the effect of these stocks, the value of $\varepsilon$ declines from 0.4 to 0.25. Additional evidence bearing on the exceedingly inelastic demand for inventories by those who held them indicates that the best estimate of $\varepsilon$ is in the neighborhood of 0.18 (Fogel, 1992).

A price elasticity of 0.18 implies that even relatively small declines in supply would lead to sharp rises in prices. Moreover, because of large differences in the elasticity of demand for grain between the upper and lower classes, a reduction in the supply of grain by as little as 5% would set off a spiral rise in prices that cut the consumption of the laboring classes by a third (Fogel, 1992). Thus the typical English subsistence crises after the ascendancy of Henry VIII took place not because there was not enough grain to go around, but because the demand for inventories pushed prices so high that laborers lacked the cash to purchase the grain (cf. Sen, 1981). Even the largest deviation of wheat prices above trend during Hoskins's entire 280-year period or Wrigley and Schofield's 331-year period involved a manageable shortfall in the supply of food. Although carryover stocks were diminished, more than two-thirds the normal amount – more than a three months supply – remained over and above all claims for seed, feed, and human consumption.

During the Tudor era authorities recognized that famines were man-made rather than natural disasters because the available surpluses were more than adequate to feed the lower classes. The basic strategy of the Crown was to leave the grain market to its own devices during times of plenty. But in years of famine for the lower classes, the state became increasingly bold in overriding the complaints of traders, merchants, brewers, bakers, and other processors about its meddling in the market. Since mere denunciations of engrossers did not work, in 1587 the Privy Council issued a "Book of Orders" which instructed local magistrates to determine the extent of private inventories of grain and to force their owners to supply grain to artificers and laborers at moderate prices. Although it took more than a decade to overcome local resistance to these orders, by 1600 local authorities were vigorously responding to the directives of the Crown. The paternalistic system began to unravel with the Civil War, when Parliament developed a legislative program aimed at unshackling farmers, producers, and merchants from the restraints that had been imposed on them (Fogel, 1992).

Whatever the motivation for the switch in policy, it was the abandonment of the Tudor–Stuart program of food relief, not natural disasters or the technological backwardness of agriculture, that subjected England to periodic famines for two extra centuries. Analysis of variance indicates that during the period from 1600 to 1640, when government relief efforts were at their apogee, the variance of wheat prices around trend declined to less than a third of the level of the preceding era. That large a drop cannot be explained plausibly by chance variations in weather, since the $F$-value is statistically significant at the 0.0001 level. Nor is it likely that the sharp rise in the variance of wheat prices during the last six decades of the seventeenth century was the result of chance variations in weather (Fogel, 1992).[12]

In the absence of government action to reduce prices during grain shortages, workers took to the streets and price-fixing riots became a standard feature of the eighteenth century. During the late 1750s, however, after food riots of unprecedented scope and intensity, proposals reemerged for the government to intervene vigorously in the

[12] The $F$-values for $S_3^2/S_2^2$ and for $S_4^2/S_2^2$ are significant at the 0.004 level (the periods referred to by the three subscripts are 1600–1640 for 2, 1641–1699 for 3 and 1700–745 for 4).

grain market (to return to the Tudor–Stuart policies), including proposals to reestablish public granaries. As the battle over these questions ebbed and flowed during the next half century, the government, at the local and the national levels, gradually shifted toward more vigorous intervention in the grain market. By the start of the nineteenth century, famines had been conquered in England, not because the weather had shifted, or because of improvements in technology, but because government policy (at least with respect to its own people)[13] had unalterably shifted back to the ideas and practices of commonweal that had prevailed during 1600–1640 (Barnes, 1930: pp. 31–45; Post, 1977).

### 4.3. Contribution of improved nutrition and health to the growth of labor productivity

The neglect of the relationship between body size and the food supply has obscured one of the principal sources of the long-term growth in labor productivity. Reconsideration of the issue starts with the first law of thermodynamics which applies as strictly to the human engine as to mechanical engines. Since, moreover, the overwhelming share of calories consumed among malnourished populations is required for BMR and essential maintenance, it is quite clear that in energy-poor populations, such as those of Europe during the second half of the eighteenth century, the typical individual in the labor force had relatively small amounts of energy available for work. This observation does not preclude the possibility that malnourished French peasants worked hard for relatively long hours at certain times of the year as at harvest time. Such work could have been sustained either by consuming more calories than normal during such periods, or by drawing on body mass to provide the needed energy. That level of work, however, could not have been sustained over the entire year. On average, the median individual in the French caloric distribution of 18-IV had only enough energy, over and above maintenance, to sustain regularly about 2.4 h of heavy work or about 4.1 h of moderate work per day.[14]

It is quite clear, then, that the increase in the amount of calories available for work over the past 200 years must have made a nontrivial contribution to the growth rate of the per capita income of countries such as France and Great Britain. That contribution

---

[13] For a more extended discussion of this point see Fogel (1992: section 2.1).

[14] I have assumed a height of 160.5 cm and a weight of about 49 kg. These assumptions imply a BMR of 1437 kcal and 1824 kcal for maintenance, leaving about 466 kcal for work. Heavy work (including rest breaks) requires 191 kcal per hour, moderate work (including breaks) 113. Hours of work per day are calculated on a basis of 365 days. If one assumes a work year of 250 days, allowing for holidays and sickness, then the figures become 3.5 h of heavy work and 6.4 h of moderate work per working day. The last pair of figures still does not standardize for slack days and inclement days, when only indoor work of a relatively sedentary nature was performed. Adjusting for such days would further increase the number of hours of heavy work and moderate work normally performed during such key seasons as planting and harvesting.

had two effects. First, it increased the labor force participation rate by bringing into the labor force the bottom 20% of the consuming units, who, even assuming highly stunted individuals and low BMIs, had had only enough energy above maintenance for a few hours of strolling each day – about the amount needed for a career in begging – but less on average than that needed for just one hour of heavy manual labor.[15] Consequently, merely the elimination of the large class of paupers and beggars, which was accomplished in England mainly during the last half of the nineteenth century (Lindert and Williamson, 1982, 1983; Himmelfarb, 1983; Williamson, 1985), contributed significantly to the growth of national product. The increase in the labor force participation rate made possible by raising the nutrition of the bottom fifth of consuming units above the threshold required for work, by itself, contributed 0.11% to the annual British growth rate between 1780 and 1980 ($1.25^{0.005} - 1 = 0.0011$).

In addition to raising the labor force participation rate, the increased supply of calories raised the average consumption of calories by those in the labor force from 2944 kcal per consuming unit in c.1790 to 3701 kcal per consuming unit in 1980. Of these amounts, 1009 kcal were available for work in c.1790 and 1569 in 1980, so that calories available for work increased by about 56% during the past two centuries. We do not know exactly how this supply of energy was divided between discretionary activities and work c.1790 but we do know that the pre-industrial and early-industrial routine had numerous holidays, absentee days, and short days (Thompson, 1967; Landes, 1969). If it is assumed that proportion of the available energy devoted to work has been unchanged between the end points of the period, then the increase in the amount of energy available for work contributed about 0.23% per annum to the annual growth rate of per capita income ($1.56^{0.0053} - 1 = 0.0023$).

Between 1780 and 1979, British per capita income grew at an annual rate of about 1.15% (Maddison, 1982; Crafts, 1985). Thus, in combination, bringing the ultra poor into the labor force and raising the energy available for work by those in the labor force, explains about 30% of the British growth in per capita income over the past two centuries.

At the present stage of research, the last figure should be considered more illustrative than substantive since it rests on two implicit assumptions that have yet to be explored adequately. The first is that the share of energy above maintenance allocated to work was the same in 1980 as in c.1790. It is difficult to measure the extent or even the net direction of the bias due to this assumption. On the one hand absenteeism appears to have been much more frequent in the past than at present, due either to poor

---

[15] It was assumed that the lowest 10% were too low on energy for any sustained work above maintenance, but that the next decile of English consuming units were 161 cm tall, with a weight of about 49 kg, which implies a BMR of about 1440 kcal and about 1829 kcal for maintenance. The estimated average of caloric intake of the second decile of the English caloric distribution in 18-IV was 2067 kcal. Strolling requires about 97 kcal above maintenance, so that such an individual could stroll for about 2.5 h. One hour of heavy manual labor, including rest breaks, requires 191 kcal above maintenance, and 297 kcal above maintenance while engaged. Computed from the requirements in FAO/WHO/UNU (1985: p. 76).

health or a lack of labor discipline (Landes, 1969). On the other hand work weeks are shorter today than in the past and a large share of energy above maintenance may be devoted to recreation or other activities whose values are excluded from the national income accounts. Although it is my guess that these two influences tend to cancel each other out, it may be that the share of energy above maintenance allocated to work (measured GNP) is lower now than in the past. In that event the estimate of the share of British economic growth accounted for by improved nutrition and health would be overstated. The other implicit assumption is that the efficiency with which tall people convert energy into work output is the same as that of short people. An enormous literature has developed on this question but the evidence amassed so far is inconclusive. However, even if both of these assumptions tend to bias upward the share of British economic growth attributed to improved nutrition, it is quite unlikely that the bias could be as much as 50%. Hence it appears that improved nutrition and health accounted for at least 20% of British economic growth and the best estimate could be as high as 30%.[16]

## 5. Conclusions and implications for current policy

Recent findings in economic and demographic history have shed new light on the European escape from hunger and high mortality since 1750. These advances have been stimulated partly by a better integration of biomedical, economic, and demographic analysis and partly by an enormous expansion of the database to which these techniques can be applied. Since we are still at an early stage of some of these investigations, current findings must be considered provisional and subject to change.

The principal findings of this paper are as follows:
(1) Crisis mortality accounted for less than 5% of total mortality in England and France in the mid-eighteenth century, and the elimination of crisis mortality accounted for under 3% of the decline in total mortality between c.1750 and 1975.

---

[16] Of course, there are biases that run in the opposite direction. As Kim has pointed out, "Depending on how the caloric requirement for BMR and basic maintenance are defined and estimated, it is possible that the actual contribution of improved nutrition and health might be greater than the estimated 30 percent. Provided that changes in height and BMI affect not only mortality but also morbidity, shorter- and lower-BMI people will have a higher incidence of disease and illness, which would increase the caloric claims against diet, leaving less calories available for work and also leading to a higher number of sick days. If BMR and basic maintenance fail to take full account of such greater caloric demands by the higher incidence of disease and illness in a shorter and lighter population, estimates of the effect of improved nutrition and health on economic growth will be biased downward.

The shorter and lighter British population of 1790 would have had a higher incidence of disease and illness than the 1980 population, requiring that a greater (negative) adjustment be made to the estimated calories available for work. This leads to a higher estimate of the increase in calories available for work between 1790 and 1980 and hence, the contribution of improved health and nutrition would be greater than the estimated 30 percent". From a memorandum by John M. Kim dated November 4, 1991.

Consequently, regardless of how large a share of crisis mortality is attributed to famines, famines only accounted for a small share of total mortality prior to 1800.

(2) The famines that plagued England and France between 1500 and 1800 were man-made – the consequence of failures in the system of food distribution related to an extremely inelastic demand for food inventories, rather than to natural calamities or inadequate technology. Not only was it within the power of government to eliminate famines, but the food distribution policies of James I and Charles I apparently succeeded in reducing the variability of annual wheat prices by over 70%.

(3) Although proper governmental policy could have eliminated famines prior to 1800, it could not have eliminated the severe chronic malnutrition that pervaded Europe. Elimination of such substantial chronic malnutrition required advances in agricultural and related technologies that permitted the per capita consumption of food to increase by about 50%.

(4) Improvements in average nutritional status (as indicated by stature and body mass indexes) appear to explain about 90% of the decline in mortality rates in England and France between 18-IV and 19-III, but only about half of the mortality decline between 19-III and 20-III.

(5) Stunting during developmental ages had a long reach, substantially increasing both morbidity and mortality rates at middle and late ages. Small males were at much higher risk of developing chronic diseases during ages 23–49, and were at much higher risk of death above age 49, even if they had optimal BMIs.

These findings indicate that the elimination of chronic malnutrition played a large role in the secular improvement in health and life expectancy. They also suggest that the elimination of stunting and wasting at early ages is of major importance in the reduction of morbidity and mortality rates at middle and late ages. Optimizing BMI at mature ages may reduce some risks faced by stunted adults but it does not eliminate the effects of stunting. It also appears that the optimal BMI may be higher for stunted than for tall adults.

The relevance of these findings for current policy issues may be more obvious for "Third World" countries than for currently industrialized countries. They call into question the "small but healthy" slogan which implies that individuals stunted or wasted early in life due to malnutrition will normally be as healthy and long-lived as those who were not. However, the Norwegian evidence embodied in Figs. 4 and 5 is supported by evidence from the United States during the 1860s (see Fig. 2) and comparable findings for Britain (Barker, 1988; Barker et al., 1989; Barker and Osmond, 1990), for Sweden (Peck et al., 1989), for the United States in the twentieth century (Andres, 1985; Costa and Steckel, 1996; Kim, 1996), for France, and for several other countries. These studies support the proposition that improvement in nutritional status during developmental ages (through a combination of better diets and improved hygiene that reduces the incidence of youthful diseases) will lower the incidence of chronic diseases at middle and late ages, increase work capacity at later ages, and increase life expectancy. These findings, therefore, suggest that payoffs later in life need to be factored into the cost–benefit analyses of programs aimed at improving nutrition and health care at younger ages.

Less obvious and perhaps more surprising are some of the implications for highly developed economies. The current height and weight of US males locates them on the 0.79 iso-mortality risk curve. If their mean height and weight shifted to the minimum point on the risk surface, their life expectancy would increase by about 20%. Assuming a corresponding development among women, such a shift would increase the joint life expectancy to about 90 years at birth. Plausible movements along the Waaler surface are not the only indicators that future increases in life expectancy may be larger than are anticipated by current official demographic forecasts (Spencer, 1989; Ahlburg and Vaupel, 1990). Studies in Britain, Norway, and Sweden indicate significant correlations between the incidence of anthropometric measures in infancy (for individuals) or infant death rates (for areas) and the incidence of chronic diseases at middle and late ages. Among the chronic diseases so linked are chronic bronchitis, ischemic heart disease, high blood pressure, stroke, and colorectal cancer (Forsdahl, 1977; Barker and Godfrey, 1984; Marmot et al., 1984; Andres, 1985; Barker and Osmond, 1986a,b, 1987; Barker, 1988, 1994; Barker et al., 1989, 1990).

Individuals who are in their sixties today were born during the 1920s or 1930s. The sharp decline in infant mortality between the mid-1930s and the mid-1980s suggests that there will be a continuing decline in the incidence of those chronic diseases at older ages that have been related to infant morbidity and mortality rates and in the death rates from such diseases. The increase in final heights between cohorts born in 1930 and in 1960 also argues in the same direction (Shapiro et al., 1968; Fogel et al., 1983; Van Wieringen, 1986; US Bureau of the Census, 1990: p. 77).

If life expectancies increase more rapidly than expected, and if height and optimal weight increase substantially during the next half century or so, various current policies may prove inadequate. An increase in life expectancy of 15 years, for example, without an appropriate policy response could lead to the bankruptcy of the Social Security system, since current set-asides and the limited proposed delays of the age at which payments begin may lead to claims against the Social Security fund that are substantially in excess of its capacity to pay (cf. Ahlburg and Vaupel, 1990). Similarly, an increase in average height to 192 cm and average weight to about 85 kg would raise baseline maintenance to about 2380 kcal per day, an increase of about 4.4%. Such an increase could easily be absorbed by the United States and Canada, but would put pressure on nations that do not produce vast food surpluses for export.

Moreover, if we extend our horizon to a century or so, it may well be that many currently underdeveloped nations will be approaching body sizes of such magnitudes. Projections of food supplies needed to meet that situation are greater than those indicated in current assessments of world food shortfalls (FAO, 1987). Such a prospect need not provoke alarm, since the capacity to increase food output by the requisite amount already exists. However, the last point calls attention to the fact that the balance between the world's food supply and the current population is still being achieved in large measure by constraining body size. The current level of food production worldwide is at least 10% lower than it would have to be if all heights and weights were optimized.[17]

## References

Ahlburg, D.A. and J.W. Vaupel (1990), "Alternative projections of the U.S. population", Demography 27: 639–652.

Aitchison, J. and J.A.C. Brown (1966), The lognormal distribution (Cambridge University Press, Cambridge).

Allen, R.C. (1994), "Agriculture during the Industrial Revolution, 1700–1850", in: R. Floud and D. McCloskey, eds., The economic history of Britain since 1700, 2nd edn., Vol. 1 (Cambridge University Press, Cambridge).

Andres, R. (1985), "Mortality and obesity: the rationale for age-specific height–weight tables", in: R. Andres, E.L. Bierman and W.R. Hazzard, eds., Principles of geriatric medicine (McGraw-Hill, New York).

Appleby, A.B. (1975), "Nutrition and disease: The case of London, 1550–1750", Journal of Interdisciplinary History 6: 1–22.

Appleby, A.B. (1979), "Diet in sixteenth-century England: Sources, problems, possibilities", in: C. Webster, ed., Health, medicine and mortality in the sixteenth century (Cambridge University Press, Cambridge).

Ashby, H.T. (1915), Infant mortality (Cambridge University Press, Cambridge).

Barker, D.J.P. (1988), "Childhood causes of adult diseases", Archives of Disease in Childhood 63: 867–869.

Barker, D.J.P., ed. (1994), Mothers, babies, and disease in later life (BMJ Publishing Group, London).

Barker, D.J.P. and K.M. Godfrey (1984), "Geographical variations in the incidence of colorectal cancer in Britain", British Journal of Cancer 50: 693–698.

Barker, D.J.P. and C. Osmond (1986a), "Infant mortality, childhood nutrition, and ischaemic heart disease in England and Wales", Lancet, i: 1077–1081.

Barker, D.J.P. and C. Osmond (1986b), "Childhood respiratory infection and adult chronic bronchitis in England and Wales", British Medical Journal 293: 1271–1275.

Barker, D.J.P. and C. Osmond (1987), "Death rates from stroke in England and Wales predicted from past maternal mortality", British Medical Journal 295: 83–86.

Barker, D.J.P., C. Osmond, J. Golding, D. Kuh and M.E.J. Wadsworth (1989), "Growth in utero, blood pressure in childhood and adult life, and mortality from cardiovascular disease", British Medical Journal 298: 564–567.

Barker, D.J.P. and C. Osmond (1990), "Height and mortality in the counties of England and Wales", Annals of Human Biology 17: 1–6.

Barnes, D.G. (1930), A history of the English corn laws from 1660 to 1846 (George Routledge, London).

Becker, G.S. (1991), A treatise on the family, 2nd edn. (Harvard University Press, Cambridge, MA).

---

[17] I have assumed that the current global averages for height and weight of an equivalent adult male are 172 cm and 67 kg and that the optimum figures are 192 cm and 85 kg. These figures imply an increase of 330 kcal per day for baseline maintenance. No allowance is made for increased energy for higher work levels. The current daily world consumption of calories is from FAO (1987: p. 3) with a factor of 0.8 used to convert kcal per capita into kcal per consuming unit. If 500 kcal are allowed for extra work output, the current food shortfall that is compensated for by small body sizes and reduced work output is equal to about 25% of the world's current annual production of food.

Bengtsson, T. and R. Ohlsson (1984), "Population and economic fluctuations in Sweden, 1749–1914", in: T. Bengtsson, G. Fridlizius and R. Ohlsson, eds., Pre-industrial population change (Almquist and Wicksell, Stockholm).

Bengtsson, T. and R. Ohlsson (1985), "Age-specific mortality and short-term changes in the standard of living: Sweden, 1751–1859", European Journal of Population 1: 309–326.

Bernard, R.-J. (1969/1975), "Peasant diet in eighteenth-century Gevaudan", in: E. Forster and R. Forster, eds., European diet from pre-industrial to modern times (Harper and Row, New York).

Billewicz, W.Z. and I.A. MacGregor (1982), "A birth to maturity longitudinal study of heights and weights in two West African (Gambian) villages, 1951–1975", Annals of Human Biology 9: 309–320.

Blayo, Y. (1975), "Mouvement naturel de la population français de 1740 à 1829", Population 30 (Numéro Spécial): 15–64.

Blum, J. (1978), The end of the old order in rural Europe (Princeton University Press, Princeton, NJ).

Bourgeois-Pichat, J. (1965), "The general development of the population of France since the eighteenth century", in: D.V. Glass and D.E.C. Eversley, eds., Population in history: essays in historical demography (Aldine, Chicago, IL).

Brownlee, J. (1916), "The history of the birth and death rates in England and Wales taken as a whole from 1570 to the present time", Public Health 29: 211–238.

Burnett, J. (1979), Plenty and want, 2nd edn. (Scholar Press, London).

Carr-Saunders, A.M. (1964), World population: past growth and present trends (Frank Cass, London).

Case, R.A.M., C. Coghill, J.L. Harley, and J.T. Pearson (1962), Chester Beatty Research Institute abridged serial life tables, England and Wales, 1841–1960, Part I (Chester Beatty Research Institute, London).

Cavalli-Sforza, L.L. and W.F. Bodmer (1971), The genetics of human populations (W.H. Freeman, San Francisco, CA).

Chamla, M.Cl. (1983), "L'évolution recente de la stature en Europe Occidentale (Période 1960–1980)", in: Bulletin et Memoire de la Société d'Anthropologie de Paris, t. 10, Serie 13: 195–224.

Chartres, J.A. (1985), "The marketing of agricultural produce", in: J. Thirsk, ed., The agrarian history of England and Wales, Vol. 5, 1640–1750, Part 2. Agrarian change (Cambridge University Press, Cambridge).

Cleland, J.G. and C. Scott, eds. (1987), The world fertility survey: an assessment (Oxford University Press, Oxford).

Coale, A.J. and S.C. Watkins, eds. (1986), The decline of fertility in Europe (Princeton University Press, Princeton, NJ).

Cole, G.D.H. and R. Postgate (1938/1976), The common people, 1746–1946 (Methuen, London).

Costa, D.L. and R.H. Steckel (1996), "Long-term trends in health, welfare, and economic growth in the United States", in: R.H. Steckel and R. Floud, eds., Health and welfare during industrialization (University of Chicago Press, Chicago, IL).

Crafts, N.F.R. (1985), British economic growth during the Industrial Revolution (Clarendon Press, Oxford).

Damon, A. (1965), "Stature increase among Italian-Americans: environmental, genetic, or both?", American Journal of Physical Anthropology 23: 401–408.

Davidson, S., R. Passmore, J.F. Brock and A.S. Truswell (1979), Human nutrition and dietetics, 7th edn. (Churchill Livingstone, Edinburgh).

Dorn, H.F. (1959), "Mortality", in: P.M. Hauser and O.D. Duncan, eds., The study of population: an inventory and appraisal (University of Chicago Press, Chicago, IL).

Drummond, J.C. and A. Wilbraham (1958), The Englishman's food: a history of five centuries of English diet, 2nd edn. (Jonathan Cape, London).

Dublin, L.I. and A.J. Lotka (1936), Length of life: a study of the life table (Ronald Press, New York).

Dublin, L.I., A.J. Lotka and M. Spiegelman (1949), Length of life: a study of the life table, Rev. edn. (Ronald Press, New York).

Dupâquier, J. (1989), "Demographic crises and subsistence crises in France, 1650–1725", in: J. Walter and

R. Schofield, eds., Famine, disease and the social order in early modern society (Cambridge University Press, Cambridge).

Durnin, J. and R. Passmore (1967), Energy, work and leisure (Heinemann, London).

Dyer, C. (1983), "English diet in the later Middle Ages", in: T.H. Aston et al., eds., Social relations and ideas: essays in honour of R.H. Hilton (Cambridge University Press, Cambridge).

Easterlin, R.A. (1968), Population, labor force, and long swings in economic growth: the American experience (Columbia University Press for NBER, New York).

Easterlin, R.A. (1980), Birth and fortune: the impact of numbers on personal welfare (Basic Books, New York).

Eckstein, Z., T.P. Schultz and K.I. Wolpin (1985), "Short-run fluctuations in fertility and mortality in pre-industrial Sweden", European Economic Review 26: 297–317.

FAO (1977), The fourth world food survey (Food and Agricultural Organization of the United Nations, Rome).

FAO (1987), The fifth world food survey (Food and Agriculture Organization of the United Nations, Rome).

FAO/WHO/UNU (1985), "Energy and protein requirements: report of a joint FAO/WHO/UNU Expert Consultation", Technical report series no. 724 (World Health Organization, Geneva).

Flinn, M.W. (1970), British population growth, 1700–1850 (Macmillan, London).

Flinn, M.W. (1974), "The stabilization of mortality in pre-industrial Western Europe", Journal of European Economic History 3: 285–318.

Flinn, M.W. (1981), The European demographic system, 1500–1820 (Johns Hopkins University Press, Baltimore, MD).

Floud, R. (1983), "The heights of Europeans since 1750: a new source for European economic history", Mimeo. (NBER, Cambridge, MA).

Floud, R., K.W. Wachter and A. Gregory (1990), Height, health, and history: nutritional status in the United Kingdom, 1750–1980 (Cambridge University Press, Cambridge).

Fogel, R.W., ed. (1986a), Long-term changes in nutrition and the standard of living, Ninth International Economic History Congress held in Bern, Switzerland.

Fogel, R.W. (1986b), "Nutrition and the decline in mortality since 1700: some preliminary findings", in: S.L. Engerman and R.E. Gallman, eds., Long term factors in American economic growth, Conference on Research in Income and Wealth, Vol. 41 (University of Chicago Press for NBER, Chicago, IL).

Fogel, R.W. (1987), "Biomedical approaches to the estimation and interpretation of secular trends in equity, morbidity, mortality, and labor productivity in Europe, 1750–1980", Typescript (University of Chicago, Chicago, IL).

Fogel, R.W. (1991), "The conquest of high mortality and hunger in Europe and America: timing and mechanisms", in: P. Higonnet, D.S. Landes and H. Rosovsky, eds., Favorites of fortune: technology, growth, and economic development since the Industrial Revolution (Harvard University Press, Cambridge, MA).

Fogel, R.W. (1992), "Second thoughts on the European escape from hunger: famines, chronic malnutrition, and mortality", in: S.R. Osmani, ed., Nutrition and poverty (Clarendon Press, Oxford).

Fogel, R.W. (1993), "New sources and new techniques for the study of secular trends in nutritional status, health, and mortality, and the process of aging", Historical Methods 26: 5–43.

Fogel, R.W. (1994), "Economic growth, population theory, and physiology: the bearing of long-term processes on the making of economic policy", American Economic Review 84: 369–395.

Fogel, R.W. (1996), "The escape from hunger and premature death, 1700–2100: Europe, American and the Third World", The Ellen McArthur lectures (Cambridge University, Cambridge) in progress.

Fogel, R.W. and S.L. Engerman (1974), Time on the cross: the economics of American Negro slavery, 2 vols. (Little-Brown, Boston, MA).

Fogel, R.W. and S.L. Engerman (1992), "The slave diet on large plantations in 1860", in: R.W. Fogel,

R.A. Galantine and R.L. Manning, eds., Without consent or contract: evidence and methods (W.W. Norton, New York).

Fogel, R.W., R.A. Galantine and R.L. Manning, eds. (1992), Without consent or contract: the rise and fall of American slavery, Vol. 2. Evidence and methods (W.W. Norton, New York).

Fogel, R.W., R. Floud, D.L. Costa and J.M. Kim (1996), "A theory of multiple equilibria between populations and food supplies: nutrition and economic growth in France, Britain and the United States, 1700–1980", Typescript (University of Chicago, Chicago, IL) in progress.

Fogel, R.W., S.L. Engerman, R. Floud, R.A. Margo, K. Sokoloff, R.H. Steckel, J. Trussell, G.C. Villaflor and K.W. Wachter (1983), "Secular changes in American and British stature and nutrition", Journal of Interdisciplinary History 14: 445–481.

Forsdahl, A. (1977), "The poor living conditions in childhood and adolescence: an important risk factor for arteriosclerotic heart disease?", British Journal of Social Medicine 31: 91–95.

Freudenberger, H. and G. Cummins (1976), "Health, work, and leisure before the industrial revolution", Explorations in Economic History 13: 1–12.

Fridlizius, G. (1979), "Sweden", in: W.R. Lee, ed., European demography and economic growth (Croom Helm, London).

Fridlizius, G. (1984), "The mortality decline in the first phase of the demographic transition: Swedish experiences", in: T. Bengtsson, G. Fridlizius and R. Ohlsson, eds., Pre-industrial population change (Almquist and Wiksell, Stockholm).

Friedman, G.C. (1982), "The heights of slaves in Trinidad", Social Science History 6: 482–515.

Frijhoff, W. and D. Julia (1979), "The diet in boarding schools at the end of the Ancien Régime", in: R. Forster and O. Ranum, eds., E. Forster and P.M. Ranum, trans., Economies, sociétés, civilisations (Johns Hopkins University Press, Baltimore, MD).

Galloway, P.R. (1986), "Differentials in demographic responses to annual price variations in pre-revolutionary France: a comparison of rich and poor areas in Rouen, 1681–1787", European Journal of Population 2: 269–305.

Galloway, P.R. (1987), "Population, prices and weather in preindustrial Europe", Ph.D. dissertation (University of California, Berkeley, CA).

Gibson, J.R. and T. McKeown (1950), "Observations on all births (23,970) in Birmingham, 1947, I: Duration of gestation", British Journal of Social Medicine 4: 221–233.

Gibson, J.R. and T. McKeown (1951), "Observations on all births (23,970) in Birmingham, 1947, III. Survival", British Journal of Social Medicine 5: 177–183.

Gille, H. (1949), "The demographic history of northern European countries in the eighteenth century", Population Studies 3: 3–70.

Glass, D.V. (1965), "Population and population movements in England and Wales, 1700 to 1850", in: D.V. Glass and D.E.C. Eversley, eds., Population in history: essays in historical demography (Aldine, Chicago, IL).

Goldin, C.D. (1990), Understanding the gender gap: an economic history of American women (Oxford University Press, New York).

Gonner, E.C.K. (1913), "The population of England in the eighteenth century", Journal of the Royal Statistical Society 76: 261–303.

Goubert, P. (1960), Beauvais et le Bauvaisis de 1600 à 1730 (S.E.V.P.E.N., Paris).

Goubert, P. (1965), "Recent theories and research in French population between 1500 and 1700", in: D.V. Glass and D.E.C. Eversley, eds., Population in history: essays in historical demography (Aldine, Chicago, IL).

Goubert, P. (1973), The ancien régime (Harper and Row, New York).

Gould, B.A. (1869), Investigations in the military and anthropological statistics of American soldiers (Riverside Press, Cambridge, MA).

Grantham, G.W. (1993), "Divisions of labour: agricultural productivity and occupational specialization in pre-industrial France", Economic History Review 46: 478–502.

Griffith, G.T. (1926), Population problems in the age of Malthus (Cambridge University Press, New York).

Habakkuk, H.J. (1974), Population growth and economic development since 1750 (Leicester University Press, Leicester).

Helleiner, K.F. (1965), "The vital revolution reconsidered", in: D.V. Glass and D.E.C. Eversley, eds., Population in history: essays in historical demography (Aldine, Chicago, IL).

Helleiner, K.F. (1967), "The population of Europe from the Black Death to the eve of vital revolution", in: E.E. Rich and C.H. Wilson, eds., The Cambridge economic history of Europe, Vol. 4: The economy of expanding Europe in the sixteenth and seventeenth centuries (Cambridge University Press, Cambridge).

Hémardinquer, J.-J. (1970), "Pour une histoire de l'alimentation", Cahiers des Annales, no. 28 (Colin, Paris).

Henry, L. (1965), "The population of France in the eighteenth century", in: D.V. Glass and D.E.C. Eversley, eds., Population in history: essays in historical demography (Aldine, Chicago, IL).

Heywood, P.F. (1983), "Growth and nutrition in Papua New Guinea", Journal of Human Evolution 12: 131–143.

Higgs, R. (1973), "Mortality in rural America, 1870–1920: estimates and conjectures", Explorations in Economic History 10: 177–195.

Higgs, R. (1979), "Cycles and trends of mortality in 18 large American cities, 1871–1900", Explorations in Economic History 16: 381–408.

Himmelfarb, G. (1983), The idea of poverty: England in the early industrial age (Random House, New York).

Holderness, B.A. (1989), "Prices, productivity, and output", in: G.E. Mingay, ed., The agrarian history of England and Wales, Vol. 6, 1750–1850 (Cambridge University Press, Cambridge).

Horton, S. (1984), "Nutritional status and living standards measurement", Mimeo. (World Bank, Washington, DC).

Hoskins, W.G. (1964), "Harvest fluctuations and English economic history, 1480–1619", Agricultural History Review 12: 28–46.

Hoskins, W.G. (1968), "Harvest fluctuations and English economic history, 1620–1759", Agricultural History Review 16: 15–31.

Hufton, O.H. (1974), The poor of eighteenth-century France (Clarendon Press, Oxford).

Hufton, O.H. (1983), "Social conflict and the grain supply in eighteenth-century France", Journal of Interdisciplinary History 14: 303–331.

INED (1977), "Sixième rapport sur la situation démographique de la France", Population 32: 253–338.

Kim, J.M. (1996), "Waaler surfaces: the economics of nutrition, body build, and health", Ph.D. dissertation (University of Chicago, Chicago, IL).

Komlos, J. (1990), "Stature, nutrition, and the economy in the eighteenth-century Habsburg monarchy", Ph.D. dissertation (University of Chicago, Chicago, IL).

Kunitz, S.J. (1986), "Mortality since Malthus", in: D. Coleman and R. Schofield, eds., The state of population theory: forward from Malthus (Blackwell, Oxford).

Labrousse, C.E. (1944), La crise de l'économie française à la fin de l'ancien régime et au debut de la révolution (Presses Universitaires de France, Paris).

Landes, D.S. (1969), The unbound Prometheus: technological change and industrial development from 1750 to the present (Cambridge University Press, Cambridge).

Langer, W.L. (1975), "American foods and Europe's population growth 1750–1850", Journal of Social History 8: 51–66.

Laslett, P. (1965). The world we have lost: England before the Industrial Age (Charles Scribner, New York).

LeBrun, F. (1971), Les hommes et la mort en Anjou aux 17e et 18e siècles (Mouton, Paris).

Lee, R. (1981), "Short-term variation: Vital rates, prices and weather", in: E.A. Wrigley and R.S. Schofield, eds., The population history of England, 1541–1871: a reconstruction (Harvard University Press, Cambridge, MA).

Lee, W.R. (1980), "The mechanism of mortality change in Germany, 1750–1850", Medizinhistorisches Journal 15: 244–268.

Lee, W.R. (1984), "Mortality levels and agrarian reforms in early 19th century Prussia: some regional evidence", in: T. Bengtsson, G. Fridlizius and R. Ohlsson, eds., Pre-industrial population change (Almquist amd Wicksell, Stockholm).

Lindert, P.H. (1983), "English living standards, population growth, and Wrigley–Schofield", Explorations in Economic History 20: 131–155.

Lindert, P.H. and J.G. Williamson (1982), "Revising England's social tables: 1688–1812", Explorations in Economic History 19: 385–408.

Lindert, P.H. and J.G. Williamson (1983), "Reinterpreting England's social tables: 1688–1913", Explorations in Economic History 20: 94–109.

Lipton, M. (1983), "Poverty, undernutrition, and hunger", World Bank Staff working paper no. 597 (World Bank, Washington, DC).

Livi-Bacci, M. (1983), "The nutrition–mortality link in past times: a comment", Journal of Interdisciplinary History 14: 293–298.

Livi-Bacci, M. (1991), Population and nutrition: an essay on European demographic history (Cambridge University Press, New York).

Maddison, A. (1982), Phases of capitalist development (Oxford University Press, Oxford).

Malthus, T.R. (1798), An essay on the principle of population (A. Flew, ed.) (Penguin, Hammondsworth, 1976).

Marmot, M.G., M.J. Shipley and G. Rose (1984), "Inequalities in death-specific explanations of a general pattern", Lancet i: 1003–1006.

Marshall, T.H. (1929), "The population problem during the Industrial Revolution", Economic History 4: 429–456

Martorell, R. (1985), "Child growth retardation: a discussion of its causes and its relationship to health", in: K. Blaxter and J.C. Waterlow, eds., Nutritional adaptation in man (John Libby, London ).

McKeown, T. (1976), The modern rise of population (Academic Press, London).

McKeown, T. (1978), "Fertility, mortality and cause of death: an examination of issues related to the modern rise of population", Population Studies 32: 535–542.

McKeown, T. and J.R. Gibson (1951), "Observations on all births (23,970) in Birmingham, 1947, II: Birth weight", British Journal of Social Medicine 5: 98–112.

McMahon, S.F. (1981), "Provisions laid up for the family", Historical Methods 14: 4–21.

Meeker, E. (1972), "The improving health of the United States, 1850–1915", Explorations in Economic History 9: 353–373.

Meerton, M.A. von. (1989), "Croissance économique en France et accroissement des français: une analyse 'Villermetrique'", Typescript (Center voor Economische Studiën, Leuven).

Mennell, S. (1985), All manners of food (Blackwell, London).

Meuvret, J. (1946), "Les crises de subsistances et la demographie de la France d'ancien regime", Population 1: 643–650.

Meuvret, J. (1965), "Demographic crisis in France from the sixteenth to the eighteenth century", in: D.V. Glass and D.E.C. Eversley, eds., Population in history: essays in historical demography (Aldine, Chicago, IL).

Mitchison, R. (1977), British population change since 1860 (Macmillan Press, New York)

Morell, M. (1983), "Food consumption among inmates of Swedish hospitals during the eighteenth and early nineteenth centuries", Paper presented at colloquium on the Standard of Living in Europe since 1850, Uppsala University, Sweden.

Mueller, W.H. (1986), "The genetics of size and shape in children and adults", in: F. Falkner and J.M. Tanner, eds., Human growth. Vol. 3, Methodology, 2nd edn. (Plenum, New York).

O'Brien, P. and C. Keyder (1978), Economic growth in Britain and France 1780–1914: two paths to the twentieth century (George Allen & Unwin, London).

Oddy, D.J. (1970), "Working-class diets in late nineteenth-century Britain", Economic History Review 23: 314–323.

Oddy, D.J. (1990), "Food, drink and nutrition", in: F.M.L. Thompson, ed., The Cambridge social history of Britain 1750–1950, Vol. 2 (Cambridge University Press, New York).

Osmani, S.R. (1992), "On some controversies in the measurement of undernutrition", in: S.R. Osmani, ed., Nutrition and poverty (Clarendon Press, Oxford).

Peck, A., M. Nyström and D.H. Vågerö (1989), "Adult body height, self perceived health and mortality in the Swedish population", Journal of Epidemiology and Community Health 43: 380–384.

Peller, S. (1948), "Mortality, past and future", Population Studies I: 405–456.

Perrenoud, A. (1984), "Mortality decline in its secular setting", in: T. Bengtsson, G. Fridlizius and R. Ohlsson, eds., Pre-industrial population change (Almquist and Wiksell, Stockholm).

Post, J.D. (1977), The last great subsistence crisis in the western world (Johns Hopkins University Press, Baltimore, MD).

Preston, S.H. and E. van de Walle (1978), "Urban French mortality in the nineteenth century", Population Studies 32: 275–297.

Pullar, P. (1970), Consuming passions: being an historic inquiry into certain English appetites (Little Brown, Boston, MA).

Quenouille, M.H., A.W. Boyne, W.B. Fisher and I. Leitch (1951), "Statistical studies of recorded energy expenditure in man", Technical communication no. 17 (Commonwealth Bureau of Animal Nutrition, Aberdeen).

Razzell, P.E. (1974), "An interpretation of the modern rise of population in Europe – a critique", Population Studies 28: 5–17.

Rebaudo, D. (1979), "Le movement annuel de la population française rurale de 1670 à 1740", Population 34: 589–650.

Richards, T. (1984), "Weather, nutrition, and the economy: the analysis of short-run fluctuations in the births, deaths and marriages, France 1740–1909", in: T. Bengtsson, G. Fridlizius and R. Ohlsson, eds., Pre-industrial population change (Almquist and Wiksell, Stockholm).

Rose, M.E. (1971), The relief of poverty, 1834–1914: studies in economic history (Macmillan, London).

Schofield, R. (1983), "The impact of scarcity and plenty on population change in England, 1541–1871", Journal of Interdisciplinary History 14: 265–291.

Schultz, T.P. (1981), Economics of population (Addison-Wesley, Reading, MA).

Scrimshaw, N.S. (1987), "The phenomenon of famine", Annual Review of Nutrition 7: 1–21.

Scrimshaw, N.S., C.E. Taylor and J.E. Gordon (1968), Interactions of nutrition and infection (World Health Organization, Geneva).

Seckler, D. (1982), "Small but healthy? A basic hypothesis in the theory, measurement and policy of malnutrition", in: P.V. Sukhatme, ed., Newer concepts in nutrition and their implications for policy (Maharashtra Association for the Cultivation of Science Research Institute, Pune, India).

Sen, A. (1981), Poverty and famines: An essay on entitlement and deprivation (Clarendon Press, Oxford).

Shammas, C. (1990), The pre-industrial consumer in England and America (Clarendon Press, Oxford).

Shapiro, S., E.R. Schlesinger and R.E.L. Nesbitt, Jr. (1968), Infant, perinatal, maternal, and childhood mortality in the United States (Harvard University Press, Cambridge, MA).

Slicher Van Bath, B.H. (1963), The agrarian history of western Europe, A.D. 500–1850 (Edward Arnold, London).

Smith, D.S. (1977), "A homeostatic demographic regime: patterns in West European family reconstitution studies", in: R.D. Lee, ed., Population patterns in the past (Academic Press, New York).

Spencer, G. (1989), "Projections of the population of the United States, by age, sex, and race: 1988 to 2080", in: Population estimates and projections, Ser. P-25, no. 1018 (US Department of Commerce, Washington, DC).

Steckel, R.H. (1986), "A peculiar population: the nutrition, health, and mortality of American slaves", Journal of Economic History 46: 721–741.

Steckel, R.H. (1987), "Growth depression and recovery: the remarkable case of American slaves", Annals of Human Biology 14: 101–110.

Stigler, G. (1954), "The early history of empirical studies of consumer behavior", Journal of Political Economy 62: 95–113.

Stolnitz, G. (1955), "A century of international mortality trends: I", Population Studies 9: 24–55.

Stolnitz, G. (1956), "A century of international mortality trends: II", Population Studies 10: 17–42.

Tanner, J.M. (1982), "The potential of auxological data for monitoring economic and social well-being", Social Science History 6: 571–581.

Thompson, E.P. (1967), "Time, work-discipline, and industrial capitalism", Past and Present 38: 57–97.

Thompson, W.S. and P.K. Whelpton (1933), Population trends in the United States (McGraw-Hill, New York).

Tilly, L.A. (1971), "The food riot as a form of political conflict in France", Journal of Interdisciplinary History 2: 23–57.

Tilly, C. (1975), "Food supply and public order in modern Europe", in: C. Tilly, ed., The formation of national states in Western Europe (Princeton University Press, Princeton, NJ).

Toutain, J. (1971), "La consommation alimentaire en France de 1789 à 1964", Economies et Sociétés, Cahiers de L'I.S.E.A., t. 5, no. 11: 1909–2049.

United Nations (1953), The determinants and consequences of population trends, Population studies, no. 17 (United Nations, New York).

United Nations (1973), The determinants and consequences of population trends. Population studies, no. 50 (United Nations, New York).

US Bureau of the Census (1990), Statistical abstract of the United States: 1990, 110th edn. (Government Printing Office, Washington, DC).

US Department of Health and Human Services (1987), "Anthropometric reference data and prevalence of overweight", Vital and Health Statistics, Series 11, no. 238 (Government Printing Office, Washington, DC).

US Nat. Cent. Health Statistics (1977), "Dietary intake findings: United States, 1971–1974", data from the Health and Nutrition Examination Survey. Health Resources Administration, Public Health Service, US Department of Health, Education and Welfare, Series 11, no. 202 (Government Printing Office, Washington, DC).

Utterström, G. (1965), "Two essays on population in eighteenth-century Scandinavia", in: D.V. Glass and D.E.C. Eversley, eds., Population in history: essays in historical demography (Aldine, Chicago, IL).

Van Wieringen, J.C. (1978), "Secular growth changes", in: F. Falkner and J.M. Tanner, eds., Human growth, Vol. 3, Methodology (Plenum, New York).

Van Wieringen, J.C. (1986), "Secular growth changes", in: F. Falkner and J.M. Tanner, eds., Human growth, Vol. 3, Methodology, 2nd edn. (Plenum, New York).

Von Tunzelman, G.N. (1986), "Malthus's 'total population system': a dynamic reinterpretation", in: D. Coleman and R. Schofield, eds., The state of population theory: forward from Malthus (Blackwell, Oxford).

Waaler, H.Th. (1984), "Height, weight, and mortality: the Norwegian experience", Acta Medica Scandinavica, Suppl. 679: 1–51.

Walter, J. and R. Schofield (1989), "Famine, disease and crisis mortality in early modern society", in: J. Walter and R. Schofield, eds., Famine, disease and the social order in early modern society (Cambridge University Press, Cambridge).

Weir, D.R. (1982), "Fertility transition in rural France, 1740–1829", Ph.D. dissertation (Stanford University, Stanford, CA).

Weir, D.R. (1984), "Life under pressure: France and England, 1670–1870", Journal of Economic History 44: 27–47.

Weir, D.R. (1989), "Markets and mortality in France, 1600–1789", in: J. Walter and R. Schofield, eds., Famine, disease and the social order in early modern society (Cambridge University Press, Cambridge).

Weir, D.R. (1993), "Parental consumption decisions and child health during the early French fertility decline, 1790–1914", Journal of Economic History 53: 259–274.

Williamson, J.G. (1985), Did British capitalism breed inequality (Allen and Unwin, Boston, MA).

Wilson, C.A. (1973), Food and drink in Britain: from the Stone Age to recent times (Constable, London).

Winter, J.M. (1982), "The decline of mortality in Britain 1870–1950", in: T. Barker and M. Drake, eds., Population and society in Britain 1850–1980 (New York University Press, New York).

World Bank (1987), World development report 1987 (Oxford University Press, Oxford).

Wrigley, E.A. (1969), Population and history (Weidenfeldt and Nicolson, London).

Wrigley, E.A. (1987a), "Some reflections on corn yields and prices in pre-industrial economies", in: People, cities and wealth: the transformation of traditional society, Ch. 5 (Blackwell, Oxford).

Wrigley, E.A. (1987b), "Urban growth and agricultural change: England and the continent in the early modern period", in: People, cities and wealth: the transformation of traditional society, Ch. 7 (Blackwell, Oxford).

Wrigley, E.A. and R.S. Schofield (1981), The population history of England, 1541–1871: a reconstruction (Harvard University Press, Cambridge, MA).

# Chapter 10

# DETERMINANTS AND CONSEQUENCES OF THE MORTALITY AND HEALTH OF INFANTS AND CHILDREN

KENNETH I. WOLPIN*

*University of Pennsylvania*

## Contents

*Support from NSF grant SES-9109607 is gratefully acknowledged. I have received helpful comments on earlier drafts from Pedro Mira, Randall Olsen, Mark Rosenzweig and an anonymous referee.

*Handbook of Population and Family Economics. Edited by M.R. Rosenzweig and O. Stark*
© *Elsevier Science B.V., 1997*

# 1. Introduction

This chapter critically surveys the literature pertaining to two central issues in population studies related to infant and child mortality. The first issue concerns the extent to which human fertility is affected by the existence of (and changes in) infant and child mortality. Interest in understanding the responsiveness of reproductive behavior to changes in infant and child mortality stems from two main sources: (1) the fertility and mortality processes are the driving forces governing population change, so an understanding of the way they are linked is crucial for the design of policies that attempt to influence the course of population change. (2) The "demographic transition", the change from a high fertility–high infant and child mortality environment to a low fertility–low mortality environment, that has occurred in all developed countries, has been conjectured to be the result of the fertility response to the improved survival chances of offspring. The second issue is concerned with the determinants of infant and child mortality. Clearly, the deaths of infant and children diminish societal welfare as evidenced by the enormous resource expenditures devoted to reducing the risk of early mortality. Knowledge of the behavioral causes of infant and child mortality is necessary for the most efficient use of those resources.

The demographic transition occurred in most European countries at the end of the nineteenth and the beginning of the twentieth centuries. France was the sole exception with the transition essentially beginning in the latter part of the eighteenth century. As an example, Table 1 illustrates the pattern of births and deaths encompassing the demographic transition period in Sweden. Without attempting to precisely date the turning points, infant mortality remained roughly constant between 1750 and 1800, declined by about 25% between 1800 and 1850, by another 42% in the next 50 years, and then by 85% over the last 40 years between 1900 and 1940. Similar patterns of decline are exhibited for the older age groups of children shown in the table. Children ever born, calculated from cross-sectional age-specific fertility rates, did not begin to decline until after 1870 and declined most rapidly after 1900. The number of surviving children, obtained by subtracting from the number of children ever born the expected number of child deaths through age 14, based on the cross-sectional age-specific mortality rates, did not begin to decline until around 1900. While the fertility decline did not begin until after the start of the decline in infant and child mortality, the fertility decline matches the period of the most rapid mortality decline. The simple correlations between the age-specific mortality rates and children ever born are in the range of 0.8–0.9.[1] The temporal pattern, that of the mortality decline preceding the fertility decline, is almost universal (Mattheisen and McCann, 1978), and is an impor-

---

[1] The positive time-series correlation exhibited in the Swedish data, and for all developed countries during the period surrounding the demographic transition, also hold cross-nationally. Less developed countries, like developed countries before the transition, have high infant and child mortality and high fertility relative to developed countries.

Table 1
Infant and child mortality and total fertility in Sweden: decade averages from 1750–1940

| Year | Mortality rate[a] | | | | Children ever born[b] | Surviving children |
|------|---------|---------|---------|-----------|-------------------|-----------|
|      | Age 0–1 | Age 0–4 | Age 5–9 | Age 10–14 |                   |           |
| 1750 | 205 | 83.9 | 12.6 | 6.4  | 5.0 | 2.9 |
| 1760 | 216 | 87.8 | 13.2 | 6.6  | 4.7 | 2.7 |
| 1770 | 202 | 88.2 | 15.7 | 8.7  | 4.2 | 2.4 |
| 1780 | 200 | 84.1 | 14.0 | 7.7  | 4.1 | 2.4 |
| 1790 | 196 | 78.4 | 10.4 | 5.1  | 4.5 | 2.7 |
| 1800 | 199 | 79.0 | 12.1 | 7.2  | 4.3 | 2.6 |
| 1810 | 183 | 76.0 | 9.7  | 5.6  | 4.3 | 2.7 |
| 1820 | 167 | 63.1 | 7.6  | 4.5  | 4.8 | 3.3 |
| 1830 | 167 | 60.3 | 7.5  | 4.7  | 4.6 | 3.2 |
| 1840 | 153 | 56.8 | 7.8  | 4.4  | 4.5 | 3.1 |
| 1850 | 146 | 60.5 | 10.9 | 5.5  | 4.3 | 2.9 |
| 1860 | 139 | 57.3 | 9.1  | 4.4  | 4.6 | 3.2 |
| 1870 | 130 | 52.3 | 8.5  | 4.2  | 4.5 | 3.3 |
| 1880 | 111 | 43.6 | 7.7  | 4.0  | 4.3 | 3.2 |
| 1890 | 102 | 36.9 | 6.0  | 3.6  | 4.1 | 3.3 |
| 1900 | 85  | 28.4 | 4.1  | 3.2  | 3.9 | 3.2 |
| 1910 | 69  | 22.0 | 3.5  | 2.9  | 3.3 | 2.9 |
| 1920 | 59  | 16.0 | 2.0  | 1.8  | 2.6 | 2.3 |
| 1930 | 46  | 12.3 | 1.4  | 1.3  | 1.8 | 1.6 |
| 1940 | 27  | 7.4  | 0.84 | 0.72 | 2.4 | 2.3 |

[a]Per 1000 live births per year of age.
[b]Based on cross-sectional age-specific fertility rates.

tant basis for the conjecture that the fertility transition was a result of the changing mortality environment.

There is a vast literature concerned with explaining the decline in infant and child mortality that occurred in Europe during the nineteenth and early twentieth centuries. The causes are still much debated, with there being two prevailing views. The first view, associated particularly with McKeown (1976), posits that the major reason for the mortality decline were improvements in nutrition. The second view argues that the most important causes of the mortality decline were improvements in public health technologies (improved public sanitation and sewage systems, the transmission of knowledge of methods for reducing the risk of death such as boiling of milk, washing hands during food preparation, etc.) brought about by advances in basic scientific knowledge about causes of death (e.g., Preston, 1976, 1991).

Interest in understanding the impact on population change of public policies that alter infant and child mortality risk as well as the desire to explain the demographic transition and cross-national data have led to considerable theoretical and empirical research into determining what are the effects of infant and child mortality risk on fertility behavior. This literature is the focus of the first half of this survey. The next section presents behavioral formulations found in the literature in which the decision-making unit (herein referred to as the family) makes a static lifetime decision about the level of fertility in an environment where survival to adulthood is uncertain. However, because such models involve a once-in-a-lifetime decision, they cannot allow for adaptation to mortality experiences. Next, a simplified model of dynamic decision-making is presented in which actual deaths are revealed sequentially and behavior is both anticipatory and adaptive. It is shown how replacement and hoarding strategies, which are prominent hypotheses about reproductive behavior in this literature, fit explicitly into the dynamic model. However, as the model makes clear, these concepts are not primitives, but are derivative from the more basic components of decision-making, namely preferences and technology.

A number of empirical methods are reviewed for estimating the quantitative effect of infant and child mortality risk on fertility, connecting them explicitly to the theoretical framework. Careful attention is paid to how what researchers have estimated is related to the effect that a hypothetical policy intervention that altered mortality risk would have on fertility. An overview of empirical results is presented and discussed.

Some of the empirical efforts at estimating fertility responses to infant and child mortality recognize explicitly that mortality risk may not be a completely uncontrollable process. In such a setting, where individuals can engage in behaviors that modify the mortality risk of their children and that are directly or indirectly related to fertility, in order to ascertain the effect of mortality on reproductive behavior requires that the part of mortality risk that is not controllable be estimated. The notion that the risk of infant and child mortality may be "produced" through parental actions leads naturally to an assessment of the literature on the determinants of infant and child mortality. The second half of this survey takes up this topic. In keeping with the focus of the first half of the survey, the issue is considered only from a micro perspective. The literature on the determinants of aggregate time-series mortality trends (see Schofield et al. (1991) for a variety of views), a topic that is extensively treated in Chapter 9 of this volume, is not addressed here. The literature addressed directly to explaining aggregate cross-country variation in infant and child mortality, a topic that is extensively treated in Chapter 7 of this volume, is also not surveyed here.[2] While the first half of the survey draws on the demographic and economics literatures, this part draws as well on the biomedical literature.

That there may be behavioral determinants of infant and child mortality is easily demonstrated by simple empirical tabulations. Table 2, adapted from Cramer (1987),

---

[2] As is well known, infant mortality in the US is among the highest in the developed world. According to the Office of International Statistics, National Center for Health Statistics, the US ranked 20th in 1989, just behind Greece and Italy, among countries classified by the UN as developed. The infant mortality rate at that time in the US was 9.8 (per 1000 live births). In contrast, Japan had the lowest rate, 4.6, and Sweden the next lowest, 5.8. The US has experienced a significant decline in infant mortality over the last 20 years, although the rate of decline has seemed to slow in the 1980s.

Table 2
Infant mortality in California in 1978 by selected characteristics and by race
(Cramer, 1978)

| Characteristic | Infant mortality rate | |
| --- | --- | --- |
| | White[a] | Black |
| All births | 8.1 | 16.2 |
| Age of mother | | |
| 15–19 | 12.7 | 19.0 |
| 20–24 | 8.1 | 15.6 |
| 25–34 | 7.1 | 14.7 |
| 35–44 | 7.8 | 18.5 |
| Birth order | | |
| First | 8.1 | 14.0 |
| Subsequent | 8.1 | 17.9 |
| Marital status | | |
| Single | 12.4 | 16.2 |
| Married | 7.6 | 16.2 |
| Education | | |
| 0–11 years | 12.2 | 23.1 |
| 12 years | 8.3 | 14.9 |
| 13 or more years | 6.3 | 12.9 |
| Prenatal care started | | |
| 1st trimester | 7.5 | 14.7 |
| 2nd trimester | 10.1 | 17.8 |
| 3rd trimester | 15.9 | 30.0 |

[a]Non-Hispanic.

which is based on linked birth and infant death records for all single live births in California in 1978, shows the relationship between several behavioral characteristics and infant mortality rates by race. The racial difference in infant mortality is obviously large, about double for blacks. The infant mortality rate is highest for teenage mothers, having either a backwards J shape (for whites) or a U shape (for blacks) with maternal age at birth. First births seem to have the same infant mortality rate as subsequent births for whites, but slightly lower mortality for blacks. Infants born to single white mothers have higher mortality than those born to married white mothers, but no difference exists for black mothers. Infant mortality declines with the mother's education and increases with prenatal care delay for both races. Evidence on the relationship of infant and child mortality with respect to other characteristics (breastfeeding, cigarette smoking, etc.) are provided when those factors are discussed.

There are several shortcomings of these models. First, although the family might be assumed to know the survival risk their children face, they cannot know with certainty the survival fraction (realized survival rate), i.e., exactly how many children will die for any given number of births. Further, if $s$ is interpreted as survival risk, i.e., the *probability* that (each) child survives to adulthood, in which case the number of surviving children for a given number of births is a random variable with mean $sB$, the formulation of the maximization problem in (1) is inconsistent with expected utility analysis unless utility is linear (Sah, 1991). Second, fertility is clearly discrete. The number of children can take only integer values. Third, fertility decision-making would seem a priori to be best described as a sequential optimization problem where one child is born at a time and in which there is, therefore, time to respond to realized deaths (O'Hara, 1972; Ben-Porath, 1976; Williams, 1977; Knodel, 1978).

Sah (1992) considered the case of an expected utility maximizing family choosing the number of discrete births to have. He showed that if there is no ex ante birth cost (a cost that is incurred regardless of whether or not the child survives), then the number of births must be a non-increasing function of the survival risk. To see the line of argument, consider the case where the choice is between having two, one, or no children. In that case, the difference in expected utilities associated with having one vs. no child is the survival risk, $s$, times the difference in utilities, i.e., $s[U(1) - U(0)]$. Similarly, the difference in expected utilities between having two children vs. having one child is $s^2\{[U(2) - U(1)] - [U(1) - U(0)]\} + s[U(1) - U(0)]$. Now, suppose that for a given $s$, it is optimal to have one child but not two, a result that requires satiation at one surviving offspring ($U(2) - U(1) < 0$). Clearly, at a higher $s$, it will still be optimal to have at least one child. However, at the higher value of $s$ it will still not be optimal to have a second child, and indeed the difference in expected utilities between having two vs. one cannot increase. As Sah demonstrates, the argument generalizes beyond a feasible set of two children to any discrete number of children.

This result, that increasing the mortality risk of children cannot reduce fertility (except in the neighborhood of certain mortality, $s = 1$), is the obvious analog to the target fertility result. However, unlike the target fertility model, it does not imply that the number of surviving children will be invariant to the survival rate. The reason is due to the discreteness (and the uncertainty). An example may be helpful. Suppose that $U(1) - U(0) = 2$ and $U(2) - U(1) = -1$. Now, assuming $s$ is non-zero, it will always be optimal to have at least one child, $s(U(1) - U(0)) = s > 0$. However, in this example, for any survival rate less than two-thirds, it will be optimal to have two children. At a survival rate just below two-thirds, the expected number of surviving children is close to 1.33, while at a survival rate just above two-thirds, the expected number of surviving children is close to 0.67. There is, thus, a decline in the expected number of surviving children as the survival rate increases in the neighborhood of two-thirds. However, the relationship is not monotonic; the higher the survival rate within the zero to two-thirds range, and again within the two-thirds to unity range, the more surviving children there will be on average because the number of births is constant within each range.

The example also illustrates what has been called hoarding behavior, having more births than would be optimal if survival were certain, which was not strictly the case in the target fertility model. Because utility is actually lower when there are two surviving children as opposed to one, if the survival rate were unity only one child would be optimal. However, when survival rates are low enough, below two-thirds in the example, the couple will bear two children because there is a significant enough chance that they will wind up with none who survive to adulthood. Indeed, at survival rates above one-half (but below two-thirds), on average the couple will have more than one surviving birth, exceeding the optimal number of births with certain survival. The key to this result, as will be apparent in the dynamic framework considered below, is that the family's fertility cannot react to actual infant and child deaths.

Sah demonstrates, however, that adding a cost of childbearing, as before, leads to ambiguity in the effect of the survival rate on fertility. He develops two sets of sufficient conditions for fertility (in the general case of any finite number of children) to decline with the survival rate (which is viewed as a necessary condition of a successful model) that depend on properties of the utility function: (i) that the utility function is sufficiently concave (in discrete numbers of children), or (ii) that for any degree of concavity the marginal utility of the last optimally chosen birth be non-positive, that is, that the marginal utility of the last child be non-positive if all of the optimally chosen children were to survive. Obviously, this second condition will fail to hold if there is no target fertility level, that is, if children always have positive marginal utility. Sah shows that these conditions are weaker than those that would be required if fertility is treated as a continuous choice within the same expected utility framework, and it is in that sense that discreteness reduces ambiguity.

### 2.1.2. Sequential decision-making

In formulating the theoretical linkages between infant and child mortality and fertility, the early contributors to this area of research clearly had in mind sequential decision-making models under uncertainty.[5] There are certainly no biological or economic constraints that would force couples to precommit to a particular level of fertility that is invariant to actual mortality experience. However, as in other areas of economics, the formalization of such dynamic models of behavior, particularly in the context of estimation, awaited further development. To illustrate the informal argumentation of that time, consider the following discussion by Ben-Porath (1976):

---

[5] Not all researchers believed that it was necessary to specify the optimization problem formally, however. In describing fertility strategy Preston (1978) states "These are obviously simplifications of what could be exceedingly complex 'inventory control' problems. But it is probably reasonable to apply no more sophisticated reasoning to the problem than parents themselves would" (p. 10).

Let us distinguish between two types of reaction to child mortality: "hoarding" and "replacement". Hoarding would be the response of fertility to expected mortality of offspring; replacement would be the response to experienced mortality. ... If children die very young and the mother can have another child, the same life cycle can be approximated by replacement. Where the age profile of deaths is such that replacement can reconstitute the family life cycle, replacement is superior to hoarding as a reaction, since the latter involves deviations from what would be the optimum family life cycle in the absence of mortality. If preferences are such that people have a rigid target of a minimum number of survivors at a given phase in the life cycle, hoarding involves a large number of births and the existence of more children than necessary who have to be supported in other phases of the life cycle.
...

The superiority of replacement is clear, but of course it is not always possible. The risks of mortality are often quite significant beyond infancy. Parents may be afraid of a possible loss of fecundity or some health hazard that will make late replacement impossible or undesirable. The reaction to mortality which is expected to come at a late phase of either the children's or the parents' life cycle may be partly in the form of hoarding.[6]

It is obvious from Ben-Porath's remarks that the replacement decision is viewed by him as a sequential process made in an environment of mortality uncertainty and that hoarding is the result of forward-looking behavior. Furthermore, Ben-Porath postulated that the essential features of the environment that lead to hoarding behavior as an optimal response are those that make replacement impossible, namely that children may die beyond the period of infancy and that the fertile period is finite (and possibly uncertain).

Although there are several sequential decision-making models of fertility in the literature which include non-negligible infant mortality risk (Wolpin, 1984; Sah, 1992; Mira, 1995), there are none that explicitly model sequential fertility behavior when there is significant mortality past infancy (probably because of its intractability in a many-period setting). However the essential behavioral implications of sequential decision-making and the intuition for them can be demonstrated in a sequential decision-making model with only three periods. Moreover, a three-period formulation is sufficient to illustrate and operationalize replacement and hoarding concepts.

Suppose that births are biologically feasible in the first two periods of a family's life cycle, but that the woman is infertile in the third. Each offspring may die in either of the first two periods of life, as an "infant" or as a "child", with probabilities given by $p_1$ (the infant mortality rate) and $p_2$ (the child mortality rate). Within periods, deaths occur subsequent to the decision about births. Thus, an offspring born in the

---

[6] Ben-Porath (1976: p. S164).

first period of the family's life cycle may die in its infancy (its first period of life), *before* the second period fertility decision is made. However, that same offspring, having survived infancy, may instead die in its childhood (its second period of life), *after* the second period fertility decision is made. Such a death cannot be "replaced" by a birth in the third period because the woman is infertile. For the same reason, a birth in period 2 is not replaceable even if its death occurs in that period (as an infant). It is assumed for simplicity that the survival probability to the adult period of life, conditional on surviving the first two non-adult periods, is unity. The family is assumed, for ease of exposition, to derive utility only from those offspring who survive to adulthood.[7] This corresponds to the notion that children are investment goods as in the old age security hypothesis (e.g., Willis, 1980); offspring provide benefits only as adults.

Formally, let $n_j = 1$ indicate a birth at the beginning of period $j = 1,2$ of the family's life cycle and zero otherwise. Likewise, let $d_j^k = 1$ indicate the death of an offspring of age $k$, $k = 0,1$, at the beginning of period $j$, zero otherwise, given that a birth occurred at the beginning of period $j - k$. By convention, an "infant" is age zero (in its first period of life) and a "child" is age one (in its second period of life). Thus, letting $N_{j-1}$ be the number of surviving offspring at the beginning of period $j = 1,2,3$ of the family's life cycle,

$$N_0 = 0,$$
$$N_1 = n_1(1 - d_1^0) = M_1^0,$$
$$N_2 = M_1^0(1 - d_2^1) + n_2(1 - d_2^0) = M_2^1 + M_2^0, \tag{1}$$
$$N_3 = M_2^1 + M_2^0(1 - d_3^1) = M_3^2 + M_3^1,$$

where $M_j^k = \{0, 1\}$ indicates the existence of an offspring of age $k = 0,1,2$ at the end of period $j$. Further, let $c$ be the fixed exogenous cost of a birth and $Y$ income per period. Finally, utility in period 1 is just period 1 consumption, $Y - cn_1$, utility in period 2 is that period's consumption, $Y - cn_2$, and period 3 utility is consumption in that period plus the utility from the number of surviving children in that period, $Y + U(N_3)$.[8] Lifetime utility is not discounted and income is normalized to zero for convenience.

Because the decision horizon is finite, the problem of optimally choosing a sequence of births so as to maximize lifetime utility is most easily solved backwards. Define $V_t^n(N_{t-1})$ to be expected lifetime utility at time $t$ if fertility decision $n_t = 1$ or 0 is made at the beginning of period $t$, given that there are $N_{t-1}$ surviving offspring at

---

[7] One can think of the third period of the couple's life as longer than a single period of life so that a birth in the second period that survives its infancy (in the couple's second period) and its childhood (the couple's third period), i.e., $d_2^0 = d_3^1 = 0$, will survive to adulthood while the couple is still alive.
[8] Note that the couple does not care about the age distribution of children.

the end of period $t - 1$. Further, define $V_t(N_{t-1}) = \max(V_t^1(N_{t-1}), V_t^0(N_{t-1}))$ to be maximal expected lifetime utility at period $t$ for given surviving offspring at the end of period $t - 1$. Because no decision is made at the beginning of period 3, consider the lifetime expected utility functions at period 2 conditional on the number of surviving children, namely

$$V_2^0(0) = U(0),$$

$$V_2^1(0) = (1 - p_1)(1 - p_2)U(1) + [(1 - p_1)p_2 + p_1]U(0) - c,$$

$$V_2^0(1) = (1 - p_2)U(1) + p_2 U(0), \tag{2}$$

$$V_2^1(1) = (1 - p_2)^2 (1 - p_1)U(2) + (1 - p_2)[2 p_2(1 - p_1) + p_1]U(1)$$
$$+ p_2[p_2(1 - p_1) + p_1]U(0) - c.$$

For either of the two states, $N_1 = 0$ or 1, the decision of whether or not to have a birth is based on a comparison of the expected lifetime utilities of the two alternatives. If the family has no surviving offspring at the beginning of period 2, either because there was no child born in period 1 or because there was a birth and the infant did not survive to period 2, then, from Eq. (2), the family will choose to have a birth in period 2 if and only if $V_2^1(0) > V_2^0(0)$, or $(1 - p_1)(1 - p_2)[U(1) - U(0)] - c > 0$. If there is a surviving offspring at the beginning of period 2, then the condition for choosing to have a birth is that $V_2^1(1) > V_2^0(1)$ or $(1 - p_1)(1 - p_2)\{(1 - p_2)[U(2) - U(1)] + p_2[U(1) - U(0)]\} - c > 0$. It is easily seen from these expressions that as long as the utility function exhibits diminishing marginal utility in the discrete stock of surviving offspring, that is, $U(2) - U(1) < U(1) - U(0)$, then, for all values of $p_1$ and $p_2$, the difference between expected lifetime utilities associated with having and not having a birth in period 2 is greater when there is no surviving offspring at the beginning of period 2 ($N_1 = 0$) than when there is a surviving offspring ($N_1 = 1$), i.e., the gain to have a birth in period 2 is larger if an offspring born in period 1 dies as an infant than if it survives to period 2. The extent to which the gain from a birth in period 2 is increased by the death of an infant born in period 1, $[V_2^1(0) - V_2^0(0)] - [(V_2^1(1) - V_2^0(1)]$ is equal to $(1 - p_2)^2(1 - p_1)\{[U(1) - U(0)] - [(U(2) - U(1)]\}$. This gain is clearly larger the more rapid is the decline in the marginal utility of surviving offspring and the smaller are age-specific mortality probabilities.

In order to isolate the impact of the infant mortality risk on second period fertility, suppose that the child mortality probability, $p_2$, is zero. In this case, the birth decision in period 2 is governed by the sign of $(1 - p_1)(U(2) - U(1)) - c$ if there is a surviving first period birth and by the sign of $(1 - p_1)(U(1) - U(0)) - c$ if there is not. Clearly, the family would not have a second birth as insurance against the child death of the first born, i.e., there would be no hoarding, because such a death given survival of infancy is impossible by assumption. However, the absence of such a hoarding motive does not imply that there is no effect of mortality risk on fertility.

An increase in first period mortality risk, $p_1$, has two effects on fertility. First, because an offspring born in period 1 is more likely to die during infancy, it is more likely that the family will enter the second period without a surviving offspring ($N_1 = 0$). In this case, according to our previous analysis the gain from a birth in period 2 would be larger. Second the value of having a second period birth is lower in the new mortality environment regardless of the existing stock of children (assuming non-satiation). The effect of a (unit) change in the infant mortality probability on the gain from having a second period birth is $-[U(N_1 + 1) - U(N_1)]$. For expositional purposes, call this the "direct" effect of mortality risk. If at an initial level of $p_1$ it were optimal for the household to have a second birth even if the first survived infancy, $(1 - p_1)(U(2) - U(1)) - c > 0$, then increasing infant mortality risk sufficiently would make it optimal to have a second birth only if the first died in infancy. Further increases in the infant mortality rate would eventually lead to optimally having zero births (at some level of $p_1$, $(1 - p_1)(U(1) - U(0)) - c < 0$).[9]

To illustrate most clearly the effect on second period fertility of increasing the probability of death in the second period of life, assume that the increase occurs from an initial state in which there is no mortality risk in either period of life, $p_1 = p_2 = 0$. It is useful to contrast that effect relative to the effect of increasing the first period mortality risk from the same state. Further, assume that in the zero mortality environment it is optimal to have only one surviving child, i.e., $[U(2) - U(1)] - c < 0$ and $[U(1) - U(0)] - c > 0$. Then, taking derivatives of the relevant expressions in Eq. (2) evaluated at zero mortality risk yields

$$\frac{d[V_2^1(1) - V_2^0(1)]}{dp_1}\bigg|_{p_1 = p_2 = 0} = -[U(2) - U(1)],$$

$$\frac{d[V_2^1(1) - V_2^0(1)]}{dp_2}\bigg|_{p_1 = p_2 = 0} = -[U(2) - U(1)] + [(U(1) - U(0)) - (U(2) - U(1))]. \tag{3}$$

The effect of a change in the "infant" mortality rate is, as previously derived, the "direct" effect, which, as noted, is negative if there is no satiation at one surviving offspring. The effect of a change in the child mortality rate is the negative direct effect plus an additional non-negative term whose magnitude depends on the degree of concavity of the utility function. Like the result in Sah, this positive offset arises because survival of the first offspring to adulthood is now uncertain and the decision about the second birth must be made prior to that realization. This hoarding effect generalizes to any levels of mortality risk in the sense that concavity is a necessary condition for its existence.

---

[9] If having a second surviving child reduces utility (there is satiation), then a second birth would only be optimal if the first died during infancy.

The analysis of the second period decision, taking the first period birth decision as given, does not provide a complete picture of the impact of infant and child mortality risk on the family's fertility profile. To see how the decision to have a birth in the first period varies with mortality risk, it is necessary to consider the relevant expected lifetime utilities in period 1, namely

$$
\begin{aligned}
V_1^0 &= \max(V_2^0(N_1 = 0), V_2^1(N_1 = 0)) \\
&= V_2(0), \\
V_1^1 &= (1 - p_1) \max(V_2^0(N_1 = 1), V_2^1(N_1 = 1)) + p_1 \max(V_2^0(N_1 = 0), V_2^1(N_1 = 0)) - c \\
&= (1 - p_1)V_2(1) + p_1 V_2(0) - c.
\end{aligned}
$$

(4)

The value (expected lifetime utility) of forgoing a first period birth is simply the maximum of the values attached to entering period 2 without a surviving offspring. The value attached to having a first period birth depends on the probability that the infant will survive. If the offspring survives infancy, the family receives the maximum of the values associated with entering the second period with an offspring and choosing either to have or not to have a birth in that period (see Eq. (2)), while if the offspring does not survive, they receive the maximum of the values associated with entering the second period without a surviving offspring (see Eq. (2)). The couple has a birth in period 1 if $V_1^1 > V_1^0$.

In order to characterize the decision rules in period 1, it is necessary to consider the types of behavior that would be optimal in period 2 under each of the two regimes, having or not having a surviving offspring at the beginning of period 2. There are three scenarios to consider: (i) it is optimal to have a birth in period 2 regardless of the value of $N_1(V_2^1(0) > V_2^0(0), V_2^1(1) > V_2^0(1))$ (ii) it is optimal to have a birth in period 2 only if $N_1 = 0$, i.e., if there is no surviving offspring ($V_2^1(0) > V_2^0(0), V_2^1(1) < V_2^0(1)$), and (iii) it is not optimal to have a birth in period 2 regardless of the value of $N_1$, ($V_2^1(0) < V_2^0(0), V_2^1(1) < V_2^0(1)$). Without providing the details, which are straightforward, the optimal behavior in period 1 is as follows: (i) if it is optimal to have a birth in period 2 when there is already a surviving offspring, then it will be optimal to have a birth in period 1, (ii) if it is optimal to have a birth in period 2 only if there is no surviving offspring, then it will be optimal to have a birth in period 1, and (iii) if it is not optimal to have a birth in period 2 regardless of whether there is a surviving offspring, then it will not be optimal to have a birth in period 1.[10]

Together, these results imply that increasing infant mortality risk cannot increase fertility. At very low mortality risk, it will be optimal (assuming the birth cost is low enough as well) to have a second birth independently of whether there is a surviving

---

[10] It should be recognized that these results are special to the assumption that offspring do not yield contemporaneous utility flows. A more general formulation is presented below.

first birth implying that case (i) holds. As infant mortality risk increases, it will eventually become optimal to have a second birth only if there is not a surviving first birth implying case (ii) holds. Finally, at some higher level of mortality risk, it will not be optimal to have a second period birth regardless of whether there is a surviving first birth implying that case (iii) holds.

The effect of increasing child mortality risk is more complex. If we assume that infant mortality risk (when child mortality risk is zero) is such that case (ii) above holds, then increasing child mortality risk will at some point produce case (iii) ( having two children regardless of the mortality experience of the first child, i.e., hoarding behavior as in Sah). Further increases in child mortality risk will lead eventually to a decline in births back to case (ii) and then to case (i).

Table 3 provides a numerical example. It presents two scenarios, one in which the infant mortality probability is varied holding the child mortality probability fixed (at zero) and the other allowing for the opposite (although the infant mortality probability is positive). In both cases, the expected number of births and the expected number of survivors to adulthood are calculated as the relevant mortality risk is varied. In the example, the values of the utility differences $U(2) - U(1)$ and $U(1) - U(1)$ are fixed, and exhibit concavity and non-satiation, as is the cost of a birth, $c$.

With respect to $p_1$, the expected number of births is piece-wise linear. Between $p_1 = 0$ and the value of $p_1$ given by the solution to $V_2^1(1) = V_2^0(1)$, i.e., the value of $p_1$ at which there is indifference between having a birth and not having a birth when there is a surviving offspring (0.1125 in the example), the family will have a birth in both periods regardless of the survival outcome of the first birth (the expected number of births is two). Between the above solution and the value of $p_1$ that makes the family indifferent between having a birth or not when there is no surviving child, the value that solves $V_2^1(0) = V_2^0(0)$ (0.606 in the example), the family will have a birth in period 1, but only have a birth in period 2 if the first offspring dies. The expected number of births is $1 + p_1$ over this range. At higher levels of infant mortality (greater than 0.606), it will not be optimal to have any births (the expected number of births and

Table 3

Dependence of the expected number of births and surviving children on infant and child mortality risk[a]

| Infant mortality risk $(p_1)$[b] | 0 | 0.025 | 0.050 | 0.075 | 0.100 | 0.125 | 0.150 | 0.175 |
|---|---|---|---|---|---|---|---|---|
| Expected births | 2 | 2 | 2 | 2 | 2 | 1.125 | 1.150 | 1.175 |
| Expected survivors | 2 | 1.95 | 1.90 | 1.85 | 1.80 | 0.984 | 0.978 | 0.969 |
| | | | | | | | | |
| Child mortality risk $(p_2)$[c] | 0 | 0.025 | 0.050 | 0.075 | 0.100 | 0.125 | 0.150 | 0.175 |
| Expected births | 1.12 | 1.12 | 2 | 2 | 2 | 2 | 2 | 1.12 |
| Expected survivors | 0.986 | 0.961 | 1.672 | 1.628 | 1.584 | 1.540 | 1.496 | 0.813 |

[a]$u(2) - u(1) = 0.8$, $u(1) - u(0) = 1.8$, $c = 0.71$.
[b]$p_2 = 0$.
[c]$p_1 = 0.12$.

survivors are zero). Thus, there is a positive relationship between the number of births and infant mortality risk over a considerable range of values of the infant mortality rate (from 0.1125 to 0.606 in the example). But, rather than being indicative of hoarding behavior, the positive relationship arises because over this range of increasing mortality risk it is optimal to "replace" infants that die. Notice, however, that the expected number of surviving children (as seen in Table 3) never declines (increases) with decreasing (increasing) infant mortality risk.

With respect to $p_2$, there may be as many as five possible piece-wise linear segments of the expected birth function over the $p_2$ domain. In the first segment, beginning from zero (and ending at 0.044 in the example), it is optimal to have a birth in both periods only if the first offspring dies (the expected number of births is $1 + p_1$). The expected number of surviving children (to adulthood) declines in this segment. In the second segment, it is optimal to have a birth in both periods and the utility gain from the second birth is an increasing function of $p_2$ (between $p_2 = 0.044$ and 0.10 in the example). The third segment repeats the second except that the gain is now declining in $p_2$ (between $p_2 = 0.10$ and 0.157 in the example). The fourth segment repeats the first with the expected number of births equal to $1 + p_1$ ($p_2 = 0.157$ to 0.552), while in the last segment the family has no births (between at $p_2 = 0.552$ and 1.0). As seen in the table, expected births first increase and then decrease as the child mortality rate increases. Notice that the jump in fertility between the first and second segments (between $p_2$ equal to 0.025 and 0.05) is exactly the hoarding response. Moreover, it is accompanied by an increase in the expected number of surviving children. Thus, increased child survival induces, over this range, a decrease in the expected number of surviving children.

As Table 3 makes clear, knowledge of the values of utility differences and of the cost of a birth are sufficient for the calculation of fertility behavior under any hypothetical mortality environment. Thus, if the model provides an accurate representation, or at least approximation, of fertility behavior, it would provide a tool for assessing the impact of health-related policy interventions and thus of the experiment postulated at the beginning of this section. Of course, the three-period model is intended to be only illustrative. For example, in a model with a longer fertile period and in which there are non-negligible age-specific mortality risks over an extended range of childhood ages, there would be a considerably more complex fertility response to a change in the mortality environment. A model is presented below that involves a much richer set of dynamic interactions. First, we turn to estimation, continuing to use the three-period model to illustrate the important issues.

## 2.2. Estimation issues

In the three-period model, the family decides deterministically in each of the two fecund periods whether or not to have a birth. A population of homogeneous families with respect to preferences (the two utility differences) and constraints (the cost of childbearing and the infant and child mortality probabilities) will all act identically. Moreover, because knowledge of preferences and constraints by the researcher would imply perfect prediction of behavior by the model (assuming for this purpose that the model is literally true), there would be no statistical estimation problem. To motivate an estimation problem, suppose that the population differs randomly in the cost of childbearing, $c$.[11] Further, assume that different values of $c$ for periods 1 and 2, $c_1$ and $c_2$, are drawn independently from the same distribution, $F(c; \theta)$, at the beginning of their respective periods. Thus, the decision in period 1 is conditioned on knowledge of $c$ only.[12] Neither period birth cost is known to the researcher, so that while each family's behavior is still deterministic (each family either decides to have a birth or not in each period), the researcher can determine behavior only probabilistically.

What can be learned from estimation obviously depends on the data that are available. In this regard, it is useful to divide the discussion of estimation issues into two cases corresponding to whether the population is homogeneous or heterogeneous with respect to mortality risk.

### 2.2.1. *Population-invariant mortality risk*

Consider a sample of families for whom we observe fertility and infant and child mortality histories. By assumption, they have the same utility function, draw their period-specific birth costs from the same distribution, and face the same mortality schedule for their offspring. In the context of the three-period model, it is sufficient for our purpose that we have information on $n_1$, $n_2$, and $N_1$, that is, that we know about all births and at least whether the first born had died in infancy.[13] In addition, let us suppose that the researcher also knows the mortality schedule faced by the sample, $p_1$ and $p_2$, and in addition, for identification purposes, knows the form and parameter values that describe the birth cost distribution $F(c; \theta)$.[14]

Then, the likelihood function for this sample is

---

[11] Alternatively, utility differences could have a random component.

[12] The assumption of imperfect foresight with respect to the future cost of childbearing is not consistent with the solution of the model presented above for the first period fertility decision. In deciding on first period fertility, the family would have to take into account the possible future actions that would be optimal for all possible values of the randomly drawn second period cost of childbearing. Changing the informational structure in this way simplifies the estimation problem and its exposition.

[13] It is not necessary to know the mortality experience in period 2 because there can be no subsequent fertility response in period 3.

[14] Knowledge by the researcher of the birth cost distribution function parameters is obviously a strong assumption. In the two-period decision context, where there are only two utility differences, adopting a specific functional form for the utility function would not reduce the number of parameters. For the longer horizon model that would realistically apply, the reader can think of placing parametric restrictions on the form of the utility function and on the distribution function for birth costs. Such assumptions would be sufficient for identification of the distribution function parameters.

$$\mathcal{L}(\omega|\text{data}) = \prod_{i=1}^{I} \Pr(n_{1i}, n_{2i}|d_{1i}, p_1, p_2, F)$$

$$= \prod_{i=1}^{I} \Pr(n_{2i}|N_{1i}, p_1, p_2, F) \, \Pr(n_{1i}|p_1, p_2, F), \tag{5}$$

where $\omega$ consists of the two utility differences. There are $I$ families in the sample with the lack of an $I$ subscript implying constancy in the population.

Now, the probability (from the researcher's perspective) that a randomly drawn family will be observed to have a birth in period 2 conditional on the two possible values of the beginning period stock of surviving offspring is:

$$\Pr(n_2 = 1|N_1 = 1) = \Pr(c_2 < (1 - p_2)(1 - p_1)[(1 - p_2)(U(2) - U(1)) + p_2(U(1) - U(0))]),$$

$$\Pr(n_2 = 1|N_1 = 0) = \Pr(c_2 < (1 - p_2)(1 - p_1)[U(1) - U(0)]). \tag{6}$$

Similarly, the probability of a first period birth is given by

$$\Pr(n_1 = 1) = \Pr(c_1 < (1 - p_1)(E_1(V_2(1)) - E_1(V_2(0)))), \tag{7}$$

where $E_1$ is the expectations operator given the information set at period 1 and is taken over the distribution of infant and child mortality and birth costs, and the value functions in the integral of Eq. (7) are given by Eq. (4). There are three sample proportions corresponding to the theoretical probabilities in Eqs. (6) and (7), from which the utility differences can be recovered.[15] Given these estimates, the response of fertility behavior in the population to variations in mortality risk can be obtained by solving the behavioral optimization problem.

Notice that in this example, there is no other way to estimate policy responses to mortality risk variation because mortality risk is assumed not to vary in the population. However, the sample proportions of births, the data analogs of Eqs. (6) and (7) used in the structural estimation, obviously provide information about behavior. Indeed, taking the difference in the probabilities in Eq. (6) provides a natural way to define a measure of replacement behavior. Specifically, define the "replacement rate", $r$, as given by

$$r = \Pr(n_2 = 1|n_1 = 1, d_1 = 1) - \Pr(n_2 = 1|n_1 = 1, d_1 = 0) \tag{8}$$

---

[15] It might appear that we could have relaxed the assumption that all of the parameters of the birth cost distribution are known, given that there are more sample proportions than unknown parameters. However, this turns out not to be the case given the structure of the model. As an example, if $F$ is assumed normal and we normalize the variance to unity, the mean of the cost distribution does not enter the decision rule in a way that allows it to be separately identified from the utility differences.

where the conditioning event in Eq. (8) is restricted to a first period birth with and without its death.[16]

Analogous to the three-period dynamic model, if there is diminishing marginal utility, then the probability of a birth is larger when there is no surviving offspring than when there is, and $r > 0$. According to Eq. (8), full replacement, $r = 1$, would require that the probability of having a second birth be unity when the first birth did not survive and zero otherwise. On the other hand, the replacement rate will be zero if the probability of a birth is independent of the number of surviving offspring, a result that requires (see Eq. (6)) that the marginal utility of surviving offspring be constant, $U(2) - U(1) = U(1) - U(0)$.

What do we learn from this transformation of the underlying probabilities, i.e., from calculating $r$? Or alternatively, for what policy experiment would calculation of $r$ be relevant? Implicit in the original policy experiment is the notion that the effect of the health program on the mortality risk of infants and children is known to families or becomes immediately obvious from its (population) impact (for example, as seems to have been the case when the polio vaccine was introduced in the US).[17] Suppose, however that, although effective, families did not alter their beliefs about mortality risks (or did so only very slowly, as might be the case with generalized improvements in nutrition). Then, we would observe families responding only to the reduced number of infant deaths as they are experienced and not to the decline in the infant and child mortality risk. In this case, the replacement rate would measure the full response to the program.

Now, the replacement rate times the number of first period infant deaths in a population yields the number of extra births that arise in that population because of the infant deaths. This result follows from the fact that the definition of $r$ in Eq. (8) is equivalent to the expected number of births given a birth and infant death in the first period, $1 + \Pr(n_2 = 1 \mid n_1 = 1, d_1 = 1)$ minus the expected number of births given a birth and no infant death $1 + \Pr(n_2 = 1 \mid n_1 = 1, d_1 = 0)$. So, suppose, for example, that the government institutes a health program that will reduce the infant mortality risk by 0.05. Following its introduction, there will be a reduction in the number of first period deaths of $0.05 \times \Pr(n_1 = 1) \times$ no. of families. If $r = 1$ at the pre-program, and perceived to be post-program, mortality risk, then all of the second period births that had resulted from the replacement of first period deaths will not occur and the number of second period births will thus decline for this reason by the same amount as the number of first period deaths. Further, the number of surviving children would be approximately unchanged. Alternatively, if $r = 0$, so that no first period deaths were re-

---

[16] As noted, this detail is unnecessary given the construction of the model, because the second period birth probability is the same regardless of why the stock of children is zero.

[17] It should be noted that the behavioral formulation assumes that the policy is itself a surprise, i.e., that families attach a zero probability to its occurrence. Otherwise, in the dynamic model, one would have to allow for a distribution over future infant and child mortality risk (conditional on current information). Introducing additional parameters would require a reconsideration of identification.

placed, the number of second period births will be unaffected by the reduction in the number of deaths, and the number of surviving children will increase by the number of averted deaths.

If the fertile stage is extended beyond two periods, the replacement rate would have to account for births, arising from a death, that occur in later periods.[18] If there are $T$ fecund periods, then the replacement rate for the specific case of a birth in the first period and its subsequent infant death is given by

$$r = \sum_{j=2}^{T}[\Pr(n_j = 1 | n_1 = 1, d_1 = 1) - \Pr(n_j = 1 | n_1 = 1, d_1 = 0)]. \tag{9}$$

Notice that in order to calculate Eq. (9) knowledge of the probabilities of *all* future birth sequences conditional on $N_1$ is required. In the $T$-period case, a replacement rate can be calculated at any period for any given birth and death sequence. For example, in a setting in which the entire birth and death sequence determined the decision rule, there would be, for example, a period 7 replacement rate given the death of a three-year-old in period 6, and conditional on other births and deaths as of the end of period 6.[19] There is thus potentially a very large set of replacement rates, all of which are determined by the parameters of the underlying behavioral model.[20]

Although perhaps less transparently than was the case in the three-period model, the expression for the replacement rate in Eq. (9) is equivalent to the difference in the expected number of births given the birth and death of a child in period 1 and the expected number of births given the birth and survival of a child in period 1. Therefore, Eq. (9) measures exactly the excess births that arise from an infant death. Analogous replacement rates would measure the excess births that would arise from the death of a child of any age given any birth and death history.

The value in estimating replacement effects for policy analysis rests on an assumption about the extent to which effective programs alter families' perceptions about mortality risk. The value in estimating the structural model does not depend on assumptions about learning because identifying the fundamental parameters allows either policy experiment to be simulated.[21] For the rest of the discussion it is assumed, as is the case in the literature, that estimating replacement rates is useful.

---

[18] Replacement births could be postponed in this model due to random fluctuations in birth costs. In richer models there could be additional reasons.

[19] Thus, replacement rates are not restricted to infant deaths.

[20] It is also possible for the replacement rate to be larger than one if children can die at older ages. A death close to the end of the fertile period might induce hoarding behavior.

[21] Mortality risk was assumed not to be changing over the family's decision period. If it were, some assumption about how families forecast future mortality risk would need to be incorporated into the behavioral model.

Longitudinal or retrospective data on birth and death histories are not always available. Often, only information on total births and deaths is reported for a cross-section of households, i.e., in the three-period model, $n_1 + n_2$ and $d_1$.[22] It would seem natural, in this case, under the assumptions of this section that mortality risk is the same for all families, to estimate a regression of the number of births on the actual number of infant and child deaths. Such a regression would determine the additional births that arise from one additional death, i.e., the replacement rate in Eq. (8) (or Eq. (9) in the $T$-period case). Thus, for the regression

$$B_j = b_0 + rD_j + v,\qquad(10)$$

where $B_j$ is the number of births in family $j$, $D_j$ the number of deaths, and $v$ is a stochastic element, the regression coefficient $r$ is the replacement rate in Eq. (8). In the three-period model, $B$ can equal only 0, 1 or 2, while $D$ can be only 0 or 1, and the only relevant deaths are those of infants.[23]

From the birth probabilities given in Eq. (6), it is possible to derive the set of probabilities for numbers of births given any number of deaths, e.g., $\Pr(B = 0 \mid D = 0)$, $\Pr(B = 1 \mid D = 0)$, etc., and, from these, the expected number of births for each number of deaths. With some tedious algebra, it can be shown that the OLS regression estimator, the difference in the expected number of births given one death and the expected number of births given zero deaths, is

$$\hat{r} = E(B \mid D = 1) - E(B \mid D = 0)$$
$$= \frac{g_1 + g_2 r}{g_1 + g_2},\qquad(11)$$

where $g_1 = \Pr(n_1 = 0)$ and $g_2 = \Pr(d_1 = 1 \mid n_1 = 1)\Pr(n_1 = 1)$. It is easy to see from Eq. (11) that the OLS regression coefficient of births on deaths in general will overstate the replacement effect.[24]

There have been several attempts to provide estimates of replacement affects that correct for the "spurious" correlation between births and deaths.[25] Olsen (1980) considers the following joint stochastic representation of total births and deaths:

---

[22] There is additional information contained in $d_1$ that results from the special nature of the three-period formulation, namely that with one total birth and one death, the timing of the birth is known. With a longer horizon, such inferences would be unavailable from total births and total deaths.

[23] Again, second period deaths are ignored because they cannot influence fertility.

[24] Notice that the replacement rate can be estimated correctly by restricting the estimation sample to couples with at least one birth ($g_1 = 0$ in that subsample). However, this is an artifact of the three-period model. In general, the number of deaths must rise with the number of births for a constant mortality rate and the resulting positive correlation between births and deaths is built into the estimated replacement effect (see below).

$$B_j = \overline{B} + r(D_j - \overline{D}) + v_j,$$
$$D_j = pB_j + \varepsilon_j, \tag{12}$$

where bars indicate means. Substituting the first equation in Eq. (12) into the second yields

$$D_j = p\overline{B} + \frac{pv_j}{1 - pr} + \frac{\varepsilon_j}{1 - pr}. \tag{13}$$

As Olsen argues, because the number of deaths is not statistically independent of $v_j$, as seen in Eq. (13), the regression coefficient estimator of $r$ from the $B_j$ equation will be biased and inconsistent. Specifically, the probability limit of the regression estimator is

$$\text{plim}(\hat{r}) = r + \frac{\text{cov}(D_j, v_j)}{\text{var}(D_j)} > r. \tag{14}$$

The OLS regression estimator overstates the true replacement rate because deaths and births are positively correlated independently of the existence of replacement; families with more births experience more deaths simply because their "sample" size is larger. Deriving expressions for the moments in Eq. (14) under the assumption that $D_j$ and $B_j$ are binomial random variables, Olsen further shows that

$$\text{plim}(\hat{r}) = r + \left\{ (1 - pr) \left[ p + \frac{(1 - p)\overline{B}}{\text{var}(B)} \right]^{-1} \right\}. \tag{15}$$

The probability limit of the OLS estimator can deviate substantially from the true replacement rate. Assuming $r = 0$, Olsen reports that the OLS regression estimate of $r$ ranges between 0.9 and 1.7 for five different populations. But, what is important is that Eq. (15) can be used to correct the replacement effect estimate using the observed mortality rate $p$ (along with the mean and variance of births). Given $\hat{r}, \overline{B}, p$, and var($B$), Eq. (15) can be solved for $r$.

---

[25] Notice that in the three-period model, knowledge of $g_1$, the proportion of families not having a child in period one, and of $g_2$, the proportion of families who both have a birth in the first period and for whom the infant dies, is sufficient to solve Eq. (11) for the true replacement effect. Of course, if one had this information it would not be necessary to estimate the replacement effect from Eq. (11) as Eq. (6) could be computed directly as previously discussed. The use of Eq. (11), as noted, is predicated on the lack of such event history data.

Mauskopf and Wallace (1984) present a somewhat different procedure for estimating the replacement rate that solves explicitly for the death distribution that is consistent with replacement behavior. To outline their method, define $B*$ to be the number of births that would occur if the family experienced no child deaths. In the three-period model $B*$ is a well-defined entity obtained by solving the sequential model for $n_1$ and $n_2$ conditional on there being no deaths. Given that $c$ varies randomly in the population, $B*$ is a random variable with expectation in the three-period model given by $1 \times \Pr(B = 1 \mid D = 0) + 2 \times \Pr(B = 2 \mid D = 0)$. In general, one can write $B* = E(B*) + u$, where $E(u) = 0$, $E(u^2) = \sigma^2$, and where $E(B*)$ is determined by the exact optimizing model that is adopted.

Because replacement children can themselves die and be replaced, Mauskopf and Wallace conceptualize the process as sequential (although they conceive of the actual decision process as being static), consisting of separate rounds of deaths, replacement births, deaths of the replacement births, replacement births of the replacement birth deaths, etc. So, in the first round, $d_0 = pB* + \varepsilon_0 = pE(B*) + \omega_0$, where $\omega_0 = pu + \varepsilon_0$ and $p$ is the (non-age-specific) mortality rate of children. First round deaths, $d_0$, conditional on $B*$, are assumed to be binomially distributed. Assuming independence between $u$ and $\varepsilon_0$, the variance of $\omega_0$ is $\text{var}(\omega_0) = p^2\sigma^2 + p(1 - p)E(B*)$. First round replacements are $r_0 = rd_0 + \eta_0 = rpE(B*) + \xi_0$, where $\xi_0 = r\omega_0 + \eta_0$ and $r$ is the replacement rate. The variance of $\xi_0$ given independence between $\eta_0$ and the other stochastic elements is $\text{var}(\xi_0) = r^2 \text{var}(\omega_0) = r(1 - r)pE(B*)$. In general, in the $i$th round, $d_i = pE(r_{i-1}) + \omega_i$ and $r_i = rE(d_1) \xi_i$. Summing over all rounds, $I = 0,1,\ldots$, they derive the following expressions for the first two moments of total deaths and total births:

$$E(D) = \frac{pE(B*)}{1 - pr},$$

$$E(B) = \frac{E(B*)}{1 - pr},$$

$$\text{var}(D) = \frac{[p^2\sigma^2 + pE(B*)(1 + pr - p)]}{(1 - pr)^2}, \tag{16}$$

$$\text{var}(B) = \frac{[\sigma^2 + prE(B*)]}{(1 - pr)^2},$$

$$\text{cov}(D, B) = \frac{[p\sigma^2 + prE(B*)]}{(1 - pr)^2}.$$

These five equations have four unknowns, $p$, $r$, $E(B*)$, $\sigma^2$, satisfying the necessary condition for identification. Mauskopf and Wallace estimate the parameters by matching the theoretical moments to the observed moments in the data.

In the $T$-period model, the replacement rate estimated from the total birth–total death relationship using either Olsen's correction or the Mauskopf and Wallace method would be an "average" of replacement rates specific to the actual birth and death sequences in the sample. Such "average" replacement rates could be quite different for samples that differ, for example, only in the age distribution of the families (women), but with the same underlying infant mortality risk, preferences, and birth costs.

### 2.2.2. Population-variant mortality risk

#### 2.2.2.1. Observable heterogeneity

Assume now that there is population variation in the mortality environment that is observable to the researcher, e.g., geographic variation in mortality rates. Structural estimation could proceed with the pooled (over geographic areas) data if utility differences (the structural parameters) were cross-sectionally invariant, or separately by geographic area if not.

A possible alternative estimation procedure is to approximate the decision rules of the optimization problem as a general function of the state variables. Birth probabilities could be approximated by

$$
\begin{aligned}
\Pr(n_2 = 1 \mid N_1) &= \Pr((h_2(N_1, p_1, p_2, c_2) > 0), \\
\Pr(n_1 = 1) &= \Pr((h_1(p_1, p_2, c_1) > 0),
\end{aligned}
\tag{17}
$$

where, as before, the $c$'s are random variables. Given distributional and functional form assumptions, the impact of a change in mortality risk can be calculated from the $h$ functions estimated with likelihood function (5). For example, linearizing the $h$ function in its arguments and assuming normality of the cost distribution leads to a standard (bivariate) probit estimation problem.[26] Although the estimates could be used to assess the impact of policy interventions that reduce mortality risks, the ability to extrapolate from Eq. (17) in order to assess "large" policy changes would depend on the global properties of the approximation of the $h$ function. And, clearly this estimation method is unavailable without population variation in mortality risk.

Non-parametric estimation of replacement rates (Eq. (8) or (9)) could be obtained for each geographic area, recalling that replacement rates depend upon the level of infant mortality risk. Because Olsen's correction factor (Eq. (15)) depends on the mortality rate, Olsen's analysis could be conducted within areas, recognizing as well the direct dependence of the replacement rate on mortality risk. Similarly, Mauskopf

---

[26] Because the second period birth probability depends on the lagged dependent variable, $N_1$, the two decision rules could be separately estimated only if $c_1$ and $c_2$ are independently drawn.

and Wallace's analysis could be conducted within geographic areas, obtaining separate location-specific estimates of replacement rates.

### 2.2.2.2. *Unobservable heterogeneity*

In this case, families differ in their underlying mortality risk to an extent not fully observed by the researcher. Structural estimation, using maximum likelihood as before, would require either that couple-specific mortality schedules be treated as estimable parameters or that they be assumed to have a known distribution whose parameters would be estimated. Suppose, for example, that $p_2 = 0$, i.e., there is no mortality risk beyond infancy. Then, because realized deaths provide information on family-specific mortality risk, the likelihood function would incorporate both fertility and mortality events, namely

$$
\begin{aligned}
\mathcal{L} &= \prod_{i=1}^{I} \Pr(n_{1i}, n_{2i}, d_{1i}^0, d_{2i}^0 \mid p_{1i}) \\
&= \prod_{i=1}^{I} \Pr(d_{1i}^0, d_{2i}^0 \mid p_{1i}) \Pr(n_{2i} \mid N_{1i}, p_{1i}) \Pr(n_{1i} \mid p_{1i}),
\end{aligned}
\tag{18}
$$

where $d_1^0$ and $d_2^0$ indicate a death of a first or second period birth in infancy as in the prior notation, and where conditioning on $p_{1i}$ indicates that the infant mortality rate is now family-specific. It is important to note that in order to implement the estimation procedure (maximize Eq. (18)) the optimization problem of the family would have to be solved for each family separately. If instead we had assumed a specific parametric distribution for $p_1$ or a non-parametric distribution having a fixed number of discrete values (a fixed number of family types), the likelihood function would contain an integration or discrete mixture over the possible values of $p_1$ that each family could be exposed to. The optimization problem would, in this case, have to be solved for each possible value of mortality risk. Notice that there are cross-equation restrictions implied by the behavioral model. Not only are birth probabilities in the two periods connected by the same fundamental parameters (the last two components of the likelihood function in the second line of Eq. (18)), but also those probabilities are functions of the mortality risk that also enters the determination of actual deaths in the first component of the likelihood function. Thus, the estimates of mortality risk would be influenced not only by observed mortality rates, but also by the fertility response to mortality risk.

Estimating approximate decision rules, Eq. (17), embedded in likelihood function (18), when there is unobserved heterogeneity in mortality risk is within the realm of models discussed, in the case of normal errors, in Heckman (1982). It differs from the structural estimation in that the cross-equation restrictions are ignored. Estimation must take into account that the unobserved heterogeneity is correlated with the existing stock of children in each period of the family's life cycle (see for example Mroz and Weir, 1990). Subject to the usual caveat about the inconsistency of fixed-effects estimates in "short" panels, one would recover an (unbiased) estimate of each family's permanent mortality risk and also obtain an estimate of the effect of mortality risk on births probabilities. However, this procedure is equivalent to a two-step procedure of estimating the family-specific mortality risk from realized family-specific mortality rates and "regressing" measures of fertility on them. Since the realized rates measure the true risk with error, these policy relevant estimates would be biased downward. Replacement effects estimated from the effect of a death on birth probabilities or total births, holding the estimated mortality risk constant, would be upwardly biased (since deaths are positively correlated with the family's true mortality risk).

Replacement rates estimated non-parametrically using sample birth probabilities would not correspond to the replacement rate for any particular family. The replacement rate in Eq. (8) or (9) holds mortality risk constant, while the sample birth proportions reflect the unobserved variation in mortality risk. The number of excess births calculated this way would also not provide the correct population effect. That calculation would have to be performed for each family separately and then summed over families to obtain the correct estimate.

Olsen suggests estimating the replacement effect from the regression equation (10) using realized sample (infant) mortality rates among families, reflecting in part variation in underlying mortality schedules and in part "luck", as an instrumental variable for total deaths (in order to correct for the spurious correlation between total births and total deaths). Although such a procedure would be valid in the case where mortality risk was constant in the population (and also unnecessary), when $p$ varies but is unobserved, the regression equation (10) is misspecified; the dynamic model, for example, implies that the expected number of births will vary with the true infant mortality risk (recall the direct effect of mortality risk demonstrated in the three-period model). If it is not included as a regressor because it is unobserved, then it enters through the regression error and the realized mortality rate, being correlated with it, cannot be a valid instrument for the number of deaths. It is important to stress that the problem with this procedure exists even if there is no "child" mortality risk; it has nothing to do with hoarding behavior. However, if there was significant child mortality and the risk varied in the population, child mortality rates would also not be a valid instrument for estimating replacement effects because they affect fertility directly (through the direct effect and the hoarding effect).

Both Olsen and Mauskopf and Wallace extended their methodologies to the case in which there is unobservable population heterogeneity in mortality risk. It is sufficient to consider the Mauskopf and Wallace paper because the problem with the method, shared by both, is more easily demonstrated. For clarity, assume that child (but, not infant) mortality risk is zero. As Mauskopf and Wallace note, one can view the moment equations (16) as conditional on a particular value of $p$ ($p_1$ under the above assumption). To get the unconditional (population) moments, Mauskopf and Wallace integrate the conditional moments over $p$ assuming that $p$ comes from the two parameter beta distribution. They then estimate the beta distribution parameters instead of $p$. However, this procedure is inconsistent with the dynamic model presented above; both the replacement rate ($r$) and $E(B^*)$, which appear in the moment equations, depend on $p$. Integrating over $p$ requires that one solve for their optimal values as $p$ changes. Ignoring this dependence leads, in principle, to incorrect estimates of the replacement effect.

## 2.3. Two biological mortality–fertility links

There are two biological links between mortality and fertility, recognized in the literature, that create special problems. The first has to do with the possibility that mortality risk can itself be influenced by the pattern of childbearing, i.e., by the timing and spacing of children, through biological mechanisms.[27] Having children spaced closer together or having children at older ages may, for example, increase the risk of infant mortality (returned to later). The second link has to do with the (seeming) contraceptive effect of breastfeeding. The death of an infant or child that is being breastfed can lead to an increased probability of a birth independently of the replacement mechanism (Preston, 1978).

To illustrate the first in the context of the three-period model, assume that the mortality rate of a child in its first period of life depends on whether a child was born in the previous period. Thus, a child born at the beginning of the first period would have an infant mortality rate $p_{11}$, while the child born in the second period would have an infant mortality rate that depended on the existence or not of a first birth, $p_{12}(n_1)$, where $p_{12}(0) < p_{12}(1)$. Note that if there is no timing (age) effect $p_{12}(0) = p_{11}$.

In the original three-period model, the relevant state space for the second period decision consisted of the two values of $N_1$. With the infant mortality rate faced by the second period child now depending on whether or not a child was born in the first period, there are three relevant values for the state space, $N_1 = 1$ and $n_1 = 1$, $N_1 = 0$ and $n_1 = 1$, $N_1 = 0$ and $n_1 = 0$. The expected utility of having a child in period 2 differs depending upon whether $N_1 = 0$ because no child was born in period 1 or because the child died. Whereas before the replacement effect could be obtained by comparing the propensity to have a child in period 2 among couples with $N_1 = 1$ and $N_1 = 0$, the replacement rate in this case can be obtained only by making such a comparison among those couples who had a child in period 1 ($n_1 = 1$), the way it was written in Eqs. (8) and (9).

This extension creates no special problem either for structural or non-structural estimation as long as there is no unobserved heterogeneity in mortality risk. In that case, and under our previous assumptions, mortality risk is weakly exogenous. However,

---

[27] There may in addition be non-biological links through resource allocation mechanisms.

when families have partial control over their mortality risk through their fertility decisions and also have unobserved traits that affect mortality risk, the estimation problem is altered considerably (mortality risk is endogenous). In this case, the likelihood function is

$$
\mathcal{L} = \prod_{i=1}^{I} \Pr(n_{1i}, n_{2i}, d_{1i}^0, d_{2i}^0 | p_{11i}, p_{12i}(n_{1i}))
$$

$$
= \prod_{i=1}^{I} \Pr(d_{1i}^0 | p_{11i}) \Pr(d_{2i}^0 | p_{12i}(n_{1i}))
$$

$$
\times \Pr(n_{2i} | N_{1i}, d_{1i}, p_{11i}, p_{12i}(n_{1i})) \Pr(n_{1i} | p_{1i}, p_{12i}(n_{1i})). \tag{19}
$$

Structural estimation would require that the optimization model that is solved now include the impact of fertility on the mortality risk function, incorporating unobserved mortality risk into the estimation as before. Identification is not possible without placing further structure on the mortality process. For example, if the first period mortality risk is actually unique to the family and period, it is obviously not possible to estimate it for families who choose not to have a first period birth (if, for example, they face a very high risk of infant mortality). This problem obviously extends to non-structural estimation and, because cross-equation restrictions are ignored, will in general be more severe.

To incorporate lactation effects without undue complication, assume that fertility control is imperfect in that a child may be born when it is not wanted, that is, when expected utility would be greater without a child than with a child, but that the parents can have a child when it is wanted with certainty. Let the conception probability when a child is not wanted, in the sense above, be $q_1$ in the first period, and let the conception probability in the second period depend on the existence of $s$ surviving first birth, $q_2 = q_2(M_1^0)$. Consistent with there being a contraceptive effect of breastfeeding, $q_2(1) < q_2(0)$.

While this modification does not affect the second period decision rule (because it is the terminal decision period), the family decides to have a child if the expected utility from the child exceeds the expected utility without the child, it does affect the probabilities associated with having a child as given in (5). In particular,

$$
\Pr(n_2 = 1 | N_1 = 1) = q_2(1) + (1 - q_2(1)) \Pr(V_2^1(1) > V_2^0(1)),
$$

$$
\Pr(n_2 = 1 | N_1 = 0) = q_2(0) + (1 - q_2(0)) \Pr(V_2^1(0) > V_2^0(0)). \tag{20}
$$

Using Eq. (20), the replacement effect as given by Eq. (8) can be broken into two parts, one that corresponds to the "behavioral" replacement rate as previously defined and one that arises from the increased conception probability when breastfeeding is terminated by an infant death, i.e.,

$$r = (1 - q_2(1))[\Pr(V_2^1(0) > V_2^0(0)) - \Pr(V_2^1(1) > V_2^0(1))]$$
$$+ [q_2(0) - q_2(1)][1 - \Pr(V_2^1(0) > V_2^0(0))].$$

(21)

Eq. (21) reduces to the behavioral replacement effect previously defined if there is perfect fertility control, $q_2(1) = q_2(0) = q_2 = 0$. If fertility control is imperfect but there is no lactation effect $q_2(1) = q_2(0) = q_2 > 0$, then only the first term is potentially non-zero and corresponds to the behavioral replacement effect with imperfect fertility control. If there is a lactation effect, then the second term in Eq. (21) is positive and the behavioral replacement effect is overstated. The magnitude of the overstatement depends on the extent to which the cessation of breastfeeding increases the conception probability and on the magnitude of the probability that a couple will not want to have a child given that they have no surviving child from the first period.

Without external knowledge or estimation of the conception probabilities $q_2(1)$ and $q_2(0)$, estimation of the behavioral replacement effect is problematic. Estimating the replacement effect non-parametrically from differences in second period birth probabilities or from total births and deaths necessarily confounds the behavioral and biological effects. The difficulty of incorporating breastfeeding into structural (and non-structural) estimation would depend on whether breastfeeding is a choice and on whether it also affects mortality risk (see below).

## 2.4. A general model

In this section a more general model is presented that combines features from a number of papers (Heckman and Willis, 1976; Newman, 1981; Wolpin, 1984; Montgomery, 1988; Mroz and Weir, 1990) and that is richer in terms of fertility–mortality links. Denote by $t = 1$ the beginning of the decision horizon, by $t = \tau + 1$ the onset of infertility, and by $t = T + 1$ the end of life. There are exactly $\tau$ fecund periods (the last fecund period begins at $t = \tau$) and $T$ periods of life (the last period of life begins at $t = T$). For convenience, all three of these dates are taken as deterministic and exogenous. In the fertility context, the exogeneity assumption for the onset of decision-making ($t = 1$) is probably the most problematic. If it is taken to be the age of menarche, then it will be necessary in most settings to model the decision to marry explicitly. Assuming the decision process to begin at marriage, however, will be correct only if marriage timing does not signify optimizing childbearing behavior.

The period length is assumed to be one month and the decision or control variable is whether or not to contracept. Let $\kappa_t^0 = 1$ if at $t$ the woman is not pregnant and contraception is not being used and equal to zero otherwise, $\kappa_t^1 = 1$ if at $t$ the woman is not pregnant and the couple chooses to contracept and equal to zero otherwise, and $\kappa_t^2 = 1$ if the woman is pregnant at $t$ and zero otherwise. A couple can be in only one of these three mutually exclusive states in any month. Because the woman becomes infertile at $t = \tau + 1$, $\kappa_t^0 = 1$ for all $t \geq \tau + g$ where $g$ is the known (non-random) gestation period.[28] Define $\kappa_t = (\kappa_t^0, \kappa_t^1)$, $\kappa_t^+ = \kappa_t, \kappa_t^2)$, and $K_t = (\kappa_{t-1}^+, \ldots, \kappa_1^+)$. Thus, $K_t$ is the month by month history of contraceptive use and pregnancies as of $t$. A birth is assumed to occur at $t$, $n_t = 1$, if the woman has been pregnant for the pre-determined gestation period ($g$). The history of births is denoted by $B_t = (n_{t-1}, \ldots, n_1)$. As before, $N_t$ is the number of children who are alive at the end of period $t$. The evolution of surviving children is given by

$$N_0 = 0,$$

$$N_1 = n_1(1 - d_1^0) = M_1^0,$$

$$N_2 = M_1^0(1 - d_2^1) + n_2(1 - d_2^0) = M_2^1 + M_2^0, \tag{22}$$

$$\vdots$$

$$N_t = \sum_{k=1}^{t} M_t^{t-k}.$$

where $M_t^{t-k}$ is equal to one if a child of age $t - k$ is alive at the end of period $t$ and is zero otherwise. The age distribution of children alive at the end of $t$ is given by the vector $M_t = (M_t^0, M_t^1, \ldots, M_t^{t-1})$ and the history of the age distribution by $M_t^+ = (M_t, M_{t-1}, \ldots, M_1)$.

Technology consists of mortality and pregnancy risk functions. The probability that a child of age $a$ ($a = 0, \ldots, t - 1$) at time $t$ will die at the beginning of period $t$, $p_t^a$, is assumed to depend on the timing and spacing of prior births, $B$, on a couple-specific frailty endowment common to all children born to the couple, $\mu_1$, and on a child-specific frailty endowment, $\mu_2$. The pregnancy probability at time (the age of the couple) $t$, $q_t$, is assumed to depend on the entire history of contraceptive choices, allowing for efficiency in use, and of pregnancies, allowing for biological dependencies, and on a couple-specific fecundity parameter, $\phi$. The frailty parameter of the mortality risk function and the fecundity parameter of the pregnancy risk function are assumed to be drawn prior to $t = 1$ and are permanent.[29]

The couple at each time $t$ is assumed to maximize the remaining discounted lifetime utility with respect to the contraception variables at $t$, $\kappa_t$, subject to a budget constraint. Per-period utility is state-dependent, namely

$$U_t = \kappa_t^0 U_t^0(N_t, X_t, \varepsilon_t^0) + \kappa_t^1 U_t^1(N_t, X_t, \varepsilon_t^1) + \kappa_t^2 U_t^2(N_t, X_t, \varepsilon_t^2), \tag{23}$$

where $X_t$ is a composite consumption good and $\varepsilon_t^j$ is a random time-varying taste parameter for each of the contraception and pregnancy states. The preference parameter

---

[28] Although a woman can be pregnant during this interval, if she is not she would never contracept.

[29] They could also depend on the mother's age at conception for biological reasons.

may have a permanent component, reflecting population taste variation for children relative to goods.

Even ignoring tractability, it is unclear exactly how to model the couple's budget constraint. The issue of whether and in what ways couples are liquidity constrained is not resolved in the literature and surely depends on the society under study. To reduce the already cumbersome notation, assume an ad hoc consumption function of the form

$$X_t = X_t(Y_t, \kappa_t, M_t, n_t), \tag{24}$$

where $Y_t$ is a stochastic exogenous income flow drawn from a known distribution. Notice that contraception is assumed to be costly as are children.

To close the model, it is necessary to specify how families forecast future economic and health conditions. For example, what do couples know about future mortality risk, an issue that is particularly relevant if health and medical technologies are evolving? Do couples know their innate frailty and fecundity endowments as of the initial period or do they learn about them as children are born? How do couples forecast future income? Given imperfect foresight, do all couples use the same forecasting rules?[30] Although one may think that these questions are only relevant if structural estimation is pursued, such a view would be incorrect. If, for example, couples learn about their infant and child mortality risk in part through experience, then the effect of a death on births will reflect not only replacement behavior but also what they learn and how they adapt to that new information (see Mira, 1995).

The general model represents, in my view, an appropriate direction for future empirical research. What components are tractable to estimate structurally given current technology is unclear. Solution and estimation methods are advancing (see Eckstein and Wolpin, 1989; Rust, 1992; Keane and Wolpin, 1994) and limits on computation are receding.

## 2.5. A brief survey of empirical results

This section is organized in the following way: first results are presented of representative studies that have had as their main goal the estimation of replacement effects. As discussed, estimates of replacement provide information about the effect of a hypothetical policy intervention, which reduces mortality risk, but for which the change in mortality risk is not perceived by families. The first set of studies in this group use

---

[30] Although economists tend to be suspicious of non-objective data, it is clear that not all individuals have the same knowledge or the same expectations about the future. The alternative to collecting such information is to make assumptions that are likely to be incorrect.

birth and death histories and the second total births and deaths. In this section a study that adopts a non-structural estimation approach is also discussed, estimating what is called approximate decision rules. In that study, mortality was only a peripheral issue and only replacement effect estimates are provided. Next, studies that estimate the effect of mortality risk on fertility are presented, providing information about the effect of an intervention when the change in mortality risk it induces is known to families. First, an example of structural estimation is given, which, although it provides answers to both of the hypothetical policy interventions, assumes that mortality risk variation is exogenous. Then several non-structural approaches are discussed which allow for mortality risk endogeneity.

### 2.5.1. Replacement effects

#### 2.5.1.1. Estimates based on birth and death history data

The definition of replacement given in Eq. (8) or (9) has rarely been adopted as the statistical measure in practice when complete fertility and mortality histories have been available. Rather, two other measures, having their roots in the demographic literature, have been more prominent, the parity progression ratio and the mean closed interval to the next birth. They are both easily defined in terms of birth probabilities. If we let $L$ equal the duration to the next birth, then conditional on the first period state, the probability that $L = t$ is

$$\Pr(L = t \mid n_t, d_1) = \Pr(n_{t+1}, n_t = 0, \ldots, n_2 = 0 \mid n_1, d_1). \tag{25}$$

These probabilities define the duration density function, say $g(L)$.[31] If there is a longest feasible duration, $L^*$, then in order for $g(L)$ to be a proper density it must include the probability of having no more children, i.e.,

$$g(\infty) = 1 - \sum_{t=1}^{L^*} \Pr(L = t \mid n_1, d_1). \tag{26}$$

(In the three-period model, $L = 1$ is the only feasible duration.) The parity progression ratio (PPR) is simply the probability that the couple will have (at least) one more birth, the next parity. A measure of replacement behavior is the difference between the PPR when there is a death and the PPR when there is not, that is, in the case where there is a birth in period 1 (as in Eq. (6)),

$$\Delta PPR = G(L^* \mid n_t = 1, d_1 = 1) - G(L^* \mid n_1 = 1, d_1 = 0), \tag{26}$$

where $G$ is the cumulative duration distribution function. PPRs can be calculated analogously for any birth and death history, and are usually calculated by conditioning

---

[31] There is actually a different density for each period and a different longest duration.

on a particular parity (rather than on age). Conditioning on parity rather than age leads to a different quantitative measure for replacement because it combines the different age-specific responses, i.e., experiencing one infant death out of three births will induce a different replacement response depending on the number of periods left until the end of the fecund horizon. However, calculating the excess number of births due to a reduction in the mortality risk for a population with homogeneous mortality risk would be identical using PPRs to that calculated from Eq. (8) or (9). For a population with heterogeneous mortality risk, the excess birth calculation using PPRs would be incorrect, as was the case with using Eq. (8) or (9).

The other prominent measure of replacement behavior, based on birth and death histories, found in the literature is the differenced mean closed interval (DMCI). The DMCI is the difference in mean birth durations, conditional on having an additional birth before the end of the fecund stage, under alternative mortality experiences. The DMCI is given by

$$
\begin{aligned}
DMCI &= \mathrm{E}(L|n_1 = 1, d_1 = 1, L \le L^*) - \mathrm{E}(L|n_1 = 1, d_1 = 0, L \le L^*) \\
&= \sum_{t=1}^{L^*} \left[ \frac{tg(t|n_1 = 1, d_t = 1)}{G(L^*|n_1 = 1, d_1 = 1)} - \frac{tg(t|n_1 = 1, d_1 = 0)}{G(L^*|n_1 = 1, d_1 = 0)} \right].
\end{aligned} \tag{27}
$$

Because the DMCI conditions on having a birth subsequent to the death, its relationship to the other replacement measures is not straightforward. For example, in the last fertile period the expected duration to the next birth, conditional on there being a birth, must be one period independent of the prior mortality experience; thus, in this case the DMCI will be zero even though the probability of an additional birth would be responsive to the mortality history ($r$ in Eq. (8) is not zero). The DMCI should be more closely related to the other replacement measures in populations of younger families and higher fertility. This measure is clearly the most problematic in calculating excess births.

Non-parametric replacement estimates based on birth and death histories can be used for policy analysis only if one can assume that mortality risk is homogeneous (or otherwise held constant). Knodel (1978) uses reconstituted birth and death information from three German villages for women who married between 1840 and 1890 and whose marriages were intact at age 45. Mean closed intervals and parity progression ratios for the three villages are shown in Table 4. All of the villages have high fertility rates; total fertility is over six. The women in the village of Mommlingen are known to have breastfed their children over extended periods, while in Schonberg and Anhausen breastfeeding was rarely practiced at all. This fact is consistent with the longer average birth interval in Mommlingen, although the prolongation of postpartum sterility due to lactation may not be the only factor.

The differences between the mean closed intervals for women who did and did not experience child deaths are clearly largest in Mommlingen, the village where breast-

Table 4
Parity progression ratios and mean closed intervals (Knodel, 1978)

|  | Mommlingen | Schonberg | Anhausen |
|---|---|---|---|
| *Mean closed intervals (months)* | | | |
| All birth intervals | | | |
| No infant deaths | 30.0 | 22.0 | 19.9 |
| One or more infant deaths | 19.4 | 20.0 | 19.2 |
| Second to third child | | | |
| First child survives | 29.0 | 23.9 | 23.4 |
| First child dies | 25.4 | 21.1 | 17.6 |
| *Parity regression ratios (%)* | | | |
| Second to third child | | | |
| No infant deaths | 96.3 | 97.4 | 84.0 |
| One or more infant deaths | 100.0 | 97.6 | 90.5 |
| Third to fourth child | | | |
| No infant deaths | 93.0 | 93.1 | 81.3 |
| One infant death | 94.5 | 87.9 | 92.9 |
| Two or more infant deaths | 85.7 | 76.5 | 90.0 |

feeding was normally practiced. For example, over all birth intervals, the mean closed interval was over ten months shorter if a woman residing in Mommlingen had experienced at least one death, but only two months shorter for women in Schonberg and less than one month shorter for women in Anhausen. The differences in parity progression ratios by infant mortality experience, however, seem to be largest in Anhausen and are therefore more suggestive of replacement behavior. But, parity progression ratios do not uniformly rise with additional deaths; indeed, the likelihood of a women moving from a third to a fourth birth declines with the number of infant deaths.[32] In an attempt to net out the lactation effect of an infant death, Knodel looks at the effect of the death of the first born on the mean closed interval between the second and third births. The differences are now largest in Anhausen, 5.8 months, and smallest in Schonberg, 2.8 months.

Vallin and Lery (1978) use a subsample of 92 000 French women who were born between 1892 and 1916 and were surveyed in 1962. As reported in Table 5, for all levels of completed family size and regardless of the birth order of the infant death, retrospectively obtained mean closed intervals are about one year less when an infant death is experienced. Parity progression ratios differ by about 16 percentage points for the movement between first and second births when the first-born did or did not die, by approximately the same amount for the movement between second and third births given that the second-born did or did not die, and by about ten percentage points for

[32] One possible explanation of this phenomenon would be that women with more deaths learn that they have a higher infant mortality rate, which reduces subsequent fertility (the direct effect).

Table 5
Parity progression ratios and mean closed intervals (Vallin and Lery, 1978)

| | Mean closed intervals | |
|---|---|---|
| | No infant death | Infant death |
| Total fertility | | |
| Two | 4.14 | 3.17 |
| Three | | |
| First birth | 3.35 | 2.43 |
| Second birth | 4.19 | 3.39 |
| Four | | |
| First birth | 2.77 | 2.16 |
| Second birth | 3.43 | 2.48 |
| Third birth | 4.06 | 3.26 |

| | Parity progression ratios ($n$ to $n + 1$) | |
|---|---|---|
| | No infant death (birth $n$) | Infant death (birth $n$) |
| First to second child | 68.5 | 84.7 |
| Second to third child | 57.6 | 72.8 |
| Third to fourth child | 56.4 | 67.4 |
| Fourth to fifth child | 57.3 | 67.9 |
| Fifth to sixth child | 59.2 | 69.2 |

higher parities. As was the case for the German historical data, the later French data reveal similarly higher fertility subsequent to an infant death. There are numerous other studies that report mean closed intervals and parity progression ratios by mortality experience. Most use cross-section data where birth and death information is collected retrospectively. Some report estimates based on regressions that hold individual characteristics constant (e.g. Ben-Porath, 1976) and in that sense are not completely non-parametric. The general findings in the literature are qualitatively the same as for the two papers discussed above.

### 2.5.1.2. *Estimates based on total births and deaths*

Table 6 reports estimates of replacement effects based on the use of total births and total deaths. The upper half of the table shows replacement effects obtained by Olsen and the lower half those by Mauskopf and Wallace. Olsen uses data from the 1973 Columbia Census Public Use Sample and reports his results for different age and residential location groups. Only the oldest age group, women who were 45–49 in 1973, are shown in Table 6. The uncorrected estimates, that is, the regression coefficient on total deaths, imply a replacement rate of over one for both urban and rural women, regardless of whether or not controls are added. The corrected estimate that assumes a homogeneous mortality rate in the population is negative, implying that there are ac-

Table 6
Replacement effects from total births regressors (Olsen, 1980; Mauskopf and Wallace, 1984)

| | Olsen | | | | | |
|---|---|---|---|---|---|---|
| | Urban 45–49 | | | Rural 45–49 | | |
| | Uncorrected | Corrected mortality rate | | Uncorrected | Corrected mortality rate | |
| | | Fixed | Random | | Fixed | Random |
| Regressors: Death only | 1.27 | −0.54 | 0.21 | 1.06 | −0.53 | 0.19 |
| Regressors: Deaths Education of wife and husband, Regional dummies | 1.21 | −0.49 | 0.20 | 1.04 | −0.51 | 0.20 |

| | Mauskopf and Wallace | | | |
|---|---|---|---|---|
| | All women | No education | 1–4 years education | ≥5 years of education |
| Replacement rate Mortality rate Fixed | 0.601 (0.03)[a] | 0.348 (0.04) | 0.592 (0.06) | 0.964 (0.13) |
| Mortality rate Random | 0.593 (0.04) | 0.437 (0.04) | 0.613 (0.05) | 0.978 (0.08) |

[a] Standard errors in parentheses.

tually fewer births when there is an infant or child death.[33] The replacement effect obtained under the assumption that the mortality rate varies in the population (independently from births) yields point estimates of around 0.2.[34] Olsen also estimates a replacement effect when the mortality rate is correlated with births. Those estimates vary between 0.13 and 0.22 depending on the joint distributional assumption for the mortality rate and total fertility.

The estimates based on the methodology developed by Mauskopf and Wallace are presented in the lower half of the table. Mauskopf and Wallace use data from the 1970 Brazilian census, restricting attention to women who were between 40 and 50 years old at the time of the survey. The replacement rate, assuming the mortality risk to be fixed in the population, was estimated to be 0.6 for the total sample. It was 0.35 for those with zero schooling, 0.6 for women with 1–4 years of schooling, and almost

[33] This result is consistent with there being a negative (income) effect of higher infant mortality risk.

[34] The independence assumption is inconsistent with optimizing behavior.

unity for women with five or more years of schooling. Allowing the mortality rate to differ in the population, using the methodology described above, only changed the estimate significantly for the lowest education group.

### 2.5.1.3. Approximate decision rules

Mroz and Weir (1990) develop a discrete-time statistical representation of the timing of births that can be viewed as an approximation to the decision rules that arise from a dynamic sequential utility maximizing model. Three stochastic processes are specified: (i) the process generating the probability of resuming ovulation after a birth, (ii) the process generating the probability of conception, and (iii) the process generating the onset of secondary sterility. The waiting time to a birth is the convolution of the waiting time to the resumption of ovulation and the waiting time to a conception, conditional on the resumption of ovulation and conditional on not becoming infecund. The probability of observing a woman with a particular sequence of births up to any given age is specified in terms of these three stochastic processes. Mroz and Weir allow for unobserved heterogeneity in each of the three waiting times; women may differ biologically in the post-anovulatory and fecund processes, and they may differ biologically and behaviorally in the conception process. However, there is neither observe nor unobserved heterogeneity in mortality risk (cross-sectionally or temporally).

Monthly probabilities are modeled as logistic functions. The fecund hazard at any month depends on duration since the start of the interval, age, age at marriage, parity attained by that month (dummy variables for each attained parity), dummy variables for whether the particular month is the first month of risk of conception in the interval, a dummy for the first month of marriage, and the number of surviving children during that month. Heterogeneity shifts the monthly probability proportionately and is assumed to take on a small number of discrete values (Heckman and Singer, 1984). Identification in this model is achieved by a combination of functional form assumptions, assumptions about biological processes (for example, exactly nine month gestation) and a clever use of data (using the timing of an infant death to tie down the beginning of the fecund period given the cessation of breastfeeding). The reader is referred to the paper for the exact details.

The model is estimated using reconstituted data between 1740 and 1819 from 39 French villages based on birth and death histories for women who were married at ages 20–24. The results provide evidence on the importance of unobserved heterogeneity (in the fertility process) in the estimation of replacement effects. Mroz and Weir report that simulations conducted prior to estimation, omitting controls for unobserved heterogeneity in the fecund hazard rate and recognizing that they accounted for the cessation of lactation due to an infant death, resulted in the probability of a birth increasing in the number of surviving children (conditional on parity, age, duration, and age at marriage). Controlling for heterogeneity in estimation, however, resulted in a negative effect as is consistent with a behavioral replacement effect. Quantitatively, Mroz and Weir found using their estimates that births increase by 13% due to the cessation of lactation alone following an infant death and by 17% overall. Given an average of about seven births, the absolute behavioral replacement effect is 0.28. Mroz and Weir essentially assume that mortality risk does not vary in the population (given covariates).

### 2.5.2. The impact of infant and child mortality risk on fertility

#### 2.5.2.1. Structural estimation

Wolpin (1984) illustrates structural estimation. Although he estimates an extended version of the three-period dynamic model, it incorporates only a few of the characteristics of the general model.[35] It has the following characteristics: (i) per-period utility is quadratic in the number of surviving children in that period and in a composite consumption good, (ii) fertility control is costless and perfect, (iii) there is a fixed cost of bearing a child and a cost of maintaining a child in its first period of life (if it survives infancy), (iv) children can die in only their first period of life subject to an exogenous time-varying (and perfectly forecasted) infant mortality rate, (v) the household has stochastic income and consumption net of the cost of children is equal to income in each period, (vi) the household's marginal utility of surviving children varies stochastically over time according to a known (to the household) probability distribution. Given this framework, the household chooses in each period whether or not to have a child.

For the purpose of estimation, Wolpin assumes that the time-varying preference parameter is drawn independently both over time and across households from a normal distribution. The mortality rate faced by the household is assumed known to the researcher, measured by the state level mortality rate in each period, and the researcher is assumed to forecast future mortality rates exactly as the household is assumed to do, namely based on the extrapolated trend in the mortality rate at the state level. Future income is forecasted from the time-series of observed household income, again under the assumption that the household uses the same forecasting method.

The data are drawn from the 1976 Malaysian Family Life Survey which contains a retrospective life history on marriages, births, child deaths, household income, etc., of each woman in the sample. Wolpin used a subsample of 188 Malay women who were over age 30 in 1976, currently married, and married only once. The period length was chosen to be 18 months, the initial period was set at age 15 (or age of marriage if it occurred first), and the final decision period was assumed to terminate at age 45, there being thus 20 decision periods. In the implementation, the cost of a birth is allowed to be age-varying as a way of capturing age variation in fecundity and in marriage rates. In addition, the woman's schooling is allowed to affect the marginal utility of surviving children.

---

[35] Mira (1995) recently extended that model to the case where families learn about the innate mortality risk they face through their realized mortality experience.

With households receiving contemporary utility flows from the stock of children, there is clearly an incentive to have children early in the life cycle, one after the other. However, with a rising income profile and no mechanism for life-cycle consumption smoothing, there will be an incentive to postpone having children until periods with higher levels of income. These two factors lead to an optimal spacing and timing pattern for births.

Parameter estimates are obtained by maximum likelihood. As already alluded to, the procedure involves solving the dynamic programming problem for each household (given their income and mortality risk profiles), and calculating the probability of the observed birth sequence. Because the woman's fertility is observed from what is assumed to be an exogenous initial decision period (either age 15 or age at marriage whichever occurs first), the likelihood function is conditioned on the initial zero stock of children that is the same for all women. The birth probability sequences that form the likelihood function can be written as products of single period birth probabilities conditional on that periods stock of surviving children, the output of the dynamic programming solution.[36]

Given parameter estimates, the replacement effect is calculated in each period and for each number of surviving children for a representative couple. The replacement effect is estimated to be small, ranging between 0.01 and 0.015 additional children ever born per additional infant death. The reason for the negligible replacement effect is that the actual fertility behavior is best fit in the context of this optimization model with utility parameters that imply essentially a constant marginal utility of children. Wolpin also calculated that an increase in the infant mortality risk by 0.05 would lead to a reduction in the number of births by about 25%. Thus, the two policy experiments would have widely different effects.[37]

### 2.5.2.2. Non-structural estimation

A number of studies have attempted to estimate the effect of mortality risk on fertility using non-structural estimation methods. As already discussed, obtaining correct estimates is challenging only if there is unobserved mortality risk variation, and particularly so when mortality risk is endogenous, as when fertility spacing affects mortality risk as discussed above. Mortality risk can also be endogenous if it is affected by behaviors that are subject to choice and if, in addition, there is population heterogeneity

---

[36] Because there is an exogenous initial condition, Wolpin is able to estimate a model in which the stochastic preference parameter contains a permanent unobservable component using the semi-parametric formulation of Heckman and Singer (1984). He did not find evidence that there exist two types of households, but did not attempt to test for the existence of more than two types.

[37] Interestingly, direct evidence about hoarding comes from my 1984 study, although I failed to recognize it at the time. Given the finding there that the marginal utility of surviving children is essentially constant, which led to the negligible estimated replacement rates, the potential hoarding response, if child mortality were significant in that environment, would also be negligible since hoarding also depends on concavity as shown in Eq. (3).

in preferences. Several studies, having recognized this problem, have attempted to estimate the effect of innate family-specific mortality risk (frailty or the $\mu$s in the previous notation) on fertility. To do so requires that one estimate the production function for child survival, accounting for all behavioral and biological determinants. The details of the methods used to estimate the survival technology as well as the findings are the subject of the next section. While the credibility of the estimates of the fertility–frailty relationship depends in part on the way that frailty estimates are obtained, let us consider the findings of studies that estimate its effect on fertility behavior assuming the frailty estimates to be credible.

Rosenzweig and Schultz (1983), using data from the 1967, 1968, and 1969 National Natality Followback Surveys (USDHEW), find that the expected number of children ever born per woman would be 0.17 greater for an infant mortality risk of 0.1 as opposed to zero. Given that in their sample the infant mortality rate is less than 3%, this experiment may be within sample variation. At the sample average of 2.5 births per woman, an additional 0.25 deaths per woman leads to 0.17 more births and therefore to 0.08 fewer surviving children. Such a finding, it should be noted, is inconsistent with the dynamic model presented above; in that model an increase in infant mortality risk cannot increase births. Of course, the underlying optimization model consistent with their estimation would be significantly more complex.

Olsen and Wolpin (1983), also using the 1976 Malaysian Family Life Survey, estimate that a couple faced with a 1% higher monthly probability of death within the first 24 months of life will have their first birth approximately two weeks earlier. This effect is rather small given that the average interval between births is 30 months. Because they also find that the result is magnified when using the actual monthly probability of death as opposed to its innate component, it appears that couples who choose, through the inputs that they control, to have higher mortality also choose to have higher fertility. Again, while inconsistent with the simple three-period model, that model is not rich enough to capture more complicated behaviors that might explain this result. For example, it is possible that the greater mortality risk induces an earlier first birth in order to increase the time over which to observe actual mortality.

Olsen (1983) adds an estimate of family-specific frailty to the regression of total births and total deaths in combination with his correction method as an attempt to separate replacement and hoarding behavior. However, as I have defined it, the effect of early age mortality risk on fertility is not a hoarding response. Controlling for innate infant frailty, however, would provide an estimate of the replacement rate that is uncontaminated by unobserved mortality risk. Using the same data as did Olsen and Wolpin, Olsen finds a replacement rate of 0.17.[38]

---

[38] Olsen contrasts this estimate to the "corrected" replacement effect estimate of 0.17.

## 3. The determinants of infant and child mortality

The three previous papers all attempted to estimate an innate frailty component by appealing to the existence of a survival technology. Their ability to isolate such a component of mortality risk draws upon a literature that is concerned with identifying the determinants of infant and child mortality, a literature that has a long history. De Sweemer (1984), in a brief chronological review of the literature on the relationship between child spacing and child survival, begins with work on the subject by Hughes in a 1923 US Government Children's Bureau publication, while Knodel and Kintner (1977) cite a 1905 paper by Howarth published in the British medical journal *Lancet* on the relationship between breastfeeding and infant mortality. A historical review of this body of research, a task that would require a book devoted only to that topic, is not attempted here. Instead a broad overview is provided of the methodological issues that arise in this literature and of the solutions that have been proposed, and a selection of empirical findings. To do that, however, requires drawing on the work of biomedical, demographic, and economic researchers. Particularly with respect to the biomedical literature, while my reading is representative, it is surely not nearly exhaustive. A noteworthy feature of that literature is its similarity with both of the other disciplines in the questions that are posed. The reason is perhaps that researchers in this area, independent of field, are most interested in providing an understanding of the phenomenon in order to formulate public policies that may lead to better outcomes. For that reason, there is a large component of the biomedical literature that concentrates on "determinants" that are behaviorally based. And, it is this focus on behavior that created an environment within which economists could contribute.

### 3.1. The framework

In order to analyze the determinants of infant and child mortality, it is necessary to provide a theoretical framework within which to distinguish between potential determining factors. How should diverse potential factors such as maternal age at birth, measures of family resources (income or wealth), the chemical balance within the uterus, the transmission of genetic materials, birth weight, or the incidence of disease be integrated into a common setting? Within a biomedical perspective, causes of infant and child mortality have been divided into what are called endogenous and exogenous categories. Endogenous causes are those that precede or are associated with birth and are biologically based, (e.g., congenital malformations, birth injury, toxemia). Exogenous causes are those attributable to the postnatal environment, (e.g., respiratory, infectious, and diarrheal diseases, accidents). This classification has led biomedical researchers to distinguish between the causes of neonatal deaths, those occurring in the first 28 days, and post-neonatal deaths, those occurring between 29 days and one year. Post-neonatal deaths, by definition, are caused by exogenous factors while neonatal deaths are caused by both exogenous and endogenous factors (Knodel and Kintner, 1977). Whether or not, as Eberstein and Parker (1984) have argued, some specific causes of death span both neonatal and post-neonatal deaths, thus making somewhat arbitrary the endogenous–exogenous distinction, specific causes of death are, in the terminology of demographers, the proximate determinants of death at any age.[39]

To fix ideas, let us assume that there is only one cause of infant death, say an infectious disease. Let us further suppose that there is a behavior (or treatment) that can be curative and a behavior that can be preventative. It is possible that these may be the same behaviors (e.g., clean drinking water both prevents diarrheal infections and cures it). Assume also that although a child is born with an innate susceptibility to acquire the disease that is time-invariant, the occurrence at any time in addition is determined by some purely random element. Overall susceptibility to the disease at any age would depend on the child's history of the disease occurrence (if there are acquired immunities for example or cumulative debilitating effects) and treatments (if susceptibility depends on the degree of recovery), on the history of the preventative behavior (if there are cumulative effects) on the child's age (biological maturity) and frailty, and on the random shock. If the child is infected, the survival outcome depends on the treatment and on the child's frailty. The survival outcome might also depend on the child's disease and treatment history if toxicity is either enhanced or diminished upon repeated occurrences and recoveries, and on the child's age. There are thus two relationships of interest: one that describes the process of disease occurrence (cause of death technology) and another that describes the mortality process conditional on the disease occurrence. It is possible to "substitute" the determinants of disease occurrence into the mortality function, substituting out current and past disease occurrence, and relate current and past behaviors (preventatives and treatments), age, frailty, and the history of the disease occurrence random shocks to an infant's or child's mortality propensity (the behavioral technology).[40] The preventative and curative effects of behaviors that provide both are confounded in this relationship.

To make the discussion more concrete (following a similar development in Rosenzweig and Schultz (1983a)), let the hazard rate of dying at age $t$, corresponding to this behavioral technology, for a child of parity $i$ born to a couple $j$ be given by

$$\lambda_{ijt} = \lambda(t_{ij}, z(t_{ij}), x_{ij}, \mu_{ij}, \varepsilon_{ijt}, \varepsilon_{ij,t-1}, \ldots, \varepsilon_{ij1}), \tag{28}$$

---

[39] Specific causes of death are assigned upon death according to the International Statistical Classification of Diseases. The endogenous–exogenous scheme consolidates causes of death into the two categories. Because all deaths must be classified and not all causes are well understood, there are residual categories like "other" or "ill-defined" conditions. There are additional categories, like SIDS (sudden infant death syndrome), that are merely descriptive of the circumstances under which death occurred.

[40] The same arguments apply to the joint set of causes of death.

where $t_{ij}$ is the duration of life of the child (age), $z(t_{ij})$ represents a vector of time-varying behaviors that denote entire histories (e.g., the number of prenatal care visits during the pregnancy), $x_{ij}$ represents a vector of behaviors that do not vary over time (e.g., maternal age at birth or child parity, reflecting components of the child's biological endowment), $\mu_{ij}$ is the (permanent) inherent frailty of the child, and the $\varepsilon_{ij\tau}$ represent the history of cause of death (disease) occurrences shocks. Notice that the effect of frailty (and indeed of all of the factors in Eq. (28)) on mortality risk can, in principle, vary with the age of the child. To maintain consistency, all of the factors in the $z$'s and $x$'s are referred to as inputs, adopting the usual production function terminology (originally applied to the household setting by Becker (1965) and specifically to health by Grossman (1972)). Some inputs are part of the behavioral decision process (behavioral inputs), while others, like gender, are beyond parental control.

Consider integrating this survival technology into the dynamic decision model of the previous section so that the behavioral inputs that affect the infant and child mortality behavioral hazard, such as whether and how long to breastfeed, when if at all during the pregnancy to obtain prenatal care, etc., would be part of the decision process. In that setting the behavioral mortality technology (Eq. (28)) acts as a constraint on the optimization problem of the family in the same way as does the budget constraint. Therefore, just as prices and (exogenous) income alter the feasible opportunity set and in that way alter the behavioral inputs, so does the inherent frailty of offspring alter opportunity sets and decisions. However, the frailty endowment of the child can influence behavior only if it is contained in the family's information set. It is, of course, not credible to suppose that a family would know with certainty child-specific frailty prior to pregnancy (or, possibly prior even to the birth). But, it is not unlikely that they have priors about the frailty of their children based on observations of other family members (mothers, sisters, etc.) and of children who are already born, and may learn about the frailty of individual children as they age (including in utero). The distinction between the component of frailty that is common to all children born to the same family and the component that is child-specific is relevant, in part, because of the existence and nature of informational constraints. As discussed below, assumptions about the content of information sets are at the root of the alternative estimation methods proposed for the technology function (Eq. (28)).

The problem that the existence of the frailty endowment creates for the estimation of the hazard function (Eq. (28)) is that while we may have measures of inputs, we do not have a complete measure of frailty, nor is it likely that we ever will (Harris, 1982).[41] Estimating Eq. (28) ignoring the existence of unobserved frailty can lead to bias in the estimates of the effects of inputs on the mortality hazard. For example, in the context of the fertility model of the previous section, families who have (or perceive themselves to have a propensity for) inherently weaker children may begin childbearing earlier. Such a response will create a negative correlation between sur-

---

[41] To do so would require that we can determine an individual's predisposition to all diseases.

vival and maternal age at birth even if none exists in the technology. Or, a woman born with a frail child may be more prone to breastfeed the child, thus creating a negative correlation between survival and breastfeeding and understating whatever survival enhancing properties breastfeeding may actually have. And, as is well known, biases in the estimated effect of one input can be transmitted to other inputs since they are jointly determined.

An additional estimation problem is created because of the existence of the cause of death shocks. The problem is that families obtain signals as to the likelihood of death that show up as potential causes of death. These signals then affect subsequent behavior and to the extent that the signals themselves are not measurable, estimates of the behavioral mortality technology is problematic. It should be recognized that prenatal behaviors are not immune from this correlation if signals about the risk of mortality are obtained during the pregnancy. Most of the literature has not explicitly considered the problem caused by the existence of dynamic behavior.

Table 7 provides a categorization of variables that belong in Eq. (28). Among the first set are biological factors, including those that are developmental (e.g. maternal age at conception), physiological (e.g., maternal height), and genetic (e.g., some component of the residual inherent frailty) in nature. All of these variables are endowments of the child in the sense that they are determined prior to the birth and unalterable, and reflect the child's innate frailty. Notice that some of these variables such as maternal age at conception or birth order are behavioral, that is, subject to parental choice, some variables such as maternal height are maternal endowments, some are characteristics of the child like gender or race, and some like the disease history of the mother prior to conception are combinations of behavior and the maternal endow-

Table 7
Inputs of the infant and child mortality production function

| | |
|---|---|
| *Biological* | |
| Birth order | |
| Maternal age at birth | |
| Prior birth spacing | |
| Gender | |
| Maternal height | |
| Maternal disease history | |
| Race | |
| Residual frailty endowment | |
| | |
| *Prenatal* | *Postnatal* |
| Substance use during pregnancy | Nutrition and feeding practices |
| Prenatal medical care visits | Well baby medical care visits |
| Maternal nutrition | Disease and accident exposure |
| Maternal time use | |
| Disease exposure | |

ment. However, it is unlikely that these factors alone capture all of the variation in the child-specific frailty endowment. The inclusion of a frailty endowment (net of these observed biological factors) tautologically accounts for this deficiency. Recall that Eq. (28) does not include experienced potential causes of death that might themselves be caused by behaviors, so diseases, congenital anomalies, low birth weight (treated as a potential cause of death) etc. are not on the list.

The interpretation of these factors as having a biological basis hinges on the inclusion of all relevant prenatal and postnatal behaviors. Prenatal behaviors include the extent of substance use during pregnancy, the quantity and types of nutrients consumed during the pregnancy, the type and extent of physical activities of the woman during the pregnancy, the timing, number and quality of prenatal care visits, and the mother's exposure to accident and health hazards.[42] Postnatal inputs include the child's nutritional intake, the timing, number and quality of well-baby care visits, exposure to accident and health hazards. All of these prenatal and postnatal inputs should be continuously measured over the pregnancy interval and over the observed lifetime of the child.

Before turning to a description of what researchers have actually estimated, it is necessary to clarify the role of variables that do not fit into the category of inputs, but which clearly play a role in the determination of mortality risk. The most obvious one is income, or more generally, financial resources. As already discussed, behaviors are determined by preferences and constraints. Depending on how one models the budget constraint, the information set, and the choice set, some aspect of financial resources will be a determinant of behavior (current income, current assets, wage rates). To understand completely the determination of mortality risk, one would need to estimate not only the behavioral technology as in Eq. (28) (and the cause-of-death technologies), but also the determinants of the behaviors that enter the behavioral technology.

As will be seen below, it has not been unusual to include measures of financial resources when they are available in addition to including measures of the behaviors. The problem with this practice, as Rosenzweig and Schultz (1983b) point out in the context of a static optimizing model, is that such a "hybrid" function does not have a simple interpretation in terms only of the technology parameters; it confounds technology and preferences. To see that, perform the thought experiment of changing a behavior for given financial resources, say using infant formula as opposed to breastfeeding. Because infant formula is costly, in order to maintain the same level of financial resources when it is chosen over the breastfeeding alternative, some other expenditure must be reduced. The exact bundle of items that will suffer a reduction in expenditures will depend on preferences (and the mortality technology). To the extent that expenditures are reduced on behaviors that affect mortality risk (for example, alcohol consumption, medical care) and that are not included in the technology speci-

---

[42] Thus, exposure to disease (e.g., German measles) during pregnancy together with prenatal behaviors and the child's frailty endowment determine the child's disease incidence without error.

fication, the effect of infant formula feeding will be a composite of both its own effect and the effect of the other behaviors that are influenced by the fall in residual resources. It is important to note that financial resources will only have an effect on mortality risk if some behaviors have been omitted from Eq. (28) or if financial resources are intergenerationally correlated with unobserved frailty. The inclusion of financial resources as a determinant of mortality risk conditional on observed behaviors is best viewed as a general specification test for omitted variables, although such a test cannot discern whether there are omitted behaviors or unobserved frailty. Everything that has been said about financial resources also holds for prices, e.g., the price of medical care, a point that will be important when discussing the estimation of the effects of public policy interventions. As with income, the inclusion of prices can at best serve as a specification test and alters the interpretation of the mortality risk function.

The issue of whether or not to include income or other measures of financial resources as determinants of mortality risk in addition to behaviors raises a closely related issue of the use of proxy variables. There is an overwhelming research bias, that seems to cross all disciplines, towards including rather than excluding variables that do not exactly measure the appropriate variables, but that may be correlated in some way with relevant variables. In some cases, as with income, it is easy to demonstrate the consequence of including a proxy because income is an explicit component of the optimizing framework. However, researchers often use proxies that are not explicitly tied to a theoretical model and so the exact interpretative difficulties that are created cannot be so easily described.

To see the problem, let us suppose that a researcher believes that an important behavioral input has been omitted, say the existence of toilet facilities within the home. Suppose, however, that the researcher does know the household's place of residence as distinguished by whether it is an urban or rural location and that rural areas are known to have fewer homes with toilet facilities. One can consider rural–urban residence to measure the existence of toilet facilities with error. Adopting the usual classical measurement error perspective, the effect of rural–urban residence will give a biased toward zero estimate of the effect of toilet facilities on mortality risk and will reduce the omitted variables bias (due to unobserved toilet facilities) that contaminates the estimates of the effects of the other inputs. Unfortunately, this is not necessarily the end of the story. One needs to know what is in the measurement error, that is, that component of rural–urban residence that is orthogonal to the existence of toilet facilities, and whether it is correlated with the other behavioral inputs. It is not difficult to establish the existence of such correlations. Because it is likely that toilet facilities are more expensive to install in rural areas than in urban areas, rural households with toilet facilities will be higher wealth households or possibly households with greater preferences for health. Thus, the other behaviors that determine mortality risk will be correlated with the measurement error component of place of residence and the exact nature of the biases that this creates depends on the correlation structure. The point is not that one should never use proxies, because it is unclear a priori whether the biases are greater when there is an omitted variable than when a proxy is used. However, in order to form an admittedly subjective judgement, it is at least necessary to present a complete framework that includes the role of proxies in the behavioral model. As a general guide, proxies that are reasonably related to only one input, e.g., sources of drinking water (well, piped, etc.) as a proxy for water's bacterial content, are more likely to ameliorate the bias from omitting the bacterial content of drinking water than are proxies that are related to many inputs simultaneously, e.g., income or region of residence. Of course, best practice is to collect the inputs accurately in the first place.

The literature is extremely heterogeneous with respect to the set of variables included as determinants of mortality risk. This is partly due to differences in the data sets that have been used; some data sets are richer in certain dimensions than others. However, in many cases it is unclear as to the criteria that are used for the inclusion or exclusion of variables in a manner that carefully accounts for the multivariate setting. Thus, it is often impossible in many cases to tell what variables would have been included had they been available. A predominant reason for inclusion seems to be that of inclusion in past studies, and that for exclusion some notion of parsimony. Table 8 summarizes some of the features of eight different studies that appear to be reasonably representative of each of the three disciplines. The first three studies are published in biomedical journals, the next three in demography journals, and the last two in economics journals. In each case the dependent variable that was studied, the estimation method, the data source, and a list of the covariates are reported. Four of the studies use US data and four use data from less developed countries.

At a superficial level, the similarities are more apparent than are the differences. The studies all use micro-data, they are all multivariate (although the Shapiro et al. (1980) study only tabulates two covariates at a time) and use standard estimation techniques (this is less true of the Olsen and Wolpin (1983) study), and the set of regressors have many in common. With respect to this latter characteristic, maternal age at birth appears in all of the studies, parity appears in all but one (note that Geronimus (1986) restricts the sample to first births), prenatal care appears in two of the four US studies, some measure of birth spacing appears in three of the studies, breastfeeding is used in four of the studies including one of the US studies, maternal education is in five, place (urban–rural) or region of residence is in three, income or proxies such as spouse's occupation, spouse's education, or the mother's marital status is in four, and a measure of the mother's prior history of fetal or child mortality appears in two. Two of the studies include tobacco use during pregnancy and another measures a characteristic of the health environment (e.g., access to piped water). In addition, three of the studies use birth weight and one includes gestation.

It is not always clear that researchers have in common the goal of estimating technology as defined above. To quote some of the authors, the aim of the Geronimus study is to "explore whether excessive neonatal mortality rates among infants with teenage mothers is attributable to young maternal age or to a translation of environ-

Table 8
Representative studies of the determinants of infant and/or child mortality: selected characteristics

| Author (source) | Dependent variable | Estimation method | Data source | Covariates |
|---|---|---|---|---|
| Geronimus (American Journal of Public Health, 1986) | Neonatal mortality | Logit with categorical explanatory variables | 1976 and 1979 linked birth and infant death certificate registers from Washington, Louisiana, and Tennessee (first births only) | Birthweight, gestations, prenatal care, maternal age at birth, place of residence, race |
| Shapiro, McCormick, Starfield, Krischner and Bross (American Journal of Obstetrics and Gynecology, 1980) | Neonatal and postnatal mortality | Cross-tabulations | Matched birth and infant death, and fetal deaths from state and local health departments for 1974 and 1975 for eight regions covered by regional prenatal centers | Birthweight, maternal age at birth, maternal education, maternal history of prior fetal loss, delivery by cesarean section |
| Kleinman, Pierce, Madans, Land and Schramm (American Journal of Epidemiology, 1988) | Fetal, neonatal and postnatal mortality | Logit with categorical explanatory variables | 1979–1983 linked birth and death certificate from Missouri | Maternal age at birth, parity, maternal education, marital status, cigarette consumption during pregnancy |
| Paloni and Tienda (Demography, 1987) | Infant and child mortality | Logit for specific age segments with categorical explanatory variables | World Fertility Survey – Peru, 1977–1978 | Previous birth interval, pace of following conception, breastfeeding, previous sibling mortality, parity, maternal age at birth, maternal education, occupation of spouse, region of residence |
| Pebley and Strupp (Demography, 1987) | Infant and child mortality | Hazard model (log-linear) | Four rural villages in Guatemala, 1974–1975 | Previous birth interval, length of following interval, breastfeeding, previous sibling mortality, parity, maternal age at birth, maternal education, family income, sex |

Table 8 (*continued*)

| Author (source) | Dependent variable | Estimation method | Data source | Covariates |
|---|---|---|---|---|
| Martin, Trussell, Salvail and Shah (Population Studies, 1983) | Infant and child mortality | Hazard model (log-linear with categorical explanatory variables | World Fertility Survey – Phillipines, Indonesia and Pakistan (1975–1980) | Maternal age at birth, maternal education, paternal education, place of residence, region of residence, parity, sex |
| Rosenzweig and Schultz[a] (Papers and Proceedings, American Economic Association, 1983) | Infant mortality | Ordinary lest squares and two-stage least squares | 1967, 1968 and 1969 National Natality Followback Surveys (USDHEW) | Maternal age at birth, breastfeeding, prenatal care, cigarette consumption during pregnancy, parity, employment after birth, race, sex |
| Olsen and Wolpin[a] (Econometrica, 1983) | Mortality in first 24 months of life | Weighted least squares derived from a nonexponential p.d.f. for the duration of life | Malaysian Family Life Survey, 1976 | Maternal age at birth, birthweight, breastfeeding, previous interval, parity, number of live siblings by age, parental home time, child care time provided by relatives, number of relatives in household by age, access to toilet facilities, electricity in house, number of sleeping rooms in house, house construction |

[a]Includes methodology to control for unobserved heterogeneity.

mental disadvantage into reproductive disadvantage" in order to determine whether the belief that "adverse pregnancy outcomes among teenage mothers are due to their inherent biological immaturity" is in fact true.[43] While this seems to be a question

[43] Geronimus (1986: p. 1416).

about the technology, because there is no statement as to the inclusion principle it is unclear for what variable(s) place of residence, birth weight, and gestation are proxies. The Shapiro et al. study attempts to determine whether "factors identified as risks for death in the first year of life also serve as risks for morbidity in surviving infants".[44] Although the paper is not explicitly concerned with the estimation of the mortality risk technology per se, it is illustrative of the types of variables that are considered in the biomedical literature on infant mortality. The preponderance of proxies, if indeed the motive is to estimate technology, is noteworthy. The same can be said of the Kleinman et al. study whose motivation is to "assess the effects of smoking in a multivariate framework with maternal race, age, parity, education and marital status".[45]

With respect to the demographic studies, Palloni and Tienda (1986) state that the "purpose of this paper is to test a set of hypotheses about the impact of both interbirth interval and lactation practices on infant and early childhood mortality in Peru".[46] A similar goal is stated by Pebley and Strupp (1987), namely to "investigate several hypotheses about the association of child mortality with maternal age, parity, and birth spacing in a sample of Guatemalan children".[47] Martin et al. (1983) consider themselves to have been "the first to examine factors in a multivariate context".[48] In contrast, the two economics papers explicitly adopt the production function framework.[49] The point is not that the behavioral production function is the only relationship of interest, which as already noted it is not, but that there seems to be little attempt in the demographic and biomedical literatures to identify the theoretical structure that embeds the relationship that is estimated.

The result of the absence of theorizing is that researchers are unrestricted in the choice of factors that are simultaneously considered.[50] Demographers intentionally control for financial resource constraints, often through proxies, even though it is arguable that they are interested in isolating the technology. Biomedical researchers generally do not control for socioeconomic factors, other than education, seemingly not because they have a well articulated reason, but because such factors are not of primary interest or are not commonly available in the data sets they use. And while the

---

[44] Shapiro et al. (1980: p. 363).

[45] Kleinman et al. (1988: p. 275).

[46] Palloni and Tienda (1986: p. 31).

[47] Pebley and Strupp (1987: p. 43).

[48] Martin et al. (1983: p. 417).

[49] Corman et al. (1987) also adopt the production function framework, but they use aggregate US county level data.

[50] There may be interdisciplinary differences in what is perceived as theory. The demographic and biomedical literatures do conceptualize differences among variables, primarily on the basis of temporal ordering. This leads to categorizing variables as antecedent, mediating or proximate factors. However, this classification scheme does not seem to lead to a set of principles governing the relationships that are estimated.

two economics examples specifically state their intention to estimate technology, there are other examples in which economists have followed the demographers' approach. Although the omission of inputs may practically be a serious problem, the use of proxies that have not been explicitly incorporated in a theoretical setting, in my view, is generally not an appropriate resolution.

The papers in Table 8 also encompass most existing estimation methods that have been used in this literature. The most popular methods of estimation either involve a logistic regression framework that recognizes the dichotomous nature of the outcome (death) or a hazard model which specifies a parametric form for the (instantaneous or discrete interval) hazard rate of death. Within these procedures, some researchers have and some have not accounted for unobserved heterogeneity (frailty). The relative merits of regression vs. hazard model approaches have been discussed at length elsewhere (see especially Flinn and Heckman, 1983) and here we concentrate on the alternative methods that have been used to control for the unobserved endowment component of mortality.

Olsen and Wolpin (1983) suppose that while the frailty endowment may be composed of a family-specific component that is common to all children and a child-specific component, only the family components known. Thus, the behavioral inputs for each child depends on the family component of frailty, but not on the child-specific permanent component. By using data on all births to the same woman, Olsen and Wolpin are able to control for the family component of frailty through a fixed-effects within-family procedure.[51]

Rosenzweig and Schultz (1983a) explicitly consider the implications for estimation of a dynamic behavioral setting similar to the one discussed above. They assume the following dynamic discrete-time representation of the evolution of child health. At birth the health of a child is determined by a set of prenatal inputs, a family-specific health endowment known prior to the birth of a child and transmitted to all of the couple's children, and a stochastic time-varying component that is observed at birth. This stochastic component corresponds, in the above terminology, to the unobserved inherent randomness in the cause-of-death technology. In the next period, the health production function depends on the prenatal inputs, the first period postnatal inputs, the past stochastic component of health at birth (because it is a determinant of the incidence of potential causes of death), the family-specific component and a new sto

---

[51] They use a regression framework derived from a continuous time hazard model in which the density function of duration is assumed to be linear in the inputs and the family-specific endowment. The uniform density assumption leads to a conditional expectation function for duration that is also linear. It is difficult to estimate more general hazard models where the unobserved heterogeneity is not independently distributed from the regressors. Ridder and Tunali (1990) develop a partial likelihood approach, which does not require the uniform distribution assumption but is in other ways restrictive.

chastic component.[52] Thus, as in the specification of Eq. (28), the health process is cumulative; past behaviors (and shocks) affect the current health outcome. Future period health outcomes are similarly determined. The input demand functions or decision rules depend on whatever factors enter the current information set as was the case in the dynamic model previously presented; these include relevant current and past prices and income, the previous pregnancy history, etc. It is, thus, possible to write the input decision rules at any time as depending only on what are assumed to be strictly exogenous variables, e.g., all past prices and shocks, and endowments. Rosenzweig and Schultz suggest a two-stage estimation procedure that accounts for the correlation of inputs with endowments and prior shocks. In the first stage, they regress inputs on prices (and income which is assumed exogenous) and then use fitted values from the first stage in estimating the production function. Under the assumption that prices are uncorrelated with endowments and shocks, the usual assumption that individuals are price-takers, the estimates of the production function parameters will be consistent.

The consistency of the estimates depends on whether the first stage regressors are actually independent of the endowment and shocks. The first stage regressors used by Rosenzweig and Schultz are: the schooling of parents, the income of the father, local government health and hospital expenditures per-capita, the local number of hospitals and health departments with family planning services per capita, the local number of obstetricians–gynecologists per capita, the state average price of cigarettes and milk, the local female and total unemployment rates, metropolitan area location and size, and the regional mix of employment by industry group. The regressors in the production function are as shown in Table 8. Notice that although Rosenzweig and Schultz argue that the relevant instruments should be the prices that enter the input decision rules, the only actual prices that are used are the tax variables. The rest of the variables, aside from income, are proxies for the theoretically appropriate entities.

Parental characteristics, such as schooling and income, depend on the parents' own endowments directly and/or because they are the result of a decision process themselves. To the extent that the frailty endowment of a child is in part inherited from parents, those characteristics would not be valid instruments.[53] Aggregate variables such as the number of hospitals or physicians in the locality of residence, are taken to represent accessibility to medical care (part of the "full" price) as well as being correlated with its market price. It is implicitly assumed that aggregate variables cannot be correlated with (unobserved) individual characteristics and so by definition must be valid instruments. However, market variables are determined in an equilibrium setting; more medical care services will be provided where the demand for medical care is

---

[52] Although they do not assume it, the existence of a permanent child-specific component of the endowment would not affect the properties of their production function parameter estimates.

[53] The illness of a child may also affect subsequent labor force decisions and, thus, household income. See Pitt et al. (1990) for an attempt to estimate this response.

higher, and the demand for medical care will be higher where, holding all else constant (such as income), the population is (on average) more frail. Such proxies for the (full) price of medical care are, therefore, also not valid instruments. It is not necessary to go through the entire list to understand the general point. The approach adopted by Rosenzweig and Schultz, while theoretically justified and the only one in the literature that can account correctly for dynamic behavior, relies on the right data being available. Because identification of the technology parameters requires the existence of a sufficient number of instruments that must on a priori grounds be judged to be valid (only overidentifying restrictions are testable) it is imperative that those instruments be contained within the theory. Only when the assumptions are understood in the context of the theory that is necessary to justify their use as instruments can the inherently subjective judgement as to their validity be made.

## 3.2. Empirical findings for selected behaviors

This section presents methodological issues that are relevant to specific behaviors and some empirical results pertaining to them. Again, there is no attempt to be exhaustive in the studies that are surveyed. They are chosen primarily because they exemplify methods and/or results.

### 3.2.1. Breastfeeding

There are a number of medically-based reasons to believe that breastfeeding will reduce the risk of infant mortality. Breastmilk is: (i) nutritious and by itself can meet nutritional requirements for up to the first six months of life (Wray, 1978), (ii) provides immunity to some infections, and (iii) is clean and can prevent the growth of bacteria. While compelling, these reasons do not provide a quantitative estimate of the value of breastfeeding in reducing mortality risk.

Historical data seem to be consistent with the medical argument. Knodel and Kintner (1977) report, using German historical data, that in cities in which breastfeeding was very uncommon, neonatal mortality rates were twice as high as in cities in which breastfeeding was relatively common, a mortality rate of 156.8 (per 1000 live births) vs. 73.7. The mortality rate differentials persisted throughout the first year of life. Such evidence, because it does not account for inputs other than breastfeeding that might have differed between cities, can at best only be suggestive.

The use of micro data to estimate the impact of breastfeeding on the risk of mortality entails serious inferential problems beyond those already mentioned. The most difficult problem arises because the duration of breastfeeding can be no longer than the duration of life; death must lead to its cessation. To understand the complication introduced, consider the experiment that would be necessary to estimate the effect of breastfeeding on the hazard function. To obtain the true effect, one would randomly assign to each woman prior to birth a duration of breastfeeding with the instruction to breastfeed for that length or until the infant died, whichever came first. Suppose that breastfeeding actually has no effect on the hazard and consider estimating the gradient of the hazard with respect to breastfeeding duration during the second day of life, conditional on surviving the first day. For the group of children surviving at least one day, some of their mothers will have never breastfed, some will have breastfed one day, and some two days. Among the women having children who die in the second day and who breastfed only one day, some would have breastfed two days had the child not died given their pre-birth assignment. We know, however, that breastfeeding has nothing to do with the hazard, so that women assigned to breastfeed at least two days would experience the same proportion of deaths in the second day as women assigned to breastfeed only one day. But, if instead of comparing hazards based on assigned breastfeeding durations, the comparison was made on observed durations, clearly those actually breastfeeding only one day would have a higher hazard than those assigned to breastfeed only one day and those breastfeeding two days would have a hazard rate of zero. This will make it appear that shorter durations of breastfeeding are associated with an increased mortality hazard, even though the true effect is zero.

This "truncation" problem is a more general one, arising whenever the input is defined to depend on the duration of life or is dependent on the achievement of a given age. Thus, for example, the effect on life expectancy of calories consumed since birth or between any ages would be truncated by death. Similarly, immunizations given after some age is reached would be truncated by death prior to the immunization age (immunized children would live longer) and thus be spuriously related to life expectancy.

A second problem, as mentioned above, arises if there is unobserved frailty heterogeneity and the behavior (breastfeeding in this case) is conditioned on it. If families breastfeed weaker children longer, engaging in compensatory behavior, the effect of breastfeeding will be understated. An additional non-behavioral reason for this correlation, special to estimating the effect of breastfeeding, is that a weak child, one who has a greater probability of dying, may be unable to suckle. This would overstate the efficacy of breastfeeding.

There have been a number of ways in which these problems have been addressed. Let us first consider papers that have ignored the issue of unobserved heterogeneity. Palloni and Tienda (1986) parameterize the log odds associated with the probability that a child dies in a discrete age interval, given that the child survived to the beginning of the interval, as linear in regressors. The age intervals are 1–2 months, 3–5 months, 6–11 months, 12–23 months, and 24–59 months. The odds ratio is assumed constant within each age interval. They resolve the problem that breastfeeding is censored at the time of death for those children who die while still being breastfed by using information on the length of breastfeeding only up to the beginning of the age at death interval. For example, for infants who die within the 3–5 month interval, the duration of breastfeeding is truncated to be at most three months. The idea is to truncate breastfeeding duration in the same way for both survivors and non-survivors. They argue that this mis-specification will attenuate the estimated breastfeeding effect on the grounds that the largest effect of breastfeeding is likely to be contemporaneous. However, although the truncation bias is eliminated, the breastfeeding variable is mismeasured in a systematic way. Breastfeeding length below the cutoff is the true duration, but breastfeeding length at the artificial maximal duration is less than the true duration. This tends to bias the breastfeeding effect upward and other inputs that are correlated with the true breastfeeding duration in an unknown direction. Perhaps more importantly, the existence of unobserved frailty heterogeneity implies that conditioning on survival to specific ages, as do Polloni and Tienda, creates a selection bias in the estimates of all of the input parameters.

This particular way of treating breastfeeding, by truncating it, seems to be the most usual method of choice. Butz et al. (1984), Pebley and Strupp (1987) and Rosenzweig and Schultz (1983a) all follow that route. Olsen and Wolpin (1983) substitute the average duration of breastfeeding of surviving children in the family for measured duration of the children that die prior to weaning. To understand whether such a procedure identifies the true breastfeeding effect, it is necessary to consider the behavioral model that Olsen and Wolpin had in mind. Because, as they assume, all decisions are made at the beginning of marriage, the optimally chosen duration of breastfeeding of each child corresponds to the length of breastfeeding that would have been observed had the child not died. However, even if the researcher knew this choice it would be correlated with the family frailty endowment and so not correspond to the appropriate experiment. But, the within-family fixed-effects estimator controls for the family-specific component of the frailty endowment (the only one recognized in the Olsen and Wolpin framework).

Now, children die for two, not necessarily mutually exclusive, reasons: they have an unhealthful mix of inputs and/or they have a poor endowment. If those who die while being breastfed have a poor endowment, then the average duration of breastfeeding for the surviving children measures the breastfeeding duration of children who died before being weaned unbiasedly, because breastfeeding is by the assumption of the model not affected by the child-specific component and the family-specific component is controlled. While the existence of measurement error causes bias of the usual kind, there is still the question of what is contained in the measurement error that accounts for differences across children in the optimal choice of breastfeeding duration. Given the assumption of the behavioral model, it must be that the input demand function for breastfeeding differs systematically by birth because, under the perfect foresight assumption, they depend on the same factors. It would, therefore, seem quite likely that the demand functions for inputs other than breastfeeding would differ systematically in ways that created differential correlations with optimal breastfeeding. Thus, as in the general proxy variable case, the measurement error would not be uncorrelated with the other regressors, contributing biases that cannot be easily signed. In the case that the children who died before weaning had a poor input mix, the correlation of those inputs with optimal breastfeeding duration would imply that the measurement error is not classical. For example, if a short duration of breastfeeding coincides with a poor input mix, then the average breastfeeding duration of surviving children will overstate systematically the duration of breastfeeding of the dead children. In either case, then, the use of this proxy does not solve the censoring problem even in the non-dynamic choice setting.

There are several other alternatives. One is to estimate a structural model in which breastfeeding is one of the decision variables. Because parents will take the technology into account in making their decision, the technology parameters are embedded in the breastfeeding decision rule (as well as in all of the other decision rules). Without specifying an explicit model that is feasible to estimate, it is difficult to assess the value of the approach in practice. It does raise an interesting potential distinction between what is the true technology and what parents believe to be the true technology. Obviously, we are attempting to estimate the true technology because we don't know what it is. Moreover, it is hard to believe that everyone has the same perception or knowledge. Thus, it would seem questionable to estimate a decision model in which the technology was assumed to be known by the agents. One approach would be to think seriously about collecting data on the perceptions that people have about the technology and embed that in the decision model. Although it can be argued that estimating structural decision models should be the goal, we are probably some time away from seeing a payoff from that approach for this problem.

A second alternative is to assume a particular structure for the technology that is sufficient for identification akin to the approach in Mroz and Weir (1990). Consider the simplest example where the mortality hazard rate is constant. If the child is not breastfed the hazard rate is $\lambda_T$, while if the child is breastfed the hazard is $1 - \alpha(b)\lambda_T$ where $b$ is the length of breastfeeding and $0 < 1 - \alpha(b) < 1$ is the effect of breastfeeding length on the mortality hazard. Presumably, the diminution in the mortality rate increases with the duration of breastfeeding (possibly at a decreasing rate), that is, $\alpha'(b) \geq 0$. Notice that breastfeeding is assumed to shift the mortality hazard rate proportionately. The breastfeeding hazard rate, the instantaneous probability of weaning, is assumed to be independent of the mortality hazard.[54]

Suppose that we have data of the following kind: there are $N_1$ children who died before being weaned and $N_2$ children who died after being weaned. For the first group we observe the duration of breastfeeding $b$ and the duration of life $t = b$, while for the second group we observe the duration of breastfeeding $b$ and the duration of life $t > b$. Suppose, first, that we do not treat the two groups differently. Then the likelihood function for the sample is the product of probabilities over sample points of the form Pr(breastfeeding terminates at $b$ and death occurs at $t$). If we simplify by assuming

---

[54] This assumption is made for illustrative purposes only. It is obviously violated if there is unobserved frailty heterogeneity.

that $\alpha(b) = \alpha b$, that is, the diminution of the mortality hazard rate is at a constant rate, then it can be shown that the maximum likelihood estimates of $\lambda_T$ and $\alpha$ solve the following equations:

$$\frac{N_1 + N_2}{\lambda_T} - \sum_{k=1}^{N_1+N_2} b_k - \sum_{k=1}^{N_1+N_2}(1 - \alpha b_k)(t_k - b_k) = 0,$$

$$-\sum_{k=1}^{N_1+N_2} \frac{b_k}{1 - \alpha b_k} + \lambda_T \sum_{k=1}^{N_1+N_2} b_k(t_k - b_k) = 0. \tag{29}$$

It should be noted that the second equation in (29) holds only if there is a non-zero breastfeeding effect. Notice also that the two equations are independent of the breastfeeding hazard function, a result of the assumed independence of the mortality and breastfeeding hazards. Although there is no closed form solution for $\alpha$ we can check to see whether its maximum likelihood estimate is zero when the true effect is zero. In that case, the first equation in (29) reduces to the well-known result that with a constant hazard the maximum likelihood estimate of the hazard rate is the inverse of average duration (of life). When the true effect of breastfeeding is zero, the second equation in (29) reduces only to the second term.[55] But that expression can only be zero if the covariance between the duration of breastfeeding and the duration of life beyond the end of breastfeeding is zero. In fact, that covariance must be positive because of the truncation of breastfeeding at the end of life for the $N_2$ observations. The result will be a non-zero and therefore biased estimate of the breastfeeding effect.

If the correct likelihood function for the sample is used, namely where the probability statements for the censored observations are of the form Pr(death occurs prior to the termination of breastfeeding), then the normal equations are

$$\frac{N_1 + N_2}{\lambda_T} - \left[\sum_{i=1}^{N_1} t_i + \sum_{j=1}^{N_2} b_j\right] - \sum_{j=1}^{N_2}(1 - \alpha b_j)(t_j - b_j) = 0,$$

$$\sum_{i=1}^{N_2} \frac{-b_j}{1 - \alpha b_j} + \lambda_T \sum_{j=1}^{N_2} b_j(t_j - b_j) = 0. \tag{30}$$

When the breastfeeding effect is zero, the maximum likelihood estimate of the constant hazard for the duration of life is again the inverse of the average duration of life over the entire sample. However, when $\alpha = 0$ the second normal equation, which again consists only of the second term, is now zero, because the covariance between

---

[55] The term in the ln likelihood from which the first term in the second equation of (27) arises is zero in this case.

the duration of breastfeeding and the additional duration of life after weaning is zero for the sample of children who were weaned before they died. Thus, the maximum likelihood estimate of the breastfeeding effect is zero when the true effect is zero.

The point is that by assuming that the hazard rate is constant and, more critically, that breastfeeding proportionately affects it, it is possible to separate the spurious correlation between breastfeeding length and the length of life that arises because of the truncation from the true effect of breastfeeding on mortality risk. The constant hazard was chosen only as an example; identification is not specific to that assumption. Adding observable regressors does not raise any fundamental issues. However, allowing for unobserved frailty that is correlated with the regressors in this setting raises daunting estimation issues that have not been adequately resolved.

Finally, the effect of breastfeeding duration can be correctly estimated if there exists an instrumental variable that mimics the random assignment experiment. Variation in the price of feeding substitutes, like the price of infant formula, would create exogenous variation in breastfeeding duration. However, truncation bias and correlations of inputs with unobserved heterogeneity are generic requiring more than a single instrumental variable for identification.

Most studies find there to be a statistically discernible beneficial effect of breastfeeding on infant mortality. Estimates are not comparable not only because of differences in specification and estimation method, but also because the effect of breastfeeding depends on the relevant feeding alternative which is often not controlled for in the estimation. And, there is no one study or small set of studies that have adequately dealt with even most of the inferential problems raised above from which a credible range of estimates can be drawn.

### 3.2.2. Prenatal care

In 1989 in the US, approximately 75% of pregnant women began receiving prenatal care in the first trimester.[56] Over the prior ten years, that figure had remained roughly constant, although there had been a significant increase in early prenatal care over the decade before that. Black–white differences in the use of prenatal care have been and continue to be large. In 1989, the utilization rate among white women was 79%, but only 60% among black women.[56] Given these figures, it is important to know to what extent increasing participation in early prenatal care would affect the risk of infant mortality. Interestingly, in a recent report of the National Commission to Prevent Infant Mortality (1992), it is claimed that "early and regular prenatal care is the best method for identifying and avoiding preventable causes of infant mortality,

---

[56] National Commission to Prevent Infant Mortality (1992: p. 31).

especially those which occur in the neonatal period".[57] One would think from that statement that there is overwhelming evidence that early prenatal care reduces infant mortality. However, Harris (1982) characterizes the literature as follows:

> The role of prenatal care has been the subject of serious dispute in the obstetric and public health literature for nearly four decades. This dispute has been fomented in great part by the nonexperimental nature of the evidence. Virtually all studies of prenatal care analyze cross-section data on the uncontrolled experience of thousands of women and their pregnancies. The subjects under study are self-selected. There are no randomized treatments. Possible confounding variables cannot be eliminated. Nor do the data reveal how the subjects actually made use of the services. (p. 15.)

There is clearly a difference of opinion, and it is not due to the decade that separates the two judgements. The same general problems alluded to by Harris still persist in more contemporaneous studies.

The problems associated with estimating prenatal care effects have much in common with those already mentioned in the discussion of estimating breastfeeding effects. In the same way that the duration of breastfeeding is bounded from above by the duration of an infant's life, the waiting time until prenatal care is sought is bounded from above by the period of gestation (Harris, 1982). The longer the time until prenatal care is obtained, the longer on average will be the length of gestation. Prenatal delay is spuriously correlated with gestation length in exactly the same way as is breastfeeding length with the duration of life. Clearly, one would not obtain a correct estimate of the effect of delaying prenatal care on gestation without somehow accounting for this spurious relationship. Whether or not the estimate of prenatal care on the mortality hazard is affected depends on whether there are omitted inputs and/or unobserved frailty heterogeneity in the estimated hazard. To the extent that gestation length influences mortality risk because it is correlated with omitted inputs, delays in seeking prenatal care will be correlated with mortality even if it has no technological effect. Rosenzweig and Schultz (1983a) estimate the effect on infant mortality of early (first trimester) relative to later prenatal care, eliminating truncation bias in much the same way as was done in the breastfeeding studies reviewed above. The effect of misspecification in this case is also similar.

The existence of unobserved frailty heterogeneity among the fetal population creates unique problems for the estimation of prenatal care effects. As with all behaviors, there is the potential behavioral response; women with troubled pregnancies or histories of such pregnancies may be more likely to seek prenatal care and more likely to seek it early. There are also, however, a number of non-behavioral relationships that confound inference. If frailty induces fetal wastage, the population of fetuses that

---

[57] National Commission to Prevent Infant Mortality (1992: p. 28).

survive to later gestations will be more robust on average. Thus, women who seek later prenatal treatment, even if randomly drawn from among women having reached that gestational length, will experience lower infant mortality than women who sought prenatal care earlier. Finally, to the extent that early prenatal care brings less healthy infants to a live birth, prenatal care will be associated with higher infant mortality.

Results on the effect of prenatal care are more varied than on breastfeeding. As with breastfeeding, this may be due to the differences in the set of "controls", sample composition, and statistical methodology. Harris, in a statistical formulation that incorporates fetal selection, found a weakly positive effect of prenatal care on perinatal mortality (the period from 20 weeks after conception to 28 days after birth).[58] However, in recognition of the problematic nature of the sources of identification, Harris (1982) is rightfully cautious about the results of his analysis. Rosenzweig and Schultz (1983a) finds that prenatal care reduces infant mortality. However, what is probably more instructive is that the result changes sign when the two-step procedure is used implying that behavioral assumptions matter. It should be recognized that the Rosenzweig and Schultz instrumental variables procedure does not produce consistent estimates of technology in the presence of fetal selection.[59]

### 3.2.3. Maternal age at birth

In the production function context, holding all other inputs and the child-specific frailty endowment constant, the interpretation of the effect of maternal age at birth on infant mortality must be biological, i.e., having to do with reproductive maturity. Indeed, this is the interpretation of almost all studies of infant mortality that include maternal age at birth as a determinant (see the discussion in Geronimus (1987)). As the data in the introduction demonstrate, the risk of infant (neonatal) mortality is considerably higher among teenage births. However, because teenagers may engage in behaviors that are deleterious to infant survival, on net, or may be drawn nonrandomly from the distribution of the frailty endowment, the simple correlation is subject to many interpretations.

As one might expect then, given the lack of consensus over what are the appropriate controls and given the differences in statistical methods and treatment of unobserved frailty, there is great variation in quantitative estimates of the maternal age at

---

[58] In the statistical formulation that does not control for fetal selection the effect of prenatal care was to increase perinatal mortality.

[59] Grossman and Joyce (1990) adopt a parametric selection model (Heckman, 1979) to correct for birth selection in estimating a birth weight production function. Lee et al. (1992) present and implement a semiparametric estimation method for incorporating post-birth survival selection in the estimation of a child health (weight) production function. Both studies account for the endogeneity of inputs in their estimation procedures.

birth–infant mortality relationship. Geronimus (1986) states that "in reviewing the literature one finds that in those studies where potentially confounding environmental risk factors are controlled, the teenage mothers in the sample do not exhibit higher rates of specific poor pregnancy outcomes than older mothers".[60] Moreover, Geronimus (1986) cites evidence from the clinical and biomedical literatures that teenagers may actually be developmentally advantaged with respect to childbearing and states that "these findings strongly suggest that teenage childbearing is not inherently risky, a conclusion that appears at odds with widespread belief".[61]

An informed judgement of the quality of the clinical evidence cannot be provided, but the non-clinical evidence neither supports nor denies Geronimus's conclusion for the reasons already stated. However, it is useful to ask, regardless of the sign of the true biological age effect, what policy implications could be drawn from either finding. Recall that what is estimated is the technology, that is, the effect of maternal age at birth holding all inputs and the frailty endowment constant. Thus, the estimate answers the question: What would be the effect of altering maternal age at birth if the woman engaged in exactly the same behaviors and had the same frailty endowment? Whether the answer to this question is of direct policy relevance depends on the policy. For example, consider the imposition of a hypothetical tax (or subsidy, depending on the desired direction of the incentive) on women who bear children at early ages.[62] Assuming that we could estimate the effect of the policy on age at birth, it is not necessary to do a complete analysis to see that the production function estimate would not be the correct estimate of the policy's impact on infant mortality. The tax, by affecting the resource constraint of the woman in the state where she has a child at a "taxable" age, will have ramifications for behaviors other than age at birth if she does have a child at a "taxable" age. Moreover, if the tax postpones the maternal age at birth for some women, one needs to know the alterations in other behaviors that will ensue for those women. That is not a simple task if young mothers are drawn self-selectively from the frailty distribution and behaviors are conditioned on frailty. The production function is only one ingredient to the analysis of policy. The evaluation of most interventionist policies, if not all, would require more than just knowledge of the technology.

### 3.2.4. Other biological determinants

As seen in the taxonomy of Table 7, there are a number of other inputs that also can be given biological interpretations. Among those that have received attention are birth

---

[60] Geronimus (1986: p. 1416). The studies cited by Geronimus come exclusively from the biomedical literature. In a survey paper, Geronimus (1987), the point is extended to studies which show weakened age of mother at birth effects and include the demographic and economic literature.

[61] Geronimus (1986: p. 1416). In the 1987 survey, Geronimus cites at least a dozen studies in support of this argument.

[62] The tax could be in the form of a reduction in the amount of welfare received in the form of AFDC.

order, prior birth spacing, gender, and race. Birth order and prior birth interval lengths reflect past fertility decisions, determined, at least as an approximation, within a dynamic optimization model like the kind previously described. The issue is whether there are biological advantages to ones placement in the birth sequence and in the distance from prior births. The biological interpretation requires that all other inputs and the residual frailty endowment be controlled. Without such controls, the number of births or the distance between births may reflect, for example, the within-family allocation of resources among children. And because they reflect past fertility-related decisions, they will be correlated with the family-specific frailty endowment.

Some researchers have included birth intervals of subsequent children in one form or another (see Table 8). While that variable does not appear in Table 7, one could argue that infectious diseases are more readily communicated within households with more children per unit of living space. Olsen and Wolpin (1983), as seen in Table 8, include the age distribution of children as well as the number of rooms in the house to measure the disease environment.[63] However, like other postnatal variables their estimates crucially rely on the assumption that dynamical considerations are absent from behavior; otherwise, postnatal inputs will depend on the child-specific frailty endowments of children who are already alive.

Ignoring the possibility of selective abortion, gender is an exogenous characteristic of a live birth. As with other biological variables it will reflect gender-based biological differences in robustness only to the extent that there are no omitted inputs, unless gender is uncorrelated with all inputs (included and omitted). Gender is often ignored in many analyses of mortality because of the assumption that it is orthogonal to all inputs.[64]

Similar issues arise in the interpretation of racial differences, although that there are differences in the behavioral inputs by race is well documented. Moreover, and possibly less well appreciated, is the question of whether or not including race ameliorates the bias in other inputs when there are acknowledged to be omitted inputs. The implicit assumption made when including race as an indicator of the omitted inputs (behaviors and/or biological) is that race accounts for a sufficiently large proportion of the variance of the omitted factors that, in spite of the altered correlation structure of the included inputs with the unobservables net of race, biases in estimated input effects are reduced (assuming that the size of the biases is what is of concern).

An admittedly extreme example may be helpful. Suppose that there are only two factors that determine mortality risk, a behavioral input and innate frailty. Further sup-

---

[63] Because a subsequent child may be more closely spaced to the observational child, if the observational child dies while being breastfed, there is a similar kind of censoring problem as with estimating the effect of breastfeeding (Palloni and Tienda, 1986; Pebley and Strupp, 1987).

[64] While prenatal inputs cannot be correlated with gender given that gender is usually unknown prior to birth, postnatal inputs could differ due to differential parental preferences for the survival of boys vs. girls. For evidence on the existence of gender survival preference, see Rosenzweig and Schultz (1982).

pose that, unknown to us, the behavior is independent of frailty so that we can obtain an unbiased estimate of its impact simply by estimating the direct relationship between the behavioral input and actual mortality. Now, consider the effect of the input holding race constant assuming that both (i) the behavior, e.g., smoking during pregnancy, differs by race, and (ii) frailty differs by race. Although the input is uncorrelated with frailty by assumption, the input will not be uncorrelated with frailty conditional on race. Thus, the estimate of the input effect will be biased if race is held constant. In the other extreme, if frailty is correlated with the behavior in the unconditional setting, the bias will be reduced to zero if the only reason that behavior is correlated with the frailty endowment is because it is correlated with race.[65] The point is, as in the case more generally of proxies, not that one should not control for race, but that the assumptions that are necessary to justify the conclusion that biases in the estimates of the effects of specific behaviors are reduced be made explicit. It should be noted that race differences in age-specific mortality risk remain statistically and substantively significant regardless of the set of inputs from those in Table 7 that are included as determinants.[66] There is no consensus explanation in the literature (see below).

### 3.2.5. Other non-biological determinants

Aside from measurement issues, the prenatal and postnatal inputs in Table 7 not previously discussed do not create any additional methodological problems. Of course, constructing measurements can itself be problematic. For example, a common measure of prenatal maternal nutrition is weight gain during pregnancy. Even assuming that subtracting out birth weight sufficiently controls for spurious correlation, weight gain will be correlated with the duration of the pregnancy for biological reasons. As with prenatal care, if increased frailty induces shorter gestation, then women who gain less weight because their gestation is shorter will experience greater infant mortality if frailty is uncontrolled. Weight gain per week of gestation may be less affected by spurious correlation with frailty, but may not be the correct measurement. Direct measures of nutrient intake are much less common (see Wolfe and Behrman (1982) for an exception).

Probably the most studied substance use factor is smoking. Results have been mixed and there is not much basis to choose among studies. There is less work on the impact of time allocation, e.g, the amount and type of physical activity of the mother during the pregnancy, nor is there much work which controls for aspects of the disease environment during the pregnancy and after the birth.

---

[65] This includes the case where race perfectly explains the variation in frailty, that is, there is no within-race variation in frailty.

[66] It does not survive the inclusion of birth weight. Small black babies have higher survival rates than do small white babies (e.g., Wilcox and Russell, 1990).

## 3.2.6. *Birth weight as a determinant*

As seen in Table 8, a number of the papers include birth weight as a determinant of mortality risk. There is certainly no question that infant mortality steeply declines with increased birth weight. Using national statistics for 1980, Buehler et al. (1987) report that the infant mortality rate per 1000 live births was 695 for infants who weighed between 500–999 g at birth, 224 for babies who weighed 1000–1499 g, 74 for those who weighed 1500–1999 g, 26 for birth weights of 2000–2499 g, and under nine for weights over 2500 g. The lowest mortality rate in 1980 was 3.4 achieved at birth weights of 4000–4499 g and mortality actually rises to 5.7 for babies over 5000 g. Because of this relationship, a low birth weight (LBW) designation is given to weights below 2500 g (5.5 pounds).[67]

As already noted, there would be no reason to include birth weight in the estimation of the mortality risk production function if all of the factors in Table 7 were measured (or controlled). Holding all of those factors constant, birth weight would not have any additional impact on mortality. The inclusion of birth weight must be taken then as a signal that there are omitted factors.[68] To understand the effect of including birth weight on the interpretation of the effects of other behavioral inputs, let us postulate the existence of a birth weight production function (Rosenzweig and Schultz, 1983b). It would seem reasonable to assume that the biological factors and prenatal factors shown in Table 7 also determine birth weight and that there are no additional factors.[69] Now, consider the case where all inputs to mortality are observed (and innate frailty is controlled) except for a single prenatal input and suppose that the mortality risk function is estimated with all observable inputs and birth weight. In this case, the effect of birth weight on infant mortality risk holding inputs constant reflects the effect of the omitted prenatal input on mortality.[70] The effect on mortality risk of any prenatal input (or biological factor) that enters the birth weight technology, however, reflects the compensating effect of the omitted prenatal input that must be made to keep birth weight constant. Thus, the effect of any input is a composite of the effects of the observed and omitted inputs on mortality risk and on birth weight, and therefore, it is necessary to know the birth weight production function in order to es-

---

[67] Infants weighing under 1500 g are given a "very low birth weight" designation. See also Sappenfield (1987) for similar cross tabulations of mortality with gestation and birth weight together.

[68] To the extent that birth weight is an indicator of inherently unobservable shocks in the cause-of-death technologies, birth weight might have an effect even if all of the factors in Table 7 were measured. Regardless, birth weight would still signal an omitted factor (it would still only be a proxy), and the arguments that follow would not be affected.

[69] One can add a second endowment factor, specific to birth weight and correlated with frailty, without altering the arguments that follow.

[70] Notice that the estimated birth weight effect will be different if a different prenatal input is omitted.

timate the mortality risk production function.[71] However, given that the unobserved prenatal input also enters the birth weight production function, its consistent estimation is not possible. It is not only impossible to estimate consistently the mortality risk technology by substituting birth weight for omitted inputs, but it is also impossible to interpret correctly the estimated input effects without specifying what are the omitted inputs.

A good example of the rather dramatic effect that including birth weight may have on interpretation is the finding reported in Meyer and Comstock (1972) that while infants born to women who smoke during the pregnancy have higher (perinatal) mortality, lower birth weight infants of women who smoke have lower mortality than comparable size infants born to women who did not smoke. If smoking reduces birth weight, as does appear to be a fairly robust result, then the effect on mortality holding birth weight constant reflects the effect of inputs on mortality that increase birth weight as well as its own effect. Similar findings appear for race. In the US, neonatal mortality rates in 1980 were about double for blacks than for whites overall. But, among low birth weight infants in 1980, neonatal mortality rates were about twice as large among whites.[72] Interestingly, this reversal does not occur for post-neonatal mortality.

A great deal of attention has been given to the estimation of the birth weight production function. If we were only interested in mortality and we had all of the inputs, that literature would be superfluous. There are two reasons to be interested in the birth weight production function. First, estimating the mortality risk function requires more information, namely data on postnatal inputs and those inputs are often unavailable. And, presumably, risk factors for reduced birth weight do not augment survival rates. Second, birth weight may be related to other outcomes of interest besides mortality (e.g., morbidity and later health, intellectual achievement).

The literature on birth weight is as large or even larger than that on infant mortality.[73] All of the points made previously concerning the estimation problems associated with biological and prenatal factors apply to this literature as well, and there is no need to repeat them. Unlike infant mortality, however, there has been a recent literature that has attempted to incorporate dynamic features of behavioral optimization more explicitly with the estimation of the birth weight technology in the presence of

---

[71] In the biomedical and demographic literature, the effect of the input itself is called the direct effect and the effect operating through its impact on birth weight the indirect effect (e.g., Bross and Shapiro, 1982; Cramer, 1987). The birth weight constant estimates are viewed as revealing something more about the underlying structure or "causal mechanisms".

[72] Buehler et al. (1987).

[73] It is, of course, impossible to give a complete enumeration. There is a fairly extensive bibliography in the aforementioned *Report to the National Commission to Prevent Infant Mortality* covering primarily the biomedical literature. Cramer (1987) is a good example of the frontier in the demographic literature as are Grossman and Joyce (1990) and Rosenzweig and Wolpin (1991) in the economics literature.

unobserved frailty. It is useful to consider such a framework because it summarizes the conditions under which alternative estimation strategies follow from basic behavioral assumptions. The statistical model, however, rather than relying on exact solutions of the optimization problem, represents an approximation to the decision rules that govern behavior.

Following Rosenzweig and Wolpin (1995), assume that the birth outcome production function for a child $k$ born to a daughter $j$ of parents $i$ is given by

$$B_{ijk} = \sum_{m=1}^{M} \alpha_m z_{mijk} + \mu_{ijk},$$ (31)

where $B_{ijk}$ is birth weight, $z_{mijk}$ are the inputs, $\mu_{ijk}$ is the (grand) child's frailty endowment, and $\alpha_m$ is the technology parameter. The three generations are linked to each other through their endowments in the following way: any child born to the same parents has a component $\mu/2$ from the mother and a component $\tilde{\mu}/2$ from the father that is the same for all siblings and a unique, child-specific, component $\phi$. A part of the common component is transmitted across generations, $\rho(\mu + \tilde{\mu})/2$. Thus, for the daughter of parents $i$,

$$\mu_{ij} = \rho\left\{\frac{\mu_i + \tilde{\mu}_i}{2}\right\} + \phi_{ij}$$ (32)

and for the child $k$ of daughter $j$,

$$\mu_{ijk} = \rho\left\{\frac{\mu_{ij} + \tilde{\mu}_{ij}}{2}\right\} + \phi_{ijk}.$$ (33)

The mother–child endowment covariance, given in Eqs. (32) and (33), is

$$\text{cov}(\mu_{ij}, \mu_{ijk}) = \frac{\rho}{2}(\sigma_\mu^2 + \sigma_{\mu\tilde{\mu}}),$$ (34)

where $\sigma_{\mu\tilde{\mu}}$ is the covariance between the endowments of mates. The covariance between the endowments of (full) siblings is

$$\text{cov}(\mu_{ijk}, \mu_{ij\kappa}) = \frac{\rho^2}{2}(\sigma_\mu^2 + \sigma_{\mu\tilde{\mu}}),$$ (35)

while the endowment covariance between cousins, children born to sisters, is

$$\text{cov}(\mu_{ijk}, \mu_{i\kappa k}) = \frac{\rho^4}{8}(\sigma_\mu^2 + \sigma_{\mu\tilde\mu}). \tag{36}$$

Returning to Eq. (31), the essence of the estimation problem is the same as in the case of mortality, namely that the unobservable endowment may be correlated with the inputs. The behavioral input decision rule for the $k$th child and the $m$th input, expressed in linear form and solely in terms of endowments (ignoring all other aspects of the relevant information set) is

$$z_{mijk} = \delta_{mk}\mu_{ij} + \sum_{n=1}^{k}\tau_{mkn}\phi_{ijn}, \tag{37}$$

where only the endowments of children already born, birth orders from $n = 1, \dots, k-1$, and possibly that of the $k$th child itself, can influence the prenatal inputs of child $k$. Notice that $\tau_{mkk} \neq 0$ implies that parents gain information about the child-specific component of the endowment during the pregnancy. In the case of child mortality, the endowments of younger children can affect postnatal inputs.

Rosenzweig and Wolpin consider a nested set of statistical models that differ based on the assumptions about behavior and the structure of endowments. They are:

(1) *Least squares*. This class of procedures produces unbiased estimates of the technology parameters in Eq. (31) under the assumption that inputs are uncorrelated with behavior. This property is consistent with a model in which endowments do not affect behavior or a model in which there is no intergenerational endowment correlation and no child-specific endowment variation. The reader will recognize that this has been the underlying assumption of most of the literature on infant and child mortality reviewed above, although least squares itself has not been the usual estimation procedure.

(2) *Instrumental variables*. If endowments affect behaviors so that a relation like Eq. (36) exists, consistent parameters of the technology can be estimated if there exist (instrumental) variables that influence behaviors but that are themselves independent of endowments. If there is no intergenerational correlation in endowments, implying that the endowments of siblings are uncorrelated, then parental characteristics, such as schooling, or family background variables, such as grandmother's schooling, may be used as instruments. This is the procedure used by Rosenzweig and Schultz (1983a) in their study of infant mortality and in their study (1983b) of birth weight.

(3) *"Sisters" fixed-effects*. There has recently been a number of papers that have used variation in the outcomes of the children of sisters (cousins) to estimate aspects of technology (Geronimus and Korenman, 1992). From Eq. (32), the difference in endowments across the $k$th child of two sisters, $ijk$ and $i\kappa k$, is $(\rho/2)[(\tilde\mu_{ij} - \tilde\mu_{i\kappa}) + (\phi_{ij} -$

$\phi_{i\kappa}$)] + ($\phi_{ijk} - \gamma_{i\kappa k}$). While this difference eliminates the common endowment component transmitted by the mother, it still contains the endowments of the husbands and the sister and child idiosyncratic components. Input differences (across cousins) will be uncorrelated with the sister (cousin) differenced endowments only if the husbands of the sisters have identical endowments and if there is no idiosyncratic component of endowments (cousins and siblings have identical endowments).

(4) *Mother fixed-effects.* Differencing the endowments of siblings eliminates the common parental endowments, but contains the child-specific components. Technology estimates based on sibling outcome and input differences will be unbiased only if the child-specific components of endowments do not alter behavior. Notice that even if only the older child's child-specific endowment affects behavior, as would be the case if parents did not obtain information about endowments during the pregnancy, sibling-differenced inputs are correlated with sibling-differenced endowments because the younger sibling's input is correlated with the older sibling's endowment in any sibling pair. Recall that this is the procedure used by Olsen and Wolpin in their study of mortality.

(5) *Instrumental variables and mother fixed-effects.* With the structure as in Eqs. (31)–(35) a more complex estimation procedure is required. Sibling-differenced inputs can be instrumented by variables that are uncorrelated with child-specific endowments. Potentially valid instruments include parental background variables and either prenatal inputs of the older child if the "own" child-specific endowment is unknown during the pregnancy or prenatal inputs of children older than the sibling pair. This procedure was first implemented in Rosenzweig (1986).

Rosenzweig and Wolpin use an estimation procedure that matches sample and theoretical moments. They demonstrate that this estimator of the technology is equivalent to the one adopted by Rosenzweig (1986), although, given its full information nature, it is more efficient. Testing the restrictions implied by the above nested behavioral assumptions, they find that the "best" estimates of technology are obtained allowing for the full scope of dynamical behavior, where behaviors are affected by both family and child-specific endowments.[74]

## 3.3. Estimating the impact of public policy interventions

Knowledge of the mortality risk technology provides useful information to families in that it enables them to make behavioral decisions more efficiently, that is, decisions that are privately welfare maximizing. Such knowledge, however, does not provide

---

[74] The requirement that the sample consist of mothers who have at least two children creates a choice-based sample if not all women in the population have at least two children. If, for example, women who have poor first birth outcomes do not have a second child, the sample of women with at least two births will have, on average, more highly endowed children. Input effects will tend to be biased unless the fertility process is explicitly modeled.

sufficient information to determine the consequences of specific policy interventions on infant and child mortality and, thus, to assess the social efficacy of alternative programs. If policy makers knew the complete behavioral model, they could determine the impact of any hypothetical program on behaviors and, therefore, on infant and child mortality. Without such information, conjectures concerning the impact of hypothetical programs must be made on the basis of extrapolations from existing programs. Obviously, the validity of such extrapolations will depend on the quality of the analyses of programs that have been adopted.

Viewed in the context of behavioral economic decision-making models, government programs aimed at altering demographic outcomes, such as infant and child mortality or fertility, are attempts to alter the structure of prices faced by decision-makers. Beyond the obvious direct influence of tax and subsidy schemes on the net price of purchased goods and services, the existence of unsubsidized goods and services, that is, those delivered at market prices, in locations that would otherwise not be serviced (or less well serviced) act to reduce the "full" price of those goods and services when the time costs of the consumer associated with obtaining access to the service are considered. The practical significance of this view for policy analysis is that policies designed for single objectives will have multiple consequences, and may ameliorate or reinforce the effects of other single-objective programs. The reason is that even a program which alters only a single price, for example, one that subsidizes the price of infant formula, (i) will affect real disposable income and thus engender income effects and (ii) will lead to cross-price effects that depend on the technology and preference structure (Rosenzweig and Wolpin, 1982).

Much of the literature on program evaluation with respect to demographic outcomes has not recognized the interconnected nature of single-objective programs (see, for example, the survey of family planning programs in Hermalin (1972) and the discussion in Easterlin (1980)). And, this perspective is still absent from the more recent demographic literature as the following statement makes clear:

Recent reviews of relevant evidence have confirmed that an increase in the practice of family planning can, theoretically, reduce infant and child mortality rates. The mechanism involved operates as follows. Births that occur at the extremes of maternal age and parity, as well as those following very short intervals, experience higher than average mortality risks. If contraceptive use leads to a reduction in the proportion of births in these high risk age, order, and interval categories, then a population's infant mortality rate would decline as its level of contraceptive prevalence rises. In addition to reducing the number of infants born, family planning practice can thus enhance their chances for survival.[75]

---

[75] Bongaarts (1987: p. 323).

While it is possible that reducing the price of contraceptives will indeed alter fertility related behaviors, such as the timing and spacing of children, for the two reasons given above it may also increase the demand for child health generally, thus increasing the usage of other non-fertility related inputs that promote child health (and survival).

Economic theory implies that to study the connection between programs specifically designed to affect infant and child mortality one must incorporate other single and multiple-objective programs that affect the prices of any of the inputs in the mortality risk technology. Moreover, in a dynamic setting in which the behavioral input decision rules depend on prior choices, one must include the history of programs if full effects are to be estimated. Perhaps because of data limitations, there do not exist studies that are sensitive to dynamic considerations.

That there are cross-program effects has been demonstrated in a number of studies. Only two are reviewed here to give a flavor of the analyses, one using data from a developing country and one using US data (see also Schultz, 1984). Rosenzweig and Wolpin (1982) use data from a household survey from rural India conducted by the National Council of Applied Economic Research over the years 1968–1971. Together with the household data on fertility and child mortality histories, the authors collected and merged district level information (fraction of villages covered) on government family planning and health facilities, educational institutions, and water sources from the 1971 Indian Census. Their results indicated that increasing the prevalence of either family planning clinics, medical dispensaries or improved water sources would have qualitatively, but not quantitatively, similar effects; they reduce fertility rates, reduce child mortality, and increase school attendance. Looking at the effect of only one program would tend to overstate its significance if programs tend to be jointly allocated to villages.

Corman and Grossman (1985) use US county-level data on neonatal mortality rates in 1977, health manpower, socio-economic characteristics, and government programs obtained from a number of sources. The programs include: Medicaid reimbursement eligibility criteria, the per-capita Medicaid payment per adult recipient in AFDC families (at the state level), the number of family planning clinics (per 1000 women age 15–44), the number of community health projects (per 1000 women age 15–44), and maternal nutrition program usage (WIC, at the state level). In addition, they include the number of newborn intensive care hospitals (per 1000 women age 15–44), the number of abortion providers (per 1000 women age 15–44), the percent of women age 15–44 who are poor, and the percent of women age 15–49 who had at least a high school education. While a few of these variables actually measure usage rather than availability, and thus belong more appropriately in a production function, the specification includes a wide variety of programs. With respect to cross-program effects, Corman and Grossman find that the prevalence of family planning programs reduces neonatal mortality rates for whites.

Both of the previous studies assume that program placement is random across geographic locations, or at least unrelated to factors that determine input decisions and that are known to policy-makers but not measured by researchers. To the extent that this assumption is violated, estimates of the effectiveness of programs will be misleading. Rosenzweig and Wolpin (1986) develop a model of the optimal placement of fertility and child health programs when there are health externalities. They show that family planning programs may be optimal (alone or in combination with direct health subsidies) in response to the health externality when (i) child health and family size are gross substitutes and/or (ii) health subsidies are on a per-child basis. Optimal subsidies depend on the inherent healthiness of the recipient child population.

In their empirical work, Rosenzweig and Wolpin find, using longitudinal data from twenty barrios in Laguna, Philippines on the height and weight of children, that program placement is indeed systematically related to (estimated) health endowments; both family planning and health programs were initiated earliest in low health endowment barrios. Further, when endogenous program placement was taken into account, both family planning and health programs appeared to improve child health.

## 4. Conclusions

This chapter has surveyed two literatures in which infant and child mortality are central. The first, the responsiveness of fertility to changes in infant and child mortality, is important both with respect to understanding historical and cross-national differences in fertility patterns and in formulating policies designed to alter the rate of population growth. The theoretical notion of a target level of fertility, leading to a positive association between fertility and infant and child mortality, was conceptualized at least as early as 1861 (see the quotation from Wappaus in Knodel (1978)). And, the notion of dynamic responsiveness of fertility to realized mortality outcomes as distinct from the mortality environment has been in the literature for at least 25 years. Importantly, the empirical literature that has attempted to quantify the extent of the fertility response has been informed by the theoretical conception of behavior. This connection between theory and data is evident both in the demographic and economics literatures and accounts, in my view, for the synergistic relationship between the two disciplines with respect to this particular issue. It may, however, be true that the progression of empirical methods in economics towards establishing even tighter links between behavioral decision rules and what is estimated, both structural estimation and the estimation of approximate decision rules, will create a greater schism between the disciplines. While far from a universally accepted view, recent developments in computationally tractable methods for the estimation of dynamic behavioral models will enable more interesting models to be estimated and will lead to quantitatively more credible estimates.[76]

[76] See Keane and Wolpin (1994).

While providing behavioral models that "fit" micro data well may be a necessary ingredient for understanding the aggregate phenomenon of the demographic transition, there is as yet little attempt to incorporate such models into behaviorally-based macro models. Overlapping generations models that consider endogenous fertility have not explicitly allowed for infant and child mortality (see the chapter by Nerlove and Raut in this volume). We do not know, for example, whether the usual pattern of delay between the mortality decline and the fertility "response" can be replicated in models that do not rely on lags in perceptions. Such an exploration would be useful.

The assumption that infant and child mortality is uncontrollable at the individual level may have a considerable impact on the way one goes about estimating the response of fertility to mortality. To the extent that behavior can affect infant and child mortality, correlations between fertility and mortality may reflect underlying household preferences. Thus, disentangling the reasons that lie behind the correlation between fertility and offspring mortality requires that one understand the mortality technology. Some researchers, therefore, have attempted to recover purely exogenous components of mortality by estimating the technology of infant and child survival.

Of course, the behavioral determinants of infant and child mortality are of interest in their own right. In the second part of the chapter, approaches to estimating the infant and child mortality technology were surveyed. The synergy between disciplines that seemed to obtain in the fertility-response literature is much less evident; in this case, owing to the subject, the preeminent literature is biomedical rather than demographic or economic. However, much of the biomedical literature seems to be only minimally guided by underlying biological models. Without such a theoretical underpinning, there is no coherent bridge between the univariate, experimentally controlled, data environment and the multivariate, non-experimental, data environment. It is certainly not unusual to see papers in the biomedical literature on the effect of factor $x$ on infant mortality without any discussion of what are the appropriate controls and what principles guide the choice of controls. The demographic literature, while perhaps somewhat more sophisticated in statistical tools, has generally followed the biomedical literature, although with greater emphasis on socio-demographic factors.

Economists have contributed (although biomedical researchers have not yet recognized it) primarily because of the sharp theoretical distinction they draw between preferences and constraints. To the extent that the behaviors that are expected to have (that is, for which there is a biological basis) an effect on mortality are determined in a choice-theoretic setting, the estimation of the mortality technology raises the same issues as does the estimation of firm production functions. Correct estimation requires that one carefully specify the behavioral model, a proposition that is generally not well appreciated by non-economists. Under behavioral models that permit dynamic response and in which there is population heterogeneity in endowed healthiness, the estimation problems are considerable. By no means does the economics literature provide all of the answers. However, there is scientific progress in that literature. Hopefully, there will also be progress in the transmission of it across disciplinary boundaries.

# References

Becker, G.S. (1965), "A theory of the allocation of time", Economic Journal 75: 493–517.

Becker, G.S. and H.G. Lewis (1975), "On the interaction between the quantity and quality of children", Journal of Political Economy 81: S279–S288.

Ben-Porath, Y. (1976), "Fertility response to child mortality: micro data from Israel", Journal of Political Economy 84 (part 2): S163–S178.

Bongaarts, J. (1987), "Does family planning reduce infant mortality rates?", Population and Development Review 13: 323–334.

Bross, D.S. and S. Shapiro (1982), "Direct and indirect associations of five factors and infant mortality", American Journal of Epidemiology 115: 78–91.

Buehler, J.W., J.C. Kleinman, C.J.R. Hogue, L.T. Strauss and J.C. Smith (1987), "Birth weight-specific infant mortality, United States, 1960 and 1980", Public Health Reports 102: 151–161.

Butz, W.P., J.P. Habicht and J. DaVanzo (1984), "Environmental factors in the relationship between breastfeeding and infant mortality: the role of water and sanitation in Malaysia", American Journal of Epidemiology 119: 516–525.

Corman, H. and M. Grossman. (1985), "Determinants of neonatal mortality rates in the U.S.: a reduced form model", Journal of Health Economics 4: 213–236.

Corman, H., T.J. Joyce and M. Grossman (1987), "Birth outcome production functions in the U.S.", Journal of Human Resources 22: 339–360.

Cramer, J.C. (1987), "Social factors and infant mortality: identifying high-risk groups and proximate causes", Demography 24: 299–322.

DeSweemer, C. (1984), "The influence of child spacing on child survival", Population Studies 38: 47–52.

Easterlin, R. (1980), "Fertility and development", Population Bulletin of ECWA 18: 1–40.

Eberstein, I.W. and J.R. Parker (1984), "Racial differences in infant mortality by cause of death: the impact of birth weight and maternal age", Demography 21: 309–321.

Eckstein, Z. and K.I. Wolpin (1989), "The specification and estimation of dynamic stochastic discrete choice models", Journal of Human Resources 24: 562–598.

Flinn, C. and J.J. Heckman (1982), "New methods for analyzing structural models of labor force dynamics", Journal of Econometrics 18: 114–142.

Fogel, R.W. (1996), Chapter 9 in this Handbook.

Geronimus, A.T. (1986), "The effects of race, residence and prenatal care on the relationship of maternal age to neonatal mortality", American Journal of Public Health 76: 1416–1421.

Geronimus, A.T. (1987), "On teenage childbearing and neonatal mortality in the United States", Population and Development Review 13: 245–280.

Geronimus, A.T. and S. Korenman (1992), "The socioeconomic consequences of teen childbearing reconsidered", Quarterly Journal of Economics 107: 1187–1214.

Grossman, M. (1972), "On the concept of health capital and the demand for health", Journal of Political Economy 80: 223–255.

Grossman, M. and T.J. Joyce (1990), "Unobservables, pregnancy resolutions, and birth weight production functions in New York City", Journal of Political Economy 98: 983–1007.

Harris, J.E. (1982), "Prenatal medical care and infant mortality", in: V.R. Fuchs, ed., Economic aspects of health (University of Chicago Press, Chicago, IL).

Heckman, J.J. (1979), "Sample selection bias as a specification error", Econometrica 47: 153–161.

Heckman, J.J. (1982), "Statistical models for discrete panel data", in: C. Manski and D. McFadden, eds., Structural analysis of discrete data with econometric applications (MIT Press, Cambridge, MA).

Heckman, J.J. and B. Singer (1984), "A method for minimizing the impact of distributional assumptions in econometric models for duration data", Econometrica 52: 271–320.

Heckman, J.J. and R.J. Willis (1976), "Estimation of a stochastic model of reproduction: an econometric approach", in: N.E. Terleckyj, ed., Household production and consumption (Columbia University Press, New York).

Hermalin, A. (1972), "Regression analysis in areal data", in: C. Chandresekaren and A. Hermalin, eds., Measuring the effects of family planning on fertility (ISSUP, Belgium Ordina Press, Liege).

Keane, M. and K.I. Wolpin (1994), "The solution and estimation of discrete choice dynamic programming models by simulation: Monte Carlo evidence", Review of Economics and Statistics.

Kleinman, J.C. et al. (1988), "The effects of maternal smoking on fetal and infant mortality", American Journal of Epidemiology 127: 274–282.

Knodel, J. (1978), "European populations in the past: family-level relations", in: S.H. Preston, ed., The effects of infant and child mortality on fertility (Academic Press, New York).

Knodel, J. and H. Kintner (1977), "The impact of breastfeeding patterns on the biometric analysis of infant mortality", Demography 14: 391–409.

Lee, L.-F., M.R. Rosenzweig and M.M. Pitt (1992), "The effects of nutrition, sanitation, and water purity on child health in high mortality environments", Mimeo. (University of Pennsylvania, Philadelphia, PA).

Martin, L.G., J. Trussell, F.R. Salvail and N. Shah (1983), "Covariates of child mortality in the Philippines, Indonesia, and Pakistan: an analysis based on hazard models", Population Studies 37: 417–432.

Matthiesson, P.C. and J.C. McCann (1976), "The role of mortality in the European fertility transition: aggregate-level relations, in: S.H. Preston, ed., The effects of infant and child mortality on fertility (Academic Press, New York).

Mauskopf, J. and T.D. Wallace (1984), "Fertility and replacement: some alternative stochastic models and results", Demography 21: 519–531.

McKeown, T. (1976), The modern rise of population (Academic Press, New York).

Meyer, M.B. and G.W. Comstock (1972), "Maternal cigarette smoking and perinatal mortality", American Journal of Epidemiology 96: 1–10.

Mira, P. (1995), Uncertain child mortality, learning, and life cycle fertility, Unpublished Ph.D. dissertation (University of Minnesota, Minneapolis, MN).

Montgomery, M. (1988), "A dynamic model of contraceptive choice", Mimeo. (Princeton University, Princeton, NJ).

Mroz, T.A. and D. Weir (1989), "Structural change in life cycle fertility during the fertility transition: France before and after the revolution of 1789", Population Studies 44: 61–87.

National Commission to Prevent Infant Mortality (1992), Troubling trends persist: shortchanging America's next generation (National Commission to Prevent Infant Mortality, Washington, DC).

Newman, J. (1981), An economic analysis of the spacing of births, Unpublished Ph.D. dissertation (Yale University, New Haven, CT).

O'Hara, D.J. (1975), "Microeconomic aspects of the demographic transition", Journal of Political Economy 83: 1203–1216.

Olsen, R.J. (1980), "Estimating the effect of child mortality on the number of births", Demography 17: 429–443.

Olsen, R.J. (1983), "Mortality rates, mortality events, and the number of births", American Economic Review 73: 29–32.

Olsen, R.J. and K.I. Wolpin (1983), "The impact of exogenous child mortality on fertility: a waiting time regression with exogenous regressions", Econometrica 51: 731–749.

Palloni, A. and M. Tienda (1986), "The effects of breastfeeding and pace of childbearing on mortality at early ages", Demography 23: 31–52.

Pebley, A.R. and P.W. Strupp (1984), "Reproductive patterns and child mortality in Guatemala", Demography 24: 43–60.

Pitt, M.M., M.R. Rosenszweig and M. Hassan (1990), "Productivity, health, and inequality in the intrahousehold distribution of food in low-income countries", American Economic Review 80: 1139–1156.

Preston, S.H. (1976), Mortality patterns in national populations with special reference to recorded causes of death (Academic Press, New York).

Preston, S.H. (1978), "Introduction", in: S.H. Preston, ed., The effects of infant and child mortality on fertility (Academic Press, New York).

Preston, S.H. (1991), Fatal years (Princeton University Press, Princeton, NJ).

Ridder, G. and I. Tunali (1990), "Analysis of related durations: a semi-parametric approach with an application to the study of child mortality in Malaysia", Mimeo. (University of Chicago, Chicago, IL).

Rosenzweig, M.R. (1986), "Birth spacing and sibling inequality: asymmetric information within the household", International Economic Review 27: 55–76.

Rosenzweig, M.R. and T.P. Schultz (1982), "Market opportunities, genetic endowments, and intrafamily resource distribution", American Economic Review 72: 803–815.

Rosenzweig, M.R. and T.P. Schultz (1983a), "Consumer demand and household production: the relationship between fertility and child mortality", American Economic Review 73: 38–42.

Rosenzweig, M.R. and T.P. Schultz (1983b), "Estimating a household production function: heterogeneity, the demand for health inputs, and their effects on birth weight", Journal of Political Economy 91: 723–746.

Rosenzweig, M.R. and K.I. Wolpin (1980), "Testing the quantity–quality model of fertility: results from a natural experiment using twins", Econometrica 48: 227–240.

Rosenzweig, M.R. and K.I. Wolpin (1982), "Governmental interventions and household behavior in a developing country", Journal of Development Economics 10: 209–225.

Rosenzweig, M.R. and K.I. Wolpin (1986), "Evaluating the effects of optimally distributed public programs: child health and family planning interventions", American Economic Review 76: 470–482.

Rosenzweig, M.R. and K.I. Wolpin (1995), "Sisters, siblings and mothers: the effects of teen-age childbearing on birth outcomes", Econometrica 63.

Rust, J. (1992), "Do people behave according to Bellman's principle of optimality?", Mimeo. (Hoover Institution, Stanford University, Stanford, CA).

Sah, R.K. (1991), "The effects of child mortality changes on fertility choice and parental welfare", Journal of Political Economy 99: 582–606.

Sappenfield, W.M. (1987), "Differences in neonatal and postneonatal mortality by race, birthweight, and gestational age", Public Health Reports 102: 182–192.

Schofield, R., D. Reher and A. Bideau (1991), The decline of mortality in Europe (Oxford University Press, Oxford).

Schultz, T.P. (1984), "Studying the impact of household economic and community variables on child mortality", Population and Development Review 10 (Suppl.): 215–235.

Schultz, T.P. (1996), Chapter 8 in this Handbook.

Shapiro, S., M.C. McCormick, B.H. Starfield, J.P. Kischer and D. Bross (1980), "Relevance of correlates of infant mortality: the challenge of low birth weight", American Journal of Obstetrics and Gynecology 136: 360–363.

Vallin, J. and A. Lery (1978), "Estimating the increase in fertility consecutive to the death of a young child", in: S.H. Preston, ed., The effect of infant and child mortality on fertility (Academic Press, New York).

Wilcox, A.J. and I.T. Russell (1986), "Birthweight and perinatal mortality: III. Towards a new method of analysis", International Journal of Epidemiology 15: 188–196.

Williams, A.D. (1977), "Measuring the impact of child mortality on fertility: a methodological note", Demography 14: 581–590.

Wolpin, K.I. (1984), "An estimable dynamic stochastic model of fertility and child mortality", Journal of Political Economy 92: 852–874.

Wray, J.D. (1978), "Maternal nutrition, breastfeeding and infant survival", in: H. Mosley, ed., Nutrition and human reproduction (Plenum Press, New York).

Chapter 11

# MORTALITY AND MORBIDITY AMONG ADULTS AND THE ELDERLY

ROBIN C. SICKLES

*Rice University*

PAUL TAUBMAN*

*University of Pennsylvania*

## Contents

*We would like to acknowledge the research assistance provided by Richard Hirth, Jenny Williams, and Abdo Yazbeck at various stages of the preparation of this chapter, to thank Mark Rosenzweig and Oded Stark for their valuable editorial oversight, and to thank Peter Hartley, Jere Behrman and an anonymous referee for insightful and helpful comments on earlier drafts. Special thanks are extended to Clayton Vernon for the essential research assistance he provided in the months following Paul's tragic death. The usual caveat applies.

*Handbook of Population and Family Economics. Edited by M.R. Rosenzweig and O. Stark*
© *Elsevier Science B.V., 1997*

In Memorial

to

Paul Taubman

(1939–1995)

He served as a friend, mentor, and colleague to all of those whose lives he touched.

## 1. Introduction

We all die, even if, as Dr. Seuss, we have an immortal corpus. The main issues are when, how, and why. Over the last several decades, health care professionals, demographers, economists and other social scientists have made great strides in their attempts to answer these questions. Interest by economists arises at least in part because of intellectual curiosity about the human condition, because a changing life expectancy affects the costs of pensions, social security, and medical care, and because changing morbidity affects the productivity of labor. Humans are indeed complex beings, and for most our eventual passing will be marked by many clinical events, some acute and others of a more chronic nature. Our medical record thus becomes an important anecdote: it tells not only of the length of our life, but also of the quality with which we lived it. Did we enjoy good health, or were we destined to live many years in pain or in a disabled state? Is it destiny that determines mortality, or do we essentially choose our fate?

The purpose of the chapter is to discuss the questions to be asked of the compiled mortality and morbidity data, paying particular attention to those data sources which are readily available and to those methods which have proven or may prove themselves particularly fruitful. In our summary of key findings from many studies, we will hopefully convince the reader as to the power of many of the newer modeling approaches to expand our understanding of the complicated nexus of mortality determinants. In the course of our survey we must keep in mind the response of a dying Gertrude Stein to the question put to her by Alice B. Tolkas: "Gertrude, what's the answer?", to which Stein's reply was "Alice, what's the question?" (Fuchs, 1992).

Section 2 of our chapter begins with a review of recent trends in mortality and morbidity in the US and in other countries and the possible roles for economic development, gender, ethnicity, migration, nutrition and anthropomorphic factors, government, and the health care system in explaining these trends, particularly in national surveillance data. In order to disentangle the structure of causality that puts into question the interpretation of such associations at the national and international level, we focus in Section 3 on static and dynamic structural models of health based on variants of the original Grossman (1972a, b) health production paradigm. We present these models within a general framework which can be utilized by researchers interested in such structural modeling without reference to particular functional forms chosen for utility and production functions. We also discuss various risk factors that researchers have found to be important determinants of mortality and morbidity at the individual level, including human capital characteristics such as schooling, behavior and lifestyles, and genetics. Section 4 provides a short discussion of the various public-use data sets in the US and elsewhere which are available for mortality and morbidity study and related self-assessed health measurement systems which have been used to fashion informative measures of health status. We turn to statistical and numerical techniques which have been employed or could be implemented to estimate reduced-form mortality hazard relations and structural models in Section 5, as well as enhancements in specifying and estimating structural dynamic models that are currently proving fruitful for researchers on this and related topics. Section 6 provides concluding remarks. Our focus will be on adults and the elderly.

## 2. Trends and sources of variations in international and US vital statistics

Throughout the twentieth century, there has been a steady rise in life expectancy throughout the world. We now live in a world where life expectancy averaged 67.2 years (Table 1). In the United States, a person born in 1900 could expect to live an average of 47.3 years. By 1995 that average had increased to 75.9 years (Fig. 1)[1,2]. There are a wide range of life expectancies throughout the world, varying by continent from a weighted average of 56.0 years in Africa to 77.6 years for Australia, and by nation from 37.5 years in Uganda to 79.3 years for Japan.[3]

Worldwide increases in longevity have shifted the age distribution toward older populations, whose morbidity patterns, and the policy implications of such, recently have been documented by the World Bank (1993). The implications of population aging are substantial at the social level (Restrepo and Rozental, 1994) and at the economic level as countries attempt to balance inter-generational transfers. Particularly problematic are the demographic shifts in Japan and Europe, where fertility rates are in decline (Bös and Von Weizsäcker, 1989).

Morbidity also varies substantially throughout the world, ranging from a low of 117 disability-adjusted life years (DALYs)[4] lost per 1000 population in established market economies in 1990 to 575 DALYs lost per 1000 population in sub-Saharan Africa (Word Bank, 1993). The number of DALYs lost worldwide in 1990 was estimated by the World Bank to be 1.36 billion, representing 42 million deaths of newborn children and 80 million deaths for those at age 50.

Fig. 2 shows the distribution of the world's population by national life expectancy based on 66 countries with over five million in population. Were there no country effects one would expect that this distribution would mirror the distribution of individual endowed life expectancies and at a heuristic level, the observed multiple modes in Fig. 2 appear to be inconsistent with a distribution of life expectancies driven by the law of large numbers.

---

[1] Recent forecasts of age-specific death rates suggest that 2065 life expectancy will increase by an additional 10.5 years (Lee and Carter, 1992).

[2] As noted by many researchers, age distributions based on Census data may overstate the portion of those in the higher age deciles due to systematic overstatement of age by the elderly (Coale and Kisker, 1985).

[3] These figures are based on the *Statistical Abstract of the United States, 1995*. For an exhaustive summary of mortality trends for low mortality countries in earlier periods see, e.g., Condran et al. (1991) and Himes et al. (1994).

[4] We provide a more detailed discussion of this and other measures of morbidity in Section 4.

Table 1
Vital statistics worldwide, 1995[a]

| Region | Population[b] | GNP[c] | Life expectancy[d] | Infant mortality[e] |
|---|---|---|---|---|
| North America | 370 | 17658 | 75.3 | 12.7 |
| Canada | 27 | 20840 | 78.1 | 6.9 |
| US | 253 | 22550 | 75.9 | 8.1 |
| Mexico | 90 | 3051 | 72.9 | 27.4 |
| Central America[f] | 23 | 1458 | 74.5 | 17.8 |
| South America | 278 | 2532 | 66.2 | 47.3 |
| Western Europe[g] | 369 | 18732 | 77.2 | 7.0 |
| Eastern Europe | 96 | 4763 | 72.4 | 13.9 |
| Asia[h] | 3343 | 2697 | 64.6 | 58.5 |
| Africa | 476 | 613 | 56.0 | 80.0 |
| Australia | 17 | 16600 | 77.6 | 7.3 |
| World[i] | 4973 (91%) | 4874 | 67.2 | 51.5 |

[a]Weighted (by population) averages for countries of more than five million people, all data are taken from *The Statistical Abstract of the United States, 1995.*
[b]Populations are in millions of persons.
[c]GNPs are expressed in terms of constant 1991 US dollars.
[d]Life expectancy is at birth, in years.
[e]Infant mortality is the rate of deaths before one year of age, per 1000 births.
[f]We have included Cuba here.
[g]We have included the new unified Germany here.
[h]We have included those states comprising the former Soviet Union here.
[i]This sample represents 91% of the world's total population.

Mortality and morbidity clearly vary by country. Can national identity serve as a proxy for the observed variations in life expectancy? Using the US as an example, if we were to approximate our white population by Canada and black population by Africa, we would predict using simple correlations a life expectancy of 75.0 years (Table 2), seemingly consistent with the observed value of 75.9 years. However, as we likewise proxy additional details regarding the ethnic distribution of the population, representing the Hispanic population by Mexico and the Asian by Asia, our prediction begins to diverge, rather than converge. The international data suggest that there are significant determinants of mortality not captured by the simple use of national origin as proxy. We discuss a number of potential determinants below.

## 2.1. Level of economic development

Worldwide data on life expectancy does appear to be strongly correlated with economic development and employment (see, for example, Brenner's (1983) and Wagstaff's (1985) surveys, and Sen (1993)). Fig. 3 displays the strong relationship between life expectancy and per capita gross national product (constant 1991 US$) for the 66

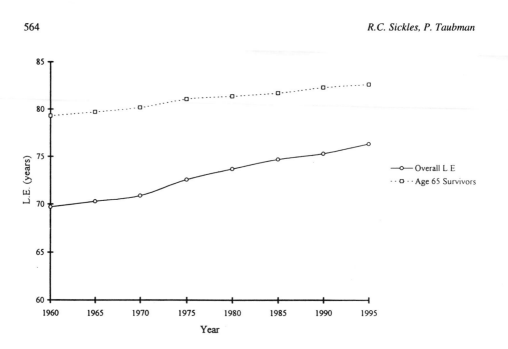

Fig. 1. Evolution of life expectancy by age cohort (US).

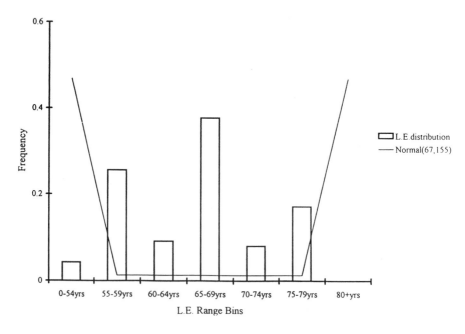

Fig. 2. Distribution of average life expectancy (World 1994).

Table 2
Ethnic group as life expectancy proxy (US 1992)[a]

| Ethnic group | Population | National origin (years) | PCI[f] | Economic agent (years) |
|---|---|---|---|---|
| Black[b] | 0.12 | 56.0 | 9300 | 75.1 |
| Hispanic[d] | 0.09 | 72.9 | 8874 | 74.5 |
| Asian[e] | 0.03 | 64.6 | (n/a) | |
| White[c] | 0.76 | 78.1 | 15981 | 77.4 |
| Interpolate | | ~74.6 | | ~76.8 |
| (actual value = 75.9 years) | | | | |

[a]All data are taken from *The Statistical Abstract of the United States, 1995.*
[b]Life expectancy approximated by weighted average for Africa for 1995.
[c]Same as above, for Canada.
[d]Same as above, for Mexico.
[e]Same as above, for Asia.
[f]Per capita income by race for 1994 (in constant 1992 US$).

nations of the world with over five million in population, representing 91% of the world population. The data strongly suggest that longevity is an economic good; evidence that life expectancy increases as a country improves its standard of living long has been recognized since the higher income typically associated with development makes possible in part the consumption of goods and services that improve health (Preston, 1976). Recent studies of the most populous country, China, reinforces this assertion (Nolan and Sender, 1992; Knight and Song, 1993), contrary to Sen's (1989) assertion that Chinese reforms have reduced China's ability to provide its population with food and health services. Other reforms in the former Soviet Union and in Eastern Europe have meant more accessibility to mortality data which is showing disturbing trends (Krúmiņš and Zvidriņš, 1992).

The relationship between economic development and mortality and morbidity is overlaid with a mosaic of other competing relationships, such as those between economic development and environmental carcinogens. As reviewed by Knudson (1992), there are known carcinogens in our ambient environment. More aggressive hypotheses concerning the relationships between pollution and cancer are found in the environmental toxicology literature (Ba Loc, 1990; Burney, 1992). The level of economic development may proxy exposure to certain environmental toxins whose proper treatment and disposal in turn requires a relatively high level of economic development.

## 2.2. Gender

The US and international census data also strongly suggest that human life expectancy

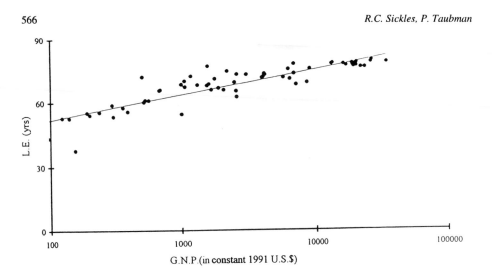

Fig. 3. Life expectancy and gross national product (World 1994).

varies by gender (Zopf, 1992)[5] as it does for other species (Retherford, 1975).[6] As seen in Fig. 4, in the US the discrepancy in life expectancy between men and women has remained fairly constant over the past 35 years, despite a conventional wisdom that the male survival disadvantage is associated with behavior patterns (such as "Type A" behaviors) which have been modified through public education and despite the substantial increase in female labor force participation rates and female adoption of predominately male lifestyle behaviors such as smoking.

There is considerable debate as to whether gender is best viewed as an instrument for behavioral and lifestyle issues, or as a proxy for an unobserved acquired survival advantage. For example, Waldron (1982) investigates the survival advantage for females, and finds that much of the advantage is related to cigarette smoking, so-called "type A behavior", alcohol, and exposure to occupational risks. While alcohol consumption among men has fallen, Waldron (1993, 1994) does not find a corresponding narrowing of sex-differences in survival rates.[7]

[5] In his comprehensive text on mortality, Zopf points out findings of Madigan (1957) which highlighted the biological differences in mortality by gender in his comparison of Roman Catholic male and female celibates living in almost identical conditions. However, Zopf also points to the work of Stolnitz (1956) who found that such factors as high rates of maternal mortality, female infanticide, and the low economic and social status of women in some societies may be significant factors in explaining gender mortality differences.

[6] Anson (1991) notes that variations in age-specific mortality between genders were sufficient to portray both the similarities and differences among 358 human life-tables.

[7] Female-specific studies of mortality have included Wolfe and Haveman (1983), using women from the Panel survey of Income Dynamics, Weatherby et al. (1983), based on life-tables from 38 countries around the world, and more recently, by Kravdal (1994), using the Norwegian Family and Occupational survey which features data on fertility, marriage, education and employment for 4000 women.

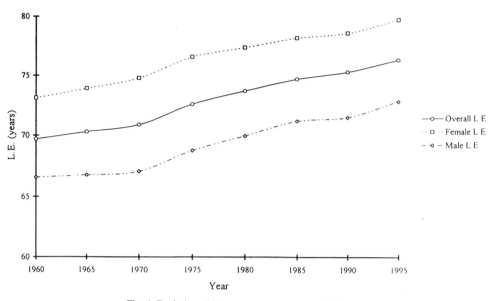

Fig. 4. Evolution of life expectancy by gender (US).

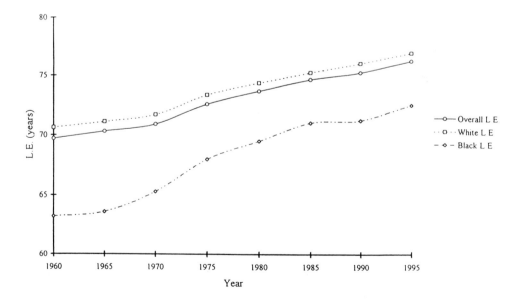

Fig. 5. Evolution of life expectancy by race (US).

## 2.3. Race

US national trends also suggest a strong source of variation in life expectancy by race. Shown in Fig. 5 is the evolution of life expectancy in the US for blacks and whites. The difference in life expectancy between the two groups narrowed substantially between 1960 and 1995, from 7.4 years to 4.5 years. Were this pattern to continue, the difference would vanish in about 50 years. A more careful review of Fig. 5 suggests that, during the ten years between 1965 and 1975, during which Medicare and Medicaid were introduced and evolved into the institutions they currently represent, the gap narrowed from 7.5 to 5.4 years, whereas during the other 25 years it narrowed by less than one year.

Throughout their lifetime, blacks in the US have higher age-specific death rates than whites. In 1960, for males aged 50 years, the death rate was 9.5 per 1000 persons for whites and 15.6 per 1000 for blacks, whereas the remaining life expectancy at age 55 for whites was 19.5 years and for blacks 18.4 years (Kitagawa and Hauser, 1973). Jaynes and Williams (1989) report that in 1984 remaining years of life at age 65 was an average of 14.8 years for white men and 13.4 for black men. Madans et al. (1986) use the NHANES follow-up to examine the differences by race (as well as gender and those living in poverty) during the 1971–1975 period of deaths during a ten-year follow-up period. They demonstrate strong differences in all of these three dimensions on the ratio of actual to expected deaths. More recently Behrman et al. (1991) show that the death hazard rate is much higher for blacks than for whites in the years covered in the Retirement History Survey (see also, Silver, 1972; Ford and DeStefano, 1991).[8]

Fig. 6 shows black life expectancy and public health care expenditures as a percentage of the gross domestic product. There is a striking correlation between the data, particularly when we consider the lagged effects of public health expenditures on life expectancy. Between 1966, two years after the Civil Rights Act of 1964, and 1976 the percentage of blacks below the poverty line fell from 41.8% to 31.1% (*Current Population Reports*, P60–185), and, with the public sector expanding health care provision to the poor, black life expectancy rose.

Most researchers in public health now disavow race per se as a contributor to mortality. Phillips and Rathwell (1986) review the subject and conclude: "It is now generally accepted in the scientific community as proven that all humans are genetically similar except in terms of susceptibility to a few rare diseases". Cooper et al. (1981), who examine differences in mortality by race and gender, conclude that environmental factors (e.g., nutrition, occupation, and income) underlie the discrepancy in death rates. He states: "...explanations based on biological determinism no longer enjoy consensus support ... there is no evidence that a major proportion of the observed

---

[8] Fuchs (1992) notes, among other things, the various problems in operationalizing a meaningful poverty measure as well as in linking low income per se with poor health.

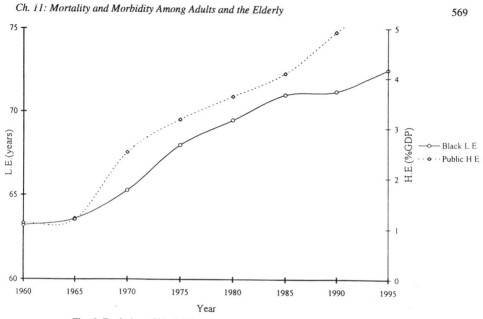

Fig. 6. Evolution of black life expectancy and public health expenditures (US).

racial differentials in health can be explained in population genetics. Environmental forces, namely social conditions, are the root cause".

While it would be naive to preclude the possibility of race as a proxy for unobserved heterogeneities, particularly given our understanding of differences in underlying susceptibilities to certain diseases (e.g., sickle-cell anemia), there is further support within the surveillance data for the race-as-proxy for socioeconomic status (Otten et al., 1990; Rogers, 1992; Menchik, 1993; McCoy et al., 1994; Zick and Smith, 1994). Moreover, differential death rates for blacks and whites based on differential socio-economic status give rise to peculiar but intuitive mortality patterns for blacks and whites, in particular the crossover of death rates. The crossover is a well-known, recurrent and consistent feature in the US mortality data. Shown in Fig. 7 are annual death rates by race and age cohorts. After 84 years of age, the black cohort has a lower death rate than the white cohort.

### 2.4. Infant mortality

One might dismiss this phenomenon because of a censoring of the black American population, that is the elimination by deaths of the lower tail of the population distribution due to particular traits within the population or due to differential rates of infant mortality which are substantially higher for blacks than for whites.

Differential rates of infant mortality among countries may also explain differential mortality and morbidity for adults and the elderly among countries. Based on the life-

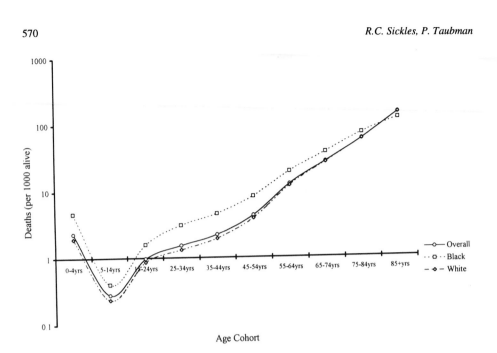

Fig. 7. Annual death rate by age cohort and race (US 1991).

table for the United States for 1991, the overall death rate during the first year of life of 9.3 per 1000 live births was exceeded by the age 55–64 and older cohorts. This death rate crossover occurs much later in life in less developed nations where the infant mortality rate may be more than ten times as high as it is in the United States. Are infant mortality rates related to economic factors? There is a wide consensus to the

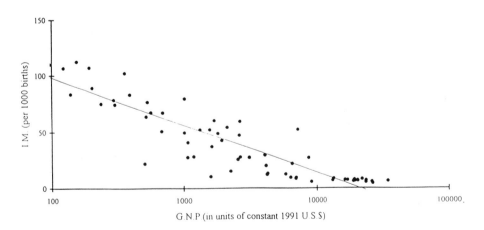

Fig. 8. Infant mortality and per capita gross national product (World 1994).

affirmative on this issue. Fig. 8 relates infant mortality rates and per capita gross national products from the sample of the 66 largest countries in the world, again noted to represent over 91% of the world's population. As was the case earlier with life expectancies, there is a strong and significant negative correlation between the rate of infant mortality and per capita GNP.

Factors which influence infant mortality, in addition to income per se, have been studied extensively. For the US, Corman and Grossman (1985) point to the importance of female education, abortion availability, neonatal intensive care facilities and Medicaid to black neonatal mortality, and note the implications of endogenous censoring of health outcomes among various ethnic groups. Rosenzweig and Schultz (1982a, b) and Thomas et al. (1990) also note the relative importance of maternal education in reducing child mortality in developing countries, although Behrman and Wolfe (1987) found that this effect is reduced when maternal endowments are properly controlled. Akin et al. (1990), Popkin et al. (1993), and their colleagues (Cebu Study Team, 1992) have pursued the estimation of child health production functions in a series of studies from the Philippines and have found important community and environmental effects. Schultz (1993) recently addressed the endogenous selection problem of infant mortality in developing countries, in particular the endogeneity of fertility control (Schultz, Chapter 8, this Handbook). The impact of selective mortality and fertility on estimates for developing countries has also been examined by Pitt and Rosenzweig (1989) and Lee et al. (1995) using parametric and robust estimators.

## 2.5. Migration

There are undoubtedly differential mortality rates within ethnic groups and among countries due to the migration selection of a population. In the US, for example, Diaz-Briquets (1991a, b) presents evidence to support a conventional wisdom that the more socioeconomically integrated Cuban-American population is advantaged in survival against other Hispanic populations. Whereas Puerto Rico is a commonwealth of the United States, with liberal entry and exit between the two, Cuba has had a very different recent immigration history. Earlier patterns were consistent with a selection bias for the "best and brightest" to the United States, and during this period this group was considered an example of successful integration. More recently, migration patterns may have been altered by the relatively large and unusual migration experiences of the late 1970s.

Bradshaw and Liese (1991) note in their analysis that survival data in the Southwestern United States and in Northern Mexican states are consistent with an acquired survival advantage for Mexican-American immigrants to the United States when compared to their particular age–sex cohort remaining in Mexico. However, these findings may be due to selection bias. Not only are there physical hardships associated with the migration from Mexico to the United States, but overall health status appears to be associated with types of employment common to these individuals. Additionally, the lack of government and employment benefits such as medical or disability insurance may adversely affect less healthy undocumented workers, decreasing their likelihood of remaining in the United States. Overall, Hispanic-Americans remain at a survival disadvantage, possibly due to an excess of early and preventable or manageable deaths (e.g., motor vehicle accidents, complications of diabetes). Censoring of the Hispanic population, which is apparently endowed with survival advantages against many of the later-onset chronic conditions, results in the same type of elderly crossover in death rates as those seen for black Americans.

## 2.6. Anthropometric factors

The secular trends that we have seen in mortality rates seem to be at odds with Malthus' (1798) predictions that "normal" life expectancy was fixed (Fogel, 1994a), although as Fogel points out, the essential point of the Malthusian thesis, that of population pressures against the constraints of available resources, is no less valid today than in Malthus' time. Indeed, the freeing up of constraints by improvements in public-health, sanitation and personal hygiene, advancements in medical technology which restrain certain pathogens (Preston, 1980), and rises in standards of living and concomitant increases in nutrition, appear to have made possible substantial increases in populations and in life expectancies. The issue of how anthropometric factors and nutritional improvements have impacted mortality rates has been taken up by Fogel (1993, 1994a, b, 1995; and Chapter 9, this volume) in a series of recent works to which we now briefly turn.

Fogel (1994b) points out that not only have nutritional advances in their own right altered life expectancies but also the nature of the dynamic between nutrition and infection (Scrimshaw et al., 1968; Preston and van de Walle, 1978) and the changing biological interaction between disease and humans (Fridlizius, 1984; Perenoud, 1984, 1991; Alter and Riley, 1989; Schofield and Reher, 1991).[9] Moreover, identification of the contribution of nutritional advancements per se to mortality hazards is clouded by the interaction, among other things, between nutrition and a set of risk factors including the level of physical activity, climate, disease exposures, and individual susceptibilities or frailties to disease. Since caloric intake must be balanced by the level of physical activity which it supports, a working definition of nutrition net of the claims on it is necessary in order to examine its particular contribution on life expectancy.

In Chapter 9, Fogel provides an extensive discussion of anthropometric indicators (e.g., stature, body mass) of nutritional changes in Europe and the US and their strong

---

[9] H.O. Lancaster's (1990) and Preston's (1976) comprehensive surveys of world mortality trends suggest that developments in the treatment of infectious diseases with antibacterials such as penicillin, and the development of effective vaccines for childhood viral conditions such as smallpox and polio, underlie much of the gains in life expectancy we have seen this century.

association with morbidity and mortality risk (Heywood, 1983; Waaler, 1984; Martorell, 1985; Osmani, 1992; Fogel, 1993; Fogel et al., 1994).[10] He also points to the ways in which variations in these anthropometric markers allowed for population size and the available food supply to equilibrate and in so doing determine life expectancy. Recent history has also shown the strong similarities between the current experiences of less developed nations and those of developed nations several centuries earlier. Fogel points out the recent debate on the fixity of life-expectancy, estimated to be 85 ± 7 years by Fries (1980) and notes that Fries' assertion that increases in life expectancy are explained by a one-hos-shay type survival curve with most deaths centered around age 85, implies that risk factors such as acute infectious diseases have been crowded out by independent chronic conditions. Compression of mortality, according to Fries (1983, 1989), would thus be possible only by changes in life-style and by medical interventions, at odds with Vaupel's (1991a) findings, using Danish twins, of a much longer life expectancy, only about 30% of the variation of which could be attributed to genetic factors. Vaupel (1991b) argues that the survivor curve will not flatten. Similar findings that argue against survival compression are found in Manton et al. (1993). These issues raised by Fogel and others frame a topical debate whose resolution remains an open research question.

## 2.7. Public policy

In his provocative book, Fuchs (1974) indicates that choices made by the government can influence who will die and from what causes by providing resources to pay for treatments in its various insurance programs and in its medical research priorities. Government influences health outcomes by way of public education, regulation of health depreciating activities and public programs (Grossman, 1982a). Governments also influence health outcomes in less obvious ways. Regulatory interventions increase the costs of the firm and thus affect individual income, and may also reduce individual incentives to invest in health by the provision of higher levels of safety (Viscusi, 1994). As noted by Newhouse (1987), about 40% of US expenditure on personal health care is provided by public programs, and for most other countries the figure is even higher.

In the United States, Medicare insures those over the age of 65, although since 1972 it has also covered the costs for those of any age who need kidney dialysis treatment or are disabled (Myers, 1981). Aside from this, most people under the age of 65 and most other diseases are not covered by government provided health care.[11] Many expensive medical procedures, considered somewhat routine, remain experi-

---

[10] We pursue issues raised in the related literature on the role of nutrition in augmenting human capital in developing countries in Section 3.

[11] Exceptions are people with limited income who are covered by Medicaid if they do not have private insurance and veterans.

mental and thus not covered under Medicare. Only very recently was cardiac transplantation added to the list of available procedures, albeit at a restricted list of medical centers. Since the mid-1970s it has been possible to protect individuals from the effects of hemophilia by providing the missing blood clotting agent. However, these shots, which cost about $20 000 per year, are not covered by Medicare.

Several investigators have explored trends between public health expenditures and life expectancy. For the US, Cutler et al. (1990) calculate that in 1960 a man aged 65 had an expected remaining life of 12.9 years, while in 1990 the corresponding figure was 15.0 years. Comparable values for women are 15.9 and 18.9 years, respectively. Much of the gain occurred by 1975, suggesting a one-time innovation in senior care between 1960 and 1975 (Medicare). Fingerhut and Rosenberg (1982) demonstrated a substantial downward shift in age-specific mortality rates among the elderly beginning around 1968, and Preston (1984), in his presidential address to the Population Association of America, asserts that this drop in death rates corresponds with the introduction of the Medicare and Medicaid programs.

The complex relationship between government and social choices is illustrated by the health care financing arrangements of the United Kingdom. In the UK, the National Health Service supposedly provides care from cradle to grave, and yet according to Aaron and Schwartz (1984), many general practitioners in the UK routinely do not tell their patients over the age of 54 that treatments are available for renal failure and other illnesses. Despite evidence of such a failure to treat, life expectancy in the UK is nearly identical to that in the United States. Aaron and Schwartz also reveal what appears to be hospital-specific utilization differences in choices of equipment and medicine as well as note the relatively low share of GNP spent on health care in the United Kingdom.[12]

Vital statistics across the world are quite consistent with the hypothesis that a more socialized system of health care delivery may be consistent with increased life expectancy. Although these comparisons are difficult to make rigorous, paradoxically due in part to our own uniqueness in terms of a private delivery sector, the literature on US–Canadian comparisons supports the hypothesis that the Canadian system may deliver longer life due to a more egalitarian allocation of resources. Infant mortality and preventable deaths underlie much of the survival disadvantage of lower socioeconomic groups. Fuchs and Hahn (1990) have argued that the costs of such public health systems are lower than private systems in place in the US and have attributed this to economies of scale, particularly preferential pricing afforded to large government purchasing agents.

In the United States, the shift towards managed care has been quite dramatic; the percentage of individuals covered by these types of plans (e.g., Health Maintenance Organizations (HMO's)) has risen from 27.3% in 1988 to 61.9% in 1993 (Employee

---

[12] There is also a bias against treating non-life threatening problems. For example, hip replacements may require a wait of up to one year. Similar problems exist in Canada.

Benefit Research Institute).[13,14] Accompanying this shift has been a substantial drop in hospitalizations; in Southern California, Medicare patients covered under an HMO were hospitalized 56% as much as those remaining on the fee-for-service plan. These types of data are frequently mentioned as outcomes in discussions of life expectancy and cost containment (Bailit et al., 1995), although often neglected are discussions of possible selection biases inherent in an individual freely choosing HMO coverage as opposed to traditional fee-for-service (Clement et al., 1994).

Governments also influence mortality by targeting research expenditures. Most (about 90%) non-drug related research in the US is funded by the National Institutes of Health whose many institutes concentrate on specific diseases. In addition, the National Science Foundation, the Veterans Administration, and the various branches of the Armed Forces also participate in the decisions to allocate health research resources. Open research issues dealing with the political economy of health research resource distribution include whether this research has had an impact on mortality rates, who determines the level and mix of funding, and for what purpose are the choices made. With respect to the National Institutes of Health, Califano (1986: pp. 47–48), former Secretary of Health, Education, and Welfare, characterizes the situation as follows: "...Much of NIH's growth has stemmed from the congressional penchant for diseases-of-the-month and the shrewd assessment of the medical research establishment and its patrons that it would be easier to get money for tragic diseases, dramatized by real-life heart-wrenching cases, than for basic research identified as such...". He then goes on to describe the growth of institutes and their research funds. For example, the budget of the first NIH institute, the Cancer Institute, increased from $400 000 in 1937 to 1.2 billion in 1984. Currently it exceeds $2 billion a year.

The use of aggregate data to infer group risk factors in mortality and morbidity determination clearly raises questions concerning which variables are endogenous and which are exogenous, a point recently remade by Manski (1993). Although aggregate level studies based on micro level decisions have been undertaken through calibration and simulation (see, for example, Auerbach et al. (1989) in their study of four OECD countries), estimation of such general equilibrium models is problematic given the enormous data requirements. In the next section we outline a structured microeconomic framework that provides explicit links between choice variables and those which can be arguably viewed as exogenous to the individual, and which can be used to estimate the parameters that characterize the structural model.

---

[13] Marder and Zuckerman (1985) have noted substantial geographical and temporal heterogeneity in the optimal scale of medical practices with scale economies evident during the period 1975–1980.

[14] Ashton et al. (1994) have also assessed the effects of aging of the veteran population on utilization rates in the Veterans Affairs medical system between 1980 and 1990. They note that the number of discharges increased by about 7% although it appeared that the utilization rate for older veterans actually declined due to shifts from hospital to ambulatory and long-term care settings.

## 3. Structural economic models of health

We now wish to outline microeconomic models of individual behavior which make explicit the causal links between mortality and morbidity, and the risk factors which give rise to changes in health. The need for such structural modeling of the risk factors which cause variations in health outcomes has been noted by many authors, a recent example being Feinstein (1992) in his survey of health outcomes and socioeconomic status. In these models, the allocation of time and the income it generates and health status are rationally chosen under constraints of scarcity, technology and uncertainty.[15] These concepts may be disconcerting at first to the non-economist. If so, consider that the dramatic growth in the relative percentage of the labor force who work part-time or are self-employed suggests that individuals increasingly make decisions to maximize their benefits resulting from their allocation of their time. As for time of death as chosen, consider suicide, living wills, the refusal by Christian Scientists of potentially life-preserving medical care, and the shortfall of deaths before personally significant dates, with a subsequent spike thereafter.[16] Simultaneity between income and death may be seen in the observation that people require higher pay to work in occupations for which more deaths occur (Thaler and Rosen, 1975).

The most widely-used framework for determining health status is the demand model originally due to Grossman (1972a, b, 1975) and utilized in numerous studies (e.g., Wolfe and Behrman, 1984, 1987; Bartel and Taubman, 1986; Behrman and Deolalikar, 1987; Behrman and Wolfe, 1987). A related but distinct framework is provided by Rosenzweig and Schultz (1983a, b, 1985), Rosenzweig and Wolpin (1980, 1988), and Wolpin (1984).

The primary differences between the two frameworks are that the latter studies concentrate on obtaining consistent estimates of the parameters of both the utility function and the health production function that underlie the demand relations, and have examined in greater detail life-cycle utility functions. Grossman-type models often have been used to estimate static reduced-form equations, sometimes dependent on previous choices so that the demand functions are conditional demand functions (Pollak, 1969, 1970). The endogeneity of some of the explanatory variables can be controlled by using instruments that affected past choices but are independent of the current disturbance term. Past shocks in market prices, for example, might serve as such instruments. Yet, as in any such instrumental variable estimation, all the past choices that directly affect current health must be observed and instrumented to obtain

---

[15] One might question the assumption that an increasingly large segment of elderly consumers, those in nursing homes, could be viewed as making the rational choices assumed in economic models of rational choice. Evidence that they do in fact behave in a manner consistent with consumer rationality can be found in Nyman (1989). For a theoretical treatment of an alternative choice problem in which individuals do not have the information processing capacity to compare all feasible allocations but rather adjust allocations myopically, see De Palma et al. (1994).

[16] Examples are birthdays, anniversaries, birth of a grandchild.

unbiased estimates of the effects of such choices. If some past choices that were affected by the same instruments as the observed choices are not observed, the instrumented values of the observed choices will represent in part the effects of the unobserved choices. Moreover, if the instruments are not sufficiently correlated with the variable being instrumented, then measurement bias may just replace the simultaneity bias (Nelson and Startz, 1990a, b; Bound et al., 1993; Staiger and Stock, 1994).

The models outlined below treat health status as endogenous to the individual's allocation of time between work and leisure, and the individual's allocation among alternative consumption items. This general framework addresses the joint determination of health choices and labor supply decisions by way of both time and consumption allocations. A number of authors have addressed this seemingly obvious link and the selection bias caused by ignoring the endogenous sample-selection of hours worked and wage rates in the health equations (see for example, Bartel and Taubman, 1979, 1986; Passmore et al., 1983; Burkhauser et al., 1986; Mitchell and Butler, 1986). We first outline the one-period model of health, pointing out that certain dynamic issues can be pursued by allowing current prices to be dependent on a distributed lag of past prices. The dynamics that this brings into the model is not specified within the model per se but is rather a statement about the evolution of exogenous variables that is independent of the one-period model's own internal static nature. We then turn to the dynamic model of health production (Grossman, 1972a, b; Grossman and Benham, 1974) and the generalizations suggested by Muurinen (1982) and Wolfe (1985) as well as more general models that address such factors as rational addictions (Becker and Murphy, 1988; Becker et al., 1994), wage endogeneity (Foster and Rosenzweig, 1994), endogenous life expectancy (Ehrlich and Chuma, 1990), uncertainty, and intertemporal nonseparability. In our treatment of economic models of health we will also provide a selected review of studies which have pointed to the importance of key risk factors in determining health outcomes at the individual level.[17,18]

## 3.1. One-period models of health demand

In the one-period static model the individual's economic problem is to allocate time to leisure, $T_t^L$, time to the production of health, $T_t^H$, and financial resources in order to[19]

---

[17] Newhouse (1987) notes the tension between robust estimators and models, such as those we outline below, which may be highly leveraged on economic assumptions and data requirements, and thus may have questionable robustness properties in empirical implementation. He points out, in particular, that robustness of model estimates is compromised by the substantial skewness of health care expenditures for the elderly.

[18] We do not pursue extended models which deal with bequests, whose treatment could itself be a chapter (see, for example, Skinner, 1985).

[19] The dual role of women as both child care providers and home care providers, neither of which is formally compensated, has been noted by many as a time allocation which has a significant negative impact on reducing women's health (see, for example, Wolfe and Haveman, 1983).

$$\max_{C_t^0, C_t^1, T_t^L, T_t^H} U(C_t^0, T_t^L, H_t), \tag{3.1}$$

where $C^0$ is the final consumption good which provides pleasure and $C^1$ is an intermediate good used to produce health. The individual works for a period of time given by $T^W = T - (T^L - T^H - T^I)$, where $T^I$ is illness time which is a function of the health stock, and given a wage $W$, has income $Y = WT^W$ from which $C^0$ and $C^1$ are purchased at prices $P^0$ and $P^1$, respectively. Let initial wealth be $A_0$. The individual's budget constraint is then

$$A_0 + [T - T_t^L - T_t^H - T_t^I(H_t)]W_t \geq P_t^0 C_t^0 + P_t^1 C_t^1. \tag{3.2}$$

Income and wealth have served as proxies for many mortality and morbidity factors for adults and the elderly, factors whose independent and dynamic effects can only be disentangled using such a structural formulation. This is because income and wealth provide for more consumption of health related goods, and by way of this, access to higher quality medical care. The importance of pension wealth and its role as an insurer of income for the elderly after retirement has long been recognized (Bodie, 1990). Rendall and Speare (1993), for example, using the Survey of Income and Program Participation (SIPP), note the importance of using the income plus wealth measure of economic well-being for the United States elderly to properly distinguish the most economically vulnerable sub-population, in particular blacks. Health can also affect labor market outcomes by altering tastes and/or the income opportunity curve. Recently, Attanasio and Hoynes (1995), using the SIPP data, point out the many shortcomings of cross-sectional analyses of mortality and wealth due to the differential effects of mortality on asset accumulation and correct for selectivity bias in survival rates using the Survey of Income and Program Participation (SIPP). Obviously, income and wealth for adults and the elderly is also influenced by whether they are in or out of the labor force. Such labor supply issues are given an exhaustive treatment in Chapter 16 by Hurd and are not pursued in this survey.

The health production function $(h_t)$ is introduced to show how health, $H_t$, is produced by the consumption of health-related goods $(C_t^1)$, time devoted to health production $(T_t^H)$, and other exogenously determined inputs, $X_t$, such as human capital characteristics, environmental factors, endowments, and individual specific heterogeneities[20]:

---

[20] Wagstaff's (1989) excellent survey of the recent British literature of empirical studies on the economics of health point out a number of issues involving how more aggregate system wide production functions can be specified to take account of allocative and technical inefficiency, the former issue having been taken up by Eakin and Kneiser (1988) and the latter by Feldstein (1967). He further points to the potential scope of stochastic frontier approaches for cross-section models (Aigner et al., 1977) and panel models (Schmidt and Sickles, 1984; Cornwell et al., 1990). These frontier methods have also been used along with polynomial-spline regressions to examine the depreciation of physical health using track and road racing data by Fair (1994). One of his more interesting findings is the relatively slow rate of physical depreciation that occurs, suggesting a bias in societal perspectives of the elderly's health potential.

$$H_t = h(C_t^1, T_t^H; X_t).$$ (3.3)

$X_t$ will usually contain such variables as education, nutrition, occupation and physical activity, marital status, behaviors and lifestyle measures, and genetic factors. Heterogeneities in preferences across individuals can be accommodated by explicitly conditioning the utility function on it as well.

### 3.1.1. Health risk factors at the individual level

*3.1.1.1. The role of human capital and other risk factors in adult health.* Grossman considered the role of wages and of human capital (i.e., education and nutrition) in the demand for health. Wage increases permit the individual to substitute time devoted to health production which reduces sick time for leisure time, until the marginal utility of leisure time increases to the new wage. Human capital, felt by Grossman to have positive wage effects, was also thought to increase the marginal product of leisure. Human capital is augmented (proxied) by education, as it is often argued that the more educated make better decisions and can process new information more effectively. When income is not controlled, education may also serve as its proxy. Specific discussion of the endogenous role of income is considered shortly. A number of studies have found human capital and its various proxies to have important impacts on adult health. Silver (1972) used 1959–1961 age-adjusted mortality rates by sex and gender for Standard Metropolitan Areas (SMAs), and found an effect upon mortality for educational attainment, marriage, and income. Kitagawa and Hauser (1973) find that among the elderly, more educated females have lower death rates than females less educated, yet there are no similar findings for elderly males. Among those of younger ages, the more educated have lower age-specific death rates for both genders. Many potentially important variables were not controlled for in their analysis, and Rosen and Taubman (1984) have shown that this methodological approach may impart a bias if the null hypothesis is false. Grossman (1975) estimated logit survival models for 1955–1969, and found that survival is positively, and significantly, related to level of education, with each year of education lowering the probability of death by 0.4 percentage points. Further, he finds that ability, earnings, and job satisfaction have significant positive associations. Rosen and Taubman (1984) use the 1973 Exact Match Sample with Social Security mortality records updated through 1976, and examine the effects of education and other variables upon age-specific death rates. Using ordinary least squares regressions, which may be a questionable statistical method, they find a significant 23% lower death rate for college graduates than for those least educated, and correspondingly strong effects for family income. Wagstaff (1986) uses the 1976 Danish Welfare Survey to model health capital as an unobservable variable in a recursive dynamic structural model and in his analysis of life-cycle effects in health production and consumption points out that structural models, such as those discussed in Heckman and MaCurdy (1980), MaCurdy (1981, 1983), and Killingsworth (1983), are essential in order to disentangle the high correlations between education and real lifetime wealth.

Women's schooling and its impact on adult health has been studied by Wolfe and Behrman (1984) and Behrman and Wolfe (1987) using adult siblings in Nicaragua. They find that control for common family background substantially changes the estimated impact of women's schooling on adult health as well as other outcomes. Strauss et al. (1993) also find strong effects of education on health for adults, consistent with their and others' findings with children. An important additional aspect of the Strauss et al. findings is that there are important gender differences between mortality and morbidity as indicators of well-being in the US and in developing countries. Feldman et al. (1989) use the National Health and Nutritional Survey (NHANES) data and the Kitagawa and Hauser study to examine trends in death rates by educational differentials and gender for the elderly, for the time periods of 1960 and 1971–1984. As with Taubman and Rosen (1982), Feldman et al. find much sharper declines over time for the more educated within each gender group, and these effects persist in their proportional hazard models even after controlling for such additional statistically significant risk factors as smoking, weight, hypertension, and high amounts of serum cholesterol. Land et al. (1994) combine Markov panel regressions with standard increment–decrement life-tables to estimate covariate effects using the Established Populations for Epidemiological Study of the Elderly (Duke University). Their methodology mitigates the standard problems in identifying covariate effects from small longitudinal panels. They find substantial and significant effects of higher education on both total life expectancy and active life expectancy (the period of life free from disability). Using data from the Health Promotion/Disease Prevention Supplement to the 1985 Health Interview Survey, Kenkel (1994) found that schooling improves individuals' choice of health inputs through improving health knowledge.

*3.1.1.2. Nutrition.* Human capital can also be augmented by better access to and knowledge about nutrition. Although the anthropometric issues taken up by Fogel in Chapter 9, which are largely devoted to the US and Europe, could be viewed as a general treatment of the human capital augmenting role that nutrition takes, we will spend a bit of time discussing how this important dimension of human capital has been treated in the extant literature on nutrition in developing countries. There is a growing literature focusing on developing countries which highlights the impact of anthropometric indicators of health and nutrition (and, to a lesser extent, direct morbidity reports) on productivity, income and wages, and which finds some effects even with efforts to control for reverse causality and unobserved heterogeneity (see, for example, Deolalikar, 1988; Behrman and Deolalikar, 1989; Haddad and Bouls, 1991; Strauss and Thomas, 1992; Schultz and Tansel, 1993; Foster and Rosenzweig, 1994; Strauss and Thomas, 1995). Strauss (1986) has shown links between health and nutrition in Sierra Leone and noted that measurement errors in both variables may cause a downward bias in their estimated effects on labor productivity. Utilizing community-level prices of food as an instrument for nutrition, Deolalikar (1988), Sahn and Alderman (1988), and Thomas and Strauss (1995) have found important impacts of nutrition on labor productivity in India, Sri Lanka, and Brazil, respectively. This literature illustrates the problems with looking at the impact of income on mortality/morbidity due to possible reverse causality and unobserved heterogeneity, the former of which might be even more important in developing countries. Many of these studies are surveyed in Behrman (1993) and Behrman and Srinivasan (1995).

*3.1.1.3. Occupation.* Perhaps no covariate more clearly illustrates the potential reverse causality between explanatory controls and health than does occupation and the reliance of certain occupations on the level of physical activity. Morris et al. (1953) examined the interrelationship between physical activity and coronary heart disease for drivers, conductors, and guards in the London Transport company in 1949 and 1950, and find conductors to have fewer coronary illnesses, speculating that this may be due to greater physical activity. They report similar findings when comparing postmen with other civil servants, admittedly with a possible selection bias for those who applied for and were accepted for positions involving more physical activity. Kitagawa and Hauser (1973) find that mortality among service workers exceeded that for agricultural workers by 80%, 1.37 compared with 0.76. These findings are somewhat specific to white workers, as they report no significant effect for non-white workers, implying that race may be acting as a proxy for occupational differences.

Sickles and Taubman (1986) estimated a model of healthiness (including death) and retirement using the Retirement History Survey and found that occupation (as well as various measures of income) is an important determinant of health. Gustman and Steinmeier (1986) analyze differences in retirement rates between blacks and whites and among more or less physically demanding jobs in the RHS. Black–white differences in retirement rates shrink with age and both health and prior occupation are important in the retirement decision. Jones and Goldblatt (1987) report that women who work outside the home have lower age-specific mortality rates than non-working women, with the lowest mortality rates found among women in relatively good socioeconomic standing who worked part time. Occupational mortality differences among men also were found, with rates the highest among laborers, miners, and construction workers, and lowest among professional workers, managers, and electrical workers. Wives of unemployed men also had death rates which were higher than wives of employed men. Burtless' (1987) study using the Retirement History Survey finds that (lifetime) employment in mining, construction, and as a labor operative, lead to worse health for the elderly, with morbidity effects greater than mortality effects.

Hayward et al. (1989) examine the influences of occupation on the nature and timing of retirement using data from National Longitudinal Survey of Older Men. They use a competing-risk hazard model with three types of exit from the labor force, retirement, disability, and death, and find that substantive complexity and physical demands of various occupations determine retirement decisions. Sorlie and Rogot (1990) estimate relative mortality risk by employment status based on life-tables for over

452 000 records in the National Death Index from 1979–1983. They find that unemployed men have standardized mortality ratios by race from 1.6 to 2.2 times those for the employed, with those unable to work having much higher ratios. Among the elderly, the employed had much lower standardized mortality ratios than those not working. Another longitudinal survey is that of Moore and Hayward (1990), who evaluated 3080 individuals from the National Longitudinal Survey who were 55 years or older. Their hazard function estimates indicate that mortality is reduced by different sets of job factors identified with the longest and most recent occupation.

*3.1.1.4. Marital status.* Marital and family status may be related to age-specific mortality for a variety of reasons, both positive (caring and companionship) and negative (stress and anxiety). Some of these effects may persist (habit formation) after the marriage has ended from death or divorce. Overall, the life-tables suggest the marriage effect to be positive, attributed to single persons leading a more dissolute lifestyle, to selection biases of persons in chronic ill health less likely to marry or stay married, and to early death due to grief on the part of widows or widowers. One might also envision negative influences due to family effects such as psychological and physical abuse or environmental hazards such as second-hand cigarette smoke. In the United States, Kitagawa and Hauser (1973) report that age-adjusted death rates maintained a consistent differential between married persons and their unmarried counterparts. Carefully correcting the data for reporting inconsistencies, they report that the mortality rate for unmarried white females was 17% higher than for married white females, and the rate for unmarried white males was 52% higher than for those married. The greater longevity and lower morbidity of married men is particularly well recognized. As Fuchs (1974) points out, "…In all developed countries, the unmarried have significantly higher death rates than the married and this differential is much greater for males than females: on the average unmarried males ages 45–54 in developed countries have double the death rate of their married counterparts. For females the marital status differential is only 30 percent…". The marriage benefit for males is, however, usually exceeded by the gender effect (Gove, 1973).

Taubman and Rosen (1982) analyze a sample drawn from the Retirement History Survey (RHS), and with models and methods similar to those discussed in Burtless (1987) based on self-reported health status, find that marital status significantly affects mortality, within and between periods, after controlling for education, family income, use of medical resources, and previous health. Their multinomial logit regressions were performed on compiled data (contingency tables), and inferences remain valid so long as the characteristics remain independent of all but random error (Goodman, 1968), criteria difficult to maintain as the number of characteristics increases. Jones and Goldblatt (1987) found that English widows had a 10% increased risk of death during the period 1971–1981, when comparing expected and actual death rates. Kaprio et al. (1987) report similar findings for both widows and widowers from Finland.

Ellwood and Kane (1990) have used the Panel Survey of Income Dynamics (PSID) to examine mortality over a 35-year simulated time span for a cohort of 65-year olds. Their comprehensive study points to a number of conclusions, among them that not being married, as well as age and disability, are associated with higher death rates for males, and that being married also has positive effects on survival for women. Smith and Waitzman (1994) have rigorously evaluated the interaction among marital status, poverty and mortality, using the NHANES 25–74-year-olds from 1971–1975 who were successfully followed between 1982–1984, applying both additive and multiplicative relative risk models. They find support for the interactive nature of these risk factors for males and less so for females. A recent study which has found negative effects of marital status on the health of women due to domestic violence can be found in Tauchen et al. (1991).

Factors such as these have been labeled socioeconomic risk factors in the demographics literature, a term which, while providing a convenient encompassing taxonomy to differentiate these risk factors from the endowment related risk factors to which we next turn, has often clouded discussion on the causal links that may determine socioeconomic risk factors themselves. Given this caveat, however, there is a growing body of evidence from studies of age-standardized mortality ratios that points to either a lack of improvement in the relative mortality experience for those of low socioeconomic status (for the US experience see, e.g., Duleep, 1986, 1989) or a widening of socioeconomic differences in mortality (see, e.g., for the US and England, Rogot et al. (1992a, b), Pappas et al. (1993), Christenson and Johnson (1995).

*3.1.1.5. Behavioral, lifestyle, genetic factors.* We next focus attention on individual behavioral and lifestyle and related genetic factors which are associated with an elevated risk of mortality. For example, alcoholics are at increased risk of motor vehicle accidents and liver diseases such as cirrhosis and chronic active hepatitis, obesity predisposes many to diseases of the circulatory system, and AIDS is now the leading cause of death for young urban males in this country.[21] Fuchs (1974) provides a simple and forceful argument for the importance of lifestyle in health outcomes. He notes that Nevada has a similar physical environment to Utah. Mormons are prevalent in Utah and are admonished not to consume alcohol, coffee, or tobacco. Utah has uniformly lower age-specific mortality rates than in Nevada.

The extent to which certain lifestyle and behavioral risk factors can be modified is, however, unclear. Li et al. (1994) note the compelling evidence for a genetic marker which predisposes the individual to alcoholism. Obesity, well known in the medical literature to predispose the individual to heart disease, hypertension, diabetes and the like, all significant contributors to mortality, is known to be accompanied by genetic markers as well (Grilo and Pogue-Guile, 1991; Stunkard, 1991). With regard to male homosexuality, there is considerable debate in the literature. Hamer et al. (1993) published findings of a genetic marker for male homosexuality, although these findings have recently been challenged. Indeed, there is growing skepticism regarding this par-

---

[21] Waldron (1993, 1994) notes that the AIDS mortality gender gap is likely to narrow.

ticular genetic-behavior link, voiced by Billings and Beckwith (1993), Byne (1994), and Greenspan (1995). Moreover, current transmission mechanisms for AIDS may be driven as much by heterosexual behavior and by IV drug use as by homosexual behavior.

Smoking behavior has long been associated with increased mortality hazards. Doll (1953) and Doll and Hill (1952, 1964) used aggregated mortality statistics to find an increase in bronchial cancer which was attributed in part to cigarette smoking. In 12 years of British data on 41 000 men and women, cigarette smokers were found to have higher death rates from lung cancer. Similar findings during this period were by Dorn (1958). With the cooperation of the Veterans Administration, Dorn mailed a short questionnaire on smoking habits to 294 000 US veterans, selected in December 1953 as holders of US government life insurance policies who served in the armed forces between 1917 and 1940, and the response rate was an overwhelming 200 000 in 1954 and another 49 000 to a second mailing in January 1957. Dorn found substantial differences in death rates by smoking status, including 14 times as many smokers dying from emphysema as compared with nonsmokers during one 16-year interval. Additional studies using the original Dorn (1958) that have corroborated his findings include Kahn (1966), Rogot (1974), Rogot and Murray (1980), and Behrman et al. (1988, 1990). Smoking behavior was also studied by Paffenberger et al. (1966) using Harvard alumni who graduated between 1916–1950, and those from the University of Pennsylvania who graduated between 1931–1940, both admittedly highly selected populations. They found that heavy cigarette smoking, as well as high blood pressure and obesity, were associated with early deaths due to coronary heart disease. Using the same population Paffenberger and Williams (1967) examined the death rate from strokes, and found the same factors, as well as early parental death and non-participation in varsity sports, associated with higher probabilities of death from stroke. Kaplan et al. (1987), evaluate mortality hazards for tobacco usage and gender, for approximately 4000 people originally living in Alameda County, California. The sample members were at least 60 years of age in 1965, and were followed for 17 years.[22] Using Cox's proportional hazard model, they find an increased risk of early death from smoking.[23] Ford and DeStefano (1991) use a proportional hazard model on the NHANES data set for 13 164 persons aged 40–77, evaluating heart disease and overall mortality, controlling for diabetes mellitus. They find age, male gender, current smoking, hypertension, and inactivity associated with occupational status are significant mortality risk factors. Obesity was also significantly associated with mortality due to coronary heart disease. Manton et al. (1993) provide a summary of the medical literature on mortality from heart attacks, which account for approximately 1/3 of all deaths and whose frequency has declined from 250 (per 100 000) for men in 1968 to 110 (per 100 000) in 1988. They find evidence of reduced risk of heart

---

[22] About 5% of their respondents' deaths are unreported.

[23] They also found increased risk associated with being male, lack of leisure time, abnormal weight to height, and not normally eating breakfast.

attack for those who cease smoking, reduce serum cholesterol and high blood pressure, exercise more, and have a more ideal body weight.

Although smoking appears to be a well-documented mortality risk factor, modifications in such behavior, as presumably with other risk factors which result in premature death, has serious implications for actuarially-based pension systems such as Social Security. Shoven et al. (1988) have concluded that the precarious state of fundability of the Social Security System would be exacerbated if premature deaths by those who pay into the system but whose benefits are cut short by early death were to be reduced.

Genetic factors, which recently have been addressed in the growing twins literature, have confounding effects on health by way of their effect on behaviors and lifestyles. For example, observed earlier deaths of smokers could occur because underlying genetic factors influence both smoking choices and mortality, in which case the true causality between smoking per se and date of death may be questioned (Fisher, 1958). Similar genetic predispositions or endowments may affect schooling and/or income and, through such channels, morbidity and mortality. Genetic endowments were found to be significant determinants of returns to schooling in Behrman et al. (1980) and several recent twins studies (Behrman et al., 1994, 1995; Miller et al., 1995) also indicate such effects, even when controlling for random measurement error in schooling, a key variable in the Ashenfelter and Krueger (1994) study of a sample of twins who attended a convention in Twinsberg, Ohio. This latter study found that measurement errors, and not endowments, are the key to explaining downward biases in the economic returns to education.

Ideally, a study to test the hypothesis that a risk factor such as smoking serves as a proxy for unobserved heterogeneities would involve stratification of a large and randomly divided sample of individuals who were either instructed to smoke or not to smoke. Although such a protocol obviously could not be institutionally approved, there remains a group of more recent studies that may serve as a reasonable substitute, involving identical twins smoking discordant. Hrubec and Neel (1981) analyze a sample of white identical and fraternal twins born between 1917 and 1927 in the US, both of whom are veterans, and study rates of "early" death for the period 1946–1975. They find slightly lower death rates among fraternal and identical twins, as compared to all veterans of the same age, and they also find a greater concordance of death rates among identical than among fraternal twins, suggesting a role for genetic endowments. Notably, they include no measured covariates in their analysis. Floderus et al. (1988) study Swedish twins born between 1886 and 1925. Using pairs discordant with respect to smoking, both still alive in 1960, the relative risk of mortality over a 21-year period beginning in 1961 ranges from 1.7 to 2.3 for males and females, respectively, with trend by cohort which may reflect the type of left censoring we discussed above in the Dorn sample. Smokers' relative risks for death from coronary heart disease are also found to be higher. Kaprio and Koskenvuo (1990) use data on Finnish identical and fraternal twins to study deaths from lung cancer and coronary disease. In a sample of 1278 smokers in 1975 and 1210 "former smokers" like-sex pairs born prior to 1958, with deaths recorded during the period 1976–1987, they find that the relative increase in risk of dying for the smoking twin was 13 in the case of identical twins and 2.4 for fraternal ones. Heavy smokers have even higher relative risks, whereas a former smoker had no excess mortality risk. The results of Akerman and Fischbein (1991), who also study Swedish twins indicate that twins are a population selected for risks for lower birth weight and birth complications, which results have implications for the health/developmental literature. Further, one must carefully distinguish between shared frailties and individual frailties. McGue et al. (1992) and Vaupel et al. (1992) show with Danish twins that a hypothesis of shared acquired longevity is inferior to one of moderate heredity with multivariate frailties, and Hougaard et al. (1992) note that the dependence of shared frailties using the Danish twins data is quite small.

Our review of the important risk factors entering the vector $X$ in Eq. (3.3) has pointed to the often subtle role that such factors have in determining health outcomes as well as to the difficulty in treating all of these risk factors as purely exogenously determined. Our pursuit of formal derivations of the demand equations for alternative single period and multiple period structural models, however, does not focus on the determination of variables in $X$. More general treatments of the variables in $X$ can be generated by rather straightforward modifications of the models we discuss below.

### 3.1.2.  Demand equations for the one-period model

The solution to the one-period model can be based on the Lagrangian function where the budget constraint is Eq. (3.2) and where the health production function is directly substituted into Eq. (3.1). The Lagrangian multiplier ($\lambda$) is interpreted as the marginal utility of wealth. First-order conditions are:

$$
\begin{aligned}
& U_{C_t^0} - \lambda P_t^0 = 0, \\
& (U_{H_t} - \lambda W_t T_{H_t}^1) h_{C_t^1} - \lambda P_t^1 = 0, \\
& U_{T_t^L} - \lambda W_t = 0, \\
& (U_{H_t} - \lambda W_t T_{H_t}^1) h_{T_{H_t}} - \lambda W_t = 0.
\end{aligned}
\tag{3.4}
$$

Note that in a one-period model $T_t^1 = f(H_{t-1})$ is a constant so that in this case $T_{H_t}^1 = 0$. Using the implicit function theorem these first-order equations are solved for the choice variables $\{C_t^0, C_t^1, T_t^L, T_t^H\}$, after substituting out $\lambda$ from, e.g., the first equation, in terms of the state variables. Choices of functional forms such as Cobb–Douglas or CES as well as assumptions such as constant returns to scale in the production of health capital provide simplifying expressions for these demand equations. However, as a general rule, choices of flexible forms such as translog or generalized

Leontief for the utility or production function may be more easily accommodated by using numerical methods to solve for the demand equations and for related elasticity measures. Dynamics can be imposed on the structure of the one-period model by specifying prices, or any of the nonchoice variables, in terms of some distributed lag of current and past values. However, no structural interpretation can be given to these dynamics since they are not specified as part of the optimizing framework.

One should immediately question a static model of health consumption. Today's exogenous variables affect tomorrow's endogenous choices, and expectations of tomorrow's exogenous variables affect today's endogenous choices. While we can, to a certain extent, overcome some of this concern in the estimation of this model, as when we employ an estimate based on instruments that affected past choices but are independent of the current disturbance term (e.g., past shocks in market prices), for any such estimation all of the past choices that directly affected current health status must be observed in order to obtain unbiased estimates.

## 3.2. Dynamic models of health demand

Two problems associated with alternatives to one-period models are simplifying assumptions usually employed for tractability, namely temporal and intertemporal separability. The first refers to the assumption that arguments of a utility function are not related to each other within a time period. This problem can be solved by choosing functional forms that model interaction between arguments at each time period. The second problem refers to treating time as a superficial barrier between an argument in time $t$ and the same argument at times $t - 1$ and $t + 1$. This is usually solved by breaking the objective function into smaller time-separable problems which allows dynamic programming techniques to be utilized to solve the maximization problem. The price for mathematical convenience is the treatment of the arguments as time separable. A number of authors have argued for the use of preference structures that incorporate forms of state dependence (e.g., Kydland and Prescott, 1982; Eichenbaum et al., 1988; Hotz et al., 1988). Accumulation of assets and retirement pensions such as Social Security that are pegged to past earnings also indicate the important role of dynamics in the timing of decisions. Burtless and Moffit (1984), for example, used the Retirement History Survey to examine the impact of Social Security benefits on labor supply of the aged and found that Social Security has important effects on the exact timing of retirement as well as the amount of labor supplied after retirement. Van de Ven and Van der Gaag (1982) in their panel study of 8000 households in the Netherlands, noted that permanent and transitory components of the income stream must be distinguished in order to properly model the positive long-run relationships between the demand for health and permanent income.

Consider a rational individual with perfect information, seeking to maximize the present discounted value of lifetime utility derived from consumption and leisure, subject to constraints of available time and resources.[24] Health for the individual is a capital stock, and the individual values health as it reduces sick time, which correspondingly increases the amount of productive time and leisure time.[25] We first represent the individual's life-cycle maximization problem in terms of the constrained dynamic programming problem where the horizon is long (see, for example, Sargent, 1987; Stokey et al., 1989) as

$$\max_{C_t^0, C_t^1, T_t^L, T_t^H} L = \sum_{t=1}^{LE} \beta(x)^{t-1} U(C_t^0, T_t^L, H_t)$$

$$+ \lambda(A_{t+1} - \gamma_t(A_t + (T - T_t^L - T_t^H - T^I(H_t))W_t - P_t^0 C_t^0 - P_t^1 C_t^1)), \tag{3.5}$$

where $\beta(X)$ is the per-period discount factor and the per-period intertemporal budget constraint is expressed in terms of the full-wage. $A_t$ are real assets at the beginning of period $t$, $\gamma_t = (1 + r_t)$, and $r_t$ is the real interest rate. Health capital evolves according to

$$H_t = h(C_t^1, T_t^H; X_t) + (1 - \delta_{t-1}(X_{t-1}))H_{t-1}, \tag{3.6}$$

where $\delta$ is the rate of depreciation. The importance of allowing for unobserved heterogeneity in the discount rate (as well as $h$ and $\delta$) has been recognized by many authors (see, for example, Fuchs, 1982).

Solutions for the life-cycle model of health investment yield the first-order conditions for maximization of constrained lifetime utility that take the form of

$$U_{C_t^0} - \lambda_t P_t^0 = 0,$$

$$(U_{H_t} - \lambda_t W_t T_{H_t}^1)h_{C_t^1} - \lambda_t P_t^1 + \beta(1 - \delta_t)(U_{H_{t+1}} - \lambda_{t+1} W_{t+1} T_{H_{t+1}}^1)h_{C_t^1} = 0,$$

$$U_{T_t^L} - \lambda_t W_t = 0, \tag{3.7}$$

$$(U_{H_t} - \lambda_t W_t T_{H_t}^1)h_{T_{H_t}} - \lambda_t W_t + \beta(1 - \delta_t)(U_{H_{t+1}} - \lambda_{t+1} W_{t+1} T_{H_{t+1}}^1)h_{T_{H_t}} = 0,$$

$$\lambda_t = \beta \gamma_t \lambda_{t+1}.$$

---

[24] Although the concept of maximization of present discounted value of future utility may appear somewhat questionable in this context, there are confirmations in the literature, most recently by Kenkel (1994), who demonstrates declining demands for health investments by the elderly as they age, consistent with an individual rationally reducing an investment in health as the "pay-off" period diminishes.

[25] If the concept of health is extended to include intellectual and emotional health as well as physical health then one can capture many other important human economic activities, in addition to those we have previously described. Deferring income by investing time in health production in order to advantage oneself of higher wages in the future has similar motives to those utilized in models of the decision-making process for higher education. Further, the substantial time many humans allocate to such activities as fraternization would suggest that human capital should be broadened to include social capital as well (Coleman, 1988 ) with careful treatment given to distributional heterogeneity that may be present within groups that define intra-individual social norms (Manski, 1993).

The last equation is the equation of motion for the marginal utility of wealth. Using the implicit function theorem the choice variables $\{C_t^0, C_t^1, T_t^L, T_t^H\}$ can be solved in terms of the state variables and $T_t^I$ after substituting out $\lambda_t$ from the first first-order condition. Illness time now has a formal role in this model and is solved by inserting $H_t$ into the functional relationship which determines $T^I = f(H_t)$.

The role of future and past wages, prices, rates of time preference, interest rates, endowments and consumer tastes as well as other state variables is now made explicit in the individual's decision model. Once functional forms for utility and production are given, the structural links that are imbedded in the individual's life-cycle decisions as well as the structured role that past and future state variables have on the dynamic demands for consumption and time allocations are specified within the model. Simplifying assumptions on functional forms such as additive separability, and on discount factors and interest rates (for example, it is often assumed that $\gamma_t \beta = 1$) provides more structure on the demand equations that may allow for more transparent analytic interpretations, but in general the derivations must be carried out numerically.

### 3.2.1. Generalizations of the Grossman-type model

At the time of the Grossman model, there was considerable interest in contrasts between health and other forms of capital. Grossman himself noted the implicit constraint against depletion (negative investment) inherent with health, as opposed to "pure" capital. Muurinen (1982) generalized Grossman's model, primarily by focusing on the depreciation factor $\delta$, which he noted was likely to be endogenously related to choices made by the individual, and by addressing the issue of length of life as a choice variable by focusing on death as an event associated with subcritical values of health capital, the Grossman death stock, which is implicitly endogenous. By incorporating education into the vector of endowments $X$, Muurinen established a relationship between education and health, in which education increases as the depreciation rate decreases for health capital. Further, Muurinen was able to clarify the dynamic relationship between wealth and health as well as income and substitution effects in health demand associated with changes in initial wealth. These findings were seen by Muurinen as able to explain the negative income elasticities often reported for health demand. Grossman's (1972a,b) model predicts health to be a normal good, a finding not always found in empirical work on the topic. This may be due to the particular form in which Grossman stated the individual's budget constraint. By assuming identical preferences and allocating time based on income, the value of leisure time for those with lower incomes may be understated. Muurinen points out that this seeming inconsistency may be due to the particular definition of wealth and/or income as permanent or transitory. Moreover, assumptions of temporal separability may cloud the relationships among long-run health consumption activities and those which are undertaken towards the end of the life-cycle when health is in decline.

Wolfe (1985) developed an extension to the Grossman model to account for retirement since the original Grossman model did not predict abrupt changes in the time allocation decision between work and leisure. Wolfe noted that in the "pure" model of Grossman, initial levels of health in excess of those whose rates of return were equal to their cost at the margin would disappear, and that a net wealth effect would be obtained by the individual instead, allowing health capital to depreciate over time. In other words, individuals work and defer substantial health investments until such time as the marginal benefits from investing in health equal the opportunity costs of forgone working time. Wolfe includes financial assets such as savings in his model, as a store for pure capital, and treats life expectancy as fixed for computational simplicity. He finds support for the observation that retirement age falls when productivity rises, since productive people work harder and thus depreciate their health capital faster, and since productive people have high wages and may have more accumulated assets, which allows them to leave the work force sooner.

### 3.2.2. Rational addictions

One may question the assumption that the rate of depreciation of health capital is exogenous since there are several choices we make, particularly the consumption of cigarettes and the excessive consumption of alcohol, which are known to negatively impact health status (see, e.g., Muurinen, 1982). In part to address this inconsistency, Becker and Murphy (1988) and Becker et al. (1991) formalized the theory of rational addictions, wherein individuals consume items such as tobacco, alcohol, or narcotics, whose future marginal utility is increased by current consumption. This model recently has been applied to cigarette smoking by Becker et al. (1994) who note that the long-run elasticity of demand with respect to price is high, and that the revenue increases to government from increased excise taxes on cigarettes may be smaller than thought, and by Chaloupka (1991, 1995). Recent applications to alcohol addiction can be found in Grossman et al. (1995).

Grossman (1972) partitioned consumption goods into those which produced health and those which did not. However, in the rational addictions model, a good such as cigarettes is considered a consumption good and a negative input into the health production function. Rational individuals smoke because they receive pleasure, despite the adverse health effects which can often be assumed known. The Grossman model can be modified to account for consumption of goods such as tobacco and alcohol, with adverse health effects by including a rationally addictive composite good, $C^2$, at price $P^2$, in addition to the composite consumption good, $C^0$, and the intermediate composite good, $C^1$. Consumption of the addictive good is accumulated into a stock of historical consumption ($N_t$) which is depreciated each period by a factor $\eta_t$. $C^2$ is a "good" in the utility function and a "bad" in the production of health.

We can incorporate these more general phenomena into the dynamic programming problem by restating Eq. (3.5) as

$$\max_{C_t^0,C_t^1,C_t^2,T_t^L,T_t^H} L = \sum_{t=1}^{LE} \beta(x)^{t-1} U(C_t^0, C_t^2, T_t^L, H_t, N_t)$$

$$+ \lambda(A_{t+1} - \gamma_t(A_t + (T - T_t^L - T_t^H - T^I(H_t))W_t$$

$$- P_t^0 C_t^0 - P_t^1 C_t^1 - P_t^2 C_t^2)), \tag{3.8}$$

where the health stock is

$$H_t = h(C_t^1, C_t^2, T_t^H; X_t) + [1 - \delta_{t-1}(X_{t-1})]H_{t-1}, \tag{3.9}$$

the stock of addictive capital (see, for example, Chaloupka, 1991) is

$$N_t = C_t^2 + (1 - \eta_{t-1})N_{t-1}, \tag{3.10}$$

and the per-period intertemporal budget constraint is modified to account for the addition of the consumption of the addictive good ($C_t^2$). The resulting first-order equations from this dynamic program are

$$U_{C_t^0} - \lambda_t P_t^0 = 0,$$

$$(U_{H_t} - \lambda_t W_t T_H^I)h_{C_t^1} - \lambda_t P_t^1 + \beta(1 - \delta_t)(U_{H_{t+1}} - \lambda_{t+1}W_{t+1}T_{H_{t+1}}^I)h_{C_t^1} = 0,$$

$$U_{C_t^2} + U_{N_t} + (U_{H_t} - \lambda_t W_t T_H^I)h_{C_t^2} + \beta(1 - \eta_t)U_{N_{t+1}}$$

$$+ \beta(1 - \delta_t)(U_{H_{t+1}} - \lambda_{t+1}W_{t+1}T_{H_{t+1}}^I)h_{C_t^2} - \lambda_t P_t^2 = 0, \tag{3.11}$$

$$U_{T_t^L} - \lambda_t W_t = 0,$$

$$(U_{H_t} - \lambda_t W_t T_{H_t}^I)h_{T_t^H} - \lambda_t W_t + \beta(1 - \delta_t)(U_{H_{t+1}} - \lambda_{t+1}W_{t+1}T_{H_{t+1}}^I)h_{T_t^H} = 0,$$

$$\lambda_t = \beta\gamma_t\lambda_{t+1}.$$

Solutions for the demand equations are obtained in the same fashion as above, albeit with the additional equation for the demand for addictive capital.

We next incorporate two endogeneities noted by Grossman, Muurinen, and Wolfe and others, but not yet formally addressed: endogenous wages and endogenous life expectancy.

### 3.2.3. Wage endogeneity

Foster and Rosenzweig (1994), in their analysis of moral hazard in the labor market for Philippino agricultural workers, recently assumed that wages were a known function of health capital (assumed in their study to be a measure of body mass), terms of employment, in particular the type of contract, and unobservable worker effort. Wage endogeneity can be brought into the Grossman-type framework by defining a wage function whose arguments are job-specific human capital ($E$), health capital, endowments, and individual-specific heterogeneity. First, define the stock of job-specific human capital as

$$E_t = T_t^W + (1 - v_{t-1}(X_{t-1}))E_{t-1},$$                    (3.12)

where $v_{t-1}$ is the depreciation of last period's stock of work experience which could in principal be allowed to vary at the individual level.

Assume that the wage $W_t$ is positive throughout life and given by

$$W_t = W(E_t, H_t; X_t).$$                                        (3.13)

Human capital is incorporated into the vector of endowments $X$ through such variables as education and nutrition. Solutions to the individual's dynamic programming problem modified by endogenous wages of this form are:

$$U_{C_t^0} - \lambda_t P_t^0 = 0,$$

$$(U_{H_t} - \lambda_t W_t T_{H_t}^I)h_{C_t^1} - \lambda_t P_t^1 + \lambda_t T_t^W(W_{H_t} - W_{E_t}T_{H_t}^I)h_{C_t^1}$$

$$+ \beta(1 - \delta_t)(U_{H_{t+1}} - \lambda_{t+1}W_{t+1}T_{H_{t+1}}^I)h_{C_t^1}$$

$$+ \beta\lambda_{t+1}T_{t+1}^W(1 - \delta_t)W_{H_{t+1}}h_{C_t^1} - \beta\lambda_{t+1}T_{t+1}^W(1 - v_t)W_{E_{t+1}}T_{H_t}^I h_{C_t^1} = 0,$$

$$U_{C_t^2} + U_{N_t} + (U_{H_t} - \lambda_t W_t T_{H_t}^I)h_{C_t^2} - \lambda_t P_t^2 + \lambda_t T_{W_t}(W_{H_t} - W_{E_t}T_{H_t}^I)h_{C_t^2}$$

$$+ \beta(1 - v_t)U_{N_t} + \beta(1 - \delta_t)(U_{H_{t+1}} - \lambda_{t+1}W_{t+1}T_{H_{t+1}}^I)h_{C_t^2}$$

$$+ \beta(1 - \delta_t)\lambda_{t+1}T_{t+1}^W W_{H_{t+1}}h_{C_t^2} - \beta(1 - v_t)\lambda_{t+1}T_{t+1}^W W_{E_{t+1}}T_{H_t}^I h_{C_t^2} = 0,$$

$$U_{T_t^L} - \lambda_t(W_t + T_t^W W_{E_{t+1}}) - \beta(1 - v_t)\lambda_{t+1}T_{t+1}^W W_{E_{t+1}} = 0,$$

$$(U_{H_t} - \lambda_t W_t T_{H_t}^I)h_{T_{H_t}} + \lambda_t T_t^W(W_{H_t} - W_{E_t}T_{H_t}^I)h_{T_t^H} - \lambda_t T_t^W W_{E_t}$$

$$+ \beta(1 - \delta_t)(U_{H_{t+1}} - \lambda_{t+1}W_{t+1}T_{H_{t+1}}^I)h_{T_t^H}$$

$$+ \beta\lambda_{t+1}T_{t+1}^W[(1 - \delta_t)W_{H_{t+1}}(1 - v_t)W_{E_{t+1}}T_{H_t}^I)h_{T_t^H}] - \beta\lambda_{t+1}T_{t+1}^W(1 - v_t)W_{E_{t+1}} = 0,$$

$$\lambda_t = \beta\gamma_t\lambda_{t+1}.$$

(3.14)

The same algorithm for solving the control variables and the marginal utility of wealth can be used here as in the above problems. The only difference is that the endogeneity of the wage now has a formal link to the solutions of the structural model by way of the functional form chosen for the wage Eq. (3.13).

### 3.2.4. Endogenous life expectancy

Shortly after the original Grossman (1972) model, Grossman and Benham (1974) began to address the issues of uncertainty which was posed in the original Grossman treatise, when they considered how wages relate to health. In their extended model, a lagged effect of health on wages was introduced. Extended treatments of uncertainty, the importance of which was noted by Grossman, with respect to economic conditions (in particular, future prices) and life expectancy have been pursued by several authors in the context of adult and elderly health. For example, Hamermesh (1984) found that in the Retirement History Survey individuals work more and consume less if they expect to live longer. Hamermesh (1985) also found that individuals extrapolate their life expectancies as life-tables change and are well informed of levels and changes in the current life-tables, although he noted that the subjective distribution of life expectancies has a larger variance than the actuarial counterpart, with the variance of the subjective distribution decreasing with age. The relative accuracy of subjective life expectancy probabilities also has been noted by Hurd and McGarry (1993) using the Health and Retirement Survey.

A formal treatment of life expectancy as a choice variable has been put forth by Ehrlich and Chuma (1990), who extended the Grossman framework by including the demand for longevity. Using a continuous-time setting, they overcame the paradox of life expectancy as both an endogenous outcome (Grossman, 1972) and as the finite horizon of the discrete-time dynamic programming problem. Ehrlich and Chuma noted that life expectancy cannot be marginalized "myopically", and must be considered as a fully endogenous variable in the life-cycle model. By so doing, they postulate an important economic consideration, that longevity itself is an economic good, as well as the dependence of the demand for longevity upon initial conditions, such as wealth. They also remind that the Fischer effect applies to health demand just like any other commodity and thus that real effects can be brought about by uncertainty about future prices. Finally, they note the importance of heterogeneity in rates of intertemporal substitution ($\beta$).

### 3.2.5. A model of uncertainty in the life-cycle health model

Decision-making under uncertainty characterizes life-cycle models of consumption and thus should characterize life-cycle models of health choice as well. Diamond and Hausman (1984) have examined the effect of two sources of uncertainty for adult workers, physical health and involuntary unemployment, on the timing of retirement using a subset of men aged 45–59 from the National Longitudinal Survey. They find health to be an important determinant of retirement while both private pensions and Social Security, whose effects are strongest at age 62 when benefits first become available, increase the probability of retirement. Anderson et al. (1986) use a life-cycle, rational expectations model to test the effect of unexpected changes in health on retirement, based on data from the Retirement History Survey, and they show that retirement plans were significantly affected by unexpected health changes. Berger et al. (1987) derive the relationship between the willingness to pay for health risk changes and the consumer surpluses associated with health changes which occur when there is certainty. They estimate this relationship empirically using survey interview data on 131 people in Denver and Chicago during 1984–1985. Bernheim (1990) has used the Retirement History Survey to test for rationality in expectations of future Social Security benefits following earlier research on the accuracy of such expectations by Bernheim (1988), and work on the accuracy of expectations concerning the timing of retirement by Burtless (1986), Anderson et al. (1986), Wolpin and Gönül (1987), and Bernheim (1989). He was unable to reject the hypothesis that innovations are unrelated to prior information and that expectations evolve as a random walk. Moreover, he notes that an implication of his findings that responses to new information just before retirement are highly rational, is that individuals recognize the links between labor supply decisions and benefit formulas at the margin, a point raised by many researchers examining the retirement decision. Uncertainty in the supply of medical care is well documented and noted by Phelps (1992) to be due in large part to the public good aspect of medical information. Information concerning the marginal productivity of medical treatments is underproduced, and the extent to which new information diffuses geographically and temporally is highly variable. Uncertainty and the demand for medical care also has been studied by Dardanoni and Wagstaff (1990), who modify Grossman's human capital model of health demand by introducing uncertainty involving illness and therapeutic efficacy. Although they do not pursue this issue empirically, in their comparative statics analysis they derive a Rothschild–Stiglitz increase in uncertainty: given that the average marginal product of medical care is unchanged or reduced as its riskiness increases, there is an increase in its demand. They conclude that health consumption is a normal good and consumers are risk-averse, consistent with the findings of Evans and Viscusi (1993) based on data on nonfatal consumer injuries. Moreover, as the expected therapeutic efficacy increases, Dardanoni and Wagstaff find that demand for medical care is reduced.

Sickles and Yazbeck (1995) have specified a modified Grossman dynamic programming model in order to evaluate the role of health, consumption, and leisure in life-cycle models with uncertainty and with exogenous wages and exogenous and known life expectancy. They use the framework of the infinite horizon programming problem subject to the usual transversality conditions. Assume that the individual faces exogenous real wages, and that at the beginning of the period realizations of the real wage, $W_t$, the real interest rate, $r_{t-1}$, and the prices of the two composite consumption goods, $P^0_{t-1}$, $P^1_{t-1}$, are known but that future realizations are unknown and random. Abstract from the possibility of addictive goods and assume that the time allocation problem is between work and leisure, the latter to improve health production, that illness time is subsumed within leisure, and that there are no bequests. The individual's economic problem is to maximize

$$E_t \left( \sum_{t=1}^{LE} \beta^{t-1} U(C_t^0, T_t^L, H_t) \right). \tag{3.15}$$

The per-period intertemporal budget constraint is

$$A_{t+1} = \gamma_t (A_t + W_t T_t^W - C_t^0 - P_t^1 C_t^1), \tag{3.16}$$

where the numeraire price is $C_t^0$. The time allocation constraint is

$$T = T_t^L + T_t^W. \tag{3.17}$$

In order to allow for intertemporal nonseparability, a convenient form for the health capital equation is

$$H_t = h(C_t^1, T_t^L; X_t) + \alpha a_t. \tag{3.18}$$

Here $\alpha$ measures the importance of past health on current health, and $a_t$ is described below. In this formulation $H_t$ is composed of two parts. The first is current investment which is created using leisure time, health related consumption and exogenous factors which could include endowments/heterogeneity. The second is the stock of past health produced over the life-cycle. In this formulation $\alpha$ measures the rate of technical substitution between current investment in health and the stock of past investment in the production of current health (Hotz et al., 1988). Alternatively, the accumulation of the stock of health could be modeled by the perpetual inventory approach used in the certainty models discussed earlier. In that specification, the level of health stock at time $t$ is an update of period $t - 1$ investment in health plus last period's depreciated health stock. The specification used in Eq. (3.18) allows for the possibility that the importance of past health relative to current health, $\alpha$, may not be unity. The distributed lag specification is in keeping with the Hotz et al. (1988) model and allows for depreciation in health independent of the lagged health effects on current utility. The law of motion for $a_t$ is given by

$$a_t = (1 - \eta)a_{t-1} + H_{t-1}, \tag{3.19}$$

where $\eta$ measures the rate of depreciation of the influence of past health on current health. Temporal nonseparability is introduced by including in health a distributed lag of past health investments in addition to the current period's health investment.

The maximization problem is stated in terms of the value function at time $t$:

$$V^t(A_t, a_t, W_t) = \max_{C_t^0, C_t^1, T_t^L} (U(C_t^0, T_t^L, H_t) + \beta E_t V^{t+1}(A_{t+1}, a_{t+1}, W_{t+1})). \tag{3.20}$$

The first-order conditions with respect to $C_t^0$, $C_t^1$, and $T_t^L$ are

$$E_t[U_{C_t^0} - \beta \gamma_t V_A^{t+1}] = 0,$$

$$E_t[U_{H_t} h_{C_t^1} - \beta \gamma_t P_t^1 V_A^{t+1} + \beta V_a^{t+1} h_{C_t^1}] = 0, \tag{3.21}$$

$$E_t[U_{T_t^L} + U_{H_t} h_{T_t^L} + \beta V_a^{t+1} h_{T_t^L} - \beta \gamma_t W_t V_A^{t+1}] = 0.$$

Using the envelope theorem and the law of iterated expectations, the Euler equations can be rewritten as

$$E_t[U_{C_t^0} - \beta \gamma_t U_{C_{t+1}^0}] = 0,$$

$$E_t\left[ U_{H_t} h_{C_t^1} - U_{C_t^0} P_t^1 + \beta h_{C_t^1}\left[ \alpha U_{H_{t+1}} - [(1-\eta)]\left[ U_{H_{t+1}} - \frac{U_{C_{t+1}^0} P_{t+1}^1}{h_{C_{t+1}^1}} \right] \right] \right] = 0, \tag{3.22}$$

$$E_t\left[ U_{T_t^L} + \frac{U_{C_t^0} P_t^1 h_{T_t^L}}{h_{C_t^1}} - W_t U_{C_t^0} \right] = 0.$$

Moreover, if one assumes that expectations are rational, then one-period ahead inno-vations $(\varepsilon_{i,t})$ can be added to the derived Euler equations, where $E_t(\varepsilon_{i,t}) = 0$, $\varepsilon_{i,t}$, $i = 1,2,3$, is orthogonal to the information set of period $t$, $\Omega_t$, and where the forecast errors for a given individual are serially uncorrelated. Realizations of future random variables imply that

$$[U_{C_t^0} - \beta \gamma_t U_{C_{t+1}^0}] = \varepsilon_{1,t+1},$$

$$\left[ U_{H_t} h_{C_t^1} - U_{C_t^0} P_t^1 + \beta h_{C_t^1}\left[ \alpha U_{H_{t+1}} - [(1-\eta)]\left[ U_{H_{t+1}} - \frac{U_{C_{t+1}^0} P_{t+1}^1}{h_{C_{t+1}^1}} \right] \right] \right] = \varepsilon_{2,t+1}, \tag{3.23}$$

$$\left[ U_{T_t^L} + \frac{U_{C_t^0} P_t^1 h_{T_t^L}}{h_{C_t^1}} - W_t U_{C_t^0} \right] = \varepsilon_{3,t+1}.$$

The model's parameters can be estimated by generalized (or simulated) method of moments (Hansen, 1982; McFadden, 1989; Pakes and Pollard, 1989), one of a set of estimators which we discuss in Section 5, once functional forms for the utility func-tion and the production function are specified.

## 3.3. Death as an exhaustive state

The economic model of health wherein life is not explicitly modeled as a choice variable can be used to express death as an exhaustive state for which the accumulated health stock fails to exceed a critical value $H^*$ (Grossman, 1972a, b; Muurinen, 1982). Although such a mortality expression is conceptually linked to structural models they are typically estimated in isolation of that structure, that is, they are estimated as unrestricted quasi-reduced-forms. Rosenzweig and Schultz (1982b, 1983b) have argued that estimation of the structural model is valuable in its own right as well as for purposes of providing a set of restricted quasi-reduced-form estimates that formally link the structural parameters to the coefficients of the determinants of the mortality equation. This allows a much richer menu of ex ante questions to be addressed concerning the role and timing of economic factors on life expectancy.

The solution to the equilibrium path of individual health stocks can be linked to mortality by introducing a stochastic rule for observing death. Define a mortality state for individual $i$ at time $t$ as

$$M_{it} = 1 \quad \text{if } H_{it} < H_{it}^* \,, \tag{3.24}$$
$$= 0 \quad \text{otherwise,}$$

where $H_{it}^*$ is an individual and time-specific threshold for the equilibrium health index. In general the mortality state will be a function of prices, income, and endowments/heterogeneity. Let the probability that an individual is alive at the beginning of the period be $[1 - F(H_{it})]$ where $F(\cdot)$ is the distribution function and assume that the mortality threshold is a shock whose arrival time follows a Poisson process. Then the probability that a new value of $H_{it}^*$ occurs during the period $(t, t + \Delta)$ is $P = \psi\Delta + o(\Delta)$.

The hazard of dying during the period is

$$\lambda_i(t) = \psi[1 - F(H_{it})] \tag{3.25}$$

and the survivor function becomes

$$S_t(t) = \exp\left(-\psi[1 - F(H_{it})]t\right). \tag{3.26}$$

The choice of $\psi$ and the distribution for the shocks determine the form of the hazard. If the level of shocks is exponential with density $f(H_{it}^*) = \exp(-H_{it}^*)$, then $F(H_{it}) = 1 - \exp(-H_{it})$ and with $\psi = \mu t^{\theta-1}$, the hazard of dying at time $t$ is given by the Weibull proportional hazard

$$\lambda_i(t) = \theta t^{\theta-1} \exp(-H_{it}). \tag{3.27}$$

Death defined in this fashion has several interpretations. In the health capital model, death might be defined as an infrathreshold value for any one of the several separable components to human capital, broadening the model to include issues such as preventable accidents caused by insufficient investment in health-education augmenting human capital and crime victimization as chosen on the basis of inadequate investment in social capital.

## 4. Sources of data on mortality and morbidity and health measurement systems

In our discussion of international mortality trends and risk factors we have pointed to particular studies, and often to particular data sets, used by researchers to study adult mortality and morbidity in countries other than the United States. In most of the industrialized countries, the health care delivery system is overseen by the federal government. Medical records data are thus centralized and are often used to conduct longitudinal mortality analyses. The earliest large-scale analyses were often conducted in Continental Europe. The United Kingdom is the source of many of the first working hypotheses concerning relationships between health and economic factors. Scandinavian countries are also the source of much data, including twins data which are crucial to many explorations of hypotheses involving the role of inherited mortality frailty. Canada frequently provides data of interest for North America. In this section, we wish to be more specific about the sources of death and mortality data, particularly those that exists in the US, in part because of the substantial body of literature that has been based on such data, including more rigorous attempts to construct better measures of quality of life, and in part because the survey instruments often used allow researchers to explore the life-cycle issues and formal structural models that we outlined in Section 3.

### 4.1. Mortality and morbidity data

The death certificate remains the official record of death and, since 1978, all US death certificates are maintained in a computerized file known as the "National Death Index". Decedents are identified by name, an identification number if available, overt demographic variables such as gender, assumed (or provided by family members) race, ethnic background, and one socioeconomic descriptor of occupation. Recently, the National Center for Health Statistics has examined the accuracy of the death certificate in the National Mortality Followback Study, calculating an effective matching rate ranging from 76% for veteran status to 86.6% for racial identity (Poe et al., 1993).

Kitagawa and Hauser (1973), in their important review of mortality differentials in the US, used the 1960 Matched Records Study of 340 000 deaths occurring over a four-month period in 1960, a collaborative effort of the Bureau of the Census, the National Center for Health Statistics, and the Population Research Center of the University of Chicago. Kliss et al. (1979) examined the general issue of accuracy of matching procedures based upon Social Security number, name, race, sex, and gender, and estimate 80–90% accuracy, with change of surname for married women the principal source of error.

More recently, Sorlie and Rogot (1990) and Sorlie et al. (1992) match deaths records with those from the Current Population Survey (CPS), which is obtained monthly and has a significant amount of demographic and economic information, to match over 452 000 death records from selected months during 1979–1983. It is important to note that Census-based matched panels may not be complete. For example, it is generally agreed that there is a Census undercount of the poor and, particularly, the undocumented Hispanic population (Tienda and Ortiz (1986); see also Ericksen and Kadane (1985) and Schirm and Preston (1987) on generic undercount problems with the Census)).

Another data source for mortality studies is the Social Security files, which must accurately track deaths in order to stop payment of certain benefits and to commence with payment of others, such as widow and surviving-child benefits. Rosen and Taubman (1984) report these data to be accurate for deaths among those over 65, and incomplete for those younger. Duleep (1986) showed that by combining several Social Security administration sources of mortality information complete death reporting may be achieved.[26]

Several other more detailed surveys of demographic, socioeconomic and behavioral issues have been matched to deaths records or Social Security files. The Retirement History Survey is a random sample of about 11 000 heads of households age 58–63, first taken in 1969 and followed up every second year through 1979. Comparable surveys such as the National Health and Nutrition Survey (NHANES), which includes the National Health Epidemiologic Follow-Up Study (NLMS) and the National Longitudinal Mortality Study (NLMS), rely upon self-assessment and survey to provide deaths data (Madans et al., 1986). Unfortunately, recent privacy legislation compromises all Social Security number-based matching protocols.

A more selected, and yet extensive, panel of records on date and cause of death are kept by the Veterans Administration (VA). Studies by DeBakey and Beebe (1952), Beebe and Simon (1969) and Rogot (1974) have each concluded that the VA's death records are nearly 100% complete. It is essential to remember that the sample of veterans is highly selected, for health, intelligence, occupation, and other potentially important mortality factors.[27]

One of the more important panels for econometric evaluation is the Panel Study of

---

[26] Still one reads of occasional fraud such as a son cashing a dead parent's check.

[27] Interestingly, World War I data are less selected than subsequent military cohorts since various health effects could not be detected then, the US IQ test was only developed during the war, and the Army was mostly drafted.

Income Dynamics (PSID) which was begun in 1968 and annually follows an original sample of 5000 households, with an oversampling of the poor, nonwhites, and elderly. This panel is felt to be representative of US households, but until recently could not be used to study longitudinal patterns of aging since records were dropped when persons died or left the sample for other reasons. This problem has recently been addressed by the provision of a nonresponse sample for all people surveyed as well as information on the reason for nonresponse (Ellwood and Kane, 1990).

A follow-up to the Retirement History Survey, ended in 1979, is the Health and Retirement Study (HRS) which is detailed in Juster and Suzman (1995). The survey is be based on 13 500 individuals and 8000 families whose head of household is 51–61 in 1993 and provides information on labor force participation and pensions, health conditions and health status, family structure and mobility, and economic status, along with detailed information on expectations. These data are to be linked to the National Death Index, Medicare files, and Social Security earnings as well as to employer health insurance benefit plans and pensions. The first two annual waves have been collected and the third is in progress. The HRS, which already has been used to examine intergenerational transfers by McGarry and Schoeni (1994) and wealth differentials by ethnicity by Smith (1995a), among others, promises to be an exciting and comprehensive data source for new and seasoned researchers in the field of aging research.

The Asset and Health Dynamics Survey of the Oldest Old (AHEAD) is a new panel of heads-of-households born in 1923 or before as well as their spouses or partners and in its current early release form contains 7911 of the eventual 8224 respondents. The AHEAD collects detailed information on income, wealth, and health status, as well as information on the children of the respondents, such as schooling, income, family structure and financial transfers and has recently been used by McGarry and Schoeni (1995) in their study of intergenerational transfers. Smith (1995b) has recently used these last two new data sets to explore wealth inequality and savings incentives for different racial and ethnic groups and their implications on retirement behavior. The PAID, HRS, and AHEAD panels are collected through the Institute for Survey Research (ISR) at the University of Michigan. The ISR works with various governmental agencies in other data collection activities, including the Labor Department's Quality of Employment Survey and the Monitoring the Future survey.

The Survey of Income and Program Participation (SIPP) is one of the largest and most comprehensive panels of Census Data in the United States and is distinguished, in part, because of the detail of data collected on participation in government programs. The data collected include demographic identification, work hours and earnings, and participation in such programs as Social Security, Worker's Compensation, Aid to Families with Dependent Children (AFDC), Women, Infants and Children (WIC). The SIPP data are commonly the source of empirical welfare analyses, often on topics dealing with the elderly and the indigent. Several thousand individuals are interviewed by CPS field representatives each month on a rotating topic of interest. For example, the March data are for income and are cited frequently. Del Bene and Vaughan (1992) note the improvements that could be made to these analyses were records from SIPP matched with Medicare files from the Health Care Financing Administration.

## 4.2. Measurement systems for health status

Arguably, there is no more active area of epidemiology currently underway than the reliable measurement of individual health status, underlying the emergent discipline of outcomes research which attempts to evaluate and compare empirically the results of various clinical interventions. There are objective health measurement systems proven to have prognostic capabilities for hospitalized patients. One such triage system is known as the Acute Physiology and Chronic Health Evaluation (APACHE) scoring system. Our interest instead lies in a reliable system for the measurement of health status for individuals who are not necessarily hospitalized and/or critically ill and one that lends itself to economic modeling. Health status measures are often developed by self-assessment, involving both objective questions as to functional status as well as subjective appraisals of perceived health status relative to others. Ferraro (1980) and Mossey and Shapiro (1982) have shown that subjective responses are highly correlated with their physicians' rating and the latter indicate that these subjective responses can actually surpass seemingly more objective findings, in terms of ability to predict and explain behaviors. Gafni and Birch (1991) provide adjustment algorithms for utility–health outcome measures detailed in Torrance (1986), which are based on the axioms of Von Neumann–Morgenstern utility theory, to correct for different valuations of health outcomes for different individuals or groups of individuals. These adjustments are meant to provide an equity neutral index of quality adjusted life-years based on individuals' preferences instead of more arbitrarily chosen weighting schemes. Idler (1992) argues that self-reported health status relative to others does not vary significantly with particular wordings of different survey instruments. Self-reported health measures in the United States and internationally have been found to have high degrees of reliability and validity by a variety of researchers. As pointed out by Strauss et al. (1993) these include the RAND health insurance study (Stewart et al., 1978; Ware et al., 1980), the RAND Medical Outcomes Study (Stewart et al., 1988), WHO surveys in Korea, Malaysia, and the Philippines (Andrews et al., 1986) and the ASEAN surveys in Indonesia, Malaysia, the Philippines, and Singapore (Ju and Jones, 1989).

### 4.2.1. Economic considerations in quality of life

Mortality studies which focus solely on the quantity of life in terms of years do not take into consideration the quality with which those years were lived. There are medical examples where quality adjustments appear warranted. Elderly individuals may

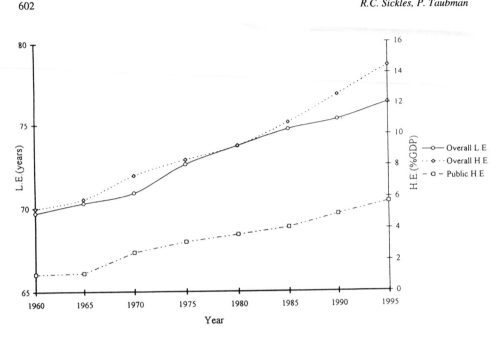

Fig. 9. Evolution of life expectancy and health expenditures (US).

elect to refuse life-prolonging therapies which are associated with severe toxicities or additional disabilities. While there are countervailing economic considerations in the case of what are referred to as "refusing medical advice" or "living wills", it would appear that a model of health in which individuals make choices in maximizing utility should account for the quality of the years of life as well as the quantity of such.

The importance of quantifying the quality with which periods of life are enjoyed, in addition to its intuitive appeal, can be motivated with recent US data. Shown in Fig. 9 are the evolution of overall life expectancy and overall health expenditures as a percentage of gross domestic product. Clearly, from 1960 until 1985, increases in health expenditures were met with increases in life expectancy. Since 1985, however, expenditures have increased much faster than life expectancy, and one might question whether these health expenditures have been valuable in terms of an increased quality of life.

Perhaps the first encounter most investigators have with quality/quantity issues concerns the reporting in the vital statistics of the "Years of (Potential) Life Lost" (YLL), which adjusts the condition-specific distribution of deaths to account for the age of the individual (Murray, 1994). Deaths past a certain average age expectancy, which is now taken to be about 75 years of age, are not counted as a loss under this measure. A more traditional economic measure, the "Years of Productive Life Lost"

Table 3
Causes of death and adjusted impact (US 1991)

| Condition | Deaths | | Expected years lost | | | Productive years lost | | | PDV earnings lost | | |
|---|---|---|---|---|---|---|---|---|---|---|---|
| | Total | (%) | Total | (%) | Per death | Total | (%) | Per death | Total | (%) | Per death |
| Heart disease | 721 | (33) | 3355 | (24) | 4.7 | 1340 | (17) | 1.9 | 32 | (19) | 90 |
| Cancers | 515 | (24) | 4275 | (31) | 8.3 | 1880 | (24) | 3.7 | 30 | (18) | 111 |
| Cerebrovascular | 144 | (7) | 535 | (4) | 3.7 | 223 | (3) | 1.6 | 4 | (2) | 72 |
| Accidents, injuries | 89 | (4) | 2800 | (20) | 31.5 | 2120 | (27) | 23.8 | 27 | (16) | 447 |
| Chronic pulmonary | 91 | (4) | 380 | (3) | 4.2 | 105 | (1) | 1.1 | | | |
| Acute pulmonary | 78 | (4) | 315 | (2) | 4.0 | 175 | (2) | 2.2 | | | |
| Diabetes mellitus | 49 | (2) | 365 | (3) | 7.5 | 165 | (2) | 3.4 | | | |
| Hepatic, cirrhosis | 25 | (1) | 418 | (3) | 16.7 | 233 | (3) | 9.3 | | | |
| Suicide | 31 | (1) | 938 | (7) | 30.2 | 678 | (9) | 21.9 | | | |
| Homicide, legal | 27 | (1) | 1153 | (8) | 43.5 | 893 | (11) | 33.7 | | | |
| All others | 400 | (19) | (−684) | (−5) | (−1.7) | 63 | (1) | 0.2 | 79 | (45) | 211 |
| Totals | 2170 | | 13850 | | 6.4 | 7875 | | 3.6 | 172 | | 153 |

(YPLL), is similar to the YLL with the exception that the productive (retirement) age cut-off age is 65 years.

Shown in Table 3 are the impacts of death by cause from the US life-table from 1991, where age-cohort deaths were collected at the age interval midpoint and adjusted impacts accordingly interpolated. Heart disease and cancer trade places between deaths and years of expected life lost, and perhaps most notably, whereas accidents and injuries accounted for only 4% of all deaths, they represented the leading cause of years of productive life lost.

### 4.2.2. Self-assessed health and mortality

Idler (1992, 1995), in her recent comprehensive reviews of the literature on self-assessed health status and mortality, proposes that subjective responses to questions soliciting self ratings of individual health status and health relative to others be complemented with "objective" controls for acute and chronic conditions, symptoms, functional status, physiology, and use of medical care.[28] Idler reviews the literature for 16 recent studies worldwide involving 49 516 subjects, followed for an (weighted) average of 6.3 years (Table 4). Self-assessed health is analyzed against mortality by computation of adjusted-odds mortality ratios, using methods of logistic regression or Cox or Weibull proportional hazards, with the superior response category receiving an odds ratio of 1.00. In Table 4, we have extracted from these studies their subjective response categories, source of objective findings, analysis technique and adjusted-odds mortality ratios by response category. Compiling weighted averages by converting response categories to a more comparable system of self-assessed health status as "excellent" "good" "fair" and "poor", we can compute the following survey estimate of the adjusted-odds mortality ratios by self-rated health status:

| Self-rated health status | Adjusted-odds mortality ratios |
|---|---|
| Excellent | 1.00 |
| Good | $1.82 \pm 0.4$ |
| Fair | $2.06 \pm 0.6$ |
| Poor | $2.87 \pm 1.3$ |

(16 studies, $n = 49\,516$)

Results appear to be quite consistent among studies and with respect to minor variations in the wording of the responses. Several other health status systems have been evaluated, as reviewed by Torrance (1986), by Donaldson et al. (1988), Nord (1992), and Murray (1994). Distinguishing these is a level of subjectivity associated with the

---

[28] Sole reliance on simple subjective health variables in the case of arthritis diagnosis was noted by Butler et al. (1987) to induce a systematic measurement bias towards better health for nonworking individuals.

Table 4
Self-rated health status and relationship with mortality (Idler, 1995)[a]

| Authors | Year | Cohort | n | F/U (years) | Analysis | Objective and controls | | Adjusted-odds ratios | | |
|---|---|---|---|---|---|---|---|---|---|---|
| | | | | | | Objective | controls | Good | Fair | Poor |
| Mossey and Shapiro | 1982 | E Canada | 3128 | 6 | LogReg | MD, self | Socio | 1.4 | 2.0 | 2.8 |
| Kaplan and Camacho | 1983 | A US | 6928 | 9 | LogReg | Self | Socio, psych | | | 1.9 |
| Kaplan et al. | 1988 | E Israel | 1078 | 5 | CoxPH | Self | Age, sex | 1.1 | 1.9 | 2.1 |
| Jagger and Clarke | 1988 | E England | 1203 | 5 | CoxPH | Self | Socio | | 1.3 | 2.1 |
| Idler et al. | 1990 | E US | 5909 | 4 | LogReg | Int, self | Socio, health | 1.9 | 2.5 | 4.0 |
| Idler and Angel | 1990 | A US | 6440 | 13 | CoxPH | MD | Socio, health | 1.9 | 2.2 | 2.8 |
| Idler and Kasl | 1991 | E US | 2812 | 4 | Cox, LR | Int, self | Socio, econo | 2.8 | 3.4 | 4.9 |
| Ho | 1991 | E Hong Kong | 1054 | 3 | LogReg | Self | Socio, health | | | 2.0* |
| Wannamethee et al. | 1991 | A England | 7725 | 4 | LogReg | Self | Socio, health | | 1.4 | |
| Wolinsky and Johnson | 1992 | A US | 5151 | 4 | LogReg | Self | Socio, health | | 1.9 | 2.2 |
| Shahtahmasebi et al. | 1992 | E Wales | 534 | 8 | Weibull | Self | Socio, psych | 1.5 | 2.0 | 2.4 |
| Pijls et al. | 1993 | A Netherlands | 783 | 5 | CoxPH | MD, self | Socio, health | 1.3 | 2.4 | 5.4 |
| Tsuji et al. | 1994 | A Japan | 2651 | 3 | CoxPH | Self | Socio | | 2.2 | 3.1 |
| McCallum et al. | 1994 | A Australia | 1050 | 7 | CoxPH | Self | Socio, psych | 1.3 | 1.7 | 2.4 |
| Schoenfeld et al. | 1994 | A US | 1192 | 3 | LogReg | Int, self | Socio, health | 1.4 | 2.0 | 2.8 |
| Dasbach et al. | 1994 | A US | 1878 | 8 | CoxPH | MD, self | Age, sex | | | 1.7* |
| Weighted averages (standard deviations) | | | 49516 | 6 | | | | 1.8(0.4) | 2.1(0.5) | 2.8(1.3) |

[a]Cohort age A = adults, E = elderly; objective Int = interviewer; (*) conversion "health relative to others" same = fair, worse = poor.

Table 5
Rosser and Watts disability–distress classification

| Index | Disability |
|-------|------------|
| 1 | No disability |
| 2 | Slight social disability |
| 3 | Severe social disability and/or slight impairment of performance at work. Able to do all household work except very heavy tasks |
| 4 | Choice of work or performance at work severely limited. Housewives and old people able to do light housework only, but able to go out shopping |
| 5 | Unable to undertake any paid employment. Unable to continue any education. Old people confined to home except for escorted outings and short walks and unable to do shopping. Housewives only able to perform a few simple tasks |
| 6 | Confined to chair or to wheelchair or able to move around the home only with support   from an assistant |
| 7 | Confined to bed |
| 8 | Unconscious |

| (Self-valuations) Disability index | Level of distress | | | |
|---|---|---|---|---|
| | None | Mild | Moderate | Severe |
| 1 | 1.000 | 0.995 | 0.990 | 0.967 |
| 2 | 0.990 | 0.986 | 0.973 | 0.932 |
| 3 | 0.980 | 0.972 | 0.956 | 0.912 |
| 4 | 0.964 | 0.956 | 0.942 | 0.870 |
| 5 | 0.946 | 0.935 | 0.900 | 0.700 |
| 6 | 0.875 | 0.845 | 0.680 | 0.000 |
| 7 | 0.677 | 0.564 | 0.000 | (−1.486) |
| 8 | (−1.028) | | | |

*Source*: Kind et al. (1982).

weights of functional status of the respondents. Perhaps one of the more interesting systems is the Rosser–Watts system (Table 5) which is discussed in Kind et al. (1982). For this system two of the (disability, distress) states, namely (unconscious,…) and (confined to bed, severe distress), are associated with a lower utility than death itself. Apparent contradictions between lifetime utility maximization and the deliberate choice of death by suicide or a living will may be rationalized within the Rosser–Watts system.

There are a number of examples of the use of health status measurement in the study of the determinants of mortality using the Retirement History Survey. Hausman and Wise (1985) study the effect of health, earnings, and Social Security payments on the retirement hazard. Their results indicate that increases in Social Security benefits between 1969 and 1975 resulted in a 3–5% increase in the probability of male retirement for those aged 62–66, while higher real earnings reduced the probability of retirement. Incentive effects of benefit cuts were also found in Fields and Mitchell (1984). Anderson and Burkhauser (1985) treat mortality and retirement as a jointly determined process and estimate the bivariate interaction effects of health and retirement. They find that health and retirement are jointly determined and that the use in empirical analysis of self-assessment measures of health instead of more objective measures exaggerates the influence of health on labor withdrawal and underestimates the importance of wages. Bazzoli (1985) focuses on the effect of a variety of health variables including a new self-evaluation of health status measures which she develops. She finds that previous studies had overestimated the effect of health on retirement and that pension and Social Security income have a larger impact on retirement than previously reported. Burtless (1987) analyzes the health status of 8131 males from the 1969–1979 waves of the RHS. Respondents were asked three self-reported questions as to health status: handicap or physical disability, relative health compared to others their own age, and the extent to which working was limited by health. Categorical responses to these three questions were ranked, and two multiperiod probit models of death were estimated by a maximum likelihood method (Butler and Moffitt, 1982). Burtless evaluates and estimates two models of death – as a continuation of subjectively reported health status below that of the lowest level reported by the respondents, and as an objective determination from deaths records. Each model is parametric for a normal distribution fit so that cumulative values (cross-sections) are consistent with the categorical responses as characteristic of an underlying continuum of health status. Burtless' findings are sensitive to the precise models of health status and death applied, particularly the relationship between occupational effects and mortality. Bound (1991) looks at the sensitivity of labor supply models to different health measures. He develops and estimates a model that incorporates self-reported measures of health and an objective measure (mortality) and finds that both measures result in biases but that the biases are in opposite directions.

In order to adjust the years of life to account for the health status, one can employ the disability- (or quality-) adjusted life-year (DALY), which relies on a determination of the health status measured for the individual during the year. Such a disability adjusted life-year measure was recently used by the World Bank (1993) in their comprehensive international study of shifts in mortality patterns and their policy implications. The quantity of life can then be defined as the sum of these year-states. Adjustments of years of life to DALY are not without ethical controversy, as reviewed by Busschbach et al. (1993) who note the work of Harris (1987) and Donaldson et al. (1988). The latter two studies contend that these adjustments result in evaluation of health care outcomes extremely unfavorable to the elderly population.

Developed by Robert Kaplan and John Anderson,[29] the Quality of Well-Being (QWB) index combines four measurement scales: mobility, physical activity, social activity, and symptom/problem complexes, building upon a body of theory in econom-

---

[29] See Kaplan and Bush (1982), Kaplan and Anderson (1988), Anderson et al. (1989).

Table 6
Quality of well-being index (Kaplan and Anderson, 1988)

| Step number | Index definition | Weight |
|---|---|---|
| *Mobility* | | |
| 1 | No limitations for health reasons | 0.0 |
| 2 | Did not drive a car, health related; did not ride in a car; and/or did not use public transportation, or had or would have used more help than usual for age to use public transportation, health related | −0.062 |
| 3 | In hospital | −0.090 |
| *Physical activity* | | |
| 1 | No limitations for health | 0.0 |
| 2 | In wheelchair, controlled movement of wheelchair without assistance; had trouble to lift, stoop, or use stairs or inclines; or limped, used a cane or had any other limitation in walking, health related | −0.060 |
| 3 | In wheelchair, did not move or control the wheelchair without help from someone else, or in bed, chair, or couch for most or all of the day, health related | −0.077 |
| *Social activity* | | |
| 1 | No limitations for health reasons | 0.0 |
| 2 | Limited in other (e.g. recreational) role activity, health related | −0.61 |
| 3 | Limited in major (primary) role activity, health related | −0.61 |
| 4 | Performed no major role activity, health related, but did perform self-care activities | −0.61 |
| 5 | Performed no major role activity, and did not perform or had more help than usual in performance of one or more self-care activities, health related | −0.106 |

ics, psychology, medicine, and public health.[30] In order to develop QWB, they evaluated the effects of disease and injuries upon behavior and role performance, constructing scales representing three aspects of daily functioning: mobility, physical activity, and social activity (Table 6), including subjective complaints by adding a symptom/problem complex. QWB reports a value between 0 and 1, defined as

$$QWB = 1 + CPX + MOB + PAC + SAC, \tag{4.1}$$

where *CPX* is individual's "score" on the Symptom/Problem scale, *MOB* is the Mobility scale, *PAC* is the Physical Activity scale, and *SAC* the Social Activity scale. Weights were estimated by data from a survey of at least eight measured days for each of 1025 subjects,[31] and these estimates have subsequently been tested across subsam-

---

[30] Rust (1990) analyzed the explanatory power of up to 75 health-related questions in the RHS and found that such health constraints on mobility as well as the subjective/objective four state health polytomy used by Sickles and Taubman were most relevant in explaining mortality hazard and the labor/leisure trade-off.

[31] A description of the empirical work can be found in Kaplan and Anderson (1988).

ples of the population. Sickles and Yazbeck (1995) augmented the QWB index with mortality information in the RHS in estimating the dynamic model life-cycle, Eqs. (3.15)–(3.19).

### 4.2.3. Aging, disability, and health status

The health status measures that we have discussed above attempt to deal in particular ways with the quality of life as mortality approaches. In attempting to quantify the quality of life in the later years, health measurement systems generally result in an index of health that is declining in age. The presence of a disability, which may also result in the placement of the individual in a nursing home, typically plays a relatively large role in weighing down health index measures. Moreover, the presence of an individual in a nursing home may also put in question the extent to which such individuals may be able to make decisions in accordance with the rational decision-making assumptions pursued in the economic models of health-augmenting allocations. A recent report by the Institute of Medicine (1990) pointed out that there was substantial scope for reducing disability in the elderly by better utilization of existing medical knowledge while Wolfe and Haveman (1990) and Stoto and Durch (1993) have noted that disability is not only becoming a more accepted condition but that better financial status has permitted an increasing number of elderly to identify themselves as disabled.

A number of studies have focused on issues such as these. Poterba and Summers (1987), using the NHIS, indicate that, between 1963 and 1982, the percentage of the elderly in nursing homes rose sharply for each age group 65–74, 75–84, and 85-and-older. For men aged 65–74, those residing in a nursing home rose from 0.68% to 1.23%, and for women 85+, from 17.5% in 1963 to 22.7% in 1982, although as pointed out by Garber and MaCurdy (1990) since the duration of stay for the high-risk elderly is relatively short, this segment of the elderly population may not be the heaviest user of long-term care. Another measure of wellness being demand for medical care, Poterba and Summers were able to show that Medicare expenditures rise sharply with age, slightly higher for women. For those aged 65–74, there was a 10% increase in restricted-activity days between 1961 and 1980, with no increase for those over 74. Multinomial analysis revealed remaining life expectancy to be significantly related to a restricted activity level. The financing of elderly long-term care is, of course, an issue seen by many as an example of market failure (see, for example Pauly, 1986; Gravelle and Taylor, 1989; Wolfe, 1993).

Manton et al. (1993) use the National Long Term Care Survey to study health utilization and mortality for about 20 000 elderly persons over the period 1982–1984. This sample initially contacted 33 000 people from Medicare's Health Insurance Master File, in order to determine if they were disabled in 1982. All of the disabled, and a subset of the non-disabled, were resurveyed in 1984. Corder and Manton examine (1) mortality and disability linkages, (2) death rates among the institutionalized, and (3) changes in patterns of mortality after a hospital stay. They find mortality rapidly increases with the level of disability and as the disabled age. Crimmins and Pramaggiore (1988) look at patterns of change in health and labor force participation between 1969 and 1981 and found no indication of improved health between 1970 and 1980 among men aged 56–64, but did find evidence of deteriorating health among the retired. Crimmins et al. (1989) update and extend the work of Poterba and Summers (1987). Using the NHIS and various Census sources, they find that for females age 65 years, 17.0 years of the expected remaining life of 18.4 years were spent outside any institution, that for 15.3 years of these years they could perform their major activity, and that for 9.3 of these years they had no long-term disability. At age 85, more than 65% of women's expected remaining life would be spent in a non-institutionalized status.

There has also been work on the implications of the disability system for labor force participation. Parsons (1980a, b) used a model of a worker's decision process under uncertainty to study the decline in male labor force participation in the US. He found evidence to confirm the hypothesis that labor force withdrawal was induced by the rapid expansion of welfare alternatives to work, principally the Social Security disability program. Fenn and Vlachonikolis (1986) develop a model of the labor force participation for the disabled using maximum likelihood techniques with a switching regression model and corrections for self-selection. Their data are taken from the 1976 Social and Community Planning Research unit in Oxford. Labor force participation varies by age, disability, and income in reduced-form equations estimated with logit methods. Holden (1988) studied the effects of ill health and employment in physically demanding occupations in the year before receipt of benefits. In the New Beneficiary Survey, employment in physically demanding jobs is associated with lower probability of work during retirement and having a work-limiting health condition decreased the probability of work. Sickles and Taubman (1986) use part of the Retirement History Survey to estimate a model of healthiness and retirement. They do not use a life-cycle model. They find a trade off in retirement between Social Security benefits and wage rates and a sharp decline in retirement before age 62, the earliest date non-disabled men are eligible for Social Security benefits. They also find that health is worse for those whose longest occupation is unskilled labor.

Liu et al. (1990) analyze 2123 participants in the Framingham sample who are 55 years or older and estimate Cox proportional hazard models over a period spanning ten years. These volunteers took a battery of eight neuropsychological tests, and Liu et al. find cognitive disparity associated with higher neuropsychological hazards, controlling for age and education. Those with marginal and poor cognitive skills had a relative risk of death of 1.37 and 1.66 respectively compared to those with no impairment in cognitive skills. Ellwood and Kane (1990) study death rates in the Panel Survey of Income Dynamics, a stratified random sample begun in 1969, with an over-representation of blacks. Focusing upon those people whose age was over 65 for at least three years, Ellwood and Kane find that disability, as well as marital status and age, is associated with higher death rates for both men and women, with the effect reversed for woman (marriage was negative for survival). Chirikos and Nestel (1991) study the extent to which occupation and impaired health explain variations in the functional capacity of older men to delay retirement. They use a competing risk framework of retirement, work disability, and death. The parameters of the hazard rate models are estimated with panel data covering a period of 17 years from the National Longitudinal Survey (NLS) of Labor Market Experience of Older Men. They find that health-related physical conditions play an important role in determining the ability of male workers to delay retirement.

The disincentive effects of programs such as the Social Security Disability Insurance program on labor force participation of older men has been studied by Bound and Waidman (1992) who extended the mostly cross-sectional studies of Leonard (1979), Parsons (1980a, b), Haveman and Wolfe (1984), Slade (1984), and Haveman et al. (1991). Building on his earlier work on identifying exogenous cross-sectional variations in replacement rates (Bound, 1989; Bound and Waidman, 1991), Bound examined these causal links using the National Health Interview Survey and found that between 1949 and 1987, as the program was substantially expanded, 25–33% of the 19.9% who dropped out of the labor force moved into the disability program. Recently, Waidmann et al. (1995) have pursued this line of research and have found, again with the National Health Interview Survey, that self-reported health limitation responses and labor force participation are jointly determined.

## 5. Statistical and numerical techniques

This section outlines developments in statistical and numerical treatments of mortality and morbidity modeling. The two broad classes of models are those which examine the duration of life or competing risks therein and those which model the healthiness of an individual.

### 5.1. Life-tables and mortality hazards

Life-table analyses of mortality are based upon an analytical framework in which death is viewed as an event whose occurrence is probabilistic in nature, although individual choices may have contributed to the relative risk of the event of death occurring.[32] These analyses require a characterization of the state of the individual as represented by various factors – acquired, environmental, or behavioral – combined with the survival status of the individual at the end of the data reporting period. Typically, a life-table analysis examines an age cohort of individuals, distinguished by a particular

---

[32] For excellent surveys of survival model methods see Kalbfeisch and Prentice (1980), Kiefer (1988), and T. Lancaster (1990).

risk factor status. Observed age-specific death rates are compared with those expected from all causes using a chi-squared contingency table approach. This is the basic approach pursued by a large body of demographic research during the last four decades (Dorn, 1958; Doll and Hill, 1964; Kitagawa and Hauser, 1973; Rogot et al., 1992b). The null hypothesis tested is usually the independence of risk-factor status and rate of death.

Although the life-table has been widely used as a survey prediction of an individual's risk of death, this technique suffers in design in that individuals are not required to survive in any consistent manner, as age-specific death rates are calculated independently of each other. We know, however, that there is an important additional structure within the data known as senescence, or increasing death rates with age[33] which, if ignored, can also bias estimates based on structural models of health. Use of known senescent trends in the survival data allows the researcher to extend the instantaneous death rates from life-tables to a model of long-term survival which can be estimated from longitudinal and panel data and which in turn allows for the effects of more complicated socioeconomic factors on mortality to be evaluated.

An important shortcoming of survival or hazard function estimates from life-tables concerns the time interval of the observations. Although events are often assumed to evolve in continuous time, data are compiled only periodically and discretely. Right-censoring (or for that matter left-censoring), due to the presence of underlying frailties undetected because of an often arbitrary choice of the data capture interval, may confound the investigator's attempt to properly deal with unobserved heterogeneity in mortality hazards (Heckman and Singer, 1984; Manton et al., 1986). A similar problem may exist in retrospective analyses of survival rates for the elderly using previous cohort experiences (Thatcher, 1992).

Assume that time is continuously distributed and that individuals at time $t$ are at instantaneous hazard of death $h(t)$. Certainty of death requires that the hazard function integrate to 1, and senescence requires that the hazard function be increasing. Denote by $s(t)$, the survival function at time $t$, that proportion of the population surviving until time $t$, which is equal to 1 minus the integral of the hazard function from time 0 until time $t$. Let $t_i$ be event time for individual $i$ and assume that life-table data are to be compiled over the interval $(t_i, t_i + \Delta t_i)$. A life-table constructed for this interval is expected to report a death rate $D(t)$ equal to the expectation of $h(t)$ over $(t_i, t_i + \Delta t_i)$, multiplied by $\Delta t_i$:

$$D(t_i, t_i + \Delta t_i) = \int_{t_i}^{\Delta t_i} h(t)\, dt \tag{5.1}$$

and the observed survival fraction at $t_i + \Delta t_i$ should represent $s(t_i + \Delta t_i)$. Estimates of the survival function (often observed to be exponential and/or logarithmic) and the

---

[33] This term has also been used by demographers and epidemiologists to apply to a list of concepts which distinguish different kinds of deaths, such as those which are caused by endogenous or exogenous factors and those which are premature instead of senescent (Stoto and Durch, 1993).

hazard function can be gotten from the Kaplan–Meier product limit estimator (Kaplan and Meier, 1958).

Aggregate data are not sufficient to test the null hypothesis of independence of risk factor status and risk of death, and cross-sectional analyses extend the analytical techniques of the demographer to the study of chosen behaviors. Recently, Foster (1991) develops a model wherein autocorrelation in cohort mortality rates can be used to estimate the extent of heterogeneity among the population, without need for strong assumptions of the distributional form of such heterogeneities, or of the hazard function itself.

Life-table analysis is distinguished by the fact that the data are inherently cross-sectional; a collection of anecdotes, if you will, of ordered pairs of state and survival status. With a null hypothesis of independence between risk factor status and risk of death, life-table analyses make a critical assumption of separability of the population into risk factor cohorts. Heterogeneities which may undoubtedly underlie particular survival advantages must remain consistently distributed within the surviving population, a questionable proposition. Human beings and their existences are complex phenomena, and exhaustive models are problematic. Inference may thus be compromised by bias associated with the classification system, and thus one cannot preclude risk status as an instrument or proxy for unobserved heterogeneities. As an example of the limitations of cross-sectional data to provide inference, consider the possible relationship between income and life expectancy. In the life-tables ordered pairs of data such as income status and life expectancy are analyzed. One causative hypothesis might be that those with higher incomes are less constrained in choices reflected in increased survival. However, the same ordered pairs of data would necessarily be consistent with the converse hypothesis that those endowed for longer survival have a choice advantage in intertemporal substitution reflected in higher socioeconomic status. Further, these same data would also be consistent with a non-causation hypothesis that socioeconomic status and life expectancy are proxies for underlying genetic endowments. Goldman (1993) has recently demonstrated the importance of this point. Using a straightforward "matching" model for marriage, she shows that cross-sectional data cannot be used to draw inference about the marriage pattern of reduced mortality as it is either reflective of a selection bias or a causal factor (e.g., a care giving factor). She proposes that the many studies which have so proceeded may be methodologically flawed.

## 5.2. Estimation of survival hazard models with heterogeneity

Consider first the continuous time duration model in which a nonnegative random variable $T$, say, time until death, has a density, $f(t)$, and a cumulative distribution, $F(t)$ (Kalbfleisch and Prentice, 1980; T. Lancaster, 1990). The hazard for $T$ is the conditional density of $T$ given $T > t$ and is given by

$$\lambda(t) = f(t| T > t) = \frac{f(t)}{[1 - F(t)]} \geq 0. \tag{5.2}$$

In terms of the integrated hazard, the density and distribution of $T$ are

$$f(t) = \lambda(t) \exp\left[-\int_0^t \lambda(\tau)\, d\tau\right], \tag{5.3}$$

$$F(t) = 1 - \exp\left[-\int_0^t \lambda(\tau)\, d\tau\right]. \tag{5.4}$$

Let $\delta = 1$ if the duration is right-censored and $\delta = 0$ otherwise. The distribution associated with realizations on $\delta$ is assumed to be independent of the survival time and is functionally independent of the survival distribution. The log likelihood function is

$$\ln L = \sum_i f(t)(1 - \delta) + \sum_i [1 - F(t)]\delta. \tag{5.5}$$

Following Vaupel et al. (1979), Heckman and Singer (1984), Manton et al. (1986), and Vaupel (1988) we can also allow for unobserved heterogeneity in genetic predispositions to death. As pointed out by a number of authors, failure to control for unobserved individual specific frailties can bias downward estimates of duration dependence in mortality hazard models, and in so doing confound the natural ordering between the propensity to die and morbidity states as well as (potentially) the impacts of other covariates. Alter and Riley (1989), for example, using mortality and morbidity data from British "friendly societies" in the nineteenth century, note that decreases in cohort age-specific mortality rates are observed over time because more frail individuals survived to reach old age due to advances in medical technology, while morbidity increased as these same individuals became more susceptible to non-fatal illnesses.

Treatments for heterogeneity which may be correlated with other covariates have utilized within type transformations of the linear probability model specification of mortality (see, for example, Rosenzweig and Schultz, 1983b) or for the alternative duration time model (Olsen and Wolpin, 1983). Instrumental variable estimators can also be used in a natural way to deal with the presence of endogenous choice variables. Because these models are linear, the complications that arise when the mortality state is linked to the covariates by the nonlinear logit or probit transformation can be circumvented and consistent standard errors can be based on a White (1980) type estimator. Fixed-effect treatments for logit type specifications (dead/not dead) have been pursued by Chamberlain (1980, 1983) and for tobit type specifications (censored length of life) by Honoré (1992).

### 5.2.1. Proportional hazard model

One of the more widely used mortality specifications is the proportional hazard model which expresses the natural logarithm of the conditional hazard of dying as a function of time. The accelerated time to failure model specifies the natural logarithm of length of life as a linear function of covariates, $\ln(T) = x\beta + \sigma\varepsilon$, where $\varepsilon$ is a random disturbance and $\sigma$ is a scale parameter. Failure time can be written as $T = \exp(x\beta)T_0^\sigma$ where $T_0$ is an event time drawn from a baseline distribution. Different parametric distributions are available to model unobserved genetic frailties $[\theta(t)]$. Also available are semiparametric estimators in which $\theta(t)$ is either factored out of the likelihood using Cox's partial likelihood (Cox, 1972) or is estimated by a finite support density estimator (Heckman and Singer, 1984). For parametric approaches, the normal distribution has an obvious genetic rationale and is parsimonious. The inverse Gaussian provides a quite flexible mixture (Manton et al., 1986), and allows for a very general description of biological risks.

To see how these statistical treatments can be implemented, consider the Weibull proportional hazard model for individual $i$:

$$h(t_i \mid x_i, \theta_i) = \exp(\gamma \ln t_i) \exp(x_i\beta + \theta_i). \tag{5.6}$$

The log hazard function is given by

$$\ln h(t_i \mid x_i, \theta_i) = \gamma \ln t_i + x_i\beta + \theta_i, \tag{5.7}$$

where $t_i$ is the continuous time of a completed spell, $x_i$ is a vector of exogenous time varying or constant covariates, and $\theta_i$ is unobserved scalar heterogeneity. Censored observations are given by

$$T_i = \min(t_i, t_c), \quad d_i = I(t_i < t_c), \tag{5.8}$$

where $t_c$ is the censored time of an incomplete spell and $I$ is an indicator function: $d_i = 1$ if $t_i < t_c$ and $d_i = 0$ otherwise.

Assuming independence over duration spells, the joint likelihood of duration times and unobserved heterogeneity is

$$L = \prod_i f(t_i, \theta_i \mid x_i), \tag{5.9}$$

where

$$f(t_i, \theta_i \mid x_i) = h(t_i, \theta_i) \exp\left[\int_0^t h(s_i, \theta_i \mid x_i)\, ds\right], \quad \text{if } d_i = 1, \tag{5.10}$$

$$f(t_i, \theta_i \mid x_i) = \exp\left[\int_0^t h(s_i, \theta_i \mid x_i)\, ds\right], \quad \text{if } d_i = 0. \tag{5.11}$$

The joint density is

$$f(t_i, \theta_i \,|\, x_i) = g(t_i \,|\, x_i, \theta_i)\mu(\theta_i) \tag{5.12}$$

and the marginal likelihood of duration times $f(t_i \,|\, x_i)$, is given by

$$L = \prod_i \int_0^t g(t_i \,|\, x_i, \theta_i)\mu(\theta_i)\, d\theta_i. \tag{5.13}$$

This likelihood function is a common form of the statistical mixture model. Control for $\mu(\theta)$ parametrically requires a distribution for $\theta$. However, an incorrect parameterization of $\mu(\theta)$ leads to estimation bias in both duration dependence effects and the parameters of included variables (Heckman and Singer, 1984).

### 5.2.2. Competing risk model

The use of single cause duration models for mortality modeling implicitly aggregates all causes of death into a single cause measure and thus may impart a misspecification due to differential risk factor effects for different types of diseases which ultimately cause death. Given the dynamic cause of death structure in the US (Manton and Stallard, 1982) this aggregation is problematic. Recently, Stoto and Durch (1993) have pointed out that age-adjusted death rates for 14 of the 15 leading causes of death in the US for 1950–1990 indicate that trends in particular competing risks of death are substantially different. The single cause duration model extends to competing risk models for cause of death (Cox, 1962; Tsiatis, 1975; Basu and Ghosh, 1978; Yashin et al., 1986). Consider two competing risks, each with a Weibull proportional hazard of mortality. Let $t_1$ be failure time were the first risk factor the only one present and let $t_2$ be failure time were the second risk factor the only one present. The density function associated with $t_j$, $j = 1,2$, takes the form

$$
\begin{aligned}
f(t_{ji}, \theta_i \,|\, x_i) &= h(t_{ji}, \theta_i)\exp\!\left[-\int_0^{t_{ji}} h(s, \theta_i \,|\, x_i)\, ds)\right], &&\text{if } t_{ji} < t_{jc}, \\
&= \exp\!\left[-\int_0^{t_{jc}} h(s, \theta_i \,|\, x_i)\, ds\right], &&\text{otherwise.}
\end{aligned}
\tag{5.14}
$$

Assume for the moment that mortality is due to risk factor 1 and that correlation between conditional proportional hazards for $t_1$ and $t_2$ is due to shared individual specific frailties, i.e. $\theta_i$ is common to the specifications of the two hazard functions for individual $i$. We observe a completed spell for $t_1$ ($t_1^*$) and calculate the contribution to the likelihood as $\Pr[t_2 > t_1^*, t_1^*]$, where

$$f(t_{1i}, t_{2i}, \theta_i \,|\, x_{1i}, x_{2i}) = g(t_{1i} \,|\, x_{1i}, \theta_i)\mu(\theta_i)g(t_{2i} \,|\, x_{2i}, \theta_i)\mu(\theta_i). \tag{5.15}$$

If the correlation between the risk factors is due to the shared frailty $\theta_i$ then $\Pr[t_2 > t_1^*, t_1^*]$ is calculated by first integrating out the heterogeneity, either by specifying the heterogeneity distribution parametrically or by using a finite support histogram method of Heckman and Singer, and then calculating the probability of observ-

gram method of Heckman and Singer, and then calculating the probability of observ-ing $t_1^*$. Heckman and Honoré (1989) and Han and Hausman (1990) have shown that even if $x_1$ and $x_2$ are identical, the competing risk model is identified so long as at least two covariates are continuous. Heckman and Taber (1994) have recently generalized these identifiability conditions. These results are quite important in light of the non-identifiability results of Cox (1962) and Tsiatis (1975) when covariates are not used.[34]

### 5.2.3. Semi-nonparametric method

Heckman and Singer's *nonparametric maximum likelihood estimator (NPMLE)* can be used to avoid the ad hoc specification of the mixing distribution $\mu(\theta)$ (Robbins, 1964; Laird, 1978; Heckman and Singer, 1982, 1984; Lindsay, 1983). Basically, this method reduces to the use of a finite support histogram to model $\mu(\theta)$. The EM algorithm (Dempster et al., 1977) has often been used to solve the likelihood equations. Appli-cation to the frailty model is accomplished by treating the sequence of unobservables $\{\theta_i\}$ as missing data. The estimator is consistent but the nature of its limiting distribu-tion is as yet not well understood. This estimator has been used in the study of adult health using the Dorn smoking sample by Behrman et al. (1990). They examine ro-bustness of estimates to functional form, individual heterogeneity, and cohort and time period variations, and note that both the Cox model and the Weibull proportional haz-ard model with no allowance for heterogeneity yield similar coefficients for the smoking variables, although the Heckman–Singer nonparametric methodology is judged best in terms of model fit.

*Maximum penalized likelihood estimation (MPLE)* provides another approach to dealing with unobserved heterogeneity but has been used less widely. It was intro-duced by Good and Gaskins (1971) and developed by De Montricher et al. (1975), and Silverman (1982). They examine the piecewise smooth estimation of an unknown density function after adding a term which penalizes unsmooth estimates:

$$\log L = \sum_{i=1}^{N} \log f(x_i) - \alpha R f(x), \tag{5.16}$$

where $f(x)$ is an unknown density, $R\{f(x)\} < \infty$, $R$ is a functional, and $\alpha$ is the smooth-ing parameter. The choice of $\alpha$ controls the trade-off between smoothness and good-ness-of-fit, while the choice of the penalty functional $R$ identifies the type of behavior considered undesirable.

Huh and Sickles (1994) detail how this model can be modified to handle unob-served variables under different assumptions about temporal and cross-sectional

---

[34] An alternative to the competing risks model is the grade-of-membership (GOM) methodology put forth by Berkman et al. (1989) and their colleagues in which fuzzy-set topology is used to catagorize heterogeneous individual health characteristics and mortality risks.

sources of heterogeneity that is uncorrelated with the observed variables. MPLE may have computational and convergence advantages over NPMLE in finite samples since roughness in the empirical heterogeneity distribution is smoothed from the likelihood by including penalty terms that take into account the degree of roughness or local variability not controlled for by covariates. MPLE is consistent as $\alpha/\sqrt{n} \rightarrow 0$ for bounded $\alpha$, if the mixing distribution can be characterized by a finite number of points of support. The NPMLE and the MPLE converge to the same function for large $N$ since the penalty term becomes negligible as estimates of unobserved heterogeneity become less rough.

Huh and Sickles compared the NPMLE and MPLE using Monte Carlo experiments. They find some discrepancies among the estimators over different experiments but estimates are similar when the underlying stochastic process is not too complicated and has been correctly modeled. Average point estimates display downward bias for both NPMLE and for MPLE. While downward bias in the duration dependence term is expected when heterogeneity is ignored and the data exhibit positive duration dependence, the source of the downward bias in the covariate effects is unclear. As the censoring rates became larger, both NPMLE and MPLE continue to underestimate the true parameter values, but NPMLE has a bigger bias. Since censoring increases the number of observations in the tails of the distribution, MPLE benefits substantially from the smoothing function of the penalty term.

### 5.2.4. Simulation methods

Simulation based probability estimators offer another approach to modeling complicated mortality experiences. Monte Carlo approaches to probability calculations are well known in the area of computer simulation and have received recent interest in econometrics (McFadden, 1989; Pakes and Pollard, 1989; Gourieroux and Monfort, 1992). As computing technology advances to handle bigger inputs with shorter processing time, computer intensive statistical methods have been introduced and developed to solve more complicated problems in stochastic process modeling. Simulation methods (Lerman and Manski, 1981; Diggle and Gratton, 1984) have many potential advantages and are seeing increasing use in econometric applications (see, for example, the special issues of the *Journal of Applied Econometrics*, 1994, and the *Review of Economics and Statistics*, 1994). Early approaches were based on frequency or density estimation. For example, the sequence of observations $\{x\}$ is used to construct an estimate of the true density, $\hat{f}$, and then independent realizations as required are drawn from $\hat{f}$. Construction of $\hat{f}$ is not an easy task and thus it may be desirable to simulate not from $\hat{f}$ itself but from the underlying data generating process (DGP) itself.

Below we outline how simulation based estimation (SIMEST) can be utilized to estimate a hazard model with unobserved heterogeneity. SIMEST is based on axioms that are assumed to govern the data generating process and does not require closed form expressions for the likelihood. The concepts of the simulation based estimation method used herein were introduced by Atkinson et al. (1983), Diggle and Gratton (1984) and Thompson et al. (1987) and are summarized in Thompson (1989).

Suppose that we wish to estimate only duration dependence ($\gamma$) without covariates. Ignoring subscripts for the moment, the hazard function for individual $i$ is

$$\lambda = t^{\gamma} \exp(\theta), \tag{5.17}$$

where $\gamma$ is the duration dependence parameter, $\theta$ is the unobserved heterogeneity component, and $t$ is time until failure.

Suppose that the transition of states follows the Poisson process. According to the Poisson axioms, the probability that failure can occur in the time interval $[0, t_i)$ is

$$\Pr[x(t+\Delta t) = 1] = \Pr[x(t) = 1]\Pr[x(\Delta t) = 0] + \Pr[x(t) = 0]\Pr[x(\Delta t) = 1)] + o(\Delta t). \tag{5.18}$$

Let the probability that one failure takes place in $[t, (t + \Delta t)]$ be $\lambda\Delta t$ for every $t$ in $[0, t)$ and the probability that more than one failure happens in $[t, (t + \Delta t)]$ be of order $o(\Delta t)$, where $\lim_{\Delta t \to 0} o(\Delta t)/\Delta t = 0$. Then

$$\Pr[x(t+\Delta t) = 1] = \Pr[x(t) = 1](1 - \lambda\Delta t) + \Pr[x(t) = 0](\lambda\Delta t) + o(\Delta t), \tag{5.19}$$

$$\frac{\Pr[x(t+\Delta t) = 1] - \Pr[x(t) = 1]}{\Delta t} = \lambda(\Pr[x(t) = 0] - \Pr[x(t) = 1]) + \frac{o(\Delta t)}{\Delta t}.$$

As $\Delta t \to 0$, $d\Pr[x(t) = 1]/dt = \lambda\{\Pr[x(t) = 0] - \Pr[x(t) = 1]\}$ and thus $\Pr[x(t) = 1] = \lambda t \exp(-\lambda t)$ and $\Pr[x(t) = 0] = \exp(-\lambda t)$. The cumulative distribution function for at least one failure on or before $t$ becomes $F(t) = 1 - \Pr[x(t) = 0] = 1 - \exp(-\lambda t)$.

A common practice is to use maximum likelihood with a parametric specification for the heterogeneity distribution and the probability density function of failure, $f(\cdot)$. An alternative approach is maximum likelihood based on a nonparametric specification of the heterogeneity distribution but with the form of the density function $f(\cdot)$ required. A third approach is to estimate the parameter $\gamma$ without formally specifying the probability density function.

First note that time to failure for all $n$ individuals is recorded as $t = (t_1 \leq t_2 \leq \cdots \leq t_n)$. Using this data we can divide the time axis into $k$ bins, the $m$th of which contains $n_m$ observations. Having an initial value for the parameter $\gamma$, the simulation mechanism is employed to generate a large number ($N$) of simulated failure times $s = (s_1 \leq s_2 \leq \cdots \leq s_N)$, where $N > n$. The simulation mechanism here is the cumulative distribution function $F(t) = 1 - \exp\{-\lambda(\cdot)f\}$ where $\lambda(\cdot) = t_i^{\gamma} \exp\{\theta_i\}$ is the Weibull proportional hazard. Then a random number $u_i$, $i = 1, \ldots, N$, is generated from the uniform distribution. Using the generated numbers, the simulated time to failure, $s_i$, can be generated by inverting $F(t)$. Let the number of simulated observations that fall into the $m$th bin be $v_{km}$. Then the simulated probability becomes $\hat{P}_{km}(\gamma_0) = v_{km}/N$. If the probability that the data fall in the corresponding bin is $P_m = n_m/N$, the natural criterion function is to minimize the distance between $\hat{P}_{km}(\gamma_0)$ and $P_m$. This turns out to be Pearson's goodness of fit. Thompson et al. suggest three possible criteria that remain unchanged when, for instance, two cells are combined into a single cell. The goodness of fit is defined as

$$S(\gamma_0) = \sum_{j=1}^{k} \frac{\hat{P}_{kj}(\gamma_0) - P_j}{P_j}, \tag{5.20}$$

where $k$ is the number of bins, and $\hat{P}_{kj}(\gamma_0)$ is the simulated probability of the $j$th bin with estimated parameter $\gamma_0$. The function is minimized when $\hat{P}_{kj}(\hat{\gamma}_0) = P_j, j = 1, \ldots, k$. Once the criterion function converges to a value $\hat{\gamma}$, confidence intervals for the true value of $\gamma$ can be derived using bootstrap methods (Thompson, 1989).

Next, suppose that the probability of failure follows the Poisson axioms and is conditional on a set of exogenous variables and duration time. Then the parameter $\lambda$ of the Poisson process is given by

$$\lambda = t^{\gamma_i} \exp(x_i \beta_i + \theta_i). \tag{5.21}$$

We wish to estimate the parameters $\delta = (\beta, \gamma)$ by SIMEST. Without loss of generality, we consider the case of one covariate $(x)$ and duration time $(t)$. Let $t = \{t_i(x_i)\}$, $i = 1, \ldots, n$, be failure time data conditional on the exogenous variable $x_i, i = 1, \ldots, n$, and let $k_1$ and $k_2$ be the number of bins dividing the time axis and the covariate axis, respectively. Let $m$ be the number of repeated simulations. Then simulated time to failure in the time axis is $0 \leq s_{11}(x_1), s_{12}(x_2), \ldots, s_{1n}(x_n), s_{21}(x_1), s_{22}(x_2), \ldots, s_{2n}(x_n), \ldots, s_{m1}(x_1), s_{m2}(x_2), \ldots, s_{mn}(x_n)$ with the corresponding value of the exogenous variable $x = \{x_i\}$ in the covariate axis. The number of these simulated times and values of a covariate which falls into the $(l_1, l_2)$th bin is denoted by $v_{l_1,l_2}$, where $l_1 = 1, \ldots, k_1$, $l_2 = 1, \ldots, k_2$. If $\delta_0$ is close to the true value, then the simulated bin probability

$$\hat{P}_{l_1 l_2}(\delta_0) = \frac{v_{l_1 l_2}}{n_m} \tag{5.22}$$

should approximate the corresponding portion of data (time and a covariate) in the same bin,

$$P_{l_1 l_2} = \frac{n_{l_1 l_2}}{n}. \tag{5.23}$$

A minor modification of the criterion is necessary since the presence of empty bins makes Pearson's goodness of fit criterion uninformative. To prevent this, the modified Pearson goodness of fit is given by

$$
S_m(\delta) = \sum_{l_1=1}^{k_1} \sum_{l_2=1}^{k_2} \frac{(\hat{P}_{l_1 l_2}(\delta) - P_{l_1 l_2})^2}{P_{l_1 l_2}}, \quad \text{if } \hat{P}_{l_1 l_2}(\delta) = 0,\ P_{l_1,l_2} \neq 0,
$$

$$
= \sum_{l_1=1}^{k_1} \sum_{l_2=1}^{k_2} \frac{(\hat{P}_{l_1 l_2}(\delta) - P_{l_1 l_2})^2}{\hat{P}_{l_1 l_2}}, \quad \text{if } \hat{P}_{l_1 l_2}(\delta) \neq 0,\ P_{l_1,l_2} = 0, \tag{5.24}
$$

$$
= 0, \qquad\qquad\qquad \text{otherwise.}
$$

The modified minimization criterion substitutes the observation probability with the simulated probability when the observed probability of a certain bin is zero. This may be possible since the simulated probability should approximate the observation probability if the estimate of parameter $\delta$ is close to the true value. The criterion is also minimized when $P_{l_1,l_2} = \hat{P}_{l_1,l_2}(\delta_0)$, $l_1 = 1, \ldots, k_1$, $l_2 = 1, \ldots, k_2$.

McFadden (1989) has pointed out that numerical breakdowns in standard algorithms can be caused by discontinuities in the simulated objective function. Thus kernel-based procedures are often pursued to smooth the discontinuities. Scott's (1979, 1985, 1992) method of average-shifted histograms has been used with success in the hazard model with heterogeneities by Huh and Sickles (1994). Other smoothing techniques for the simulated frequency, maximum simulated likelihood, and simulated method of moments estimators are discussed in McFadden (1989), Stern (1992), McFadden and Ruud (1994), Geweke et al. (1994), and Hajivassiliou et al. (1996).

Conditions for consistency and asymptotic normality of the simulation-based estimator are shown in Lerman and Manski (1981). McFadden (1989) and Pakes and Pollard (1988) prove similar results for alternative simulation estimators for finite numbers of simulations.

### 5.3. Estimation of models of morbidity with heterogeneity/classical MLE

We next turn to *classical maximum likelihood estimators*. As an example we choose the simultaneous static model of morbidity which can be linked to labor force participation or to the labor supply decision based on a model considered in Lee (1982), Sickles and Taubman (1986), Burtless (1987) and Sickles (1989). The model is an extension of the single equation limited dependent variable model of Heckman (1976). The longitudinal nature of the data set is accommodated by using a conventional error components specification in which heterogeneity among individuals is modeled as a random effect. There are two equations in the system: the first models the unobservable health stock while the second links the observed health status to the retirement decision. The system can be written as

$$y_{it}^{*(1)} = x_{it}^{(1)} \beta_1 + \varepsilon_{it}^{(1)},$$

$$y_{it}^{*(2)} = \gamma_2 y_{it}^{(1)} + x_{it}^{(2)} \beta_2 + \varepsilon_{it}^{(2)},$$

$$(5.25)$$

for $i = 1, \ldots, N$; $t = 1, \ldots, T$,

$$\varepsilon_{it}^{(j)} = \mu_i^{(j)} + \nu_{it}^{(j)}, \quad j = 1,2,$$

$$(5.26)$$

and where

$$
\begin{aligned}
E[\varepsilon_{it}^{(j)} \varepsilon_{ks}^{(\ell)}] &= \sigma_\mu^{(j)} + \sigma_\varepsilon^{(j)}, & j = l,\ i = k,\ t = s, \\
&= \sigma_\mu^{(j)}, & j = l,\ i = k,\ t \neq s, \\
&= \sigma_{\nu^{(1)}} \sigma_{\nu^{(2)}}, & j \neq l,\ i = k,\ t = s, \\
&= 0, & \text{elsewhere.}
\end{aligned}
$$

$$(5.27)$$

Here $x_{it}^{(1)}$ and $x_{it}^{(2)}$ are $(1 \times k_1)$ and $(1 \times k_2)$ vectors of exogenous variables, $\beta_1$ and $\beta_2$ are conformable vectors of structural coefficients, $\gamma_2$ is a scalar, $j_{it}^{*(1)}$ and $j_{it}^{*(2)}$ are the latent variables for healthiness and leisure, respectively, and $y_{it}^{(1)}$ and $y_{it}^{(2)}$ are their observed counterparts; $\varepsilon_{it}^{(1)}$ and $\varepsilon_{it}^{(2)}$ are the structural disturbances that are decomposed by the rule in Eq. (5.26). The latent variables are linked to the observed indicators by the following rules:

$$y_{it}^{(1)} = j, \quad \text{if } A_{j-1}^{(1)} - x_1 \beta_1 < \varepsilon_{it}^{(1)} \leq A_j^{(1)} - x_1 \beta_1, \quad j = 1,\ldots,J_1,$$

$$(5.28)$$

with $A_0^{(1)}$, $A_{J_1}^{(1)}$, normalized at $-\infty$ and $+\infty$, respectively, and

$$y_{it}^{(2)} = j, \quad \text{if } A_{j-1}^{(2)} - x_2 \beta_2 < \varepsilon_{it}^{(2)} \leq A_j^{(2)} - x_2 \beta_2, \quad j = 1,\ldots,J_2,$$

$$(5.29)$$

with $A_0^{(2)}$, $A_{J_2}^{(1)}$, normalized at $-\infty$ and $+\infty$, respectively.

The data Sickles and Taubman analyzed was a panel of five biennial waves of about 800 males drawn from the approximately 11 000 individuals in the Retirement History Survey. A computational issue arises when implementing maximum likelihood since calculation of the joint probabilities of observing differing configurations of health–retirement states for the same individual over the $T$ time periods of health–retirement states is problematic if the number of time periods is large. Numerical methods for handling the ten-period integration problem are available (Clark, 1964) but are both computationally burdensome and have an approximation error that is difficult to bound. Although moment based alternatives to maximum likelihood exist (McFadden, 1989; Pakes and Pollard, 1989) the direct evaluation of multidimensional integral is practical due to the particular structure of the correlation pattern of disturbances implied by the variance components model, a point which was originally noted by Butler and Moffitt (1982) and applied to the univariate probit model. Computational details for utilizing Gaussian quadrature techniques can be found in Butler and Moffitt (1982) and in Sickles and Taubman (1986).

Because computation of the joint probabilities is problematic when different correlation patterns and/or limited dependent variable structures are used, a more attractive alternative to classical maximum likelihood is *simulated maximum likelihood* (Albright et al., 1977), Hajivassiliou and McFadden (1990), Geweke (1991), Keane (1994), and Geweke et al. (1994) have demonstrated the appeal of this estimator using the GHK probability simulator in the multinomial probit model. Semiparametric maximum likelihood alternatives to exact maximum likelihood of the simultaneous latent variable model have been pursued by Ichimura (1993), Klein and Spady (1993), Lee (1995), and have been pursued empirically by Lee et al. (1995) in their structural equations semi-parametric study of family allocations and child health.

### 5.4. Alternative estimators for structural dynamic models of health

*Generalized method of moments* (Hansen, 1982) or *simulated method of moments* (McFadden, 1989; Pakes and Pollard, 1989) are natural approaches to estimate the dynamic model in Section 3.2.5. Recently, Haveman et al. (1994) utilized the former estimator to investigate a three-equation simultaneous model of health, work-time, and wages using panel data from the PSID. To proceed with estimation, one first selects a parametric form for the utility and production function which is specified in terms of a set of parameters ($\beta$). Letting $X_{it}$ be the vector of variables entering the $i$th individual's ($G$) first-order conditions in period $t$, the ($1 \times G$) system can be expressed as $f(X_{it}, \beta) = \varepsilon_{i,t+1}$. Rationality and its implication that information in $\Omega_{it}$ is of no help in forecasting future shocks implies that $E[f(X_{it}, \beta) \otimes Z_{it}] = 0$, where $Z_{it}$ is a ($1 \times h$) matrix of elements of $\Omega_{it}$. The population orthogonality conditions for the years that the panel data are available can be derived by averaging over time

$$\mathrm{E}\left(\frac{1}{T}\sum_{t=1}^{T}[f(X_{it}, \beta) \otimes Z_{it}]\right) = \mathrm{E}[M(X_i, Z_i, \beta)]. \tag{5.30}$$

Sample analogues are then constructed by averaging over the sample of $N$ individuals,

$$O_N(\beta) = \mathrm{E}\left(\frac{1}{N}\sum_{i=1}^{N}[M(X_i, Z_i, \beta)]\right) \tag{5.31}$$

and generalized method of moments estimates of $\beta$ are defined as the

$$\text{argmin}[O_N(\beta)W_N O'_N(\beta)],\tag{5.32}$$

where $W_N$ is the symmetric positive definite weighting matrix

$$W_N = W_N^* = S_N^{-1} = \left(\sum_{i=1}^{N} M(X_i, Z_i, \hat{\beta})' M(X_i, Z_i, \hat{\beta})\right)^{-1}\tag{5.33}$$

and where consistent first step estimates of $\beta$ are based on setting the weighting matrix $W_N$ to the identity matrix.

The asymptotic covariance matrix for the gmm estimator is

$$\Phi = (D_N^1 S_N^{-1} D_N)^{-1}, \quad D_N = \sum_{i=1}^{N}(\partial M(X_i, Z_i, \hat{\beta})/\partial\beta).\tag{5.34}$$

This approach has great appeal as well as considerable overlap with the estimation theory behind the simulated score estimator based on distributional instead of moment assumptions (McFadden and Ruud, 1994).

There are a rich set of extended model specifications and empirical approaches that have been pursued and can be utilized to deal with particular aspects of matching the theoretical models of health with empirical methodologies. As noted above, individual specific heterogeneity can be included directly in the production or utility function, either of which can be specified in terms of a set of observable individual specific variables or unobservable frailties/heterogeneities. Moreover, other types of latent structures can be dealt with in the context of this estimator by utilizing a finite draw from the heterogeneity or latent structure distribution and averaging the moments, essentially integrating out the heterogeneity or latent structure from the Euler equations (McFadden, 1989; Pakes and Pollard, 1989). This is computationally intensive but promises to be more widely used as computing cycles become increasingly less expensive. McFadden and Ruud (1994) recently extended the simulated method of moments to more general cases by utilizing simulated bias corrections. Distributional assumptions can also be the basis for estimation, either using exact maximum likelihood or simulated maximum likelihood. Geweke et al. (1994) have pursued alternative sampling algorithms for the simulated maximum likelihood estimator as well as the kernel-smoothed frequency estimator considered in Huh and Sickles (1994) and elsewhere. The Geweke et al. results point to the advantage of Gibbs sampling in the simulation exercise. Moreover, because such key variables as leisure choice are often constrained or are categorical for adults and the elderly due to retirement or various states of labor force status, dynamic discrete methods are often employed as opposed to Kuhn–Tucker constraints on leisure or an explicit construction of virtual wage rates that correspond to the observed limit observations (Wales and Woodland, 1983; Lee and Pitt, 1986; Ransom, 1987; and Hurd, 1990, Chapter 16, this volume, with respect to retirement specifically). In different contexts, exact and approximate solutions for the dynamic discrete model have been explored by, among others, Gotz and McCall (1984), Miller (1984), Wolpin (1987), Pakes (1987), Rust (1987, 1989), Eckstein and Wolpin (1989), Berkovec and Stern (1991), Hotz and Miller (1993), Hotz et al. (1994), Keane (1994), and Stern (1994).

A particularly appealing approach to estimating the discrete-state/discrete-time case of the dynamic programming model outlined in Section 3 has been put forth by Rust (1989, 1990, 1995). With estimates of the Markov transition probability densities for the stochastic laws of motion as inputs, Rust is able to estimate the underlying utility structure using his nested fixed point maximum likelihood algorithm (Rust, 1989). Rust analyses a model in which the control variables are consumption, a trichotomous work decision (full time, part time, retired), and a Social Security decision, with health status, among other variables, as a state variable, and with the augmented mortality data supplied by Taubman and utilized by Sickles and Taubman (1986) in their retirement-health model. A formal treatment of unobserved heterogeneity is not undertaken although reduced-form proxies for "worker beliefs" are included in his analyses. His findings are intuitive and offer an important computationally-intensive alternative to standard closed form approaches to dynamic optimization found in the literature. Backward recursion is the main method for solving this problem. When there is a finite number of states, the value function represents a finite list of options for each given state. One then maximizes the value function in each period starting from the last period and works backward through each prior period. A problem with this method is the total number of computing operations required. The number of operations depends on the number of time periods, states, and actions. The bulk of computations occurs in the evaluation of conditional expectations of the value function for each possible combination of state, action, and time. Rust implements a method which exploits the special sparsity structure of the transition probability matrix to speed up the procedure which is described in detail in Rust (1989, 1995). The solution algorithm is modified somewhat when the planning horizon is infinite. There are two main methods for numerical solutions in this case: successive approximation and policy iteration. These methods take advantage of the fact that the solution to the infinite horizon problem can be found by computing a fixed point of the Bellman operator.

Successive approximation, also referred to as value function iteration, starts with an arbitrary guess for a solution of Bellman's equation and the Bellman operator is simply iterated. By the contraction mapping theorem, this algorithm will find a fixed point and thus a solution to the problem. An initial guess of the Bellman equation equal to zero is equivalent to solving an approximate finite-horizon problem by backward induction. It is important to note that successive approximation converges linearly and is thus a relatively slow procedure.

The policy iteration method starts by choosing an arbitrary initial policy function which is used to update the value function in the following period. In infinite horizon problems, one is interested only in the stationary optimal policy of the problem. In the policy iteration, each time a new policy function is computed a new value function is computed as if that policy were used forever. Then, with this new value function, one derives a new policy function and again computes the value function. This procedure is repeated until convergence of the policy function, and thus the value function.

A final procedure that we discuss is related to the work of Rust but utilizes computational methods to approximate the Bellman equation using continuous time models. This avoids the necessity of deriving explicit Euler equations and may allow for a richer menu of stochastic assumptions concerning, among others, heterogeneity and discrete control variates. Judd (1994, 1995) and others have pursued this approach based on orthogonal polynomial approximations to the Bellman equation. Instead of discretization methods used for solving problems of continuous state problems, the value function is approximated with continuous functions. The only restrictions that enter into the value function are imposed through the state and control variables. In this method, one considers a finitely parameterizable collection of functions, where the functional form could be a linear combination of orthogonal polynomials. The value function $V(x)$ is approximated by $\hat{v}(X; \alpha)$ where $\alpha$ is a vector of coefficients. Once the basic functional forms are determined, e.g., a linear combination of orthogonal polynomials, splines, or neural networks, one focuses on finding the coefficients $\alpha$ so that the function $\hat{v}(X; \alpha)$ approximately satisfies the Bellman equation by choosing a residual function to estimate coefficients. For more detail on these procedures see Judd and Solnick (1994) and Judd (1995). Keane and Wolpin (1994) have recently also pursued simulation approaches to solve the dynamic discrete choice model using a combination of Monte Carlo integration and regression based interpolations as alternatives to the polynomial approximations suggested in Bellman et al. (1963). These and other alternatives, such as those proposed by Judd (1995) which utilize orthogonal polynomials or other series approximations for Bellman's equation, appear particularly attractive for future research on health using highly structured models which consider such issues as heterogeneity, discrete state and control variables, and constraints.

Although the statistical and numerical treatments covered in this section are not exhaustive, they do cover most of the generic approaches to modeling mortality and morbidity, and offer up alternatives to univariate approaches that have typically been used in biostatistics. The lack of a controlled experimental setting in survey research on mortality and morbidity pushes the researcher away from univariate methods such as the Kaplan–Meier product limit estimator of simple life-tables and toward the multivariate techniques we have outlined.

## 6. Comments and conclusions

This chapter has pointed to the converging paths that demographic, epidemiologic, biological, and socio-economic paradigms must take in order for the study of mortality and morbidity of adults and the elderly to bear fruitful results. It is clear that central to the study of such a complex issue is the availability of data monitoring systems that provide accurate information on disease etiology and specific causes-of-death as well as the plethora of economic, biological, lifestyle and behavioral, and other risk factors whose relevance to mortality and morbidity outcomes we have discussed in this chapter. Grossman's (1982b) commentary on the width of scope for theoretical work to guide future empirical study on the topic of mortality and morbidity of adults and the elderly (Gravelle, 1984) appears just as relevant today as it was a decade ago, augmented with the additional comment that the scope for emerging empirical and computational methods to implement the theoretical advances is just as wide.

# References

Aaron, H. and W. Schwartz (1984), The painful prescription (Brookings Institute, Washington, DC).

Aigner, D., C.A.K. Lovell and P. Schmidt (1977), "Formulation and estimation of stochastic production function models", Journal of Econometrics 6: 21–37.

Akerman, A. and S. Fischbein (1991), "Twins: are they at risk?", Acta Geneticae Medicae et Gemellologiae 40: 29–40.

Akin, J., D.K. Guilkey and B. Popkin (1990), "The production of infant health: input demand and health status differences related to gender of the infant", in: T. Schultz, ed., Research in population economics, Vol. 7 (J.A.I. Press, Greenwich, CT).

Albright, R., S. Lerman and C. Manski (1977), Report on the development of an estimation program for the multinomial probit model, Report prepared by Cambridge Systematics for the Federal Highway Administration.

Alter, G. and J. Riley (1989), "Frailty, sickness and death: models of morbidity and mortality in historical populations", Population Studies 43: 25–46.

Anderson, K. and R. Burkhauser (1985), "The retirement health nexus: a new measure of an old puzzle", Journal of Human Resources 20: 315–333.

Anderson, K., R. Burkhauser and J. Quinn (1986), "Do retirement dreams come true? The effect of unanticipated events on retirement plans", Industrial Labor Relations Review 39: 518–526.

Anderson, J.P., R.M. Kaplan, C.C. Berry, J.W. Bush and R.G. Rumbaut (1989), "Interday reliability of function assessment for a health status measure", Medical Care 27: 1076–1084.

Andrews, G., A. Esterman, A. Braunack-Mayer and C. Rungie (1986), "Aging in the Western Pacific" (World Health Organization Regional Office for the Western Pacific, Manila).

Anson, J. (1991), "Demographic indices as social indicators", Environmental Planning A 23: 433–446.

Ashenfelter, O. and A. Krueger (1994), "Estimates of the economic return to schooling from a new sample of twins", American Economic Review 84: 1157–1174.

Ashton, C., T. Weiss, N. Peterson, N. Wray, T. Menke and R.C. Sickles (1994), "Changes in VA hospital use, 1980–1990", Medical Care 32: 447–458.

Atkinson, E., R. Bartoszynski, B. Brown and J. Thompson (1983), "Simulation techniques for parameter estimation in tumor-related stochastic processes", Proceedings of the 1983 Computer Simulation Conference (North-Holland, New York).

Attanasio, O.P. and H.W. Hoynes (1995), "Differential mortality and wealth accumulation", Working paper no. 5126 (NBER, Cambridge, MA).

Auerbach, A.J., L.J. Kotlikoff, R.P. Hagemann and G. Nicoletti (1989), "The economic dynamics of an ageing population: The case of four OECD countries", OECD Economic Studies 12: 97–130.

Bailit, H., J. Federico and W. McGivney (1995), "Use of outcomes studies by a managed care organization: Valuing measured treatment effects", Medical Care 33: S216.

Ba Loc, P. (1990), "The environment and cancer", Journal of Environmental Pathology 10: 273.

Bartel, A. and P. Taubman (1979), "Health and labor market success: the role of various diseases", Review of Economics and Statistics 61: 1–8.

Bartel, A. and P. Taubman (1986), "Some economic and demographic consequences of mental illness", Journal of Labor Economics 4: 243–256.

Basu, A.P. and J.K. Ghosh (1978), "Identifiability of the multinormal and other distributions under competing risks model", Journal of Multivariate Analysis 8: 413–429.

Bazzoli, G. (1985), "Does educational indebtedness affect physician specialty choice?", Journal of Health Economics 4: 1–19.

Becker, G.S. and K.M. Murphy (1988), "A theory of rational addiction", Journal of Political Economy 96: 675–700.

Becker, G.S., M. Grossman and K.M. Murphy (1991), "Rational addiction and the effect of price on consumption", American Economic Review 81: 237–241.

Becker, G.S., M. Grossman and K.M. Murphy (1994), "An empirical analysis of cigarette addiction", American Economic Review 84: 396–418.

Beebe, G. and A. Simon (1969), "Ascertainment of mortality in the U.S. veteran population", American Journal of Epidemiology 89: 636–643.

Behrman, J.R. (1993), "The economic rationale for investing in developing countries", World Development 21: 1749–1772.

Behrman, J.R. and A. Deolalikar (1987), "Will developing country nutrition improve with income? A case study for rural South Africa", Journal of Political Economy 95: 108–138.

Behrman, J.R. and A. Deolalikar (1989), "Wages and labor supply in rural India: the role of health, nutrition and seasonality", in: D.E. Sahn, ed., Causes and implications of seasonal variability in household food security (Johns Hopkins University Press, Baltimore, MD).

Behrman, J.R. and T. Srinivasan, eds. (1995), Handbook of development economics, Vol. 3 (North-Holland, Amsterdam).

Behrman, J.R. and B. Wolfe (1987), "How does mother's schooling affect family health, nutrition, medical care usage, and household sanitation?", Journal of Econometrics 36: 185–204.

Behrman, J.R., M. Rosenzweig and P. Taubman (1994), "Endowments and the allocation of schooling in the family and in the marriage market: the twins experiment", Journal of Political Economy 102: 1131–1174.

Berhman, J.R., M. Rosenzweig and P. Taubman (1995), "Individual endowments, college choice and wages: estimates using data on female twins", Mimeo.

Behrman, J.R., R.C. Sickles and P. Taubman (1988), "Age specific death rates", in: E. Lazear and R. Ricardo-Campbell, eds., Issues in contemporary retirement (Hoover Institution, Stanford, CA).

Behrman, J.R., R.C. Sickles and P. Taubman (1990), "Age specific death rates with tobacco smoking and occupational activity: sensitivity to sample length, functional form, and unobserved frailty", Demography 27: 267–284.

Behrman, J.R., R.C. Sickles, P. Taubman and A. Yazbeck (1991), "Black–white mortality inequalities", Journal of Econometrics 50: 183–204.

Behrman, J.R., Z. Hrubec, P. Taubman and T. Wales (1980), Socioeconomic success: a study of the effects of genetic endowments, family environment and schooling (North-Holland, Amsterdam).

Bellman, R., R. Kalaba and B. Kotkin (1963), "Polynomial approximation: a new computational technique in dynamic programming allocation processes", Mathematics of Computation 1: 155–161.

Berger, M., G. Bloomquist, D. Kenkel and G. Tolley (1987), "Valuing changes in health risks: comparison of alternative measures", Southern Economic Journal 53: 967–984.

Berkman, L., B. Singer and K. Manton (1989), "Black/white differences in health status and mortality among the elderly", Demography 26: 661–678.

Berkovec, J. and S. Stern (1991), "Job exit behavior of older men", Econometrica 59: 189–210.

Bernheim, B.D. (1988), "Social security benefits: an empirical study of expectations and realizations", in: E. Lazear and R. Ricardo-Campbell, eds., Issues in contemporary retirement (Hoover Institution, Palo Alto, CA).

Bernheim, B.D. (1989), "The timing of retirement: a comparison of expectations and realizations", in: D. Wise, ed., The economics of aging (University of Chicago Press, Chicago, IL).

Bernheim, B.D. (1990), "How do the elderly form expectations? An analysis of responses to new information", in: D. Wise, ed., Issues in the economics of aging (University of Chicago Press, Chicago, IL).

Billings, P. and J. Beckwith (1993), "Studies that purport to show a genetic basis for homosexuality, or any other pattern of human behavior, are flawed", Technology Review 96: 60–62.

Bodie, Z. (1990), "Pension as retirement income insurance", Journal of Economic Literature 28: 28–49.

Bös, D. and R.K. Von Weizsäcker (1989), "Economic consequences of an aging population", European Economic Review 33: 345–354.

Bound, J. (1989), "The health and earnings of rejected disability insurance applicants", American Economic Review 79: 482–503.

Bound, J. (1991), "Self-reported versus objective measures of health in retirement models", Journal of Human Resources 26: 106–138.

Bound, J. and T. Waidman (1991), "Accounting for trends in self-reported disability", Mimeo.

Bound, J. and T. Waidman (1992), "Disability transfers, self-reported health and the labor force attachment of older men: evidence from the historical record", Quarterly Journal of Economics 107: 1393–1420.

Bound, J., D.A. Jaeger and R. Baker (1993), "The cure can be worse than the disease: a cautionary tale regarding instrumental variables", Working paper no. 137 (NBER, Cambridge, MA).

Bradshaw, B.S. and K. Liese (1991), "Mortality of Mexican-origin persons in the southwestern United States", in: I. Rosenwaike, ed., Mortality of Hispanic populations (Greenwood, Westport, CT).

Brenner, M. (1983), "Mortality and economic instability: detailed analyses for Britain", in: J. John, ed., Influence of economic instability on health (Springer, Berlin).

Burkhauser, R.V., J.S. Butler, J.M. Mitchell and T.P. Pincus (1986), "Effects of arthritis on wage earnings", Journal of Gerontology 41: 277–281.

Burney, M. (1992), "The role of environment in cancer incidence in Pakistan", Journal of Environmental Pathology 11: 355.

Burtless, G. (1986), "Social security, unanticipated benefit increases, and the timing of retirement", Review of Economic Studies 53: 781–806.

Burtless, G. (1987), "Occupational effects on the health and work capacity of older men", in: G. Burtless, ed., Work, health and income among the elderly (Brookings Institution, Washington, DC).

Burtless, G. and R. Moffitt (1984), "The effect of social security benefits on the labor supply of the aged", in: H. Aaron and G. Burtless, eds., Retirement and economic behavior (Brookings Institution, Washington, DC).

Busschbach, J., D. Hessing and F. Charro (1993), "The utility of health at different stages in life: a quantitative approach", Social Science and Medicine 37: 153–158.

Butler, J.S., R.V. Burkhauser, J.M. Mitchell and T.P. Pincus (1987), "Measurement error in self-reported health variables", Review of Economics and Statistics 69: 644–650.

Butler, J.S. and R. Moffitt (1982), "A computationally efficient quadrature procedure for the one-factor multinomial probit", Econometrica 50: 861–864.

Byne, W. (1994), "The biological evidence challenged", Scientific American 270: 50–56.

Califano, J. (1986), America's health care revolution: who lives? who dies? who pays? (Random House, New York).

Cebu Study Team (1992), "A child health production function estimated from longitudinal data", Journal of Development Economics 38: 323–351.

Chaloupka, F.J. (1991), "Rational addictive behavior and cigarette smoking", Journal of Political Economy 99: 722–742.

Chaloupka, F.J. (1995), "Economic models of habitual and addictive behavior: empirical applications to cigarette smoking", in: L. Green, ed., Advances in behavioral economics, Vol. 3 (JAI Press, Greenwich, CT).

Chamberlain, G. (1980), "Analysis of covariance with qualitative data", Review of Economic Studies 47: 225–238.

Chamberlain, G. (1983), "Panel data", in: Z. Griliches and M. Intriligator, eds., Handbook of econometrics (North-Holland, Amsterdam).

Chirikos, T. and G. Nestel (1991), "Occupational differences in the ability of men to delay retirement", Journal of Human Resources 26: 1–26.

Christenson, B. and N. Johnson (1995), "Educational inequality in adult mortality: an assessment with death certificate data from Michigan", Demography 32: 215–229.

Clark, C. (1964), "The greatest of a finite set of random variables", Operations Research 9: 145–162.

Clement, D.G., S.M. Retchin, R.S. Brown and M.H. Stegall (1994), "Access and outcomes of elderly patients enrolled in managed care", Journal of the American Medical Association 271: 1487–1492.

Coale, A.J. and E.E. Kisker (1985), "Mortality crossovers: reality or bad data?", Population Studies 40: 389–401.

Coleman, J. (1988), "Social capital in the creation of human capital", American Journal of Sociology 94: S95–S120.

Condran, G., C. Himes and S. Preston (1991), "Old age mortality patterns in low-mortality countries: an evaluation of population and death data at advanced ages, 1950 to present", Population Bulletin of the United Nations no. 30: 23–61 (UN, New York).

Cooper, R., M. Steinhauser, A. Schatzkin and W. Miller (1981), "Improved mortality among U.S. blacks, 1968–1978: the role of antiracist struggle", International Journal of Health Services 11: 511–522.

Corman, H. and M. Grossman (1985), "Determinants of neonatal mortality rates in the U.S.", Journal of Health Economics 4: 213–236.

Cornwell, C., P. Schmidt and R.C. Sickles (1990), "Production frontiers with cross-sectional and time-series variation in efficiency levels", Journal of Econometrics 46: 185–200.

Cox, D.R. (1962), Renewal theory (Methuen, London).

Cox, D.R. (1972), "Regression models and life tables", Journal of the Royal Statistical Society, Series B, 34: 187–200 (with discussion).

Crimmins, E. and M. Pramaggiore (1988), "Changing health of older working age population and retirement patterns over time", in: E. Lazear and R. Ricardo-Campbell, eds., Issues in contemporary retirement (Hoover Institution, Stanford, CA).

Crimmins, E., A. Saito and D. Ingegneri (1989), "Changes in life expectancy and disability-free life expectancy in the United States", Population Development Review 15: 235–267.

Cutler, D., J. Poterba, L. Sheiner and L. Summers (1990), "An aging society: opportunity or challenge?", Brookings Papers on Economic Activity 1: 1–56, 71–73.

Dardanoni, V. and A. Wagstaff (1990), "Uncertainty and the demand for medical care", Journal of Health Economics 9: 23–38.

Dasbach, E., R. Klein, B. Klein and S. Moss (1994), "Self-rated health and mortality in people with diabetes", American Journal of Public Health 84: 1775–1779.

DeBakey, M. and G. Beebe (1952), "Medical follow-up studies on veterans", Journal of the American Medical Association 182: 1103–1109.

Del Bene, L. and D.R. Vaughan (1992), "Income, assets, and health insurance: economic resources for meeting acute health care needs of the aged", Social Security Bulletin 55: 3–25.

DeMontricher, G., R. Tapia and J. Thompson (1975), "Nonparametric maximum likelihood estimation of probability densities by penalty function methods", The Annals of Statistics 3: 1329–1348.

Dempster, A., N. Laird and D. Rubin (1977), "Maximum likelihood from incomplete data via the EM algorithm", Journal of the Royal Statistical Society, Series B, 39: 1–38.

Deolalikar, A. (1988), "Nutrition and labor productivity in agriculture: estimates for rural south India", Review of Economics and Statistics 70: 406–413.

De Palma, A., G.M. Myers and Y.Y. Papageorgiou (1994), "Rational choice under an imperfect ability to choose", American Economic Review 84: 419–440.

Diamond, P. and J. Hausman (1984), "The retirement and unemployment behavior of older men", in: H. Aaron and G. Burtless, eds., Retirement and economic behavior (Brookings Institution, Washington, DC).

Diaz-Briquets, S. (1991a), "Mortality in Cuba", in: I. Rosenwaike, ed., Mortality of Hispanic populations (Greenwood Press, Westport, CT).

Diaz-Briquets, S. (1991b), "Mortality patterns of Cubans in the United States", in: I. Rosenwaike, ed., Mortality of Hispanic populations (Greenwood Press, Westport, CT).

Diggle, P. and R. Gratton (1984), "Monte Carlo methods of inference for implicit statistical methods", Journal of the Royal Statistical Society, Series B, 46: 193–227.

Doll, R. (1953), "Bronchial carcinoma: incidence and aetiology", British Medical Journal 2: 521–527, 585–590.

Doll, R. and A. Hill (1952), "A study of the aetiology of carcinoma of the lung", British Medical Journal 2: 1271–1286.

Doll, R. and A. Hill (1964), "Mortality in relation to smoking: ten years' observations of British doctors", British Medical Journal 1: 1399–1410.

Donaldson, C., A. Atkinson, J. Bond and K. Wright (1988), "Should QALY's be programme-specific?", Journal of Health Economics 7: 239–258.

Dorn, H.F. (1958), "The mortality of smokers and non-smokers", Proceedings Social Statistics Section American Statistical Association 53: 34–71.

Duleep, H.O. (1986), "Measuring income's effect on adult mortality", Journal of Human Resources 21: 238–251.

Duleep, H.O. (1989), "Measuring socioeconomic mortality differentials over time", Demography 26: 345–351.

Eakin, K.B. and T.J. Kniesner (1988), "Estimating a non-minimum cost function for hospitals", Southern Economic Journal 54: 583–597.

Eckstein, Z. and K. Wolpin (1989), "The specification and estimation of dynamic stochastic discrete choice models", Journal of Human Resources 24: 562–598.

Ehrlich, I. and H. Chuma (1990), "A model of the demand for longevity and the value of life extension", Journal of Political Economy 98: 761–782.

Eichenbaum, M., L.P. Hansen and K. Singleton (1988), "A time-series analysis of representative agent models of consumption and leisure decisions under nonseparable utility", Quarterly Journal of Economics 103: 51–78.

Ellwood, D. and T. Kane (1990), "The American way of aging: an event history analysis", in: D. Wise, ed., Issues in the economics of aging (University of Chicago Press, Chicago, IL).

Ericksen, E. and J. Kadane (1985), "Estimating the population in a census year: 1980 and beyond", Journal of the American Statistical Association 80, 98–108.

Evans, W. and W. Viscusi (1993), "Income effects and the value of health", Journal of Human Resources 28: 497–517.

Fair, R.C. (1994), "How fast do old men slow down?", Review of Economics and Statistics 76: 103–118.

Feinstein, J.F. (1992), "The relationship between socioeconomic status and health: a review of the literature", Additional papers (NBER, Cambridge, MA).

Feldman, J.J., D.M. Makuc, J.C. Kleinman and J. Cornoni-Huntley (1989), "National trends in educational differentials in mortality", American Journal of Epidemiology 129: 919–933.

Feldstein, M. (1967), Economic analysis for health service efficiency: econometric studies of the British National Health Service (North-Holland, Amsterdam).

Fenn, P. and I. Vlachonikolis (1986), "Male labour force participation following illness or injury", Economica 53: 379–391.

Ferraro, K. (1980), "Self-ratings of health among the old and the old-old", Journal of Health and Social Behavior 21: 377–383.

Fields, G. and O. Mitchell (1984), "The effects of social security reforms on retirement ages and retirement incomes", Working paper 1348 (NBER, Cambridge, MA).

Fingerhut, L. and H. Rosenberg (1982), "Mortality among the elderly", in: Health, United States, 1981, Department of Health and Human Services Publication (PHS), 82–1221 (December), (United States Department of Health and Human Services, Washington, DC).

Fisher, R. (1958), "Cancer and smoking", Nature 182: 596.

Floderus, B., R. Cederlof and L. Friberg (1988), "Smoking and mortality: a 21-year follow-up based on the Swedish twin registry", International Journal of Epidemiology 17: 332–340.

Fogel, R. (1993), "New sources and new techniques for the study of secular trends in nutritional status, health, mortality, and the process of aging", Historical Methods 26: 5–43.

Fogel, R. (1994a), "Economic growth, population theory, and physiology: the bearing of long-term process on the making of economic policy", American Economic Review 84: 369–395.

Fogel, R. (1994b), "Malthus and the study of mortality today", in: K. Lindahl-Kiessling and H. Landberg, eds., Population, economic development, and the environment (Oxford University Press, Oxford).

Fogel, R. (1995), The escape from hunger and high mortality: Europe, America, and the Third World, 1700–2050, in press.

Fogel, R., D. Costa and J. Kim (1994), "Secular trends in the distribution of chronic conditions and disabilities at young adult and late ages, 1860–1988: some preliminary findings", Mimeo.

Ford, E. and F. DeStefano (1991), "Risk factors for mortality from all causes and from coronary heart disease among persons with diabetes", American Journal of Epidemiology 133: 1220–1230.

Foster, A. (1991), "Are cohort mortality rates autocorrelated?", Demography 28: 619–634.

Foster, A. and M. Rosenzweig (1994), "A test for moral hazard in the labor market: contractual arrangements, effort and health", Review of Economics and Statistics 76: 213–227.

Fridlizius, G. (1984), "The mortality decline in the first phase of the demographic transition: Swedish experiences", in: T. Bengtsson, G. Fridlizius and R. Ohlsson, eds., Pre-Industrial population change (Almquist and Wiksell, Stockholm).

Fries, J. (1980), "Ageing, natural death, and the compression of morbidity", New England Journal of Medicine 303: 130–136.

Fries, J. (1983), "The compression of morbidity", Milbank Quarterly 61: 397–419.

Fries, J. (1989), "The compression of morbidity: near or far?", Milbank Quarterly 67: 208–232.

Fuchs, V. (1974), Who shall live? Health, economics, and social choice (Basic Books, New York).

Fuchs, V. (1982), "Time preference and health: an explanatory study", in: V.R. Fuchs, ed., Economic aspects of health (University of Chicago for the National Bureau of Economic Research, Chicago, IL).

Fuchs, V. (1992), "Poverty and health: asking the right questions", The American Economist 36: 12–18.

Fuchs, V. and J. Hahn (1990), "How does Canada do it? A comparison of expenditures for physicians' services in the United States and Canada", New England Journal of Medicine 323: 884–890.

Gafni, A. and S. Birch (1991), "Equity considerations in utility-based measures of health outcomes in economic appraisals: an adjustment algorithm", Journal of Health Economics 10: 329–342.

Garber, A.M. and T. MaCurdy (1990), "Predicting nursing home utilization among the high-risk elderly", in: D. Wise, ed., Issues in the economics of aging (University of Chicago Press, Chicago, IL).

Geweke, J. (1991), "Efficient simulation from the multivariate normal and student-t distributions subject to linear constraints", Computer Science and Statistics: Proceedings of the 23rd Symposium on the Interface, pp. 571–578.

Geweke, J., M. Keane and D. Runkle (1994), "Alternative computational approaches to inference in the multinomial probability model", Review of Economics and Statistics 76: 609–632.

Goldman, N. (1993), "Marriage selection and mortality patterns: inferences and fallacies", Demography 30: 189–195.

Good, J. and R. Gaskins (1971), "Nonparametric roughness penalties for probability densities", Biometrika 58: 255–277.

Goodman, L. (1968), "The analysis of cross-classified data: independence, quasi-independence, and interaction in contingency tables with missing entries", Journal of the American Statistical Association 63: 1091–1131.

Gotz, G.A. and J.J. McCall (1984), "A dynamic retention model for air force officers", Report R-3028-AF (RAND Corporation, Santa Monica, CA).

Gourieroux, C. and A. Monfort (1989), "Simulation based inference in models with heterogeneity", Journal of Econometrics 52: 159–199.

Gove, W. (1973), "Sex, marital status, and mortality", American Journal of Sociology 79: 45–65.

Gravelle, H.S.E. (1984), "Time-series analysis of mortality and unemployment", Journal of Health Economics 3: 297–306.

Gravelle, J.G. and J. Taylor (1989), "Financing long-term care for the elderly", National Tax Journal 42: 219–232.

Greenspan, R. (1995), "Understanding the genetic construction of behavior", Scientific American 272: 72.

Grilo, C. and M. Pogue-Geile (1991), "The nature of environmental influences on weight and obesity", Psychological Bulletin 110: 520.

Grossman, M. (1972a), The demand for health: a theoretical and empirical investigation (National Bureau of Economic Research, New York).

Grossman, M. (1972b), "On the concept of health capital and the demand for health", Journal of Political Economy 80: 223–225.

Grossman, M. (1975), "The correlation between health and schooling", in: N. Terleckyj, ed., Household production and consumption (Columbia University Press, New York).

Grossman, M. (1982a), "Government and health outcomes", American Economic Review 72: 191–196.

Grossman, M. (1982b), "The demand for health after a decade", Journal of Health Economics 1: 1–3.

Grossman, M. and L. Benham (1974), "Health, hours, and wages", in: M. Perlman, ed., The economics of health and medical care (Macmillan, London).

Grossman, M., F.J. Chaloupka and I. Sirtalan (1995), "An empirical analysis of alcohol addiction: results from the monitoring the future panels", Mimeo.

Gustman, A. and T. Steinmeier (1986), "A disaggregated, structural analysis of retirement by race, difficulty of work and health", The Review of Economics and Statistics 68: 509–513.

Haddad, L. and H. Bouis (1991), "The impact of nutritional status on agricultural productivity: wage evidence from the Philippines", Oxford Bulletin of Economics and Statistics 53: 45–68.

Hajivassiliou, V. and D. McFadden (1990), "The method of simulated scores for the estimation of ldv models with an application to external debt crises", Mimeo.

Hajivassiliou, V., D. McFadden and P.A. Ruud (1996), "Simulation of multivariate normal rectangle probabilities and derivatives: theory and computational results", Journal of Econometrics, in press.

Hamer, D., S. Hu, V. Magnuson, N. Hu and A. Pattatucci (1993), "A linkage between DNA markers on the X chromosome and male sexual orientation", Science 261: 321.

Hamermesh, D.S. (1984), "Life-cycle effects on consumption and retirement", Journal of Labor Economics 2: 353–370.

Hamermesh, D.S. (1985), "Expectations, life expectancy, and economic behavior", Quarterly Journal of Economics 100: 389–408.

Han, A. and J. Hausman (1990), "Semiparametric estimation of duration and competing risk models", Journal of Applied Econometrics 5: 1–28.

Hansen, L.P. (1982), "Large sample properties of generalized method of moments estimators", Econometrica 50: 1029–1054.

Harris, J. (1987), "QALYfying the value of life", Journal of Medical Ethics 13: 117.

Hausman, J. and D. Wise (1985), "Social security, health status and retirement", in: D. Wise, ed., Pensions, labor, and individual choice (University of Chicago Press, Chicago, IL, for NBER).

Haveman, R. and B. Wolfe (1984), "Disability transfers and early retirement: a causal relationship", Journal of Public Economics 24: 47–66.

Haveman, R., H. De Jong and B. Wolfe (1991), "Disability transfers and the work decision of older men", Quarterly Journal of Economics 106: 939–950.

Haveman, R., B. Wolfe, B. Kreider and M. Stone (1994), "Market work, wages, and men's health", Journal of Health Economics 13: 163–182.

Hayward, M.D., W.R. Grady, M.A. Ardy and D. Sommers (1989), "Occupational influences on retirement and death", Demography 26: 393–409.

Heckman, J.J. (1976), "The common structure of statistical models of truncation, sample selection, and limited dependent variables and a simple estimator for such models", Annals of Economic and Social Measurement 5: 475–492.

Heckman, J.J. and B. Honoré (1989), "The identifiability of the competing risks model", Biometrika 76: 325–330.

Heckman, J.J. and T. MaCurdy (1980), "A lifecycle model of female labor supply", Review of Economic Studies 47: 47–74.

Heckman, J.J. and B. Singer (1982), "The identification problems in econometric models for duration data", in: W. Hildenbrand, ed., Advances in econometrics (Cambridge University Press, Cambridge).

Heckman, J.J. and B. Singer (1984), "A method for minimizing the impact of distributional assumptions in econometric models for duration data", Econometrica 52: 271–320.

Heckman, J.J. and C.R. Taber (1994), "Econometric mixture models and more general models for unobservables in duration analysis", Technical working paper no. 157 (NBER, Cambridge, MA).

Heywood, P.F. (1983), "Growth and nutrition in Papua New Guinea", Journal of Human Evolution 12: 131–143.

Himes, C.L., S.H. Preston and G.A. Condran (1994), "A relational model of mortality at older ages in low mortality countries", Population Studies 48: 269–291.

Holden, K. (1988), "Physically demanding occupations, health, and work after retirement: findings from the new beneficiary survey", Social Security Bulletin 51: 3–15.

Honoré, B.E. (1992), "Trimmed lad and least squares estimation of truncated and censored regression models with fixed-effects", Econometrica 60: 533–567.

Hotz, V.J. and R. Miller (1993), "Conditional choice probabilities and the estimation of dynamic programming models", Review of Economic Studies 60: 497–530.

Hotz, V.J., F. Kydland and G. Sedlacek (1988), "Intertemporal preferences and labor supply", Econometrica 56: 335–360.

Hotz, V.J., R. Miller, S. Sanders and J. Smith (1994), "A simulation estimator for dynamic models of discrete choice", Review of Economic Studies 61: 265–290.

Hougaard, P., B. Harvald and N.V. Holm (1992), "Measuring the similarities between the lifetimes of adult Danish twins born between 1881–1930", Journal of the American Statistical Association 87: 17–24.

Hrubec, Z. and J. Neel (1981), "Familial factors in early deaths: twins followed 30 years to ages 51–61", Human Genetics 59: 39–46.

Huh, K. and R.C. Sickles (1994), "Estimation of the duration model by nonparametric maximum likelihood, maximum penalized likelihood, and probability simulators", Review of Economics and Statistics 76: 683–694.

Hurd, M. (1990), "Research on the elderly: Economic status, retirement, and consumption and saving", Journal of Economic Literature 28: 565–637.

Hurd, M. and K. McGarry (1993), "Evaluation of subjective probability distributions in the HRS", Working paper no. 4560 (NBER, Cambridge, MA).

Ichimura, H. (1993), "Semiparametric least squares (sls), and weighted sls estimation of single-index models", Journal of Econometrics 58: 71–120.

Idler, E.L. (1992), "Self-assessed health and mortality: a review of studies", International Review of Health Psychology 1: 33–54.

Idler, E. (1995), "Self-rated health and mortality studies", Mimeo.

Idler, E. and R. Angel (1990), "Self-rated health and mortality in the NHAMES-1 epidemiologic follow-up study", American Journal of Public Health 80: 446–452.

Idler, E. and S. Kasl (1991), "Health perceptions and survival: do global evaluations of health status really predict mortality?", Journal of Gerontology: Social Sciences 46: 555–565.

Idler, E., S. Kasl and J. Lemke (1990), "Self-evaluated health and mortality among the elderly in New Haven, Connecticut and Iowa and Washington counties, Iowa, 1982–1986", American Journal of Epidemiology 131: 91–103.

Jagger, C. and M. Clarke (1988), "Mortality risks in the elderly: five-year follow-up of a total population", International Journal of Epidemiology 17: 111–114.

Jaynes, G.D. and R.M. Williams Jr. (1989), A common destiny: Blacks and American society (National Academy Press, Washington, DC).

Jones, D.R. and P.O. Goldblatt (1987), "Cause of death in widow(er)s and spouses", Journal of Biosocial Sciences 19: 107–121.

Ju, A. and G. Jones (1989), Aging in ASEAN and its socio-economic consequences (Institute of Southeast Asian Studies, Singapore).

Judd, K.L. (1994), "Approximation, perturbation, and projection methods in economic analysis", in: H. Amman, D. Kendrick and J. Rust, eds., Handbook of computation economics (North-Holland, Amsterdam).

Judd, K.L. (1995), Numerical methods in economics (MIT Press, Cambridge, MA).

Judd, K.L. and A. Solnick (1994), "Numerical dynamic programming with shape-preserving splines", Mimeo.

Juster, F.T. and R. Suzman (1995), "The health and retirement study: an overview", Health and retirement study working paper series, Core paper no. 94-1001 (rev.) (Institute for Social Research, Ann Arbor, MI).

Kahn, H. (1966), "The Dorn study of smoking and mortality among U.S. veterans: report of 8 and 1/2 years of observation", in: W. Haenszel, ed., Epidemiological approaches to the study of cancer and other diseases, U.S.P.H.S. National Cancer Institute Monograph, Vol. 19 (National Cancer Institute, Bethesda, MD).

Kalbfleisch, J.D. and R.L. Prentice (1980), The statistical analysis of failure time data (Wiley, New York).

Kaplan, E.L. and P. Meier (1958), "Nonparametric estimation from incomplete observations", Journal of the American Statistical Association 53: 457–481.

Kaplan, G.A. and T. Camacho (1983), "Perceived health and mortality: a nine-year follow-up of the human population laboratory cohort", American Journal of Epidemiology 117: 292–304.

Kaplan, G., V. Bartell and A. Lusky (1988), "Subjective state of health and survival in elderly adults", Journal of Gerontology 43: S114–S120.

Kaplan, G.A., T.E. Seeman, R.D. Cohen, L.P. Knudesen and J. Guralnik (1987), "Mortality among the elderly in the Alameda County study: behavioral and demographic risk factors", American Journal of Public Health 77: 307–312.

Kaplan, R.M. and J.P. Anderson (1988), "A general health policy model: update and applications", Health Services Research 23: 203–235.

Kaplan, R.M. and J.W. Bush (1982), "Health-related quality of life measurement for evaluation research and policy analysis", Health Psychology 1: 61–80.

Kaprio, J. and M. Koskenvuo (1990), "Cigarette smoking as a cause of lung cancer and coronary heart disease: a study of smoking discordant twin pairs", Acta Geneticae Medicae et Gemellologiae 39: 25–70.

Keane, M. (1994), "A computationally practical simulation estimator for panel data", Econometrica 62: 95–116.

Keane, M. and K. Wolpin (1994), "The solution and estimation of discrete choice dynamic programming models by simulation and interpolation: Monte Carlo evidence", Review of Economics and Statistics 76: 648–672.

Kiefer, N.M. (1988), "Economic duration data and hazard functions", Journal of Economic Literature 26: 646–679.

Killingsworth, M. (1983), Labor supply (Cambridge University Press, Cambridge).

Kind, P., R. Rosser and A. Williams (1982), "Valuation of quality of life: some psychometric evidence", in: M.W. Jones-Lee, ed., The value of life and safety (North-Holland, Amsterdam).

Kitagawa, E. and P. Hauser (1973), Differential mortality in the United States of America: a study of socioeconomic epidemiology (Harvard University Press, Cambridge, MA).

Klein, R.W. and R.H. Spady (1993), "An efficient semiparametric estimator for binary response models", Econometrica 61: 387–421.

Kliss, B. et al. (1979), "The 1973 CPS-IRS-SAA-Exact Match Study: past, present and future", Policy Analysis with Social Security Research Files (US Social Security Administration, Washington, DC).

Knight, J. and L. Song (1993), "The length of life and the standard of living: economic influences on premature death in China", Journal of Development Studies 30: 58–91.

Knudson, A. (1992), "Heredity and environment in the origin of cancer", Progress in Clinical and Biological Research 376: 31–40.

Kravdal, Ø. (1994), "The importance of economic activity, economic potential and economic resources for the timing of first births in Norway", Population Studies 48: 249–267.

Krúmiņš, J. and P. Zvidriņš (1992), "Recent mortality trends in the three Baltic republics", Population Studies 46: 2459–2473.

Kydland, F. and E. Prescott (1982), "Time to build and aggregate fluctuations", Econometrica 50: 1345–1371.

Laird, N. (1978), "Nonparametric maximum likelihood estimation of a mixing distribution", Journal of American Statistical Association 73: 805–811.

Lancaster, H.O. (1990), Expectations of life: a study in the demography, statistics, and history of world mortality (Springer-Verlag, Berlin).

Lancaster, T. (1990), The econometric analysis of transition data (Cambridge University Press, New York).

Land, K., J. Guralnik and D. Blazer (1994), "Estimating increment–decrement life tables with multiple covariates from panel data: the case of active life expectancy", Demography 31: 297–319.

Lee, L.-F. (1982), "Health and wage: a simultaneous equation model with multiple discrete indicators", International Economic Review 23: 199–221.

Lee, L.-F. and M. Pitt (1986), "Microeconomic demand systems with binding non-negativity constraints: the dual approach", Econometrica 54: 1237–1242.

Lee, L.-F. (1995), "Semiparametric maximum likelihood estimation of polychotomous and sequential choice models", Journal of Econometrics 65: 381–428.

Lee, L.-F., M.R. Rosenzweig and M.M. Pitt (1995), "The effects of improved nutrition, sanitation and water purity on child health in high-mortality populations", Mimeo.

Lee, R. and L. Carter (1992), "Modelling and forecasting U.S. mortality", Journal of the American Statistical Association 87: 659–672.

Leonard, J. (1979), "The social security disability program and labor force participation", Working paper no. 392 (NBER, Cambridge, MA).

Lerman, S. and Manski, C. (1981), "On the use of simulated frequencies to approximate choice probabilities", in: C. Manski and D. McFadden, eds., Structural analysis of discrete data with econometric applications (MIT Press, Cambridge, MA).

Li, T., L. Lumeng, W. McBride, and J. Murphy (1994), "Genetic and neurobiological basis of alcohol-seeking behavior", Alcohol and Alcoholism 29: 697.

Lindsay, B.G. (1983), "The geometry of mixture likelihoods: a general theory", The Annals of Statistics 11: 86–94.

Liu, I.Y., A.Z. LaCroix, L.R. White, S.J. Kittner and P.A. Wolf (1990), "Cognitive impairment and mortality: a study of possible confounders", American Journal of Epidemiology 132: 136–143.

MaCurdy, T. (1981), "An empirical model of labor supply in a lifecycle setting", Journal of Political Economy 89: 1058–1085.

MaCurdy, T. (1983), "A simple scheme for estimating an intertemporal model of labor supply in the presence of uncertainty", International Economic Review 24: 265–289.

Madans, J.H., C.S. Cox, J.C. Kleinman, D. Makuc, J.J. Feldman, F.F. Finucane, H.E. Barbano and J. Coronni-Huntley (1986), "10 years after NHANES 1: Mortality experience at initial followup, 1982–1984", Public Health Reports 101: 465–473.

Madigan, F. (1957), "Are sex mortality differentials biologically caused?", Milbank Memorial Fund Quarterly 35: 129–130.

Malthus, T.R. (1798), An essay on the principle of population, 7th edn. (Kelley, New York, 1971).

Manski, C.F. (1993), "Identification of endogenous social effects: the reflection problem", Review of Economic Studies 60: 531–542.

Manton, K.G. and E. Stallard (1982), "Temporal trends in U.S. multiple cause of death mortality data: 1968 to 1977", Demography 19: 527–547.

Manton, K.G., E. Stallard and J.W. Vaupel (1986), "Alternative models for the heterogeneity of mortality risks among the aged", Journal of the American Statistical Association 81: 635–644.

Manton, K., L. Corder and E. Stallard (1993), "Estimates of changes in chronic disability and institutional medicine and prevalence rates in the U.S. elderly population from the 1982, 1984, and 1989 national long-term care survey", Journal of Gerontology 48: S153–S167.

Marder, W.D. and S. Zuckerman (1985), "Competition and medical groups", Journal of Health Economics 4, 167–176.

Martorell, R. (1985), "Child growth retardation: a discussion of its causes and its relationship to health", in: K. Blaxter and J.C. Waterlow, eds., Nutritional adaptation in man (Libby, London).

McCallum, J., B. Shadbolt and D. Wang (1994), "Self-rated health and survival: a 7-year follow-up study of Australian elderly", American Journal of Public Health 84: 1100–1105.

McCoy, J., H. Iams and T. Armstrong (1994), "The hazard of mortality among aging retired and disabled worker men: a comparative sociodemographic and health status analysis", Social Security Bulletin 57: 76–87.

McFadden, D. (1989), "A method of simulated moments for estimation of discrete response models without numerical integration", Econometrica 57: 995–1026.

McFadden, D. and P. Ruud (1994), "Estimation by simulation", Review of Economics and Statistics 76: 591–608.

McGarry, K. and R.F. Schoeni (1994), "Transfer behavior: measurement, and the redistribution of resources within the family", Journal of Human Resources, in press.

McGarry, K. and R.F. Schoeni (1995), "Transfer behavior within the family: results from the asset and health dynamics survey", Working paper no. 5099 (NBER, Cambridge, MA).

McGue, M., J. Vaupel and B. Harvald (1992), "Longevity is moderately heritable in a sample of Danish born twins", Mimeo.

Menchik, P.L. (1993), "Economic status as a determinant of mortality among black and white older men: does poverty kill?", Population Studies 47, 427–436.

Miller, P., C. Mulvey and N. Martin (1995), "What do twins studies reveal about the economic returns to education?: a comparison of Australian and U.S. findings", American Economic Review 85: 586–600.

Miller, R. (1984), "Job matching and occupational choice", Journal of Political Economy 92: 1086–1120.

Mitchell, J. and J. Butler (1986), "Arthritis and the earnings of men", Journal of Health Economics 5: 81–98.

Moore, D. and M. Hayward (1990), "Occupational careers and mortality of older men", Demography 27: 31–48.

Morris, J.N., J.A. Heady, P.A. Raffle, C. Roberts and J. Parks (1953), "Coronary heart disease and physical activity of work", Lancet ii: 1053–1057, 1111–1120.

Mossey, J. and E. Shapiro (1982), "Self-rated health: a predictor of mortality among the elderly", American Journal of Public Health 72: 800–808.

Murray, C. (1994), "Quantifying the burden of disease: the technical basis for disability-adjusted life years", Bulletin of the World Health Organization 72: 429–445.

Muurinen, J.M. (1982), "Demand for health: a generalized Grossman model", Journal of Health Economics 1: 5–28.

Myers, R. (1981), Social security, 2nd edn. (McChan Foundation, Bryn Mawr).

Nelson, C. and R. Startz (1990a), "The distribution of the instrumental variables estimator and the t-ratios when the instrument is a poor one", Journal of Business 63: S125–S140.

Nelson, C. and R. Startz (1990b), "Some further results on the exact small sample properties of the instrumental variables estimator", Econometrica 58: 967–976.

Newhouse, J.P. (1987), "Health economics and econometrics", American Economic Review 77: 269–274.

Nolan, P. and J. Sender (1992), "Death rates, life expectancy and China's economic reforms: a critique of A.K. Sen", World Development 20: 1279–1303.

Nord, E. (1992), "Methods for quality adjustment of life years", Social Science and Medicine 34: 559–569.

Nyman, J. (1989), "The private demand for nursing home care", Journal of Health Economics 8: 209–231.

Olsen, R.J. and K.I. Wolpin (1983), "The impact of exogenous child mortality on fertility: a waiting time regression with dynamic regressors", Econometrica 51: 731–749.

Osmani, S.R. (1992), "On some controversies in the measurement of undernutrition", in: S.R. Osmani, ed., Nutrition and poverty (Oxford University Press, Oxford).

Otten, M.W., Jr., S.M. Teutsch, D.F. Williamson and J.S. Marks (1990), "The effect of known risk factors on the excess mortality of black adults in the United States", Journal of the American Medical Association 263: 845–850.

Paffenberger, R. and J. Williams (1967), "Chronic disease in former college students, V: early precursors of fatal stroke", American Journal of Public Health 57: 1290–1299.

Paffenberger, R., P. Wolf, J. Notkin and M. Thorne (1966), "Chronic disease in former college students, I: Early precursors of fatal coronary heart disease", American Journal of Epidemiology 83: 314–328.

Pakes, A. (1987), "Patents as options: some estimates of the value of holding European patent stocks", Econometrica 54: 755–784.

Pakes, A. and D. Pollard (1989), "Simulation and the asymptotics of optimization estimates", Econometrica 57: 1027–1058.

Pappas, G., S. Queen, W. Hadden and G. Fisher (1993), "The increasing disparity in mortality between socioeconomic groups in the United States, 1960 and 1986", New England Journal of Medicine 329: 103–109.

Parsons, D. (1980a), "The decline in male labor force participation", Journal of Political Economy 88: 117–139.

Parsons, D. (1980b), "Recent trends in male labor force participation", American Economic Review 70: 911–920.

Passmore, D.L., U.A. Ay, S. Rockel, B. Wade and J. Wise (1983), "Health and youth unemployment", Applied Economics 15: 715–729.

Pauly, M.V. (1986), "Taxation, health insurance, and market failure in the medical economy", Journal of Economic Literature 24: 629–675.

Perrenoud, A. (1984), "The mortality decline in a long-term perspective", in: T. Bengtsson, G. Fridlizius and R. Ohlsson, eds., Pre-industrial population change (Almquist and Wiksell, Stockholm).

Perrenoud, A. (1991), "The attenuation of mortality crises and the decline of mortality", in: R. Schofield, D. Reher and A. Bideau, eds., The decline of mortality (Oxford University Press, Oxford).

Phelps, C.E. (1992), "Diffusion of information in medical care", Journal of Economic Perspectives 6: 23–42.

Phillips, D. and T. Rathwell (1986), Health, race, and ethnicity (Croom Helm, London).

Pijls, L., E. Feskens and D. Kromhout (1993), "Self-rated health, mortality, and diseases in elderly men: The Zutphen study 1985–1990", American Journal of Epidemiology 138: 840–848.

Pitt, M.M. and M.R. Rosenzweig (1989), "The selectivity of fertility and the determinants of human capital investments: Parametric and semi-parametric estimates", Mimeo.

Poe, G., E. Powell-Griner, J. McLaughlin, P. Placek, G. Thompson and K. Robinson (1993), "Comparability of the death certificate and the 1986 national mortality followback survey", Vital and Health Statistics, Series 2, no. 118 (National Center for Health Statistics, Washington, DC).

Pollak, R.A. (1969), "Conditional demand functions and consumption theory", Quarterly Journal of Economics 83: 60–78.

Pollak, R.A. (1970), "Habit formation and dynamic demand functions", Journal of Political Economy 78: 745–763.

Popkin, B.M., D.K. Guilkey, J.B. Schwartz and W. Flieger (1993), "Survival in the perinatal period: a prospective analysis", Journal of Biosocial Sciences 25, 359–370.

Poterba, J. and L. Summers (1987), "Public policy implications of declining old age mortality", in: G. Burtless, ed., Work, health, and income among the elderly (Brookings Institution, Washington, DC)

Preston, S.H. (1976), Mortality patterns in national populations (Academic Press, New York).

Preston, S.H. (1980), "Causes and consequences of mortality decline in LDC's during the twentieth century", in: R.A. Easterlin, ed., Population and economic change in developing countries (University of Chicago Press, Chicago, IL).

Preston, S.H. (1984), "Children and the elderly: divergent paths for America's dependents", Demography 21: 435–457.

Preston, S.H. and E. van de Walle (1978), "Urban French mortality in the nineteenth century", Population Studies 32, 275–297.

Ransom, M.R. (1987), "A comment on consumer demand systems with binding non-negativity constraints", Journal of Econometrics 34: 355–359.

Rendall, M.S. and A. Speare, Jr. (1993), "Comparing economic well-being among elderly Americans", Review of Income and Wealth 39: 1–21.

Restrepo, H.A. and M. Rozental (1994), "The social impact of aging populations: some major issues", Social Science in Medicine 39: 1323–1338.

Retherford, R. (1975), The changing sex differential in mortality (Greenwood, Westport, CT).

Robbins, H. (1964), "The empirical Bayes approach to statistical decision problems", Annals of Mathematical Statistics 35: 1–20.

Rogers, R. (1992), "Living and dying in the USA: sociodemographic determinants of death among blacks and whites", Demography 29: 287–296.

Rogot, E. (1974), Smoking and general mortality among U.S. veterans 1954–1969 (United States Department of Health, Education and Welfare, Washington, DC).

Rogot, E. and J. Murray (1980), "Smoking and causes of death among U.S. veterans: 16 years of observation", Public Health Reports 95: 213–222.

Rogot, E., P.D. Sorlie and N.J. Johnson (1992a), "Life expectancy by employment status, income, and education in the national longitudinal mortality study", Public Health Reports 107: 457–461.

Rogot, E., P.D. Sorlie, N.J. Johnson and C. Schmidt (1992b), A mortality study of 1.3 million persons by demographic, social, and economic factors: 1979–85 follow-up (National Heart, Lung, and Blood Institute, Bethesda, MD).

Rosen, S. and P. Taubman (1984), "Changes in the impact of education and income on mortality in the U.S.", in: Statistical uses of administrative records with emphasis on mortality and disability research (United States Department of Health, Education and Welfare, Washington, DC).

Rosenzweig, M.R. and T.P. Schultz (1982a), "Child mortality and fertility in Columbia", in: Health policy and fertility in Columbia (Elsevier, Amsterdam).

Rosenzweig, M.R. and T.P. Schultz (1982b), "The behavior of mothers as inputs to child health: the determinants of birth weight, gestation, and rate of fetal growth", in: V. Fuchs, ed., Economic aspects of health (University of Chicago Press, Chicago, IL).

Rosenzweig, M.R. and T.P. Schultz (1983a), "Estimating a household production function: heterogeneity, the demand for health inputs, and their effects on birth weight", Journal of Political Economy 91: 723–746.

Rosenzweig, M.R. and T.P. Schultz (1983b), "Consumer demand and household production: the relationship between fertility and child mortality", American Economic Review 73: 38–42.

Rosenzweig, M.R. and T.P. Schultz (1985), "The demand for and supply of births: fertility and its life-cycle consequences", American Economic Review 75: 992–1015.

Rosenzweig, M.R. and K.I. Wolpin (1980), "Life-cycle labor supply and fertility: causal inferences from household models", Journal of Political Economy 88: 328–348.

Rosenzweig, M.R. and K.I. Wolpin (1988), "Heterogeneity, intrafamily distribution, and child health", Journal of Human Resources 23: 437–461.

Rust, J. (1987), "Optimal replacement of GMC bus engines: an empirical model of Harold Zurcher", Econometrica 55: 999–1035.

Rust, J. (1989), "A dynamic programming model of retirement behavior", in: D.A. Wise, ed., The economics of aging (University of Chicago Press, Chicago, IL, for the NBER).

Rust, J. (1990), "Behavior of male workers at the end of the life-cycle: an empirical analysis of states and controls", in: D.A. Wise, ed., Issues in the economics of aging (University of Chicago Press, Chicago, IL, for the NBER).

Rust, J. (1995), "Numerical dynamic programming in economics", in: H. Amman, D. Kendrick and J. Rust, eds., Handbook of computational economics (North-Holland, Amsterdam).

Sahn, D.E. and H. Alderman (1988), "The effect of human capital on wages and the determinants of labor supply in a developing country", Journal of Development Economics 29: 157–183.

Sargent, T.J. (1987), Dynamic macroeconomic theory (Harvard University Press, Cambridge, MA).

Schirm, A.L. and S.H. Preston (1987), "Census undercount adjustment and the quality of geographic population distributions", Journal of the American Statistical Association 82: 965–977.

Schmidt, P. and R.C. Sickles (1984), "Production frontiers and panel data", Journal of Business and Economic Statistics 2: 367–374.

Schoenfeld, D., L. Malmrose, D. Blazer, D. Gold and T. Seeman (1994), "Self-rated health and mortality in the high-functioning elderly: a closer look at healthy individuals: MacArthur field study of successful aging", Journal of Gerontology: Medical Sciences 49: M109–M115.

Schofield, R. and D. Reher (1991), "The decline of mortality in Europe", in: R. Schofield, D. Reher and A. Bideau, eds., The decline of mortality in Europe (Oxford University Press, Oxford).

Schultz, T. (1993), "Mortality decline in the low income world: causes and consequences", American Economic Review 83: 337–341.

Schultz, T.P. and A. Tansel (1993), "Estimates of wage returns to adult health in Cote d'Ivoire and Ghana", Mimeo. (Yale University, New Haven, CT).

Scott, D.W. (1979), "On optimal and data based histograms", Biometrika 66: 605–610.

Scott, D.W. (1985), "Average shifted histograms: effective nonparametric density estimators in several dimensions", Annals of Statistics 13: 1024–1040.

Scott, D.W. (1992), Multivariate density estimation (Wiley, New York).

Scrimshaw, N.S., C.E. Taylor and J.E. Gordon (1968), Interactions of nutrition and infection (World Health Organization, Geneva).

Sen, A. (1989), "Food and freedom", World Development 17: 769–781.

Sen, A. (1993), "The economics of life and death", Scientific American, May: 40–47.

Shahtahmasebi, S., R. Davies and G. Wenger (1992), "A longitudinal analysis of factors related to survival in old age", Gerontologist 32: 404–413.

Shoven, J.B., J.O. Sundberg and J.P. Bunker (1988), "The social security cost of smoking", in: D. Wise, ed., The economics of aging (University of Chicago Press, Chicago, IL).

Sickles, R.C. (1989), "An analysis of simultaneous limited dependent variable models and some nonstandard cases", in: R. Mariano, ed., Advances in statistical computing: theory and applications, Vol. 2 (JAI Press, Greenwich).

Sickles, R.C. and P. Taubman (1986), "An analysis of the health and retirement status of the elderly", Econometrica 54: 1339–1356.

Sickles, R.C. and A. Yazbeck (1995), "On the dynamics of demand for leisure and the production of health", Mimeo.

Silver, M. (1972), "An econometric analysis of spatial variations in mortality rates by race and sex", in: V. Fuchs, ed., Essays in the economics of health and medical care (National Bureau of Economic Research, Cambridge, MA).

Silverman, B.W. (1982), "On the estimation of a probability density function by the maximum penalized likelihood method", The Annals of Statistics 10: 795–810.

Skinner, J. (1985), "The effect of increased longevity on capital accumulation", American Economic Review 75, 1143–1150.

Slade, F. (1984), "Older men: disability insurance and the incentive to work", Industrial Relations 23: 260–269.

Smith, J.P. (1995a), "Unequal wealth and incentives to save", Documented briefing (RAND Corporation, Santa Monica, CA).

Smith, J.P. (1995b), Racial and ethnic differences in wealth (RAND Corporation, Santa Monica, CA).

Smith, K. and N. Waitzman (1994), "Double jeopardy: Interaction effects of marital and poverty status on the risk of mortality", Demography 31: 487–493.

Sorlie, P. and E. Rogot (1990), "Mortality by employment status in the National Longitudinal Mortality Study", American Journal of Epidemiology 132: 983–992.

Sorlie, P., E. Rogot and N. Johnson (1992), "Validity of demographic characteristics on the death certificate", Epidemiology 3: 181–184.

Staiger, D. and J.H. Stock (1994), "Instrumental variables regression with weak instruments", Technical working paper no. 151 (NBER, Cambridge, MA).

Stern, S. (1992), "A method for smoothing simulated moments of discrete probabilities in multinomial probit models", Econometrica 60: 943–952.

Stern, S. (1994), "Two dynamic discrete choice estimation problems and simulation method solutions", Review of Economics and Statistics 76: 695–702.

Stewart, A., R. Hays and J. Ware (1988), "The medical outcome study short form general health survey: reliability and validity in a patient population", Medical Care 26: 724–735.

Stewart, A., J. Ware, R. Brook and A. Davies-Avery (1978), Conceptualization and measurement of health status for adults in the health insurance study, Vol. VI: Physical health in terms of functioning, R-1987/2-HEW (RAND Corporation, Santa Monica, CA).

Stokey, N.L., R.E. Lucas, Jr. and E.C. Prescott (1989), Recursive methods in economic dynamics (Harvard University Press, Cambridge, MA).

Stolnitz, G.J. (1956), "A century of international mortality trends: II", Population Studies 10: 22–32.

Stoto, M.A. and J.S. Durch (1993), "Forecasting, survival, health, and disability: Report on a workshop", Population and Development Review 19: 557–581.

Strauss, J. (1986), "Does better nutrition raise farm productivity?", Journal of Political Economy 94: 297–320.

Strauss, J. and D. Thomas (1992), "Health, wealth and wages of men and women in urban Brazil", Mimeo. (RAND Corporation, Santa Monica, CA).

Strauss, J. and D. Thomas (1995), "Human resources: empirical modeling of household and family decisions", in: J.R. Behrman and T.N. Srinivasan, eds., Handbook of development economics, Vol. 3 (North-Holland, Amsterdam).

Strauss, J., P. Gertler, O. Rahman and K. Fox (1993), "Gender and life-cycle differentials in the patterns and determinants of adult health", Journal of Human Resources 28: 791–837.

Stunkard, A. (1991), "Genetic contributions to human obesity", Research Publications: Association for Research in Nervous and Mental Disease 69: 205–218.

Taubman, P. and S. Rosen (1982), "Healthiness, education and marital status", in: V. Fuchs, ed., Economic aspects of health (University of Chicago Press, Chicago, IL).

Tauchen, H., A. Witte and S. Long (1991), "Violence in the family: a non-random affair", International Economic Review 32: 491–511.

Thaler, R. and S. Rosen (1975), "The value of saving a life: evidence from the labor market", in: N. Terleckyj, ed., Household production and consumption (National Bureau of Economic Research, New York).

Thatcher, A.R. (1992), "Trends in numbers and mortality at high ages in England and Wales", Population Studies 46, 411–426.

The World Bank (1993), World development report (Oxford University Press, Oxford, for the World Bank).

Thomas, D., J. Strauss and M.-H. Henriques (1990), "Child survival, height for age and household characteristics in Brazil", Journal of Development Economics 33: 197–234.

Thompson, J. (1989), Empirical model building (Wiley, New York).

Thompson, J., E. Atkinson and B. Brown (1987), "SIMEST: an algorithm for simulation-based estimation of parameters characterizing a stochastic process", in: J. Thompson and B. Brown, eds., Cancer modelling (Marcel Dekker, New York).

Tienda, M. and V. Ortiz (1986), "Hispanicity and the 1980 census", Social Science Quarterly 67: 3–20.

Torrance, G.W. (1986), "Measurement of health state utilities for economic appraisal: a review", Journal of Health Economics 5: 1–30.

Tsiatis, A. (1975), "A nonidentifiability aspect of the problem of competing risks", Proceedings of the National Academy of Sciences 72: 20–22.

Tsuji, I., Y. Minami, P. Keyl, S. Hisamichi, H. Asano, M. Sato and K. Shinoda (1994), "The predictive power of self-rated health, activities of daily living, and ambulatory activity for cause-specific mortality among the elderly: a three-year follow-up in urban Japan", Journal of the American Geriatrics Society 42: 153–156.

Van de Ven, W. and J. Van der Gaag (1982), "Health as an unobservable", Journal of Health Economics 1: 157–183.

Vaupel, J.W. (1988), "Inherited frailty and longevity", Demography 25: 277–287.

Vaupel, J.W. (1991a), "The impact of population aging on health and health care costs: Uncertainties and new evidence about life expectancy", Mimeo.

Vaupel, J.W. (1991b), "Prospects for a longer life expectancy", Mimeo.

Vaupel, J.W., K.G. Manton and E. Stallard (1979), "The impact of heterogeneity in individual frailty on the dynamics of mortality", Demography 16: 439–454.

Vaupel, J., A. Yashin, L. Xue, N. Holm and B. Harvald (1992), "Strategies for modelling genetics in survival analysis", Mimeo.

Viscusi, W.K. (1994), "Mortality effects of regulatory costs and policy evaluation criteria", RAND Journal of Economics 25, 94–109.

Waaler, H.T. (1984), "Height, weight and mortality: the Norwegian experience", Acta Medica Scandinavica, Supplement, 679: 1–51.

Wagstaff, A. (1985), "Time-series analysis of the relationships between unemployment and mortality: a survey of econometric critiques and replications of Brenner's studies", Social Science and Medicine 21: 985–996.

Wagstaff, A. (1986), "The demand for health", Journal of Health Economics 5: 195–233.

Wagstaff, A. (1989), "Econometric studies in health economics", Journal of Health Economics 8: 1–51.

Waidman, T., M. Schoenbaum and J. Bound (1995), "The illusion of failure: trends in the self-reported health of the U.S. elderly", Working paper no. 5017 (NBER, Cambridge, MA).

Waldron, I. (1982), "An analysis of causes of sex differences in mortality and morbidity", in: W.R. Gove and G.R. Carpenter, eds., The fundamental connection between nature and nurture (Heath and Company, Lexington, DC).

Waldron, I. (1993), "Recent trends in sex mortality ratios for adults in developed countries", Social Science and Medicine 36: 451–462.

Waldron, I. (1994), "Contributions of biological and behavioral factors to changing sex differences in ischemic heart disease mortality", in: A. Lopez, T. Valkonen and G. Caselli, eds., Premature adult mortality in developed countries (Oxford University Press, London).

Wales, T.J. and A.D. Woodland (1983), "Estimation of consumer demand systems with binding non-negativity constraints", Journal of Econometrics 21: 263–285.

Wannamethee, G. and A. Shaper (1991), "Self-assessment of health status and mortality in middle-aged British men", International Journal of Epidemiology 20: 239–245.

Ware, J., A. Davies-Avery and R. Brook (1980), Conceptualization and measurement of health status for adults in the health insurance study, Vol. VII: Analysis of relationships among health status measures, R-1987/6-HEW (RAND Corporation, Santa Monica, CA).

Weatherby, N.L., C.B. Nam and L.W. Isaac (1983), "Development, inequality, health-care, and mortality at the older ages: a cross-national analysis", Demography 20: 27–43.

White, H. (1980), "A heteroscedasticity-consistent covariance matrix estimator and a direct test for heteroscedasticity", Econometrica 48: 817–838.

Wolfe, J.R. (1985), "A model of declining health and retirement", Journal of Political Economy 93: 1258–1267.

Wolfe, J.R. (1993), The coming health crisis (University of Chicago Press, Chicago, IL).

Wolfe, B.L. and J.R. Behrman (1984), "Determinants of women's health status and health-care utilization in a developing country: a latent variable approach", Review of Economics and Statistics 56: 696–703.

Wolfe, B.L. and J.R. Behrman (1987), "Woman's schooling and children's health: are the effects robust with adult sibling control for the women's childhood background?", Journal of Health Economics 6: 239–254.

Wolfe, B.L. and R. Haveman (1983), "Time allocation, market work, and changes in female health", American Economic Review 73: 134–139.

Wolfe, B.L. and R. Haveman (1990), "Trends in the prevalence of work disability from 1962 to 1984 and their correlates", The Milbank Quarterly 61: 53–80.

Wolinsky, F. and R. Johnson (1992), "Perceived health status and mortality among older men and women", Journal of Gerontology: Social Sciences 47: S304–S312.

Wolpin, K.I. (1984), "An estimable dynamic stochastic model of fertility and child mortality", Journal of Political Economy 92: 852–874.

Wolpin, K.I. (1987), "Estimating a structural search model: the transition from school to work", Econometrica 55: 852–874.

Wolpin, K.I. and F. Gönül (1987), "On the use of expectations data in micro surveys: the case of retirement", Mimeo. (Ohio State University, Columbus, OH).

Yashin, A.I., K.G. Manton and E. Stallard (1986), "Dependent competing risks: a stochastic process model", Journal of Mathematical Biology 24: 119–164.

Zick, C. and K. Smith (1994), "Marital transitions, poverty, and gender differences in mortality", Journal of Marriage and the Family 53: 327–336.

Zopf, P. (1992), Mortality patterns and trends in the United States (Greenwood, Westport, CT).

# INDEX TO VOLUMES 1A AND 1B